HANDBOOK
of
PUBLIC POLICY

HANDBOOK
of
PUBLIC POLICY

Edited by
B. GUY PETERS
and JON PIERRE

SAGE Publications
London ● Thousand Oaks ● New Delhi

First published 2006

SAGE Publications Ltd
1 Oliver's Yard
55 City Road
London EC1Y 1SP

SAGE Publications Inc.
2455 Teller Road
Thousand Oaks, California 91320

SAGE Publications India Pvt Ltd
B-42, Panchsheel Enclave
Post Box 4109
New Delhi 110 017

British Library Cataloguing in Publication data

A catalogue record for this book is available from
the British Library

ISBN-10 0-7619-4061-8   ISBN-13 978-0-7619-4061-6

Library of Congress Control Number available

Typeset by C&M Digitals (P) Ltd., Chennai, India
Printed in Great Britain by Cromwell Press Ltd, Trowbridge, Wiltshire
Printer on paper from sustainable resources

Contents

List of Contributors

Richard D. Bingham is a Professor of Public Administration and Urban Studies at the Maxine Goodman Levin College of Urban Affairs, Cleveland State University, USA.

Davis B. Bobrow is Professor at the Graduate School of Public and International Affairs, University of Pittsburgh, USA.

Peter Bogason is Professor of Public Administration at the Department of Social Sciences, Roskilde University, Denmark.

Geert Bouckaert is Professor and Director of the Public Management Institute, Katholieke Universiteit Leuven, Belgium.

Graeme Boushey is a Graduate Research Fellow in the Center for American Politics and Public Policy at the University of Washington, USA.

Gary Bryner is Professor at the Department of Political Science, Brigham Young University, USA

Kenneth Button is Professor of Public Policy at the School of Public Policy, George Mason University, USA

Walter Carlsnaes is Professor of Political Science at the Department of Government, Uppsala University, Sweden.

Peter DeLeon is Professor at the Graduate School of Public Affairs, University of Colorado at Denver, USA.

Helen Fawcett is Lecturer at the Department of Government, University of Strathclyde, UK.

Herbert Gottweis is Professor at the Department of Political Science, University of Vienna, Austria.

Wyn Grant is Professor in the Department of Politics and International Studies at the University of Warwick, UK

John Halligan is Professor at the School of Management and Policy, University of Canberra, Australia.

Michael Hill is Emeritus Professor, University of Newcastle upon Tyne, UK.

Peter L. Hupe is Associate Professor in the Department of Public Administration at Erasmus University, Rotterdam, The Netherlands.

Bryan D. Jones is Donald R. Matthews Distinguished Professor of American Politics, and Director of the Center for American Politics and Public Policy at the University of Washington, USA.

Christoph Knill is Professor in the Department of Political Science and Administration, University of Konstanz, Germany.

Christine R. Martell is Assistant Professor at the Graduate School of Public Affairs, University of Colorado at Denver, USA.

Susan Marton is Assistant Professor at the Department of Political Science, Karlstad University, Sweden.

Michael Moran is Professor of Government in the Department of Government and International Politics, University of Manchester, UK.

Kevin V. Mulcahy is Sheldon Beychok Distinguished Professor at the Department of Political Science, Louisiana State University, USA

Tim Newburn is Professor of Criminology and Social Policy and Director, Mannheim Centre for Criminology, London School of Economics, UK.

B. Guy Peters is Maurice Falk Professor of Government in the Department of Political Science at the University of Pittsburgh, USA.

Jon Pierre is Professor in the Department of Political Science at the University of Gothenburg, Sweden.

Irene S. Rubin is Professor Emeritus of Political Science in the Division of Public Administration at Northern Illinois University, Dekalb, USA.

Ian Thynne is in the Governance Program, Faculty of Law, Business and Arts, Charles Darwin University, Australia.

John Uhr is Senior Fellow in the Political Science Program, Research School of Social Sciences, at the Australian National University, Canberra.

David L. Weimer is Professor of Public Affairs and Political Science at the University of Wisconsin-Madison, USA.

Harold L. Wilensky is Professor Emeritus of Political Science at the Department of Political Science, University of California at Berkeley, USA.

Søren C. Winter is Research Professor, Danish National Institute of Social Research, Copenhagen, Denmark.

Samuel Workman is a Graduate Research Fellow in the Center for American Politics and Public Policy at the University of Washington, USA.

Evert Verdung is Professor of Political Science at the Institute for Housing and Urban Research (IBF) and Department of Government, Uppsala University, Sweden.

Aiden R. Vining is the CNABS Professor of Government and Business Relations, Faculty of Business Administration, Simon Fraser University, Vancouver, Canada.

Introduction

B. GUY PETERS AND JON PIERRE

The **Handbook of Public Policy** is an attempt
to cover the area of public policy studies. That
is an ambitious goal, and perhaps a too ambitious one. Both the real world of public policy
and the academic study of policy are sizeable,
complex and differentiated bodies of practice
and of knowledge. If anything the body of
information that any treatment of public
policy must attempt to cover has been increasing. On the one hand, governments have
altered the manner in which they consider
policies substantively, changing some established fields such as economic policy to
become "competitiveness policy", and/or "sustainable development policy", and also are
attempting to integrate better the range of
policies that have existed in the past to generate more strategic approaches to governing.

The academic study of public policy has also
been expanding to include a wider range of
academic disciplines and approaches. For
example, anthropology has become a more
central player in understanding the processes
by which policies are selected, as well as understanding some substantive aspects of policy
such as those directed toward immigrants.
Further, the range of theoretical approaches to
public policy has expanded as the limits of the
more conventional ways of thinking about
policy have become more apparent. For example, the chapter on constructivist approaches
to policy (Gottweis, this volume) reflects the
emergence of a strong strand of theorizing that
has been developing to supplement, and to
contradict, to more rationalist perspectives on
policy.[1]

The final major question that faces policy
studies is how to put together the practical and
the academic aspects of this area of inquiry.
Practitioners generally want answers to their
day to day problems, are little concerned with
theory, and think that academics are hopelessly
enisled in their ivory towers. On the other
hand, however, academics often argue that the
experts in particular policy areas are obsessed
with those policies and cannot see the bigger
political and economic picture about the
impact and meaning of those policies. We have
attempted to balance these various perspectives
within the *Handbook* as a whole, but relatively
few of the individual chapters have been able to
strike the balance between these two poles.

THE COMPLEXITY OF PUBLIC POLICY

The study of public policy is a very complex
topic, and any attempt to force policy into any
narrow theoretical frame should be considered
with some skepticism. On the one hand there
are some real virtues for policy as an area of
inquiry for the social sciences, given that it is
amenable to so many different perspectives.
On the other hand, however, this complexity
requires bringing together a wide range of
theoretical and analytical perspectives to gain
any sort of understanding of what is happening in any policy area. Both academic disciplines and substantive policy concerns tend to
narrow the vision and to limit the ability of
analysts to understand the underlying complexity of most policies.

The typical manner of approaching public
policy is to consider the various areas of government activity one by one – health, defense,

taxation. Studies of that sort are certainly valuable, but the first important aspect of the complexity of public policy is that focussing on the "single lonely policy" may vastly over-simplify the interactions of multiple policies in producing outcomes for citizens. For example, if government wants to improve the quality of health for its population, the obvious area for investment is in hospitals and other aspects of the "health care industry". On the other hand, however, improving nutrition, or enhancing opportunities for exercise, may actually produce greater health benefits. Therefore, there is a need to think carefully about the interactions of policies and means of coordinating policies to create more effective, if more complex, responses to policy problems.

A second dimension of complexity in public policy studies is the need to examine policy questions from a range of theoretical perspectives. For example, in his classic study of international politics and foreign policy in the Cuban missile crisis, Graham Allison (1971) discussed the virtues of "triangulation" and the use of multiple theoretical perspectives to understand decisions. His more comprehensive[2] approach has rarely been used for other policy areas, but would make a major contribution to understanding exactly what is happening in the policy area. The difficulty may be that few individuals are able to bring a wide-ranging theoretical grounding for the study of policy in this manner, so we all focus on what we know best and attempt to do it well. Scholars and practitioners may be able to build triangulated understandings of policies by cumulating the work of individuals using their own approaches, but this assumes that those individuals will have examined exactly the same policies and have made their findings sufficiently transparent to do that sort of comparison.[3]

A third complexity involved in the study of public policy arises from the word "public". There has been a tendency in the analysis of policy to consider primarily, or solely, the role of the public sector and official actors in the process, and to ignore the role of private sector actors. In fairness, that tendency has been less apparent in recent years than in the past, especially in Northern European countries in which the policy networks (Sorenson and Torfing, 2003) and corporatism (Wiarda, 1997) institutionalize the involvement of a variety of social actors in making and implementing public (sic?) policies. Even in the less-developed countries there is growing evidence of the use of social actors as a means of assisting government to make and deliver public policies, and that this involvement of non-government actors has enhanced the legitimacy of the State.

A final complexity concerns what do we study when we attempt to study public policy? Do we focus only on the decisions that are made and the processes that produce them, the programs that governments develop to deliver services and to influence the society, or the tools that governments use in their implementation? Ultimately, as Harold Lasswell (1935) pointed out some 70 years ago, that politics is about "who gets what", and if that is true of politics then it is certainly true for public policies. Therefore, in the end we should be concerned with the impacts of policy choices on people, and the distribution of benefits in the society. As numerous students of government performance have pointed out, however, assessing those impacts is difficult. Some impacts, for example the benefits of education, may not be fully apparent until many years later, and some may be so diffuse (culture and arts policy?) that measurement for other than academic purposes may not be particularly valuable.[4]

THE ELUSIVENESS OF PUBLIC POLICY AS OBJECT AND THEORY

To gain some understanding of public policy, which – as this volume will show – is both a very heterogeneous concept and also a field of the social sciences that displays a number of different approaches, we must first remind ourselves of the significance of the substantive and analytical dimensions of public policy. Substantively, public policy has undergone some rather fundamental changes over the past couple of decades in terms of policy design, selection of policy instruments and the role of the state in society more broadly. As we will discuss later in this Introduction, public policy in general has become less interventionist, controlling and obtrusive. Instead, there is today a stronger emphasis of the regulatory role of the state. The *Zeitgeist* of much of the 1980s and 1990s has been that of rolling back the state, unleashing markets, cutting taxes and public spending and reducing control. Globalization – real or imagined – has continued to fuel this model of public policy.

Analytically, a number of approaches have emerged, highlighting different elements of public policy and offering different types of explanations to policy design and efficiency. This volume presents the leading approaches in policy research but it does so without detailing the chronological development of this research field. Policy researchers have, rightly, been concerned with process throughout most of the post-war period. Indeed, even when institutional analysis has been the predominant theoretical perspective on public policy there has been an undercurrent of studies calling for "process-tracing" to supplement the institutional perspective. Process remains extremely important; actors' assessment of policy challenges and various strategies to ameliorate those problems today are largely a reflection of decisions and assessments made yesterday. Policy evolves through process, hence it is difficult for studies that ignore process to arrive at a deeper understanding of policy. We will return to these issues later in this chapter.

The tool kit of policy analysts includes an impressing number of theories, models and frameworks. Unlike many other subfields of the social sciences, however, these approaches seem to be complementary much more than they are contending, mainly because of many different types of questions which scholars raise in policy analysis. As a result, much of the controversy that has evolved in political science over rational choice versus other theories never made much of an imprint in the field of public policy.

These trends and developments raise two sets of questions. First, we need to know more

about what causes changes in public policy. The growing interest in policy diffusion and policy learning depends in part on its claim to be a rewarding avenue into these issues. Most observers would, however, probably argue that such patterns of policy transfer among states offer only a limited explanation to the broader question of policy change. If anything, policy transfer probably occurs once a changed course of policy has been decided and is not so much part of the drive for change per se. Instead, it appears as if the main sources of policy change are either economic or related to voters' demands. The economic drivers of policy change – either in terms of changes in the tax base and the public budget or in terms of global pressures on tax levels and public spending – represent a powerful pressure on policy makers. Voters' preferences matter too, but probably less in terms of policy instrument selection and policy design than in the relationship between taxes and benefits for the main constituencies in society. People are probably not very concerned with how services and programs are delivered as long as they are provided.

Most importantly, there is plenty of proof that politics matters in shaping policy choice. That means that governments of different ideological orientations tend to make different choices with respect to how the state should allocate its resources and how those resources should be mobilized. These observations hold true even in an era where it is often said that policy challenges are becoming more similar among different countries, whether because of demographic patterns, economic modernization or global economic pressures (see, for instance, Castles, 1998). National political and institutional contexts still offer much in terms of explanation of policy choice. Those choices are made in the context of national systems of structures and values that have proven quite resilient in the midst of globalization and economic deregulation.

The second question we need to address has to do with the development of policy analysis as a social science research field. Public policy research has been concerned with changes in public policy across time and space. This applies to the entire range of variables in policy research, from theories of societal problems to selection of policy instruments. Students of public policy, like all social scientists, have fads and fashions with respect to what theories and models are "in" and which are not.

It could well be argued that institutional approaches, ideational approaches or, indeed, most or all of the approaches covered in this *Handbook* are to a large extent more a reflection of changes in the preferences among the observers of public policy than a reflection of changes in policy itself. That having been said, however, these linkages do exist between the dimensions, i.e. between what is studied and how it is studied. Thus, for instance, the growing interest in implementation followed fairly logically on the expansion of federal programs in the mid- and late 1960s under the heading of the Strong Society. Similarly, there has been an increasing interest among scholars in regulation, or even in the emergence of a "regulatory state", partly as a result of states' increasing use of regulation and less emphasis on using more costly policy instruments.

Another example of the linkage between substance and theory can be found in the study of policy change. Adaptation to changing economic preconditions is a surprisingly slow process, and although politics matters in the aggregate, changes in individual programs can be a frustrating experience for incoming governments because of the inertia in the public sector. This has drawn scholars' attention to the significance of different types of obstacles to policy changes. Such obstacles are typically believed to be institutions or processes which, de facto if not de jure, lock in or protect areas of public spending from reassessment. Again, it appears as if the increasing interest in institutions has generated a broader and more inclusive understanding of what shapes and sustains public policy. In some ways, it could be that social scientists are just beginning to discover what practitioners in the policy process have known for a long time; politics matters but institutions mitigate the impact of changes in the political leadership.

Thus, the study of public policy could be described as shooting at a mobile target with a somewhat malfunctioning rifle. The target is changing course frequently – or does not change course when we expect it to – and our weapon is far from perfect in composition and robustness. However, it is safe to say that the diversity of approaches to public policy that we have seen develop has helped us understand public policy to a greater extent than would have been the case had the discipline been more homogenous.

THE DEVELOPMENT OF PUBLIC POLICY PROPER

The debate among students of public policy about how to best approach this topic has evolved alongside significant developments in public policy itself. A quick look back in time suggests that over the past several decades we have seen profound changes in policy objectives and instruments. The 1960s and 1970s saw most Western governments expanding the public sector. The preferred policy instruments tended to be fairly coercive. New public programs were launched to address societal problems. The growth in the economy generated increasing incomes to the state which provided the financial base for expanding programs in sectors like education, social welfare, housing policy and research and development. With only slight exaggeration we could say that the Western societies of the 1960s and 1970s were more state-centric compared to those of the 1980s and 1990s. This applies – with significant variation – to jurisdictions on both sides of the Atlantic; in the case of the United States we need only compare the Strong Society programs under Lyndon Johnson with the more market-embracing policy style of Reagan to note how much has changed in a rather short period of time.

Although many policy objectives have not been abandoned, contemporary public policy tends to draw on other instruments and institutional models compared to twenty years ago. Indeed, one could argue that in some cases the social theory underlying public policy has been reassessed. In the early post-war period, the predominant social theory of public policy emphasized the positive contribution of policy and state action to resolve societal problems. In the contemporary policy vernacular, there is a much greater awareness of the contingencies and complexities surrounding policy design and implementation.

Looking more broadly at these issues, there seem to be three types of changes that summarize the developments over the past couple of decades. The first of these changes is a shift away from a policy style characterized by command and control by the state towards a regulatory state (Moran, 2003). The budgetary cutbacks in welfare programs that represent a rather uniform pattern across the western hemisphere have been accompanied by a growing emphasis on the regulatory role of the state. This development has also been driven by the tendency to open up for market-based systems of resource allocations and the relationship between the providers and consumers of public services. Thus, if the previously predominant policy emphasized political solutions to societal problems, the current strategy is more based on a notion of rolling back the state, allowing the market to play a greater role in society.

Another overarching development in policy style could be described as "back to basics". During the first couple of decades following World War II, most western states – as well as subnational institutions – assumed roles and responsibilities that could not be said to belong to the core roles of the state in society. Thus, many states owned enterprises providing collective good such as electricity, railway transportation, telecommunication services, and the like. Also, states provided financial support to an array of functions and activities in civil society and the culture sector. The 1980s and 1990s saw somewhat of a reversal of this expansion of the scope of the state. The previously mentioned stronger emphasis on the regulatory role of the state is one element of this "purification" of the state (see Premfors, 1999). The state should no longer own enterprises, not even if the services produced were collective goods. Instead, the state should return to its core role in society; any function beyond that role should be carefully assessed and, if possible, transferred to the market or to civil society. In the United States, the Reagan administration sought to rid the federal level of all responsibilities and functions which could not be defined as part of the core role of government. Similarly, in Britain, Mrs. Thatcher embarked on a project aiming at drastically reducing the scope of government in society and to "unleash" the market. While these types of reform helped the state to curb budget deficits and to stimulate the economy, they also caused considerable political friction as constituencies deprived of financial support took to political arms.

The third and final change in policy style which we will discuss here is in many ways derived from the former two; the so-called shift from government to governance. Sometimes labelled "the new governance", this development refers to a tendency among most west European governments during the late 1980s and 1990s to produce and deliver public service in concert with the market and civil society. The role of the state in the governance model is not to produce all those services itself but rather to coordinate public and private action so as to ensure that those services and programs are delivered. Collective goals and objectives remain defined by political institutions but the pursuit of those goals needs not be a matter solely for the state. Thus, the governance perspective highlights concerted action, shared resources and negotiation as an alternative to the state-centric model which features a clear separation of state and society and a state strategy primarily based on command and control.

The increasing interest in "new governance" is part of a cluster of issues which we and many others have discussed elsewhere (Pierre and Peters, 2000, 2004; Pierre, 2000; see also Kjaer, 2004; Rhodes, 1997). The significance of the governance model in the current analysis is that it represents a very different foundation of public policy compared to the traditional government model. In a governance perspective, public policy is to a large extent the outcome of bargaining among political institutions and societal actors. Students of neo-corporatism find little news in this observation and, to be sure, what has been labelled "new governance" is not very new in many European national contexts. What does appear to be novel about the model of governance which evolved during the 1990s is that it involves the market to a larger extent than the neo-corporatist model, which mainly saw peak organizations engage in deliberation with the state. If anything, the "new governance" is more contextual and messier than most previous models of governance. That development poses a significant challenge to observers of policy making and public policy. While the state remains the undisputed center of representation, accountability and coordination, it faces a more complex environment with which it interacts.

These three developments in the role of the state have redefined the range and scope of public policy and, more broadly, have reformulated the social theory which public policy rests on. That development, in turn, redefines policy objectives and influences the selection of policy instruments. Most importantly, perhaps, is that all models of state-society exchanges become institutionalized; citizens and organized interests learn what to expect from the state in terms of problem-solving and resource mobilization. In societies with "weak states" (Migdal, 1998), expectations on the state are low and societal actors develop non-political solutions to various problems. Similarly, in countries with "strong states", people become socialized into turning to the state for help with almost any problem. This institutionalization makes a transition from a government-centered model of governance to a market-based or network-based governance model difficult and politically quite complex.

THE STUDY OF PUBLIC POLICY

A key purpose of this volume is to present the multitude of approaches to public policy. In much of the public policy analysis of the past several decades, the focus has been on the process through which public policy is designed and implemented. By studying the different stages of the policy process – agenda setting, decision making, legitimation, implementation, and so on – observers develop an understanding of why policy looks the way it does (see, for instance, Dye, 1987; Kingdon, 1995). Each stage has its own set of actors; for instance, decision makers are rarely involved in the implementation of policy. Also, each individual stage displays its own types of potential conflict and political opportunity structures. The overall rationale of the stages approach is that what actors do at one stage of the policy process is to a large extent framed by what other actors have done earlier in the process. Historical institutionalists rightly point out that the first stages in any process have a major influence on what happens next. We should, however, recognize that, although there are powerful lock-in factors in the policy process, there is some room for political and strategic consideration at all the stages of the process. For instance, as the implementation literature tells us, identical policies can be implemented in a number of different ways – with different outcomes – in different institutional settings.

There is a great deal of logic in the process approach. What happens at a particular stage is very much shaped by decisions and actions at the previous stages. Policy makers probably assess policy alternatives and political strategies in a process stage model and, indeed, the formal procedure of policy making defines in great detail the process. These formal rules of policy making shape actors' behavior and it therefore also makes sense for policy analysts to structure their observations according to that perspective. On the other hand, however, individuals also play a role in the process, and act as policy entrepreneurs to attempt to have their own policy preferences enacted into law. Thus, policy making represents a complex interaction of individuals, institutions, ideas and interests.

In addition to looking at policy, the process by which policies are formed and implemented, we can also ask a number of other questions about policy. One of the more important components of the study of public policy is the use of analytic techniques that can be used to assist decision-makers in choosing policies. These techniques are often based on assumptions of optimality and rationality derived from economics, and therefore often confront the political realities that may make presumably optimal solutions impossible. Rationalist modes of analysis are not alone, however, and other methods (reflecting their theoretical underpinnings) such as bounded rationality, discourse analysis, and humanist approaches to policy, do contend for attention, and offer alternative answers to questions about public policy.

Yet another means of thinking about policy is to focus on the various policy areas and types of policy. The most obvious way to engage in this form of analysis is to use the familiar functional names of policy – defense, agriculture, etc. These names are helpful, and there may be as much variance across policy areas than there is across countries in the manner in which policies are processed. Still, there is a great deal of internal variance within each of these areas,[5] so that a more analytic way of thinking about policy types may be needed. Theodore Lowi (1972) has supplied the most commonly used of these analytic schemes, but there are other ways of thinking about policy types and their impact on policy analysis (Peters and Hoornbeek, 2005).

The fourth significant dimension of public policy research has been the rapidly growing interest in the role of political institutions in shaping and sustaining public policy. A couple of seminal studies published during the 1980s (March and Olsen 1995, 1999; Hall, 1986) delivered a powerful argument that public policy, state-society relationships and political behavior more broadly are "shaped and constrained" by institutions. Institutions should not only be understood in the narrow, structural sense; institutions are carriers and transmitters of norms and values which define a "logic of appropriateness" for political and social behavior. Applied to public policy research, institutional analysis has highlighted the significance of structure and norm in defining policy objectives. Once a policy is in place, it stays in place. The institutionalization of public policy creates a "path dependency"

which makes competing policy options unattractive because of high political or economic costs. Thus, institutional analysis has offered significant help in understanding lock-in effects in public policy and different types of obstacles to policy change.

The institutional approach to policy analysis thus appears to cut the proverbial pie in a different way than does the stages model. To be sure, the increasing dominance of institutional analysis over the process approach has left some researchers looking for analytical models which combine attention to institutions with an understanding of the logics of the policy process *qua* process (Sabatier, 1999). Although the institutional approach draws on a different logic than the stages model, there is some overlap between the two approaches; for instance, scholars can investigate the role of institutions in the policy process. That said, institutional analysis has problems understanding agency, something which the stages model is better geared to conceptualize and explain.

Different academic disciplines conceptualize public policy and policymaking differently. Political science focuses on the processes, institutions and the power struggles among competing interests in having their wishes enacted into policy. Economics is concerned more with the economic effects of policies and with designing optimal policy solutions. Philosophy is concerned with the profound but knotty normative questions involved in policy choices. This list could be extended, but the basic point is that a number of academic disciplines bring something to the table when the discussion of public policy begins.

The contribution of different academic disciplines also can be assessed with regard to different stages of the policy process (see Pierres's chapter in this volume). More broadly, the influence of different disciplines plays out, not only in the scholarly debate on how to best understand public policy, but also in the substantive issues that the discipline helps to identify. Any unidimensional analysis of policy therefore should be somewhat suspect, although each scholar will remain a prisoner of his or her academic training.

CONCLUSIONS: THE FUTURE OF PUBLIC POLICY RESEARCH

The study of public policy is now a well-established component of several academic disciplines, as well as having a literature, professional associations, journals, and theories of its own. One of the questions about the future, therefore, is whether the eclecticism that has characterized the development of this area of study in the past will persist, or whether there will be the development of a paradigm for policy studies. Our own preference would be to continue with a more eclectic approach, emphasizing the range of alternative means of addressing the same concerns and learning from those multiple perspectives.

The future of policy studies will almost certainly be more international and comparative. The diffusion of policies among nations, and the importance of international regimes and international organizations on national policy choices, appears only likely to increase. That having been said, however, we must remain cognizant of the persistence of national policy styles and national policy problems that can not be subsumed under a large international umbrella.

We hope that this volume will contribute both to the understanding of public policy of those who come to it as novices, and to the increased understanding of veterans in the area. The coverage is extensive, but could always have been larger. The range of scholars and the range of issues should make clear that this is a multi-faceted and international enterprise, and further that the study of public policy has importance, not just as an academic enterprise, but also has real impacts on the lives of citizens.

NOTES

1. This approach to policy is not really that new. See Fischer (2003) for an excellent restatement.
2. Although Allison did use three approaches there may well be still others that could have been used to illuminate these decisions even further.

3. The increasing use of Bayesian methods to bring together studies (Ragin, 1987) done in different ways is
4. That having been said, however, arts organizations have been increasingly sophisticated in making arguments for the economic benefits of their programs and the economic utility of public sector subsidies, never mind the real cultural benefits.
5. Think, for example, of the differences between kindergarten and higher educational policy issues, although they both are education policy in the functional classification.

REFERENCES

Allison, G. T. (1971) *Essence of Decision* (Boston: Little, Brown).
Castles, F. G. (1998) *Comparative Public Policy: Patterns of Post-War Transformation* (Cheltenham: Edward Elgar).
Dye, T. R. (1987) Understanding Public Policy, 6th Ed. (Englewood Cliffs, NJ: Prentice-Hall).
Fischer, F. (2003) *Reframing Public Policy* (Oxford: Oxford University Press).
Hall, P. A. (1986) Governing the Economy: The Politics of State Intervention in Britain and France (Oxford: Oxford University Press).
Kingdon, J. W. (1995) Agendas, Alternative and Public Policies, 2nd. Ed (New York: Harper Collins).
Kjaer, A. M. (2004) *Governance* (Cambridge: Polity Press).
Lasswell, H. (1935) *Politics: Who Gets What, When, How* (New York: McGraw Hill).
Lowi, T. J. (1972) Four Systems of Policy, Politics and Choice, *Public Administration Review* 32, 298–310.
March, J. G. and J. P. Olsen (1989) Rediscovering Institutions (New York: Free Press).
March, J. G. and J. P. Olsen (1995) *Democratic Governance* (New York: Free Press).
Migdal, J. S. (1988) *Strong Societies and Weak States* (Princeton, NJ: Princeton University Press).
Moran, M. (2003) The British Regulatory State (Oxford: Oxford University Press).
Peters, B. G. and J. A. Hoornbeek (2005) The Problem of Policy Problems, in P. Eliadia, M. M. Hill and M. Howlett, eds., *Designing Government* (Montreal: McGill-Queens University Press).
Pierre, J. (ed.) (2000) Debating Governance (Oxford: Oxford University Press).
Pierre, J. and B. G. Peters (2000), Governance, Politics and the State (Basingstoke: Macmillan).

Pierre, J. and B. G. Peters (2004) Governing Complex Societies: Trajectories and Scenarios (Basingstoke: Palgrave).

Premfors, R. (1999) "Organisationsförändringar och förvaltningspolitik – Sverige", in P. Laegreid and O. K. Pedersen (eds), Fra opbyning till ombygning i staten: Organisationsforandringer i tre nordiske lande (Copenhagen: Jurist-og Ökonomforbundets Forlag), 145–68.

Ragin, C. (1987) The Comparative Method: Moving Beyond Qualitative and Quantitative Strategies (Berkeley: University of California Press).

Rhodes, R. A. W. (1997) Understanding Governance (Buckingham: Open University Press).

Sabatier, P. A. (1999) Theories of the Policy Process (Boulder, CO: Westivew).

Sorenson, E. and J. Torfing (2003) "Network Politics, Political Capital and Democracy", International Journal of Public Administration 26, 609–43.

Wiarda, H. (1997) Corporatism and Comparative Politics: The Other Great "ism" (Armonk, NY: M. E. Sharpe).

Section One

Making Policy

1

The Three Action Levels of Governance: Re-framing the Policy Process Beyond the Stages Model

PETER L. HUPE AND MICHAEL J. HILL

1. INTRODUCTION

The state of the art

> Mountain islands of theoretical structure, intermingled with, and occasionally attached together by foothills of shared methods and concepts, and empirical work, all of which is surrounded by oceans of descriptive work not attached to any mountain of theory.

Thus Schlager (1997: 14) characterises the present landscape of the study of the policy process[1]. This varied landscape partly mirrors the complexities of the object of study itself. A key element in many approaches to describing this landscape is the stages model of the policy process. In this chapter we will review the functionality of that so called 'model'.

Sabatier (1999: 1–2) specifies the elements of the policy process as 'an extremely complex set', consisting of:

(a) a multiplicity of actors (both individual and corporate) each of which have different interests, values, perceptions and policy preferences;

(b) a time span of a decade or more;

(c) within a policy domain there are normally dozens of different programmes involving multiple layers of government;

(d) a variety of debates about the policy involved, partly of a highly technical character and held in different fora;

(e) the high stakes involved give rise to 'politics' and power political behaviour in and around a policy process.

These complexities of the object form the background to the fact that the contemporary study of the policy process appears to go in various directions. In his textbook *Public Policy* Wayne Parsons gives a broad overview of the conceptual wealth present in the field of policy analysis. He calls this field 'rich in different approaches, academic disciplines, models (heuristic and causal), metaphors and maps' (Parsons, 1995: 64). One of the striking aspects of the almost 700 pages of Parsons' book is not only the scope of the insights about the policy process available, but also the variety of labels these insights are presented under. Starting from the first pages the reader encounters terms like 'approach' (p. xv), 'frames of analysis'

(p. xvi), 'frameworks and methods or approaches' (p. xvii), 'analytical frameworks' (p. 32, heading), 'theoretical frameworks' (p. 32, text). Under the heading 'Models, maps and metaphors' Parsons explicitly addresses the question of how to label the different ways of organizing one's ideas in the study of the policy process. As an overarching and most general term he chooses 'frameworks', 'within which and through which we can think and explain' (p. 57). Parsons distinguishes here between explanatory, 'ideal-type' and normative frameworks (pp. 57–8).

> We begin with theories, models, mental maps, metaphors; and to think analytically about public policy we have to be sensitive to the existence of 'reality' as a construction within a multiplicity of frameworks. The activity of theorizing about public policy is, therefore, like drawing a map... (p. 58).

Given the varied landscape as pictured there is more than reason to have adequate maps. For, since the founding fathers of the study of public administration, the discourse has developed in diverging ways that in many respects can be described as a 'dialogue of the deaf'. On the one hand, the rational assumptions about public decision making, as once postulated by authors like Wilson (1887) and Simon (1945), seem to remain persistent. While implying 'stagist' relationships between sets of activities within the realm of politics and administration, these assumptions above all refer to a clear division of labour. The way in which practising politicians and administrators in many countries, for example, have adopted contracting out and similar meta-policies, aiming at the separation of 'implementation' from 'policy', resembles those assumptions. At the same time, reporting on 'policy fiascos', journalists tend to confront what is happening at the implementation level of a policy straightforwardly with what has been agreed upon in the legislative stage. Moreover, many academics are quite happy to do work which would seem to share assumptions of this kind. We have in mind here the substantial evaluation literature, particularly the current concern to explore ways to make policy more evidence based. In the UK this trend is visible under the slogan 'What works?' (Davies et al., 2000).

Meanwhile, on the other hand, we see theoretical work which suggests that the policy process departs so far from rationality that the most appropriate model is a 'garbage can' (Cohen, March and Olsen, 1972) or that at least parts of the policy process, such as agenda setting, are 'dynamic, fluid and loosely jointed' (Kingdon, 1995: 230). Post-modernist theory goes even further, not merely to unmask the rationalist discourse, but indeed to suggest the impossibility of rational processes at all (Fox and Miller, 1995; see also Fischer, 2003). The argument we will develop is obviously closely linked with the former of the alternative perspectives just mentioned. At the same time we consider there can be a reconciliation between these apparent extremes.

Our point of departure is the view that in Western countries in many fields public policies are working. Such policies are only given public attention when there is a crisis, or even a disaster. For academics there has been a tendency to take their leads from publicity about the negative aspects of government performance. Since Selznick published *TVA and the Grass Roots* in 1949, many social science studies, certainly ones concentrating on implementation, have found disappointing results of public policies in practise. Often this disappointment about what happened to good intentions has been expressed in more or less straightforwardly gloomy titles. Setting the tone were *New Towns in Town: Why a Federal Program Failed* (Derthick, 1972) and *Implementation: How Great Expectations Are Dashed in Oakland* (...) (Pressman and Wildavsky, 1973; see Hill and Hupe, 2003, for a further discussion of the issues about 'implementation failure'). In this context Linder and Peters speak of the 'horrors of war' approach to the study of public policy (1987: 460). This approach, with its emphasis on 'failures', has turned many of these studies into what Rothstein calls 'misery research' (1998: 62–5).

Before we move to look at the stages model more precisely, it is important to highlight a problem about the study of the policy process, which has made the debate about that model both complex and intense. As indicated, the systematic study of the policy process has its roots in the classical literature on public administration. The founding elements in that literature had two contentious characteristics. One was the notion that there could be a clear separation between politics and administration, making the latter the careful formulation of specific activities based upon the policy goals set by democratically accountable politicians (Wilson, 1887). The other was that the policy process could, or should, be a rational one, in the sense in which that term was used by Simon (1945). This would mean that a careful and thorough examination of the relationship between ends and means is carried out by those required to translate policies into action. Both of these notions, of course, came under attack. It was argued that Wilson's ideal of the separation of administration from politics was unattainable, that administration is inevitably a political process (Waldo, 1946) and that the translation of policies into action is a very much more haphazard process than Simon suggested (Lindblom, 1959).

Systematic study requires a general map

We put aside here the arguments, particularly used on the 'rationalist side', that their models represent ways policy process *should* occur. Rather our stance is based upon a view that both sides in the argument tend to distort reality. The case against the rational actor can be easily made: indeed much of the work of its opponents deploys good evidence of haphazard and irrational decision making processes and of the manipulative deployment of discourses. The case that needs to be made more clearly, however, is on the other side, that there is a tendency for contemporary analyses of policy processes to focus upon mistakes and disasters and to disregard the large number of examples of stable, successful policy processes, involving deliberate design work worthy of Simon's model. Frederickson and Smith speak of 'the high-reliability systems; the best examples include commercial air travel, the provision of electricity, gas, and cable television services; and the operation of nuclear power plants, aircraft carriers and submarines' (2003: 80). Quoting Perrow (1999) on 'normal accidents' they say: 'There will be failures and there will be accidents, simple probability demonstrates that it is so … But every day we enjoy the modern miracle of high-reliability systems' (Ibid.: 81). We could similarly refer to social policy systems. All over the world complex systems have been designed to deliver social benefits, in accordance with explicit rules, which function uncontroversially much of the time. Debate focuses upon either their occasional failures or upon those (often marginal) parts of the systems where rules are hard to operate.

If we try to take a balanced view between the positive and the negative image of policy processes we need a way of theorising about both its more systematic aspects and about the phenomena that may undermine that. In our stance we join the many students of the policy process who want to try to sort out approaches to specifying the issues at stake and the scope for their systematic study. One key element in debates about how to do this has involved sharp differences of view about the extent to which it is possible to separate the policy process into 'stages'. The so called 'stages model' has been offered as a map, around which a consensus about theory building may be developed. A question then is whether this map building can be a shared process, as is implicit in the positivist model of social science, or whether we have a series of competing maps (or at worst each our own map) which cannot be reconciled with each other.

Our objective here is first to explore the nature, functions and limitations of what has been called the stages model, and then to see whether an alternative general framework for the analysis of policy processes may be built upon it. The central questions are:

- What functions does the so called 'stages model' fulfil in the study of the policy process?
- Which limitations to its use can be identified?
- And how may these limitations be overcome in an alternative framework for analysis?

Hence, in the following discussion we first look at various versions of the stages model and at criticisms of it (second section). Next, an assessment is given: Is it a 'model' or something else? – while also the methodological pitfalls arising out of an unreflecting use get attention (third section). From there we proceed to set out an alternative analytical framework built upon notions of alternative aspects of governance, aiming to offer suggestions for dealing with the identified limitations of the model (fourth section). We then go on to explore the analytical gains that may be made by approaching policy processes in terms of our framework (fifth section). The chapter ends with some conclusions (sixth section).

2.   THE STAGES MODEL OF THE POLICY PROCESS

Variants in the literature

The study of the policy process owes a lot to Harold Lasswell, the American political scientist who was active during the second half of the twentieth century. Parsons sees Lasswell as the originator of what the latter himself called 'the policy orientation' (1951a). Overviewing Lasswell's work (1951b, 1968, 1970, 1971) Parsons gives the following characterisation of that 'policy orientation': 'multi-method, multi-disciplinary, problem-focused, concerned to map the contextuality of the policy process, policy options and policy outcomes; and whose goal is to integrate knowledge into an overarching discipline to analyse public choices and decision making and thereby contribute to the democratization of society' (Parsons, 1995: xvi). Lasswell (1956) was one of the first to approach the overall process of the making of public policy explicitly in terms of 'phases' or 'stages'. He uses that term to refer to a set of separate and successive steps, thought of as in principle taken in a chronological order, from initiative via formulation and decision to evaluation and termination. More specifically, Lasswell (1956) distinguishes between what he calls the seven 'stages' of 'the decision process':

- intelligence
- promotion
- prescription
- invocation
- application
- termination
- appraisal

In doing this Lasswell argues that he is framing a 'conceptual map (that) must provide a guide to obtaining a generalised image of the major phases of any collective act' (Lasswell, 1971: 28). Lasswell was by no means the only scholar to see the policy process as involving stages; indeed Wilson's politics/administration dichotomy can be seen as containing the seeds of such an approach. In 1945 Herbert Simon (1945) had formulated the logic of the way people reach decisions in terms of three successive stages: intelligence, design and choice.

Since Lasswell's specification of seven stages there have been many variants, altering the number of stages or specifying them a little differently (Mack, 1971; Rose 1973; Brewer, 1974; Jenkins, 1978; Hogwood and Gunn, 1984). Probably the most complex elaboration of the stages heuristic is provided by Dror (1989: 163–4). He distinguishes three major stages: the metapolicy-making stage, the policy-making stage, and the post-policy making stage. Within each of those Dror specifies four to seven substages; all adding up to a total number of 18 successive (sub-) stages. In numerous policy textbooks published since the 1970s, the stages heuristic has been used to structure accounts of the policy process (see, for example, Jones, 1970; Anderson, 1975; May and Wildavsky (eds.), 1978; Hoogerwerf (ed.), 1978; Kuypers, 1980; Brewer and DeLeon, 1983; Hogwood and Gunn, 1984; Palumbo, 1988; Van de Graaf and Hoppe, 1989; Howlett and Ramesh, 2003).

Even amongst contemporary writers, eager to stress the complexity of the policy process, we still find that the idea of stages is influential. Thus Sabatier, in his edited book on the policy process, provides the following definition:

> The process of public policy making includes the manner in which problems get conceptualized and brought to government for solution; governmental institutions formulate alternatives and select policy solutions; and those solutions get implemented, evaluated, and revised (1999: 3).

Criticisms

Despite the perfectly 'stagist' definition just quoted, Sabatier argues:

> The conclusion seems inescapable: The stages heuristic has outlived its usefulness and needs to be replaced with better theoretical frameworks (1999: 7).

Nakamura (1987) criticizes the stages model of the policy process, portraying it as unrealistic, calling it the 'textbook approach'. Lindblom (1968) was one of the first to emphasise the sometimes blurred borders between the stages; later he and Woodhouse stress that 'policy making is (…) a complexly inter-active process without beginning or end' (1993: 11). Jenkins-Smith and Sabatier make the following points in a more detailed critique of what they call the stages 'heuristic':

(a) That it is not a causal model.
(b) That it '*does not provide a clear basis for empirical hypothesis testing*'.
(c) That it is descriptively inaccurate.
(d) That is has a 'built-in *legalistic, top-down focus*'.
(e) That it gives an inappropriate emphasis to '*the policy cycle as the temporal unit of analysis*'.
(f) That it 'fails to provide a good vehicle for integrating the roles of policy analysis and *policy-oriented learning throughout the public policy process*' (1993: 3–4, italics from the original).

Similar arguments had been set out in Sabatier (1991) and in Stone (1989).

3. THE FUNCTIONALITY OF THE STAGES MODEL

An assessment of the stages heuristic

In order to find out if these seemingly definitive judgements can be justified it is worthwhile to look more precisely at the nature of the stages heuristic or stages notion – neutral terms that, indeed, beforehand seem more appropriate. What is the 'stages model' and what not? What can it do and what not? And what should it do? One of its proponents of the first hour who has stayed an advocate, is Peter DeLeon. He outlines a few characteristics of the heuristic, and the functions it fulfils (1999: 20–3). First, stages 'offer a way to think about public policy in concept and (…) in operation' (Ibid.: 21). Hence, by giving attention to the characteristics of related sets of activities the stages notion not only gave rise to textbook knowledge of the policy process, but also directed an entire generation of theoretical-empirical research. DeLeon points out a sequence of 'policy classics' that focused upon crucial stages in the policy process rather than on specific issue areas. He argues that these works brought a new richness to the policy sciences, because they emphasized the complexities of policy processes and researched these in greater depth than political scientists and economists, using more rigorous models, had done before. Even John (1998: 36), a critic of what has been called the stages model, concedes that 'Researchers can apply it because it imposes some order on the research process'.

DeLeon goes on to argue that analysing the policy process, while doing such in terms of stages, has enabled a move away from the study of legal-juridical institutions as practised in public administration and from the study of quasi-markets exercised by economists. This innovative emphasis 'helped to rationalize a new problem oriented perspective' (Ibid.: 22). In offering such a defence of the stages heuristic DeLeon considers it important to make clear that he does not regard it as a 'theory', in the sense implied by the first three points against it mentioned by Jenkins-Smith and Sabatier. DeLeon argues:

> Brewer and DeLeon (and, by implication, Lasswell) (…) realized that it was not suitable to formal hypothesis testing or prediction with much precision (…). Rather, they viewed the policy process as a device (a heuristic, as it were) to help disaggregate an otherwise seamless web of public policy transactions. They proposed that each segment and transition were distinguished by differentiated actions and purposes (DeLeon, 1999: 24).

Accordingly, DeLeon argues that frameworks like the 'advocacy coalition framework' of Sabatier and Jenkins-Smith and the 'punctuated equilibrium framework' of Baumgartner and Jones (1993) can be positioned as referring to policy initiation, an early part in the stages heuristic (though that hardly seems fair to the former). DeLeon gives more examples of perceived alternative approaches to the stages heuristic (for instance Fischer, 1995, on evaluation), which, in fact, relate well to it instead of replacing it. If this is so, may it be then perhaps that the stages heuristic is something of a different order?

It seems useful to note here how carelessly notions of theory are used in policy studies. Elinor Ostrom (1999) argues that it is important to distinguish within theoretical work three levels of specificity, which are often confused: frameworks, theories and models. Hence she identifies these as follows:

- A framework helps to identify the elements needed for more systematic analysis, providing a list of variables and 'metaphorical language that can be used to compare theories' (Ibid.: 40).
- Theories 'enable the analyst to specify which elements of the framework are particularly relevant to certain kinds of questions and to make general working assumptions about these elements. Thus, theories focus on a framework and make specific assumptions that are necessary for an analyst to diagnose a phenomenon, explain its processes, and predict outcomes. Several theories are usually compatible with any framework' (Ibid.).
- Models 'make precise assumptions about a limited set of parameters and variables' (Ibid.).

Therefore, perhaps we may argue that the stages heuristic is a framework rather than a theory. This seems the obvious position to take about the value of the heuristic as a device to facilitate research, and, as John (1998) adds, teaching.

Schlager, however, offers a slightly different approach to this issue. She sees the stages notion as a 'useful categorization of behaviour and action within entire policy processes' but not a framework because 'general classes of variables, or "universal elements", and general relationships among them' are lacking. She thus describes it as 'a typology that completely describes policy decisions and actions that occur around a policy' (Schlager, 1999: 239). But if it is a typology, what then are the parameters? In our view the key to understanding the nature of the stages heuristic must be sought in its origins: Lasswell's 'policy orientation' (1951a). Focusing on what Dewey (1927) once described as 'the public and its problems', public policy is an object of scholarly inquiry with a scope going beyond scientific theory. This implies that the stages heuristic can be seen as part of a widespread, in fact pre-scientific, general conception of public policy. The term 'public policy' seems to imply a set of underlying assumptions of which, in an ideal-typical form, the following construction can be made.

Within the *trias politica* the executive power executes what the legislative power has formulated and decided upon. Actors other than the designer/decision maker execute public policies according to the intentions legitimately laid down in laws or other official documents. Preconditions for effective policy are adequate knowledge and information, a solid basis of power and cooperation, and an obedient field of application (Van Gunsteren, 1980). Through the implementation process the intentions of a public policy are, literally, realised. Overall, the realisation of these intentions takes the form of what is called a policy process: a series of orderly staged successive sequences, going from articulation via formation and implementation to evaluation (and back). A policy is seen as 'a hypothesis containing initial conditions and predicted consequences. If X is done at time *t1*, then Y will result at time *t2*' (Pressman and Wildavsky, 1973: xiii). Despite the use of the term 'policy cycle', actually the more appropriate metaphor is that of a chain: both in time and often in space, vertically linking various 'clearances'. Public servants, especially those with an implementation task, fulfil their jobs within a hierarchical setting, with fixed competences, led by documents and guided by rules. If what is achieved is not what was expected, shortcomings in implementation are to blame, particularly insufficient rule compliance.

For policy researchers a few consequences follow (for an elaboration see Hill and Hupe,

2003): Policy determines action, while policy intentions predict policy performance in a 1:1 relationship.

With the general conception of public policy, as constructed here, we obviously are back to the idea of the administrative process described in our introduction as the traditional model linked with the work of Wilson, Simon and many others. We accept then the way in which researchers have in various respects argued that this ideal-typical 'image' does not represent the real world of public policy. Yet people continue to hold this conception of public policy, founded as it is in institutionalised normative views on democracy and the rule of law, as highly attractive. The conception seems so widespread, not only because it is rooted in the political-administrative culture and institutions of the Western *Rechtsstaat*, but also because it appeals to both a general *quest for control* (Van Gunsteren, 1976) and a psychological desire for a rational order of things[2]. In this context there is no need to be surprised about the persistency of the stages heuristic. If that is the perspective, is the heuristic then suited for the study of the policy process as it is, after all; or should it be adapted?

DeLeon, though an advocate, acknowledges that the negative aspect of the invitation from the stages heuristic to researchers to look at 'just one stage at a time' is the neglect of the policy process as a whole (1999: 23). Furthermore, the heuristic may lead to a view of the policy process as 'disjointed' and 'episodic', taking place in the relatively short term (a key aspect of Sabatier's critique from the point of view of his 'advocacy coalition framework'). Besides, the picture of stages inappropriately implies a certain linearity to many, instead of 'feedback actions and recursive loops' (Ibid.). Also, when one takes the stages heuristic as a general map for the analysis of policy processes, as indicated above, it potentially gives rise to some misunderstandings that may have consequences for research findings.

First, the picture of stages seems *to reify the scope of each separate stage*. This conflicts with a view taken for a long while, and particularly since Lipsky's seminal work (1980), that policy making goes on even at the street-level. While, in fact, there is nothing implicit to the stages

model which denies that policy making goes on at later stages, nevertheless this is the implication of its casual or uncritical use. It may, indeed, be 'implementation'; but it could also be ongoing 'policy formation'. While it may have been originally inherent to the stages heuristic that there was a fixed, *a priori* localisation of specific stages to certain administrative layers, this empirically needs not be the case. Second, related to this problem is what has been designated as 'the fallacy of the wrong layer' (Hill and Hupe, 2003). If at a 'lower' layer the stage of 'policy formation' *de facto* can be observed, this must not be seen as implying a judgement about the legitimacy of that participation in the policy process. The latter is a normative question that should be distinguished from the empirical observation. The stages heuristic seems to imply for each stage *a specific, presupposed set of actors*, a third methodological limitation. Where empirical and normative matters thus are confused, one may fall into a pitfall which could be called the 'control trap' (Hill and Hupe, 2003).

Our position is that the stages heuristic is rooted in the logically defensible assumption that decisions are followed by actions, which require a cumulative process if anything is to occur at all. But such a view does not preclude the idea that there will be subsequent decisions that may undermine the original one. Then does this imply a need to abandon the stages notion or to use it with care?

Despite his criticism of the stages heuristic Sabatier observes 'Given the staggering complexity of the policy process, the analyst *must* find some way of simplifying the situation in order to have any chance of understanding it' (1999: 4). Parsons sees the value of the stages heuristic to cope with 'multi-framed activity' (1995: 80), but at the same time underlines the necessity to look beyond it towards

the mapping of the wider contexts of problems, social process, values and institutions within which policy-making and policy analysis (take) place (p. 81).

Hence he argues

Given the existence of a complex policy reality framed by a range of theories, models, explanations, values and ideologies, the problem is not with the policy cycle [stages may be substituted in this context – the authors] *per se*, as with the need to incorporate or include models and approaches which are or may be deployed in policy analysis (Parsons, 1995: 81).

In other words, given the need for a relatively 'empty' framework general enough to comprise multiple theoretical approaches, Parsons sees a remaining function for the, perhaps amended, stages heuristic.

On the basis of this overview we suggest the following criteria for a 'framework' as a 'general map'. First, the latter must have the capacity to encompass conceptually the 'multiple multiplicity' character of public policy processes. This involves both a variety of actors and very often a variety of administrative layers, and horizontally linked organisations. The scholarly analysis of these uses a variety of disciplinary perspectives, 'lenses', and focuses specifically on various parts of the policy process. Second, a 'general map' or framework must enable specified ('localised') theory formation around selected sets of variables, rather than compel the building of one grand theory. Third, while the first criterion requires the framework to be as comprehensive as possible, it at the same time needs to be open in the empirical sense. Rather than implying a 'managerialist' or 'top-down' view of the policy process (Parsons, 1995: 81), a general framework for analysis must facilitate systematic and normatively open empirical research.

Assessing the stages heuristic according to these criteria we may conclude that it has difficulty in meeting the first and third criteria. DeLeon's reference to the way in which it has facilitated some classic pieces of research indicates that it meets the second one. Overall, we may characterise the stages heuristic as a multidimensional framework for the analysis of policy processes, of which not all relevant dimensions have been articulated. Can we build on it to produce a more helpful overarching framework?

Alternative analytical frameworks as 'general maps'

Though the stages heuristic seems a widely used general framework for the study of the policy process, some alternatives have been developed. We will look at these here. But in doing so, it is important to recognise that in some respects these still involve a 'stages' perspective, albeit a modified one.

Lynn (1981: 146–9; 1987) uses the concept of 'nested games' to assign the various parts of the policy process. There is the 'high game', in which it is decided whether or not a policy will be made. Then, in the 'middle game', the direction of the policy is determined. The 'low game' is about the practical side of the policy making; implementation is central here.

Parsons (1995: xvii) distinguishes 'three broad and overlapping levels or dimensions of analysis'. Each of those 'may be seen through a variety of different frameworks and approaches' (p. 82). The way in which issues and problems are defined and policy agendas are set Parsons calls 'meso-analysis'. As a level of analysis cutting through the various phases of the policy process, it is 'meso' because it:

> explores approaches which link the input side of the policy-making process with the policy/decision-making and output process focusing on the relationship between the 'pre-decisional' dimensions of policy-making and its decisional and post-decisional contexts (Parsons, 1995: 82).

The analysis of 'how decisions are taken and policies are made and how analysis is used within the decision-making process' Parsons calls 'decision analysis' (p. 82). Then 'delivery analysis' refers to 'how policies are administered, managed, implemented, evaluated and terminated' (p. 82).

Finally, there is the 'institutional analysis and development' (IAD) framework developed by Elinor Ostrom and her colleagues, presented as such for the first time in 1982 by her and Larry Kiser. Stemming from micro-institutional analysis Kiser and Ostrom (1982: 184) specify three related but distinct levels of analysis.

> The *operational level*, which explains the world of action. The *collective choice level*, which explains the world of 'authoritative decision-making'. The third is the *constitutional level*, explaining 'the design of collective choice mechanisms' (p. 184). It may be noted that these are listed in the original formulation in an order that reverses the conventional order of the stages model.
>
> Individuals at the operational level 'either take direct action or adopt a strategy for future actions, depending on expected contingencies.' They are often 'authorized to take a wide variety of actions at this level without prior agreement with other individuals' (pp. 207–8).

Collective decisions are made 'by officials (including citizens acting as officials) to determine, enforce, continue, or alter actions authorized within institutional arrangements'. These collective decisions are plans for future action. 'Unlike individual strategies, collective decisions are enforceable against nonconforming individuals … The authority to impose sanctions is a key attribute of the collective choice level of decision-making' (p. 208).

On the third level 'Constitutional decisions are collective choices about rules governing future collective decisions to authorize actions. Constitutional choices, in other words, are decisions about decision rules' (p. 208).

In the framework institutional arrangements are 'linking each level of decision making to the next level. Constitutional decisions establish institutional arrangements and their enforcement for collective choice. Collective decisions, in turn, establish institutional arrangements and their enforcement for individual action' (p. 209).

In this framework it is only at the operational level where an action in the physical world flows directly from a decision.

In an updated discussion of the framework, Ostrom (1999: 36–9) elaborates some 'key difficulties' in the study of institutions. They involve the multiple meanings of the term institution, the invisibility of institutions, the multiplicity of inputs coming from various disciplines and the corresponding need to develop a specific 'language', and the configuration character of relationships. An additional matter Ostrom mentions is the multiplicity of levels of analysis. Particularly important here is the analytical treatment of the nested structure of the framework (1999: 38–9).

Further to these ways of specifying a framework for policy analysis we think there is room for an additional framework as another alternative for the stages heuristic, driven by the aim of all three but particularly inspired conceptually by Ostrom's framework. In our view for that purpose some amending of that framework is necessary. Specifically, there is a need to make an explicit link with the concept of 'governance'.

4.   THE POLICY PROCESS AS MULTIPLE GOVERNANCE

Governance

Various authors have given definitions of the concept of 'governance'. Richards and Smith, for instance, say:

Governance 'is a descriptive label that is used to highlight the changing nature of the policy process in recent decades. In particular, it sensitizes us to the ever-increasing variety of terrains and actors involved in the making of public policy. Thus, it demands that we consider all the actors and locations beyond the "core executive" involved in the policy making process' (2002: 3).

While for Milward and Provan

'Governance (…) is concerned with creating the conditions for ordered rules and collective action, often including agents in the private and nonprofits sectors, as well as within the public sector. The essence of governance is its focus on governing mechanisms – grants, contracts, agreements – that do not rest solely on the authority and sanctions of government' (1999: 3; for other definitions see also Kooiman, ed., 1993; 1999; 2003; Pierre and Peters, 2000; Heinrich and Lynn, eds, 2000; Lynn et al., 2001).

A contribution towards developing a governance perspective to the study of policy processes, founding and grounding their conceptualisation in relation to the state of the art of implementation theory and research, was made by Hill and Hupe (2002). What follows in this section is partly based on that but offers a further elaboration of the insights presented there. The concept of governance is designed 'to incorporate a more complete understanding of the multiple levels of action and kinds of variables that can be expected to influence performance' (O'Toole, 2000: 276). That makes the concept well suited to incorporation into a general framework for the multi-dimensional analysis of policy processes. Thus, such analysis can be seen as 'governance research' (see Heinrich and Lynn, eds, 2000; Lynn et al., 2001). Hill and Hupe (2002: 15) sketch the consequences of that. First, a clear distinction is made between the *how* and the *what* of scholarly attention. Focusing upon *governing* as action, rather than as *government* as institution, leaves empirically open who is the acting actor (may be a public, may be a private one). Second, differentiating between administrative layers is important. Third, the act of management is taken seriously; in principle it can be observed in all the loci of political-societal relations. Therefore levels of analysis have to be specified.

Summarising, the stucture of a policy process can be seen as consisting of various elements: actors, sets of activities, action situations, and layers. Each concept will be elaborated here.

Actors

Ostrom's definitions of an actor ('a single individual or a group functioning as a corporate actor') and of action ('those human behaviors to which the acting individual attaches a subjective and instrumental meaning') cannot be improved (1999: 43). Taking the concept of governance seriously means that the answer to the question who is the 'governing actor' is empirically open. This implies that the number and legitimacy of actors actually involved in a particular policy process may differ from what on normative grounds may be expected.

Action levels

Taking our lead from Kiser and Ostrom's (1982) 'three worlds of action', outlined above, we see the policy process as governance as consisting of three broad sets of activities that we call *constitutive*, *directive* and *operational* governance. The notion of *constitutive governance* derives from Kiser and Ostrom's notion of constitutional choice, which they define as the framing of rules that 'affect operational activities and their effects in determining who is eligible' together with rules 'to be used in crafting the set of collective-choice rules that in turn affect the set of operational rules' (Ostrom, 1999: 59). This somewhat ambiguous formulation, defined elsewhere, as noted above, as 'decisions about decision rules' seems to embrace both fundamental decisions about the content of policy and about the organizational arrangements for its delivery. This distinction is important; for example, a major policy innovation in the field of health care delivery will contain both rules on who is to be entitled to new health benefits together with rules about how those benefits are to be delivered. In that respect it may be a bit misleading to speak of 'constitutional choice', directing the reader's attention to the latter when that has little significance without the former. Hence our preference for the term 'constitutive'[3].

The direction in *directive governance*, our alternative to Kiser and Ostrom's 'collective choice', stands for the formulation of and decision making about collectively desired outcomes. Facilitating the conditions for the realisation of these situations belongs to this part of governance. *Operational governance* concerns the actual managing of that realisation process.

Respectively these three action levels refer to structure-oriented, content-oriented, and process-oriented sets of activities. Ostrom's illustration of a shift of action levels is worthwhile quoting here.

> (W)hen a 'boss' says to an 'employee', 'How about changing the way we do X?' and the two discuss options and jointly agree upon a better way, they have shifted from taking actions *within* previously established rules to making decisions *about* the rules structuring future actions (Ostrom, 1999: 47).

In the terminology of the Multiple Governance Framework presented in this chapter, what is at stake here is a shift from the level of operational governance to the level of directive governance. Speaking of 'a policy (or collective–choice) tier' (Ibid.: 41) and even of 'policy-making (or governance)' (Ibid.: 59), it looks as if Ostrom, though only casually, unintendedly anticipates the kind of explicit policy process-as-governance conception proposed in this chapter. At one place she calls policy subsystems 'multiple linked action arenas at all three levels of analysis' (Ibid.: 58). What Ostrom then states about the nested character of her framework also goes – of course with an amended terminology – for ours. Ostrom thus specifies the way institutional rules (a central concept in the substance of her framework) cumulatively affect the actions taken and outcomes obtained in any setting.

Though the centrality of the concept of 'rules' is specific, the working of the nesting mechanism could not be better pictured, and is very similar to the consequences of the nested character of the Multiple Governance Framework. Schlager (1999: 238) interprets this as follows: '(T)he rules-in-use that structure the operational level originate from the other two levels'. In the same paragraph she concludes: 'Although the analyst can choose to keep the analysis focused on a single level, the other two levels are always implicitly included'.

Table 1.1   *The Multiple Governance Framework*

	Action levels		
Scale of action situations	Constitutive Governance	Directive Governance	Operational Governance
System	Institutional design	General rule setting	Managing trajectories
Organisation	Designing contextual relations	Context maintenance	Managing relations
Individual	Developing professional norms	Situation bound rule application	Managing contacts

Adaptation of: Hill and Hupe, 2002, p. 183.

Action situations

The three sets of activities generally distinguished above as action levels get a specific form dependent on the locus observed. When we speak of 'locus' our definition is comparable to (though perhaps less refined than) the one Ostrom gives of her concept 'action situation':

> An analytic concept that enables an analyst to isolate the immediate structure affecting a process of interest to the analyst for the purpose of explaining regularities in human actions and results, and potentially to reform them (Ostrom, 1999: 43).

Empirically, both the number of acting actors and that of the potential action situations in which they act – as Elinor Ostrom has pointed out – can be thought of as infinite. Since the latter category does not coincide with the former, can a usable taxonomy be devised? Here, too, a threefold distinction can be made: irrespective of the kind of formal administrative layer looked at, an actor there can be seen performing specific activities in action situations on a scale that can vary from action of and between individuals (in practice called 'the street-level'), via action of and between organisations, to action on the system-scale. This varying degree of aggregation can be labelled in a summarising way as, respectively, the locus of the Individual, of the Organisation, and of the System.

Administrative layers

Going 'downwards' in a system of vertical public administration, a policy process encounters a range of actors and loci as action situations. Within that empirical range as a specific assembly of such actors and actor situations

normatively cut out are one or more layers. The term 'layers' refers to a specific kind of action locations: the formal, legitimate political-administrative institutions, including representative organs, with certain territorial competences. While the term 'locus' concerns action situations in political–societal relations designated in the threefold aggregated distinction mentioned above, it refers to a series of spots on a line of vertical public administration from which 'real' actors participate in a particular policy process. Related to each other in a nested configuration, like Russian dolls, both the number of real persons actually involved in a given policy process and the variety of action situations in which they act, usually is larger than implied by the specific formal administrative layer. When we examine the latter we are (only) looking at legitimate constitutional settings within a specific political-administrative system, while the study of the policy process needs a broader perspective on relevant variables.

We call this 'the Multiple Governance Framework'. Its nested character implies that, conceptually, one action level is not necessarily confined to one administrative layer. Whether, for instance, in a given policy process at the layer of local government just 'implementation' or rather 'policy co-formation' is practised, is, to begin with, an empirical question, resting upon an interpretation of the extent of change. Drawing the line between goal setting and goal realisation seems at stake here. Any judgement about whether the specific empirically observed action is desirable is a normative matter. Similarly, there are various acts of 'operational governance' – consisting of managing trajectories, managing inter-organisational relations, and managing external and internal

Table 1.2   *Alternative general analytical frameworks for the study of the policy process*

Nested games *Lynn (1981)*	Institutional rational choice *Kiser and Ostrom* *(1982; Ostrom, 1999)*	Multiple stages *(Parsons, 1995)*	Multiple governance *(Hill and Hupe, 2002)*
High game	Constitutional level	Meso analysis	Constitutive governance
Middle game	Collective choice level	Decision analysis	Directive governance
Low game	Operational level	Delivery analysis	Operational governance

contacts – which can be regarded as sublevels of action and are not confined to one specific layer of government. Thus, the connections between actors, acts and action spots are of an empirical instead of an *a priori* nature. Rather than supposing them, they are to be investigated[4].

Positioning the framework

We acknowledge that the Multiple Governance Framework as presented here is partly intellectually derivative from the IAD-framework. At the same time, however, there are some major differences that amount to more than the terminological amendments and justify the development of a separate framework. First, the framework links the study of the policy process explicitly with the concept of governance. Essential to this is the shared focus on action rather than (only) on institutions in the traditional-legalistic sense of the word; the combination of a 'vertical' and 'horizontal' orientation; the stress on specifying levels of analysis and on distinguishing empirical from normative matters. Second, a specific characteristic of the framework outlined here is the localisation of the various governance activities, in the variety of action situations within a range of political-societal relations. The general 'employee' of Elinor Ostrom becomes, for instance, a street-level bureaucrat, may be a fire officer, while his or her 'boss' may be the head of the local Fire Brigade. Third, the Multiple Governance Framework draws the micro-economically rooted assumptions of the IAD-framework into mainstream social science, making links with the classical scholarly

themes of public administration. Thus, a framework has been devised which is particularly suitable for the study of the policy process. Fourth, Ostrom's formulation has a strong institutional emphasis whilst, as we pointed out above to explain our adaptation of the concept of 'constitutional choice', we see 'content' issues in respect of policy innovations as of great importance in structuring subsequent decisions.

We set out in Table 1.2 our categories to describe levels of analysis, comparing them with some of the alternative approaches.

5.   THE USE OF THE MULTIPLE GOVERNANCE FRAMEWORK

When we leave the concept of actors aside the singularity of the notion of stages has been differentiated into three concepts: action levels, action situations and layers in a politico-administrative system. If a stages perspective were adopted each of them might be seen to designate alternative approaches to exploring the development of policy. Indeed, the more simplistic approaches to the stages perspective go further to equate and confuse these three concepts. Our approach instead is to suggest that, while of course what we have called nesting occurs, one cannot presume either any explicit uni-directional progress through the designated categories or a taken for granted equation between successive levels, loci and layers. In a given situation one may hypothesize that either or both of these relationships do occur, and accordingly test whether this is true. Furthermore, and this is a particular source of confusion in many discussions of public administration, one may encounter views, often strongly held, that the supposed relationships *should* occur.

By using a matrix form any reference of verticalisation seems to have been avoided. And yet, despite the grid character, even this framework could be read in a 'stagist' way. Such reading would imply that constitutive governance establishes the structural dimensions, that directive governance determines the detailed contents and that operational governance is concerned with the process side of public policies. Readers may react to this, saying that this is indeed what they would expect to find. But if they do so, are they providing a hypothesis, or a statement about what they *should* find?

This question highlights the relationship between the various activities in a policy process taking place at different moments, at different spots, by different actors. Leaving aside the empirical question about who are the acting actors on one hand, and the similar question which administrative layer is looked at, on the other, the framework as pictured in Table 1.1 in the boxes, shows the kind of activities that may occur as a result of specified action level/action situation combinations. Could it, indeed, be, that an activity cluster ('stage'), identified here as one specific level of action and usually associated with one particular layer, along the line of vertical administration, is going on not only (legitimately or not) practised by actors at other layers but in a variety of action situations as well? It is then crucial, repeating our key observations about hypotheses and 'ought' statements, to recognise both that there is great variation in the extent to which these activities as a result of certain action level/action situation combinations do occur and that there can be debate about the extent to which policy outputs *should* be affected by these activities. Clear examples of this can be found in controversies about the determination of health or education policy. Reality in these systems will, we hypothesize (following our own recommendation for caution in this respect), be a combination of an explicitly and not easily amended system, conveying certain expectations of the system as a whole, together with locally determined management arrangements and rules affecting discretion at the street-level. But not only is there likely to be great variation around these themes, there will also be controversy about the appropriateness or inappropriateness of the structuring involved. The latter will take the form of arguments about professional prerogatives and about the rights of patients, pupils and parents to influence the system. Such arguments will not be merely about discretion at the street-level but also about the adequateness of 'prior' structuring decisions.

Hence, we suggest, our alternative analytical framework offers two contributions to the study of the policy process while avoiding the methodological limitations of the stages heuristic. We set these two out below: enhancing 'localised' theory formation and helping the identification of action possibilities.

Enabling contextual theory formation

The primary function of the Multiple Governance Framework is to provide a conceptual (meta-) basis for contextual theory-building in the study of the policy process. At a meta-level it designates organising concepts that enable the formation of specific low- or middle range theories of a more 'localised', in the sense of locus-related, character. Like DeLeon (1999: 29), Hill and Hupe (2003) advise against reaching for a 'grand unifying theory'. Rather, we suggest that for mainstream comparative-empirical research projects it is desirable to look at a subject at one administrative layer and no more than two action levels at a time. After all, in the study of the policy process, many more hypotheses have been formulated than tested.

In the specification of a research question the framework guides the selection of variables. Looking at the dependent variables used in policy research so far it is possible to distinguish the aim of explaining:

- policy change within a given political system;
- adoption of a policy or set of policies;
- variation in policy outputs or outcomes (Sabatier, ed., 1999).

The framework provides flexibility to choose the appropriate unit of analysis. On the side of the independent variables, too, the Multiple Governance Framework offers a way of structuring these rather than prescribing what they should be. O'Toole's (1986) scan of the implementation literature suggested a massive list of variables, attracting the criticism that here is a subject in need of parsimony (see Matland, 1995; also Meier, 1999). The identification of the framework within which action may occur brings this list down to a limited range; Hill and Hupe (2002: 123) have suggested about seven categories of independent variables[5]. This narrower range makes it possible to select a small number of variables thought relevant to the research question at hand.

Aiding the identification of action choices

A great deal of the implementation literature has been preoccupied with a normative argument between 'top-down' and 'bottom-up' perspectives. Both stem from deeply held views about democratic accountability. Faced with what they regard as defects in the implementation process both perspectives concern themselves with efforts to increase the capacity to steer the policy processes, either from the top or the bottom. By contrast, an analytical perspective that recognises that influencing the policy process can involve adjustments to a complex nested system of levels, loci and layers, may help actors to identify alternatives for action. Those with a strong top-down perspective may be assisted by recognising that they have choices between fundamental restructuring, the adjustment of specific arrangements, or new ways of curbing street-level discretion. Conversely, from a bottom-up perspective there will be questions about whether what is crucial is to devise new ways of making street-level decisions, or whether there are institutional and/or structural modifications that would need to be made before these would be feasible.

Between those strong ideological positions many will, following Day and Klein (1987),

argue that public policy processes need to be able to hold in tension multiple 'accountabilities'. In this respect, as in the cases of public policy for health and education mentioned above, it may be important to try to develop policies so that they follow complex pathways across the items in Table 1.1. The issues about how, and by whom, the overall structure and funding should be determined may differ from those about local arrangements for policy delivery, whilst each again may differ from the concerns about the discretionary behaviour of practitioners. All are connected, but there are many options about how those connections may be made: this goes for policy research as well as in policy practise.

6.   CONCLUSIONS

Hardly any other insight from public administration or political science has been so generally adopted by practitioners as the so-called stages model of the policy process. This seems to exemplify Lasswell's stress on the extended scope of what he called the 'policy orientation', going beyond the borders of science. The idea of policy making as proceeding in successive stages influenced Pressman and Wildavsky in formulating their 'chain' hypothesis, implying the likelihood of 'implementation gaps' (Bowen, 1982). By consequence it invited the kind of 'misery research' we mentioned above. The stages notion is an important element in a broader conception of public policy that is both persistent and, in empirical research, to a certain extent misleading. That it is persistent has to do, as we have shown, with three factors. First, the conception is normatively attractive because it has been founded on the principles of democracy and the trias politica. Second, it appeals to what Van Gunsteren (1976) describes as a general quest for control in public affairs. Third, the orderly neatness of particularly the stages notion seems psychologically attractive.

At the same time, especially inasmuch as this conception of public policy points automatically to the 'black box' of the implementation of a specific policy as 'explaining' why the results of that policy are judged as disappointing or worse, it is misleading. In this respect this conception may keep away from open and systematic research into what has happened, how and why. This 'control trap' seems to lay at the basis of much of the failure discourse around public policy processes. It is particularly this restricted explanatory power that forms the heart of the criticisms frequently expressed with regard to the stages 'model'.

We accept the case for the stages heuristic functioning as a general map for the analysis of policy processes. As such it is a very general map – not a 'model' and certainly not a causal 'theory' – that has been used to good effect in some classic policy studies. At the same time, according to the standards of a moderate positivism in social science, it is conceptually neither multi-dimensional nor empirically open enough to enable and enhance systematic theoretical-empirical research in the study of the policy process. Given the varied landscape of the study of the policy process, our stance is that such research is both necessary and possible.

Therefore, building further upon Elinor Ostrom's Institutional Analysis and Development framework, we have linked that framework into the mainstream of the politics-and-administration focused policy sciences connecting it to an explicit governance orientation. As such the Multiple Governance Framework has a multidimensional as well as a nested character. It provides organising concepts that can assist low- or middle-range theory formation and systematic empirical research with a 'localised' character. Among other things this means that one level of action, such as the 'stage' of implementation, is not seen as *a priori* confined to one administrative layer.

The framework presented here does not break altogether with the concerns of the many scholars who have recognised the logical 'nesting' or 'institutional pathways' affecting many decision processes. In that respect it can still be said to embody an idea of stages, though a loose one. When the framework is put forward as a conceptual device to assist with the framing of subsequent theoretical-empirical

studies, empirical questions about its validity are to be answered. Apart from enabling contextual theory formation we have indicated that it may aid contextual reflection by practitioners. Furthermore, the Multiple Governance Framework may also fulfil institutional functions; one could think of a research programmatic use or a function as a map for public agendas. In fact, the framework is designed to combine two essential tasks: one within social science, and one in a broader societal context. The first task is providing what Ostrom (1999: 41) calls a 'multi-tier conceptual map'. The other task goes beyond that: to function as a multiple heuristic in an institutional sense. Then, after all, we are back again with the essence of Lasswell's 'policy orientation'; double bound as it is.

NOTES

1. Following up *Implementing Public Policy* that Michael Hill and Peter Hupe published in 2002, this chapter elaborates on some of the insights developed in that book. The major work on it was done during a stay of the latter as a visiting fellow, March and April 2003, at the Public Management Institute, Katholieke Universiteit Leuven. He thanks Geert Bouckaert, the director of the Institute, and Rudolf Maes for their generosity. Wim Hafkamp, the Dean of the School of Social Sciences, Erasmus University Rotterdam, and Victor Bekkers and Jan Hakvoort, of the Department of Public Administration, are thanked for their support of Peter Hupe's two months stay in Leuven.

On the 10th of June 2003 Peter Hupe presented a draft of this chapter in the *Centre for Public Governance*, research group of the Department of Public Administration, Erasmus University Rotterdam. He thanks the participants in that session, particularly Menno Fenger, for their comments. On a later version comments were given by Elinor Ostrom and George Frederickson, which were highly appreciated by the authors.

2. It is against this background that we could formulate the *implementation follows formulation and decision theorem*. This says nothing about who and where, but is a matter of logic (Hill and Hupe, 2002: 4).

3. Originally (Hill and Hupe, 2002) we used the term 'constitutional governance' here. Now we think the possible reference to 'the constitution' – though not intended – may make the connotation of this term too fixed and formal. Essential is the general notion of the Latin verb 'constituere': forming, building, designing. Therefore we propose here, instead, to speak of *constitutive governance*.

4. Acknowledging two things seems appropriate here. First, the labels used in this chapter purposely are made

more 'empty' or abstract than in the book (2002) version. Aiming at maximal analytical applicability, in the designation of the dimensions of the analytical framework any connotation with real world epitheta (cf. 'street-level') has been avoided. Eliminating connotations with real layers within the framework makes the latter more applicable in research, in principle, at any layer. Second, at the same time the nested character is reconfirmed: the distinguished loci and actors can be observed at each empirical layer in the real world of public administration, formal or not.

5. On the basis of an updated extensive literature scan Hill and Hupe (2002: 123) identified seven categories of independent variables seen as having an impact on the results of policy processes. These categories are the following: a) variables dealing with policy characteristics; b) variables on the policy formation sub process; c) variables about the kind of 'vertical public administration' concerned (number of layers; their legitimate competence, actual relationships, etc.); d) variables regarding the response from implementers to the policy involved; e) variables dealing with the horizontal inter-organizational relationships; f) variables on the response from those affected by the policy, and g) variables regarding the configuration of wider macro-environmental factors.

REFERENCES

Anderson, J.E. (1975) *Public Policy-making*. New York: Holt, Praeger.

Baumgartner, F.R. and B.D. Jones (1993) *Agendas and Instability in American Politics*. Chicago: University of Chicago Press.

Bowen, E.R. (1982) 'The Pressman-Wildavsky paradox'. *Journal of Public Policy*, 2 (1): 1–21.

Brewer, G.D. (1974) 'The policy sciences emerge: To nurture and structure a discipline'. *Policy Sciences*, 5 (3) (September): 239–44.

Brewer, G.D. and P. DeLeon (1983) *The Foundation of Policy Analysis*. Monterey, California: Brooks/Cole.

Cohen, M.D., March, J.G. and Olsen, J.P. (1972) 'A garbage can model of organizational choice', *Administrative Science Quarterly*, 17 (1): 1–25.

Day, P. and R. Klein (1987) *Accountabilities*. London: Tavistock.

Davies, H.T.O., S.M. Nutley and P.C. Smith (eds.) (2000) *What Works?* Bristol: Policy Press.

DeLeon, P. (1999) The Stages Approach to the Policy Process: What Has it Done? Where Is It Going? in: P.A. Sabatier (ed.) (1999) *Theories of the Policy Process*. Boulder, Colorado: Westview Press, 19–32.

Derthick, M. (1972) *New Towns in Town: Why a Federal Program Failed*. Washington, D.C.: Urban Institute.

Dewey, J. (1927) *The Public and its Problems*. New York: Holt.

Dror, Y. (1989) *Public Policymaking Reexamined*, second edition (first edition: 1968). New Brunswick, N.J.: Transaction Publishers.

Fischer, F. (1995) *Evaluating Public Policy*. Chicago: Nelson Hall.

Fischer, F. (2003) *Reframing Public Policy*, Oxford: Oxford University Press.

Fox, C.J. and H.T. Miller (1995) *Postmodern Public Administration: Towards Discourse*. Thousand Oaks Calif.: Sage.

Frederickson, H.G. and K.B. Smith (2003) *The Public Administration Theory Primer*. Boulder, Colorado: Westview Press.

Graaf, H., van de and R. Hoppe (1989) *Beleid en politiek*. Bussum: Coutinho.

Gunsteren, H.R. van (1976) *The Quest for Control: A Critique of the Rational Central Rule-Approach in Public Affairs*. London: John Wiley and Sons.

Gunsteren, H.R. van (1980) 'Planning in de verzorgingsstaat: Van chaotisch naar systematisch falen' in J.K.M. Gevers and R.J. in 't Veld (eds.), *Planning als maatschappelijke vormgeving* Deventer: Van Loghum Slaterus: 15–32.

Heinrich, C.J. and L.E. Lynn, Jr (eds.) (2000) *Governance and Performance; New Perspectives*. Washington, D.C.: Georgetown University Press.

Hill, M.J. and P.L. Hupe (2002) *Implementing Public Policy: Governance in Theory and Practice*. London: Sage.

Hill, M.J. and P.L. Hupe (2003) 'The multi-layer problem in implementation research'. *Public Management Review*, 5 (4): 469–488.

Hogwood, B.W. and L. Gunn (1984) *Policy Analysis for the Real World*. Oxford: Oxford University Press.

Hoogerwerf, A. (ed.) (1978) *Overheidsbeleid: Een inleiding in de beleidswetenschap*. Alphen aan den Rijn: Samsom.

Howlett, M. and M. Ramesh (2003) *Studying Public Policy: Policy Cycles and Policy Subsystems*. Second edition, Ontario: Oxford University Press.

Jenkins, W.I. (1978) *Policy Analysis: A Political and Organisational Perspective*. London: Martin Robertson.

Jenkins-Smith, H. and P.A. Sabatier (1993) 'The study of the public policy process' in P.A. Sabatier and H.C. Jenkins-Smith (eds.) (1993) *Policy Change and Learning: An Advocacy Coalition Approach*. Boulder, Colorado: Westview Press.

John, P. (1998) *Analysing Public Policy*. London: Pinter.

Jones, Ch. (1970) *An Introduction to the Study of Public Policy* (first edition). Belmont, California: Wadsworth.

Kingdon, J.D. (1995) *Agendas, Alternatives and Public Policies* (second edition). Boston: Little, Brown and Company.

Kiser, L.L. and E. Ostrom (1982) 'The Three Worlds of Action: A Metatheoretical Synthesis of Institutional Approaches' in E. Ostrom (ed.) (1982) *Strategies of Political Inquiry*. Beverly Hills, California: Sage.

Kooiman, J. (ed.) (1993) *Modern Governance: New Government-Society Interactions*. London: Sage.

Kooiman, J. (1999) 'Social-Political Governance: Overview, Reflections and Design', *Public Management (Review)*, 1 (1): 67–92.

Kooiman, J. (2003) *Governing as Governance*. London: Sage.

Kuypers, G. (1980) *Beginselen van beleidsontwikkeling* (two volumes). Muiderberg: Coutinho.

Lasswell, H.D. (1951a) 'The policy orientation' in Lerner, D. and H.D. Laswell (eds.) (1951) *The Policy Sciences*. Stanford, California: Stanford University Press.

Lasswell, H.D. (1951b) 'Democratic character' in *The Political Writings of Harold D. Lasswell*. Glencoe, Illinois: Free Press.

Lasswell, H.D. (1956) *The Decision Process: Seven Categories of Functional Analysis*. College Park, Maryland: University of Maryland.

Lasswell, H.D. (1968) 'The policy sciences' in *The Encyclopedia of the Social Sciences*, vol. 12. New York: Macmillan/Free Press.

Lasswell, H.D. (1970) 'The emerging conception of the policy sciences'. *Policy Sciences*, 1: 3–14.

Lasswell, H.D. (1971) *A Pre-view of Policy Sciences*. New York: Elsevier.

Linder, S.H. and B.G. Peters (1987) 'A design perspective on policy implementation: The fallacies of misplaced prescription'. *Policy Studies Review*, 6 (3): 459–75.

Lindblom, C.E. (1959) The science of muddling through, *Public Administration Review*, 19: 78–88.

Lindblom, C.E. (1968) *The Policy-making Process*. Englewood Cliffs, N.J.: Prentice-Hall.

Lindblom, C.E. and E.J. Woodhouse (1993) *The Policy-making Process*, third edition. Englewood Cliffs, N.J.: Prentice-Hall.

Lipsky, M. (1980) *Street-level Bureaucracy: Dilemmas of the individual in public services*. New York: Russell Sage Foundation.

Lynn, L.E., Jr (1981) *Managing the Public's Business*. New York: Free Press.

Lynn, L.E., Jr (1987) *Managing Public Policy*. Boston, Mass.: Little, Brown and Company.

Lynn, L.E., Jr, C. Heinrich and C.J. Hill (2001) *Improving Governance: A New Logic for Empirical Research*. Washington DC: Georgetown University Press.

Mack, R. (1971) *Planning and Uncertainty*. New York: John Wiley.

Matland, R.E. (1995) 'Synthesizing the implementation literature: The ambiguity-conflict model of policy implementation', *Journal of Public Administration Research and Theory*, 5 (2): 145–74.

May, J. and A.B. Wildavsky (eds.) (1978) *The Policy Cycle*. Beverly Hills, California: Sage Publications.

Meier, K.J. (1999) 'Are we sure Lasswell did it this way? Lester, Goggin and implementation research', *Policy Currents*, 9 (1): 5–8.

Milward, H.B. and K.G. Provan (1999) 'How networks are governed', unpublished paper.

Nakamura, R. (1987) 'The textbook policy process and implementation research'. *Policy Studies Review*, 7 (2) (Autumn): 142–54.

Ostrom, E. (1999) 'Institutional Rational Choice: An Assessment of the Institutional Analysis and Development Framework' in P.A. Sabatier (ed.) (1999) *Theories of the Policy Process*. Boulder, Colorado: Westview Press, 35–71.

O'Toole, L.J., Jr (1986) 'Policy recommendations for multi-actor implementation: An assessment of the field'. *Journal of Public Policy*, 6 (2): 181–210.

O'Toole, L.J., Jr (2000) 'Research on Policy Implementation: Assessment and Prospects'. *Journal of Public Administration Research and Theory*, 10 (2): 263–88.

Palumbo, D. (1988) *Public Policy in America*. New York: Harcourt, Brace, Jovanovich.

Parsons, W. (1995) *Public Policy: An Introduction to the Theory and Practice of Policy Analysis*. Cheltenham, UK: Edward Elgar.

Perrow, C. (1999) *Normal Accidents: Living with High Risk Technologies*. Princeton: Princeton University Press.

Pierre, J. and B.G. Peters (2000) *Governance, Politics and the State*. New York: St Martin's Press.

Pressman J. and A. Wildavsky (1973, first edition) *Implementation: How Great Expectations Are Dashed in Oakland; Or, Why It's Amazing that Federal Programs Work at All, This Being a Saga of the Economic Development Administration as Told by Two Sympathetic Observers Who seek to Build Morals on a Foundation of Ruined Hopes*. Berkeley: University of California Press.

Richards, D. and M.J. Smith (2002) *Governance and Public Policy in the UK*. Oxford: Oxford University Press.

Rose, R. (1973) 'Comparing public policy: An overview'. *European Journal of Political Research*, 1: 67–94.

Rothstein, B. (1998) *Just Institutions Matter: The Moral and Political Logic of the Universal Welfare State*. Cambridge: Cambridge University Press.

Sabatier, P.A. (1991) 'Towards better theories of the policy process'. *Political Science and Politics*, 24 (2) (June): 147–56.

Sabatier, P.A. (1999) 'The need for better theories' in P.A. Sabatier (ed.) (1999) *Theories of the Policy Process*. Boulder, Colorado: Westview Press, 3–17.

Sabatier, P.A. (ed.) (1999) *Theories of the Policy Process*. Boulder, Colorado: Westview Press.

Sabatier, P.A. and H. Jenkins-Smith (1999) 'The Advocacy Coalition Framework: An Assessment' in P.A. Sabatier (ed.) (1999) *Theories of the Policy Process*. Boulder, Colorado: Westview Press, 117–66.

Schlager, E. (1997) 'A response to Kim Quaile Hill's In Search of Policy Theory', *Policy Currents*, 7 (June): 14–5.

Schlager, E. (1999) 'A Comparison of Frameworks, Theories, and Models of Policy Processes' in P.A. Sabatier (ed.) (1999), *Theories of the Policy Process*. Boulder, Colorado: Westview Press, 233–60.

Selznick, P. (1949) *TVA and the Grass Roots*. Berkeley: University of California Press.

Simon, H.A. (1945) *Administrative Behavior*. First edition. New York: Free Press.

Stone D.A. (1989) 'Causal stories and the formation of policy agendas', *Political Science Quarterly*, 104: 281–300.

Waldo, D. (1946) *The Administrative State: A Study of the Political Theory of American Public Administration*. New York: The Ronald Press Company.

Wilson, W. (1887) 'The study of administration', *Political Science Quarterly*, 2: 197–222.

2

The Policy Sciences: Past, Present, and Future

PETER DELEON AND CHRISTINE R. MARTELL

INTRODUCTION

The Policy Sciences orientation has primarily been attributed to Harold D. Lasswell, writing in the late 1940s and early 1950s, most prominently articulated in his essay 'The Policy Orientation' as the opening chapter to *The Policy Sciences* (1951a; also see Lasswell 1971).[1] The Policy Sciences approach was explicitly focused on the rigorous application of a variety of science endeavors (hence, the plural usage of 'sciences') to issues affecting the processes of governance; along these lines, Lasswell wrote of the knowledge 'in and of' the act of governing; that is, the process and substance of governance (respectively). In addition, there was a clear understanding of the necessity of democratic processes or what he defined as the 'policy sciences of democracy' (e.g., Lasswell 1951b).

Since this time, however, the policy sciences, as both an academic discipline and an applied craft, have experienced a checkered pattern of growth, application, and contraction. This essay will briefly delineate the initial purposes of the policy sciences, indicate their development and frustrations, and offer some areas for potential future growth in light of their past.

THE CONCEPT OF THE POLICY SCIENCES

If the study of public policy and providing advice to policymakers has a relatively short academic lineage, from a practitioner standpoint, it reflects a storied legacy. Rulers have been the recipient of policy advice since at least the recording of history (see Goldhamer 1978 for details); advisers to whomever ruled were rarely lacking for reasons easy to imagine. However, there is a clear distinction between the earlier purveyors of policy advice and what later came to be known as the policy sciences, namely that advisers to rulers rarely relied on extensive policy research nor carefully crafted reports. Their advice, whatever its merits, was usually shaped by their 'power behind the throne' experience. For this reason, policy advisers were invariably members of the royalty or the ruler's personal attendants; there is scant record of laypersons serving in an advisory capacity.[2]

In contrast, the American university at the turn of the 20th century housed a number of disciplinary approaches, such as political science, anthropology, geography, law, psychology, sociology, and public health, that were the natural precursors to the study of public affairs in general and the activities of government in particular. Heineman et al. 2002 (also Fischer 2003) have singled out public administration and political science as progenitors in this particular focus. However, the policy sciences approach and their authors have carefully distinguished themselves from these early disciplinary contributions by offering three defining characteristics of the approach:

1. The policy sciences are explicitly *problem-oriented*, rejecting the study of a specific phenomenon per se; the societal or political question of 'so what' has always been integral to the policy sciences. Likewise, problems occur in particular contexts that must be considered in terms of both the analysis and later recommendations.
2. The policy sciences are distinctively *multidisciplinary* in their intellectual and practical approaches; virtually every social or political problem has components tied to varying academic disciplines without falling clearly into any one discipline's exclusive domain.
3. The policy sciences' approach is explicitly *value oriented*; in many cases, the central theme deals with the democratic ethos and human dignity, thus denying the strictures of logical positivism that were so prevalent in the American social sciences in the 20th century.[3] This value orientation recognizes that no social problem is without a value component. As such, in order to understand a problem, one must acknowledge its value components. Similarly, no policy analyst is without her/his own values, which also must be addressed (Amy 1984; Stone 1998).[4]

The policy sciences have been operationalized as a process delineated in terms of discrete stages in the policy process. The decision process originally proposed by Lasswell (1956),[5] later articulated by Brewer (1974) and, subsequently, Brewer and DeLeon (1983) (also see Anderson 1975/1979 and Jones 1970/1984) includes Policy Initiation, Policy Estimation, Selection, Program Implementation, Program Evaluation, and Policy Termination. Providing a conceptual breakdown of policy formulation and execution, with each stage possessing unique characteristics, the stages approach (referred to as a 'heuristic' by Sabatier 1999 and Fischer 2003) offers a mechanism to achieve a multidisciplinary and value-oriented approach to policy. In practice, however, researchers have broken the stages into disjointed units, as we shall see below, betraying the holistic intent of Lasswell's process and resulting in an implied linear rationality devoid of idea and value (DeLeon 1999).

Paul Sabatier (1993 and 1999), along with Robert Nakamura (1987) and others, have been very critical of the stages process, noting, among other things, that it neglects 'the role of ideas – particularly ideas involving the relatively technical aspects of the policy debates – in policy evolution' (Sabatier 1993: 15). He (and co-author Hank Jenkins-Smith) have severely criticized the policy process framework for its *theoretic* shortcomings, specifically (Jenkins-Smith and Sabatier 1993: 3–4; emphases in original):

-   'The stages model is not really a *causal model at all.*' That is, it did not lend itself to prediction or even how one stage transitioned to another.
-   'The stages model *does not provide a clear basis for empirical hypothesis testing.*' That is, it is not amenable to amendment, confirmation, or verification.
-   'The stages heuristic suffers from *descriptive inaccuracy* in posing a series of stages ...'
-   'The stages metaphor suffers from a built-in *legalistic, top-down focus.*'
-   'The stages metaphor inappropriately *emphasizes the policy cycle as the temporal unit of analysis.*'
-   'The stages metaphor fails to provide a good vehicle for integrating the roles of policy analysis and *policy-oriented learning throughout the public policy process.*'

Many of Sabatier's observations are correct when one views the policy process approach (or what Sabatier labels a 'metaphor' or 'heuristic') but there is little evidence that such a set of criteria was ever intended (DeLeon 1999: 24 and Brunner 1991) or even appropriate. Rather, the stages approach is designed to feature different stages of the policy process, highlighting their distinct functions and features, ranging from Policy Initiation to Policy Termination, and provide the necessary guidelines. For example, different mechanisms attend policy estimation compared to policy implementation. A review of the policy literature over the past forty years indicates that the stages approach has done precisely that (see DeLeon 1999: 22). In that sense, Lasswell's model continues as a beacon, although, as we will see below, the stages' particular roles have been amended by lessons drawn from various political events.

THE APPLICATION OF THE POLICY SCIENCES

Moving the policy sciences from the halls of academe to the offices of government largely occurred on the federal level during the 1960s (see Radin 2000), such that, by the 1980s, virtually every federal office had an analytic office. Since then, many states (including memberships in inter-state consortia, such as the National Conference of State Legislatures) have built up policy analysis shops to the extent budgets permit. In addition, for-hire 'think tanks' of most every political orientation have proliferated. Every public sector official would agree that more information on which to base decisions and policies is better than less. To serve that demand, virtually every university has a graduate program in public affairs (or has re-tooled its public administration program) to fill the apparent need for sophisticated policy analysis. Yet the turn of the 21st century has hardly ushered in a Golden Age of Policy Advice. One needs to ask why policy scientists increasingly voice the perception that their work is not being utilized (Weiss 1980;

Lindblom and Cohen 1979), or, if it is, to what effect or purpose, as David Kirp (1991) talks semi-facetiously (one hopes) about the 'end of policy analysis'? Heineman and his colleagues (2002, 1, 9) speak of this concern:

> … despite the development of sophisticated methods of inquiry, policy analysis has not had a major substantive impact on policymakers. Policy analysts have remained distant from power centers where policy decisions are made…. In this environment, the values of analytical rigor and logic have given way to political necessities.

Radin (2000) provides a counter to these charges of despair, arguing that policy analysis has not only produced excellent and effective policy research but has had a distinct effect on policymaking, although not as much as a proponent would have preferred. And the policy 'market' place would be supportive, in terms of the number of policy analysts employed in a lengthy list of policy agencies.

We need not necessarily agree with all of the claims of the demise of the policy sciences and certainly not the utility of policy research in general. Still, one can assert that the Lasswellian charge for the policy sciences in either application or concept has not been universally realized. Let us take, then, a moment to chronicle the political events that have had a noticeable effect on the policy sciences to better appreciate their evolution.

THE GROWTH OF THE POLICY SCIENCES

In general, two paths have been proposed to outline the development of the policy sciences. Beryl Radin (2000) has characterized the institutional growth of the policy approach, largely relying on the (fictional) histories of an 'old school' economist *cum* policy analyst juxtaposed with a 'younger,' university-trained policy analyst. Through them, she casts an institutional framework on the policy sciences, indicating their march from a limited analytic approach, practiced by relatively few practitioners, to a growing number of government institutions. Specifically, Radin notes the emergence of analytic studies from the RAND Corporation to the US Department of Defense (DoD) in the early

1960s (under the guise of 'systems analysis' and a Programmed Planning and Budget System, PPBS). From its apparent success in the Defense Department, President Lyndon Johnson mandated the government-wide diffusion of PPBS, most visibly in the Department of Health, Education, and Welfare, in the mid-1960s. Although success in the DoD of PPBS's DoD was never duplicated elsewhere (see Wildavsky 1984; Schick 1973), the analysis orientation soon was adopted by a number of federal offices, state agencies, and a number of analytic consultant groups (see Fischer 1993 and Ricci 1984). Thus, Radin views the growth of the policy sciences as a 'growth industry,' in which a few select government agencies first adopted an explicitly innovative analytic approach, others adopted similar approaches, and a corresponding industry developed.

DeLeon (1988) has cast the growth of the policy analysis in a consonant but more complicated manner, in which he ties the growth of specific analytic 'lessons learned' to given political events. In his view, political conditions effectively supplied analysts with particular scenarios and data to which they could turn their skills, thus impressing both their immediate policymaking clients and the larger population, as well with the perspicacity of the approach. In particular, he suggested that the resulting policy initiatives (which he termed 'supply') and policymakers' requirements ('demand') collaborated to define the specific development of the policy sciences. The two, he posits, must be synchronous for a synergistic relationship to develop.

DeLeon (1988) initially set forth five political conditions that articulated the policy sciences: the Second World War; Lyndon Johnson's 'War on Poverty;' America's involvement in the Vietnam War; the 'Watergate Affair' and the ensuing impeachment of President Richard Nixon; and the 1970's Energy Crisis.

During the Second World War, the United States marshaled an unprecedented array of social scientists – economists, political scientists, psychologists, etc. – to support the war effort, ranging from managing the domestic economy to coordinating the strategic bombing campaign. However, after the war, while the 'supply' side of the policy equation was ready, there was little on the 'demand' side. Policymakers, perhaps tired of the wartime exigencies or perhaps enveloped with a return to peacetime 'normalcy,' did not take these newly honed skills into consideration.

Still, these wartime activities established an important illustration of the ability of the social sciences to direct problem-oriented analysis to urgent public issues, in this case assuring victory over the Axis powers. As a point of interest, Lasswell and Kaplan spent the war with the Library of Congress studying how to best utilize (and protect against) propaganda. These realizations led directly to the formation of the National Science Foundation and the Council of Economic Advisors (see Polsby 1984), as well as research facilities such as The RAND Corporation (Smith 1966). Yet, as a result of the imbalance of supply and demand, the policy analytic approach was more or less quiescent until the 1960s, when the assassination of President John Kennedy and the succession of President Lyndon Johnson conspired to declare a War on Poverty.

The policy sciences faced another opportunity to practice their skills during the War on Poverty, namely the need to confront social complexity and identify the central problem, namely, the pervasive poverty – largely fueled by the emerging civil rights demonstrations – afflicting what Harrington (1960) called 'the other America.' Even though poverty had always been a part of the American fabric, US policymakers found that they were remarkably uninformed about the conditions and extent of poverty in America. Social scientists moved aggressively into this knowledge gap with unbridled enthusiasm, if not always relevant insights, producing what Moynihan (1969) called 'maximum feasible misunderstanding.' Policymakers proved to be inherently limited in their views by their unique set of experiences.

To engage the campaign against poverty, a vast (if not necessarily coordinated) number of social programs (Model Cities, VISTA, Headstart, and a host of programs out of the Office of Economic Opportunity, OEO) was initiated, with important milestones being achieved, especially in the improved statistical measures of what constituted poverty and evaluation measures to assess the various anti-poverty programs (Rivlin 1970), but poverty was insistently endemic. Walter Williams (1998), looking back on his days in the OEO, has suggested that these were the 'glory days' of policy analysis. Other OEO veterans, such as Robert Levine (1970), were more reserved, while some, such as Murray (1984), indicated that, with the advent of the anti-poverty programs, the American poor was actually 'losing ground.' At best, policy analysts were forced to confront the immense complexity of the social condition. Later, DeLeon was to ask 'if ten years and billions of dollars had produced any discernible, let alone effective, relief' (DeLeon 1988: 61).

The 'policy lessons' ascribed to the War on Poverty were three-fold. In the first place, the policy sciences were thwarted by policymakers' inability to understand and respond to the complexity of poverty as presented to them. There was an inability to formulate persuasive arguments in the policy initiation stage. Second, policymakers and analysts 'discovered' the vagaries of implementation (see Pressman and Wildavsky 1984 for a particularly cogent example); in retrospect, this 'implementation blinder' could have been foretold by the public administration scholars had they been engaged, but the difficulties encountered eviscerated many programs (see Derthick 1972). Finally, and arguably the most successful learning experience, policymakers learned to demand thorough evaluations of a variety of policy programs, even though, at that time, evaluators were still methodologically naïve; more to the point, however, both parties failed to realize the political nature inherent in these exercises. In effect, policy soldiers in the War on Poverty failed to frame the right questions, account for the factors that affected implementation, and were unable to evaluate the programs with discernment. In short, the War on Poverty served as an annealing agent for policy research.

The disappointment of the policy sciences recurred with the unfortunate experiences in Vietnam from the early 1960s until the early 1970s. The decade-long Vietnam war brought the detached policy analysis instruments, including applied systems analytic techniques, to the intimate horrors of combat, with political conditions exacerbated by the growing domestic civil unrest as to its conduct and, of course, the loss of lives. The war was closely monitored and managed by the Secretary of Defense's office, with close oversight from a succession of presidents. It became increasingly obvious that analytic rigor – specified in terms such as 'body counts,' sorties flown, and hamlets 'pacified' – and 'rational' decisionmaking were not indicative of the growing rancor of the war. There was repeated evidence that 'hard and fast' numbers were being manipulated to serve political purposes. Moreover, systems analysis was not intellectually able to capture analytically the almost daily changes in the war's activities, occurring on both the international and domestic arenas (see Gelb and Betts 1979).

To return to DeLeon's metaphor, during the Vietnam War and its domestic ramifications, the policy 'supply' could not square with the political 'demand.' In terms of policy estimation, systems analysis, one of the apparent US advantages of defense policymaking, was surprisingly myopic and was a partial contributor to the ultimate US failures in Vietnam (Gray 1971). Department of Defense analysts could not reflect the required (and respective) political wills necessary to triumph, as *The Pentagon Papers* (Sheehan 1971) subsequently showed. On the other hand, Frances FitzGerald's *Fire in the Lake* (1972) foretold the inevitable American military disaster, as the North Vietnamese were willing to incur whatever losses were needed in what they saw as the defense of their nation. Even if the war effort itself had been well conducted (surely an arguable point), the manner in which the war was visualized and projected by the analytic community left much to be desired, a shortcoming widely noted in the domestic anti-war community and, ultimately, in policymaking circles.

The policy sciences learned that, in spite of the best analysis, good policy analysis is inseparable from values. The events surrounding the re-election of President Richard Nixon in 1968, his Administration's heavy-handed attempts to 'cover up' the incriminating evidence, and his willingness to covertly prosecute Vietnam war protester Daniel Ellsberg, combined to lead the Congress to the potential impeachment of a sitting American, averted only because the President chose to resign in ignominy rather than face certain impeachment proceedings (Olson, 2003). The overwhelming evidence of foul play in the highest councils of the US government brought home the idea that moral norms and values were central to the activities of government. The Ethics in Government Act (1978) was only the most manifest recognition that normative standards were central to governance processes, validating, as it were, one of the central tenets of the policy sciences. Regardless, however, few will ever forget the President of the United States protesting, 'I am not a crook,' and its effect of the public's trust in its elected government.

The energy crises of the 1970s provided a virtual test bed for the best analytic efforts the country could offer. Partially as a result of an Arab boycott on petroleum production, record-high gasoline prices spiraled throughout the nation. As a result, the public was inundated with analyses and formulae regarding the level of petroleum reserves (domestic and world-wide), competing energy sources (e.g., nuclear vs. petroleum vs. coal) over differing (projected) time frames, with a backdrop of threatened national security. With this plethora of technical data, the analytic community was seemingly prepared to bring light out of the darkness (for example, see Landsberg 1972). But, this was not to be the case; as Weyant was later to note, 'perhaps as many as two-thirds of the [energy] models failed to achieve their avowed purposes in the form of direct application to policy problems' (quoted in Weyant 1980: 212). Aaron Wildavsky and Ellen Tannenbaum (1981) poignantly referred to this period as 'the politics of mistrust.' Faced with a chorus of demands to 'fix the problem,' the research community was unable to provide an acceptable supply.

The contrast was both remarkable and apparent: Energy policy was awash in technical considerations (e.g., untapped petroleum reserves and complex technical modeling; see Commoner 1979 and Greenberger et al. 1984) but the basic decisions were decidedly political (that is, *not* driven by analysis), as President Nixon declared 'Project Independence,' President Carter intoned that energy independence represented the 'moral equivalency of war,' and President Ford created a new Department of Energy. Policy estimation was particularly found to be lacking, partially because of the inherent technical demand of the problem, but also because of the imputed political positions implied by the various energy options. There was seemingly a convergence between 'analytic supply' and 'government demand,' yet no policy consensus was forthcoming, a condition that did little to enshrine the policy sciences approach with either its immediate clients (government officials) or its ultimate ones (the citizenry). The experience of the energy crisis highlighted the lack of negotiation and resolution.

Since DeLeon (1988) first posed that these historical events shaped the development of the policy sciences, there have been two additional 'events' that, arguably, have been equally definitive: The impeachment of President Bill Clinton (in the late 1990s); and the horrific terrorist attacks on the United States in September 2001, with the subsequent decisions by President George W. Bush to declare war on world-wide terrorist movements, and, in keeping with this charge, to go to war against Afghanistan and Iraq. Without pretending to offer exhaustive histories of these actions (indeed, the latter is on-going and, as such, impossible to put into perspective), let us indicate their broad outlines and effects.[6]

The policy sciences approach was seemingly well represented in the Clinton White House as President Clinton was widely (and glowingly) acknowledged to be the presidential prototype of a 'policy wonk' (Woodward 1994). But, as events transpired over the course of his Presidency, politics, pure and simple, trumped analysis during the administration, as partisan agenda and personal norms assumed more importance than policy development. For whatever reasons, President Bill Clinton was a political lightning rod, an almost constant target of personal calumny, from the day of his inauguration in 1992 until he left office in January 2000. Minor peccadilloes (like the furor over the so-called White House 'travelgate' incident, in which Clinton staffers bureaucratically hijacked the travel arrangements for the White House press; see Drew 1994), unfortunate tragedies (the suicide of White House Counselor Vincent Foster), and the curse of a few proposals that were downright ill-fated (the Clinton Health Care initiatives; see Skocpal 1997) constantly plagued the Administration. These tended to overshadow some very major successes (e.g., presiding over the reversal of the Federal deficit to a position of surplus) and the continued faith accorded him by the voting public. Taken in combination, they all contributed to a rich political legacy.

Regardless of these political comings and goings, his Administration will mostly be remembered for his intemperate acts with a young White House female intern and his subsequent attempts to hide these acts from the American members of his administration, his own family, and the voting public. Especially in light of his vehement initial denials, Clinton's remarkable parsing concerning the meaning of 'is' and his later admissions of these events will become the unfortunate signature moments of his second term in office.

President Clinton was the first American President in well over 100 years to be brought before the Congress in an act of impeachment. Although he was eventually found by the US Senate to be innocent of the charges leveled for impeachment (see Johnson 2001 and Baker 2001 for particulars), the proceedings were as politically value laden as few events in recent American history. Thus, mirroring in many ways Nixon's Watergate scandal, the impeachment of President Clinton, although conducted under a full canopy of legal proceedings and media attention, was a reminder that moral considerations can dictate seemingly analytic decisions, as Clinton's subsequent autobiography (2004) indicates.

An inherent shortcoming for most policy recommendations has been the inability to prepare for future contingencies, even in the presence of mounting information, due to prior belief preferences and misunderstandings, possibly multiplied by what Janis (1983) earlier labeled 'groupthink.' The September 11th air-borne attacks on New York City and Washington DC, followed shortly thereafter by the subsequent retaliatory American attacks on Afghanistan and (less directly) Iraq, can be viewed in terms of shortcomings in the 'rational' policy advice, representing a failure to presciently see looming disasters and to act accordingly. Thousands of lives were lost, leading citizen to later disagree over whether the intelligence communities should have been able to 'follow the dots' that would have revealed the plans of Al Qaeda. Others have argued whether US spokespersons callously misrepresented (or seriously politicized) the evidence at hand, or, more probably, ignored the possibility that the evidence was sketchy at best (Woodward 2004 and Clarke 2004). Core values once held dearly (e.g., *habeas corpus*) or acknowledged by international conventions (such as the Geneva Conventions regarding prisoner of war treatment) are being challenged as little more than bothersome inconveniences when confronted with possible issues of national survival.

At the very least, the United States finds itself engaged in a second war in the Persian Gulf in a decade with serious loss of life, with goals that are increasingly questioned, restated, and debated. The situation has been exacerbated by the partisanship expected in a presidential election, making an 'objective' reading of the 'facts' more nettlesome than usual. The one clear lesson, however, from this commitment resonates from Vietnam, namely, an understanding of the 'human element,' i.e., nations are more susceptible to being 'liberated,' not 'occupied,' and it is *their* (rather than the CIA or DoD's) reading of the visceral tea leaves that makes the difference. The Selection stage seems especially vulnerable to this episode, as earlier positions seemed to color the evidence at hand. In many ways, policy analysis failed to marshal the evidence that policymakers could have gleaned from past policy failures, suggesting a bigger human challenge to the policy sciences.

These constellations of events have manifested themselves in a worrisome position for the policy sciences, that is, a general disillusion in the way in which the American people view their government and its processes and, as a result, the role of the policy sciences. From the immense national pride that characterized the victory over totalitarian forces in the Second World War, the American voter has suffered a series of on-going disappointments, ranging from what many consider to be a failed War on Poverty to a failed war in Southeast Asia, to the unprecedented (in living memory) attacks on Washington DC and New York City, to the failure of US troops to be treated as 'liberators' in Iraq. Watergate cast a darkening pall on the American body politic; the Clinton Administration did little to dispel those clouds; and President Bush – who was elected in 2000 on a platform of lowering political dissonance in Washington – has not been able to reduce the partisan tensions. Thus, scholars like E.J. Dionne writes *Why Americans Hate Politics* (1991) or Joseph Nye (and colleagues) edit a book *Why Americans Don't Trust Their Government* (1997) disparaging the American body politic and, with it, the policy advice industry. Most damaging to the policy sciences' tradition is Christopher Lasch's pointed and hardly irrelevant question: 'does democracy have a future? ... It isn't a question of whether democracy *can* survive ... [it] is whether democracy *deserves* to survive' (Lasch 1995: 1 and 85; emphases added).

To be sure, political activities are not synonymous with the practice of the policy sciences. But the two indisputably reside in the same policy space. For the policy sciences to meet the goals of improving the processes and results of government through a rigorous application of its central themes, the failures of the body politics naturally must be at least partially ascribed to the policy advice industry, which includes the policy sciences. Historical examples have shown that the supply and demand conditions for the policy sciences are necessary but not sufficient for good policy. Supply and demand for policy analysis needs to be coordinated around the right issue at the right time to the right person/agency. As such,

context *always* matters. And policymakers must be willing to see and accept the products of the policy sciences and their proponents.

Confronting complex problems not only requires a multidisciplinary approach. Many have held that the key to the policy process basically must accommodate a broad understanding with accurate problem framing (Schön and Rein 1994). In spite of a set of strong analytic skills, the policy sciences are inseparable from values, normative concepts, and political ideology. Yet, the policy sciences have not regularly integrated complexity and values with policymaking. One needs to ask: Why should the nominal recipients of the policy sciences subscribe to them if they do not manifest the values and intuitions of the client policymaker? To this question, one needs to add the question of democratic procedures, a tenet virtually everybody would agree upon until the important issues of detail emerge (see DeLeon 1997; Barber 1984; Dahl 1970/1990), e.g., does direct democracy have a realistic place in a representative democracy?

THERE ARE NO EASY ANSWERS

Let us submit the following proposition: that, on face value, the policy sciences approach has inherent strengths, both in 'knowledge of' government (i.e., understanding the processes), and 'knowledge in government' (what they offer policymakers in terms of substance). But what we have seen above is that the juncture of the Lasswellian vision of the policy sciences with workaday policymaking has not been realized, often because the analytic 'supply' has not coincided with the policymaking 'demand.' So how can one best prescribe the policy analytic skills that policymakers request from their advisors and how can the policy sciences best respond with integrity? Inherent in this question is a principal assumption: policy scientists, in the words of Aaron Wildavsky (1979), must 'speak truth to power.' Without access to and trust from policymakers, the policy sciences lose their *sine quo non*. They are, from their earliest iteration, an *applied* discipline; if the policy sciences become irrelevant through lack of application or, to borrow another metaphor, if (policy) advice does not match (political) consent, then the policy sciences will have failed to meet the challenges spelled out by its earliest advocates.

Of course, we should not necessarily abide by a counsel of despair. As policy scientists, we need to recognize that a variety of conditions have changed (witness, for one, the revolution in technologies that directly affect the productivity levels of the American worker) and, moreover, that no one has ever suggested that the policy sciences must remain constant to their original vision; *mutatis mutandis* in terms of context and processes must be part of the policy sciences. In this section, then, let us outline a postpositivist approach to enhance the policy sciences and a few relatively new methodologies and approaches (e.g., social network analysis, participatory policy analysis, and Q-methodology) that the policy sciences might wish to apply to a changing world. But, as we will show, none of these (or the combination) will act as an analytic Rosetta Stone; the policy community, its issues, and its membership are too diverse and, in some cases, oppositional. There are, in short, no easy answers.

Let us first offer a few milestones from which to view the landscape as a means to assess in what ways conditions have changed since Lasswell. The early twenty-first century brings a world that is increasingly interdependent, where regional issues have global reach. Economies and social systems are inextricably connected and interdependent, as transnational economic activities spur local responses; for instance, basically invisible (and all but invulnerable) life forms called 'prions' can result in 'bovine spongiform encephalopathy' (a degenerative and fatal brain disease, or Creutzfeldt-Jacob syndrome in cattle, or what is popularly referred to as 'mad cow' disease), a local event that affects the food supply of nations oceans away, upsetting international commerce and threatening public health regimes. While in general the end of the Cold War has brought a shift from communistic to democratic thought, the realization of these benefits is challenged by issues of ethnic identity, economic instability, environmental degradation, militaristic ideals, and a history and fears of marginalization, or what Samuel Huntington (1996) has referred to a as 'clash of civilizations and the remaking of world order.' The ideological debates between public and private sectors continue, with the relatively new infusion of the nonprofit sector (both nationally and internationally) assuming an increasingly important role in service provision. The resulting process makes it clear that no specific sector has a monopoly on the processes or products of governance. Moreover, the bifurcation of the American body politic along largely partisan lines often makes agreement on specific policy issues problematic.

Postpositivism and the Policy Sciences

The policy sciences community has never been blind to the presence of and competition between competing values, but perhaps values have been under-represented in policy research taken as a whole. This amendment, then, is to find conceptual approaches and tools that accommodate the diversity. To that end, numerous authors (Fischer 1998; Schneider and Ingram 1997; Bobrow and Dryzek 1987; Schön and Rein 1994; Dryzek 1990; Hajer and Wagenaar 2003; Forester 1999) have advanced a postpostivist perspective. Although not universally accepted (see Sabatier 1999 and Lynn 1999), its advantages warrant discussion.

In response to the shortcomings of framing and issue understanding, as well as presenting a more encompassing epistemological perspective, the postpositivist perspective – which includes a variety of differing methodologies, such as 'deliberative' (Forester 1999), policy discourse (Hajer 1993), argumentation (Fischer and Forester 1993), interpretative, and narrative (Roe 1994) – provides a more thorough prescription for dealing with diverse, interconnected, value-laden policy issues.[7] We will deal with two arguments in order, the first being a rejection of the positivist orientation, the second being more constructive (dare we say 'positive'?) in nature.

Regarding the first assessment, Fischer (1998: 143; also see Fischer 2003) provides a model postpositivist rationale when he writes that 'Postpositivism ... not only offer[s] a theory of the social sciences that is identifiable readily in our existing practices, it also constitutes an incorporation of new methods and approaches rather than a simple rejection of old ones.' While empirical or behavioral approaches which have been lumped under a positivist label identify causal relationships as a means of deriving an aggregated, *predictive* relationship, postpositivist approaches identify causal mechanisms as a means *understanding* a relationship (DeLeon 1998). Ann Chin Lin suggests that '[I]nterpretive work reconstructs categories that are organic to the context it studies, and thus is much less likely to be led astray by preconceived notions that stem from inappropriate generalizations' (Lin 1998: 164).

Other authors – Frank Fischer (2003), John Dryzek (1990 and 2000), Ronald Brunner (1991), Maarten Hajer (with Wagenaar 2003) – are more strident in their criticisms and have identified what they describe as serious epistemological shortcomings of the positivist approach, assumptions, and results, offering historical examples that attest to its deficiencies. Dryzek (1990: 4–6) has been particularly outspoken in his assessments of positivism, especially of what he (and others) call 'instrumental rationality,' which he claims,

> destroys the more congenial, spontaneous, egalitarian, and intrinsically meaningful aspects of human association ... represses individuals ... is ineffective when confronted with complex social problems ... makes effective and appropriate policy analysis impossible ... [and, most critically] is antidemocratic.

In a more constructive sense, a postpositivist approach, particularly in terms of 'policy discourse' (see Hajer 1993), provides a more complete understanding of values and relationships (among both organizations and personal perceptions). As we will argue below, the postpositivist orientation is more conductive to the democratic strain in policy research. Just as important, policy discourse is more conducive to understanding the policy process results because research findings 'only have meaning if they have a theory attached to them' (Coleman 1991: 432).

The policy researcher must recognize that not all empirical research is to be discarded in the postpositivist dustbin of policy analysis. An immense corpus of analytic research over the past half-century, as well as highly skilled analysts, have added greatly to our knowledge; in many cases, we should be loathe to relinquish these contributions and to deny them, in Lynn's (1999) words, a 'place at the table.' Edward Lawlor (1996) poses the hard questions that policy scientists need to ask themselves before professionally signing on the any new research orientation: 'What separates the analyst from the journalist or consumer advocate under this new argumentative turn? What separates the policy analyst from literary theorist and critic in the case of narrative policy analysis?' He continues:

> To disconnect policy analysts from their disciplinary roots and charge them with the general communicative functions espoused by the new argumentative school would not only remove 'tools' as a defining feature of the field, it would further undermine the already shaky intellectual identity of the field. Postpositivism and so-called postmodernism in policy analysis is a swamp of ambiguity, relativism, and self-doubt ... creating more problems for the policy analysis business than it solves (Lawlor 1996: 120).

Thus, without abandoning the positivist tools that are appropriate for specific situations – remember, context always counts (see, for example, DeLeon 1998) – let us explore some research tools that move the policy sciences forward in the postpositivist direction.

Social Network Theory, Participatory Policy and Q-Methodology

In response to the shortcomings of complexity, multidisciplinary nature of issues, social network theory offers a conceptual approach for understanding interconnectivity among various actors. In many ways, networks have succeeded governmental units as an appropriate unit of analysis, because, for most, any contemporary policy issue – be it criminal justice, human rights, education, or health care – specific policy problems are attended by social congeries or a network of concerned actors representing the public, private, and nonprofit sectors, working (hopefully but not always) cooperatively towards a consensus resolution. As such, networks reflect interconnectedness among actors, issues, or groups and provide a mechanism to conceptualize the complex relationships among these societal elements (Coleman and Skogstad 1990; Heclo 1978; Rhodes 1990). Castells (1996: 468) summarizes: 'Networks constitute the new social morphology of our societies and the diffusion of network logic substantially modifies the operation and outcomes in processes of production, experience, power, and culture.'

As with other approaches, social network analysis imposes a semblance of order on a chaotic reality. It provides form and identity to relationships and analysis, yet recognizes the dynamic nature of boundaries. Networks strive to address who will participate in which event. That is, whereas other policy analysis approaches tend to focus on the *hierarchical* processes that have characterized the process in the past, a network approach examines the policy process in terms of the *horizontal* relationships that increasingly describe policy issues. As Heclo (1978: 104) notes, 'it is through networks of people who regard each other as knowledgeable, or at least needing to be answered, that public policy issues tend to be refined, evidence debated, and alternative options worked out – though rarely in any controlled, well-organized way.'

To address Sabatier's (1999) criticisms that the stages associated with the policy sciences are disjointed, networks provide a more fluid view of the policy process and the contingent actors, as well as addressing the complexity created by conditions of reciprocal interdependence (Atkinson and Coleman 1992; Scharpf 1990). Hajer and Wagenaar (2003: 13) place network analysis at a key juncture of future policy research when they ask 'what kind of policy analysis might be relevant to understanding governance in the emerging network society.'

While the identification of network actors and relationships is, in and of itself, important, its real value to the policy sciences is the identification of the content (if not the intensity) of relationships. Policy research has paid less

attention to the structural context and content of exchange, in favor of research on transactions. Previous research shows a separation of the connection of networks and the process and outcome variables (Scharpf 1990: 161). Atkinson and Coleman (1992: 160) pose the question: 'Are there relationships of power and dependency that transcend and color individual transactions?' Answers to this and similar questions would go far to build a predictive theory of policy outcomes.

As all theories are refined over time, network theory will continue to be developed. A future research agenda would address some outstanding issues. The first is how policy networks change and how that change affects the policy outcomes, whereby research would address the variables of boundary shifts and inclusion and exclusion (Atkinson and Coleman 1992). In this vein, a similar agendum considers the connections between policy communities and policy networks, where the former represent a variety of actors and potential actors who are interested in the policy issue and share interest and beliefs, though not necessarily concordant, about the policy solution. Policy networks are a subset of policy communities.[8] They are formed on the basis of exchange, of primarily information and resources, and influence and represent the body of actors that interacts regularly (Fischer 2003). Howlett and Rayner (1995) hypothesize that policy change occurs most readily when the policy community and networks are unified.

A second area of study is to understand the ways in which network and community actors develop, ascribe, and share meaning of background assumptions, ideas towards scientific knowledge, and their role of involvement (Fischer 2003). This area is premised on an interpretive community, where knowledge is created not just by the relationships among selected data and variables, but by the interpretation and situational context in which those variables are applied (Innes 1998).

The third deals with the impact of political ideas and theories about policies. Particularly, attention must shift to 'the dominant values guiding public policy, the knowledge base available to policymakers, and the norms that legitimize various approaches to policy'

(Atkinson and Coleman 1992: 174). Norms and values may change over time or differ per actor. As such, 'analysts must seek to ascertain the more general principles and norms underlying interpretation of the policy field' (Atkinson and Coleman 1992: 175).

As a conceptual and methodological tool, networks offer promise. Interestingly enough, the injection needed to remedy and develop this approach is consistent with a postpositivist prescription. The value of postpositivism over positivistic approaches is the ability to discern context, power, and the answer to 'why'. Thus, structural interpretations, change processes, and norms and values of networks can possibly be handled with postpositivist approaches.

Within the policy tool kit should be mechanisms to enhance participatory policy analysis (DeLeon 1997), discourse analysis (Torgerson 2003; Hajer 1993), and policy learning. Fischer (1998: 143) posed the issue directly: 'Holding out the possibility of redeeming or realizing a policy science of democracy, [postpositivism] calls for participatory institutions and practices that open spaces for citizen deliberation on contextual assumptions, empirical outcomes, and the social meaning of conclusions' (also see Fischer 2003). But just how one operationally reaches the saddle point between participation and governing has been a question for eternities. Still, participatory policy at least explicitly addresses the issue. Indeed, Torgerson (2003) makes the argument that increased efforts in participatory policy analysis would narrow the perceived gap between politics and policy, since both parties will be able to address their preferences more openly and deliberatively. A participative approach has the potential to provide better information that may ultimately open the door to broader and more appropriate policy solutions. Thus, a participatory discourse or inquiry allows for decreased conflict, increased trust, multiple viewpoints, and normative interpretations, and portends towards a greater democratic underpinning, along the lines of a 'one person, one vote' direct democracy (Barber 1984).

A participatory approach opens the door to interpretive policy analysis, whereby the artifacts that carry meaning to the policy community are identified and meaning ascribed to the artifacts is discerned for different members of the community so that points of conflict, reflecting different interpretations, can be identified (Fischer 2003; also see Stone 1998). In this way, stakeholders help analysts understand the context of analysis (Durning 1999), in theory, on a more equitable, discursive basis, or what Habermas (1983) refers to as an 'ideal speech situation.' In a complementary basis, Emery Roe (1994) has indicated that 'narrative' policy analyses can examine competing narratives and help frame problems differently, especially in the context of a highly uncertain, charged, or power-laden issue. The methodology places an emphasis on learning from ambiguity, but one needs to carefully extrapolate to other policy situations (Schram 1995).

Still, one needs to caution that deliberative democracy must be treated with the same skepticism that underlies all policy methodology (see Lynn 1999), especially from its proponents. Certainly greater public participation will threaten the extant bureaucracies and their proponents, but the democratic promises of the initiative and referenda have been sorely undercut by highly organized political groups (Broder 2000; Ellis 2002). Torgerson (2003: 119) cautions: 'The institutionalization of a discursive design … has the potential to influence the power context from which it emerges and may … be opposed because of this. Both the feasibility of discursive designs and their co-optive tendencies thus need to be considered in terms of the power relationships found in a particular setting.' Moreover, few would advocate for a policy discourse in which sheer volume and empty rhetoric outweighed deliberation (DeLeon 1997), but the prevalence of that behavior is seen daily in the public media and its effects on the body politic.

Of the postpositivist tools, Q-methodology is consistent with narrative analysis that gets beyond the polarized framing of issues by reframing policy issues in ways not initially perceived, largely by subverting the assumptions of objectivism. The method provides information on public values and positions, providing policy makers with a broader range of policy options (Durning 1999; van Eeten

2001). 'Q-methodology is useful in the prescription context because it can allow a public dialogue to take place regarding values and can then contribute to the stabilization of expectations needed to achieve prescription outcomes' (Steelman and Maguire 1999: 365). Q-methodology identifies patterns of subjective perspectives across individuals. It groups individuals with like views to discern how that subgroup perceives an issue (Durning 1999). Important to its application is to conceptualize the relationship between the policy analyst and the decisionmaker – as consultative or participative – and the stage of the policy process for which information is gathered (Steelman and Maguire 1999; Durning 1999; Roberts 1995; Lasswell 1971). The technique offers policymakers a tool to increase the knowledge base and understanding of a situation's context and meaning. The challenge to Q-methodology will be to aggregate preferences to survive a collective process of deliberation (Lynn 1999).

IN CLOSING …

The policy sciences are unquestionably an approach in transition, but it is not clear what the end point will resemble. The past has been promising in many ways, but the policy sciences have not achieved the prominence in policymaking circles that its early proponents might have wished; in addition, at times, the means to these ends have been problematic. Part of this was due to the policy-defining conditions that have proven to be remarkably complex and analytically unwieldy, a situation only worsened by the wholesale movement of the policy analysis community to economics and behavioralism, or what we have called here 'positivism.' But part of this dyspepsia is that the policy sciences' offerings were consistently not timely nor resonant with the requirement of the policymaking community. Thus, neither the policy advising nor the policymaking communities have been satisfied with the applications of the policy sciences, hardly an encouraging condition.

The history of the policy sciences naturally affects the present day analyst/client relationships. We can further say that a continuation of the status quo will not be to the benefit of either party. The 'promise' then of the policy sciences is that, to gain in stature and acceptance, some important new directions must be grafted to the policy sciences' approach. Moreover, most observers can agree that the policy sciences cannot surrender their dedication to a democratic ethos. As Hajer and Wagenaar (2003: 15) state, 'Whatever we have to say about the nature and foundation of the policy sciences, its litmus test will be that it must 'work' for the everyday reality of modern democracy' (also see Torgerson 2003). Given the three defining characteristics of the policy sciences – problem oriented, multidisciplinary, and normative – we propose that these directions will more clearly articulate the value-orientation vector. It is important that the value component of policy decisions be understood and made more transparent for all concerned.

To these ends, we have suggested ways in which this avenue can be accommodated most readily, through the use of a more ecumenical postpositivist approach, a more participatory set of guidelines, the application of social network analysis, and perhaps a greater use of tools such as Q-methodology for specific purposes. The common denominator among these approaches is that all encourage a less reductionist, more democratic voice in the policy process. These will not come particularly easy, as they require skill sets somewhat different from those currently practiced. For instance, participatory policy analysis requires a certain adroitness at group processes and mediation.

We would not want to suggest that these are the only new avenues for the policy sciences to consider; surely there is a world of alternatives to ponder. However, we do wish to make the point that, if the policy sciences are to legitimately aspire to their original claims, featuring 'knowledge of and knowledge in' government, then the 'same old same old' will only lead to the marginalization of the policy sciences, a fate Lasswell and succeeding generations of policy scientists *and* policymakers can only regret.

NOTES

1. The attribution is not universal. Beryl Radin (2000) traces the development of policy analysis with Yehezkel Dror (see Dror 1971) as the principal early contributor to the field.

2. An anecdote to this effect. In 1707, a fleet of British ships of the line was returning to England; during a particularly foggy night, a seaman, who knew the area, suggested to the British admiral that the fleet was approaching dangerous shoals. The seaman was immediately hung for his impertinence; shortly thereafter, the fleet was destroyed when it ran aground of the shoals and thousands of lives were lost (Sobel 1995).

3. Lasswell and Kaplan (1950, xii and xxiv) dedicate the policy sciences to provide the 'intelligence pertinent to the integration of values realized by and embodied in interpersonal relations,' which 'prizes not the glory of a depersonalized state of the efficiency of a social mechanism, but human dignity and the realization of human capabilities.'

4. A moment should be set aside to distinguish 'policy analysis' from the 'policy sciences.' Many (e.g., Radin 2000, Dunn 1981, and Heineman et al. 2002) reference the former. DeLeon (1988: 9) indicated that 'Policy analysis is the most noted derivative and application of the tools and methodologies of the policy sciences' approach.' For the purposes of this essay, the terms are largely interchangeable.

5. Lasswell's original stages are intelligence, promotion, prescription, invocation, application, termination, and appraisal (1956).

6. Nor is this to suggest that there have not been other significant political events, such as the complete collapse of Communism in 1989, the 1996 Welfare Reform Act, or the globalization/telecommunication phenomena.

7. Fischer (2003), among others, has used the terms 'postpositivism,' 'postmodernism,' and 'postempiricism' as synonyms. In this essay, we will use the first as a collective term.

8. For more work on policy subsystems, see Milward and Walmsley (1984).

REFERENCES

Amy, Douglas J. (1984). 'Why Policy Analysis and Ethics are Incompatible.' *Journal of Policy Analysis and Management.* Vol. 3, No. 4 (Summer). Pp. 573–591.

Anderson, James E. (1975/1979). *Public Policy Making.* New York: Holt, Rinehard, and Winston. 2nd edition.

Atkinson, Michael M. and William D. Coleman (1992). 'Policy Networks, Policy Communities and the Problems of Governance.' *Governance: An International Journal of Policy and Administration.* Vol. 5, No. 2. Pp. 154–180.

Baker, Peter (2001). *The Breach: Inside the Impeachment and Trial of William Jefferson Clinton.* New York: Berkeley Books.

Barber, Benjamin (1984). *Strong Democracy: Participatory Politics for a New Age.* Berkeley: University of California Press.

Bobrow, Davis B., and John Dryzek S. (1987). *Policy Analysis by Design.* Pittsburgh, PA: University of Pittsburgh Press.

Brewer, Garry D. (1974). 'The Policy Sciences Emerge: To Nurture and Structure a Discipline.' *Policy Sciences.* Vol. 5, No. 3. Pp. 239–244.

——, and Peter DeLeon (1983). *The Foundations of Policy Analysis.* Belmont, CA: Wadsworth Publishing.

Broder, David S. (2000). *Democracy Derailed: The Initiative Movement and Power of Money.* New York: Harcourt.

Brunner, Ronald D. (1991). 'The Policy Movement as a Policy Problem.' *Policy Sciences.* Vol. 24, No. 1 (February). Pp. 295–331.

Castells, Manuel (1996). *The Rise of the Network Society.* Oxford: Blackwell.

Clarke, Richard A. (2004). *Against All Enemies.* New York: The Free Press.

Clinton, Bill (2004). *My Life.* New York: Alfred A. Knopf.

Coleman, David A. (1991). 'Policy Research—Who Needs It?' *Governance: An International Journal of Policy and Administration.* Vol. 4, No. 4. Pp. 420–455.

Coleman, William D. and Grace Skogstad (1990). 'Policy Communities and Policy Networks: A Structural Approach.' In William D. Coleman and Grace Skogstad (eds.), *Policy Communities and Public Policy in Canada.* Toronto: Copp Clark Pitman.

Commoner, Barry (1979). *The Politics of Energy.* New York: Alfred A. Knopf.

Dahl, Robert A. (1970/1999). *After the Revolution.* New Haven, CT: Yale University Press.

DeLeon, Peter (1988). *Advice and Consent: The Development of the Policy Sciences.* New York: Russell Sage Foundation.

—— (1997). *Democracy and the Policy Sciences.* Albany NY: SUNY Press.

—— (1998). 'Models of Policy Discourse: Insights vs. Prediction.' *Policy Studies Journal.* Vol. 26, No. 1 (Spring). Pp. 147–161.

—— (1999). 'The Stages Approach to the Policy Process: What Has it Done? Where Is it Going?' In Paul A. Sabatier (ed.), *Theories of the Policy Process.* Boulder, CO: Westview Press.

Derthick, Martha (1972). *New Towns In-Town.* Washington DC: The Urban Institute.

Dionne, E.J. (1991). *Why Americans Hate Politics.* New York: Simon & Schuster.

Dunn, William N. (1981). *Public Policy Analysis.* Englewood Cliffs, NJ: Prentice-Hall.

Durning, Dan (1999). 'The transition from traditional to postpositivist policy analysis: A role for Q-methodology.' *Journal of Policy Analysis and Management*. Vol. 18, No. 33. Pp. 389–410.

Drew, Elizabeth (1994). *On the Edge: The Clinton Presidency*. New York: Simon & Schuster/ Touchstone.

Dror, Yezekhel (1971). *Design for the Policy Sciences*. New York: American Elsevier.

Dryzek, John S. (1990). *Discursive Democracy: Politics, Policy, and Political Science*. Cambridge, UK: Cambridge University Press.

—— (2000). *Deliberative Democracy and Beyond*. Oxford, UK: Oxford University Press.

Ellis, Richard J. (2002). *Democratic Delusions: The Initiative Process in America*. Lawrence: University of Kansas Press.

Fischer, Frank (1993). 'Policy Discourse and the Politics of Washington Think Tanks.' In Frank Fischer and John Forester (eds.), *The Argumentative Turn in Policy Analysis and Planning*. Durham, NC: Duke University Press. Pp. 21–42.

—— (1998). 'Beyond Empiricism: Policy Inquiry in Postpositivist Perspective.' *Policy Sciences Journal*. Vol. 26, No. 1 (Spring). Pp. 129–146.

—— (2003). *Reframing Public Policy*. Oxford: Oxford University Press.

—— and John Forester (eds.) (1993). *The Argumentative Turn in Policy Analysis and Planning*. Durham, NC: Duke University Press.

FitzGerald, Frances (1972). *Fire in the Lake*. Boston: Little, Brown.

Forester, John (1999). *The Deliberative Practitioner: Encouraging Participative Planning Processes*. Cambridge, MA: The MIT Press.

Gelb, Leslie, with Richard K. Betts (1979). *The Irony of Vietnam: The System Worked*. Washington DC: The Brookings Institution.

Goldhamer, Herbert (1978). *The Adviser*. New York: American Elsevier.

Gray, Colin (1971). 'What Has Rand Wrought?' *Foreign Policy*. No. 4 (Fall). Pp. 111–129.

Greenberger, Martin, Garry D. Brewer, and Thomas Schelling (1984). *Caught Unawares: The Energy Decade in Retrospect*. Cambridge, MA: Ballinger.

Habermas, Jürgen (1983). *The Theory of Communicative Action: Reasons and the Rationalization of Society*. Thomas McCarthy (Trans.). Boston: Beacon Press.

Hajer, Maarten A. (1993). 'Discourse Coalitions and the Institutionalization of Practice: The Case of Acid Rain in Great Britain.' In Frank Fischer and John Forester (eds.), *The Argumentative Turn in Policy Analysis and Planning*. Durham, NC: Duke University Press. Pp. 43–76.

Hajer, Maarten A., and Hendrik Wagenaar (2003). 'Introduction.' In Maarten A. Hajer and Hendrik Wagenaar (eds.), *Deliberative Policy Analysis: Understanding Governance in the Network Society*. Cambridge, NY: Cambridge University Press. Pp. 1–33.

Hajer, Maarten A., and Hendrik Wagenaar (eds.) (2003) *Deliberative Policy Analysis: Understanding Governance in the Network Society*. Cambridge, NY: Cambridge University Press.

Harrington, Michael (1960). *The Other America: Poverty in the United States*. New York: Penguin.

Heclo, Hugh (1978). 'Issue Networks and the Executive Establishment.' In *The American Political System*, Anthony King (ed.). Washington: American Enterprise Institute.

Heineman, Robert A., William T. Bluhm, Steven A. Peterson, and Edward N. Kearny (2002). *The World of the Policy Analyst*. Chatham, NJ: Chatham House Publishers. Third Edition.

Howlett, Michael and Jeremy Rayner (1995). 'Do ideas matter? Policy network configurations and resistance to policy change in the Canadian forest sector.' *Canadian Public Administration*. Vol. 38, No. 3. Pp. 382–410.

Huntington, Samuel P. (1996). *The Clash of Civilizations and the Remaking of World Order*. New York: Simon & Schuster.

Innes, Judith J. (1998). 'Information on Communicative Planning.' *Journal of the American Planning Association*, Vol. 64, No. 1. Pp. 52–63.

Janis, Irving (1983). *GroupThink*. Boston: Houghton Mifflin. 2nd Edition.

Jones, Charles (1970/1984). *An Introduction to the Study of Public Policy*. Belmont, CA: Wadsworth. 3rd Edition.

Jenkins-Smith, Hank C., and Paul A. Sabatier (1993). 'The Study of the Policy Process.' In Paul A. Sabatier and Hank C. Jenkins-Smith (eds.), *Policy Change and Learning*. Boulder, CO: Westview Press. Chap. 1.

Johnson, Hayes (2001). *The Best of Times: America in the Clinton Years*. New York: Harcourt.

Kirp, David L. (1991). 'The End of Policy Analysis: With Apologies to Daniel (*The End of Ideology*) and Frank (The End of History) Fukuyama.' *Journal of Policy Analysis and Management*. Vol. 11, No. 4 (Fall). Pp. 693–696.

Landsberg, Hans (1979). *Energy: The Next Twenty Years*. Cambridge: Ballinger for Resources for the Future.

Lasch, Christopher (1995). *The Revolt of the Elites and the Betrayal of Democracy*. New York: W.W. Norton.

Lasswell, Harold D. (1951a). 'The Policy Orientation.' In Daniel Lerner and Harold D. Lasswell (eds.), *The Policy Sciences*. Palo Alto, CA: Stanford University Press. Chap. 1.

—— (1951b). *The World Revolution of Our Time: A Framework for Basic Policy Research*. Palo Alto, CA: Stanford University Press. Reprinted in Harold D. Lasswell and Daniel Lerner (eds.), *World Revolutionary Elites*. Cambridge, MA: The MIT Press 1965. Chap. 2.

—— (1956). *The Decision Process*. College Park: University of Maryland Press.

—— (1971). *A Pre-View of Policy Sciences*. New York: American Elsevier.

—— and Abraham Kaplan (1950*). Power and Society*. New Haven, CT: Yale University Press.

Lawlor, Edward F. (1996). 'Book Review.' *Journal of Policy Analysis and Management*. Vol. 15, No. 1 (Winter). Pp. 110–121.

Levine, Robert A. (1970). *The Poor Ye Need Not Have With You: Lessons from the War on Poverty*. Cambridge, MA: The MIT Press.

Lin, Ann Chih (1998). 'Bridging Positivist and Interpretivist Approaches to Qualitative Methods.' *Policy Studies Journal*. Vol. 26, No. 1 (Spring). Pp. 162–180.

Lindblom, Charles E. and David K. Cohen, (1979). *Usable Knowledge: Social Science and Social Problem Solving*. New Haven: Yale University Press.

Lynn, Laurence E., Jr. (1999). 'A Place at the Table: Policy Analysis, Its Postpositive Critics, and the Future of Practice.' *Journal of Policy Analysis and Management*. Vol. 16, No. 3 (Summer). Pp. 411–425.

Milward, H. Brinton and Gary L. Walmsley (1984). 'Policy Subsystems, Networks and the Tools of Public Management.' In R. Eyestone (ed.), *Public Policy Formation*. Greenwich, CT: JAI Press.

Moynihan, Daniel P. (1969). *Maximum Feasible Misunderstanding: Community Action in the War on Poverty*. New York: The Free Press.

Murray, Charles (1984). *Losing Ground*. New York: BasicBooks.

Nakaruma, Robert (1987). 'The Textbook Polic Process and Implementation Research.' *Policy Studies Research*. Vol 7, No. 2 (Autumn). Pp. 142–154.

Nye, Joseph S., Jr., Philip D. Zelikow, and David C. King (1997) (eds.). *Why People Don't Trust Government*. Cambridge, MA: Harvard University Press.

Olson, Keith W. (2003). *Watergate: The Presidential Scandal that Shook America*. Lawrence, KS: The University Press of Kansas.

Polsby, Nelson W. (1984). *Political Innovation in America*. New Haven: Yale University Press.

Pressman, Jeffrey, and Aaron Wildavsky (1984). *Implementation*, Berkeley: University of California Press. 3rd Edition.

Radin, Beryl A. (2000). *Beyond Machiavelli: Policy Analysis Comes of Age*. Washington, DC: Georgetown University Press.

Rhodes, R.A.W. (1990).'Policy Networks: A British Perspective.' *Journal of Theoretical Politics*. Vol. 2. Pp. 293–317.

Ricci, David M. (1984). *The Transformation of American Politics: The New Washington and the Rise of Think Tanks*. New Haven, CT: Yale University Press.

Rivlin, Alice M. (1970). *Systematic Thinking for Social Action*. Washington DC: The Brookings Institution.

Roberts, R. (1995). 'Public Involvement: From Consultation to Participation.' In F. Vanclay and D.A. Bronstein (eds.). *Environmental and Social Impact Assessment*. New York: John Wiley & Sons.

Roe, Emery (1994). *Narrative Policy Analysis*. Durham, NC: Duke University Press.

Sabatier, Paul A. (1993). 'Policy Change over a Decade or More.' In Paul A. Sabatier and Hank C. Jenkins-Smith (eds.), *Policy Change and Learning*. Boulder, CO: Westview Press. Chap. 2.

—— (ed.) (1999). *Theories of the Policy Process*. Boulder, CO: Westview Press.

——, and Hank C. Jenkins-Smith (eds.) (1993). *Policy Change and Learning*. Boulder, CO: Westview Press.

Scharpf, Fritz (1990). 'Games Real Actors Could Play: The Problem of Connectedness.' Köln: Max-Planck-Institute für Gesellschaftsforschung, Paper 90/8.

Schick, Allen (1973). 'A Death in the Bureaucracy: The Demise of Federal PPB.' *Public Administration Review*. Vol. 33, No. 2 (March/April). Pp. 146–156.

Schneider, Anne Larason and Helen Ingram (1997). Policy Design for Democracy. Lawrence, KS: University of Kansas.

Schön, Donald and Martin Rein (1994). *Frame Reflection*. New York, NY: Basic Books.

Schram, Stanford F. (1995). 'Against Policy Analysis: Critical Reason and Poststructural Resistance.' *Policy Sciences*. Vol. 28, No. 4 (November). Pp. 375–384.

Sckopal, Theda (1997). *Boomerang: Health Care Reform and the Turn Against Government*. New York: W.W. Norton.

Sheehan, Neil (1971). *The Pentagon Papers*. New York: Bantam and the *New York Times*.

Smith, Bruce L.R. (1966). *The RAND Corporation*. Cambridge, MA: Harvard University Press.

Sobel, Dava (1995). *Longitude*. New York: Walker and Co.

Steelman, Toddi A. and Lynn A. Maguire (1999). 'Understanding Participant Perspectives: Q-Methodology in National Forest Management.'

Journal of Policy Analysis and Management. Vol. 16, No. 3 (Summer). Pp. 361–388.

Stone, Deborah (1998). *Policy Paradox.* New York: Norton.

Torgerson, Douglas (2003). 'Democracy through Policy Discourse.' In Maarten A. Hajer and Hendrik Wagenaar (eds.), *Deliberative Policy Analysis: Understanding Governance in the Network Society.* Cambridge: Cambridge University Press. Chap 4.

van Eeten, Michel J. G. (2001). 'Recasting Intractable Policy Issues: The Wider Implications of The Netherlands Civil Aviation Controversy.' *Journal of Policy Analysis and Management,* Vol. 20, No. 3. Pp. 391–414.

Weyant, John P. (1980). 'Quantitative Models in Energy Policy.' *Policy Analysis.* Vol. 6, No. 2 (Spring). Pp. 221–234.

Weiss, Carol H. (1980). 'Knowledge creep and decision accretion.' *Knowledge.* Vol. 1, No. 3. Pp. 341–404.

Wildavsky, Aaron (1979). *Speaking Truth to Power.* Boston: Little, Brown.

—— (1984). *The Politics of the Budgetary Process.* Boston: Little Brown.

——, and Ellen Tanenbaum (1981). *The Politics of Mistrust.* Beverly Hills: Sage.

Williams, Walter (1998). *Honest Numbers and Democracy.* Washington DC: Georgetown University Press.

Woodward, Bob (1994). *The Agenda.* New York: Simon & Schuster.

—— (2004). *Plan of Attack.* New York: Simon & Schuster.

3

Behavioral Rationality and the Policy Processes: Toward A New Model of Organizational Information Processing

BRYAN D. JONES, GRAEME BOUSHEY, AND
SAMUEL WORKMAN

INTRODUCTION

Behind any study of public policy processes is a theory of organizations. Policy is made by organizations, but organizations are made up of interacting human decision-makers. As a consequence, any theory of organizations harbors a theory of individual choice.

This chapter considers the analysis of organizations from the competing perspectives of rational choice theory and bounded rationality. Our essay is divided into four parts. The first section surveys the broad characteristics of these behavioral models in the study of public policy. Although both begin with a common goal of connecting individual choice to macropolitical outcomes, they disagree fundamentally over how *individual* behavior should be understood. Rational choice theory claims analytical rigor and theoretical parsimony, holding that individuals behave *as if* they were pure utility maximizers to deduce patterns of outputs from social systems (Friedman 1953). There is no scientific analysis to support this assumption; it is simply an assumption, presumably validated by its

deductive power. Bounded rationality insists that any model of choice be based in scientific analysis of the cognitive architecture of humans, even if that scientific analysis implies less parsimony.

In the second part, we survey recent empirical assessments of behavioral rationality—how people actually behave in experimental and observational situations where comprehensive rationality makes precise predictions about outcomes. Findings across disciplines of decision making not only point to the theoretical inadequacies of the rational choice framework, but also provide the important tools for constructing more realistic models of human choice.

The third part of this essay examines policy implementation and administration in light of studies of principal-agent dilemmas in organizations to highlight key differences between rational choice theory and bounded rationality. While rational choice theory has evolved to provide a more accurate portrayal of human behavior and preferences (Ostrom 1999a; Ostrom 1999b; Levi 1997), research in this paradigm nonetheless continues to overemphasize the problems of delegation and control in bureaucracy. The obsession with control is symptomatic of the larger pathologies of rational choice theory – the core assumptions of individual utility maximization simply do not capture the complexities of human decision-making. By focusing narrowly on questions generated from the control trap, rational choice theory ignores a wide range of intriguing questions about information processing and policy dynamics in bureaucratic decision-making.

In the final part of this essay, we point toward an information-processing model of the policy process that avoids the obsession with control that permeates rational theories of policymaking. We argue that it is both more scientifically sound and fundamentally more parsimonious than models based on rational choice.

PART I: BOUNDED RATIONALITY AND RATIONAL CHOICE THEORY: AN OVERVIEW

In the behavioral sciences, such as psychology and behavioral biology, the major topic of inquiry is individual behavior. In the social sciences, such as political science and economics, the aim is to understand social systems of interacting individuals. Social scientists need both a model of individual behavior and an understanding of how individuals interact to produce social outcomes, such as those produced by free markets or policymaking processes in government. As a consequence, social scientists cannot dally with the nuances of human behavior that do not impact on the interactions of people in organizations. Any model of individual choice in policymaking processes must be parsimonious, and they must link individual level actions to policymaking outcomes.

The behavioral models of *comprehensive rationality* and *bounded rationality,* which today divide the theories of public policy, were driven by a common desire to improve the rigor of political analysis. Applications of both rational choice theory and bounded rationality in the study of public policy and administration

evolved from the efforts of such diverse theorists as Herbert Simon, Mancur Olson, and Anthony Downs to link individual human decision-making with broader macropolitical outcomes (Simon 1947; Olson 1982; Downs 1957). Although the competing models of rationality disagreed about the fundamental motivations behind individual choice, they were unified in their belief that the processes and policy outcomes be most powerfully understood through exploring the role of individual behavior in collective decision-making. A theory of rationality which anticipated individual choices in the context of the larger political process would present a significant advancement in the study of government – such a set of assumptions would act as a theoretical tool-box that could be used, not only to cut through the complexity of public decision-making, but also to locate areas of conflict within organizations, and potentially predict future political outcomes. Both rational choice theory and bounded rationality pushed the study of public policy away from case studies and atheoretical descriptions of public administration toward a generalized theory of public policy.

Despite these common aims, the theories of rationality are deeply divided over the most basic assumptions of individual choice. Rational choice theory borrows heavily from economic assumptions of individual preferences, and believes that a sufficient behavioral model could be drawn from deductions of an individual's self interested utility maximization. Bounded rationality began as a critique of comprehensive rationality, and grew from an effort to reconcile the reductionist economic assumptions of rational choice with observed psychological constraints on human decision-making. The following sections outline the distinguishing characteristics of both rational choice theory and bounded rationality as applied to the study of public policy. This critique intends not only to cast light on the major differences between the two theories, but also calls attention to exciting empirical findings which we believe are fueling increasing theoretical convergence around a single positive theory of human choice.

COMPREHENSIVE RATIONALITY AND THE THEORY OF POLICY PROCESSES

In recent decades rational choice theory has been widely applied to the study of government. This dominance extends in no small part from the model's theoretical parsimony. Rational choice theorists have explored some of the most complex aspects of politics by making relatively few core assumptions about individual behavior. As in neoclassical economic models, the theory of comprehensive rationality posits that political decision-makers are self-interested utility maximizers who hold stable preferences and objectives, and make strategic decisions to maximize the personal benefits of a given choice. To understand politics at the aggregate level, researchers need only to understand ordered preferences of individual actors who populate a specific institution or political sphere and the formal rules by which these fixed preferences are combined. In this approach, preferences + rules = policy outcomes.

Important distinctions can be drawn between rational choice models in public policy, political science, and economics; however, all rational choice models share common characteristics. First, decision-makers hold stable *ranked* and *ordered* preferences for outcomes. Given three possible alternatives – options A, B, and C, a rational chooser will form clear preferences between each of the three given alternatives. These preferences are transitive, meaning that if an individual prefers option A to B, and prefers option B to C, he also prefers option A to C. Second, a decision-maker possesses necessary *information* to connect choices to outcomes. With this information, individuals then *optimize* when making decisions – they make strategic choices in order to achieve their most preferred outcome. "Thick" rationality adds the assumption of individual *self-interest* in determining preferences. For example – preferences for a higher tax rate to fund public education over a lower overall tax rate suggest that an individual will receive greater personal *utility* for increased funding in public education than from lower taxes. Regardless of the underlying reasons for this preference, rational choice scholars reduce it to a question of self-interest. Their behaviors reflect only their effort to maximize the utility of their choice.

Even the staunchest proponents of rational choice theory regard this characterization of the model as more of an ideal type than a realistic portrayal of human behavior. Decisions made under conditions of complete certainty – when specific strategic choices are known to lead to explicit outcomes – are rarely found in political or economic life. More powerful insights have evolved from rational choice theory when theorists have examined decision-making under *risk* – where a strategy might lead to several different outcomes with known probability, or conditions of *uncertainty* – where outcomes are known but the probabilities associated with those outcomes are not, and must be estimated.

Rational choice theorists use *expected utility theory* to approximate how individuals make calculations that rank alternatives by their *expected value* (under risk or uncertainty) rather than their known value. Under conditions of risk, individuals form strategic preferences probabilistically – they compare the probability that their most preferred outcome will occur against the probability that their less preferred outcome will occur, and both against the cost of making a decision.

It is not enough that individuals calculate the probabilities that outcomes will occur if they take a particular action; they must also calculate the likelihood that their choice will yield the outcome against the probability that their choice will have no bearing on the outcome. Individuals must not only predict the probability that an event will occur, but also the chance that an event would occur without their participation, or that their less preferred outcome would occur in spite of their participation. A classic example is rational voter models, where people are predicted to vote only if their expectation that their vote will make a difference exceeds the marginal cost of voting.

Comprehensive rationality holds great appeal as a model of choice for three basic reasons. First, rational choice promises a parsimonious method for studying complex political behavior. By assuming that actors are singularly motivated to maximize gains available in political decisions, a wide range of considerations that have long complicated the study of political science – social class, partisanship, or cultural values – become peripheral to a decision-maker's preferences. The challenge of rational choice theory is to characterize accurately the payoffs available to political actors in a given arena. A classic example of this approach can be drawn from David Mayhew's study of congressional voting behavior in *Congress: the Electoral Connection*. In his analysis, democratic representation is motivated singularly by a congressman's desire to retain political power (Mayhew 1974). Ideology and policy-making matter only insomuch as they instruct a politician as to where his source of political power is located, and how to make appropriate votes to retain electoral support.

The second advantage of the rational choice method is its broad theoretical generalizability. Unlike descriptive studies of political behavior, the baseline assumptions of rational choice methods are characterized by a 'universalism that reveals generalizable implications beyond those under immediate investigation' (Levi 1997, 20). Deductions from rational choice theory are not specific to a particular time and case, but should offer insights wherever similar conditions can be observed. Mancur Olson argues that 'the persuasiveness of a theory depends not only on how many facts are explained, but also how diverse are the kinds of facts explained'. In Olson's view, the rational choice approach has the double benefit of preserving the parsimony of a theory by removing 'any inessential premises or complexities that ought to be removed from an argument,' while retaining a high degree of explanatory power (Olson 1982: 12–13). Drawing upon a relatively small set of assumptions about human behavior, Olson is able to advance a series of predictions that serve as the basis of a theory of how the formation of interest groups in democratic societies detract economic growth. That democratic nations have sustained high levels of growth, even as interest groups have proliferated, means that Olson's theory was wrong, but

that is not the point. It was clearly and cleanly stated in a generalized manner that facilitated testing against empirical observation.

This leads to the third advantage. The rational choice method is a comparably rigorous approach to the study of political processes. Rational choice researchers derive formal mathematical models from a set of assumptions about individual preferences. These models derive a set of hypotheses of anticipating a specific outcome in politics, and then test them against the self interested behavior of actors put forward in the theoretical assumptions of rational choice theory—in this regard, rational choice hypotheses are verified or falsified. This approach forces researchers to advance well-specified models of political choice. Rational choice models focus only on those most crucial elements of the political process that are necessary to explain outcomes.

Both the simplicity and the promise of theoretical generalizablity have made rational choice theory a popular tool for the study of government. The rational choice approach has been applied to such subfields as organizational behavior (Bendor and Moe 1985; Moe 1984) congress (Mayhew 1974; Arnold 1990), parties and elections (Downs 1967) and collective action problems (Olson 1982). The breadth of this research is suggestive of the theoretical power of the model. By exploring the strategic behavior of self-interested individuals, rational choice theorists have produced a rich and theoretically unified body of research in a discipline once marked by methodological eclecticism.

BOUNDED RATIONALITY AND THE THEORY OF POLICY PROCESSES

Perhaps because rational choice theory takes a decidedly reductionist approach to the study of government—one which is 'willing to sacrifice nuance for generalizability, detail for logic' (Levi 1997: 21)—dissenting researchers have long charged that these sparse assumptions of individual utility maximization distort the complexity of both individual behavior and organizational decision-making. Field researchers complain that observations of individual behavior rarely match the calculating self-interested actor posited in rational choice theory (Brehm and Gates 1997; Lipsky 1980). The behavioral norm of individual utility maximization simply does not seem to reflect accurately the actions of politicians, bureaucrats and voters, whose choices so often seem to be motivated by risk aversion, sense of mission, identity, fairness, or altruism. For these critics, rational choice theory is at best idiosyncratic—applicable only to discrete institutions such as the US congress where political behavior can be safely matched to self-interest (Rockman 2000). At worst rational choice theory is misleading, as it reduces potentially interesting social behavior such as altruism to an individual's self-interest (Monroe 1996).

Researchers who actually study individual decision making find the rational choice approach curious. Cognitive psychologists find the economic assumptions of stable ordered preferences, transitivity, and utility maximization to be a strange abstraction of human decision-making. Findings in psychology indicate that people are poor at forming preferences, generating alternatives, and making decisions (Sniderman et al. 1991; Tetlock 2000; Jones 2001). Studies show that individuals often lack even the most basic tools with which to make informed rational decisions. Preferences and choices are bounded more by emotion and environmental context than by rational analysis (Jones 2001). Research in cognitive psychology makes one wonder how people are able to form preferences or make decisions at all.

Herbert Simon (1947) developed bounded rationality as an effort to reconcile the strict economic assumptions of comprehensive rationality with actual decision-making revealed by the empirical study of organizations. Preferences and choices seemed bounded by cognitive and emotional constraints that interfered with the process of purely rational decision-making. Much like comprehensive rationality, bounded rationality offers an efficient method for moving between individual decisions and organizational outcomes. Bounded rationality retains the hallmarks of a theoretical model—it captures only those aspects of human behavior needed to understand collective decision-making.

As with so many researchers who followed him, Simon noticed that the assumptions of expected utility analysis failed to match his own observations of real world economic decision-making (Simon 1999). Looking at budgeting in Milwaukee, Simon observed that relatively little individual behavior matched 'substantive or objective rationality, that is, behavior that can be adjudged to be optimally adapted to the situation' (Simon 1985, 294). He instead found that the processes of both individual and organizational decision-making were a good deal messier than rational expectations would have us believe. Bureaucratic budgets were often adjusted incrementally, using the prior year's budgeting as a benchmark for future spending needs (Thompson and Green 2001; Simon 1991). Organizational decisions were made more through horse trading and bargaining than a process even remotely resembling fully rational decision-making (Simon 1999). Organizations and individuals proved poor at generating complex alternatives or making trade-offs. Environmental factors, such as issue salience, individual attention, and time constraints, shaped the depth of solution searches in organizations.

Simon (1985) believed the most glaring problem with comprehensive rationality was its focus on outcomes rather than the process of individual decision-making. By ignoring the procedures of choice, rational choice theory blithely accepted that 'rational' outcome emerged from self-interested behavior. Such an approach is especially dangerous when attempting to understand the broader mechanisms of collective policy-making, where the motivations for preference formation and political behavior are at least as important as the outcome itself. Simon (1985: 294) explains:

There is a fundamental difference between substantive and procedural rationality. To deduce substantively, or objectively, rational choice in a given situation, we need to know only the choosing organism's goals and the objective characteristics of the situation. We need know absolutely nothing else about the organism, nor would such information be of any use to us, for it could not affect the objectively rational behavior in any way.

To deduce the procedurally or boundedly rational choice in a situation, we must know the choosing organism's goals, the information and conceptualization it has of the situation, and its abilities to draw inferences from the information it possesses. We need know nothing about the objective situation in which the organism finds itself, except insofar as that situation influences the subjective representation.

Simon argued that a theoretical model oriented toward understanding procedurally or boundedly rational decision-making would provide a more realistic bridge between individual and collective choice. A 'behavioral' model of rationality would take a decidedly scientific and inductive approach to understanding decision-making. In order to make efficient generalizations connecting individual psychological processes to collective political and economic choice, research needed to follow strict scientific guidelines. Underlying theoretical assumptions of human behavior needed to be tested and retested. Those assumptions that were verified through scientific research would be preserved in the scientific model, while others would be modified or abandoned. What bounded rationality lost in parsimony it would gain in accuracy. Unlike the artificial behavioral assumptions of comprehensive rationality, bounded rationality would capture the biological, emotional, and environmental constraints that constrained the procedures of decision-making.

As with rational choice theory, bounded rationality has been widely applied in the study of public policy. While bounded rationalists might emphasize different elements of behavioral model in their research, virtually all research in bounded rationality draws from four core principles: the Principal of Intended Rationality, the Principal of Adaptation, the Principle of Uncertainty and the Principle of Trade-offs (Jones 2003). From these principles, modern researchers have advanced a vigorous research program that explores how both people and institutions behave. As we will see, even though experimental and empirical

research have improved our understanding of the behavioral model of choice, these four central tenets remain largely valid.

The Principle of Intended Rationality

The principle of intentionality suggests that we look at the goal directed behavior of people, and investigate the manner in which their cognitive and emotional constitutions either help or hinder their goal-seeking. This distinguishes bounded rationality from psychological theories, which generally focus only on the limitations of individual choice-makers. While comprehensive rationality assumes single-minded maximization, the principle of intended rationality allows researchers to distinguish between careful cost benefit analysis that closely approximates utility maximizing decision-making, quick decisions based on heuristic cues, unthinking reliance on past strategies, or even spontaneous decisions that seem to make no reference to potential gains or losses. Given the time, costs, and demands of a specific decision, humans may rely on hard-wired biological responses, generalized decision-making strategies, or full information searches. 'Cognitive architecture is most obvious when action occurs at short time scales. As one moves toward actions that take longer times, cognitive architecture is less and less evident, and the nature of the task takes on more and more importance in explaining action' (Jones 2001, 56). Humans may intend to be rational, but their decision-making capabilities break down under time constraints or very high information costs. Moreover, there is no good evidence that people are more rational when the stakes are high, as some rational choice theorists have maintained. In direct defiance of that claim, state lotteries sell more tickets when the pot is large, lowering the probabilities and the expected return.

Principle of Adaptation

The principle of adaptation is closely related to the notion of intentionality. Much of human behavior is explained by the nature of the 'task environment' surrounding a decision. With time, human decision-making adapts to the specific nature of the problems they face in a specific circumstance. The more time and learning an individual invests in a specific problem, the less constrained they become by environmental or biological constraints. This notion of adaptation accounts for changes in decision-making efficiency in a single problem space over time. When a problem is iterated over time, people learn or develop coping strategies. Even more intuitively, the principle of adaptation may explain why organizations encourage specialization in areas of complexity, and routinization in decisions under severe time constraints.

A rich tradition of research in political science and psychology explores the use of heuristics in political decision-making—attempting to identify cost-cutting cues individuals rely upon in order to limit investment costs from making complex decisions in low-information environments. The key issue is whether these heuristics are maximally adaptive (Lupia, McCubbins and Popkin 2000; Gigerenzer et al. 1999). While some have argued that heuristics invariably follow what a fully rational individual would choose, that is quite clearly not the case. 'Buy a lottery ticket when the stakes are high' is a classic heuristic that leads to lower expected returns than not buying at all, or buying when the stakes are low. It is likely that some heuristics are adaptive calculational crutches and some are misleading and even mal-adaptive.

The Principle of Uncertainty

Individuals operate in an environment of almost constant risk and uncertainty. Because of human cognitive architecture, uncertainty is far more fundamental to choice than expected utility theory admits. Not only are individuals unaware of the outcomes that will result from strategic choices, but they are uncertain of the procedures of choice themselves and are even uncertain about their own preferences. Uncertain outcomes may produce dependence on procedures, and may explain instances of extremely risk adverse behavior.

The Principle of Trade-Offs

The final notion central to models of bounded rationality is the principle of trade-offs. Unlike comprehensive rationality, which suggests that individuals are able to move seamlessly between ranked goals, bounded rationalists argue that people find it difficult to trade off one goal against another when forming preferences and making choices (Slovak 1990; Tetlock 2000). This critique is a major shift away from the transitivity assumption in rational choice theory; however it is important to capture the volatile shifts in preferences observed by both behavioral economists (Kahneman and Tversky 1986) and public opinion researchers (Zaller 1992). Preferences are determined by emotional and cognitive cues, and are rarely as stable as rational choice theorists have us believe. Because of these trade-off difficulties, Simon argued that individuals, and by extension organizations, 'satisfice,' quickly choosing an option that is 'good enough' rather than searching for one that weighs the payoff of every possible choice.

Because bounded rationality is concerned with the procedures of individual choice, the school of thought tends to approach the study of politics by looking to how individuals and organizations respond to changes in their problem environments. Because individual decision-makers have limited attention for problem solving, they must address problems serially, one-at-a-time, which means they are forever juggling inputs, prioritizing them via the allocation of attention and the sense of urgency that inputs generate. The salience of a particular problem is almost always generated by non-rational elements in politics—by scandal, by crisis, by the mobilization of critics—rather than calm decision to allocate the scarce resource of attentiveness.

In governments, as well as in all organizations, attention is allocated in a process political scientists call *agenda setting*. Organizations also suffer from limited attention spans, and must process at least major problems serially. Routine problems may be delegated and handled according to rules, but fresh problems cannot be handled this way. It is common for many problems to press forward on the governmental agenda, and whether the most severe problems receive the most attention is an empirical question. In individuals, as well as in organizations, the allocation of decision-making attention is crucial for understanding the immediate and future behavior of an organization.

Because it is explicitly oriented toward understanding the processes of decision-making, bounded rationality has been widely applied to the study of public policy and public administration. Bounded rationalists have explored a range of policy problems, ranging from agenda setting (Kingdon 1995; Baumgartner and Jones 1993), congressional decision-making (Kingdon 1973), federal budgets (Padgett 1980), incrementalism (Wildavsky 1964; Davis, Murray, Dempster and Widalsky 1966) and risk aversion (Kahneman and Tversky 2000). As a model of choice, bounded rationality is at least as broadly applicable as comprehensive rationality.

PART II: BEHAVIORAL DECISION THEORY AND THE SHORTCOMINGS OF RATIONALITY

Concerns over competing models of political choice are by no means limited to researchers in political science. Some of the most hostile critiques of the rational choice model have come from pioneering work by behavioral decision theorists, who have struggled to reconcile the assumptions of the rational calculating economic man with research in cognitive psychology that insists that human decision-making is frequently neither optimizing nor rational. The most intriguing contributions from behavioral decision theory have come from efforts to answer two basic questions about decision-making. First—how do individual preferences respond to changes in the framing or emotional stimuli of the problem? Second—how do game theoretic strategies based on rational choice assumptions compare

to actual human strategies in real world games?

FRAMING EFFECTS AND PUBLIC POLICY

Studies linking framing effects present an especially intriguing challenge to our understanding of rational political behavior. Framing studies have demonstrated that an individual's understanding of a policy idea depends heavily on the context and heuristic cues surrounding a policy problem (Garrett 2003; Jones 1994; Kahneman and Tversky 2000). Rather than holding stable opinions about public policies, individual opinions are volatile, and shift according to the framing of the political issue (Zaller 1992). The relationship between a voter and a policy idea is thus at least partially contingent on the context in which the voter is presented the policy choice. By 'directing attention to one attribute in a complex problem space,' policy entrepreneurs can produce desired changes to public responses to policy problems (Jones 1994, 104). Public receptivity to public policies seems highly responsive to shifts in the framing of a policy problem.

PROSPECT THEORY AND RISKY CHOICE

Daniel Kahneman and Amos Tversky's research in prospect theory provides one interesting framework for understanding how framing effects limit rational behavior. As a response to errors they saw in Bernoulli's expected utility assessment of choice under risk (Kahneman 2002) prospect theory advances a boundedly rational model of risky choice, by focusing on the reference point and framing of decisions rather than the strict utility of 'final asset positions' put forward by rational choice theorists (Kahneman 2002, 460). The approach grew from a series of studies in decision-making that demonstrated how individual preferences were shaped by environmental context. People would hold different preferences for virtually identical decisions based on how the problem was presented. Kahneman explains:

> Preferences appeared to be determined by attitudes to gains and losses, defined relative to a reference point, but Bernoulli's theory and its successors did not incorporate a reference point. We therefore proposed an alternative theory of risk, in which the carriers of utility are gains and losses—changes of wealth rather than states of wealth. Prospect theory (Kahneman and Tversky, 1979) embraces the idea that preferences are reference dependent. (461–462).

Approaching the study of risky choice from the perspective of changes in wealth rather than overall states of wealth, Kahneman and Tversky arrive at the intuitively appealing notion that humans cope with gains and losses differently—that people 'are risk adverse in the domain of gains, and risk seeking in the domain of losses' (Quattrone and Tversky 1988, 723). Prospect theory further demonstrates that people make different choices depending on how decisions are framed—the weights they give in decision-making shift in response to how their attention is directed. 'An individual would prefer a sure gain of $80 over an 85% chance to win $100. The same individual would prefer a gamble offering an 85% chance of losing $100 to a certain loss of $80' (Berejikian 2002, 762.) Although the chance to win $100 is the same as the chance of losing the $100, individuals generally make different choices. In the domain of gains people value certain gains over possible gains. In the domain of losses, people will make riskier decisions in the hopes of avoiding any loss. These findings clearly contradict the tenets of rational choice theory, which would assume that a rational chooser would prefer certain gains or certain losses equally.

In a similar vein, Richard Thaler's research on mental accounting further suggests that individual preferences and expectations are shaped by emotional cues. Basic economic theory suggests that money is *fungible*, that money 'has no labels' and is treated the same way regardless of how it is earned (Thaler 1992, 108). However, Richard Thaler draws a series of hypothetical scenarios to show that the manner in which people *receive* and then psychologically *allocate* the use of money has an important bearing on how the money is perceived and spent. 'The effect on current consumption … of winning the $300 football pool should be the same as having a stock in which I own 100 shares increase by 3 dollars a share, or having the value of my pension increase by $300. The marginal propensity to consume all types of wealth is supposed to be equal' (Thaler 1992, 108–109).

Yet people do not approach the gain of $300 equally. The $300 won in lottery or betting is seen as a sudden windfall, and might be spent with clear conscience on celebration. A sudden $300 increase in the pension plan will be treated with miserly caution, an essential part of a savings account linked to concerns for future financial stability. Although the amount is the same, people *perceive* it differently because it was *accounted for* differently. Money can thus be better thought of as placed in various mental accounts. Money appropriated for one use is spent or saved differently than money appropriated for another (Thaler 1992).

Findings from prospect theory and mental accounts are compelling because they provide empirical evidence that individual decision-making is strongly constrained by framing cues which illicit emotional responses. Unlike the calculating maximizer posited by rational choice theory, 'in real life, generating maximum utility is neither simple nor smooth, and is affected by the cognitive and emotional constitution of the decision maker' (Jones 2001, 26). The strategic choices pursued by individuals may not reflect calculations of optimality, but rather their disposition towards loss aversion or risk acceptance, or even their emotional response to a sudden windfall.

EXPERIMENTAL GAME THEORY

Unlike studies of framing effects, which examine how individual preferences shift in response to external emotional cues, experimental game theory began by asking if people behave in a manner consistent with game theoretic expectations of rational self-interest. To test accurately assumptions of economic choice, individuals must be given clear guidelines and all relevant information with which to form strategic preferences. In spite of this convention, the most popular experimental games have provided mixed evidence at best that individuals behave in a manner consistent with game theoretic assumptions of strategic preferences. Players with full information about the rules and objectives of the game frequently prove themselves to be inefficient in forming game theoretic strategies (Fudenberg and Levine 1997).

By far the most intriguing findings have come from research in the now famous 'divide-the-dollar' games, which captured the imagination of decision theorists exactly because they have failed to substantiate the most basic hypothesis drawn from expected utility theory.[1] In the simplest form of the game, *the ultimatum game*, a proposer and a responder are asked to share a sum of money. The proposer must divide the sum however he sees fit with the responder. Because neither player receives any money if the responder rejects the offer, rational choice theory would lead us to predict that the smallest permissible offers would be made and accepted. The proposer would rationally seek to maximize the monetary gains available in game play, while the responder would prefer even an incremental gain over no gain at all.

Yet mounting evidence suggests that individuals rarely if ever play as pure income maximizers. Proposers frequently offer up to half of the sum being divided, while responders routinely reject offers of under one-third of the total—even when neither player knows the other, and often simply play against a computer (Nowak, Page and Sigmund 2000). Even in the *dictator* form of the divide-the-dollar game, where the responder is required to accept any offer made by the proposer, an impressive 76% of responders chose to divide the money equally (Kahneman, Knetsch and Thaler 1986).

Ultimatum game experiments not only routinely fail to reproduce purely rational utility maximizing behavior in individuals in the lab, but they also provide strong evidence that human decision-making cannot be fit neatly into economic assumptions of comprehensive rationality. Individual trading behavior in ultimatum games has been shown to be highly context-specific. Repeated play games suggest that learning, social interaction, and norms of reciprocity strongly shape ultimatum trading (Nowak, Page and Sigmund 2000; Goeree and Holt 2000). A sense of entitlement seems to shape how a proposer or responder plays the game. Players who *earn* the responsibility of proposer engage in distinctly different trading behavior than those who are simply *designated* the role of proposer (Hoffman and Spitzer 1985). Researchers have demonstrated the influences of culture (Roth et al. 1991; Henrich 2000), and proposer and respondent characteristics such as sex (Solnick 2001) and age (Murnigham and Saxon 1994) in ultimatum trading strategies. Post-game surveys of players suggest that norms of fairness, reciprocity, cooperation, and generosity express themselves strongly, even in single shot anonymous trading.

The brunt of experimental research in divide-the-dollar games has remained narrowly focused, first on revealing the pathologies of comprehensive rationality, and then in revealing altruistic, fair or other 'anomalous' behavior in research subjects. The discussion and conclusion sections of most ultimatum game research almost invariably speculate that evolutionary norms of fairness, cooperation, or rational risk aversion constrain responders from making decidedly one-sided offers. This points to a common complaint of experimental research—it is a powerful critique of one model of rationality, but so far the tradition has done little to generate and test new and scientifically realistic alternatives of choice. Experiments are fantastic devices for testing particular behavioral assumptions, but they are less useful in generating new ones.

Despite these limitations, efforts to replicate assumptions of comprehensive rationality have succeeded in fueling a movement to integrate findings of actual behavior into a more realistic model of human choice. Findings from cognitive psychology, cultural anthropology, political science, and behavioral economics, demonstrate how considerations outside of strategic rationality influence the procedures of individual decision-making. Experts across disciplines increasingly agree that a successful model of human choice must integrate empirical findings about the effects of culture, attention streams and issue salience, emotional cues, framing effects, and identity and social perspective into a parsimonious model of decision-making. This research agenda has led to renewed interest in established theories of decision-making, such as bounded rationality and prospect theory, as well as a wealth of new and modified theories from the rational choice tradition.

RATIONAL RESPONSE: THIN RATIONALITY AND NEW INSTITUTIONALISM

Although a few dogmatic economists and political scientists have continued to conduct research through assumptions of comprehensive rationality, most recent rational choice studies in political science have attempted to integrate empirical findings of individual preferences into renewed models of individual rationality. It is clear that the traditional rational choice assumption of self-interest has failed—that the self-interest axiom cannot explain instances of altruism, ethical restraint, or fairness—has lead an increasing number of theorists to allow maximization for any goal. The analyst refuses to make assumptions about motives for maximization. These steps may complicate the model or limit broad theoretical generalizability; however, the growing evidence documenting inconsistencies between rational choice assumptions and actual human behavior warrants a revision of the theory to include the potential rewards outside of material or status gain. Margaret Levi points out:

> The addition of non-egoistic considerations or motivational norms [as community standards or fairness principles] does increase the complexity and difficulty of analysis... . The advantage of an assumption in which actors consider net payoffs that include both material and ethical factors is that it may better approximate reality albeit at the sacrifice of a neater and more parsimonious model. Nonetheless, as the maximand more closely approximates reality, the more reality it should capture' (Levi 1997, 24–25).

Individual preferences may be modified to capture not only an individual's desire to maximize gains, but an equally strong 'ethical' belief that the individual's behavior harms no other individual's. These rational choice models integrate assumptions of fairness, altruism, reciprocity, justice, etc., into the ordered preferences of their rational actor. The individual continues to hold ordered preferences, and continue to make decisions based on whatever will yield their most preferred outcome. The problem, of course, is that trade-offs among these various goals must be explicitly built into the model, and one of the primary findings of behavioral decision theory centers on the difficulties people have with such trade-offs.

Another hallmark of recent research in rational choice theory has been to give greater attention to the institutions in which political actors make choices. *Institutional Rational Choice Theory* examines how institutions provide specific information about the gains and losses available to actors in a given sphere. Institutional rational choice theory is especially concerned with understanding how organizational cultures permit cooperation in places where selfish maximization might prove problematic (Miller 1992; Ostrom 1998). In many situations, rational maximization at the individual level leads to collective disaster—as in Garret Hardin's (1968) tragedy of the commons, where unlimited common grazing rights lead to destruction of the common pasture illustrates. Through learning or experimentation, organizational rules may develop that encourage collective outcomes that overcome the "tragedy" of individual self-maximization (Ostrom 1999a). Once in place, these rules are enforced through a system of formal and informal incentives that control selfish behavior. This framework provides 'a general language about how rules, physical and material conditions, and attributes of the community affect the structure of action arenas, the incentives individuals face, and the resulting outcomes' (Ostrom 1999b, 59).

These institutional and cultural extensions are the most important additions to rational choice theory to be put forward in recent years. Yet, by incorporating so many "soft" variables they move quite briskly away from the traditional approach. How can one predict whether an organizational culture will emerge to overcome rational self-interest? Clearly not always, and hence the institutional structure is dependent on some other context that is left unspecified in the model.

PART III: PRINCIPAL AGENCY AND ORGANIZATIONAL BEHAVIOR

In spite of improvements, rational choice models simply are insufficient to capture critical aspects of organizational behavior. Because this research remains focused on outcomes rather than processes, rational choice theories are overwhelmingly focused on problems of collective action and individual utility maximization, which provide only limited insights into organizational behavior. Bounded rationality can examine the roots of collective action problems, but it also can shift research attention toward the more interesting questions of attention allocation and organizational information processing.

Recent studies in public administration have focused a good deal of attention on problems of delegation and control in organizational decision-making. Indeed, virtually all theoretical discussions of policy implementation have centered on these questions to the exclusion of such important topics as adaptive problem-solving and information-processing. While principal-agent dilemmas illuminate some important aspects of bureaucratic behavior, its prominence in studies of public policy is partially an artifact of the rational choice model of behavior. The fundamental problems of principal-agent dilemmas—those of information asymmetries, moral hazards, and incentive structures—are those that map neatly onto the most basic assumptions of individual utility maximization. Pioneering work in principal-agent models have spurred a rich discussion in public

management; however we fear the privileged place such research now holds in the study of organizations provides students with a simplistic and misleading view of the dynamics of bureaucratic policy-making.

A more comprehensive understanding of bureaucratic decision-making can be gained through the lens of bounded rationality, which offers a scientifically sound alternative model of behavior while sacrificing little parsimony. Rather than focusing exclusively on control, bounded rationality focuses on how changes in the external environment shape information processing both within and across organizations. This approach to the study of organizations will invariably yield a more sophisticated understanding of bureaucracy, as it is better suited to link the procedures of human choice with broader policy processes.

POLICY IMPLEMENTATION AND AGENCY THEORY

Rational choice decision-making as applied to the implementation stage of the policy process generally takes the form of principal-agent models of the bureaucracy's interactions with the legislative, executive, and judicial branches of government. In this section we argue that the underlying assumptions of the principal-agent model of politico-bureaucratic relations render it inaccurate, not only in terms of adequately explaining the relationship, but also as a description of the relationship and policy processes more generally at the implementation stage.

Principal-agent models of behavior were originally developed in the economic analysis of firms (Alchian and Demsetz 1972); although an emphasis on efficient production and incentive structures in organizations dates much earlier (Taylor 1911). The principal-agent relationship is essentially a contract. In order to increase production, the principal enters into an agreement with the agent for the production of the good. The principal's goal is to ensure the efficient production of the good; meanwhile, the agent's goal is to avoid time, effort, and resources necessary for producing the good.

For example, if we were examining a business firm, we might consider the employer the principal and the employees as agents. In the model, employees have incentive to "shirk", that is, loaf. This means that managers must closely monitor them to insure efficient production of a given good. No system of monitoring can completely eliminate all free-riding, because the resources for such monitoring face the law of diminishing marginal returns. This is the essence of the principal-agent problem.

Why do principals face the problem of free riding? The answer lies in information asymmetries found in the relationship between the principal and the agent. In the principal-agent model, the agent holds two key informational advantages over the principal. The first informational advantage lies in the selection process. Principals cannot know *a priori* the exact qualifications of a given agent, while the agent has a better idea of his or her competence. The agent may exaggerate her ability in order to attain the position, and even if most exaggerations are caught by the employer's personnel policies, some incompetents will slip through. This first informational asymmetry is usually termed *adverse selection*. The second informational advantage held by the agent involves the monitoring of the agent after the contract has been established. *Moral hazard* results when the principal lacks the resources or ability to engage in constant monitoring of the agent. The agent is then able to shirk, reducing the efficiency of the firm. The task of the principal is to induce compliance on the part of the agent through a system of incentives.

In order to invoke the principal-agent framework, the analyst must assume goal incongruence. The goal of the principal is the production of some good, while the goal of the agent is to reap the rewards of the contract with the principal without expending the effort to produce the good. To put it simply, the goal of the agent is to shirk. If goal incongruence does not exist, then principal-agent models are inappropriate for examining the relationship. Underlying the assumption of goal incongruence is a further assumption about the relationship of the actors to their goals. The principal-agent model assumes that a given actor's goals are known. Formal principal-agent modeling has rightly recognized that there exists uncertainty about the goals of the other actors in the relationship (Bendor and Moe 1985; Bendor, Taylor and Van Gaalen 1985; Bendor, Taylor and Van Gaalen 1987a; Bendor, Taylor and Van Gaalen 1987b; Moe 1984), but this does not take account of the uncertainty that shrouds an actor's knowledge of her own goals. Actors may not be able to define their own goals, especially in contexts in which trade-offs must be made between competing goals.

The model also assumes that strategies for attaining given goals are easily attached to the goals. The principal's goal of efficient production is attained by developing the appropriate incentive structure such that it is to the agent's material disadvantage to shirk rather than work. Likewise, the agent's goal is to maximize the benefit to be gained from the contractual relationship with the principal through manipulation or information. The final assumption concerning goal oriented behavior is complete information. The model assumes that if the principal is able to observe agent outputs, the principal is able to judge whether or not these outputs conform to the goal of efficient production (Worsham, Eisner and Ringquist 1997).

Finally, the principal-agent approach makes certain assumptions about the nature of the principal-agent relationship over time. The principal-agent approach is based in comparative statics (Bendor and Moe 1985). Relationships change only when exogenous 'shocks' to a system disturb a system otherwise in equilibrium. It should be noted that this is not entirely a problem of principal-agent theory per se. Comparative statics and equilibrium analysis also has roots in systems theories in both political science and sociology (Eisner, Worsham and Ringquist 1996; Worsham, Eisner and Ringquist 1997; Worsham, Rinquist and Eisner 1998).

Given these assumptions, it is imperative to the success of the contractual relationship that the principal *control* the behavior of the agent. There is no room for shared goals or learning and adaptation of behavior over time, or the potential counterproductive results on productivity of an environment of continual distrust and suspicion fostered by monitoring. The theme of control has been central in subsequent scholarship on the implementation stage of the policy process.

Rational choice approaches were used in the study of public policy long before the advent of the now-dominant principal-agent approach, most notably in Niskanen's (1968; 1971; 1975) model of the budget-maximizing bureaucrat and Anthony Downs' (1967) study of information limitations and bureaucracies. The principal-agent model really burst onto the scene in political science with works by Mitnick (1980; see also Mitnick 1973) and Miller and Moe (1983a; 1983b). This culminated in an article by Moe (1984), *The New Economics of Organization*, which formally introduced principal-agent approaches to the study of policy implementation to political scientists. Moe insightfully unified principal-agency from the economic analyses of business firms to the issue of how democratically elected officials can control unelected public bureaucrats; hence principal-agency could be used to illuminate a critical problem in democratic theory. Unfortunately, it altered the perspective on bureaucracy from one of balancing problem-solving, information-acquisition, and the advantages and disadvantages of delegation, to one stressing a single- minded emphasis on formal procedures of monitoring and control.

It also reversed the old normative emphasis in public administration on keeping politics out of administration. At least since Woodrow Wilson (1887), political scientists have been concerned with the distinction between politics and administration, mostly from the perspective of trying to keep politicians from interfering with professional implementation by demanding special favors from supposedly neutral bureaucrats. Principal-agency suggests that all independent behavior of bureaucrats is not motivated by professional problem-solving, but is based in the desire to shirk. Principal-agency assumes that all attempts by politicians at control are motivated by "efficient production" rather than crass political gains that add inefficiencies to public production.

Moe (1984) argues that for principal-agent theory to be useful in the study of implementation, we must take account of the fact that politicians are not necessarily motivated by the efficient production of public service; they may be more concerned with political efficiency rather than production efficiency. Moreover, the major problem of control might not be shirking, but could involve several different possibilities, including material benefit of some sort, ranging from budgetary slack to promotion, but might also be policy related. At a minimum, scholars utilizing the principal-agent frameworks would need to grapple with the issues of political efficiency and diversity of goals—not trivial alterations.

EX ANTE CONTROL OF IMPLEMENTATION

With the formal introduction of principal-agent theory, work on policy implementation collapsed to analyses of how a political principal is to control a shirking bureaucracy. One group of scholars argues that political control of the bureaucracy is achieved ex ante (McCubbins 1985; McCubbins, Noll and Weingast 1989). Democratically elected officials gain control of the bureaucracy through setting the 'structure and process' of organizations before their actual creation through detailed legislation specifying administrative procedure, personnel, and organizational structure (McCubbins, Noll and Weingast 1989; Banks and Weingast 1992). In this view, Congress 'stacks the deck' against the agency during its creation in order to ensure subservience to Congress or organized interests at later periods. The deck-stacking thesis focuses on political efficiency—the political coalition in control wishes to continue its advantage through later implementation. Other scholars argued that the political branches of government could also achieve ex post control of the bureaucracy through budgeting, personnel, staffing, political appointments, ongoing interactions with the bureau, and congressional oversight hearings (Bendor and Moe 1985; Bendor, Taylor and Van Gaalen 1987a; Miller and Moe 1983b).

But is congress the principal in the American system of divided powers? Both congress and the president attempt to influence the bureaucracy (not to mention the judiciary). Some scholars argue that congress is the institution wielding the most influence or control on the bureaucracy (McCubbins 1985; McCubbins, Noll, and Weingast 1989; Weingast and Moran 1983). Other scholars see the president, with his ability to influence the bureaucracy through budgets, OMB, and political appointments, as the abler of the two branches to achieve control and focus their theoretical and empirical attention on him (Golden 2000; Wood 1988; Wood and Waterman 1991).

McCubbins, Noll, and Weingast (1989) put forth three hypotheses concerning agency structure and process and its effects on the subsequent regulatory environment. First, the agency's design should, 'create a political environment that mirrors the politics at the time of enactment' (McCubbins, Noll, and Weingast 1988, 444). That is to say, winners and losers at the formulation stage of the policy process should benefit or lose in the same relative proportions at the implementation stage due to institutional design. Second, agency structure and process will favor those constituencies of the winning coalition at the formulation stage. Finally, agencies will exhibit an 'autopilot' characteristic (McCubbins, Noll, and Weingast 1988, 444). As the preferences of the favored constituency change, so will the preferences and thus behavior of the agency.

More recent scholarship is divided on the efficacy of structure and process as a means for controlling the bureaucracy. Balla (1998) finds that the open comment procedures for the new pay schedule and rules regarding Medicare did not favor the groups presumably favored by the dominant coalition in congress. Balla and Wright (2001) did find that advisory commissions correctly represented the political factions involved in the legislation of drinking water, but these authors did not examine the actions of these commissions.

Note that in the development of the principal-agent literature, the descriptive fit of the principal-agent model is somewhat strained. For example, in the deck-stacking thesis there is no room for politicians to prefer neutral competence in administration—the major aim of the Progressive Movement so important in American political life during the first quarter of the 20th Century. To the extent that Progressives were successful (and in many respects they were very successful), they left a legacy of removing political control and the politicized administration that the deck-stacking thesis suggests.

DESCRIPTIVE CRITIQUES

Beginning in the 1990s, scholars began to argue that descriptive flaws led agency theorists to explanations of bureaucratic behavior that were less than adequate (Eisner, Worsham, and Ringquist 1996; Hindera and Young 1998; Krause 1996; Meier, Pennington, and Eller 2001; Potoski and Nemacheck 2001; Worsham, Eisner, and Ringquist 1997). Principal-agent analysis generally has difficulty accounting for the fragmented nature of policy processes in the American system of government. That is, there are multiple, competing principals in the American system of separated powers (Choi 2001). Moreover bureaucracies themselves have constituencies and engage in advocacy policy-wise for these constituencies (Hindera and Young 1998; Meier, Pennington, and Eller 2001; Potoski and Nemacheck 2001). These bureaucratic constituencies could also be considered the principals.

All of these potential principals compete to influence or control the bureaucracy. These competing principals often have multiple, conflicting goals, especially under divided government. Once the political context of multiple, competing principals is taken into account, bureaucratic intransigence becomes much harder to pin down conceptually. To whom should the agency respond? Why should the agency respond to one principal to the exclusion of others? We argue that the more appropriate question to ask is, how do bureaucracies make trade-offs among the competing and contradictory demands of their political environment? Answering this question requires that we take an information processing approach to the study of bureaucratic behavior.

A second descriptive criticism of agency theory involves the goals of the agent. The goals of the agency are assumed to be adverse to those of the principal. Principal-agent modeling has difficulty addressing agents whose goals are not consistently adverse to those of the principal. Recent research at the street level calls into question the assumption that bureaucrats are primarily motivated by the goal of shirking (Brehm and Gates 1997). Krause (1996) argues that the development of goals over time is a two-way process. Agencies influence and even help to refine the goals of political principals. Second, using principal-agent models requires the researcher to acknowledge that both the principals' and agents' goals are known and easily prioritized. Bender and Moe (1985) note that the relationship between the bureaucracy and its political principals is likely dynamic, and the goals of the actors are likely to evolve and are clarified over time, both by the interactions of the bureaucracy with the political principals as well as through organizational factors. Worsham, Eisner, and Ringquist (1997) have argued that we cannot assume that bureaucratic agents are motivated to maximize material return to themselves; they may have other goals—some of which may correspond to those of the policymaking branches. This raises several questions concerning the type of behavior we should expect from the bureaucracy.

When confronted with a choice between attaining one of many possible goals, how does an actor choose? We are back to a serious problem in all rational theories of choice: to make any progress, some very strong assumptions must be made about what goals are used in the process of maximization. A bounded rational view of individual decision-making takes account of the difficulties of making trade-offs among multiple and competing goals. Principal-agent theories of policy processes also assume that the strategies, or means for attaining goals, are easily attached to the goals themselves. Although the studies outlined above all note that goals are not easily achieved, the uncertainty that surrounds the means to achieve the goals is rarely modeled.

How do principals know which strategies will lead to the desired outcomes?

Furthermore, it was argued long before principal-agent theory came to dominate implementation studies that success in terms of goals is difficult to measure (Lipsky 1980; Worsham, Eisner, and Ringquist 1997). How do principals know desirable outputs when they see them? Monitoring outputs can be counterproductive as agents shift away from productive problem-solving (as well as shirking) toward the goal that is monitored. This is a classic critique of standardized testing in schools as teachers "teach to the test". The linkage between strategies and goals cannot be understood outside a dynamic relationship. This suggests that bureaucratic outcomes, rather than outputs, are the more important indicators of goal success, which, in turn, suggests the efficacy of a problem solving approach to implementation.

If bureaucrats' interests are not necessarily adverse to those of the principal, an emphasis on control as a description of the process of implementation may be misleading. Golden (2000) finds that bureaucrats in various regulatory agencies in the Reagan administration for the most part were responsive to the policy directions of the administration, even in the absence of formal control procedures. Brehm and Gates (1997) find that bureaucrats are not fundamentally interested in shirking. They argue that functional motivations and peers are the prime influences on intra-organizational behavior to the exclusion of influence by superiors within the organization. Bureaucrats, for the most part, work. Their research adds a strong empirical foundation to arguments advocating taking organizational context seriously (Lipsky 1980; March and Simon 1958; Simon 1947; Wilson 1989).

PART IV: INFORMATION-PROCESSING AND PUBLIC POLICY

How are we to come to grips with the fact that bureaucrats are often predisposed to be responsive, but that policy outcomes are not always exactly as political principals would have them? If organizational decision-making is our focus, then we should approach the problem by asking how organizations process information from both their political and task environments (see Wilson 1989), and how this information is used in making trade-offs among competing demands and functional requirements (Jones 2001; Jones 2003).

An information-processing approach would analyze the ways in which administrative structure and processes are developed in ways that aid in focusing attention on particular problems and types of information. It would need to rely on bounded rationality as a decisional underpinning, because the cognitive limits of individuals and organizations color how they process information. This approach would view hierarchies or organizational structures as mechanisms for focusing attention (Jones 2001). Normatively, an information-processing approach sees structure and process aimed at enhancing the problem-solving capacity of both agencies and Congress more generally, not just enhancing one partner at the expense of the other. Constraining agency decision-making renders the agency less able to adjust both to its task environment and its political environment (Jones 2001; Wilson 1989). Keeping politicians completely out of implementation can cause agencies to cut off an important source of feedback.

It is reasonable to argue that members of congress might well prefer a flexible agency that is adaptable both to its political and task environment; delay may be desirable in order to maintain policy stability (Carpenter 1996). Agencies are rightly cautious in responding too quickly to demands from their environments. Agency delay is a result of the agency reducing the uncertainty in its environment. Once the agency is sure that a given signal is meant to influence policy in a given direction, the agency adjusts accordingly.

This approach calls into question a theory of bureaucratic behavior that fails to consider the uncertainties inherent in the environments of agencies and questions the amount of resources that are devoted to questions of control without actually specifying how agencies go about making decisions—decisions made

in environments characterized by ambiguity and uncertainty (Jones 2001; Jones 2003; Krause 2003). An emphasis on discovering the ways in which agencies balance competing, contradictory demands in their environments mandates that scholarly attention be turned toward specifying agency decision-making processes. It also mandates that scholarly attention be turned toward explaining bureaucratic behavior more broadly, rather than one facet of the relationship between bureaucracy and the elected branches of government.

BOUNDED RATIONALITY AND POLICY IMPLEMENTATION

If we adopt a problem-solving, information-processing perspective based in bounded rationality, we are equipped to examine both scientific and normative questions in a more productive light than if we begin with a rigid principal-agent model based in rational choice. Because bounded rationality begins with the assumption that both "principals" and "agents" are goal-seeking entities with multiple potential objectives, and assumes that both are fallible in the pursuit of these goals, it leads to normative analyses that neither treat the "professional bureaucrats" as invariably correct, as did the Progressives, nor the elected politicians, as do the proponents of principal-agency. Scientifically, it is much less likely to "get stuck" on one partial and incomplete understanding of legislative-bureaucratic relationships, because it has a much stronger inductive component than does principal-agency or any other models derived from rational choice.

Because bounded rationality begins by looking to the procedures of individual choices, it is well equipped to explore endogenous dynamics of interpersonal and hierarchical relationships at the heart of principal-agent dilemmas. But the approach isn't limited to the internal dynamics of public administration. Because bounded rationality looks to how decision-makers interact with exogenous environmental changes in time, information flows, and attention—it is also able to understand dynamic change in the policy outputs of organizations. In this regard, we find it curious that researchers in public administration are calling to expand principal-agent models of bureaucratic behavior (Waterman and Meier 1998; Bendor, Glazer and Hammond 2001).

A scientifically sound and parsimonious alternative approach connecting individual and organizational behavior already exists. To demonstrate the value of bounded rationality in the study of organizations, we describe first how the model might be applied to principal-agent dilemmas and to broader and more interesting questions about bureaucratic information processing. We contend that bounded rationality actually provides a more robust understanding of principal agency. More importantly, we argue that those researchers who study organizational behavior through the lens of bounded rationality look to a greater and more appealing range of research questions than the problems of delegation and control.

BOUNDED RATIONALITY AND PRINCIPAL-AGENT MODELS

Recent empirical challenges to the central assumptions of comprehensive rationality have spurred calls for reform in either the method or the behavioral model employed in studies of interpersonal relationships. In their elegant review *Theories of Delegation*, Bendor, Glazer, and Hamond (2001) conclude with a challenge to improve the study of principal-agent dilemmas, complaining in part that too little attention is given to a) the 'real world' institutional context of principal-agent dilemmas (266–267); b) pre-existing information and policy programs that might constrain an actor's behavior; and c) the complexity of the task environment facing actors in a given environment (267). Waterman and Meier (1998) attack the limitations of standard principal-agent dilemmas from another direction, deriving an interesting set of hypotheses by relaxing assumptions of information asymmetries and goal incongruence. They argue 'all political-bureaucratic

relationships are not a caldron of conflict. The environment is dynamic and conflict varies according to both the level of information that principals and agents posses and the level of goal conflict' (197).

Perhaps the most troubling set of problems identified by critics of principal-agent models have been that they are founded in artificial and even incorrect assumptions of human behavior. Under empirical scrutiny, the assumption of goal incongruence generally, and agent shirking specifically, is less pronounced than principal-agent theory would have us believe. In many organizations, agent behavior is determined more by the organizational culture and feelings of agent solidarity than through incentive structures and principal monitoring (Brehm and Gates 1993). The importance of institutional norms and cultures inspired Gary Miller's *Managerial Dilemmas*, one of the most exciting innovations in modern organization theory (Miller 1992). Miller's work challenged the Skinnerian notion that workers in agency were most effectively induced to work through incentives and punishment, arguing instead that an organizational culture is far more effective in establishing worker compliance or noncompliance with principal goals (Miller 1992). Nothing in bounded rationality rejects that incentives and monitoring within organizations can shape individual behavior—and Miller's interest in organizational culture is entirely consistent with procedural rationality's interest in the influence of external factors in individual choice.

Yet bounded rationality is not merely as good as new institutionalism in explaining principal-agent relationships—it performs better. This superiority stems from the considerable attention bounded rationality places in the cognitive constraints on decision-making. New institutionalism is an enormous improvement over traditional principal-agent studies because it built such exogenous factors as culture into the decision-making model. Unfortunately it adds, in an ad hoc way, whatever the analyst thinks actors are "maximizing", and generally ignores the trade-offs implied between the standard assumption of self-interest and the other imputed goals that might get maximized. Find a deficit in the theory, and a new goal is added.

Bounded rationality takes but one additional step by showing how biological hardwiring and psychological traits shape how individuals act within organizations, including the complex relationship between incentives and response. Having moved so rapidly away from simple models of self-interest maximization, and having recognized that "informal norms" such as a sense of fairness can be maximized, why do rational choice theorists not simply take the next small step and introduce the individual and organizational cognitive architectures that bounded rationality emphasizes?

Bruno Frey's research on 'the crowding out effect' (Frey 1993; Osterloh and Frey 2000) is an excellent example of how bounded rationality might improve models of principal-agent relationships, and it shows the practical danger of believing that agents simply respond to incentives provided by the principal. Drawing from psychological studies that show individuals respond negatively to control, Frey argues that 'under readily identifiable conditions, increased monitoring reduces an agents overall work effort' (1993, 663). Increased monitoring breaks the 'psychological contract' with the agent, lowering his or her incentive to respond to incentives or punishment. Not only is increased monitoring not terribly effective, but it might prove harmful to organizational productivity—a blunder based on theory rather than analysis. Frey then compares behavior across organizations to identify which types of organizations will produce a positive (increased productivity) or a negative (decreased productivity) by increasing monitoring—a much more scientific and inductive approach than the standard deductive stance taken by principal-agent theorists.

By looking to the psychological and environmental constraints on individual choice, bounded rationality allows researchers to capture realistic and counter-intuitive behavior that escapes rational choice analysis. New institutionalism and bounded rationality have both discovered the importance of organizational rules and norms in delineating individual preferences; however, bounded rationality distinguishes itself by capturing psychological as well as environmental constraints on choice. Although inductive research is more time consuming, such an approach will ultimately yield a more compelling portrayal of principal-agent dilemmas. In bounded rationality, individual responses to monitoring, incentive structures, routines, and organizational mission are no longer abstracted from artificial models, they are grounded in the science of observation.

BOUNDED RATIONALITY AND POLICY OUTPUTS

While bounded rationality may well improve research in principal-agent dilemmas, the thrust of this argument is not to rescue principal-agent theory. Instead, we hold that starting with the assumption of bounded rationality will stimulate a wide range of interesting research questions in organizational information processing, which will ultimately provide us with a far more robust understanding of bureaucratic behavior. This final section looks to the unique emphasis of bounded rationality on how individuals and organizations receive, process, and act upon a variety of information cues.

The promise of bounded rationality is that it allows researchers to connect individual behavior to organizational output without the rigid and misleading constraints of rational choice. For the study of public policy processes, such a model is enormously appealing. It allows researchers to explore political behavior in the aggregate by making assumptions about the behavior of the individual.

The earliest advances in organizational processing models emerged from the study of public budgeting (Simon 1947; Wildavsky 1964; Davis, Murray, Dempster and Wilasky 1966); see Thompson and Green 2001 for a critical review). Bounded rationality was used to explain incremental changes in public budgets. The high costs of generating alternatives and making fully optimal decisions, coupled with the uncertainty of outcomes, led to what might be best characterized as risk averse policy incrementalism. At the core of many explanations of budget incrementalism was Simon's notion of satisficing. To limit the costs of making decisions, both individuals and organizations looked to alternatives that were good enough. Budget incrementalism emerged from the risk averse convention of referring to the prior-year's budget when creating a new one. 'Because the reference point for decision-making is always some point decision made in the past, the outcomes of local search, combined with a propensity to limit bargaining and enforcement costs, are small or incremental changes in policy' (Thompson and Green 2001: 3).

While early models of organizational information processing focused on the politics of incrementalism, more recent studies of bounded rationality have focused on the dynamics of policy change. Behavioral models here have been driven by an intriguing empirical reality—neither budgets specifically (Padgett 1980; Carpenter 1996) nor policy agendas more generally (Baumgartner and Jones 1993) adhere to the strict pattern of incrementalism. Instead, budgets and agendas follow the trajectory of punctuated equilibriums—periods of incrementalism followed by a sudden flurry of policy activity (Baumgartner and Jones 1993). These recent studies have improved our understanding of the policy processes by integrating the role of shifting attention into models of organizational behavior (Jones 2003). Students of how governments set policy agendas emphasize the role of the allocation of attention in determining the behavior of policy makers (Cohen, March, and Olsen 1972; Kingdon 1995; Baumgartner and Jones 1993). Shifts in the external environment produce shifts in the preferences and goals of policy-makers. When an institution or organization's attention is squarely focused on a specific policy domain, we might anticipate increased activity, legislation, and spending. However, because the allocation of attention is limited to a few select issues, many policy programs continue incrementally—and follow the conservative, risk averse path outlined by prior research in public budgeting.

Low salience issues will generally follow an incremental pattern—little new information or alternatives will be integrated into the solution searches. When attention is focused on a high salience policy problem, we anticipate a broader solution search, greater generation of alternatives, and increased legislative activity. However, even when attention is squarely focused on a problem, decision-making will be bounded by cognitive and emotional constraints.

TOWARD AN INFORMATION-PROCESSING MODEL OF POLICY MAKING

In The Politics of Attention, Bryan Jones and Frank Baumgartner (2005) outline the components of a comprehensive model connecting individual and organizational behavior. This model is drawn from bounded rationality, and attempts to capture both the dynamics of individual and collective choice at each stage of the policy process.

Figure 3.1 depicts their information-processing model. Notice at each stage the authors have characterized the decision-making process at the individual and the systems level, because organizations fall prey to the same kinds of cognitive limits as do individuals (Jones 2001).

At the core of the model is the problem of *issue attention*. Organizational agendas reflect what actors believe to be the most salient or pressing concerns. Because both organizational and individual attention is limited, agenda setting necessitates that organizations prioritize political problems, focusing first and foremost on the most urgent concerns. These concerns may be dictated less by informed reasoning and more by emotional responses to political problems, 'as emotions are critical in determining priorities' (Jones 2001: 73–74). In organizations, the high priority issues will receive the brunt of attention, while less salient concerns will fall to the wayside. If these less salient issues demand political action, they may follow the path of incrementalism and emphasis on 'pre-packaged' solutions.

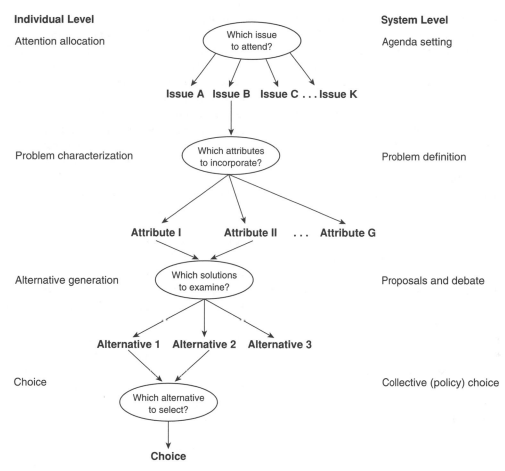

Figure 3.1 *An information-processing model of choice*

The next step in the information-processing model takes the form of *problem characterization* and organizational *problem definition*. Received information is rarely neutral—individuals and organizations must decide how to characterize and approach a particular problem. Understanding how individuals characterize and organizations define the nature of a political task is essential in the policy process. For example, failing students in public education might be seen primarily as a problem of waning parental involvement, or it might be seen as a systemic failure of the school system. The received information may be characterized in any number of ways, depending on the preconceived attitudes of the decision-maker, or the larger organizational culture.

The final two stages of the model describe how individuals and institutions reduce a problem to a manageable set of *alternatives*, and then *select a policy solution*. For example—policy proscriptions addressing failing schools might take any number of forms—smaller class sizes, increased funding, increased oversight, school and student accountability, curriculum overhaul, etc. Because decision-makers struggle at evaluating and making trade-offs (Sniderman et al., 1991; Tetlock 2000; Jones 2001), choices must be reduced to a few actionable alternatives. In organizations, this is often done through debate. Failing schools can be solved through increasing funding, or through increasing accountability and oversight. The choice is then made according to institutional procedures.

It is important to note that political decisions may not represent individual responses to politically neutral information. People often become attached to preferred solutions beyond their direct utility—a process Herbert Simon referred to as 'identification with the means' (Jones 2001). The emotional orientation toward a solution or particular set of solutions bounds the alternatives a decision-maker is willing to consider. In politics, political ideology affects how people prioritize problems, construct problem spaces, and organize solutions. Because ideologies help define "the self" the solution implied by the ideology will be very resistant to information.

The entire process of attention allocation, problem definition, and attaching solutions to problems must of necessity be a disjoint and episodic process. Governmental response will not be proportionate to the severity of the problem—the "exogenous shocks" of rational choice's favored comparative statics. One of the major empirical predictions of bounded rationality is that, taken in dynamic terms, policy responses will be far more punctuated than would be predicted from a fully rational response alone (Jones and Baumgartner 2005).

CONCLUSION

This essay has distinguished between rational choice and bounded rationality in studies of public policy. We began with a comparison between the two approaches, then detailed the objections to rational choice stemming from the laboratory experiments in behavioral decision theory. Taking principal-agent theory as the major perspective used today to analyze policy implementation, we showed how it has mis-directed scholarly attention to one issue in bureaucratic behavior to the exclusion of many others, and produced a questionable approach to understanding how to improve bureaucratic performance. We briefly examined the information-processing approach, based in bounded rationality, which insists that we focus both on the complex and uncertain environment of policy-makers and on their cognitive capacities that channel how they respond to the uncertain and ambiguous information pressing down on them.

A growing body of evidence criticizing the empirical and theoretic inadequacies of comprehensive rationality has led an increasing number of researchers to call for a renewed model of choice in public decision-making. In political science, rational theorists have admitted to a variety of organizational and cultural constraints on the maximization of self-interest, to the extent that even altruism can be "rational". This destroys parsimony and the deductive method, for one never knows what is being maximized without empirical examination. Yet rational choice theorists still refuse to take the final step, the admission that cognitive limits of individuals also affects the decision-making process.

A full return to bounded rationality is necessary to carry forward the new demands for realistic yet theoretically tractable models of individual and organizational choice. Only by dropping the increasingly weighty baggage of rational choice and its misleading theories represented by principal-agency can we proceed productively, with an increased appreciation for observation as well as theory. After all, the approach was born in the disciplines of political science, organization theory, and public administration. Instead of borrowing from economists, poorly equipped to study politics, we are simply re-acquainting ourselves with our past.

NOTE

1. For a good review, see Colin Camerer and Richard Thaler's 'Anomalies: Ultimatums, Dictators and Manners,' *Journal of Economic Perspectives* (1995) 9: 209–219

REFERENCES

Alchian, Armen A., and Harold Demsetz. 1972. Production, Information Costs, and Economic Organization. *American Economic Review* 62 (December): 777–795.

Arnold, R. Douglas. 1990. *The Logic of Congressional Action.* Yale University Press.

Balla, Steven J. 1998. Administrative Procedure and Political Control of the Bureaucracy. *The American Political Science Review* 92 (3): 663–673.

Balla, Steven J., and John R. Wright. 2001. Interest Groups, Advisory Committees, and Congressional Control of the Bureaucracy. *American Journal of Political Science* 45 (4): 799–812.

Banks, Jeffrey S., and Barry R. Weingast. 1992. The Political Control of Bureaucracies Under Assymetric Information. *American Journal of Political Science* 36 (2): 509–524.

Baumgartner, Frank R. and Bryan D. Jones. 1993. Agendas and Instability in American Politics. Chicago: University of Chicago Press.

Bendor, Jonathan, and Terry M. Moe. 1985. An Adaptive Model of Bureaucratic Politics. *The American Political Science Review* 79 (3): 755–774.

Bendor, Jonathan, Serge Taylor and Roland Van Gaalen. 1985. Bureaucratic Expertise Versus Legislative Authority: A Model of Deception and Monitoring in Budgeting. *The American Political Science Review* 79 (4): 1041–1060.

Bendor, Jonathan, Serge Taylor, and Roland Van Gaalen. 1987a. Politicians, Bureaucrats, and Asymmetric Information. *American Journal of Political Science* 31 (4): 796–828.

Bendor, Jonathan, Serge Taylor, and Roland Van Gaalen. 1987b. Stacking the Deck: Bureaucratic Missions and Policy Design. *The American Political Science Review* 81 (3): 873–896.

Bendor, Jonathan, Glazer, A, and T. Hammond. 2001. 'Theories of Delegation. In Nelson Polsby, ed., *Annual Review of Political Science*. Palo Alto, CA: Annual Reviews.

Berejekian, Jeffrey D. 2002. 'Model Building with Prospect Theory: A Cognitive Approach to International Relations.' *Political Psychology* 23: 759–786.

Brehm, John, and Scott Gates. 1993. 'Donut Shops and Speed Traps: Evaluating Models of Supervision on Police Behavior.' *American Journal of Political Science* 37: 555–81.

Brehm, John, and Scott Gates. 1997. *Working, Shirking, and Sabotage*. Ann Arbor: University of Michigan Press.

Brehm, John, and Scott Gates. 1997. *Working, Shirking, and Sabotage: Bureaucratic Response to a Democratic Public*. Ann Arbor: University of Michigan Press.

Camerer, Colin and Richard Thaler. 1995. 'Anomalies: Ultimatums, Dictators and Manners.' *Journal of Economic Perspectives* 9: 209–219.

Carpenter, Daniel P. 1996. Adaptive Signal Processing, Hierarchy, and Budgetary Control in Federal Regulation. *The American Political Science Review* 90 (2): 283–302.

Choi, Jin-Wook. 2001. Rethinking Political Control Over Independent Regulatory Agencies: The Case of SEC. Paper read at The Annual Meeting of the American Political Science Association, August 30–September 2, 2001, at San Francisco, CA.

Cohen, Michael, James G. March, and Johan P. Olsen. 1972. A Garbage Can Theory of Organizational Choice. *Administrative Science Quarterly* 17: 1–25.

Davis, Otto A., Murray A. H. Dempster, and Aaron Wildavsky. 1966. A Theory of Budget Process. *American Political Science Review* 60: 529–547.

Downs, Anthony. 1957. An *Economic Theory of Democracy*. New York: Harper.

Downs, Anthony. 1967. *Inside Bureaucracy*. Edited by A. R. C. R. Study. New York: Harper-Collins.

Eisner, Marc, Jeff Worsham, and Evan Ringquist. 1996. Crossing the Organizational Void: The Limits of Agency Theory in the Analysis of Regulatory Control. *Governance* (October).

Frey, Bruno. 1993. 'Does Monitoring Increase Work Effort? The Rivalry with Trust and Loyalty.' *Economic Inquiry* 31: 663–670.

Friedman, Milton. 1953. 'The Methodology of Positive Economics.' In Milton Friedman, Essays in Positive Economics. Chicago: The University of Chicago Press.

Fudenberg, Drew and David Levine. 1997. 'Measuring players' losses in experimental games.' *Quarterly Journal of Economics* 112 (2): 507–536.

Garrett, Elizabeth. 'The Law and Economics of Elections: The Law and Economics of 'Informed Voter' Ballot Notations' (Symposium). *Virginia Law Review* 85 (November 2003): 1553.

Gigerenzer, Gerd, Peter Todd, and the ABC Research Group. 1999. Simple HeuristicsThat Make Us Smart. Oxford University Press.

Goeree, Jacob K. and Charles Holt. 2000. 'Asymetric inequality aversion and noisy behavior in alternating-offer bargaining games,' *European Economic Review* 44: 1079–1089.

Golden, Marissa Martino. 2000. *What Motivates Bureaucrats? Politics and Administration During the Reagan Years*. New York: Columbia University Press.

Hardin, Garrett. 1968. 'The Tragedy of the Commons.' *Science* 162: 1243–1248.

Henrich, Joseph. 2000. 'Does Culture Matter in Economic Behavior? Ultimatum Game Bargaining among the Machiguenga of the Peruvian Amazon.' *The American Economic Review* 90: 973–980.

Hindera, John J., and Cheryl D. Young. 1998. Representative Bureaucracy: The Theoretical Implications of Statistical Interaction. *Political Science Quarterly* 51 (3): 655–671.

Hoffman, Elizabeth, and Mathew L. Spitzer. 1985. 'Entitlements, Rights and Fairness: An Experimental

Examination of Subjects' Concepts of Distributive Justice.' *Journal of Legal Studies* 14: 259–97.

John, Peter. 2003. 'Is There Life After Policy Streams, Advocacy Coalitions, and Punctuations? Using Evolutionary Theory to Explain Policy Change.' *Policy Studies Journal* 31 (4): 481–498.

Jones, Bryan D. 1994. *Reconceiving Decision Making in Democratic Politics: Attention, Choice, and Public Policy.* Chicago: The University of Chicago Press.

Jones, Bryan D. 2001. *Politics and the Architecture of Choice: Bounded Rationality and Governance.* Chicago: The University of Chicago Press.

Jones, Bryan D. 2003. Bounded Rationality and Political Science: Lessons from Public Administration and Public Policy. *Journal of Public Administration Research and Theory* 13 (4): 395–412.

Jones, Bryan D. and Frank R. Baumgartner 2005. The Politics of Attention: How the Government Prioritizes Problems. Chicago: University of Chicago Press.

Jones, Bryan D. and Frank R. Baumgartner. 2005. *The Politics of Attention: How the Government Prioritizes Problems.* Chicago: University of Chicago Press.

Jones, Bryan D., Tracy Sulkin, and Heather A. Larsen. 2003. Policy Punctuations in American Political Institutions. *American Political Science Review* 97 (1): 151–169.

Kahneman, Daniel and Amos Tversky. 1979. 'Prospect theory: An analysis of decisions under risk.' *Econometrica* 47: 313–327.

Kahneman, Daniel and Amos Tversky. 1986. 'Rational Choice and the Framing of Decisions.' In Daniel Kahneman and Amos Tversky, eds. 2000. *Choices, Values and Frames.* Cambridge University Press.

Kahneman, Daniel and Amos Tversky, eds. 2000. *Choices, Values and Frames.* Cambridge University Press.

Kahneman, Daniel. 2002. 'Maps of Bounded Rationality: A Perspective on Intuitive Judgement and Choice.' *Nobel Prize Lecture, December 8th, 2002.*

Kahneman, Daniel, Jack Knetsch, and Richard H. Thaler. 1986. 'Fairness and the Assumptions of Economics.' *Journal of Business* 59: S283–S300.

Kingdon, John. 1995. Agendas, Alternatives, and Public Policies, 2nd. Ed. Boston: Little, Brown.

Kingdon, John. 1973. *Congressmen's Voting Decisions.* New York: Harper & Row.

Krause, George A. 1996. The Institutional Dynamics of Policy Administration: Bureaucratic Influence Over Securities Regulation. *American Journal of Political Science* 40 (4): 1083–1121.

Krause, George A. 2003. Coping with Uncertainty: Analyzing Risk Propensities of SEC Budgetary

Decisions, 1949–97. *American Political Science Review* 97 (1): 171–188.

Levi, Margaret. 1997. 'A Model, A Method, and a Map: Rational Choice in Comparative and Historical Analysis'. In *Comparative Politics: Rationality, Culture, and Structure*, Mark Lichbach and Alan Zuckerman, eds, pp. 19–41. New York: Cambridge University Press.

Lupia, Arthur, Mathew McCubbins, and Samuel L. Popkin, eds., *Elements of Reason.* Cambridge: Cambridge University Press.

Lupia, Arthur, Mathew D. McCubbins, and Samuel L. Popkin. 2000. 'Beyond Rationality: Reason and the Study of Politics'. In Lupia, Arthur, Mathew D. McCubbins, and Samuel L. Popkin, eds., *Elements of Reason.* Cambridge: Cambridge University Press.

Lipsky, Michael. 1980. *Street-Level Bureaucracy: Dilemmas of the Individual in Public Services.* New York: Russell Sage Foundation.

March, James G., and Herbert A. Simon. 1958. *Organizations.* New York: Free Press.

Mayhew, David. 1974. *Congress: The Electoral Connection.* New Haven: Yale University Press.

McCubbins, Matthew D. 1985. The Legislative Design of Regulatory Structure. *American Journal of Political Science* 29 (4): 721–748.

McCubbins, Matthew D., Roger G. Noll, and Barry R. Weingast. 1989. Structure and Process: Politics and Policy: Administrative Arrangements and the Political Control of Agencies. *Virginia Law Review* 75: 431.

Meier, Kenneth J., Michael S. Pennington, and Warren S. Eller. 2001. The Effect of New Goals and Priorities on Agency Responsiveness to Traditional Clientele: An Examination of the EEOC. Paper read at The Annual Meeting of the American Political Science Association, August 29–September 2, 2001, at San Francisco, CA.

Miller, Gary J., and Terry M. Moe. 1983a. Bureaucrats, Legislators, and the Size of Government. *American Political Science Review* 77 (June): 297–322.

Miller, Gary J., and Terry M. Moe. 1983b. The Positive Theory of Hierarchies. Paper read at The Annual Meeting of the American Political Science Association, at Chicago.

Miller, Gary. 1992. *Managerial Dilemmas: The Political Economy of Hierarchy.* Cambridge: Cambridge University Press.

Mitnick, Barry M. 1973. Fiduciary Rationality and Public Policy: The Theory of Agency and Some Consequences. Paper read at The Annual Meeting of the American Political Science Association, at New Orleans, LA.

Mitnick, Barry M. 1980. *The Political Economy of Regulation.* New York: Columbia University Press.

Moe, Terry M. 1984. The New Economics of Organization. *American Journal of Political Science* 28 (4): 739–777.

Monroe, Kristen R. 1996. *The Heart of Altruism: Perceptions of a Common Humanity.* Princeton University Press.

Muringhan, Keith J. and Michael S. Saxon. 1994. 'Ultimatum Bargaining by Children and Adults,' unpublished working paper, *University of British Columbia Faculty of Commerce.* (Cited in Thaler 1992).

Muringhan, Keith J. and Madan Pillutla. 1995. 'Being Fair or Appearing Fair: Strategic Behavior in Ultimatum Bargaining.' *Academy of Management Journal* 38: 1408–1427.

Newell, Allen. 1990. Unified Theories of Cognition. Cambridge, MA: Harvard University Press.

Niskanen, William A. 1968. The Peculiar Economics of Bureaucracy. *Papers and Proceedings of the Eightieth Annuel Meeting of the American Economic Association* 58 (2): 293–305.

Niskanen, William A. 1971. *Bureaucracy and Representative Government.* Chicago: Aldine-Atherton, Inc.

Niskanen, William A. 1975. Bureaucrats and Politicians. *Journal of Law and Economics* 18: 617–644.

Nowak, Martin A., Karen Page and Karl Sigmund. 2000. 'Fairness versus Reason in the Ultimatum Game' *Science* 289: 1773.

Olson, Mancur. 1982. *The Rise and Decline of Nations.* Yale University Press.

Osterloh, Margeret and Bruno Frey. 2000. 'Motivation, Knowledge Transfer, and Organizational Forms.' *Organization Science* 11: 538–550.

Ostrom, Elinor. 1998. 'A Behavioral Approach to the Rational Choice Theory of Collective Action'. *American Political Science Review* 92: 1–22.

Ostrom, Elinor. 1999a. 'Coping with Tragedies of the Commons'. In Nelson Polsby, ed., *Annual Review of Political Science* 2. Palo Alto, CA: Annual Reviews.

Ostrom, Elinor. 1999b. 'Institutional Rational Choice: An Assessment of the Institutional Analysis and Development Framework.' In *Theories of the Policy Process,* Paul A. Sabatier, ed. Boulder, CO: Westview.

Padgett, John F. 1980. Bounded Rationality in Budgetary Research. *American Political Science Review* 74: 354–372.

Potoski, Matthew, and Christine L. Nemacheck. 2001. Bureaucratic Influence in the Legislative Arena: 1984 Drug Price Competition-Patent Restoration Act and FDA Distributive Program

Awards. Paper read at The Annual Meeting of the American Political Science Association, August 30–September 2, 2001, at San Francisco, CA.

Quattrone, George and Amos Tversky. 1988. 'Contrasting Rational and Psychological Analyses of Political Choice,' *American Political Science Review* 82: 719–736.

Rockman, Bert. 2000. 'Theory and Influence in the Study of Bureaucracy: Micro- and Neoinstitutional Foundations of Choice.' *Journal of Public Administration Research and Theory* 11 (1): 3–27.

Roth, Alvn, Vesna Prasknikar, Masahiro Okuno-Fujiwara and Shmuel Zamir. 1991. 'Bargaining and Market Behavior in Jerusalem Ljubljana, Pittsburgh, and Tokyo: An experimental study.' *American Economic Review* 81: 1068–95.

Simon, Herbert A. 1947. *Administrative Behavior: A Study of Decision-Making Processes in Administrative Organizations.* 4th ed. New York: Simon and Schuster, Inc.

Simon, Herbert A. 1985. 'Human Nature in Politics: The Dialogue of Psychology with Political Science.' *The American Political Science Review* 79: 293–304.

Simon, Herbert A. 1991. *Models of My Life.* New York: Basic Books.

Simon H.A. 1999. The potlatch between political science and economics. In *Competition and Cooperation: Conversations with Nobelistsabout Economics and Political Science,* J Alt, M Levi, E Ostrom, eds. Cambridge, UK: Cambridge University Press.

Slovak, Paul. 1990. Choice. In Thinking: An invitation to cognitive science, vol. 3. Daniel Osherson and Edward E. Smith, eds. Cambridge, Mass: MIT Press.

Sniderman, Paul, et al. 1991. *Reasoning and Choice.* Cambridge: Cambridge University Press.

Solnick, Sara. 2001. 'Gender Differences in the Ultimatum Game.' *Economic Inquiry* 39: 189.

Taylor, Frederick W. 1911. *The Principles of Scientific Management.* New York: W. W. Norton.

Tetlock, Philip. 2000. 'Coping with Trade-offs: Psychological Constraints and Political Implications'. In Lupia, Arthur, Mathew D. McCubbins, and Samuel L. Popkin, eds., *Elements of Reason.* Cambridge: Cambridge University Press.

Thaler, Richard H. 1992. *The Winner's Curse; Paradoxes and Anomalies of Economic Life.* Princeton University Press.

Thompson, Fred and Mark Green. 2001. Organizational Process Models of Budgeting, *Research in Public Administration,* 55–81.

True James L., 2000. 'Avalanches and Incrementalism: Making Policy and Budgets in the

United States.' *American Review of Public Administration* 30: 3–18.

Waterman, Richard and Kenneth Meier. 1998. Principal-agent Models: An Expansion? *Journal of Public Administration Research and* Theory 2: 173–202.

Weingast, Barry R., and Mark J. Moran. 1983. Bureaucratic Discretion or Congressional Control?: Regulatory Policymaking by the Federal Trade Commission. *Journal of Political Economy* 91: 765–800.

Wildavsky, Aaron. 1964. *The Politics of the Budgetary Process*. Boston: Little, Brown.

Wilson, James Q. 1989. *Bureaucracy: What Government Agencies Do Why They Do It*. New York: Basic Books, Inc.

Wilson, Woodrow. 1887. The Study of Administration. *Political Science Quarterly* 2: 197–222.

Wood, B. Dan. 1988. Principals, Bureaucrats, and Responsiveness in Clean Air Enforcements. *American Political Science Review* 82: 213–234.

Wood, B. Dan, and Richard W. Waterman. 1991. The Dynamics of Political Control of the Bureaucracy. *The American Political Science Review* 85 (3): 801–828.

Worsham, Jeff, Marc Allen Eisner, and Evan J. Ringquist. 1997. Assessing the Assumptions: A Critical Analysis of Agency Theory. *Administration and Society* 28 (4): 419–440.

Worsham, Jeff, Evan Rinquist, and Marc Eisner, eds. 1998. *A Theory of Political Influence of the Bureaucracy*. Edited by J. D. White, *Research in Public Administration*. Stamford, CT: JAI Press.

Zaller, John R. 1992. *The Nature and Origins of Mass Opinion*. Cambridge University Press.

4

Policy Design: Ubiquitous, Necessary and Difficult

DAVIS B. BOBROW

INTRODUCTION

The familiar function of a handbook for a professional community is to provide a survey of the state of the art in some pertinent aspect of professional practice. A handbook typically identifies the major instruments of a professional repertoire, and assesses their strengths and weaknesses to suggest best practices. In doing so, it cites known regularities or patterns, established theories, and well-tested techniques. That is usually done with the explicit or tacit claim that they are either the specialized property of the field or used especially well by its members.

It is hard to argue that policy design has much in the way of such possessions other than borrowing from other specializations and often relaxing their standards for advanced professional practice. Why then does policy design warrant inclusion in a handbook on public policy?

One possible answer is a sociology of the profession's presence of a more or less organized group of specialist experts. Yet, unlike policy analysis, policy design shows few of the trappings of a professional community: self-identification as a policy designer; a professional association and journal; standards for certification; broader social attribution of special expertise; consensually shared views of core foundation knowledge; or a widely accepted program for improving capabilities.

Policy design merits attention, nevertheless, because it is ubiquitous, necessary, and difficult. For better or ill, it has and does go on and is explicitly so labeled for public policies in areas as diverse as: foreign affairs (e.g., Hoag, 1976); trade policy (e.g., Brainard and Martimort, 1996); international exchange rate coordination (e.g., Cohen and Wyplosz, 1995); industrial policy (e.g., Cody Kitchen and Weiss, 1990); environmental quality (e.g., Pellikan and van der Veen, 2002); food stamps (e.g., Ohls and Beebout, 1993); national information systems (e.g., Laudon, 1986); government spurred innovation (e.g., Roessner, 1988); International Monetary Fund programs (e.g., Killick, 1995); managed health care (e.g., Hurley, Freund, and Paul, 1993); child health care (e.g., Goggin, 1987); health insurance (e.g., Oliver, 1999); internal migration (e.g., Castro et al., 1978); macroeconomic policy (e.g., Taylor, 1993); homeland security (e.g., Demchak, 2002); and democratic governance (e.g., Schneider and Ingram, 1997).

Further, the instances of work explicitly labeled policy design are far outnumbered by those in which designs are prescribed or evaluated without bearing that label in a prominent and explicit way. With or without a policy design title, policy assessments by lay people and "policy wonks" applaud or bemoan the consequences attributed to such efforts. That is no less the case for international concerns than for the dominant focus of the literature, quintessential domestic policy. We are, of course, well into a world in which designs which assume that consequences, causes, and policy options can be neatly segregated by national borders are doomed to disappointment.

Subsequent sections of this chapter address: policy design as a messy imperative; root conceptions of policy design; subsequent elaborations and differentiations of its conception; and core strategies for its conduct – a suggested ten commandments.

Before turning to those matters, it seems helpful to recognize the core metaphors for policy design, and the core activities of policy designers they imply. As an initial orientation for subsequent modification, central metaphors are those of architectural drawings or engineering blueprints, i.e., the products of the design sciences (Perlmutter, 1965; Alexander, 1964; Alexander, 1982). Policy designs are representations of what might be turned into realities. The analogy with architecture and architects should be taken seriously, if only because it appears again and again (e.g., Schon, 1983; Weimer, 1992: 136; Meier and Smith, 1994: 440).

Architectural metaphors have in many quarters gained favor over the engineering ones for several reasons. One is the view of 'social engineering' as inappropriately and inherently a matter of arrogant command by those in control of positions of power, be they in Washington, Moscow, or Brussels, i.e., anti-democratic. A second is the not necessarily warranted view of it as a failure in practice, e.g., some constructions of what has happened with efforts to engineer a welfare state in the U.S. and elsewhere. Social engineers are not as wise or smart as they and those who employ them might like to think about picking winners and rejecting losers. Related to

both reasons is the notion that engineering, unlike architecture, denies the possibilities for unwanted responses by those who must go along for the design to materialize and work as envisioned by its engineers. Such an assumption of a lack of voice, exit options, resistance strategies, and bargaining power is of course more often than not extremely unrealistic (Stewart and Ayres, 2001).

Under either metaphor, designs are representations of sets of choices and instructions to select and apply materials sufficient to produce an intended result. 'Designers put things together and bring new things into being, dealing in the process with many variables and constraints' (Schon, 1987: 42). Architecture of course draws on available scientific knowledge, but does so in the pursuit of normative standards and makes use of a lot of intuitive craft and creativity. Policy designers do so as well, and the quality of their endeavors does not depend only on the technical robustness of the "policy sciences" (Lerner and Lasswell, 1951; Dror, 1971).

A grossly over-simplified skeleton which a stereotypic designer of policies qua engineer might flesh out in a representation appears in Figure 4.1. Note it's linear, mechanical, and non-reflective appearance.

A policy design is stipulated in the expectation that adopting it will produce particular patterns of human or organizational activity and chains of consequences. Individually, or in combination, they will suffice to achieve certain predicted desirable changes in targets (intermediate products) which as a set will provide the necessary and sufficient conditions for a valued outcome.

This skeleton of course raises more questions than it answers. Why bother? Can we flesh it out adequately if at all? What ingredients go into a policy? How do we specify a valued outcome? Who are relevant persons, organizations, and collectivities? What are the pertinent human and organizational actions and socially relevant chains of consequences? What determines them? What policies will have what effects on those determinants? What are the targets to be achieved? What human actions and chains will do that? What determines if those in a position to decide to pick a particular representation will

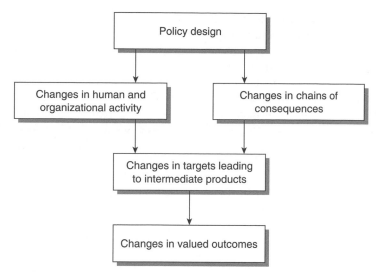

Figure 4.1   *An initial visualization*

Source: Modified from Dorfman, 1986: 108.

choose a particular one? Even if they do, will the sketch or blueprint be followed as building or implementation proceed? What body of theory, strategies, techniques, procedures and processes will enable us to answer these and other questions in ways which are consistent, ethically appropriate, and pragmatically feasible? There are then prima-facie grounds for doubt about the normative and pragmatic status of the approach in the strawman of Figure 4.1. Those are far from sufficient grounds for turning one's back on policy design.

POLICY DESIGN AS A MESSY IMPERATIVE

We often are far from indifferent about our personal and collective futures as individuals, members of social groupings, and citizens of political entities. We act, and delegate to others the responsibility to act and induce us to act, in ways which hold normative and pragmatic promise in our eyes. That promise lies in forestalling, or limiting the damage potentially posed by, distressing outcomes and achieving or at least improving the odds of appealing ones.

We tend to hold those in positions of collective responsibility accountable for the actual or prospective occurrence of unwelcome eventualities, and the failure to materialize of attractive ones we expected. We look to ruling elites to design or at least adopt designs for a desirable future and invent or at least implement ways of bringing it about. We may well reward and punish them accordingly within our understanding of their responsibilities and policy possibilities. On their part, ruling elites usually try to anticipate what will trigger particular punishments and rewards. The market for ways to pursue preferred or at least tolerable futures never closes with the attendant incentives for purveyors to enter and stay in that market. Applied social scientists have long been among those purveyors, or at least staffed them and tried to influence them and their customers.

When those ways involve more or less explicit ensembles of material and nonmaterial ingredients, context conditions, and processes, we can think of them as designs. They can appropriately be thought of as public policy designs when they involve government units or officials acting directly, or as a target of or motivator for actions by others. In a common-language sense, designs are recommended plans, but ones not at all necessarily involving *dirigiste* central planning.

Public policy design is ubiquitous since organized social and political action always involves ingredients, always has a context, always contains processes, and in modern society always involves some aspect of governance. That is no less true for those who believe in a benign or unavoidable, "invisible hand" economic or theological. For them, policy designing is still warranted if only to let the invisible hand come closer to functioning at its ostensible best rather than its imaginable worst. Policy design attempts are not the monopoly of those who buy into any one particular notion of the role of the state or embrace any particular view of desirable and just distributions of power, wealth, status or rectitude.

Policy design then claims our attention if two conditions are met. The first is that we are not indifferent to 'who gets what, when, and how' (Lasswell, 1961), a range of concern which includes processes, and aggregate and distributional outcomes. The second is that we acknowledge the existence of more than one possible positively or negatively valued state of affairs in some slice of the future, rather than granting inevitability to a particular prospect (Dror, 1986). Defeating prophets of inevitability, e.g., about inequality, may be facilitated by showing that a present state of affairs was not itself inevitable but rather results from a set of previous actions, be they ones of commission and omission (e.g., Fischer et al., 1996). Those actions could follow from an integrated, purposeful plan (deliberate intent) or merely follow from unintended second or third order effects from foreseeable or unforeseeable relevant events.

In sum, when both conditions seem to be met, the responsible course becomes to try to 'tilt the odds' toward more preferable outcomes. Preferences can be for a previously unexperienced future, maintenance of the status quo, or even resurrection of an ostensibly attractive past. They, alternatively, can be to forestall some envisioned future, erode or shatter the status quo, or forestall reversion to some past. Policy elites and publics have then little choice but to frame and choose among alternative policy designs. That is hardly new, even if it may in pre-industrial societies have emphasized an accommodation to spirits and nature, as with the Navajo Indian

"way", and never been labeled policy design. In the contemporary world, the difference is massive broadening in the range of others and phenomena whose impacts affect us, acceleration in the speed with which they do so, and near instant information about and media reporting of ostensibly outcome relevant developments.

Those secular trends increase the incentives to engage in policy design while making the endeavor more difficult. The difficulties involve: 1) greater complexity in terms of the number and variety of actors and factors; 2) rapid changes raising the risks of designs being rendered obsolete or seriously flawed before they are finished; and 3) extreme vulnerability to a loss of support due to declines in issue priority and "from the get-go" exposure to organized opposition.

The feasibility of relatively attractive paths into the future seems then to depend in increasingly important ways on interdependencies with and sensitivities to others and on contextual factors. From this perspective, policy design is necessary for timely anticipation of and accommodation to what we cannot control, as well as for making the most of what we can control. A ship's captain must steer in the face of expected or unexpected bad weather just as he or she must in a benign sea. The wise captain, naval architect and engineer tries to have built in resilience to shocking circumstances imaginable and unknowable (Demchak, 2002). Policy design tries to help "captains" and citizens by providing courses of action and material aids which can be used and retain their efficacy in 'turbulent environments' (Ackoff, 1979).

Policy design also is necessary for anticipatory policy analysis. Policy analysis broadly conceived is fundamentally the "scoring" of possible behaviors in terms of value criteria. Policy analysts are in search of at least one set of behaviors which seems likely to be at least satisfactory or ideally optimal. That quest is hostage to: the possible behaviors we envision; the foresight with which we specify sequences and quantities and qualities of behaviors; and the extent to which we encompass the range of considerations and priorities of outcomes and their associated valuations. Anticipatory policy analysis can be no better than the policy designs it considers. Unfortunately, the necessity of policy design may often only be the mother of invention and not of success. Like even the best batters in baseball or strikers in soccer, the harsh statistical reality is that the vast majority of the time our best efforts will not achieve a hit or a goal. Even when they do, that is no guarantee of future successful performance by repeating the previously successful moves (counter to Chung, 1993).

Many of the inherent difficulties are well known – the lack of stable and fully revealed goal preferences; limited understanding of causality; at best partial knowledge of the future; counter-measures deliberate and unintentional of unanticipated vigor, skill and type; the presence of residual designs, institutional interests, legacies, and memories rather than a clean slate; and hard to fathom complexity. Policy design is a "game of failure" and disappointment, and thus not for the easily discouraged or those who do not find the act of participation inherently gratifying compared to only being a spectator.

That is not to say that technique and strategy do not matter for achievement, that all failures must be repeated, or that an unsuccessful specific effort cannot set the stage for subsequent relative success. At least in the long-run, the odds for both positive achievements and avoiding failures can be improved, if only at the margin. Since policy design is a game that will be played, it makes sense to seek ways to play more effectively. What those are and the capacity to put them into use will of course vary. Some strategies and techniques may have merit almost generically and others only for particular situational factors and available resources. An implication is that policy designers need to be adept at generically useful skills and situational diagnosis, command a broad repertoire to draw on for particular situations, and be realistic about available resources.

Some final prefatory implications of a team sport metaphor are worth noting as they bear on policy design. First, while the designer is a player at the stage of suggesting what to do, he or she is most of the time not in a position to adopt or implement policy designs. The role is more that of a coach who, through analysis and intuition, determines what behaviors on the field are desirable, and tries to prepare and persuade players (as agents) to make them. Like even the wisest coach, a policy designer has to live with the possibility of the actual players putting advice into action well, poorly, or not at all. The designer can, however, be more or less competent at fitting strategies and techniques to the available players, the nature of the opposition, field conditions, and the time remaining in a game, series, or season. And, of course, like changing coaches, firing and replacing designers may be a more common response to disappointment than changing those who adopt or implement policy designs.

Second, policy design is often a competitive sport. Experts compete for the chance to design policies. If they get it, their designs are pitted against alternatives. When designs go into the white water of the policy process they are placed in the hands of individuals who may well be competing for personal success, and of teams (e.g., political parties and bureaus) who compete to improve or at least do as well for themselves as they have before. Ultimately, designs in practice and the political entities who have put them more or less into practice are competing against benchmarks used by relevant audiences.

The policy designer has reason to take into account the benchmarking criteria at work and their interpretation, while recognizing his or her limited (but perhaps not non-existent) capacity to stipulate them. Flying in the face of prevalent benchmarks and interpretations increases the chances that designs will be ignored, rejected, or distorted in implementation. Even if fulfilled, a design may be deprived of the status of a model for emulation in other jurisdictions or time periods. In effect a policy design provides a promise, albeit a hedged one. The promise competes with held images of the past, present, and future to elicit "gambles" or bets from elites and general populations.

Further, there is no guarantee that: a) the design teams and their employers or sponsors are all playing the same game, or b) if they are, accept the same rules, or c) if they do, accept the same measures and standards of performance. This lack of homogeneity can lead to "design wars" between experts rooted in different disciplines, ideologies, and intellectual traditions (see Bobrow and Dryzek, 1987; Linder and Peters, 1992). It can also lead in the world outside the design studio, think-tank, or policy planning bureau to profound disappointments, surprises, and conflicts.

More encouragingly, a policy design and the activities associated with designing need not move fully from paper or hard drive into practice, or fully achieve their promise, to provide benefits. Efforts at designing or applying a policy can raise performance norms for policy content and process. Those experiences can enlighten us about what does not work as desired, and focus us on vulnerabilities for future amelioration. More arguably, they can leave satisfaction with the benefits of the endeavor ("a game well-played") even if one's favorite loses and thus maintain or increase enthusiasm for trying again. If policy design is ubiquitous and necessary, it makes sense to think of it as being played not only in a long season, but for many seasons.

CONCEPTIONS OF POLICY DESIGN

More than four decades ago, Jan Tinbergen (1958) addressed policy design. His specific concern was with development, which can be thought of more broadly as progress toward a preferred but yet to be realized collective future. His perspective continues to echo in subsequent conceptions of the motivation for and fundamental characteristics of policy design. He advocated a turn to design as a replacement for 'decisions ... taken on the basis of vague ideas of general progress, and often somewhat haphazardly ... a process of trial and error ... [marked by] ... setbacks and crises, and probably a good deal of misplaced energy and effort ...' (Tinbergen, 1958: 3). Policy design effort follows from dissatisfaction with a record of behavior including its efficiency.

Motivated by that dissatisfaction, the policy designer builds on awareness that ultimate, broad goals require achieving 'certain general

conditions ... an economy must possess certain basic characteristics ... and some government activity.' A government must have at hand 'a minimum of instruments of economic policy ... and these must be properly used.' Because the goals or values sought are never in reality singular but always multiple (a multi-attribute utility function), the instruments should be multiple as well.

Beyond those basics, design is informed by an 'awareness of ... [goal related] ... potentialities and advantages' derived from descriptions of the past and present, and projections. It also should be informed by awareness of 'varying circumstances. Depending on circumstances some elements of ... policy will require more emphasis and attention or will appear more or less promising than others.' Further, the action elements of designs ('programs' and their component 'projects') 'by their very nature have to be guesses and must be revised periodically.' (Tinbergen, 1958: 4–7). In sum, Tinbergen called attention to the starting points of universal requirements or necessary conditions, government policy instruments as means, recognition of alternative possible outcomes, situational diagnosis, uncertainty, and sufficient flexibility for revision in light of experience.

While Tinbergen did emphasize economic matters and governmental instruments, he made it quite clear that a far broader set of actors and factors should be considered in policy design. These include the private sector, general population attitudes, the administrative organs of government with their varied proclivities and capabilities, current economic structure, natural resources, geographic situation, particularly strong personalities, the size of the entity involved, and its sensitivity to behavior external to it. Policy design then is the 'solution of a jig-saw puzzle of considerable complexity.' (Tinbergen, 1958: 35)

In light of these considerations, the challenges to the policy designer are to devise a set of steps which together make up a 'coherent and coordinated whole.' That, in turn, calls for avoiding the pitfalls of sole reliance on quantitative data, wishful thinking about available resources, omission of interactive effects, and inattentiveness to time-lags and sequences of action. Policy designs are working drafts to be scrutinized and modified, based on eclectic information, internal consistency, completeness, and the direct and primary as well as indirect and secondary consequences of their constituent programs and projects (Tinbergen, 1958: 9–33). Given the importance of what will not be known with certainty, the responsible designer will consider offering 'alternative programs,' each with a somewhat different base of assumptions. Failures will still result because of factors such as the ignorance of politicians, pressure from vested interests, ministerial rivalries, incentives offered by legislatures, and external interference.

Policy designers should be modest about the 'role to be played by scientific knowledge and insight … The relevant facts of life are too many and too varied to make it possible to reach decisions without a strong intuitive feeling for human relations' (Tinbergen, 1958: 68–69). Policy designers engage more in a craft than a science. Policy design *a la* Tinbergen stands in contrast to 'an interventionist perspective, requiring a precise forecast of events so an external hand can intervene to assure meeting of the exogenously determined targets' (Saeed, 1994: 11).

ELABORATIONS AND DIFFERENTIATIONS

Since Tinbergen's volume appeared, much has been written in several intellectual communities about what policy design should and can be. In large measure, these contributions amount to elaborating and differentiating elements explicit or implicit in his perspective. Elaboration and differentiation do not necessarily carry with them implications of universal superiority, or exclusive, most quintessential status. They can instead suggest the opposite – a broadening of the scope of policy design rather than a narrowing. After Schon's 'reflective practitioner' who engages in a conversation with a design situation (Schon, 1983, 1987), the elaborations and differentiations may as a whole suggest an enriched and more varied, rather than a more circumscribed and narrowly focused conversation.

The Tinbergian perspective surely can encompass many more recently offered conceptions. Herbert Simon's view of design as the process of 'changing existing situations into preferred ones' (Simon, 1972: 55) becomes compatible when one invokes his conception of satisficing. If a current situation, and current prospects for the future, are satisfactory there need be only limited interest in design. If they are not, designers need quest after only what would make them satisfactory, and not after what would make them optimum. Reconciliation for inclusion is not even required for conceptions such as those of Linder and Peters (1988) 'the purposive or goal-directed rearrangement of a problem's manipulable features'; May's (1981) 'identification and manipulation of key design variables to create viable alternatives'; or Wildavsky's art of finding solutions to policy problems that specify desirable relationships between 'manipulable means and attainable objectives' (Wildavsky, 1979: 15–16 in Weimer, 1993: 111). Tinbergen's recognition of situational variety is a harbinger of the emphasis on it in 'case-wise' prescriptions for policy analysis and design (Bruner, 1986, 1983).

Nevertheless, Tinbergen's perspective, wise as it was and is, leaves open a wide and difficult range of issues about the practice of policy design. Some of these are about steps in the creation of a meritorious design. Others are about what its contents should be. Still others are about the intellectual sources of or approaches to providing those contents. Taken to exclusive extremes, the different positions in these debates amount to different conceptions of policy design (for comparisons of some of the major contenders, see Bobrow and Dryzek, 1987; Linder and Peters, 1992). Yet we need not, and should not, treat them as either/or choices.

Continued contention about what aspects of the policy design elephant to emphasize is then about claims to shares in a mix, rather than something to be resolved by giving the mix a more homogenous, less multi-faceted character. Those claims or suggestions may contribute to an 'armamentarium' of 'frames with which to envisage' coherent designs and 'tools with which to impose … [designer's] … images on situations' (Schon, 1987: 218).

This position, applied to political entities and not just economic ones and to designs for outcomes not limited to economic ones, adopts and generalizes the counsel of Adelman and Taylor (1986: 84) 'Ultimately, appropriate forms … need to evolve which can be adapted flexibly to economies and societies at vastly different levels of development, having different objectives and constraints, operating with different information and power structures, and having differing social norms and values. The evolution of such planning technologies requires melding a historical and socio-political perspective with the tools of operations research in a much more flexible and synergistic manner …'

Major elaborations and differentiations modify, almost always by complicating, the visualization introduced in Figure 4.1. I will first consider two major sorts of elaborations which are by no means incompatible with each other. One proliferates elements of a policy design, and thus tasks to be dealt with in the design process. A second provides maxims, wise guidance, for the undertaking of those tasks. Neither sort is the particular property of a single technical discipline. Each introduces "cascades" of questions to be dealt with.

ADDITIONAL TASKS

Some of the additional tasks involve problem definition (DeLeon, 1994; Schneider and Ingram, 1989). What are we proposing the design to remedy? A wrong or incomplete answer will lead to designs which are social failures, either because they deal with a remedy for a different malady altogether or yield an outcome which the ostensible beneficiaries view more as a threat or harm than as a remedy or benefit.

From this angle, problem definition involves value clarification and identifying dissatisfactions or as yet unmet or endangered desires as goals (Lasswell, 1971). These are certainly matters of moral philosophy – the warranted claims of the poor, the rich, nationals, foreigners, the living, future generations. They call for judgments about whose fate should have how much standing in defining what are positive and negative outcomes (issues of representation) and the quantity and distribution of a varity of benefits (goods) received and costs (bads) borne (e.g., for indigenous knowledge as intellectual property in Norchi, 2000, or for wealth creation and public health and welfare in Daniere and Takahashi, 1999).

From another angle, problem definition involves a grasp of causality. What brings about particular human or organizational actions and chains of consequences? Why do they produce particular intermediate products or performance on target phenomena? Why do particular sets of products and performances produce one or another outcome? With weak and partial answers to these questions, we simply cannot know with confidence answers to a host of very practical questions. What needs to be changed? By how much and how quickly? What will induce those changes without triggering responses which countervail them? Consideration of causality in policy design also raises issues about factors external to a particular policy system which can affect its behavior, the triggers of the bad weather or turbulence to which we referred earlier.

Context altering events and developments may be unanticipated in their entirety or magnitude. We may be unable to specify their frequency, time of onset, and duration. Consider the impacts of the collapse of the Soviet Union on the foreign policy designs of most other nations, of a tide of refugees on welfare delivery systems, of assassination or atrocity on inter-group relations, or of an agricultural blight on food provision. The "exogeneous" cannot be relied on to remain helpfully walled off. Yet some possibilities are surely imaginable, and thus can be accommodated in a robust design. Others are not, but such possibilities can be accommodated at least in part by building in slack and redundancy, even at a sacrifice of efficiency. Still, other changes can only be handled by a quick and thorough reversion to a reconsideration of problem redefinition (after Demchak, 2002).

From a third angle, problem definition involves a reasonably accurate description of a current situation, including its probably irreversible trends. That may seem rather mundane, but descriptive reality is often not well known or a matter of consensus. For major policy matters, domestic and international, it more often is contested ground. And it is fought over or obscured in large measure because our understandings of it affect what even the best processes of value clarification and causality determination will find or have found. This aspect of problem definition can take a lot of hard work. Reflect for a moment on the difficulties of: listing the relevant shapers and shakers of foreign trade conduct in particular industries and flows as more than general categories; determining the percentage of welfare recipients who genuinely would prefer to have jobs under varying conditions; estimating the current national costs of mental illness let alone its incidence; or assessing the closeness in time (imminence) of any particular country having ready-to-use weapons of mass destruction (as with Iraq, Iran and North Korea). If we don't know where we are, how can we determine a course to move from there to someplace else or even to maintain the status quo?

To compound matters further, the problem may not be an absence of good designs in the compass of Figure 4.1 but lie with some of the factors and actors which pose themselves between the design as representation and the design in practice. Such obstacles involve adoption and implementation (Bardach, 1977; Pressman and Wildavsky, 1973) and interpretation (Edelman, 1977, 1971). Will the design be adopted in full or in part by authorized authorities and processes and sustained in that status for its intended life? Even if it is, will those persons, organizations, and social groupings, who must act to make the adoption more than a piece of paper, do so in ways the design assumes? How will the policy be portrayed along the way from design to adoption to implementation to a verdict on its results? At least by now few policy experts would deny the importance of adoption and implementation. The pertinent issues for a conception of policy design are whether those matters are part of it, and if so what role they should play in it. Interpretation is less discussed with relation to policy design, and even abhorrent to some given its connotations of "spin" and deception.

Yet neglect of it flies in the face of the reality of the attention to presentation and public and media relations which take a large part of the time of policy-makers and takers, and of those who would influence them.

I suggest that adoption, implementation, and interpretation usually should be integral parts of policy design. An architect adapts his design to the proclivities of those who must agree to buy it, use it, and build it – while trying to influence their notions of what they want and can have. This caveated position accepts that on occasion it may be useful to formulate a design simply as a utopian, aspirations raising endeavor. Far more frequently, adoption or implementation or interpretation failure are fates to be avoided. What is in, and interpreted to be in, a Figure 4.1 type design will affect the chances of adoption, and the fidelity of implementation in spirit and letter. That does not argue for taking the design course with the most popular "face" and established odds of adoption and implementation. Doing so could vitiate the reason for undertaking the design effort in the first place – to improve what would otherwise be outcomes. It does call for steps in design which will serve several purposes.

The first is to give a design thought to be commendable in terms of valued outcomes the best possible chance of being realized. The second is to help focus design efforts on critical obstacles to preferred outcomes. The 'bottleneck' obstacles may lie with the processes of and incentives at work for adoption and implementation and predominant interpretations. In that case, adoption and implementation institutions and symbolic costumes are important parts of policy designs. If those in being are problematic, design efforts should re-invent them. The third is to filter alternative proto-designs thought to hold equivalent promise for preferred outcomes. Adoption and implementation feasibility and interpretative ease can provide a reasoned basis for selecting the design to be developed in detail, to be transformed from a sketch into a blueprint. The fourth is that what goes on in adoption and implementation will affect interpretation of the differences made in beneficial results and in valued outcomes. We often care about processes and not just outcomes.

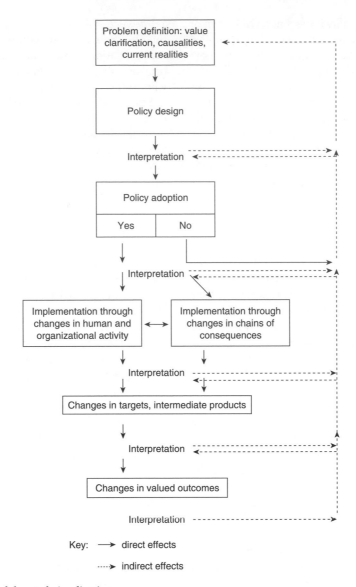

Figure 4.2   *An elaborated visualization*

Acceptance of this inclusionary position on adoption, implementation, and interpretation, of course increases the burden of problem definition. It adds more about which we need to ascertain values, understand causality, and know current reality.

An appealing feature of Figure 4.1 is its sequential quality. Policy designers are like many of us in liking to cross tasks off of their to-do lists and move on. Unfortunately, reality is rarely so permissive. Human and organizational actions are influenced by changes in chains of consequences and vice-versa. Achievements or shortfalls in targets affect subsequent actions and chains. Perceptions that valued outcomes are being realized, exceeded, or placed at increased risk do matter for subsequent human and organizational actions and chains of consequences. We can and should add adoption and implementation experiences into that world of feedbacks. The feedbacks are seldom without intermediating interpretations.

We then arrive at a visualization more like Figure 4.2.

The spaghetti in this picture contrasts with the neatness of Figure 4.1. Rather than linear movement, we have chronic recursiveness to one or more previous tasks. Rather than unfiltered impacts on subsequent stages we have intervening interpretative processes, often highly contested about their main content. This template is a far more realistic skeleton of what goes on in and around public policy systems than that of Figure 4.1. Even so, making the visualization directly useful for specific policies, located specifically as to place and time, involves unpacking the elements and the flows and filters between them to an extent that defies representation in a single picture. To return to the architectural analogy, consider how a sketch of a building on a single page proliferates into increasingly detailed, voluminous representations of parts of it.

GUIDING MAXIMS

We can readily agree on the design situation most conducive to sound problem definition and thus to high confidence policy design. The fortunate policy designer would have a well-filled physical or electronic shelf. It would contain reasonably clear specifications of values, based on widely accepted patterns of actor representation. It would provide strong causal theories and empirically established sensitivities to legislation, administrative guidance, judicial decisions, resource inputs, organizational reforms, and public relations campaigns – together with their temporal leads and lags. It would make available detailed, timely and accurate profiles of current states of affairs. Dream on.

Part of the policy design problematique deals then with what to do in the substantial absence of such attractive resources. One possibility defers policy design altogether, since it amounts to laboring on "bound to fail" (or only to succeed by chance) illusions. This "further research is needed" position stands aside for an indeterminate period of time from the pursuit of valued collective outcomes. It is tolerable only

with reason to be rather sanguine about what will result while we wait for the research to pan out. Another possibility is to "do" policy design in ways which take deficits in problem definition; and setting into account, a "yellow-light" position. That position does not gainsay the need for better foundations for problem definition, indeed it may amount to advocacy for efforts to "hold the fort" until those improvements are available and provide openings to take advantage of them as they become available.

Tinbergen of course took the "proceed with caution" position. The wisdom to which we now turn elaborates his position and has implications for designing as an activity. It emphasizes exploration, making provision for "post-launch" adjustments or even "mission" cancellation, and hedging.

Exploratory activities include interactions and pre-negotiations with the parties who will "live" in the design (e.g., users, clients, stakeholders, adopters, implementors, target populations) and best judgment impact statements about policy consequences. Explorations include attempts to understand the dynamics of the current system and its participants. An example is the 'reference mode' in systems dynamics models capturing the 'important feedback loops existing between the … elements in the system that create the particular time variant patterns' already present (Saeed, 1994: 22). Others feature probes to illuminate how the parties will behave if placed into one or another designed future ("what if" games, exercises, simulations and even "trial balloons") under a range of possible conditions, and with what results (e.g., labor market measures in response to changes in technology and external competition, as in Ho, 2000, or welfare reform financial incentives as in Robins, Michalopoulos, and Pan, 2001).

Still others, as circumstances permit, include "trying out" all or parts of the policy design (prototypes in pilot studies) to determine its performance (field experiments) or examining situations where it in effect has been tried out (natural experiments). (See the classic work of Campbell, 1969; and Cook and Campbell, 1979, and recent examples with respect to rural development programs in Fox and Gershman, 2000, welfare to work programs, as in Loeb and Corcoran, 2001 and Bloom et al., 2001, occupational safety, as in Murphy-Greene and Leip, 2002, and home financing to check urban sprawl, as in Blackman and Krupnick, 2001.) Even if systematic try-out data are not available, a more informal scrutiny by experts knowledgeable about previous design efforts may be undertaken (e.g., for international economic sanctions, as in Miljkovic 2002, or the "murder boards" to which intelligence estimates and weapons designs are sometimes subjected).

Provisions for adjustment bear on avoiding locked-in commitment to all or part of a design, and the supply of and responsiveness to "back-talk from the situation", as the design is followed. The former amounts to recommending flexibility in the design, keeping options open for choice as the design unfolds in practice. That can be done by delegation in place of specification, for example, granting administrative discretion. It can be done by building conditionalities into the design to be triggered by specified states of affairs. It can be done by structuring the design in terms of diversified "stages of choices," each one of which is selective while maintaining more than one alternative (competitors) to be selected from at a later point when uncertainty reducing additional information will be available.

Back-talk (feedback) provision at its simplest involves designing in transparency through such "sunshine" devices as public access to information, whistle-blower protections, and reporting and review requirements. At another and more demanding level, it benefits from the design containing explicit 'flags' relevant to a need for adjustment. These may be milestones (what should have happened by a certain point as the design was put into practice) or indicators confirming or disconfirming that the design is performing as intended. It often is desirable and necessary to design in organizational cells empowered to collect and process such information.[1]

Yet even if designs have ample provision for the supply of feedback, other considerations merit attention to increase the chances of responsiveness to it. These are more matters of the design management situation than of the design itself and the incentives that situation

poses. Policy designers are usually invested at least psychologically in their products. So too are those who adopted them and have gained rents by a prominent role in implementing them. So too are the beneficiaries of the intermediate products. Getting any or all of them to respond constructively to adjustment signals takes forethought about how to hold up to them persuasive prospects of reward and punishment.

Adjustment is more likely when designs are pursued on the basis of a widely shared premise that adjustment is their normal and appropriate fate, given imperfect forecasting capacities (as argued in Aaron, 2000). It is less likely when doing so invokes an attribution of incompetence or evil. In the first situation, adjustments amount to 'upgrades' or 'product improvements' which usefully take into account experiences and changes in opportunities. In the second, they are confessions of defects which call into question the basic merit of the design itself. Such confessions simply provide an enemy with weapons.

Of course, the ultimate in avoiding excessive commitments is not to make commitments at all, or only the most modest and limited ones. Extreme incrementalism is the ultimate hedge. It argues for narrow and thin designs as they involve changes from what will otherwise be the case. The chances of disappointment are less if one tries to change too little, than if one tries to change too much. One is less likely to propound designs which will worsen matters. The chances of designs being realized in practice benefit from "going with the flow" rather than challenging most prevailing norms and standard operating procedures – or the incentives which support them. The counsel of incrementalism also implies placing policy designs on a "short leash" (e.g., through such mechanisms as sunset provisions, or one-year funding, or institutional "checks and balances"). Go through the yellow light very slowly and, after that, consider what to do at the next intersection.

An incremental approach surely can be part of a "learning strategy" but in that case it too requires some of the same information providing and responsiveness encouraging features as the adjustment emphasis discussed previously and blurs into it.

Another form of hedging is 'compromise' (Arrow, 1986). The design can still be broad and deep, but does not try to optimize in terms of intermediate target products or valued outcomes. Designers 'respect the uncertainty of their basic premises' by trying to 'strike a balance between meeting all contingencies, with great waste of resources for the contingencies that do not arise, and meeting none, with the penalties that follow. How the balance between safety and daring is struck depends on the probabilities of the different possibilities, the costs of providing against them, and the penalties for failure to meet them' (Arrow, 1986: 162, 165–66).

These maxims all have strong arguments in their favor. Unfortunately, they also tend to have several drawbacks. First, they increase the tasks involved with policy design and thus the resources and time it takes. That is reasonably self-evident for the exploratory and adjustment providing features and for hedging through compromise. Less self-evidently, it is also true for incrementalism. That road leads to endless, short, and tight deadline policy design cycles. Each one involves a full set of tasks, as in Figure 4.2. The parties to policies in practice have ample reason to act in their own sweet time as their bargaining power increases as deadlines approach. The proliferation of design tasks, and increases in the resources and time they consume, raise the chances of policy design fatigue and lessen the energies and speed of actually moving out to realize a design.

Second, for reasons mentioned earlier, it is not obvious that many of the envisioned tasks are any more capable of successful completion than those discussed with reference to problem definition. Consider the determinations involved in Arrow's compromising. Nor is it any clearer than it was for problem definition as to when we will have done these tasks well enough to give us warranted confidence in proceeding.

Third, delay in making major policy design commitments has its own risks (as with U.S. health insurance reforms in Oliver, 1999, or the "Oslo process" intended to resolve the Israeli–Palestinian conflict). Windows of opportunity can close. Situations can deteriorate and unwanted ones can become either more difficult to reverse or require more time and effort to do so. Opponents can mobilize and engage in blocking actions. Stances of adjustment and hedging limit the incentives to the parties to bet strongly on a particular design, or to accept it more than superficially. While such stances do avoid the discrediting risks of unfulfilled grand promises, they also work against the sorts of appeals that can mobilize enthusiastic, intense support.

PRIMACY FOR PROCESSES AND PROCEDURES

Other than further research, there are three non-fatalistic responses to the challenges of policy design *a la* Tinbergen introduced previously. One is of course to proceed with due humility, convinced that there is no other socially responsible course and with modest hopes about improvement in the tools available to us. A second, which does not buy into inevitable policy failure, is to drop a "pretentious" rhetoric of design in favor of the "old-fashioned way" to deal with policy problems. Get a bunch of smart, motivated, and knowledgeable people together and hope that they will be creative, politically agile, and lucky. The problem is that even the "best and the brightest" can turn out to be wrong or lack the mandate for effective agency. A third, design with a fundamental difference, is that to which we now turn.

Design with a difference does not directly address policies as choices for classic content areas (e.g., social welfare, public health, economic growth, defense). What it designs instead are processes and procedures for generic purposes of problem definition, value clarification, and policy adoption, implementation, and interpretation. Normative positions and pragmatic judgments come together to make process and procedure design the road to better policy performance. While oversimplified, it is helpful to distinguish two strands – institutionalists and, after Linder and Peters (1992), 'deliberationists.'

Pragmatically, both are impressed by the difficulties noted in meeting the demands of

Figure 4.2, the requisite "matching" of policy design elements to current and altered characteristics of the world in which the design is to be put into practice. They are pessimistic about our ever having the control or foresight to do so well enough. Normatively, institutionalists and deliberationists see the need for protections against exploitation of the roles of problem definer, policy designer, adopter, implementer, and interpreter by special interests. Where they differ is in how to deal with those pragmatic and normative problems.

Institutionalists, after Douglas North (1990: 3), attempt to prescribe the 'rules of the game' designs include and the mechanisms to make those rules operational, that is, institutional designs. One example is the formation of partnerships to contain and resolve what would otherwise be policy, program, and project paralyzing conflicts, as with the World Commission on Dams (Brinkerhoff, 2002).

A more general example is that of the turn in development thinking toward governance to emphasize actions to bring about 'accountability, a conducive legal framework, and transparency' (World Bank, 1991: ii) drawing on general principles about conducive conditions and necessary properties of each. Accountability, it is claimed, has a better chance when procedures and processes make for continuing competition, e.g., through full or partial privatization. Participatory opportunities for affected publics to articulate their interests are helped by designing in NGO roles and decentralizing responsibility to more proximate bureaucracies and elected office-holders. A legal framework is as it should be when 'rules are known in advance … [and are] … actually in force, mechanisms … ensure application of the rules, conflicts … [are] … resolved through binding decisions of an independent judicial body or through arbitration, there are known procedures for amending the rules when they no longer serve their purpose.' A design which provides for these conditions will be more likely to 'prevent predatory government actions and agent rent-seeking' (World Bank, 1991: iii).

How to get institutions to behave as desired fundamentally amounts to taking advantage of the incentives they already have and ones provided by "reforms" in procedures and processes

(Weimer, 1992). Those reforms ostensibly will shift distributions of power and information so that the relevant parties behave better. That will, however, only happen if the incentives cross a hard to discern strength threshold and include clear signals about their future application, as with pro-environment technology efforts by firms in Norberg-Bohm, 1999.

Deliberationists focus more on the quality of the discourse from which policy emerges than on what in particular emerges. To "get the discourse right", some recommend 'explicit standards of discourse' (MacRae, 1988; Anderson, 1987). Others concentrate on particular 'models of deliberation' (Fischer, 1981; Paris and Reynolds, 1983; Linder and Peters, 1992: 226–7). The former focus on what ought to be discussed; the latter on who will participate and their freedom to raise matters they care about. The latter places in the hands of the parties who will be involved and affected the tasks of value and option formation, context appraisal and choice, rather than stipulating them in the design. That empowerment ostensibly will bring to bear creativity, information, diagnostic skills, value clarifications, and a sense of ownership which a temporally or situationally distant professional elite of policy designers cannot muster. Interactions between the parties along process and procedure lines provided by a designer will itself make for 'matching' and is likely to do so better.

These recipes seem very different from those of Tinbergen and his descendants. Yet three questions remain to be answered. Can institutionalist and deliberationist approaches be married with his in ways which compliment each others' strengths and compensate for each others' weaknesses? Would institutionalist and deliberationist recommendations necessarily work as envisioned or are some additional properties required? Is making those properties available and getting the procedures to be realized into practice similar to some of the challenges posed in Figure 4.2?

The answer to the first question is largely positive. For institutional design, that is implied by our previous discussion of adoption, implementation and interpretation. Tinbergen after all recognized the importance of the targets of institutional design. Yet he also recognized that policy satisfaction also includes policy results in terms of particular tangible and psychic benefits and costs and not just processes and procedures. Most assessments of policy performance find it to be the joint product of both policies and institutions involved with them (e.g., Keiser and Meier, 1996). Satisfaction can be denied by getting institutions wrong (Meier and Smith, 1994), but achieving satisfaction takes more than getting them right. Even if, for example, one can make implementing bureaucracies quite compliant in a Weberian fashion, we may still find abhorrent or stupid the policy they are complying with.

Deliberationists' communicative suggestions could certainly contribute to an improved grasp of the values at work, defining policy problems, knowing current realities, and understanding the reasons for human and organizational actions (e.g., Berger, 1977). What would be conducive interpretations and conditions for adoption and effective implementation might be made clearer. At the same time, communicative discourse could be improved by the sorts of analyses and information at the heart of Tinbergian policy design, and be substantially disappointing in their absence.

Whether the institutionalists' or the deliberationists' recommendations would have the benefits they envision seems contingent. The former pose recipes which experience suggests are less than guaranteed in their consequences across situations. That is why we see alternating cycles of centralization and decentralization (Montias, 1986). Institutionalists' recipes may fail to acknowledge how learning from one pass at them may lead to behavior which deprives them of subsequent efficacy. For example, rationalizing closing of U.S. military bases was helped in one pass by establishing closing procedures "behind a veil of ignorance" where individual legislators did not know if and how their district would be affected (Weimer, 1992). While the procedures have remained in place for subsequent rounds, legislators became fully aware of the potential for adverse district consequences and moved to block further closings.

The deliberationist approach depends on who gets to participate, the skills they bring to the

discourse, the investment they are willing to make in it, and how binding the understandings reached will be. One can imagine cases in which the participants would be diverse and representative, have substantial if not identical communicative skills, give high priority to the dialogues, and have substantial influence with those they represent (as illustrated in Walters, Aydelotte, and Miller, 2000). One can also imagine cases of the opposite (as illustrated in Pelletier et al., 1999). Relevant parties are advertently or inadvertently left out. Some participants, for all sorts of reasons, are highly effective communicators and others are "bumps on the log." Attendance is a pro-forma or watchdog activity rather than a constructive engagement. Those who go to the meeting are the people their home group neither trusts or respects.

The differentiations from Tinbergen's position of institutionalists and deliberationists call for different rules of the policy design and policy process game than often prevail. How to get that to happen and meet relevant conditionalities involves a system of constructions, actions and consequences, rather like those in Figure 4.2.

Institutionalists would be wise to consider the variety in what has happened in light of their rather similar prescriptions for post-Communist nations. They also might well consider the implications of historical experience, which shows that nations with 'basic success stories … [with respect to meeting basic human needs] … have had very different economies from an institutional and political point of view' (Streeten, 1986: 29).

Deliberationists would do well to note the particular circumstances apparently needed to get a process of evolving policy through a more cooperative dialogue in place for environmentalists with ranchers and agriculturalists in the American West under Department of Interior sponsorship. They may find sobering how some steps in line with a shared information, transparency standard can, in particular, contexts countervail other parts of their prescriptions. Consider uses of courts and legislatures to obstruct or enhance pursuit of data sought by those already holding negative views about the effects of smoking or particular industrial products and processes. In those instances, greater achievement of transparency could and has had the consequence of deterring "emancipatory" policy dialogue (Hilts, 1999).

Institutionalist and deliberationist approaches are potentially important and useful. They are not sufficient unto themselves, automatically successful, or devoid of the challenges facing other approaches to policy design.

STRATEGIES – THE TEN COMMANDMENTS

When we consider the intellectual instruments available to policy designers, it is possible to find abundance or a rather thin portfolio.

If one includes the bodies of instruments used in the relevant sciences and professions – by no means limited to the social sciences – abundance seems an accurate description. Consider Dorfman's (1986: 108) list of relevant specialties for environmental policy: engineering; agronomy; meteorology; hydrology; chemistry; soil sciences; epidemiology; toxicology; oncology; zoology; biology; forestry; geology; economics; social sciences. Of course, the social sciences themselves contain many disciplines and we can and should also recognize the pertinence of law, the information sciences, and political and social philosophy. If we consider the wealth of different policy issues for which there is some demand for policy design the list would get much longer still. Each has its instruments which are potentially applicable and examples can be found of their use in policy design (e.g., for economics Cody, Kitchen and Weiss, 1990; Henderson, 1986; Cohen and Wyplosz, 1995; Brainard and Martimort, 1996). There are far too many strategies and techniques to review here, particularly if considered with responsible cautions about the appropriateness of their theoretical assumptions and feasibility of their information requirements.

The long-standing abundance just discussed for practical purposes contrasts with a much smaller repertoire of options when we limit our consideration to strategies formulated, with a special focus on policy design and generically applicable to it (Weimer, 1992: 135;

Linder and Peters, 1988, 1984). From this perspective, the rules for inclusion in the policy designer's basic repertoire emphasize relevance to the challenges posed by Figure 4.2 and to a wide range of policy domains in terms of both issue areas and levels and forms of governance.

Any selection on those bases is of course open to argument, but I suggest ten core strategies. They belong if only because going entirely without any one of them exposes the designer and his or her designs to substantial, hard to avoid grief. The core ten are then in effect a necessary part of the repertoire, not to be confused with a complete one. For convenience they can be labeled as: discipline breakout; minimum necessary conditions; safeguards; placement; oppositional analysis; borrowing; tinkering; backward mapping; forward mapping; and judgment shaping. They may seem banal, until one reflects on how often they are slighted with, at least in retrospect, disappointing results.

Discipline breakout rejects as more than stimulating grist for the designer's mill the framing provided by any single technical and professional disciplines. The designer must break out from the constrained definitions of problems, lists of actors, patterns of causation and correlation, and inventories of policy moves set by any single such discipline. Reality always is more complicated than that and policy designs are instruments to deal with reality rather than scholastic gymnastics. The most efficacious designs will then be full of what are tangential matters from any orthodox single frame perspective, as argued in Ascher, 2002 and exemplified in Brewer and Kakalik, 1979.

A **minimum necessary conditions** strategy has the policy designer identify and address what has to be the case, or be made the case, for a preferred outcome or range of outcomes to have much of a chance of realization. If those conditions are not met, the design should be a non-starter. If those necessary conditions seem in reach via the design, it should receive serious consideration and warrants elaboration to enrich it with sufficient conditions. This strategy involves thinking through how to avoid well-known, chronically possible failure by key elements in any policy design, e.g., recurrent types of government and market failure. It also involves dealing with what are for the outcome the design pursues crucial parties, and crucial desiderata for them.

For example, in addressing the necessary conditions for Israeli–Palestinian peace, Yorke (1990) focuses on the need to meet minimum Israeli requirements ('full peace and security') and Palestinian ones ('an independent state'). She reasons that those minima can only be provided with normalization between Israel and some other states in the region. Given the established suspicions and grievances, sustained movement toward peace requires simultaneous judgments by the parties that the advantages of peace outweigh the advantages of a continuation of the status quo … all have a stake in keeping the peace and … that peace holds fewer risks than the status quo' (Yorke, 1990: 117).

That last phrase illustrates the third strategy, safeguards. The risks in following through with a policy design do not fall primarily on its designers but on the affected parties. Realization of the design in practice requires their tolerance and often active steps on their part. They are more likely to entrust their fate to the design when it provides and is seen by them to provide means to limit damage should it go awry or break down. For Yorke, those provisions involve guarantees and commitments by third parties external to the Middle East. Also, given the very mixed record of policy design results, the responsible designer recognizes a similar need whatever the affected parties may think. The strategy of safeguards, it should be noted, is not equivalent to incrementalism, which carries its own risks.

Placement begins from awareness that policy designs apply to systems with histories. That is true for the actors in them (individuals, organizations, social groupings, politico-legal entities) and policy issues and options. The designer starts not from a clean slate but from a clutter. Placement (Neustadt and May, 1986) develops chronologies for pertinent actors and issues of major experiences in their past. Those provide no precise causal guidance as to precedents which will be used in the present and future, but they are suggestive of how policy designs alternatives will be treated differently from actor to actor and issue area to issue area,

including by legacy policy networks, e.g., for agricultural environmental regulations, as in Montpettit, 2002.

Oppositional analysis assumes that attempts to pursue a policy design in practice will be the target of deliberate foiling moves by adversaries at one or more points in Figure 4.2 (Wohlstetter, 1964, 1968). Thus, it becomes important to envision the stimulus the policy as designed will itself pose to those who would object to it (measure/counter-measure sequences). The active nature of the environment also calls for anticipation of secular trends and changes, for example, in technology, which may enhance the opportunities available to opponents. Still further, attention should go to the possibility of situational changes (shocks), unplanned by any of the affected parties, which may provide attractive opportunities for opposition. Imagining such changes in the 'terms of competition' usually requires very detailed analysis of the end-to-end chains of developments encompassed in a Figure 4.2 design and thus of the complete life-cycle of a policy design in practice.

Design work usually rests on faith that there are unachieved but, in principle, possible opportunities to do better than the status quo and the looming future. It remains to go from faith to credible demonstration of what those are and the realistic availability of means to achieve a more preferred future. **Borrowing** is a strategy for doing so (Rose, 1993; Schneider and Ingram, 1988; Weimer, 1993). It embraces what seems to have worked well elsewhere in circumstances sufficiently analogous to those facing the policy designer. The premise is that such "solutions" or "best practices" worked on similar problems in similar contexts, so they should work for me.[2] The wheel need not be reinvented but only emulated. Warranted borrowing clearly involves a host of judgments about performance elsewhere, and similarities to the situation facing the designer.

The greater the scope of what is borrowed, the harder it will be to get it into practice in the relevant situation. Even if what is borrowed is quite limited and narrow, no two situations will be precisely alike in all pertinent respects. These realities, plus the persistent appeal of incrementalism, argue for a strategy of tinkering (Weimer, 1993). The idea is to tune or tweak what exists, or what is borrowed and the context to receive it, without challenging most of what is in place. Designers go for relatively 'feasible manipulations' of what already exists (May, 1981). The policy world, even its reformist elements, usually is full of those who prefer tinkering. It then will be hard to follow a less incremental design before considering such options and discrediting them.

Backward-mapping and forward-mapping each start from the same premise that "end-to-end", full life cycle treatment is needed for robust design, a premise shared with oppositional analysis. The backward and forward strategies differ in where they would have a designer start (Elmore, 1985). In backward mapping the idea is to start just before the end in the production of outcomes and work toward the beginning, identifying who must do what and what must be the case all along the way (Elmore, 1979–80). Forward-mapping starts at the initial point of realizing a policy design and works toward its conclusion. It lays out the transition from what exists, or is currently "programmed" by man and nature to exist, to a more preferable outcome. Think of backward or forward mapping as yielding a set of stripmaps which together span the journey from origin to destination, but which can be produced and read, starting with the last strip or the first. These strategies call for moving briskly from generalized principles to the detailed particulars of a policy context, taking into account possible changes in it, such as those highlighted by oppositional analysis.

The final strategy, judgment shaping, draws on research in behavioral decision theory (Tversky and Kahneman, 1974; Kahneman and Tversky, 1979; Kahneman and Lovallo, 1993; Tversky and Simonson, 1993). That research yields human tendencies in making judgments. They imply correctives policy designs should supply, and design moves to shape the judgments of those involved in their adoption, implementation and interpretation. The tendencies differ from traditional models of rational judgment.

Tendencies to correct for include: treating problems as isolated unique instances; denial of uncertainties which would damp optimism; attraction to sure gains and underweighting of only probable ones; and favoring small steps, and aggregates of small steps, away from status quo behavior over large steps singly and in aggregate. A particularly misleading tendency is to extrapolate the ease or difficulty of the initial steps in a policy to that of the critical for outcomes later steps, e.g., as in much of the Bush Administration responses to 9/11, including the Afghan and Iraq ventures (Bobrow, 2003).

Moves to shape responses to designs include possibilities to take advantage of the ways in which preferences are context-dependent. Support for a particular policy design becomes contingent on the presence of alternative designs. By presenting an increased number of alternatives, the designer calls into action the dynamics of "tradeoff contrast" and "extremeness aversion". For the former, imagine two policy designs one of which offers both greater benefits and costs than the other. Introducing a third design with the greater benefit but at a much higher cost will increase preferences for the first design at the expense of the second. For extremeness aversion, imagine two policy designs, each of which has a great positive putative consequence and a great negative one. If a third design with more limited positive and negative consequences is introduced, it will pull support away from one or both of the first two.

These tendencies operate for designers and not just for the parties affected by policy design.[3] In sum, understanding judgment shaping has substantial implications for how we develop policy designs, for their quality, and for their chances of acceptance.

At their extremes, any one of the ten commandment strategies is in some tension with one or more of the others. Balanced and judicious attention to all of them can, however, improve capacity to deal with the challenges of policy design.

NOTES

1. Of course, pledges for continuing assessment may not actually have been implemented, as with the waivers

granted to American states for departures from previous federal health care program guidelines.

2. Related to this strategy is a filtering one of "counter-borrowing". In it, the search is for failures in similar contexts and what is found should then be rejected as a design alternative.

3. The implications for the self-awareness and discipline of policy designers are significant, with implications analogous to those incorporated into the professional preparation of psychiatrists.

REFERENCES

Aaron, Henry J. (2000). 'Seeing Through the Fog: Policymaking with Uncertain Forecasts.' *Journal of Policy Analysis and Management*, 19: 193–206.

Ackoff, Russell (1979). 'The Future of Operational Research is Past.' *Journal of the Operational Research Society*, 30: 93–104.

Adelman, Irma and J. Edward Taylor, eds. (1986). *The Design of Alternative Development Strategies*. Rohtak, India: Jan Tinbergen Institute of Development Planning.

Alexander, Christopher (1964). *Notes on the Synthesis of Form*. Cambridge: Harvard University Press.

Alexander, Ernst A. (1982). 'Design in the Decision-Making Process.' *Policy Sciences*, 14: 279–92.

Anderson, Charles (1987). 'Political Philosophy, Practical Reason, and Policy Analysis,' In Frank Fischer and John Forester, eds. *Confronting Values in Policy Analysis*. Beverly Hills: Sage, 22–44.

Arrow, Kenneth J. (1986). 'Planning and Uncertainty,' In Adelman and Taylor, *op.cit.*, 161–70.

Ascher, William (2002). 'The Brewer-Kakalik Research on Services for Handicapped Children: A Paradigm of Applied Policy Sciences.' *Policy Sciences*, 35: 305–10.

Bardach, Eugene (1977). *The Implementation Game*. Cambridge: MIT Press.

Berger, Thomas R. (1977). *Northern Frontier, Northern Homeland: Report of the Mackenzie River Inquiry*. Toronto: James Lorimer.

Blackman, Allen and Alan Krupnick (2001). 'Location-Efficient Mortgages: Is the Rationale Sound?' *Journal of Policy Analysis And Management*, 20: 633–49.

Bloom, Howard S., et al. (2001). 'Testing a Financial Incentive to Promote Re-employment among Displaced Workers: The Canadian Earnings Supplement Project (ESP).' *Journal of Policy Analysis and Management*, 20: 505–23.

Bobrow, Davis B. (2003). 'Losing to Terrorism: An American Work in Progress.' *Metaphilosophy*, 34: 387–406.

Bobrow, Davis B. and John S. Dryzek (1987). *Policy Analysis by Design*. Pittsburgh: University of Pittsburgh Press.

Brainard, S. Lael and David Martimort (1996). 'Strategic Trade Policy Design with Asymmetric Information and Public Contracts.' *Review of Economic Studies*, 63: 81–105.

Brewer, Gary D. and James S. Kakalik (1979). *Handicapped Children: Strategies for Improving Services*. New York: McGraw-Hill.

Brinkerhoff, J.M. (2002). 'Global Public Policy, Partnership, and the Case of the World Commission on Dams.' *Public Administration Review*, 62: 324–36.

Bruner, Ronald D. (1986). 'Case-wise Policy Information Systems: Redefining Poverty.' *Policy Sciences*, 19: 201–23.

—— (1983). 'Case-Wise Policy Analysis: Another Look at the Burden of High Energy Costs.' *Policy Sciences*, 16: 97–125.

Campbell, Donald T. (1969). 'Reforms as Experiments.' *American Psychologist*, 24: 409–29.

Castro, Mary and International Labor Office. (1978). *Migration in Brazil: Approaches to Analysis and Policy Design*. Liege: Ordina.

Chung, Kyong Won (1993). 'The Miracle of Han River: Government Policy and Design Management in the Motor Industry.' *Design Management Journal*, 4: 41–47.

Cody, John, Richard Kitchen and John Weiss (1990). *Policy Design and Price Reform in Developing Countries: Guidelines with Special Reference to Industry*. New York: St. Martin's.

Cohen, Daniel and Charles Wyplosz (1995). 'Price and Trade Effects of Exchange Rate Fluctuations and the Design of Policy Coordination.' *Journal of International Money and Finance*, 14: 331–47.

Cook, Thomas D. and Donald T. Campbell (1979). *Quasi-Experimentation: Design and Analysis for Field Settings*. Boston: Houghton Mifflin.

Daniere, Amrita G. and Lois M. Takahashi (1999). 'Public Policy and Human Dignity in Thailand: Environmental Policies and Human Values in Bangkok.' *Policy Sciences*, 32: 247–68.

DeLeon, Peter (1994). 'Reinventing the Policy Sciences: Three Steps Back to the Future.' *Policy Sciences*, 27: 77–95.

Demchak, Chris C. (2002). 'Un-Muddling Homeland Security: Design Principles for National Security in a Complex World.' *The Forum*, 1. www.bepress.com/forum.

Dorfman, Robert (1986). 'Benefit/Cost Analysis of Environmental Problems,' In Adelman and Taylor, *op.cit.*, 103–23.

Dror, Yehezkel (1986). *Policy Making Under Adversity*. New Brunswick, NJ: Transaction.

—— (1971). *Design for Policy Sciences*. New York: American Elsevier.

Edelman, Murray (1977). *Political Language: Words that Succeed and Policies that Fail*. New York: Academic.

—— (1971). *Politics as Symbolic Action*. New York: Academic.

Elmore, Richard F. (1985). 'Forward and Backward Mapping: Reversible Logic,' In Kenneth Hanf and Theo A.J. Toonen, eds. *Policy Implementation in Federal and Unitary Systems*. Boston: Martinus Nijhoff, 33–70.

—— (1979–80). 'Backward Mapping: Implementation Research and Policy Design.' *Political Science Quarterly*, 94: 601–16.

Fischer, Claude S., Michael Hout, Martine Sanchez Jankowski, Samuel R. Lucas, Ann Swidler, and Kim Voss (1996). *Inequality by Design: Cracking the Bell Curve Myth*. Princeton: Princeton University Press.

Fischer, Frank (1992). 'Participatory Expertise: Toward the Democratization of Policy Science,' In William N. Dunn and Rita Mae Kelly, eds. *Advances in Policy Studies Since 1950*, Policy Studies Review Annual Volume 10. New Brunswick: Transaction, 351–76.

—— (1981). *Politics, Values and Public Policy*. Boulder: Westview.

Fox, Jonathan and John Gershman (2000). 'The World Bank and Social Capital: Lessons from Ten Rural Development Projects in the Philippines and Mexico.' *Policy Sciences*, 33: 399–419.

Goggin, Malcolm L. (1987). *Policy Design and the Politics of Implementation: The Case of Child Health Care in the American States*. Knoxville: University of Tennessee Press.

Henderson, David (1986). *Innocence and Design: The Influence of Economic Ideas on Policy*. Oxford: Blackwell.

Hilts, Philip J. (1999). 'Law on Access to Research Data Pleases Business, Alarms Science.' *New York Times*, July 31, A1ff.

Ho, Lok Sang (2000). 'Wage Subsidies as a Labour Market Policy Tool.' *Policy Sciences*, 33: 89–100.

Hoag, Malcolm W. (1976). *United States Foreign Policy: Why Not Project Interdependence by Design?*; Los Angeles: International Institute for Economic Research.

Hurley, Robert E., Deborah A. Freund, and John E. Paul. (1993). *Managed Care in Medicaid: Lessons for Policy and Program Design*. Ann Arbor: Health Administration Press.

Kahneman, Daniel and Dan Lovallo (1993). 'Timid Choices and Bold Forecasts: A Cognitive Perspective on Risk Taking.' *Management Science*, 39: 17–31.

—— and Amos Tversky (1979). 'Intuitive Prediction: Biases and Corrective Procedures.' *Management Science*, 12: 313–27.

Keiser, Lael R. and Kenneth J. Meier (1996). 'Policy Design, Bureaucratic Incentives, and Public Management: The Case of Child Support Enforcement.' *Journal of Public Administration Research and Theory*, 6: 337–64.

Killick, Tony (1995). *IMF Programmes in Developing Countries: Design and Impact*. New York: Routledge.

Lasswell, Harold D. (1971). *A Pre-View of the Policy Sciences*. New York: Elsevier.

—— (1961). *Politics: Who Gets What, When, and How*. Cleveland: World.

Laudon, Kenneth C. (1986). *Dossier Society: Value Choices in of the Design of National Information Systems*. New York: Columbia University Press.

Lerner, Daniel and Harold D. Lasswell, eds. (1951). *The Policy Sciences: Recent Developments in Scope and Methods*. Stanford: Stanford University Press.

Linder, Stephen H. and B. Guy Peters (1992). 'A Metatheoretic Analysis of Policy Design.' In Dunn and Kelly, *op.cit.*, 201–37.

—— (1988). 'The Analysis of Design or the Design of Analysis.' *Policy Studies Review*, 7: 738–50.

—— (1984). 'From Social Theory to Policy Design.' *Journal of Public Policy*, 9: 237–59.

Loeb, Susanna and Mary Corcoran (2001). 'Welfare, Work Experience, and Economic Self-Sufficiency.' *Journal of Policy Analysis and Management*, 20: 1–20.

MacRae, Duncan (1988). 'Professional Knowledge for Policy Discourse.' *Knowledge in Society*, 1: 6–24.

May, Peter J. (1981). 'Hints for Crafting Alternative Policies.' *Policy Analysis*, 7: 227–44.

Meier, Kenneth J. and Kevin B. Smith (1994). 'Say It Ain't So, Moe: Institutional Design, Policy Effectiveness, and Drug Policy.' *Journal of Public Administration Research and Theory*, 4: 429–42.

Miljkovic, Dragan (2002). 'Economic Sanctions as the Propositional Sustainability Problem.' *Policy Sciences*, 35: 1–15.

Montias, J. Michael (1986). 'On the Centralization and Decentralization of Economic Activities,' In Adelman and Taylor, *op.cit.*, 171–90.

Montpetit, Eric (2002). 'Policy Networks, Federal Arrangements, and the Development of Environmental Regulations: A Comparison of the Canadian and American Agricultural Sectors.' *Governance*, 15: 1–20.

Murphy-Greene, C. and L.A. Leip (2002). 'Assessing the Effectiveness of Executive Order 12898: Environmental Justice for All?' *Public Administration Review*, 62: 679–87.

Neustadt, Richard E. and Ernest R. May (1986). *Thinking in Time: The Uses of History for Decision Makers*. New York: Free Press.

Norberg-Bohm, Vicki (1999). 'Stimulating "Green" Technological Innovation: An Analysis of Alternative Policy Mechanisms.' *Policy Sciences*, 32: 13–38.

Norchi, Charles H. (2000). 'Indigenous Knowledge as Intellectual Property.' *Policy Sciences*, Vol. 33 no. 3–4, pp. 387–398.

North, Douglas (1990). *Institutions, Institutional Change, and Economic Performance*. New York: Cambridge University Press.

Ohls, James C. and Harold Beebout. (1993). *The Food Stamp Program: Design Tradeoffs, Policy, and Impact: A Mathematica Policy Research Study*. Washington: Urban Institute Press.

Oliver, Thomas R. (1999) 'The Dilemmas of Incrementalism: Logical and Political Constraints in the Design of Health Insurance Reforms.' *Journal of Policy Analysis and Management*, 18: 652–83.

Paris, David C. and James F. Reynolds (1983). *The Logic of Policy Enquiry*. New York: Longman.

Pelletier, David et al. (1999). 'The Shaping of Collective Values through Deliberative Democracy: An Empirical Study from New York's North Country.' *Policy Sciences*, 32: 103–31.

Pellikan, Huib and Robert J. van der Veen. (2002). *Environmental Dilemmas and Policy Design*. New York: Cambridge University Press.

Perlmutter, Howard V. (1965). *Toward a Theory of Social Architecture*, Tavistock Pamphlet 12. London: Tavistock.

Pressman, Jeffrey and Aaron Wildavsky (1973). *Implementation*. Berkeley: University of California Press.

Roessner, J. David, ed. (1988) *Government Innovation Policy: Design, Implementation*, Evaluation. New York: St. Martin's.

Robins, Philip K., Charles Michalopoulos, Elsie Pan. 'Financial Incentives and Welfare Reform in the United States.' *Journal of Policy Analysis and Management*, 20: 129–50.

Rose, Richard (1993). *Lesson-Drawing in Public Policy: A Guide to Learning Across Time and Space*. Chatham, NJ: Chatham House.

Saeed, Khalid (1994). *Development Planning and Policy Design: A System Dynamics Approach*. Aldershot: Avebury.

Schneider, Anne and Helen Ingram. (1997). Policy Design for Democracy. Lawrence: University Press of Kansas.

—— (1989). 'The Powers of Problem Definition: The Case of Government Paperwork.' *Policy Sciences*, 22: 97–121.

—— (1988). 'Systematically Pinching Ideas: A Comparative Approach to Policy Design.' *Journal of Public Policy*, 8: 61–80.

Schon, Donald A. (1987). *Educating the Reflective Practitioner: Toward a New Design for Teaching and Learning in the Professions*. San Francisco: Jossey-Bass.

—— (1983). *The Reflective Practitioner: How Professionals Think in Action*. New York: Basic Books.

Simon, Herbert A. (1972). *The Sciences of the Artificial*. Cambridge: MIT Press.

Stewart, Jenny and Russell Ayres (2001). 'Systems Theory and Policy Practice: An Exploration.' *Policy Sciences*, 34: 79–94.

Streeten, Paul (1986). 'Basic Needs: The Lessons,' In Adelman and Taylor, *op.cit.*, 27–37.

Taylor, John B. (1993). *Macroeconomic Policy in a World Economy: From Econometric Design to Practical Operation*. New York: W.W. Norton.

Tinbergen, Jan (1958). *The Design of Development*. Baltimore: Johns Hopkins University Press.

Tversky, Amos and Itamar Simonson (1993). 'Context-Dependent Preferences.' *Management Science*, 39: 1179–89.

—— and Daniel Kahneman (1974). 'Judgment Under Uncertainty: Heuristics and Biases,' In Richard Zeckhauser, et al., eds., *Benefit-Cost and Policy Analysis*. Chicago: Aldine, 295–307.

Walters, Lawrence C., James Aydelotte, and Messica Miller (2000). 'Putting More Public in Policy Analysis.' *Public Administration Review*, 60: 349–59.

Weimer, David L. (1993). 'The Current State of Design Craft: Borrowing, Tinkering, and Problem Solving.' *Public Administration Review*, 53: 110–20.

—— (1992). 'Claiming Races, Broiler Contracts, Heresthetics, and Habits: Ten Concepts for Policy Design.' *Policy Sciences*, 25: 135–59.

Wildavsky, Aaron (1979). *Speaking Truth to Power*. Boston: Little, Brown.

Wohlstetter, Albert (1968). 'Theory and Opposed Systems Design,' In Morton A. Kaplan, ed., *New Approaches to International Relations*. New York: St. Martin's, 19–53.

—— (1964). 'Analysis and Design of Conflict Systems,' In Edward S. Quade, ed., *Analysis for Military Decisions*. Santa Monica: RAND, P-387-PR, 103–48.

World Bank (1991). *Managing Development: the Governance Dimension*, Discussion Paper. Washington: The World Bank.

Yorke, Valerie (1990). 'Imagining a Palestinian State: An International Security Plan.' *International Affairs*, 66: 115–36.

5

Networks and Bargaining in Policy Analysis

PETER BOGASON

INTRODUCTION

This chapter[1] tells how scientific calls for rationalism and for understanding non-rational behavior have fought visible, but at times less conspicuous, wars over the use of various models of interaction in policy processes. The concept of *network* (depicting various types of linkages between actors) has been quite victorious, but that does not mean that the features it covers are new.

Robert Hoppe has expressed the transformation of policy analysis over time well: It has gone from "Speaking Truth to Power" to "Making Sense Together" (Hoppe 1999, 201). In this chapter, the difference between the two statements is illustrated by the models of the rational actor and of mutual adjustment. We analyze some core features of these models, and from there we shall discuss a number of developments within the literature in the second half of the 20th century, in order to gain a better understanding of how theorists have dealt with human interaction in the policy process. Subsequently, we shall go through the way in which various schools of thought have dealt with the resulting pattern

of interaction, a pattern that in the early years of the third millennium A.D. is conceptualized as a *network* by most theorists. It is a story of how the rational model has conceded to interactive theories of political and administrative processes, and how the conceptions of policy processes have been broadened from being based on the polity and politics in a narrow sense to being a societal affair involving many types of actors.

However, the general ideas of networks have been present in the literature on mutual adjustment for many years. Earlier on, however, there was less agreement about the right term. This article establishes common themes on the variation. The approach is systematized historically. In the view of this author, social theories do not exist in any abstract sense. They are constructed by scholars who interact with one another and inspire one another in complex, international research networks, more or less in a Kuhnian (Kuhn 1962) way. However, real paradigm shifts are rare in the social sciences (Lakatos 1974), while marginal shifts in theoretical approaches are frequent. Scholars are subject to fads and fashions, they apply explicit and implicit comparisons, they compete for attention within their scholarly community. Policy analysts also react to and analyze the same empirical phenomena in society. Thus, they create competition, innovation and the diffusion of ideas, which often bear considerable resemblance to one another, and which are discussed in groups of scholars who share some fundamental views on social theory. They then apply the theories with some variation, according to the circumstances of their empirical research.

In short, theory is contingent on time and space, and thus the present *network* understanding of policy has come about as a result of scholars interacting and discussing the possible interpretations of social phenomena – in this case policy processes. This chapter explores some trends that have been present for the last 30 years or so without pretending any full coverage, since the theme of policy networks is vast. And since the author was present most of the time, participating in several networks, the critical reader may find some autobiographical biases. The reader will find other recent accounts of the development of the theme in Hoppe (1999), Hajer and Wagenaar (2003), and Fischer (2003), each tailored to a specific context (and all critical of traditional policy analysis). In addition, Hill and Hupe (2002) provide a general discussion from the angle of implementation, particularly the tensions between *top-downers* and *bottom-uppers* (explained below).

The discussion will be selective, it is not possible to digest all types of network policy analysis within one short chapter. We have omitted the trends towards a *transnationalization* of domestic policies, which has been due to international regimes, like the EU, the UN, the WTO etc., discussing how policies are negotiated in complex settings involving many actors, including various NGOs; see for example *Linkage Politics* (Rosenau 1969). Following patterns towards institutionalization within the EU, there has been a merge of literature on intra- and inter-state relations, to some degree captured by the concept of *multi-level governance* (Hooghe and Marks 2001). We also ignored the *evaluation* literature which, of course, is relevant for methodology within

policy analysis. In particular, the fourth generation of evaluation (Guba and Lincoln 1989) is closely linked to governance and deliberative policy analysis. Fischer (1995) brings some of the pieces together nicely.

ORGANIZED ORDER VERSUS MUDDLED PROCESSES

The classical, rational and the mutual adjustment models form the backbone of this chapter. In this chapter, we shall focus on how these models treat the decision-making processes and the interaction between actors.

Rational Policy-making

"Speaking Truth to Power" (Wildawsky 1979) indicates a troubled relationship between science and politics, between those finding the true state of the world and those wanting to rule it. Indeed, much of the policy literature is concerned with *authority, expertise and order* (Colebatch 1998). First, the policy literature deals with core activities of governments, setting up authority relations to back up the ideas of the policy principles so that they may be carried through authoritatively. Second, it discusses that policy principles do not come from an empty space, they are based on in-depth knowledge of the affairs the policy aims at regulating. This knowledge may come from governmental or external sources, but it is brought together in the contents of the policy. And third, the literature expects the policy to aim at solving a number of important problems within the target area, thus creating some sort of order in that segment of society. In the end, the policy may not be successful, but still, problem-solving is an important aspect of the general understanding of policy.

Mostly authority, expertise and order has been dealt with in the orderly fashion brought about by a top-down perspective, using a sequential model of policy-making. Policy is created, decided upon and implemented step by step by collecting information, weighing the pros and cons of various possible ways of acting, and then deciding on the course of action that – in the vein of Pareto-equilibrium – will provide most people with most happiness for the lowest costs. Public (sub)agencies then execute the policy without much further ado.

This model, often named *rational*,[2] constitutes a core in the sequential model of policy-making (see chapter by Charles O. Jones), a model with good heuristic qualities, and a model that fits the picture which has dominated constitutions separating politics and administration, as well as the minds of managers, and their supporting management consultants and also much of the literature on management. It is a model of leaders being in control at the apex of the organization, from where they can design the processes desired to obtain the goals of the organization. A good example of how these lines of thought have been used in the literature is provided by Yehezkel Dror, who in 1968 published his *Public Policymaking Reexamined* (Dror 1968), followed in 1971 by two companion books (Dror 1971; Dror 1971) to substantiate some of the contentions of the first book. His aim was twofold: to advance the study of policy-making and to contribute to the improvement of public policymaking – which lacks the proper use of knowledge.

Dror's optimal model has three major stages (Dror 1968, 163–196): Metapolicy-making, policy-making and post-policy-making, and within those there are eighteen sub-stages, one of which is continuous communication and feedback channels interconnecting all phases. *Metapolicy-making* involves seven stages of processing values, processing reality, processing problems, developing resources, designing the policy-making system, allocating problems, values and resources, and finally determining the policy-making strategy. *Policy-making* involves another seven stages of suballocating resources, making and prioritizing operational goals, ditto for other significant values, preparing a set of major alternative policies (including some "good" ones), predicting benefits and costs of those policies, identifying the best policies in that light, and then deciding whether the best alternatives are "good" policies. *Post-policy-making* involves motivating the

execution of the policy, executing it, and evaluating the results.

The feedback elements of the model give it a dynamic feature, and Dror stresses the demands for iterative processes. He also leaves room for "extra-rational" behavior based on limited resources, uncertainty, and lack of knowledge as well as creativity and intuition (Dror 1968, 157–158), but the aim of the model is to limit the importance of such elements in order to enhance optimal policy-making – understood as "one that is not distorted by the noise that is in fact inherent in all, and especially complex, structures" (Dror 1968, 200). The task, then, is to organize processes so that at least one unit contributes to each phase, and so that the contributions of various units add up to an overall optimal operation at low costs and with little distortion. However, there is no one single model for organizing – one may use hierarchy or polycentric structures in various forms, depending on the demands of the situation. The judgment of success or failure rests on the contribution of the participants to the process, not to a particular organizational form.

In other words, Dror does not subscribe to a monolithic hierarchy. Nevertheless, he emphasizes the need for overall systems management, metapolicy-making and comprehensive public policy-making in order to promote adjustment and take advantage of new knowledge, and to prevent sub-optimization by single units. The key to such a demand is better personnel: professional staffs, units to survey and retrieve knowledge, and units for policy-oriented research. This form of manpower is to be supported by computerized systems and it must be managed in new ways (this is 1968), "in order to stimulate interprofessional teamwork and creativity" (Dror 1968, 274). In addition, there must be some systematic evaluation and learning feedback from experience.

The model, then, relies on our capabilities to produce knowledge based on science, and to feed it into the policy-making process in order to enhance enlightened choices within a comprehensive system, and in order to avoid incremental policy-making (see next section) which in Dror's opinion amounts to nothing but conservatism in disguise. In a later edition of the book (Dror 1983), Dror has added an introduction in which he laments the lack of advance of the policy sciences in the direction he has recommended. He also acknowledges that active participation in governmental roles has, in the meantime, taught him some important lessons about policymaking: "Social science studies from the outside do not penetrate into the realities of central high-level decision making", and "… ominous policy-making weaknesses are built-in into core components of governance, with present policy predicaments overtaxing maximum policy-making capacities." (Dror 1983, x–xi). The problem he faces is that of research and advice versus politics of all sorts. The original book is based on the ideal of science as an integral part of the desired model optimal policy-making, and the political dimensions were not treated in-depth – a problem Dror did not solve, no matter how many times he paid heed to other sources of information, including extra-rational forms[3].

Mutual adjustment in policy-making

This line of argumentation in the policy literature is concerned with the empirical characteristics of the policy process in a political setting. Analysis of policy cannot be understood in isolation from the ways politicians, administrators and representatives of interest in society at large interact about themes of common interest. One core argument, promulgated by Charles E. Lindblom, is that the information rendered in and by such processes has as much value as information produced by researchers and other experts. So, where proponents of the rational model recommend problem-solving based on the authority of expertise, followers of mutual adjustment advise problem-solving based on the authority of agreements reached among interested parties.

Lindblom's most famous text is, undoubtedly, "The Science of Muddling Through" (Lindblom 1959), originally published in *Public Administration Review*, but reprinted in numerous Readers. The message is relatively simple, but also highly contested; instead of making a comprehensive analysis of all possible means to obtain an end, the administrator resorts to comparing only a few which often do not deviate much from past uses, and the one selected is the one that creates agreement among the participants in the policy-making process, no matter what their ideological standpoints might have told them to do.

For the purposes of this article, Lindblom's discussion of *how agreement comes about* is crucial. It is not a long or even deep analysis. It is a short, nearly an ideal type description of how almost every interest in the USA has its watchdog, and that in the formation of a policy a process of mutual adjustment takes place among various interest groups and public agencies; and even though all these actors may not have an explicit focus on a particular policy goal, the result of the processes will be a viable policy. Thus there is no comprehensive income policy in the USA, but "a process of mutual adjustment among … (various actors) … accomplishes a distribution of income, in which particular income problems neglected at one point in the decision process becomes central at another point." (Lindblom 1959). Furthermore, policies are not made once and for all, but changed and adapted in a never-ending and continuous process in which those who lost at one point may gain at another. Moreover, since changes are incremental, losses (and gains) for each policy process are endurable.

The underlying understanding of this process is one of a large number of actors, continuously interacting about a host of themes, rarely coordinated by any central agency, but rather performing according to some analogy of the *hidden hand* of the economic market. Lindblom indicates this without really conceptualizing it in footnote number 7 in the article: "The link between the practice of successive limited comparisons and mutual adjustment of interests in a highly fragmented decision-making process adds a new facet to pluralist theories of government and administration." Lindblom expanded this line of thinking in his *The intelligence of Democracy* (Lindblom 1965) with the subtitle *Decision making through mutual adjustment*. The book sets the tone on page 3: "… people can coordinate with each other without anyone's coordinating them, without a dominant common purpose, and without rules that fully prescribe their relations to each other."

The principles of this argument are found in a much earlier paper from 1955, "Bargaining. The hidden hand in Government" (Lindblom 1988), and it is a largely un-referenced, but insightful, discussion of how bargaining coordinates policy, how it takes place in and among public agencies, and how actors are motivated for that particular behavior. The key is that no one trusts hierarchy to bring forward "every fact and value favorable to him. We want a social mechanism in which every man can speak for himself or find someone to speak for him." So bargaining involves actors and brings forward more aspects to a matter. In other words, the policy-making process is a matter of politics in the broadest sense, and in politics there is not only one truth available. Researchers mostly follow the political master designated by the hierarchy, but other parties interested in the matter may contribute with other views.

In the quote above, we find one clue to Lindblom's subsequent career of advocating for pluralism in policy analysis. There is more, of course; the arguments are unfolded in *The Intelligence of Democracy* and used in Lindblom's and Cohens' *Usable Knowledge* (Lindblom and Cohen 1979). One basic message is that there is no privileged knowledge in the policy process,[4] and another is that the process can only be successful if agreement (not only compromise) is reached: then the process has acquired a rationality which serves a democratic solution.

The two models compared

The two models are, indeed, adversaries. Dror explicitly renounced incrementalism, and Lindblom, of course, wrote to warn against any belief in the rational model. Dror is not a rationalist in the classic sense, but his model should be seen as an approximation to rational decision-making.

The models share an interest for the role of knowledge in the policy-making process. But they differ sharply in their interpretation: the rational model subscribes to comprehensive uses of scientific knowledge, whenever possible, the model of mutual adjustment puts science on a par with any other type of knowledge. This does not mean that Dror's model ignores other means of acquiring knowledge, but any information should be put into a context of priorities set beforehand. The model of mutual adjustment does not rely on pre-set goals, but on agreement acquired during the process.

Both models are created for Western democratic and pluralistic societies. Therefore, they both contain elements of communication and interaction which are useful for our subsequent discussion of networks. However, their understanding of how to play a role in a democracy is quite different. One is based on technocratic knowledge, depending on how politicians allow it to be expressed. The other one is based on knowledge in the *demos*, depending on how it may express itself.

Rational models are often seen as command-and-control systems, featuring the (democratic and elected) top. Dror does not subscribe to such a view, but recommends interaction between stages and between actors in the process – within the frames of goal-setting. The model presupposes that the politicians ultimately are in control of the bureaucracy and hence, in Dror's terms, they control meta-policy-making. The bureaucrats provide politicians with documentation for any verifiable statement and they substantiate that all relevant information has been scrutinized. In turn, the politicians are controlled by the voters at the general elections and by the watchdog function provided by a free press. So, the rational model is also to be applied in a pluralistic setting.

The model of *mutual adjustment* is basically one of interaction, but the number of actors is an open question, dependent on the democratic procedures of society. It requires a pluralistic society and a political system that allows various societal interests to enter the policy-making processes and participate with a prospect to win attention and influence now and then. Who exactly will win and when is then an open (empirical) question. These conditions should be fulfilled in a polity in a pluralistic society like the USA. But 18 years after his seminal article (Lindblom 1959) was published, Lindblom conceded in a much acclaimed book (Lindblom 1977) that there might be a bias in the policy system which provided certain actors with more clout than others – in the American case, big business. In a later book (Lindblom 1990), Lindblom stated that, although imperfect, he saw no alternative to pluralism; instead the challenge was to cope openly with the problems to reduce adverse consequences as much as possible.

TOWARDS NETWORK ANALYSIS

Policy analysis has its main roots in American political science – with a little help from friends in economics and sociology – and in public administration, which, however, for most policy purposes itself is rooted in political science. Political science developed a strong platform in the 1950s and 1960s based on various versions of systems analysis – David Easton (e.g. Easton 1965) and Karl Deutsch (Deutsch 1963) are examples of mainstream thinking in the field. And, regardless of the potentials for other ways of doing analysis in, for instance, Deutsch's cybernetic ideas, political scientists focused their interest on organizations within the political systems, often conceptualized as *institutions*, meaning interest organizations, political parties, parliaments, the executive, local government and other organizational forms of political life. Their aim was to theorize about these components of the political system – an example of such a partial analysis is Sjöblom (1968) on political parties in a multiparty system, strongly influenced by David Easton and Anthony Downs (1957).

However, most *policy* analysts were not so interested in theorizing about components within the political system. The systematic policy movement started in the second half of the 1960s (e.g. Ranney 1968) and became a thriving field in the 1970s, first of all as *policy implementation research*. Many policy analysts

used the systems approach and wanted to explain the outputs and outcomes of the political system without really analyzing the contents of the policy processes (Sharkansky and Hofferbert 1969). But empirical analyses coming closer to the dynamics of the policy process led to the conclusion that focus on the outcomes of single organizations like the legislature was not really helpful: ideas and principles in parliamentary law were often changed during processes of adaptation in the executive branches and in implementing organizations at the regional and local levels.

Pressman and Wildawsky's examination of the fate of a federal program in a local setting is a classic example (Pressman and Wildawsky 1973). One main explanation of the changes was the long chain of decision-makers from Washington, DC, to Oakland, CA, which they called the *decision path*, and they viewed each decision-maker as a relatively autonomous actor who could in effect block progress. In a second edition in 1979 (Pressman and Wildawsky 1979), Wildawsky wrote a new chapter on "Implementation in context", and referred to Hugh Heclo's use of *issue network* as a heuristic device to understand how policies were coordinated.

Heclo had coined the term network much earlier. In a review article on policy analysis he wrote that one should be careful "not to reify collectivities into individual deciders but to understand the networks of interaction by which policies result" (Heclo 1972, 106), and he recommended analyzing within programs (instead of analyzing organizations). This he did himself in Britain, in Sweden and in the USA, research which led him to core concepts within policy analysis: *policy communities and issue networks* (Heclo and Wildawsky 1975). Policy communities were more stable interaction patterns among policy interests, issue networks were mostly *ad hoc* mode.

Heclo was not alone in such research. In a number of research settings, scholars were searching for theoretical and conceptual solutions to their observations of multiple actors interacting in policy formulation and implementation. Many of them share empirical observations, but their point of departure in various disciplines means that their analytical interests and concerns differ.

Within research on interest organizations and their relations to the state, the term *neo-corporatism* (Schmitter 1974) was created to indicate a particular and generalizable pattern of interaction in society, giving industrial interests in a crucial role in politics, but without much formal representation in decision-making bodies, and mostly without formally delegated powers. This was in contrast to corporatism proper (as was the case in Fascist Italy), where organized interests would have formal state powers, Schmitter's ideas were followed up on by various projects which lead to theorizing about the *segmented state* or *state sectors*, indicating much of what Heclo had termed policy communities. But there was an important difference in their view on the degree of integration within the networks. While Heclo, Wildawsky and others supported a pluralist view of politics and hence looked for alternation in the importance of actors within the network, researchers analyzing policy sectors worked within a tradition looking for closed interrelations among actors.

Schmitter's ideas became very influential in research in North European countries, primarily regarding relations between interest organizations and the state. In Europe he influenced several research agendas regarding collective action and interest organizations (Czada and Windhoff-Héritier 1991) as well as the borderline between public and private (Streeck and Schmitter 1985). In Norway, a research program on *power* led to theorizing about new segmented forms of state power within policy sectors, with voters and the parliament in less prominent positions than the constitutional design would lead you to think (Olsen 1978), and government, administration and interest organizations in strong positions. Within broader social theory, Norwegian researchers coined the phrases of the *negotiated economy* (Hernes 1978), a concept indicating that market forces were replaced by negotiations between social organized interests and the state (Pedersen and Nielsen 1988). These results led to an increased interest in analyzing *institutional aspects* of society, based on a mix of macro- and

micro-theoretical foundations in economics (Williamson 1975) and sociology (Selznick 1957). We shall return to institutionalism below.

Planning researchers found a need for conceptualizing coordinators in town planning based on multiple agencies in local government. One conceptual solution to these findings was the invention of the *reticulist* (Friend, Power and Yewlett 1974) as an actor that links other actors together in networks. These authors drew on organization theory, whose practitioners observed inter-organizational phenomena in many settings. Some were seen to reduce the importance of market relations and hence a break with some elements of economic theory of the market. Examples were *interlocking directorates*, where corporations shared a number of individuals on boards of directors and hence were able to coordinate policies (Pennings 1980); an early and socially broader oriented example of this line of thinking was Wright Mills' book on the *Power Elite* (Mills 1956).

Other relations were seen as variations in features of the *organizational society* where private organizations communicated with one another about common purposes and engaged in new relations with the state in order to influence public policies. And, likewise, since the state engaged in more and more policies and programs that would affect various organizational interests, it had concerns and needs for coordination which could be satisfied by better communication with organized interests. As a consequence, the state and private organizations became interdependent, and there was a need to conceptualize the relations.

One line of such inter-organizational research was based on resource exchange as the medium for sustaining interorganizational relations, but the focus was on the macro-aspects of exchange; one influential source was Benson (1975) who used the (Marxist) logic of substructure and superstructure from political economy to tease out basic forces like money and authority, which were then brought into play in a superstructure of organizational interactions. He developed his first model into an analytical model of a two-leveled policy sector – understood as a subset of a large number of interorganizational networks in society (Benson 1982). In Europe, Rod Rhodes used these and other sources in organization theory as inspiration for developing his models of state-local government relationships (Rhodes 1979; Rhodes 1986) which he continued to use for an extensive discussion of policy networks and policy communities as organizing factors in British politics and administration (Rhodes 1997).

Another line of inter-organizational research had a micro focus and could be said to have some inspiration from literature dealing with increased division of labor in society. How can such sectors be understood? Most rationales in such analysis are based on theories of public choice, which lead to the conception of a *service industry* (Ostrom and Ostrom 1977; Ostrom, Parks and Whitaker 1978) – which had many common features with a policy sector. The basic idea was to counter theories of (large) bureaucratic organization by theories of (small) organizational cooperation, making a case for small-scale government and governmental agencies which would pool resources for larger tasks, if necessary. The basic ideas were developed into game theoretical frameworks and applied in various forms of self-government (Ostrom 1990) and in intergovernmental relations in Germany (Scharpf 1997).

Both the resource based and rational choice models were presented in an often-quoted anthology on inter-organizational policy-making in 1978 (Hanf and Scharpf 1978). It fulfilled at that time the need implementation scholars had for analytical models, which at the same time caught interaction *among* levels of administration as well as *at* each level. It was to be the first volume of the soon after rapidly growing literature on the *fragmentation of the state apparatus*. The fragmentation was due to decentralization of powers to lower levels and sharing powers with various organizations in the "gray" zone. This created new and intensified possibilities to exercise influence on separate decision-makers. Following this tendency, the borders between public and private tend to become blurred, and the exchanges of information make the various actors dependent on one another for updating and development of their understanding of the environment.

SUBSEQUENT TRENDS IN POLICY NETWORK ANALYSIS

Above we inspected some of the roots of policy network analysis and its development in the 1970s and early 1980s. We shall now discuss the subsequent development of analytical perspectives, which include traditionalists, institutionalism, governance, and trends towards deliberative discourse analysis. They have developed historically, of course, so they overlap, and to some degree they both react to and build upon one another in the sequence of institutionalism in the 1980s, governance in the 1990s and deliberative analysis in the late 1990s and now under further development in the 2000s. Traditionalists were found all the time – but some of them changed with the currents.

What were those trends about? Grossly oversimplifying, one can say that there has been a move from system and hierarchy (rational models) towards fragmentation and empowerment (mutual adjustment). Institutionalists were concerned with how political systems fared and they worked to re-conceptualize the modernistic state apparatus into something less monolithic in processes involving various stakeholders in society. Governance scholars continued this work and conceptualized the workings of various parts of the systems and helped us understand better how network policy processes took place. Discourse and deliberation scholars cashed in on further changes in society towards involving citizens in policy processes, and they also were part of the general movement among some social scientists towards social constructivism and pragmatism.

These three forms constitute some of the "forefront" in research during those years. But that is not to say that every one participated. Of course, many policy analysts proceeded in more traditional veins and challenged the newbees, or approached the new ideas without buying them wholesale. So, first, we'll review some of the main arguments among them.

Traditionalists

The essence of the development of traditional policy analysis is caught by referring to the struggles between *top-down* and *bottom-up analysis*. In many ways, this was a discussion between the rational model and muddling through, between Dror and Lindblom – without their being present in direct confrontations.

An example of the top-down perspective is given by a model of Intergovernmental Implementation by Van Horn (1979, 15). The problem is to get National priorities implemented at the local level, and the remedy is, first of all, to get clearer policy goals and standards at the federal level – the more specific, the better. This must be supplemented by better, i.e. clear, accurate, consistent and timely communication. All these elements are part of the rational model, as is the distinction between policy and implementation, which is maintained. However, Van Horn does recognize that local attitudes of political actors and interest groups are important, as are the skills of agencies and the need for adequate resources. The policy problem is how to overcome such hindrances for successful implementation. One can find similar understandings of the policy process in the literature (Bardach 1977; Mazmanian and Sabatier 1983).

This way of understanding the policy process was countered by various scholars, claiming that enhanced control from the top simply would not be enough. One must understand what is going on among the various agencies, and such understanding cannot be won by focusing on the top, one has to unwrap what goes on locally (Hjern and Hull 1982; Hjern and Hull 1984). The critics developed the concept of an *implementation structure* (Hjern and Porter 1983), an analytical tool to map the interactions between actors involved in the policy process, inspired by – among others – Elmore (1979) and Lipsky (1980). A core *dictum* was that actors, *a priori*, should be put on a higher position in the policy process if one were to truly realize what goes on – namely the creation of a policy network instead of a system of authority.

A thorough mapping and discussion of the various positions is found in Hill and Hupe (2002, 41–84). Several attempts to create a compromise between the two schools have been made over the years, and even the most ardent proponents of either side have conceded that a pure paradigm is not tenable (Sabatier 1986; Hjern and Hull 1987). There is some authority present in most systems, but it may be dormant – negotiations take place "in the shadow of hierarchy" (Scharpf 1997, 197–205). Whatever the case, most of those taking part in the discussion on top-down versus bottom-up did fairly traditional analysis in methodological terms; they used statistics, interviewed actors and followed the mainstream tradition in their empirical analysis. Several of them also took part in the discussions leading to the new institutionalism, which is the subject of the next section.

New institutionalism

The most dominant trend of the 1980s involved *new institutionalism*. There are several versions within policy analysis – and many more outside, which we shall ignore. Most of them share a dissatisfaction with the American behavioral revolution (Easton 1953; Simon 1945; Truman 1951), but they have different cures for the malady. The main distinction relates to micro- and macro-perspectives on actors, respectively (Scharpf 1997; March and Olsen 1989). Many of the attempts to theorize about policy networks ended up with delineating some sort of subsystem, probably with some inspiration from Heclo (1972) and his predecessors in American analysis of subgovernments (e.g. Lowi 1964). One theme was the degree of autonomy policy networks enjoyed vis-á-vis more inclusive systems like the political systems (Lehner 1991; Rhodes 1986). Another theme concerned the policy network as such: how was it organized, how were powers distributed (Scharpf 1991; Rhodes and Marsh 1992). A third theme concerned the role of networks at a societal level: How could one understand the politics and administration of societies with many policy networks (Lehmbruch 1991; Campbell, Hollingsworth and Lindberg 1991)?

Whatever the case, policy analysts found that the formal organizational system of government often did not adequately describe the patterns of interaction they found in policy formation and implementation. Moreover, the alternative, "American" behavioral analysis, lacked a foundation in or a link to what organizations meant in political life. If one structures the field in terms of Richard Scott's three types of institutional theory – regulative, normative and cognitive (Scott 1995), three types of questions interested policy analysts. First, they found themselves confronted with questions of what systems of rules that might really apply to the actions of both organizations and individuals. Furthermore, they asked themselves what social obligations the actors wanted to adhere to when they set standards for future policies, or when they implemented policies in ways that were not always in close accordance with the stated, formal policy principles. Third, they found a need for identifying norms for proper behavior in networks across organizational boundaries – how did actors perceive one another, and how did they come to terms when their organizational backgrounds differed?

Such questions are to some degree answered by various institutional theories. Scott's distinctions were not part of the discussions of policy scholars in the 1980s, at least not explicitly, so they articulated their institutional theories differently. There was a relatively clear cleavage between scholars working on the basis of rational choice theory and those who were more interested in structural analysis. In a way, their interest was much about the same. They realized that it would be no use only to focus on formal organizations like parliaments or bureaucracies to analyze policy processes. *Rational choice* theorists then asked themselves how variations in structural conditions would affect various types of rational actors. Examples are various ways of organizing the police force (Ostrom, Parks and Whitaker 1978), or ways of organizing local governments in metropolitan areas (Oakerson 1987). The rationale behind this was that small organizations could be effective if they cooperated with other ones about certain tasks in a rational way, based on self-interest,

thus consciously waiving their formal autonomy in such fields, replacing it by mutual dependence. *Structuralists* likewise asked themselves about the role of institutional settings, but their interest was, more or less, to make plausible a claim that organizational actors do not decide as rational actors, they rather follow standard operating procedures, and normative facets of the organization as they appear in myths, symbols and even rituals – in short, the organizational culture which would define appropriate behavior of actors. Therefore, organizational factors would be important, but in other ways than traditional political science had used them in the past (March and Olsen 1989).

The main difference between the two types of new institutionalism, then, was rooted in opposite hypotheses about the behavior of actors. In addition, there were strong normative differences, in that most rational theorists did not much care about how services were provided and therefore might advocate for privatization; structuralists to a much greater extent adhered to maintaining the particular democratic values provided by public sector organization of services. In policy terms, this became very visible in normative discussions, e.g. about the pros and cons of *new public management* (Hood 1991; Barzelay 1992).

Governance

A second major trend came in the 1990s, and its theme was labeled *governance*. In many ways it was a natural sequel to the focus on institutionalism in the 1980s. There was an enduring competition between macro- and micro-analytical approaches to conquer the right to be called *new* institutionalists (Selznick 1996), and there were tensions between new and old institutionalists, to say nothing about those who still saw formal organizations as institutions (Aberbach and Rockman 1987). So the more the field of analyzing policy networks developed, the more the search for more adequate concepts intensified. Increasingly, the concept of governance gained momentum: it could be seen as something other than govern*ment*, and it had a processual flavor to it.

Nevertheless, governance turned out to get some comparable problems to institutionalism. It has become a somewhat fuzzy concept, covering a vast territory and therefore maybe less useful as a discriminating concept. Rhodes (1997, 47) refers to six meanings: the minimal state, corporate governance (of enterprises), new public management, "good governance" (for developing countries), socio-cybernetic system (overall characteristics), and self-organizing networks. More categories probably can be found. But let us venture to capture some core meanings which will then form the backbone of the discussions in this chapter.

The most general use of governance covers new forms of government-society relations – as an example the socio-cybernetic system mentioned above. This comprehensive interpretation of governance suggests that the principles of modern society, with its division of labor between state, market and civil society, is under siege and, in particular, hierarchical state-society relations are being replaced by other forms of interrelationships, which often imply some "co"-action between public and private (Kooiman 1993, 4–6). Such an interpretation invites us to reconceptualize modern theories of the state; there is little agreement about how to do this, examples are theories of reflexivity (Beck, Giddens and Lash 1994) and of postmodern conditions (Bogason 2000; Miller 2002). Such theoretical constructs open up possibilities for understanding the state as a network mingled with the greater society and, consequently, political action changes in its meaning. Analytical interest goes away from a focus on parliamentary and bureaucratic processes of negotiation, and instead scholars identify interaction patterns between various interests, the results of which then get recognition as public policies. The precise organizational pattern is not defined, it is an empirical question within a dynamic system, much like Giddens' ideas of structuration (Giddens 1984).

A second and related, but less comprehensive meaning of governance, implies only the fall of clear organizational boundaries of public and private organizations, and the wider context (like state theory) is not really addressed. One example is that "*governance refers to self-organizing, inter-organizational networks* characterized by interdependence, resource exchange, rules of the game, and significant autonomy from the state." (Rhodes 1997, 15, italics in original). Such a definition sets rather clear boundaries for the analytical interest of scholars, and it invites a specific way of theorizing, based on inter-organizational assumptions. It puts networks into the center of our analytical interest, and other forms of governing are, consequently, left out of sight.

Policy scholars have taken part actively in the development of governance theory. Early on, their empirical findings pointed to problems with traditional political theory in explaining what went on in policy formation and implementation. Their findings on policy networks called for alternatives to the received view of the modern state. It became very clear when facets of policy networks were discussed in a management perspective – here the obvious lack of traditional control instruments belonging to the manager of the closed organization (Gage and Mandell 1990; Kickert, Klijn and Koppenjahn 1997); the primary role of the network manager then becomes to facilitate communication.

Deliberative policy analysis

The third major trend in policy analysis began in the 1990s and is gaining momentum in these first years of the third millennium. It is very comprehensive since it involves both theory and methodology, not to say foundations of social science. It concerns *deliberation and discourse* in policy processes, and thus it has one leg in the governance tradition, but it also reflects something more. Echoing the *linguistic turn* in the philosophy, one signal was the publication of the anthology entitled *The Argumentative Turn in Policy Analysis and Planning* (Fischer and Forester 1993), whose editors were inspired by Deborah Stone (1988) to state that "policy-making is a constant discursive struggle over the criteria of social classification, the boundaries of problem categories, the intersubjective interpretation of common experiences, the conceptual framing of problems, and the definitions of ideas that guide the ways people create the shared meanings which motivate them to act." So: "Policy analysis and planning are practical processes of argumentation." (Fischer and Forester 1993, 1–2).

No reference to networks in those sentences, but of course the development of policy analysis towards networks had unveiled processes which were hidden in the organizations of the 1960s and before. So they were closed to the type of scholarly scrutiny which was, after all, easier to perform in the networked policy processes of communication researchers followed in the 1970s and 1980s. And, sure enough, about half of the articles in the anthology discuss various forms of deliberation in the policy process, and hence indirectly network settings.

Discourse thus relates to language, and a primer on narrative policy analysis was written by Emery Roe (1994). But there are also roots in institutionalism: "From this perspective acid rain is a story-line that, potentially, brings out the institutional dimensions of the ecological problematique." (Hajer 1995, 265). This means that the author has an analytical interest in how discourse is structured or embedded in society, while at the same time it structures society – in other words, not unlike Giddens' ideas of structuration, which has the concept of institution at the core of the analysis (Giddens 1984).

Speaking metaphorically, the deliberative policy analysis brings the scholar down from the ivory tower to the people. The institutionalists and most governance theorists kept the privileged status of researchers to analyze currents in society and to work for a better theoretical understanding of how policy came about. But the 1990s gradually saw changes in the social sciences, which meant that the privileged and isolated status of scholars was meant to be revoked, and their roles to be changed from observers to participants in research processes that stressed dialogue instead of observation and reporting (Guba and Lincoln 1989; Erlandson, Harris, Skipper et al. 1993). Thus, the advocates of change mirrored societal developments towards more public participation in policy processes in their own

research practices: "… a close practical and conceptual connection exists between a post-positivist policy analysis and today's decentered world of governance" (Hajer and Wagenaar 2003, xiv).

This statement, then, reflects that, in most Western countries, the public sector has been opened up for more participation in policy processes. One may doubt the sincerity of this (Miller 2002, vii–viii), but measured on the surface – by the sheer growth in the number of new channels for participation – this is a fact (OECD 2001). In policy analysis, this has consequences for the role and use of expertise (Fischer 1999) which increasingly becomes part of an ongoing discourse with less and less elevated status for policy analysts; instead they have to make their points of view understood by a broader public. Deliberation also means that organized interests get more legitimate access to the policy process, but in the light of the research on institutionalism and governance, that is hardly surprising. But the consequences for the roles of ordinary citizens may be more profound, in that citizens get access to participate in ways that earlier on might have been seen as counterproductive to an efficient public sector. Some of the development may be conceptualized as empowerment of citizens (Sørensen 1997); an interesting research question is to what degree formal rights to participate actually are brought into use for influencing policy decisions. If that is the case, other researchers speak of a strengthening of social capital in society (Putnam, Leonardi and Nanetti 1993). In more radical versions, one can say that the citizens decide about the future of their communities (Ostrom 1995) instead of, for example, relying on a benign but bureaucratic welfare state.

The research, then, stresses the features of deliberation, dialogue, collaboration and mediation. Much of it should be understood as part of the scientific development towards postempiricist social science. Empiricists, or traditional policy analysts, have tried to minimize social and interpretative judgments, postempiricists recognize their basic, constitutive role in any form of analysis (Fischer 2003, 226). Postempiricist policy analysts do not speak truth to power, they collaborate with power holders and mediate with diverse interests. In that sense, they have become part of the network society.

NETWORK ANALYSIS – A STATUS

Where is network analysis at now? We have followed a historical trajectory from rational policy analysis to analysis integrating a broader conception of the processes involved. So scholars involved in such analysis have all participated in a battle between rational decision-making and muddling through – maybe not in the open, and maybe not even as a conscious choice by the analyst, but still the theme of doing things rationally or not pops up everywhere. At the very least, as a pedagogic means to illustrate what we are not doing. More seriously, as a theme that has to be addressed in order to persuade the reader that rationalism is or is not applicable in this case – and it seems that rationalism is on the decline.[5] That is not to say that Lindblom's mutual adjustment is the only answer to non-rational demands. But his ideas are hovering over many of the solutions we face.

The outline given above about the changes in policy analysis stresses a transition towards network analysis, but that does not mean that former types of policy analysis are gone. "Network" is still a debated term, to say nothing of network analysis. Have we not seen it all before? Of course we have in some sense, our predecessors in political analysis were not idiots. In a more narrow sense, things are new, but, as Keith Dowding (1994) has shown, the literature then tends to become bogged down because of definitional fights between academic camps. So more energy is used for fights than for sensible analysis of one's own results as well as of the results from colleagues. Christopher Pollitt's critique that there are tendencies towards ahistorical comprehension, and that it is hardly proven that networks form a new and better type of democracy, are also worth considering (Pollitt 2003, 65–67). That said, I think that one should interpret the focus on networks and process as a consequence of a

more and more complicated, or at least comprehensive, policy process everywhere in the Western world. The point, then, does not concern the exact definition of the phenomena under scrutiny, but the general recognition that we are observing qualitatively different policy processes. The challenge is to show how they differ from the past, and what measures then should be taken.

What, then, may we find in common among the different camps of policy network analysis? It seems to me that one main distinguishing feature of the advanced policy analysts of today is that they apply a *new* version of *pragmatism*. The classic Deweyan pragmatist was interested in theory as a vehicle for promoting change in societal affairs. The pragmatist of today has less faith in theory. To put it crudely, pragmatists of today are interested in conceivable practical consequences of affirming an idea or taking an action – consequences that are satisfying and desirable in the light of power relations (Cherryholmes 1999, 124–125). They follow a pragmatism which is anticipatory and hence inductive and fallible; today's pragmatists construct their reality socially and perform analysis critically; they are skeptics and hence not believers of a final Truth. They see the world as contingent, and thus they are contextualists. They are holists and reject distinctions like fact/value, objective/subjective, theory/practice, ends/means, analytic/synthetic. This *credo* I will call the "new pragmatism." It certainly covers the postpositivists within policy analysis, and to a degree it covers many other network analysts – of whom some still subscribe to a distinction of fact and value, and of objective and subjective.

New pragmatists do not see *evidence* in the classic sense of getting the data straight, preferably in some version of statistical analysis. They beg the question of the existence of a network and involve themselves in processes of argumentation and power – resource exchange or not, "science" or not. They base their action on some form of hermeneutic analysis, and many of them do not mind using supplementary information based on some strand of positivism. Nevertheless, they see such evidence as one out of many channels of information for their craft. Hoppe characterizes two types of analysts which I would count under the new pragmatists: Forensic policy analysts and participatory policy analysts (Hoppe 1999, 207–208).

The *forensic* policy analysts see a cacophony of competing thinking styles, ideologies, paradigms, perspectives, etc. in policy analysis, and hence they advocate for first distinguishing between the various sorts of frames of thinking that can be found pertaining to a policy problem. Then they want to create a new sort of frame, combining plausible and robust arguments (frame-reflection, following, for example, Schön and Rein (1994)) into a new policy design. This may be done with various stakeholders and hence the barrier between analyst and policy-maker is torn down (Guba and Lincoln 1989; Erlandson, Harris, Skipper et al. 1993) in a creative process of finding solutions to the problems at hand. As with Lindblom, the differences between means and goals disappear in a world of continuous change.

The *participatory* policy analyst may be in agreement with the forensic analyst, but does not stop with the question of how to understand policy frames. S/he broadens the perspective even more and emphasizes the importance of involving citizens in the policy processes – to include local knowledge, to make obvious themes of ethics, or to cut through disagreements among experts. Or, to make up for the increase in distance between politicians and the demos, and the strengthening of the administrative apparatus (Fischer 2003, 15–16). Some critics argue that the quality of the debate and/or solution is not guaranteed by citizen involvement. The counter question of the pragmatists is: Who is to be the umpire of such quality? For new pragmatists there is no absolute standard to use as truth medium.

Analysts following the rational paradigm cannot possibly agree with this. Followers of Lindblom would feel closer, particularly since science is not awarded any pedestal, but probably they would package this form of truth with a conception of the political process which creates winners. Those winners, then, are in a position to define the truth for the time being, that is until some one else comes into power. Cynical, maybe, but political analysis never was for someone with a feeble heart.

NOTES

1. The author wants to thank Anders Berg-Sørensen, Allan Dreyer Hansen, Eva Sørensen, Jacob Magnussen and Peter Triantafillou for helpful comments on a draft version.

2. Not all users of sequential models adhere to the strictly rational version, though. For instance, Wildawsky wanted us to speak truth to power, but his own model of decision-making was less demanding than the rational version, he was closer to incrementalism.

3. Dror is no naivist. In the second edition of his book (Dror 1983), he makes explicit his history of learning as an Israeli scholar and a Zionist in political terms, and he discusses the values that come out of such a past, thereby setting what he considers an example for other scholars involved in policymaking. He thus follows the stance that; although no one is value free – which would be desirable – one can make up for it by making values explicit to the reader.

4. From the introduction to *Democracy and Market System*: "I cannot think of any human accomplishment that unambiguously and undeniably could not not have been achieved without social science." (Lindblom 1988, 21)

5. If one tries to get an overview of university course literature on policy analysis, it seems that rational and statistical analysis dominates – Amazon.com's three most popular books on policy analysis are Bardach (2000), Weimer, Vining and Vining (1998) and Patton and Sawicki (1993). But in conferences and anthologies purporting to mirror the state of the art, such techniques do not take many pages.

REFERENCES

Aberbach, J. D. and Rockman, B. A. (1987) Comparative Administration – Methods, Muddles and Models. *Administration and Society* 18(4), 473–506.

Bardach, E. (1977) *The Implementation Game: What Happens After a Bill Becomes a Law.* Cambridge, MA: MIT Press.

Bardach, E. (2000) *A Practical Guide for Policy Analysis: The Eightfold Path to More Effective Problem Solving.* New York: Chatham House Publishers.

Barzelay, M. (1992) *Breaking Through Bureaucracy. A New Vision for Managing in Government*, in collaboration with B. J. Armajani. Berkeley: University of California Press.

Beck, U., Giddens, A. and Lash, S. (1994) *Reflexive Modernization. Politics, Tradition and Aesthetics in the Modern Social Order.* Cambridge: Polity Press.

Benson, J. K. (1975) The interorganisational network as a political economy. *Administrative Science Quarterly*, 20, 230–49.

Benson, J. K. (1982) A framework for policy analysis. In *Interorganizational Coordination: Theory, Research and Implementation*, eds D. L. Rogers and D. A. Whetten, pp. 137–76. Ames, Iowa: Iowa State University Press.

Bogason, P. (2000) *Public Policy and Local Governance: Institutions in Postmodern Society*, New Horizons in Public Policy. Cheltenham: Edward Elgar.

Campbell, J. L., Hollingsworth, J. R. and Lindberg, L., eds. (1991) *Governance of the American Economy*. Cambridge: Cambridge University Press.

Cherryholmes, C. H. (1999) *Reading Pragmatism*. New York: Teachers College Press.

Colebatch, H. K. (1998) *Policy*. Buckingham: Open University Press.

Czada, R. M. and Windhoff-Héritier, A., eds (1991) *Political Choice. Institutions, Rules and the Limits of Rationality*. Frankfurt am Main: Campus Verlag.

Deutsch, K. W. (1963) *The Nerves of Government. Models of Political Communication and Control*. New York: The Free Press of Glencoe.

Dowding, K. (1994) Policy networks: Don't stretch a good idea too far. In *Contemporary Political Studies*, eds P. Dunleavy and J. Stayrer, pp. 59–78. Exeter: Shortrun Press.

Downs, A. (1957) *An Economic Theory of Democracy*. New York: Harper & Row.

Dror, Y. (1968) *Public Policymaking Reexamined*. Pennsylvania: Chandler Publishing Company.

Dror, Y. (1971) *Design for Policy Sciences*. New York: American Elsevier.

Dror, Y. (1971) *Ventures in Policy Sciences*. New York: Elsevier.

Dror, Y. (1983) *Public Policymaking Reexamined*. New Brunswick, N.J.: Transaction Books.

Easton, D. (1953) *The Political System. An Inquiry Into the State of Political Science*. New York: Alfred A. Knopf.

Easton, D. (1965) *A Framework for Political Analysis*. Englewood Cliffs, NJ: Princeton University Press.

Elmore, R. E. (1979) Backward mapping: Implementation research and policy decisions. *Political Science Quarterly*, 94(4), 601–16.

Erlandson, D. A., Harris, E. L., Skipper, B. L. and Allen, S. D. (1993) *Doing Naturalistic Inquiry: A Guide to Methods*. London: Sage.

Fischer, F. (1995) *Evaluating Public Policy*. Chicago: Nelson-Hall Publishers.

Fischer, F. (1999) *Technocracy and the Politics of Expertise: Managerial and Policy Perspectives*. London: Sage.

Fischer, F. (2003) Beyond empiricism: Policy analysis and deliberative practice. In *Deliberative Policy Analysis. Understanding Governance in the Network Society*, eds M. A. Hajer and H. Wagenaar, Theories of Institutional Design, pp. 209–27. Cambridge: Cambridge University Press.

Fischer, F. (2003) *Reframing Public Policy. Discursive Politics and Deliberative Practices*. Oxford: Oxford University Press.

Fischer, F. and Forester, J. (1993) Editors' introduction. In *The Argumentative Turn in Policy Analysis and Planning*, ed. F. Fischer and J. Forester, pp. 1–17. London: UCL Press.

Friend, J., Power, J. and Yewlett, C. (1974) *Public Planning: The Inter-Corporate Dimension*. London: Tavistock Publications.

Gage, R. W. and Mandell, M. P. (1990) *Strategies for Managing Intergovernmental Policies and Networks*. Praeger: New York.

Giddens, A. (1984) *The Constitution of Society. Outline of the Theory of Structuration*. Cambridge: Polity Press.

Guba, E. G. and Lincoln, Y. S. (1989) *Fourth Generation Evaluation*. London: Sage.

Hajer, M. A. and Wagenaar, H., eds (2003) *Deliberative Policy Analysis. Understanding Governance in the Network Society*, Theories of Institutional Design. Cambridge: Cambridge University Press.

Hajer, M. A. and Wagenaar, H. (2003) Introduction. In *Deliberative Policy Analysis. Understanding Governance in the Network Society*, eds M. A. Hajer and H. Wagenaar, Theories of Institutional Design, pp. 1–30. Cambridge: Cambridge University Press.

Hajer, M. (1995) *The Politics of Environmental Discourse. Ecological Modernization and the Policy Process*. Oxford: Clarendon Press.

Hanf, K. and Scharpf, F. W., eds (1978) *Interorganizational Policy Making. Limits to Coordination and Central Control*, SAGE Modern Politics Series, 1. London: Sage.

Heclo, H. (1972) Review article: Policy analysis. *British Journal of Political Science*, 2, 83–108.

Heclo, H. and Wildawsky, A. (1975) *The Private Government of Public Money: Community and Policy Inside British Politics*. London: Macmillan.

Hernes, G., ed. (1978) *Forhandlingsøkonomi og blandingsadministration*. Oslo: Universitetsforlaget.

Hill, M. and Hupe, P. (2002) *Implementation*. London: Sage Publications.

Hjern, B. and Hull, C. (1982) Implementation research as empirical constitutionalism. *European Journal of Political Research*, 10(2), 105–17.

Hjern, B. and Porter, D. O. (1983) Implementation structures: A new unit of administrative analysis. In *Realizing Social Science Knowledge*, eds B. Holzner, K. D. Knorr and H. Strasser, pp. 265–77. Wien-Würzberg: Physica-Verlag.

Hjern, B. and Hull, C. (1984) Going interorganisa-tional: Weber meets Durkheim. *Scandinavian Political Studies*, 7(3), 197–212.

Hjern, B. and Hull, C. (1987) *Helping Small Firms Grow: An Implementation Approach*. Beckenham, Kent: Croom Helm.

Hood, C. (1991) A public management for all sea-sons? *Public Administration*, 69 (Spring), 3–19.

Hooghe, L. and Marks, G. (2001) *Multi-Level Governance and European Integration*. Boulder: Rowman & Littlefield.

Hoppe, R. (1999) Policy analysis, science and poli-tics: From 'speaking truth to power' to 'making sense together'. *Science and Public Policy*, 26(3), June, 201–10.

Kickert, W. J. M., Klijn, E.-H. and Koppenjahn, J. F. M., eds (1997) *Managing Complex Networks. Strategies for the Public Sector*. London: Sage.

Kooiman, J. (1993) Social-political governance: introduction. In *Modern Governance: New Government-Society Interactions*, ed. J. Kooiman, pp. 1–6. London: SAGE Publications.

Kuhn, T. S. (1962) *The Structure of Scientific Revolutions*. Chicago: Chicago University Press.

Lakatos, I. (1974) Falsification and the methodology of scientific research programmes. In *Criticism and the Growth of Knowledge*, ed. I. Latakos and A. Musgrave, pp. 91–196. Cambridge: Cambridge University Press.

Lehmbruch, G. (1991) The organization of society, administrative strategies, and policy networks. In *Political Choice. Institutions, Rules and the Limits of Rationality*, eds R. Czada and A. Windhoff-Héritier, pp. 121–58. Frankfurt am Main: Campus.

Lehner, F. (1991) The institutional control of orga-nized interest intermediation: A political perspec-tive. In *Political Choice. Institutions, Rules and the Limits of Rationality*, eds. R. Czada and A. Windhoff-Héritier, pp. 233–56. Frankfurt am Main: Campus.

Lindblom, C. E. (1959) The science of muddling through. *Public Administration Review*, 19, 79–99.

Lindblom, C. E. (1965) *The Intelligence of Democracy. Decision Making Through Mutual Adjustment*. New York: The Free Press.

Lindblom, C. E. (1977) *Politics and Markets*. New York: Basic Books.

Lindblom, C. E. (1988) Bargaining: The hidden hand in government. In *Democracy and Market System*, C. E. Lindblom, pp. 139–70. Oslo: Norwegian University Press.

Lindblom, C. E. (1988) Introduction. In *Democracy and Market System*, C. E. Lindblom, pp. 9–21. Oslo: Norwegian University Press.

Lindblom, C. E. (1990) *Inquiry and Change. The Troubled Attempt to Understand and Shape Society*. New Haven: Yale University Press.

Lindblom, C. E. and Cohen, D. (1979) *Usable Knowledge. Social Science and Social Science Solving*. New Haven: Yale University Press.

Lipsky, M. (1980) *Street-Level Bureaucracy: Dilemmas of the Individual in Public Services*. New York: Russell Sage.

Lowi, T. J. (1964) American business, public policy, case studies, and political theory. *World Politics*, 16 (July), 686–715.

March, J. G. and Olsen, J. P. (1989) *Rediscovering Institutions. The Organizational Basis of Politics*. New York: Free Press.

Mazmanian, D. A. and Sabatier, P. A. (1983) *Implementation and Public Policy*. Glenview, IL: Scott & Foresman.

Miller, H. T. (2002) *Postmodern Public Policy*. Albany, NY: State University of New York Press.

Mills, C. W. (1956) *The Power Elite*. New York: Oxford University Press.

Oakerson, R. J. et al. (1987) *How Fragmentation Works – St Louis Style*. ACIR: Washington DC.

OECD (2001) *Citizens as Partners. Information, Consultation and Public Participation in Public Decision-Making*. Paris: OECD.

Olsen, J. P., ed. (1978) *Politisk organisering*. Oslo: Universitetsforlaget.

Ostrom, E. (1990) *Governing the Commons: The Evolution of Institutions for Collective Action*. Cambridge: Cambridge University Press.

Ostrom, E. (1995) Self-organization and social capital. *Industrial and Corporate Change*, 4(1), 131–59.

Ostrom, E., Parks, R. and Whitaker, G. (1978) *Patterns of Metropolitan Policing*. Cambridge, MA: Ballinger Publishing Company.

Ostrom, V. and Ostrom, E. (1977) Public goods and public choices. In *Alternatives for Delivering Public Services*, ed. E. S. Savas. Boulder, CO: Westview.

Patton, C. V. and Sawicki, D. S. (1993) *Policy Analysis: Concepts and Practice*. Englewood Cliffs, NJ: Prentice-Hall.

Pedersen, O. K. and Nielsen, K. (1988) The Negotiated Economy: Ideal and History. *Scandinavian Political Studies*, 11(2), 79–101.

Pennings, J. M. (1980) *Interlocking Directorates*. San Francisco: Jossey Bass.

Pollitt, C. (2003) *The Essential Public Manager*. Maidenhead: Open University Press.

Pressman, J. L. and Wildawsky, A. B. (1973) *Imple-mentation*. Berkeley, CA: University of California Press.

Pressman, J. L. and Wildawsky, A. B. (1979) *Implementation*. Berkeley, CA: University of California Press.

Putnam, R., Leonardi, R. and Nanetti, R. Y. (1993) *Making Democracy Work: Civic Traditions in Modern Italy*. Princeton, NJ: Princeton University Press.

Ranney, A. (1968) *Political Science and Public Policy*. Chicago: Markham.

Rhodes, R. A. W. (1979) *Central-Local Government Relationships*. London: Social Science Research Council.

Rhodes, R. A. W. (1986) *The National World of Local Government*. London: Allan & Unwin.

Rhodes, R. A. W. (1997) *Understanding Governance. Policy Networks, Governance, Reflexivity and Accountability*. Buckingham: Open University Press.

Rhodes, R. and Marsh, D. (1992) New directions in the study of policy networks. *European Journal of Political Research*, 21, 181–205.

Roe, E. (1994) *Narrative Policy Analysis. Theory and Practice*. Durham, NC: Duke University Press.

Rosenau, J. N., ed. (1969) *Linkage Politics. Essays on the Convergence of National and International Systems*. New York: Free Press.

Sabatier, P. A. (1986) Top-Down and Bottom-Up approaches to implementation research: a critical analysis and suggested synthesis. *Journal of Public Policy*, 6(1), 21–48.

Scharpf, F. W. (1991) Political institutions, decision styles, and policy choices. In *Political Choice. Institutions, Rules and the Limits of Rationality*, ed. R. Czada and A. Windhoff-Héritier, pp. 53–86. Frankfurt am Main: Campus.

Scharpf, F. W. (1997) *Games Real Actors Play. Actor-Centered Institutionalism in Policy Research*. Boulder, CO: Westview Press.

Schmitter, P. C. (1974) Still the century of corporatism? *The Review of Politics*, 36, 85–131.

Schön, D. A. and Rein, M. (1994) *Frame Reflection. Toward the Resolution of Intractable Policy Controversies*. New York: Basic Books.

Scott, R. W. (1995) *Institutions and Organizations*. London: SAGE Publications.

Selznick, P. (1957) *Leadership in Administration*. New York: Harper & Row.

Selznick, P. (1996) Institutionalism "old" and "new". *Administrative Science Quarterly*, 41, 270–77.

Sharkansky, I. and Hofferbert, R. I. (1969) Dimensions of State Politics, Economics and Public Policy. *American Political Science Review*, 63, 867–79.

Simon, H. A. (1945) *Administrative Behavior*. New York: Free Press.

Sjöblom, G. (1968) *Party Strategies in a Multiparty System*. Lund: Studentlitteratur.

Sørensen, E. (1997) Democracy and empowerment. *Public Administration*, 75(3), 553–68.

Stone, D. (1988) *Policy Paradox and Political Reason*. Glenview, IL: Scott, Foresman and Co.

Streeck, W. and Schmitter, P. C., eds (1985) *Private Interest Government. Beyond Market and State*. London: Sage Publications.

Truman, H. S. (1951) *The Governmental Process. Political Interest and Public Opinion*. New York: Alfred E. Knopf.

Van Horn, C. E. (1979) *Policy Implementation in the Federal System: National Goals and Local Implementors*. Lexington, MA: Lexington Books.

Weimer, D. L., Vining, A. R. and Vining, A. (1998) *Policy Analysis: Concepts and Practice*. Englewood Cliffs, NJ: Prentice-Hall.

Wildawsky, A. (1979) *Speaking Truth to Power. The Art and Craft of Policy Analysis*. London: MacMillan.

Williamson, O. (1975) *Markets and Hierarchies: Analysis and Antitrust Implications*. New York: Free Press.

6

Concepts and Theories of Horizontal Policy Management

B. GUY PETERS

Coordination and coherence are familiar themes in the discussion of shortcomings of public administration and public policy. Governments have long sought to discover means of making the policies adopted in one department or agency correspond with, or at least not conflict with, those adopted in other departments. Likewise, governments have sought for mechanisms to ensure that there are not major lacunae in their policy regimens, so that all potential clients are served and citizens do not fall through holes in the various safety nets of government, or escape adequate economic regulation. Unfortunately, as Pressman and Wildavsky (1984) argued some years ago, much more has been said about creating coordination than actually has been done about it, and coordination remains a principal "philosophers' stone" in the analysis of good public administration (Jennings and Crane, 1994).

It is indeed difficult to do anything about coordination, given the way in which governments tend to be structured and given the entrenched patterns of thinking about public policy and about governing. The Blair government in the United Kingdom, for example, has made a great ruckus about creating "joined up government" but there is no real evidence that

the vertical nature of governing has changed substantially in the UK (6, 2004). The Finnish government has developed an elaborate system for managing cross-cutting policy priorities (Peters, 2006). Likewise, the Canadian government has come to recognize the need for enhanced coordination but there has not yet been the level of change desired, despite investment of a good deal of energy by senior officials through a variety of organizations and procedures. We could go on adding examples of government attempts to create more effective horizontal structures but the general point remains that governments are faced with significant challenges in creating greater policy coherence.

Asian governments are no different from those on other continents in confronting the challenge of coherence. Attempting to typify government in Asia is in some ways ridiculous, given the diversity of governing forms and experiences, so we will need to examine differences perhaps more than similarities. For some Asian governments the need to create coordination may be more pressing for Asian governments, given that the lower levels of economic development produce fewer slack resources to be wasted on redundant programs. On the other hand, some governments in Asia may have greater capabilities for producing coordination, given the existence of strong political parties (China) or strong central agencies within the bureaucracy (Japan). Likewise, the absence of strong civil society institutions in most Asian countries (Callender and Johnston, 1998) eliminates another source of effective if informal coordination of public programs.

MANAGING HORIZONTAL GOVERNMENT

Governments need to find mechanisms to manage more effectively in the horizontal as well as the vertical direction. Reforms such as those associated with the New Public Management have improved vertical management, but if anything have weakened the horizontal management capacity of governments (see below). There are any number of examples of governance failures resulting from inadequate policy coordination and a reluctance to expend the political capital necessary to manage government in a more horizontal manner. These failures include excessive costs because of duplication of programs, firms having to go to numerous different regulatory organizations in order to get needed permits to go into business, "poverty traps" for less advantaged citizens resulting from an unwillingness to coordinate taxation and expenditure programs, and citizens not receiving needed services because their particular set of socio-economic characteristics were not covered by a patchwork of laws attempting to provide for all groups within the society. All these failings result in governments costing more, and/or providing less high-quality services, than they might under a more coordinated system.

The vertical nature of government

Politically and administratively public policy appears to function better vertically, so that the "stovepipes" that define policy within governments are perpetuated and reinforced. It is crucial to recognize that this vertical structuring of the public sector is as much a function of political as administrative characteristics within government. Perhaps most importantly, the vertical character of policy and administration is maintained by clientele politics, as well as by the desire of government to serve particular components of the public. Clientele groups that are involved in the public sector often believe that they have the right to their own organization to serve them. Government organizations that stray too far from serving their clientele encounter the risk of losing necessary political support. Sometimes maintaining the separate organizations to serve the clientele appears important, even if the services themselves might be retained, or even enhanced, in a larger and more heterogeneous organization.[1]

The organizations serving clients have many of the same interests in maintaining their exclusive position as do the clientele groups, and perhaps even more. Bureaucratic organizations want to maintain their client base and their close relationships with their clients in order to maintain their budgets and their influence within political circles. In this part of the game of bureaucratic politics clients are a resource and a source of power. Therefore, coordinating programs, and possibly diluting that relationship between clients and the organization, is usually not considered good politics in these circles.[2] Somewhat paradoxically, some research has indicated that coordination with less-closely allied activities is easier than with more similar programs – the more remote types of programs are not conceived of as being the potential threat that the more similar programs are. In coalition governments these differences among ministries may be accentuated by ministers from different parties controlling ministries that need to cooperate.

Although it is easy to characterize bureaucratic politics in the above totally self-serving manner, we should also remember that most employees of public programs believe in the benefits of their program for clients. The organizations therefore argue (and often believe) that they protect their programs as much in the perceived interest of the clients as that of the organization itself. This belief in the centrality and efficacy of their programs by employees of public organizations makes achieving coordination more difficult, given that members of an organization believe that they are in actuality supplying what the citizen needs. Members of a public organization may realize that their clients do require a variety of services, but may still believe that the most efficient way to provide for those needs is to place additional funds and responsibility within the one organization.

Further, in addition to the commitments to serve their clients, the vertical nature of administrative structures is reinforced by the different types of expertise held by different ministries, and the linkage of those organizations with different professional networks. As Martin Painter (1987, 12) put it:

> ... powerful political and intellectual reasons contribute to perpetuating and reinforcing the self-containment of functional and organizational compartments. Each policy sector – health, transport, town planning industrial development, employment and so forth – exists in a jurisdictional shelter of organizational structures where actors develop their own partial perspectives and where specialized relationships of support and opposition develop connecting, bureaucratic and outside interests in distinct arenas of sectoral policymaking.

Finally, legislative politics also helps to maintain vertical politics and to make coordination among programs, even closely related programs, more difficult. Some of this effect is a result of the same type of politics described for clientele groups and bureaucratic organizations. Legislatures have similar contacts with clients, as do the bureaucratic organizations, although the clients are usually referred to as "constituents" in the legislative milieu. The vertical nature of these relationships may be exacerbated through having strong legislative committees that correspond directly with the ministerial structure of government. Vertically defined ministerial structures also are considered important by legislatures for maintaining accountability for programs and funds. If funds and responsibility are commingled through horizontal structures then those oversight functions become more difficult, and accountability for both programs and finances may be diminished.

The above discussion sounds much like traditional discussions of "iron triangles" in American government, and to some extent it is, but many of these same vertical patterns emerge without the peculiar features of American government.[3] Indeed, the pressing need to manage government in a more horizontal fashion appears in virtually every country for which I can find information. Thus, even in Scandinavian countries with corporate pluralist structures and networks surrounding their ministries (Olsen, 1987), coordination often is identified as a significant administrative issue.[4] These systems are cooperative and to some extent network based in how they administer programs (Marton, 2000), but still have difficulty in working across ministries, or at times working across divisions within the same ministry. On the latter point, one common strategy for attempting to improve horizontal management has been to create "superministries" within which numerous closely related programs are all included. In many cases all this effort has done is to move the coordination problems within the one ministry, and to make the issue less visible and therefore less likely to be addressed directly.[5]

Alternative Views of Coordination

Although coordination is often discussed as a single concept, it actually may mean several different things. The most common distinction made is between positive and negative versions of coordination, with the former term implying avoiding direct conflicts among programs, while the latter implies a more active stance of assuring that the programs work together effectively, and support each other. So, negative coordination might be achieved through attempting to reduce the number of conflicting regulations on businesses, while the latter might be achieved by providing business the opportunity to do "one-stop shopping" and receive all their needed licenses at once at a single location.

While the former conception of coordination is much easier to attain, it is a rather minimalist version of horizontality, and may not produce the types of benefits expected. That is, eliminating overlaps may be desirable politically given the amount of complaint and

Table 6.1   *Thinking about horizontal government*

Activity		
Means/ends	Coordination	Integration
Joined-up (ends)	Joined-up coordination	Joined-up integration
Holistic (means)	Holistic coordination	Holistic integration

obvious difficulties created, but may not address the more fundamental questions of achieving integrated and coherent conceptions of public policy. Achieving that level of integration will require more positive approaches to coordination, involving implementing common conceptions and negotiating differences among policymaking organizations. Achieving that level of coordination tends to involve imposition of political power from above, or the creation of a strong network of actors that develop shared conceptions of appropriate policy.

The ideas of "joined up government" advanced by the Blair government in the United Kingdom is an indication of the desirability of achieving more positive levels of coordination. Perri,[6] a scholar who has worked in Number 10, has pointed to two dimensions in the analysis of coordination activities in government (see Table 6.1). One dimension is the simple question of whether government is attempting to have its numerous departments merely take into account the activities of other organizations, or whether there is more of an attempt to force real integration of the purposes and actions of the programs. The second dimension is a bit more complex, implying the existence of a means/ends dichotomy in the management of programs. That is, it may be easier to agree on ends for programs and for coordination than it is to agree upon the mechanisms that will generate that coordination. Politically, agreement on means may involve one or more parties having to cede some aspects of their program (and budget).

Policy and administration

Following from the above classification of actions meant to produce enhanced coherence in government, we can ask whether the emphasis in coordination and horizontality in the public sector should be on policy or on administration (Regens, 1988, 138). The title of this conference contains both the words "policy" and "management", and both of these concepts have some relationship to the capacity to make government work better horizontally. These two issues are indeed certainly related, but they also have important differences. Further addressing one issue without the other can solve only a portion of the coordination problems usually identified in public service delivery. Administrative coordination is in essence coordination from the bottom-up, and is focussed on service delivery issues. This bottom-up orientation toward making government more effective assumes that the important questions about governing are implementation questions. A policy orientation to coordination assumes, on the other hand, that if policies are formulated well initially then there will be few (or at least fewer) problems in putting them into effect. The policy perspective is more of a "top-down", politically-centered conception about how to make government perform better than is administrative coordination.

The choice between administrative and policy coordination is to some degree a false dilemma; to be truly effective in generating coherence governments will require both forms of coordination. The question then becomes one of the balance between coordinating the two elements of the policy cycle: formulation and implementation. Some scholars (Elmore, 1979; Barrett and Fudge, 1981) have argued that policy formulation should be guided by implementation concerns and that policy should be "backwards-mapped". In the context of coordination, this strategy involves thinking about the potential duplication problems at the implementation stage implied by the policies that are being designed, and designing around the implementation problems. Other analysts have argued (Linder and Peters, 1987; Hogwood and Gunn, 1984) that, although implementation is important, it should not be so dominant in initial policy formulation. Governments should first decide what they want to do and then decide how those goals can be achieved efficiently and effectively (Bogason, 1991). For the coordination question these decisions will require deciding what priorities the governing system as a whole has, in contrast to the multiple priorities that exist with each individual program and organization.

Asian governments may have less capacity to depend upon coordination at the bottom than do governments in European or North American systems. To depend upon lower level bureaucrats to coordinate, or to engage in what is to some extent self-effacing behavior, when they are not as well integrated as career structures, or may depend upon external sources of income to survive economically, is to ask perhaps too much. Descriptions of several of these bureaucracies (Indonesia, Philippines) indicates that there is less commitment to public service goals than might be expected for civil servants in other political systems. Further, in some systems (Thailand, India) there is a great deal of internal fragmentation in the administrative system that may make coordination more difficult.

Top-down versus bottom-up

Related to the above question about politics and administration is a second question of whether coordination can best be achieved at the beginning of the policy process or whether it should be more focussed at the "bottom" of government. In other words, do the people who actually deliver services know more about those services, and their clients, than individuals at the top of organizational hierarchies? If they do, then it would make sense to have services coordinated around their targets, whether they are individuals, organizations, or areas, rather than impose the coordination from the center of government. If the bottom-up approach to coordination is emphasized then bargaining over coordination would be done not by ministers and senior civil servants in central agencies but rather by lower level administrators.

This latter strategy corresponds well to the "empowerment" ideologies now being implemented within many governments (Peters, 1996), but it also requires the initial creation of clear policy frameworks at the highest reaches

of government. It appears that the highest reaches of government can not avoid responsibility for creating and delivering integrated policies, especially if there is to be an attempt to produce some redefinition of a policy area to include the cross-cutting dimensions. That having been said, the importance of emerging, cross-cutting issues, and the absence of as yet clear definitions of those issues, will require high levels of interaction between top and bottom of organizations.

Again, the dichotomy between top-down and bottom-up being discussed here is to some extent false. In many concrete examples of coordination, the need for greater cooperation among policy-making organizations at the top first becomes apparent as difficult cases present themselves in the field. Likewise, the failures of coordination at the bottom of the structures become apparent as the results of policy-making and administration are assessed by evaluators at the centers of the political systems. As well as becoming apparent of the problems through interactions of top and bottom, it is likely that the problems can only be addressed through interactions up and down the hierarchies within government.

Horizontal or Vertical?

The coordination question is generally, conceptualized in terms of making government function in a more "horizontal" manner, and, indeed, many of the most important contemporary issues concerning coordination are those of working across programs within a single level of government. These problems of managing horizontally are compounded when the issue of coordination among levels of government is added, especially in federal regimes such as Canada, Germany, or the United States (Derlien, 1991). Even in unitary regimes, however, many of the same inter-governmental coordination problems among political and administrative levels of government arise, albeit usually without the political intensity that can characterize federal-provincial disputes in a federal regime (Toonen, 1985). These problems may be confounded to an even greater extent when, as in most countries, central government ministries have field structures that do not correspond to the structure of sub-national government.

The fundamental root of the coordination problem in federal systems is that most federal regimes have evolved in ways that permit all levels of government to be involved in almost all policy areas. Thus, to be capable of addressing problems of redundancy and incompatibility requires that all governments agree on some basic approaches to the policy and work to make their means of service provision more compatible. This agreement is often easier said than done, but it has been done. For example, several respondents in a series of interviews on coordination in Canada pointed out that the federal government and the provinces have come to agreements to coordinate and integrate their efforts at food inspection as a precursor to further attempts to coordinate policies among the levels of government. These agreements may appear to be simple matters – negative coordination only – but should be seen as an accomplishment in light of the difficulties involved in achieving those agreements. One respondent pointed out that these agreements were gained only after days of discussion and then had to be validated at the level of the provincial prime ministers. Further, these vertical coordination concerns were compounded by the need to coordinate food safety issues across various ministries, such as agriculture, trade and industry, and increasingly foreign affairs. Thus, one of the more common functions of government – ensuring that the food sold in the market – is safe for the consumer actually involves a significant level of inter-organizational and intergovernmental bargaining to become compatible.[6]

Further, in most federal systems the central government utilizes sub-national governments to implement many or most of their policies. This implementation strategy means that, even if policies are effectively coordinated in the national capital, that integration may fall apart once those policies begin to be implemented. If the central government is not particularly concerned about how their policies are implemented, as appears true under the block grant provisions becoming so common in the United States (Katz, 1995), then there is no particular cause for concern. If the central government does care, as most do, then vertical coordination becomes a *sine qua non* for successful horizontal coordination (Derlien, 1991). The reverse is probably also true, and it would be difficult for sub-national implementors to compensate for fundamental design errors occurring at the central government level (Linder and Peters, 1987). Perhaps the most important point here is that almost all governing now is multi-level governance, requiring blending not only the perspectives of different levels of the public sector, but also blending different functional policy communities existing at all levels of the system.

PRESSURES FOR HORIZONTALITY

Coordination and coherence have been problems for as long as there have been governments, but the need for improved coordination appears to be more manifest in the early 21st century than in the past. This emphasis on coordination appears to have arisen for a number of reasons. These pressures for horizontal government reflect political demands for a range of actors, including changes in political ideologies about the role of public sector. In addition, administrative reforms over the past several decades have resulted in the need for increased coordination interventions in order to address new problems that have emerged as a result of attempts to solve problems of efficiency and effectiveness in government.

Fiscal pressures

Perhaps the dominant pressure for enhanced organizational coordination in the public sector comes from the need to save public money. For both political and strictly financial reasons governments have less money to spend than in the past and must attempt to control public spending as effectively as possible. One way of controlling expenditures is through eliminating redundancy and ensuring that services will be provided in the most cost-efficient manner. The examples of contradictions and duplications in public programs are familiar and make good copy for the exposes of inefficiency and outright incompetence in the public sector. Further, for governments intent on saving money, eliminating redundant programs is a way to do so without necessarily reducing the level of services being delivered to the public.

Although familiar to people inside and outside of government, the existence of these coordination problems and their fiscal impacts are often exaggerated for political purposes. These coordination failures certainly do exist, but generally represent very minor amounts of money, compared with the political benefits that the programs involved may generate for their governments. Further, coordination itself is far from a costless activity. To impose coordination on an existing ministerial structure requires utilizing resources to monitor overlaps and perhaps even more political capital to impose sufficient political "clout" to eliminate those overlaps. Creating coordination may also require creating new programs to close gaps in program structures, and with that will generate increased expenditures by government.

Strategic management

One positive consequence for coordination arising out of the management reforms during the past several decades is the emphasis on strategic management and the selection of clear objectives for the public sector. One of the first things that any politician or administrator engaged in such an undertaking discovers is that most of the important strategic objectives for governments cut across conventional organizational boundaries and therefore require working horizontally across the "stovepipes" of government. So, exercises such as implementing Strategic Results Areas in New Zealand, Strategic Portfolios in Finland and (to a more limited degree) the Government Performance and Results Act in the United States[7] require those governments to think collectively and horizontally about what they want to do, and how they are going to

accomplish their goals. These programs are never easy tasks to implement, and the mechanisms as yet in place are often inadequate to create genuine strategic management. Still, these represent movements in the appropriate direction for enhanced policy coordination. As governments continue to develop programs of performance management and stress the results of their programs, then questions of the contributions of numerous programs to the achievement of the desired outcomes will become more apparent.

Issues

The issues that governments must now confront also call for greater attention to horizontal management. Governments have invested a great deal of effort at finding ways to make individual programs work more effectively, but the policy issues that are emerging tend to transcend the usual boundaries of those ministries and programs. For example, a principal economic issue confronting contemporary governments has been defined as "competitiveness". This is certainly an economic issue but also involves education, labor, social policy, regulation and a host of other policy considerations. Likewise, issues are being defined in terms of client groups – women, the elderly, immigrants – whose needs cut across conventional boundaries of ministries and require greater integration of existing programs. There is every reason to expect issues to continue to defy the boundaries of conventional ministerial structures, so that the needs for coordination are not likely to diminish. Likewise, it does not seem that simply moving "boxes" in order to capture a particular set of problems will solve the problems – the next issue may only cut across the new administrative boxes that have been created to solve the previous problem.

Earlier administrative reforms

Although some earlier reforms have emphasized strategic management and integration of policies, a more common pattern of reform has been to decentralize, devolve and disaggregate the public sector (deMontricher, 1999; Peters and Pierre, 2000). These reforms may have generated some efficiency benefits for the public sector (although those benefits are often difficult to demonstrate) but they have made governments that were already fragmented vertically even more diverse and fragmented institutions. As well as creating autonomous or semi-autonomous agencies within the public sector, these reforms have created a number of organizations – referred to as quangos and quagos – that have some characteristics of both public and private sector organizations. Therefore, a subsequent round of reform has been instituted that stresses the need for restoring some greater integration among the component structures of the public sector, and creating greater coherence. These reforms include strengthening central agencies, strengthening offices of presidents and prime ministers (Peters, Rhodes and Wright, 2000) and creating "super-ministries" that pull together a range of relevant ministries. In some instances the simplest response has been to reinstitute the traditional ministerial structures and reduce emphasis on decentralization.

Globalization/Europeanization

Globalization is something of a cliché, but it is also a reality for governments. Even governments that have been relatively insulated from international pressures find that almost all their policies have an international dimension, and that those international pressures tend to force broader consideration of the issues. Education may have been primarily a national concern, even in the recent past, but it is now centrally connected with issues of international competitiveness, thereby requiring closer associations with labor, industry and foreign affairs ministries. Agriculture is now centrally connected with international affairs, certainly in Europe, but also in most other countries. The list of connections among ministries could be extended but the basic point remains the same – international involvement creates more interconnections among policies

and therefore greater need for horizontal government structures.

The impact of international forces on coordination requirements is nowhere clearer than in the European Union. These fifteen countries are finding that they must develop coordination mechanisms in their national capitals, as well as in Brussels, if they are to be successful participants in the game of European policy-making (Kassim, Peters and Wright, 2000; Kassim, Menon, Peters and Wright, 2001). Although some countries have chosen not to invest heavily in coordination activities and to permit ministries to bargain relatively autonomously in a variety of settings, the typical response to EU membership has been to create significant structures for coordination. Some, such as the United Kingdom, have regarded policy coherence vis-à-vis Europe as essential to their capacity to extract as much as possible from the policy system, and also to be able to defend the national interest effectively in what is often assumed by the British to be a relatively hostile environment.

Cross-cutting concerns

Coordination is also being driven by a range of cross-cutting concerns of modern governments and contemporary public opinion. For example, the environment has become a common concern for a range of policies, and environmental agencies have become in essence another set of central agencies. Just as all policies must be approved by ministries of finance for their fiscal implications so too must these policies also be vetted by environmental agencies (Doern, 1993). Rights and equality for minorities, women and other designated groups are also becoming concerns for coordination and common consideration across a range of specific policy choices. Finally, as noted above, the international implications of most if not all issues are also now a matter of common concern.[8] In short, policies are no longer seen as just operating within their own defined policy domain; the full range of their implications is now understood and becomes part of a broader consideration of the issues.

MANAGING HORIZONTAL GOVERNMENT

The above discussions of the nature of policy coordination and the contemporary motivations for enhancing coordination then lead rather naturally to question how this Holy Grail of administration can be created in the real world of governing. The conventional answer would be to impose greater control from the upper reaches of government. This is certainly one solution, and often an effective one, but it is by no means the only available solution to the problem. The general style of governing has changed in the majority of industrialized democracies, with much greater reliance on indirect instruments and diminished reliance on direct government provision and command and control regulations. As those changes have occurred so have changes in the ways in which coordination is approached. Therefore, we will look at markets, networks and hierarchies as alternative means of achieving coordination. This classification of social processes has by now become quite conventional in the social sciences (see Thompson, Frances, Levacic and Mitchell, 1991) but is still a useful scheme through which to approach issues of categorizing and assessing coordination mechanisms. Further, this threefold classification emphasizes the extent to which contemporary governance ideas have moved away from thinking about hierarchy as the only, or even the dominant, approach to coordination (not to mention other aspects of governing (Pierre and Peters, 2000)).

Markets

The economic theory of markets assumes that coordination will occur almost automatically if competitive forces are permitted to function without interference. The "hidden hand" that is assumed to function in other aspects of market relationships is also expected to operate in the coordination of programs. Indeed, in many ways, markets are fundamentally institutions for coordination, with the institution presumed to assure that sellers and buyers will find each other, and find each other at an acceptable price level for both. Thus, while most of the means of producing coordination that we discuss conventionally require the *imposition* of coordination on government structures by law and authority, the market approach to coordination would substitute more indirect and virtually autonomous modes of coordination. The actors will be involved with each other for purposes of mutually advantageous exchange, and their involvement will be episodic and partial, rather than the more comprehensive style of interaction typical of actors entirely within the public sector itself.

In the case of coordination through markets within the public sector, the necessary bargaining may come about, with money being the medium of exchange. One clear example is the creation of internal markets (Jerome-Forget, White and Wiener, 1995; OECD, 1993) as a means of coordinating actions and imposing market discipline on organizations that otherwise would be governed strictly through hierarchy. The assumption of internal markets is that there are some components of service delivery that can be conceptualized as "selling" their services, while other actors within government are the "buyers" of those services. These artificial markets function as mechanisms of getting these actors together in the most efficient manner, without having to use formal authority. Also, we should remember that, to some extent, the budgetary process has always been something of a coordination process based on money, but the increasing reliance on internal markets has made the role of money and exchange in coordination more explicit than in conventional patterns of governance.

Likewise, contracts among public organizations are increasingly being employed as a means of coordinating their activities, replacing previous coordination through hierarchy with mutually acceptable "deals" (Fortin, 2000). Contracts in the public sector combine some features of markets with an otherwise legally based instrument (Peters, 2002). As with internal markets the bargaining in internal contracting is also "quasi", given that it is all public money and there may be a legal requirement for the delivery of the service.[9] Further, contracting in the public sector may be restricted in the number of possible bidders and in the range of alternative patterns of service delivery possible under the law. Despite those constraints, contracting is a market-based idea for coordination that may be applicable to a wide range of service areas.

Finally, the market can be utilized to coordinate economic policy, especially within the European Union. The increased linkage of these countries and their fiscal and monetary policies means that the operations of the market places pressures on all the countries to make their policies compatible (Jacquet, 1998). Further, the Maastricht Treaty and the Amsterdam Treaty place strong demands on the member governments to coordinate their fiscal policies. Arguably, some of the same pressure for coordination is arising, perhaps less directly than in the EU, in all the industrialized democracies as they must compete with one another in an international marketplace. This coordination may extend not just to monetary and fiscal policy but also to tax policy (see Hallerberg and Basinger, 1998) social policy (Adema, 1997) and a range of other public policies contributing to economic competitiveness.[10] Further, the close financial connections now are necessitating closer coordination of financial and even criminal laws (Laronche, 2000).

In summary, the market does provide some instruments to promote the coordination of policies, but it may not be an all-purpose solution. For the market to be effective there must be something for the participants to exchange, and that is not always the case in public programs. Thus, this approach may work when the programs involve goods and services that are in principle marketable, but almost certainly not for all. Not all relationships among multiple organizations can be coordinated effectively through markets and exchange. In some instances there are mutual complementary goals, rather than the somewhat contradictory goals implied in market exchanges. Further, the goals that might be achieved through mutual adjustment among the interested parties might be different from those sought by the legislators who wrote the law, or even

perhaps the tops of hierarchies responsible for implementing the law. The very decentralization that makes markets so valuable in some situations also may limit their effectiveness. Those limits on markets may be especially damaging for policies that contain a strong legal or entitlement basis for citizens, and hence will not be effective for the vast range of social policies in which government is placed in the position of providing services to clients. On the other hand, market-based instruments such as taxation may be able to replace command and control regulation in a variety of areas.[11]

Networks

Networks are another bargained mechanism for producing policy coordination. Rather than the exchange relationships implied by the market, networks themselves are defined much as individual organizations would be, though patterns of interaction. For organizations those interactions occur primarily among individuals, while for networks they are among other organizations as well as individuals. Networks have many virtues as mechanisms for coordination, and to some extent depend upon natural patterns of interaction that emerge among organizations and individuals concerned with the same policy issues. These may be "epistemic communities" (Zito, 1999) defined by common intellectual position and common patterns of training. Networks depend upon the interests and commitment of individuals and groups to be successful; most of these participants (inside and outside the public sector) want to do their jobs as well as possible and find networks convenient for enhancing their effectiveness (Chisholm, 1989).

The term "network" is to some extent a short-hand term for a variety of patterns of interactions between state and society, and within the public sector itself (Olsen, 1987; Kickert, 1995). In general, these network relationships involve the State relinquishing some of its authoritative powers in order to achieve greater agreement among the interested and affected parties within a policy area (Marin, 1990). This is a natural mechanism for coordination, given that bargaining tends to create agreement on proposals and tends also to involve a wide range of actors. Network bargaining can be effective at both the formulation and implementation stages of the policy process (see Considine, 1992). In both aspects of the process of governing networks can be used to avoid turf-battles over policies and clients, and to create a common perception of the policy issues and a common reaction to the issues. Networks need not exist only in the national capital around the design of policy, but often are crucial at the lowest level. That is, networks organized around clients (classes or even individuals) can be the most effective form of coordination in the social services. For many Asian countries the absence of networks of organizations in the civil society that can provide the external network may be a serious impediment to using non-governmental methods for coordination. Perhaps especially important for coordination and coherence is the relative absence of social groups that cut across conventional policy sectors.

Professionalism creates a ready-made network for coordinating some types of public policies. One virtue of the professions in their classical definition (see Wolgast, 1992) is their function as a reference group for their members and, in most instances, professionals will have their own network of fellow professionals that can supplement the networks created through the organization itself. Although in many ways beneficial, professional networks also can limit coordination. In the first place, these networks are relatively closed to outsiders, so that there is less capacity for objective scrutiny of policies than is true for other forms of decision-making. In addition, each profession tends to define problems and solutions in their own terms so that there may be very effective coordination within each profession and therefore (usually) within each single program, but coordination across programs may actually be more difficult.[12]

Other networks could be structured more vertically, with most interactions being upward to the relevant government organization, rather than organizations in the network solving problems among themselves. This is one emerging role for central agencies that may eschew their traditional role of imposing coordination in favor of bargaining over issues with a range of organizations. Further, certain public sector organizations have an emerging role in creating coordination, particularly when utilizing popular ideas and issues, particularly environmentalism, as a means of promoting common values (Doern, 1993). Ideas like environmentalism, even in the absence of an institutional basis, can be used to produce coordination across programs.

Despite their virtues, networks also have some weaknesses intellectually (Dowding, 1995) and as a means for producing public sector coordination. One of these is an analytic problem; once you have said that a network exists in a policy area, what do you say next? It is difficult to argue that networks do not exist, but it also appears difficult at times to say much more about them and to use them in any predictive manner. This weakness is especially true given that networks can have rather different internal dynamics. For example, Paul Sabatier (1988) conceives of multiple networks existing around many policy areas, with the principal dynamic being conflict over the definition of the policy problem and over finding the appropriate solution to the issue. This clash of ideas is, however, a form of coordination, since it tends to eliminate conflicting ideas about policy and with that conflicting and probably wasteful duplication. Still, the behavior of networks, especially those structured without a central position to government, may be too indeterminate to permit government to be particularly effective in coordinating programs.

Interest groups

Political groups advocating the interests of those segments of society presenting government with cross-cutting policy issues can function as a means of identifying needs and pressing for their solution. In many countries the target populations for major cross-cutting policy issues – the elderly, women – are well-organized and are positive political symbols.

Other populations, however, are less well-organized and in the case of immigrants are often conceptualized as pariah groups with few political rights and resources. Depending upon the political power of the groups requiring service may not be the most effective means of generating coordination and policy coherence. For example, one of my British respondents pointed to the recent attempts to coordinate and integrate government responses to racial attacks in British cities. In this case the leadership had to be from within the bureaucracy itself – the Home Office and the Crown Prosecution Service – as opposed to coming in response to the political power of the groups in question. The various immigrant groups and ethnic organizations simply did not have sufficient legitimacy and political "clout" to provoke the desired response from the political system themselves.

Interest groups may have many of the same problems as political parties in coping with cross-cutting issues. Many political parties work with particular definitions of the issue areas that have been functional for them in the past but which have outlived their utility, or which are not widely shared by other actors involved in the issue areas. To be successful they may have to broker deals with other groups with complementary if not contradictory definitions of issues (Sabatier, 1988; Page, 2003). This need to compromise and negotiate often contrasts with their need to serve their members directly. That service may be oriented toward the separation of separate programs for their constituents rather than accepting the interdependencies among policies and issues.

The civil service network

Another important network mechanism for producing greater coordination within government is structuring the careers of civil servants so that they have broad experience and a broad conception of government and policy. Countries such as the United States, Finland or Norway, in which civil servants spend most or all of their careers within a single agency or department will, everything else being equal, encounter greater difficulties in coordinating policies than will other countries. Civil service systems such as those of the United Kingdom and other Westminster democracies, in which there are relatively frequent movements among departments as a civil servant works his or her way up through the hierarchy during their career, should produce a somewhat better possibility of adequate policy coordination. Civil servants who have worked in a variety of different programs should have a better idea of the perspectives of other departments, and tend to have a sense of belonging to a government rather than to a particular organization within that government. They should also have a better idea of the total range of services delivered by government and how they could be made available to clients.

Canadian respondents in a set of international interviews about coordination expressed growing concern about the loss of this important informal mechanism for generating coordination within the public sector. They noted that the down-sizing of the public service is reducing the opportunities for movement within government so that individuals tend to remain in one post for much longer. Their vision of what government does and is about has narrowed accordingly. Further, the increasing technical content of most programs means that greater expertise is required, and with that individual civil servants may have fewer fungible skills that can be applied in other settings. While the public service may be becoming more expert it also may be lessening the chances of effective coordination from within the public service itself.

The absence of a career, professional civil service may be an impediment to effective coordination within government. The problems are as significant for European and North American countries that have opened their senior civil service to non-career appointments as it is for Asian, African, and Latin American countries that have not successfully institutionalized civil service systems. The absence of a civil service may be compensated for by the connections of the "in and outers" with policy networks that can provide them with both substantive policy information and a range of connections within government.

Hierarchy

We will now turn to the most common mechanism used to achieve coordination in the public sector – hierarchy. The most common pattern is for coordination problems to be addressed from the top by authority and legal provisions. Even after several decades of intensive administrative reforms, driven to a great extent by ideas of the market (Peters, 1996), when issues of coordination arise the most common response is still to use authority and hierarchy. This is to some extent a recognition of established patterns, or path dependency, of using this type of coordination device. This also reflects the relative effectiveness of these devices when dealing with the full range of policy issues, while markets tend to be restricted in their applicability, and networks depend perhaps excessively upon the good will of the participants.

Another virtue of the hierarchical approach to coordination is that there is a wide range of responses available within the broad category of hierarchical methods. Governments have been rather creative in the ways in which they respond to the necessity of coordinating, and have a repertoire of ways to confront overlap and duplication. As noted above, some of these depend upon political power and others depend more upon administrative procedures and inter-organizational relationships, but all have at times enjoyed some success in bringing together program that were by structure and culture different, competitive and perhaps even hostile.

The core executive

The locus for horizontal policy coordination and issues management is usually assumed to be at the very center of government – the chief executive and the central agencies that serve that executive. The ultimate responsibility for policies, and the coordination of those policies, lies with prime ministers in parliamentary regimes. The situation of the American President is somewhat more complex, but even there the President bears ultimate responsibility for the execution of policy. These chief executives are now attempting to provide themselves with the means for promoting coordination, whether it is done primarily by the executive or through the use of cabinet and powerful administrative agencies (see Peters, Rhodes and Wright, 2000).

Chief executive staff. By themselves prime ministers and presidents do not have much capacity to produce effective coordination. They tend to be extremely overworked and have little time to spend on coordinating the activities of the numerous ministries under their overall control. They can, however, develop staffs and organizations that can assist them in coordination. The most developed organizations of this type are in the Executive Office of the President in the United States. This office contains not only the personal staff of the President but a number of monitoring and coordinating organizations such as the Office of Management and Budget, the Council of Economic Advisors and the National Security Council as well. All recent presidents also have had some organization in the White House for coordinating domestic policy, although the name and responsibilities of those organizations have varied. Although similar offices exist in other governments, e.g. the Bundeskanzlersamt in Germany and Austria (Mueller-Rommel, 2000), the Kansli in Sweden (Larsson, 1988), and the Department of Prime Minister and Cabinet in Australia (Davis, 1998), they tend not be as fully articulated as in the United States.

One virtue of these executive organizations for managing cross-cutting policy issues is that they tend to be flexible and do not have to be concerned with delivering services to existing clients (other than advice to the chief executive). They can thus create internal task forces or temporary structures to cope with changing issues and interpretations of issues. Further, they do not have as much policy "turf" to defend as do line agencies. On the other hand, relying on this level of government for coordination is likely to be highly centralizing. Further, it can overload the office of the chief executive at a time when the prevailing ethos of governance is decentralization. Those problems can be compounded if definitions of issues and policies are more clearly identified at the lower echelons of government.

Central agencies. A more general strategy for achieving coordination from the center of government is to rely upon central agencies. By this term we refer to budgetary, policy, and personnel management organizations that report directly to the chief executive, or which are assigned principal responsibility for policy coordination and central management of issues (Campbell and Szablowski, 1979; Savoie, 1995b). Examples of central agencies are the Treasury in Britain, the Treasury Board Secretariat in Canada, and Departments of the Public Service and Ministries of Finance in a number of countries. These organizations can be employed to enforce the priorities of the chief executive, but they also tend to develop priorities and managerial styles of their own, and to develop substantial power over policy.

Central agencies can play a significant role in creating coordination, but they also can generate substantial conflict with the line organizations actually providing public services. These frictions reflect the conflicts between "line" and "staff" organizations that are typical of inter-organizational politics within the public sector. The former type of organizations resent the power exercised by control organizations that do not directly serve the public and which, it is argued, know little about the programs being delivered. Staff organizations (including central agencies) tend to believe that line agencies have extremely narrow views on policy and do not understand the need to impose overall priorities on government.

The role of central agencies has been increasing in most contemporary political systems, despite the general *Zeitgeist* of decentralization and deconcentration. The political dynamic has been that as programs are decentralized the conventional mechanisms of political control are devalued. The one major control instrument that remains in place is the budget, so that ministries of finance in particular become crucial in the process of controlling administration. Further, as performance management becomes a central component of managing the public sector, then ministries of finance become even more central to processes

of control and accountability. Again, however, to be fully effective, the central agencies must be strongly supported by the prime minister.

Cabinet itself, especially with strong Prime Minister or Minister of Finance. Cabinet itself is another locus for the management of cross-cutting policy issues. In some ways it is the most logical institution to perform this task; all the principal actors in policy-making and service provision are represented. On the other hand, cabinet may be a place in which the ministers must protect the interests of their departments. Those interests may well not be best served (in the short term at least) by excessive cooperation with other agencies, or by examining the broader implications of groups of policies. The cabinet can serve as the locus for the examination of cross-cutting issues if there is adequate leadership, both from the Prime Minister and from the civil service that serves the cabinet. With that leadership there can be a capacity to redirect the discussion of issues and enhance policy coordination. Even with a strong prime minister, a close link with the minister of finance appears to be crucial in creating coherent government, so that, as Donald Savoie (1999) said, there is a need to ensure that "no light shines between them".

Cabinet committees. A cabinet may be too large an organization to coordinate programs effectively. This is especially true given that each minister usually will feel compelled to defend the interests of his or her own department, and this need may make the necessary cooperation difficult to obtain. Many cabinets have been reduced drastically in size (Bouckaert, Ormond and Peters, 2000), but may still be too large to function effectively as a single decision-making entity. In the case of problems that are not well defined and which cut across a range of ministries ministers may feel compelled to defend the claims of their department over control of the issue, with some loss of necessary cooperation across departments.

Most cabinet systems therefore have developed working "inner cabinet" systems, or some committees within cabinet that can establish collective priorities and coordinate policies across portfolios (Mackie and Hogwood,

1985). One approach to achieving this goal is to create an overarching "priorities and planning committee" within cabinet, as in Canada. This approach can coordinate policies across the entire range of public programs, but often will push too many decisions upwards to a few senior officials of government. The alternative approach is to develop a series of cabinet committees, each responsible for a particular segment of policy. This approach has the advantage of bringing the relevant departmental ministers to the table to coordinate their own activities. This has been particularly evident in the budgetary process, with envelope budgeting in Canada and Sweden as examples. This approach also has its disadvantages. In particular, the boundaries between policy areas, and therefore between cabinet committees, are not always clear. The boundaries between policy areas may be becoming even less clear; for example social policies, labor market policies, and even education policies, have become intertwined through competitiveness concerns to a degree not previously experienced. Therefore, there may be a proliferation of coordinating committees, and the consequent need to coordinate the coordinators.

Ministers without portfolio, or with additional coordinative portfolio. Another means of generating improved coordination within a cabinet system is to utilize ministers without portfolio tasked to coordinate programs within a broad policy area. Another related method would be to assign departmental ministers additional coordinating portfolios. For example, in the Netherlands one minister has been assigned the additional responsibility for coordinating all programs being delivered to immigrants, as well as programs designed to regulate their entry and their participation in the labor market. In other cases ministers have been assigned the responsibility for integrating the services provided to women, or in one case to provide a range of services for the middle class.

While this system has the advantage of designating someone to be responsible for coordination of a policy area, it also has several important drawbacks. The most obvious is that it can overload an already busy minister. Further, although the minister is responsible for coordinating a range of other programs, this is unlikely to receive the same priority as running the programs within his or her own department. In the case of a minister without portfolio assigned primary responsibility for coordinating programs, such an individual may have more time to spend on this activity but may not have other necessary resources. In particular, cabinet ministers without a departmental power base may not have sufficient clout within the cabinet to bring his or her colleagues along if there is a need to coordinate their policies. This, however, may be counteracted by assigning politicians with strong political links to the prime minister these roles.

Junior ministers. Rather than have a minister accept additional responsibilities and add to an already extensive range of duties, governments can instead develop a system of junior ministers that can help coordinate their ministries, and perhaps accept responsibility for services to designated groups or for other special functions. To some degree junior ministers will have some of the same problems encountered by ministers without portfolio. Being designated "junior" these officials almost certainly have less power in government than will ministers, or probably senior civil servants. If these aspiring political leaders are asked to coordinate a range of services and manage crosscutting issues controlled by powerful ministers they may have only limited success. Further, they may be placed in confrontational positions with the senior ministers and may perceive the job as a political detriment rather than a step up the political career ladder.

Ministerial organizations themselves. We have been discussing the need to coordinate across cabinet portfolios or their equivalents, but cabinet departments can themselves develop mechanisms for policy coordination. One that has been tried in a number of countries is the creation of "superministries" that would incorporate within their own structures a wide range of programs that otherwise would have to be made compatible across departmental structures. At one extreme the Swiss government is limited to seven government departments, so that if their portfolios are relatively homogenous they should be able to produce substantial internal congruence of policy. At less of an extreme, in Australia, the Hawke government in 1983 reorganized government to create a smaller number of large ministries and created an inner cabinet that had some capacity to coordinate policies across the entire range of government services. The British government had tried a similar strategy much earlier, and the Nixon administration in the United States had proposed creating four "super-departments" in the federal government (Nathan, 1975).

While it may appear logical to locate as many similar programs as possible within a single ministry, the coordination gains from that structural decision may be more apparent than real. First, there will have to be a significant sub-ministerial structure which may engender its own difficulties in coordination. Likewise, if a minister has a too large a ministry with too many internal divisions, he or she may encounter the same problems in producing coordination as might a prime minister with an equal number of ministries to coordinate. Finally, the location of all the apparently related programs within the single department may lead to complacency and the assumption that the problems have been solved while the problems actually persist.

Placing a number of programs together within a single ministry also may have other effects on policy and management. By placing the principal coordinative responsibility within a department, the decisions tend to be taken more by career officials than by political officials. If departments remained more fragmented, politicians would have to debate those issues in at the cabinet level in order to produce better policy coordination. Developing larger departments, in turn, may free up the cabinet to make more fundamental decisions about policy priorities. On the other hand, however, ministers will always have priorities, so creating the large departments may assist some interests and leave many others without advocates in cabinet.

Advisory committees. One way to approach the problem of coordination of programs is to have a means of mutually representing the interests of relevant programs. This can be done through the creation of broad advisory committees for departments or bureaus containing representatives of other organizations. For example, in the Scandinavian countries (Norway in particular) each ministry will have an advisory committee composed of representatives of interest groups, as well as from other ministerial departments. Any significant policy initiative by the ministry must be referred to this advisory committee. This system works well in these countries, with their traditions of consensual decision-making and well-developed interest group universes. Even without that tradition this method can at least inform interested departments of actions and perhaps allow them to be settled (in cabinet or by other means) earlier than they might otherwise be. Further, like most other existing mechanisms for coordination, the agenda for these committees is set by existing organizations using conventional conceptualizations of policy.

One variant of the advisory committee mechanism is the use of management boards. With the increasing use of disaggregated government organizations (e.g. agencies in the United Kingdom) in a number of countries there may be a need to use the same governance system as was developed for organizations of this type in Scandinavia. In the Scandinavian countries from which this model of organization was derived, the use of boards composed of government and lay personnel is a means for providing a broad perspective on the functions and role of the organization, and hence a broader perception of the policies being developed. To the extent that other government organizations are represented on these boards they can help produce enhanced coordination. For example, the boards used for policy direction and oversight in Sweden contain a variety of government officials who can advance the ideas and interests of their own organization and hence produce a certain amount of coordination without formalized interventions.

Agencies with portfolios relevant to coordination. Ministries or agencies can be developed that have direct responsibility for coordinating services for a specific target population or geographical area. At a minimum these organizations can act as advocates within government for the interests of those segments of the population. Examples of organizations of this type serving particular demographic groups are the Administration on Aging in the United States, the Ministry for Family and Seniors and the Ministry for Women and Youth in Germany, and the former Ministry for the Middle Class in France. Examples of these organizations serving geographical areas are the "regional ministries" in Canada, for example the Atlantic Canada Opportunities Agency, the Ministry for Macedonia and Thrace in Greece, and the Ministry for the Mezzogiorno in Italy.

The development of organizations of this type does bring attention to the needs of demographic or regional groups, but it is far from a guarantee that those interests will be served in the way in which they need to be. These ministries and agencies often are not perceived as central players in government, so that, even though they may sit at the cabinet table, they may not have much influence over major players such as the principal large social and economic ministries. In addition, these ministries may provide some services for the target groups but still must ensure that services provided from other ministries are compatible. In other words this may be just another version of the division of services among departments. Further, as cross-cutting issues become more significant, the more traditional definitions and limitations characteristic of existing programs may not push consideration of the issues ahead quickly enough.

Interministerial organizations. Another obvious means for coordinating the activities of existing programs and to explore the needs for new structures to cope with cross-cutting issues is to develop organizations within the interstices of existing organizations. All governments have some forms of inter-ministerial governance, although they differ in the extent to which those structures are articulated and the power they can exercise over policies. What follows here is a brief enumeration of some of those mechanisms.

Task forces, working groups, etc. When government is going to enter a policy area for the first time, or when there is a great deal of confusion about the best way to conceptualize a cross-cutting policy issue, a standard response is to create a temporary "task force" or "working group". These are sometimes given executive authority, for example some *projets de mission* in France or *Projektgruppen* in Germany, but generally these organizations are oriented toward problem identification and clarification – a central need for cross-cutting policy issues (Timsit, 1988). A major recent example is the establishment of major agency, program and expenditure reviews in Canada (including one in social policy on pensions). These appear to be very much recognitions of the need to think more broadly about the issues facing an aging population and the governments that provide them services.

If the cross-cutting issues can be "solved" in a limited period of time, or if a clear definition of the issues can be developed in the limited time span allowed for most of these special organizations, then this approach is perhaps the most desirable manner to address the coordination problem. They can provide a clear focus and perhaps clear answers to a limited problem. If that success is not possible – and that is usually the case – then these organizations either go out of business with little being accomplished or become simply another set of players in the complex network that will surround these issues.

Another way to think about interministerial organizations is as "virtual organizations" – organizations that may have no permanent structure and/or membership. This style of organization has been advocated by some Canadian civil servants interviewed in this project as a mechanism for generating coordination without creating yet another permanent structure. The argument is, in part, that creating another permanent organization with the goal of enhancing coordinate will itself soon require additional coordination as issues change and new patterns of interaction among organization become the dominant concerns. Still, reaching agreements about when and under what circumstances an organization will cease to exist is not the most pleasant thing for most public officials – for them it is thinking about death.

Interministerial committees. Another flexible means for attempting to deal with cross-cutting issues is to employ committees of the organizations affected. Almost all governments use some form or another of these committees. This practice is perhaps best developed in France with committees existing at the level of officials, ministers (or their *cabinets*), and finally to coordinate between the Prime Minister and the President. Coordinative committees of this sort have also been well-developed in the Antipodean systems. Like all committees formed to link existing organizations, committees of this type will have a difficult time in advancing the definitions of policy far beyond those that already exist. If, as argued, there is a need in many policy areas for some potentially sweeping redefinition of the issues to be considered then these committees are unlikely to change policies significantly (Schon and Rein, 1994). Granted broader powers than is usually the case, committees of this type might be able to advance more innovative ideas about policy, but would tend to be only as effective as their most committed member.

Coordinating organizations. Another approach to policy coordination is to develop special organizations with the task of ensuring coordination for clients. One example of this was the Model Cities program in the United States which, during the War on Poverty in the 1960s and early 1970s, sought to identify the range of services available to residents of poor inner city neighborhoods and to coordinate them in order to provide the full range of services to clients. The time at which Model Cities was in operation was in many ways very much like the present, in terms of the perceived need to rethink an area of policy and to attack social policy questions differently. For a variety of reasons (financial, bureaucratic among others) Model Cities enjoyed only limited success, but it was one means of incorporating both some rethinking of the problems with service delivery. In particular, it forced a number of organizations delivering services to think about how they could cooperate more effectively with organizations having similar objectives.

Processes

The above discussion has centered on the impacts of structural remedies for creating greater effectiveness of coordination activities. Coordination also could be enhanced by a variety of procedures. Procedures may not appear to be hierarchical in the same way as structural changes, but do definitely rely on authority for their capacity to make organizations comply. If nothing else, procedures can force organizations to consider the implications of their policy choices for other organizations and for clients. Just as structures cannot guarantee success in coordination, these processes depend upon the commitment of the principal participants to the goals of coordination. Otherwise, the processes may only perpetuate or reinforce the independence of programs and justify that perpetuation as the result of careful policy analysis.

Budgeting. Budgeting reflects the priorities of government in dollar terms. Therefore, it can be a central process for improving coordination of government priorities and programs. Given the tight fiscal constraints under which governments now function, budgeting may be the most important mechanism for setting priorities and coordinating activities. The goals of priority setting and policy coordination can be achieved in at least two ways. One would be through the use of relatively technocratic approaches such as those associated historically with program budgeting. This involves assessment of the relative costs and benefits of any expenditures and their relationship with other spending programs. The alternative approach is "Star Chamber" proceedings in which senior political and/or administrative officials examine expenditure requests, requiring the advocates of programs to justify their expenditures, and then impose some collective priorities on public spending.

Budgeting in the contemporary political and fiscal environment implies reducing spending as well as allocating resources among competing purposes. This change in the culture of budgeting, in turn, tends to reduce the willingness of organizations to invest in policy coordination. When there is reduced funding organizations tend to retreat to their "heartlands" (Downs, 1967) and do not want to use resources to extend their domains or to help achieve broader, government-wide, goals. The constant threat of reductions and cutbacks makes agencies hunker down and wait for better days. On the other hand, the changing managerial culture in government also means that it is difficult for public sector organizations to avoid demands for greater attention to coordination and policy coherence.

Regulatory review. The Office of Management and Budget in the United States exercises regulatory reviews over the activities of the executive branch (McGarrity, 1991; Stevens, 1995). Whenever an agency wants to issue regulations (secondary legislation) OMB reviews these regulations in terms of their compatibility with the program of the president, their cost, and their relationship to other, existing sets of regulations. This is but one of several mechanisms that governments use to monitor and control secondary legislation to both ensure the protection of individual rights and to coordinate regulations being issued by government organizations.

Central agencies in several other countries also exercise similar forms of regulatory review and attempts to coordinate the activities of their bureaucracies (see Pullen, 1994). This control is often not as great a problem, given that in cabinet governments a good deal of this regulatory clearance is done at the cabinet level itself, or through the Prime Minister's office. In general, the greater the autonomy granted to administrative agencies, as is the case for the Scandinavian countries, the greater will be the need to institutionalize some mechanisms of coordinating issuance of secondary legislation. The question then becomes whether economic, policy or political criteria will dominate the coordinating decisions, and how will the values be structured.

Evaluation. The evaluation of public policies can be another process for producing coordination, although it is usually directed toward other ends. Evaluation tends to be directed at a single program rather than at complexes of programs. Even then, it can point to programs whose effectiveness is limited by failure to coordinate with other programs, or by the absence of needed programs. If evaluation can be oriented around target populations (Rossi and Freeman, 1989), rather than to specific programs, it can be a means for pointing to the needs for coordination. Further, the definition of the relevant target population should, perhaps, be made external to the program itself if the greatest benefits for managing cross-cutting issues is to be obtained (Schneider and Ingram, 1993).

Evaluation will tend to be less useful in the case of cross-cutting policy issues because the goals and interdependencies within the constellation of policies may be less clearly established than in more linearly-defined policy areas. Conventional program evaluation may find that a program is working effectively, while from a broader, systemic perspective it is seriously deficient. Existing social insurance programs, for example, may provide pensions to the elderly efficiently and effectively but yet not address at all the range of services a graying population requires, nor effectively relate the skills of aging population to a changing labor market.

"Coordination comments." In Australia the procedure of "coordination comments" has been designed and institutionalized in order to prevent members of cabinet from proceeding with departmental policies without adequate coordination with their peers. Cabinet members are required to circulate for comment any proposals they will bring to cabinet at least several days prior to the meeting. Other cabinet systems have rules to avoid surprises in cabinet, but this method in Australia goes the furthest in generating coordination. Although occurring at a lower level, one Canadian respondent in our study pointed out that, in the large departments created after the 1993 reorganization, one of the emerging forms of coordination among sections within some departments is a formalized comments procedure for the component organizations. Again, we can see that creating very large structures tends to

induce managerial problems of its own, even if the strategy does make some contributions to enhanced coordination.

Another not unrelated, procedure can be found in the Finnish government. In that system every month the cabinet meets informally in a so-called "evening school" to discuss collectively a major policy issue. Given the informality of that setting, and the absence of formal decision-taking at the meeting, this procedure promotes full discussion of the issues and makes substantive coordination possible in a less threatening manner. The formal decision-making for government still must take place within the Council of State, but some of the more difficult issues may be decided ahead of time in a setting in which informal bargaining rather than defense of departmental turf can be more possible.

Summary

The relatively greater attention to mechanisms of hierarchical control in this paper does not imply any greater intellectual appeal of these mechanisms of coordination. What it does indicate, however, is the relative level of attention of governments to these as opposed to other forms of coordination. Governments continue to develop and implement means of coordination using their own powers, even when there are network and even market mechanisms operating at the same time. On the one hand this may appear wasteful, but it does indicate both that governments retain rather old-fashioned commitment to authority and hierarchy and that they also recognize their legal and political responsibilities to provide the best possible government to their citizens. Their emphasis on law and authority also indicates that they continue to think of the public as citizens as well as merely economic consumers of services.

CAVEATS

To this point in the paper I have been rather unambiguous in singing hymns of praise to coordination and coherence in government. That is certainly the conventional stance in public administration and it is for the most part also the most appropriate stance from my perspective on governing. On the other hand, however, there are some questions that should be asked about coordination as a value in administration, especially about the cost/benefit ratio that program designed to enhance coordination may have for government. That is, there are multiple goals that must be pursued through the public sector and coherence may be only one among many.

Is Coordination Always the Answer?

We have been pursuing coordination as if it were always the answer to problems facing the public sector. We should, however, at least entertain the possibility that enhancing coordination and coherence is not always a positive contribution to resolving policy problems. There may be some circumstances in which competing and incoherent approaches are functional, rather than dysfunctional, for both government and the governed. For example, even though government funds a great deal of scientific research, it almost certainly should not attempt to impose a single line of research or establish an orthodoxy (Salbu, 1994). Drawing the line between funding "good science" and establishing such an orthodoxy may be difficult, but also may be necessary. For example, the "War on Cancer" in the United States demonstrated that settling on a single line of research too quickly can waste resources with little result.

In addition to research funding, there may be other policy areas in which coordination is not especially desirable for government. For example, in many policy areas there is far less than certain knowledge (Dror, 1992) about how to produce desired changes in the behavior of individuals in society. The debates over welfare policy and criminal justice in the United States and numerous other countries are extreme but not isolated examples of this knowledge problem. Therefore, government may be well-advised at times to adopt an explicitly experimental approach to policy and to minimize coordination and coherence. Some scholars have advocated such an experimental approach (Campbell, 1982; 1988), and at times even some politicians have argued that there is insufficient evidence to make a long-term commitment to any particular policy option. In addition, some program areas can benefit from redundancy and duplication and excessive coordination can make the policy area more prone to error (Landau, 1969).

Accountability and Coordination

We also must consider the classical question of public accountability and the impact of attempts to enhance coordination on the capacity of governments to enforce accountability. While greater coordination generally should enhance the efficiency and effectiveness of government programs, there are instances in which it does not, and within a complex multi-organizational policy environment it may be difficult to identify where the system has broken down. Accountability, at least in its *ex post facto* sense, depends upon the capacity of politicians and the public to identify who is responsible for any failures in a program. The danger with coordination is that by making everyone to some extent responsible for programs in the end no one is actually responsible and it becomes much easier to evade responsibility.

The dangers to accountability may arise through several of the methods used for improving coordination. For example, financial accountability becomes difficult to enforce when funds from several departments are mingled in order to create adequate resources for comprehensive attacks on major cross-cutting policy problems, for example drug enforcement or urban regeneration. How does government ensure that money is being spent in the ways intended when it was appropriated? If it is not, who should be held responsible for the misallocation? Perhaps even more fundamentally, are conventional ideas about parliamentary accountability the best ways to think about accountability in the emerging world of the more complex delivery of public service, and if not, what principles are better suited for this task?

SUMMARY AND CONCLUSIONS

We began by noting that coordination is one of the major goals of public administration, and has been so for some time. This paper has discussed a number of the issues that arise when that seemingly simple goal of improving coordination is advanced. These problems are intellectual as well as practical, and require thinking about a number of alternative ways of achieving the same policy and administrative goals. Formal mechanisms of coordination are often the best ways of achieving those goals, but more informal methods also have their place, even within the public sector itself. The changing nature of government, with the emergence of the "New Public Management" and a range of other innovations in public policy and administration, tend to place a greater emphasis on the informal and market-based ideas, rather than the formal.

One of the challenges – analytically and for government itself – is to determine when different approaches to coordination are most appropriate, and develop an understanding of the contingencies that may be operative. The three approaches we have discussed here reflect different concepts and different locations in the political process. The hierarchical approach, the most common approach, appears crucial in program areas that are peculiarly public, e.g. defense, foreign affairs, revenue collection and the like. The other two approaches appear more applicable to that other large range of public programs that are (at least in principle) marketable or which are surrounded by significant networks of private actors. This is as yet a gross generalization, and substantial refinement is needed to make it at all useful. Still, it may point to ways of addressing coordination and improving both the practice and the analysis.

NOTES

1. For example, President Jimmy Carter attempted to divide the (then) Veterans Administration by moving the educational components into the Department of Education, the health and social service components into the Department of Health and Human Services, and the residual elements into the Department of Defense. He failed rather abjectly at this rationalization and coordination in the face of pressure from veterans' organizations.

2. In a study I did with several colleagues over 25 years ago we found that social service agencies tended to hang on to clients and not to refer them for needed services. This was true even in the context of the Model Cities Program, an attempt to provide more comprehensive services to the residents of poor neighborhoods in American cities. When interviewed agency leaders argued that it was too "dangerous" for them to risk losing clients.

3. For example, the "Resortsprinzip" in German government is another indication of this segmentation of government.

4. For example, in recent consulting work for the Finnish government creating policy integration emerged as a dominant issue. This was true even though this government has a long tradition of cooperative management and policy development.

5. One common pattern has been to create very large ministries for health and social services. This single ministry may have several ministers and be responsible for up to half of the total public budget. This creates a tremendous managerial overload for the senior public servants, and may do so with little real improvement in coordination.

6. The Canadian Food Inspection Agency was created in 1997 to bring together related activities from Agriculture, Fisheries, Health and Industry ministries. It also absorbed some functions that had been largely provincial.

7. The Office of Management and Budget prepares each year a government-wide set of priorities to correspond to the more specific priorities coming from the agencies. The OMB document tends to be long on pious hopes and short on specifics.

8. In some ways ministries of foreign affairs have not become central agencies so much as all ministries have developed their own international sections and international political views. This is in contrast to the role of environmental agencies.

9. In a "real" contracting arrangement the actors involved would have more of an opportunity to walk away if an acceptable deal could not be reached. In the public sector the legal mandates restrict the exit option.

10. There is, however, evidence that countries are still behaving more autonomously than the proponents of globalization might lead us to believe.

11. This can be seen most clearly from the "instruments" perspective on public policy (Salamon, 2000).

12. For example, in my earlier research on the Model Cities program in the United States, professionals tended to refer clients to others in the same profession rather than serving the "whole client" as intended by the program.

REFERENCES

6. P. (2004) Joined-Up Government in the Western World in Comparative Perspecitve: A Preliminary Literature Review and Exploration, *Journal of Public Administration Research and Theory* 14, 103–39.

6, P. (2001) Joined Up Government Around the World, paper presented at Conference on Joined-Up Government, Oxford, October 30.

Adema, W. (1997) What Do Countries Really Spend on Social Policies: A Comparative Note, *OECD Economic Studies* 28, 153–67.

Alexander, E. R. (1993) Interorganizational Coordination: Theory and Practice, *Journal of Planning Literature* 7, 328–43.

Allard, C. K. (1990) *Command, Control and the Common Defense* (New Haven: Yale University Press).

Barrett, S. and C. Fudge (1981) *Policy and Action: Essays on the Implementation of Public Policy* (London: Methuen).

Bogason, P. (1991) Control for Whom?: Recent Adventures on Governmental Guidance and Control, *European Journal of Political Research* 20, 189–208.

Bouckaert, G., D. Ormond and B. G. Peters (2000) *A New Governance Agenda* (Helsinki: Ministry of Finance).

Callender, G. and J. Johnston (1998) Governments and Governance: Examining Social and Economic Autonomy in Malaysia and Singapore, *Asian Journal of Public Administration* 20, 151–72.

Campbell, C. and G. Szablowski (1979) *The Superbureaucrats: Structure and Behaviour in Central Agencies* (Toronto: Macmillan of Canada).

Campbell, D. T. (1982) Experiments and Arguments, *Knowledge: Creation, Diffusion, Utilization* 3, 327–37.

Campbell, D. T. (1988) The Experimenting Society, in Campbell, *Methodology and Epistemology in the Social Sciences: Selected Essays* (Chicago: University of Chicago Press).

Chisholm, D. (1989) *Coordination Without Hierarchy* (Berkeley: University of California Press).

Commission on Social Justice (1994) *Social Justice: Strategies for National Renewal* (London: Vintage).

Considine, M. (1992) Alternatives to Hierarchy: The Role and Performance of Lateral Structures Inside Bureaucracy, *Australian Journal of Public Administration* 51, 309–20.

Davis, G. (1998) Executive Coordination Mechanisms, in P. Weller, H. Bakvis and R. A. W. Rhodes, eds., *The Hollow Crown: Countervailing Trends in Core Executives* (London: Macmillan).

de Montricher, N. (1999) *L'amenagement du territoire* (Paris: La Decouverte).

Derlien, H.-U. (1991) Horizontal and Vertical Coordination of German EC-Policy, *Hallinnon Tutkimus*, 3–10.

Doern, G. B. (1993) From Sectoral to Macro Green Governance: The Canadian Department of the Environment as an Aspiring Central Agency, *Governance* 6, 172–94.

Dowding, K. (1995) Model or Metaphor? A Critical Review of the Policy Network Approach, *Political Studies* 43, 136–58.

Downs, A. (1967) Inside Bureaucracy (Boston: Little, Brown).

Elmore, R. F. (1979) Backward mapping: Implementation Research and Policy Decisions, *Political Science Quarterly* 94, 601–16.

Dror, Y. (1992) Policymaking Under Adversity (New Brunswick, NJ: Transaction Books).

Fortin, Y. (2000) *Contractualisation dans le secteur public* (Paris: Decouvert).

Greer, P. (1994) *Transforming Central Government: The Next Steps Initiative* (Buckingham: Open University Press).

Hall, R. et al. (1978) Interorganizational Coordination in the Delivery of Social Services, in L. Karpik, ed., *Organization and Environment: Theory, Issues and Reality* (Beverly Hills: Sage).

Hallerberg, M. and S. Basinger (1998) Internationalization and Changes in Tax Policy in OECD Countries, *Comparative Political Studies* 31, 321–52.

Hogwood, B. W. and L. Gunn (1984) *Policy Analysis for the Real World* (Oxford: Oxford University Press).

Jacquet, P. (1998) L'union monetaire et la coordination des politiques macroeconomiques, in Conseil d'Analyse Economique, *Coordination europeenne des politiques economiques* (Paris: La documentation francaise).

Jennings, E. T. and D. Crane (1994) Coordination and Welfare Reform: The Quest for the Philosopher's Stone, *Public Administration Review* 54, 341–8.

Jerome-Forget, M., J. White and J. M. Wiener (1995) *Health Care Reform Through Internal Markets* (Washington, DC: The Brookings Institution).

Katz, J. L. (1995) Key Members Seek to Expand State Role in Welfare Plan, *Congressional Quarterly Weekly Report* 53 (2), 159–62.

Kassim, H., B. G. Peters and V. Wright (2000) *Policy Coordination in the European Union; The National Dimension* (Oxford: Oxford University Press).

Kassim, H., A. Menon, B. G. Peters and V. Wright (2001) *Policy Coordination in the European Union:*

The Brussels Dimension (Oxford: Oxford University Press).

Kickert, W. J. M. (1995) Public Governance in the Netherlands: An Alternative to Anglo-American Managerialism, Public Administration 75, 731–53.

Landau, M. (1969) Redundancy, Rationality and the Problem of Duplication and Overlap, *Public Administration Review* 29, 346–58.

Laronche, M. (2000) Quarante pratiques fiscales deloyales repertoirees au sein de la seule Union, *Le Monde*, 23 Mai.

Larsson, T. (1986) *Regeringen och des kansli* (Stockholm: Studentlitteratur).

McGarrity, T. (1991) *Reinventing Rationality: The Role of Regulatory Analysis in the Federal Bureaucracy* (Cambridge: Cambridge University Press).

Mackie, T. T. and B. W. Hogwood (1985) *Unlocking the Cabinet: Cabinet Structures in Comparative Perspective* (London: Sage).

Marin, B. (1990) Generalized Political Exchange: Preliminary Considerations, in B. Marin, ed., *Generalized Political Exchange: Antagonistic Cooperation and Integrated Policy Circuits* (Frankfurt: Campus Verlag).

Marton, S. (2000) *The Mind of the State* (Gothenberg: University of Gothenberg).

Metcalfe, L. (1994) International Policy Co-ordination and Public Management Reform, *International Review of Administrative Sciences* 60, 271–90.

Miller, G. J. (1992) *Managerial Dilemmas: The Political Economy of Hierarchy* (Cambridge: Cambridge University Press).

Mueller-Rommel, F. (2000) Germany, in Peters, Rhodes and Wright, *Administering the Summit* (London: Macmillan).

Nathan, R. P. (1975) *The Plot That Failed: Nixon and the Administrative Presidency* (New York: Wiley).

Niskanen, W. (1994) *Bureaucracy and Public Economics* (Cheltenham: Edward Elgar).

OECD (1993) *Internal Markets* (Paris: Organization for Economic Cooperation and Development), Market–Type Mechanisms, Vol. 6.

Olsen, J. P. (1987) *Organized Democracy* (Oslo: Universitetsforlaget).

Page, S. (2003) Entrepreneurial Strategies for Managing Interagency Collaboration, *Journal of Public Administration Research and Theory* 13, 311–40.

Painter, M. (1987) *Steering the Modern State: Changes in Central Coordination in Three Australian State Governments* (Sydney: Sydney University Press).

Peters, B. G. (1996) *The Future of Governing; Four Emerging Models* (Lawrence: University Press of Kansas).

Peters, B. G. (2002) Contracts and Resource Allocation in Public Governance, In A. Heritier, ed., *Common Goods: Reinventing European and International Governance* (Lanham, Md: Rowman and Littlefield).

Peters, B. G. (2006) *Horizontal Governance: The Search for Coordination and Coherence* (Lawrence: University Press of Kansas).

Peters, B. G. and J. Pierre (2000) *Administrative Reform and the Civil Service* (London: Routledge).

Peters, B. G., R. A. W. Rhodes and V. Wright (2000) *Administering the Summit: Support for Presidents and Prime Ministers* (London: Macmillan).

Pierre, J. and B. G. Peters (2000) *Governance, Policy and the State* (Basingstoke: Macmillan).

Pressman, J. L. and A. Wildavsky (1984) *Implementation*, 2nd ed. (Berkeley: University of California Press).

Pullen, W. (1994) Eyes on the Prize, *International Journal of Public Sector Management* 7, 5–14.

Regens, J. L. (1988) Institutional Coordination of Program Action: A Conceptual Analysis, *International Journal of Public Administration* 11, 135–54.

Sabatier, P. A. (1988) An Advocacy-Coalition Model of Policy Change and the Role of Policy-Oriented Learning Therein, *Policy Sciences* 27, 123–35.

Salamon, L. M. (2000) *Handbook of Policy Instruments* (New York: Oxford University Press).

Salbu, S. R. (1994) Regulation of Drug Treatments for HIV and AIDS, *Yale Journal of Regulation* 11, 401–52.

Savoie, D. J. (1995a) Globalization, Nation States and the Civil Service in B. G. Peters and D. J. Savoie, eds., *Governance in a Changing Environment* (Montreal: McGill/Queens University Press).

Savoie, D. J. (1995b) *Central Agencies: Looking Backward* (Ottawa: Canadian Centre for Management Development).

Savoie, D. J. (1999) *Governing from the Centre.* (Toronto: University of Toronto Press).

Schneider, A. B. and H. Ingram (1993) Social Construction of Target Populations: Implications for Politics and Policy, *American Political Science Review* 87, 334–47.

Schon, D. and M. Rein (1994) *Frame Reflection: Resolving Intractable Policy Issues* (New York: Basic Books).

Smith, G. (1991) The Resources of a German Chancellor, in G. Jones, ed., *West European Prime Ministers* (London: Frank Cass).

Smith, M. J., D. Marsh and D. Richards (1993) Central Government Departments and the Policy Process, *Public Administration* 71, 567–94.

Stevens, L. N. (1995) *Regulatory Reform: How Can Congress Assess the Administration's Initiatives* (Washington, DC: General Accounting Office, July 18) GAO/T-95–206.

Taylor, S. (1984) *Making Bureaucracies Think: The Environmental Impact Statement Strategy of Administrative Reform* (Stanford: Stanford University Press).

Thompson, G., J. Frances, R. Levacic and J. Mitchell (1991) *Markets, Hierarchies and Networks* (London: Sage).

Timsit, G. (1988) *Les autorites independents administratives* (Paris: Presses Universitaires de France).

Toonen, T. A. J. (1985) Implementation Research and Institutional Design: The Quest for Structure, in K. Hanf and T. A. J. Toonen, eds., *Policy Implementation in Federal and Unitary Systems* (Dordrecht: Martinus Nijhoff).

Wolgast, E. (1992) *Ethics of an Artificial Person: Lost Responsibility in Professions and Organizations* (Stanford: Stanford University Press).

Zito, A. (1999) *Making European Environmental Policy* (London: Macmillan).

7

Budgeting

IRENE S. RUBIN

Political science has long wrestled with the question of whether the characteristics of decision-making processes affect the outcomes of those decisions. There are usually many other factors contributing to outcomes besides processes, which means that any given process may have different outcomes at different times or in different circumstances. As a result, it has been difficult for political scientists to demonstrate that decision-making processes impact outcomes. This chapter examines the question of the impact of process on outcomes, using as an example budget process in the United States at the national level, with particular attention to the post 1998 changes and recent budgetary outcomes. While this case does not provide an airtight design, it does provide a kind of natural experiment.

Although the focus will be on the United States, there will be some comparisons with process reforms in other industrialized democracies. All the countries in the OECD world, and indeed in the world more broadly, are struggling to find budget processes that produce efficient allocation of funds but yet are not dominated by technical considerations. The "ideas in good currency" about budgeting appear to cycle between highly rationalistic solutions, such as PPBS, to simple, if effective, mechanisms to reduce public expenditure (Gray, Jenkins and Segsworth, 2002). The United

States has certainly had its share of both of these types of solutions, but is not alone in its attempt to find a solution for one of the central set of policy decisions for government.

BUDGET RULES AS ILLUSTRATION OF PROCESS

What are budget process rules? What is their function? Budget process rules describe the order in which budget decisions will be made, the timeliness of the decision-making, which actors make which decisions, and the constraints under which the decisions will be made. These rules provide definitions, for example, how balance will be defined. Budget rules determine what budget claims will be compared with what other claims, what evidence and whose evidence will be brought to bear on the decision, and how much time there will be for deliberation on those decisions.

A good budget process is stable from year to year, it provides necessary definitions that are known to and used by all parties, and it ensures discipline, so that revenues do not exceed expenditures over the long haul. Budgets may include borrowing, but are not balanced unless there is a plan and revenue sources to pay off that debt as it comes due. To ensure discipline, the process normally outlines steps to estimate (and revise) revenue estimates, and breaks up pieces of the decisions on spending and gives them separate limits, so that, when added up, they do not exceed the total revenue available. A good process is reasonably neutral among policy goals and political interests, providing a forum for the articulation, discussion and resolution of necessary policy issues without biasing the results in advance. It combines information coming up from programs and professional staff with centrally determined policy and discipline. Further, in a democracy, budget process must assure that minority parties are heard, and that decisions are not made that prevent different factions that might come to power in the future from also making policy decisions.

Maintenance of neutral rules allows the decision-making to proceed *in a politically charged environment*. Without it, conflicts may bring the budget to a standstill, as often occurs in less stable democratic systems. Without neutral rules, minorities may feel that they cannot win or influence decisions, and hence cease to participate or work at disrupting the process. Politicians are often tempted to bias the rules to facilitate some immediate policy goal rather than maintaining neutral rules. For example, the requirements of the stability pact in the Eurozone have been used not only to stabilize the budget but also to disadvantage some social interests (Stolfi, 2006).

Some rules can be changed without damaging the collective policy framework necessary for democratic decision-making, others cannot. There must be time to consider legislation, there must be thoughtful prioritization, there must be a role for the minority as well as majority; there must not be decisions that lock in current policy priorities and prevent future democratically elected officials from making changes. Perhaps one exception to that generalization is the use of earmarked taxes and trust funds as a means of justifying certain types of taxation (Patashnik, 2000). There must be good quality information provided in a timely fashion, to decision makers and to the media and public. The process must be firmly enough in place that it is predictable from year to year

for all the participants, who must have a chance to learn and use the process. The process must be visible to the public.

In evaluating the consequences of rules changes, one has to look initially at the rules themselves. They can be described in terms of how they compare to the idealized process described here. For example, how neutral are they with respect to outcomes? How consistent and predictable are they from year to year? What steps are included in the budget process to assure that spending is controlled by a revenue estimate? Is there a procedure for prioritization of expenditures? Second, one has to look at the changes. Did new rules supplement or supplant the old ones? Were the old rules kept but their intent evaded? Were the rules "gamed"? Was it a minor rule that was avoided or voided, or a major one, was it one rule or a cluster of them, was the change informal and temporary, or formal and long term? Budget process change is a complex variable, but it must be understood in some detail if its consequences are to be examined.

BUDGET CHANGE IN THE UNITED STATES

This study focuses on the federal budget process in the United States, with particular attention to the period from 1998 to the end of 2004. However, in order to see a rule change, one must also examine what budget rules preceded the change and what outcomes were associated with the period in which the preceding process was in effect. One also needs to know the degree to which those prior rules were implemented. Thus, the study of budgeting in the United States compares three periods, one from 1986 to 1990, when Gramm Rudman Hollings was in place, one from 1990 to 1998 (when the Budget Enforcement Act was in place), and the final one, from 1998 to 2004, during the decline and termination of the BEA and the rise (return?) of *ad hoc* budgeting. Innovations in budget practices in the United States have been diffused widely in the past, and some of these same ideas have been used in other countries to address similar issues. Thus, this one case study is just that but it also illustrates some generalities about budgets and the impact of rules on performance.

Data Sources

The information on budget process and implementation comes from laws, journal articles, newspaper accounts, newsletters from public interest research groups, and reports from think tanks and advocacy groups. Efforts were made to draw on both sides of the political spectrum as well as some sources closer to the middle. Data also comes from government publications, such as the *Historical Tables of the U.S. Budget* and budget hearings, and from on-line news magazines focusing on the federal government, such as *Government Executive* and *The Hill.*

Assumptions

Several assumptions underlie the analysis. First, budget processes do not determine outcomes, they influence them, making certain outcomes easier to achieve and others harder. This influence may be greater and more visible at some times than others. Since it is difficult to either prove or falsify influence or measure it in any precise fashion, the conclusions in this essay are inferential.

The logic of the analysis depends on four kinds of argument. First, there were three phases of budget process change, each associated with a set of outcomes. If deficits increase during the first phase, decrease and disappear during the second, and reappear, almost instantly, in the third, even if there are many other things going on during those time periods, there would be evidence of a *likely* relationship between process and outcomes. Second, if the actors who want to accomplish a particular policy goal first change the process and then accomplish their goal, it looks as if they believe they had to change the process, formally or informally, to accomplish their goal. Such behavior provides additional strength to the argument for a linkage between process and outcomes. Third, if mechanism can

be demonstrated, such that the process addresses issue A and the outcome for issue A changes when the process changes, this should be construed as further evidence supporting a relationship. Finally, if alternative explanations besides the changes in budget process can be ruled out, in part or in whole, the case would be even stronger.

A second assumption is that processes can be more or less formal, with informal processes easier to change and less durable or predictable. Informal processes may carry out the intent of the formal rules or contradict them or supplant them. Budget rules may be more or less actively enforced, mechanisms of enforcement may exist, but be seldom used, or may be actively evaded, through distorted data (gaming the system) or definitional changes or various kinds of budget gimmicks or accounting rules changes. The impact of budget rules on outcomes depends to some extent on the degree of enforcement in practice. Budget processes do not enforce themselves, they require the consent and will of the actors to give them life and force. For the purposes of this study, a shift from rule enforcement to rule non-enforcement is considered a change in budget process, even without a formal, legal change.

The Intervention

This study is about a natural experiment, a set of changes in budget rules. Budget processes are often overlaid on each other, rather than completely removed and started afresh, but key features may be added or subtracted. All later budget processes were overlaid on the 1921 Budget and Accounting Act, which created executive budgeting, so that the president and his budget office prepared a budget request for legislative consideration. Similarly, the changes inherent in the 1974 Congressional Budget and Impoundment Control Act, in which the Congress enhanced its ability to question that presidential proposal and come up with its own if it wished, underlay the later changes. From the point of view of budget process, the central feature of the 1974 Congressional Budget and Impoundment Control Act was the preparation by Congress of an annual budget resolution to guide committee decisions and assure some fiscal discipline.

In 1986, a new set of procedures was laid on top of the preceding laws to try to reduce the level of deficits. Its central feature was an effort to force spending reductions in order to reduce the annual deficit by a targeted amount. To do this, the process, named after its legislative sponsors Gramm, Rudman, and Hollings, provided for an automatic, across-the-board cut if more targeted and selective cuts were not made or were not deep enough. The threat of such across-the-board cuts, affecting both Republican and Democratic priorities, was intended to force spending reductions. Gramm, Rudman, and Hollings did not work well from a variety of perspectives, including the exemption of many major programs from the threat of across-the-board cuts, so that so called across-the-board cuts fell on relatively few programs, and those were hit disproportionately hard, and could not effectively be cut year after year. The rules of Gramm, Rudman, and Hollings were generally evaded.

In 1990, a new process was instituted, the Budget Enforcement Act, which had a different approach to deficit reduction. It was more even-handed, in that it included controls not only over spending but also over revenue. The central features of the Budget Enforcement Act were spending caps in the discretionary side of the budget and required offsets for increases in entitlement spending or decreases in revenues (Meyers, 1992). It was forbidden to reduce revenue without increasing it somewhere else or reducing mandatory spending to compensate.

By 1998, partly as a result of a booming economy and partly the result of the budget discipline required by the budget enforcement act, the federal government achieved budgetary balance, (more or less), removing the pressure to maintain the spending caps, which were then widely ignored (see Palazzolo, 1999). In 2002, the Budget Enforcement Act lapsed, and it was not renewed. During this period, Congress has also had difficulty enforcing or carrying out some of the key provisions of the 1974 act. What were the consequences of these rules changes?

Dependent variables

This study of budgeting in the United States examines two sets of outcomes of the budget process. One is traditional budgetary outcomes, such as budgetary balance and the size of and the composition of public spending. The other is the degree to which the budget process is consistent with, and implements, democratic governance.

One of the most basic aims of budget process is to match resources to expenditures. On one end of this continuum would be budgetary balance, defined in some consistent manner, and at the other, uncontrolled and huge deficits, representing not so much spending for real emergencies as a loss of discipline. Somewhere near the midpoint would be controlled deficits, for specified policy purposes and true unforeseeable emergencies. Indicators of this continuum include changes in the size of the deficit, in absolute and relative terms, and the amount and purpose of borrowing.

A second outcome can be labeled the private versus public benefit continuum. It is anchored by spending for narrow interest or constituency group benefits or short-term partisan purposes, on one end, and by broad-based benefits for society on the other. Most outcomes fall between the ends of the continuum, but different budget processes or differential enforcement of the rules can facilitate a shift more in one direction or the other. It may be difficult to come to agreement on what a broad-based policy outcome for the public good looks like, but, even with some noted differences in definition, it has been possible to track the amount of pork in the budget over time, where pork is an indicator of narrow, often partisan, benefits. Earmarking in legislation is used here (and by policy analysts more generally) as an indicator of these narrower benefits.

A third outcome of the budget process is the size of and composition of public spending, the scope of government. On the one end is small government, low taxes, limited regulatory powers, and few entitlements; on the other, larger government, higher taxes, more active regulatory functions, and many substantial entitlements. Budget rules can influence the ease of moving in one direction or the other.

These three outcomes are traditionally thought of as budgetary outcomes, but there is a sense also in which the budget process is itself an outcome. Because it is itself such an important part of public policy-making, the way the budget is put together says much about governance. On the one hand, budget process has a direct effect on the quality of decision-making and, on the other hand, it has a direct effect on democratic processes.

Budget process influences the quality of decisions to the degree that it frames appropriate comparisons and trade-offs and does an effective job at prioritization. The quality of information provided to decision-makers and the timeliness of that information, combined with the time allowed for decisions to be made, all influence the quality of budgetary decision making. If assumptions are watered down, revenue projections distorted up or down, the degree of feedback from decisions on the economy, and hence on future revenues, is pulled out of the air, then the quality of decisions will suffer. If accounting rules are changed or definitions blurred, or if there is a difference in assumptions or rules between decision-makers, so that all are not acting from the same set rules or assumptions and are talking past each other, then the quality of decision-making declines. If the balance between political policy goals on one hand and technical input on needs on the other gets out of whack, in either direction, the quality of decisions will suffer.

If the rules are fair, neutral, and allow all parties to introduce legislation, propose amendments, and have a say, if the process does not lock in outcomes that prevent future political coalitions from making changes according to the wishes of their constituencies, if there is sufficient accurate information presented in a timely fashion and there is time to deliberate on proposals, then the process helps implement democracy. If it fails to do those things, if decisions are made in secret, if the process is not open and not accountable, if the rules are not made known in advance, if some are kept out, then the processes of representation and accountability are corroded, and democratic governance is compromised.

Comparative Perspectives

In 2005 the federal deficit in the United States was among the highest in the world, perhaps a function of the absence of clear rules for controlling expenditure increases and revenue reductions. A number of other countries that in the past had had significant budget deficits – for example Italy, Belgium and Canada – are now managing their budgets much better and, in the case of Canada, have been amassing significant budget surpluses. Is this just good fortune, or does the presence of clear controls and rules give some backbone to public officials who might otherwise find deficits more palatable politically? Or have there been changes in the fiscal cultures of countries that now stress the importance of maintaining fiscal discipline and using market-type forces to control the public sector (see HM Treasury, 2005)

The Maastricht Treaty and the Stability and Growth Pact have helped governments in many European countries stand up to special interests and to control spending. Even countries who are not members of the Eurozone have had their budgeting behaviors influenced by the central place of Brussels in public finance (Albert-Roulhac, 1998). One major study of budgeting (Wanna, Jensen and deVries, 2003) argues, however, that rules and structures have become less important than in the past in controlling budgets. Rather, their central finding is that evidence and argument tend to dominate over formality and power. If this is the case then the failures of American budgeteers in recent years may be more a function of their inability in coming up with good arguments, or, perhaps even more so, their commitment to ideas about reducing taxation rather than to ideas about controlling deficits.

It may well be, of course, that the United States is different. The complexity of the political system and the magnitude of the budget process may make reliance on argument and the culture of organizations a less viable solution than in parliamentary democracies, especially small, homogenous, parliamentary democracies. Somewhat paradoxically for a country often priding itself on being opposed to strong regulations and bureaucracy, its own internal governance processes may require just those types of controls if they are to resist the centrifugal pressures within the political system.

CHANGES AND OUTCOMES

1986 to 1990: Gramm Rudman Hollings and Deficit Reduction Targets

Gramm Rudman Hollings set annual targets for deficit reduction, but those targets were routinely missed. Efforts to avoid sequestration, the technical term for across-the-board cuts, led to intense gaming of the system, pushing expenditures into following years to make the budget look more balanced than it was, and then pushing them back when the next year arrived, for example. The legislation was not even handed, it approached the issue of deficits from the perspective of forcing deep spending cuts, but there was little consensus on which programs to cut or how deeply to cut them, so the unthinkable, the sequester process, was supposed to be invoked. The sequester process was supposed to be neutral, in the sense of affecting all programs, but while it didn't have a political bias, it tended to cut some programs disproportionately because they hadn't been exempted. The result was illogical, without serious prioritization. The process might have reduced deficits if it had in fact been implemented, but, with widespread evasion of its rules, Gramm Rudman Hollings proved unable to control deficits.

From 1990 to 1998, under the Budget Enforcement Act, the norms of budgetary balance were strengthened. Spending caps were generally treated seriously, forcing a number of difficult trade-offs, many in full public view. The always present temptation to reduce taxes was curtailed; taxes were actually increased to help balance the budget. By 1998, with the help of a growing economy, the budget was more or less balanced; surpluses were projected for many years in the future. Public debate focused on what to do with the surpluses, whether to reduce taxes or fix social security, or buy down the national debt.

After 1998, because of the surpluses, the consensus to adhere to the spending caps in the Budget Enforcement Act quickly eroded. Spending exceeded the caps by a wide margin. The key features of the BEA rules were ignored or gamed. One common practice was to treat some routine expenditures as if they were emergencies, since emergencies were not required to be offset by revenue increases or other decreases in spending. By calling the expenditure, such as the census, an emergency (which it was not except in political terms) budgeteers did not have to find revenue to cover the expense, which then added to the deficit.

As budget scholar Allen Schick observed,

> The arrival of a surplus a few years ago triggered a spending frenzy that vitiated the discretionary spending caps established by the 1990 Budget Enforcement Act and made a mockery of the BEA requirement that increased spending be offset by cuts in other spending or by revenue increases. In 2000 and 2001, discretionary spending soared more than $200 billion above the legal limits on annual appropriations. The caps expire at the end of 2002 – which will at least enable politicians to be more honest about what they are doing. They no longer have to pretend that the census and other ongoing operations of government are national emergencies. (Allen Schick, *The Brookings Review*, Spring, 2002. Vol. 20 No. 2 pp. 45–48. The Deficit That Didn't Just Happen: A Sober Perspective on the Budget)

Huge surpluses turned nearly immediately into large and growing deficits. This process began before 9/11/2001 and hence cannot be attributed solely to responses to that event. OMB reports in the Historical Tables of the U.S. Budget for 2005 that the on-budget surplus for fy 2000 was 86.626 billion dollars, but by 2001 there was a deficit of 33.257 billion (fiscal year 2001 spending is controlled by decision-making that occurs the previous year). Figures for deficits for 2002, 2003, and 2004 were reported as 317.456 billion, 536.128 billion, and 674.766 billion. These numbers are so huge and growing so rapidly as to suggest they are out of control. Deficits are listed in Table 7.1, along with the budget process in effect at the time.

As former CBO staffer Phil Joyce observed, there was insufficient consensus after 1998 to come up with congressional targets and adhere to them. The lack of agreement meant that the budget process was operating without a notional budget constraint. As a result, Joyce claimed "no one knows how much is enough – or

Table 7.1 *Deficits/surpluses, on budget, from 1980 through 2004 (millions)*

Budget process in place	year	deficit/surplus
Congressional budget and Impoundment Control	1980	−72,710
	1981	−73,948
	1982	−120,040
	1983	−208,014
	1984	−185,629
	1985	−221,671
Gramm Rudman Hollings	1986	−237,946
	1987	−169,298
	1988	−193,951
	1989	−205,910
Budget Enforcement Act	1990	−277,786
	1991	−321,525
	1992	−340,463
	1993	−300,434
	1994	−258,904
	1995	−226,387
	1996	−174,061
	1997	−103,322
	1998	−29,982
BEA key provisions not enforced	1999	+1,873
	2000	+86,626
	2001	−33,257
BEA expires	2002	−317,456
	2003	536,128
	2004	−674,766 (est)

Source: Historical tables of the U.S. Budget, 2005, table 1–1.

too much – spending. And nobody knows – or everybody knows, but nobody agrees – when the deficit is too large or the surplus too small" (Philip Joyce "Federal Budgeting After September 11th: A Whole New Ballgame, or is it Déjà vu All Over Again?" in Public Budgeting & Finance (Winter, 2005).

To the extent that the increase in deficits since 1998 resulted from 9/11 and terrorism related expenditures, one could argue that they are not related to the budget process and would have occurred no matter what the budget rules were. However, as Brian Reidl from the conservative Heritage Foundation has argued, most of the spending increase since 2001 was not for terrorism related expenses. The recent round of deficits was the result of tax cuts that were not offset by reductions in spending, and by spending increases not only for the war in Afghanistan, and later in Iraq, but also for domestic spending, including pork, which began to surge after 1998. The

wars in Afghanistan and Iraq were paid for primarily through supplemental appropriations, which were not offset by reductions in spending elsewhere, and added to the deficit, but they were in the range of 60 to 80 billion a year, nowhere near the total of the deficit.

Three sources are often cited as the cause of deficits, a slow growing economy, increases in spending, and reductions in tax rates. Of these, the slow growing economy had the least impact, because while revenue growth may have slowed down some, so did interest rates, which lowered the costs of government borrowing. Expenditures did increase, but not just for the wars and intelligence efforts; entitlements also grew rapidly, especially for Medicare and Medicaid. Other spending increased as well. Overall, spending increased from 18.4 percent of GDP in fiscal year 2000 to 19.8 percent in 2004, a startling increase in the size of government spending. But this increase would have been more than offset if revenues had been allowed to remain the same percent of GDP they had been in 2000. If taxes had not been reduced as a proportion of the economy, there would have been no deficit in 2004, instead there would have been a surplus of more than 100 billion dollars (Center for American Progress, An analysis of the recent deterioration of the fiscal condition of the U.S. Government. Washington, DC September 2004, p. 9, accessed online at http://www.americanprogress.org). Increases in entitlement spending for Medicare and Medicaid should not be laid at the feet of the budget process, nor probably should the increases in spending on the military post 9/11; but the reductions in taxation were made decidedly easier by the removal of the constraint that required either spending reductions or alternative revenue increases to compensate for tax reductions. These tax reductions contributed in a major way to the rise of deficits.

While some of the spending increases were not related to the budget process and would have occurred even if there had been no changes in the budget process, some of it may well have been related to the changing process. Many observers noted the increase in the amount of pork type spending, or earmarks after 1998.

Brian Reidl of the Heritage foundation reported the number of pork projects skyrocketed from under 2,000 five years ago [1998] to 9,362 in the 2003 budget. Total spending on pork projects has correspondingly increased to over $23 billion. This trend continued in the fiscal year (FY) 2004 appropriations bills, which include approximately 10,000 earmarks (Another Omnibus Spending Bill Loaded with Pork. The Heritage Foundation by Brian M. Riedl WebMemo #377 December 2, 2003).

Reidl described what he saw as the legions of interest group lobbyists asking for these funds, and a shift from program funds for general programmatic purposes, often awarded on the basis of technical merit through open competitions, to these earmarked projects, which he argued went to the highest bidder. To finish up the process, he argued, Congress then had to appropriate more money for the initial program and then in turn earmarked more of that money.

During the period of the Budget Enforcement Act, while the caps were closely observed, appropriations subcommittees had to make painful trade-offs for each item of spending. Pork projects were obvious and required a publicly acknowledged cut in some other worthy project. Because the caps were binding, the amount of pork was low during this period. When pork spending no longer required an explicit trade-off, the budget process made it easier to include them. Moreover, policy deadlocks, particularly over whether the rules still required offsets to tax reductions, delayed appropriations, resulting in omnibus appropriations, easy vehicles to slip pork into. The omnibus appropriations bills were often so large and so quickly passed that legislators did not have time to read them, let alone pull back the pork projects from them. The successes of the BEA exacerbated the demand for pork, but the failures of budget process after 1998 facilitated this growth in spending and moved the budget more in the direction of short-term, personal or partisan benefit and away from collective benefit.

The growth in earmarks was noted by many other observers, and had begun well before 9/11. In fiscal year 2000, OMB counted 6,183 legislative earmarks. That number represented a considerable increase from prior years.

"People say earmarks are part of the grease that makes government work, and to some extent, that's true," said John Cogan, a Stanford University economist and former OMB deputy director who headed the initial drafting of Bush's budget blueprint as a member of the transition team. "But 6,183 earmarks is an awful lot of grease." Government Executive Magazine – 2/13/01 Bush team eyes earmarks, may push biennial budget plan, February 13, 2001, James Barnes, National Journal 2002: Expiration of the BEA and Ad Hoc Budgeting

When the budget enforcement act of 1990 expired in 2002, it was not renewed. Congress could have fallen back on the 1974 process, but with lack of consensus on balance, tax cuts, and offsets, it was difficult to put a budget resolution together that both houses and both parties could agree on. The result can best be described as *ad hoc* budgeting, unpredictable, marked by stalemates, and noted for huge omnibus appropriations that no one could read in the time allotted. The omnibus appropriations were laden with pork and special interest legislation. War was funded by supplemental appropriations that added to the deficits, and obscured the fact that the budget as passed seriously and systematically underestimated expenditures and the size of the deficit. Deficits continued to grow, despite promises to curtail them.

The quality of budgetary decision-making deteriorated in this environment. The administration supported new budget rules that were one sided, that required offsets for new expenditures or program expansions, but not for tax reductions. This proposed rule would make it easy to reduce taxes almost at will and without regard for budgetary consequences. This proposed rule was attached to the House version of the budget resolution for the 2005 fiscal year budget. It was not only biased toward one policy, it was unlikely to actually reduce or control the burgeoning deficit since both revenues and expenditures need to be controlled to reduce or eliminate deficits. The Senate refused to go along with the House rules proposal and hence was unable to pass the budget resolution. Consideration of budget issues in the Senate went forward without a resolution but few of the appropriations bills were passed by the end of the fiscal year, necessitating an omnibus appropriation of the remaining appropriations bills. The omnibus legislation was huge, no one was given a chance to read it before passage, violating some basic democratic values and process. Moreover, there is little indication that the omnibus legislation represented considered evaluation of competing projects, programs, or budgetary claims. The pork that was stuffed into this mammoth appropriation act prompted mocking editorials in newspapers.

Under the 1974 act, both houses of Congress agree to not only totals in the budget resolution, and revenues necessary to fund those totals, but also to how those totals will be allocated to different functions of government. The committees work within these targets, so they will not have to do their work only to find out at the end that their decisions and carefully worked out compromises would be undone by further cuts to come in under limits. By allocating targets up front, the process provides some financial discipline. In addition, Congress collectively prioritizes spending at the macro rather than the micro level. The subcommittees make prioritization decisions within their areas, deciding between program requests as long as they stay within their allocations. Prioritization is the heart of budgeting; when Congress does not come up with a budget resolution or automatically accept the president's proposal, the committees may go over the totals (which may not even be known or agreed to in advance) and then make across-the-board cuts later, to get down to the maximum which has by then been determined. This process allows for a minimum of prioritization. This is in fact what happened in 2004, for the fy 2005 budget. In fact, Congress failed to pass a budget resolution in three of the last five recent years.

The deficits were largely a function (though not exclusively) of the tax reductions ardently desired by the president. The president wanted the tax cuts, but did not want to take responsibility for either programmatic reductions or the deficit. The result was a series of rules that would make it look as if the tax reductions cost less than they actually do. Budget observers call these *ad hoc* accounting rules "gimmicky scoring."

The administration first argued that its tax cuts would be temporary, so that, under the rules, they would only have to count a few years of the consequences, even though the financial impact increased after the end of that period. Then, a couple of years later, the administration argued that the tax cuts should be treated as permanent, so that an extension of the tax cuts would not be scored as having any increased costs. The administration sought to dodge the implications of the tax cuts first one way, and then serpentined back to dodge the implications the other way (Budget Rule Change Would Make The Cost Of Extending The Tax Cuts Disappear, 2/27/04 Robert Greenstein and Joel Friedman The Center for Budget and Policy Priorities, on line at http://www.cbpp.org/2-27-04bud4.htm).

It was not only the executive branch that engaged in creative scoring and rules changes to make deficits look smaller or vanish in order to justify the policy of tax cuts without replacement of the revenues or compensating reductions in spending. House Republicans adopted what has been called dynamic scoring as a way of measuring the impact of revenue cuts. Dynamic scoring tries to take into consideration the increase in economic activity, and hence the increase in federal revenue, that would result from any tax cut. The problem is that no one knows how big that effect might be, and the temptation is to make it as big as necessary to wipe out the apparent negative effects of a tax cut. CBO, the Congressional Budget Office, has not adopted dynamic scoring, and neither did the Senate, meaning that budget estimates are likely to differ between committees and between houses.

INFLUENCE OF BUDGET PROCESS (AND DETERIORATION)

Budget processes do not stand alone, they do not reduce spending, or increase deficits, they are a set of rules used by people making decisions. When the consensus that underlies the rules evaporates, the rules may remain in place while implementation erodes. When that happens, the effect of the rules is either watered down or eliminated. Gramm Rudman Hollings did not eliminate or reduce deficits in the manner predicted by the rules, in large part because Gramm Rudman Hollings was not enforced. Similarly, the Budget Enforcement Act had major impact on holding down expenditure growth and reducing the amount of pork in the budget, as long as there was consensus that the process was needed and should be enforced. When that consensus evaporated in 1998, the rules were no longer enforced and spending surged, tax reductions were passed, and deficits grew at a very fast pace. When decision-makers agree that they want a particular outcome, particular features of budget processes can make it easier to bring about those outcomes.

This chapter has argued that there are two classes of outcomes of the budget process. The first is this indirect impact or influence on the size of the deficit, the growth of expenditures (as a measure of the size of government) and the degree to which spending is constituent related (to satisfy requests from either individual or companies in a legislator's district) or for narrow partisan purposes. The second is a direct effect on the quality of decision-making and on democratic decision-making.

The chapter makes the case that deficits and spending respond to budget rules, since deficits grew during GRH and, after a couple of years of growth, began to and continued to decline under the Budget Enforcement Act, and then when BEA was no longer enforced and allowed to lapse, and the features of the 1974 Congressional Budget and Impoundment Control Act were only used episodically, spending surged and deficits rebounded. The effectiveness of the BEA in controlling earmarks may have built up demands to the point that, when the controls were relaxed, earmarking too took a major upswing.

It is not only the case that these outcomes correlated with the periods when various budget process rules were in place, and implemented or not implemented, but also that the specific features of the process that were or were not being implemented spoke directly to the results. In other words, there is a mechanism linking the budget process with these three outcomes. The spending controls in GRH were not implemented fully and were frequently gamed; deficit reduction targets were missed. BEAs caps and offset requirements were implemented and, even though they did not control the cost increases due to existing legislation, they provided a kind of discipline and consciousness of the impact of spending decisions. BEA also forced trade-offs, making earmarks not only visible but politically expensive, as legislators had to say what they would cut (and who else's earmarks they would cut) in order to fund their constituency-based projects. When these constraints ended, spending, including for earmarks, surged. BEA required explicit offsets for revenue reductions; when the BEA fell into disuse, the president proposed and Congress passed large and repeated tax breaks. House efforts to reform the budget process by asking for offsets for increased spending, but not for tax reductions, suggests that they felt such rules facilitated their policy goals of reducing tax levels. There would be no procedural obstacles to doing so.

Are there any rival hypotheses that could explain these results other than the influence of budget process? There is little doubt that the growth of the economy in the later 1990s helped to balance the budget, but the growth of the economy was not sufficient in and of itself to reach balance. In addition, spending rates were controlled. The two together helped restore balance. Similarly, the slow down of the economy in the early 2000s had some effect on reducing revenue, but tax reductions and spending increases had a much larger impact. A second possible rival hypothesis is that the amount of pork spending was increasing anyway, possibly due to a changeover in leadership and determination to build new coalitions of supporters in many tightly contested races. However, the long term trend was a reduction in geographically based spending, and although there have always been some earmarks in the budget, BEA seemed to hold down the level, which then jumped after the BEA constraints were over. It may well be that the reduction in the number of programs that can be used distributively has increased the demand for pork, but, even within this model, BEA spending controls and explicit and public trade-offs held it down for a while. In the post BEA world, trade-offs, when they occur, are invisible; tax reductions occur seemingly without the necessity of cutting spending programs.

The effect of budget process rules on the quality of decision-making is less inferential and there is no need to rule out alternative hypotheses. The process is the outcome. The deterioration of scoring rules, altering them to gain short term policy advantages, and then changing them back again, to get additional benefits in the short run, the adoption of accounting rules that obscure present and future costs, the huge and quick omnibus spending bills that bypass the committee process and that legislators are unable to read, the inability to implement the budget resolutions that force some prioritization, all suggest a deterioration of the quality of decision-making.

Perhaps most seriously, the budget process has become less democratic. The processes have become *ad hoc*, to produce a budget in the face of policy stalemates. Rules are made and remade, often in the service of particular immediate policy goals, not known in advance, not neutral, and not agreed to by all parties. They do not allow for a forum in which disagreements can be discussed and worked out, exaggerating the tendency toward stalemate, contributing to the lack of budget resolutions. The administration is not content merely to lower taxes, but also seeks to lock in those reductions for years to come, and has increased borrowing to an extent that will burden the next generation, and reduce its ability to prioritize.

With the end of divided government as a result of the elections in 2004, policy stalemates should be reduced. It should be easier to pass budget resolutions and hence to prioritize the budget because the administration will control a majority of both Houses of Congress. It should be easier to pass appropriations bills, and hence the need for huge, last minute omnibus appropriations should be reduced. The quality of decision-making should therefore improve and the process should become more predictable and open. But when the same political party controls the White House and both Houses of Congress, there is an increased chance of passing budget rules with marked policy biases. As yet, there is no evidence that political actors are aware that there are minimum requirements for a budget process, that collective rules are necessary for functioning, that they must be agreed on by all parties, and be perceived as fair. Both Democrats and Republicans have become more ideological in recent years, the differences between them have become more acute. The resulting policy quarrels need to be fought on a level playing field so the public trusts and accepts the outcomes. If the process does not seem fair, legitimate, or neutral with respect to partisan policy outcomes, or if it is not open to scrutiny, public mistrust grows, participation continues to decline, and democracy itself erodes. In this sense, budget process not only matters, it may be fundamental to governing in the United States. That having been said, however, rules are but one part of the equation of budget control in most industrialized democracies, and a range of factors must be considered for a more complete understanding.

REFERENCES

Albert-Roulhac, C. (1998) The Influence of EU membership on Methods and Processes of Budgeting in Britain and France, *Governance* 11, 209–30.

Gray, A., W. I. Jenkins and B. Segsworth (2002) Budgeting, Auditing and Evaluation (New Brunswick, Transaction).

HM Treasury (2005) *Public Expenditure Planning and Control in the United Kingdom* (London: HM Treasury).

Meyers, R. (1992) Federal Budgeting and Finance; The Future is Now, *Public Budgeting and Finance*, 4, 2–14.

Palazzolo, D. (1999) *Done Deal?: The Politics of the 1997 Budget Agreement* (New York: Chatham House).

Patashnik, E. M. (2000) *Putting Trust in the US Budget* (Cambridge: Cambridge University Press).

Stolfi, F. (2006) Reforming the Italian State: Administrative Modernization and Fiscal Management (Unpublished Ph.D. Dissertation, Department of Political Science, University of Pittsburgh).

Wanna, J., L. Jensen and J. de Vries (2003) *Controlling Public Expenditure* (Cheltenham: Edward Elgar).

8

Implementation

SØREN C. WINTER

Although the field of implementation research is barely 30 years old, implementation has already been analyzed from many different perspectives representing different research strategies, evaluation standards, concepts, focal subject areas, and methodologies. This chapter first performs a critical review of some of the major contributions to the literature. This examination will follow the development of the field over three generations of research (Goggin, 1986).

Second, based on a critical examination of the development and status of the research field, the chapter will suggest promising ways of moving ahead. It claims that implementation research can be improved by accepting theoretical diversity and partial theories and hypotheses, rather than looking for one common and general theoretical framework, seeking conceptual clarification, including focusing on output (performance of implementers) as well as outcomes as dependent variables in implementation research, and applying more comparative and statistical research designs, rather than relying on single case-studies in order to sort out the influence of different implementation variables.

THE PIONEERS

In several respects the book, *Implementation*, by Pressman and Wildavsky (1973) sets the stage for later implementation research. Most implementation research has focused on implementation problems, barriers, and failures, and this pessimistic view of implementation was already reflected in the subtitle of this seminal work, 'How great expectations in Washington are dashed in Oakland; or, Why it's amazing that federal programs work at all....'.

This case study focused on the local implementation of a federal economic development program to increase employment among ethnic minority groups in Oakland in California. Its guiding research questions were: 'How well was this authoritative mandate (law, regulation, program, official pronouncement) implemented?' and 'How might it have been better implemented?' Later research redefined the question to focus on achieving the explicit or implicit values in a given mandate rather than its prescriptive details (Bardach, 2001). Accordingly, goal achievement has been the dominating standard and dependent variable for implementation research since the 1970s.

Pressman and Wildavsky focused on the 'complexity of joint action' as the key implementation problem. In their Oakland economic development case – as in many others – federal, regional, state, and local government actors, courts, affected interest groups, private firms, and media had a role and stake in policy implementation. Implementation problems were amplified not only by the many actors but also by the many decision and veto points, which must typically be passed during the implementation process. Although they probably over-emphasized the lack of conflict in their case, Pressman and Wildavsky convincingly showed that merely slightly different perspectives, priorities, and time horizons among multiple actors with different missions in repeated and sequential decisions could cause delay, distortion, and even failures in policy implementation.

However, the two authors also demonstrated that failures are not only caused by bad implementation but also by bad policy instruments. Many of the problems in the Oakland case would have been avoided had policy makers chosen a more direct economic instrument that would *ex post* have tied spending of public expenditures to the actual number of minority workers employed, rather than relying on endless *ex ante* negotiations with affected parties and authorities.

Pressman and Wildavsky are good representatives for the first generation of implementation studies, which were typically explorative and inductive case studies with a theory-generating aim. Very few central theoretical variables were in focus, in this case the number of actors and decision points and the validity of the causal theory. Another outstanding example is Eugene Bardach's (1977) *The Implementation Game,* which placed more emphasis on the aspects of conflict in implementation, seeing implementation as a continuation of the political game from the policy adoption stage, although partly with other actors and other relations among actors. Bardach analyzed the types of games that various actors apply in the implementation process in order to pursue their own interests. However, these games tend to distort implementation from the legislative goals. Among other representatives from what has later been called the first generation of implementation research we find Erwin Hargrove (1975), who called implementation research 'the missing link' in the study of the policy process, and Walter Williams and Richard Elmore (1976).

SECOND GENERATION MODEL BUILDERS: TOP-DOWN, BOTTOM-UP AND SYNTHESES

Second generation implementation studies began in the early 1980s. While the first generation studies had been explorative and theory generating, the ambition of the second generation was to take a next step in theory development by constructing theoretical models, or rather frameworks of analysis, which could guide empirical analysis. Some of these studies had more optimistic views on successful implementation.

The construction of models and research strategies, however, immediately led to a major confrontation between the so-called *top-down* and *bottom-up* perspectives on policy implementation. The predominant top-down researchers focused on a specific political decision, normally a law. On the background of its official purpose they followed the implementation down through the system, often with special interest in upper level decision-makers. They would typically assume a control perspective on implementation, trying to give good advice on how to structure the implementation process from above in order to achieve the purpose of the legislation and to minimize the number of decision points that could be vetoed.

The best-known and most frequently used (Sabatier 1986) top-down analysis framework was developed by Mazmanian and Sabatier (1981). It contains 17 variables placed in 3 main groups concerning the tractability of the problems addressed by the legislation, the social and political context, and the ability of the legislation to structure the implementation process. This structuring can be made by means of, for example, hierarchy, appointing of authorities and staff with a positive attitude towards the legislation/program, and use of incentives including competition among providers. By adding a long-term perspective of 10–15 years to implementation, the authors show that, over time, start-up problems are often ameliorated by better structuring of the implementation by policy advocates (see also Kirst and Jung, 1982). This gave rise to much more optimistic views of implementation in contrast to the pessimism introduced by Pressman and Wildavsky (1973) and joined by most implementation analysts.

Mazmanian and Sabatier's framework was met by two different kinds of criticism. According to one strand, the model was naive and unrealistic because it overemphasized the ability of policy proponents to structure implementation, thus ignoring the ability of policy opponents to interfere in this structuring process (Moe, 1989). Often policy opponents are able to make policy goals less clear and to increase their own long-term influence in the implementation process in order to avoid some of the effects intended by policy proponents. Conceptually, the model ignored the politics of policy-formulation and policy design (Winter, 1986b; May, 2003).

Another strand of criticism came from the bottom-up researchers who took special interest in 'the bottom' of the implementation system, the place where public policies are delivered to citizens or firms. They all emphasized the influence that front-line staff have on the delivery of policies such as social services, income transfers and law enforcement in relation to citizens and firms. Front-line workers are crucial decision-makers in these studies that emphasize the weak control that politicians and administrative managers have of control front-line staffs.

Like top-down researchers (and also most evaluation researchers), some bottom-up researchers use the official objectives of a given legislation as the standard of evaluation (Lipsky, 1980; Winter, 1986a). Michael Lipsky (1980) developed a theory on 'Street-level Bureaucracy.' It focuses on the discretionary decisions that each front-line worker – or 'street-level bureaucrat' as Lipsky prefers to call them – make when delivering policies to individual citizens. This discretionary role in delivering services or enforcing regulations makes street-level bureaucrats essential actors in implementing public policies. Indeed, Lipsky (1980) turns the policy process upside-down by claiming that street-level bureaucrats are the real *policy makers*. However, one ironic aspect of the theory is that, although Lipsky emphasizes the individual role of street-level bureaucrats in implementing

public policies, their similar working conditions make them all apply similar behavior. This means that street-level bureaucrats even across policy-types, tend to apply similar types of practices, whether they are teachers, policemen, nurses, doctors, or social workers. It also means that their individual attitudes are not expected to have important implications for their behaviors.

Although trying to do their best, street-level bureaucrats experience a gap between the demands made on them by legislative mandates, managers and citizens on one side and their high workload on the other. In this situation they all apply a number of coping mechanisms that systematically distort their work in relation to the intentions of the legislation. They ration services, make priorities between their tasks, apply simple standardized processing of clients, which tends to be in the favor of more easy cases and resourceful clients (creaming), they seek to control clients, and over time street-level bureaucrats develop more cynical perceptions of clients and modify the policy objectives that are the basis of their work. According to Lipsky, increasing staff resources is no cure to coping as more resources will merely lead to more demand for services.

Other *bottom-up* researchers go the whole length, rejecting the objective of policy mandates as an evaluation standard. Instead their analysis departs from a specific problem (Elmore, 1982) such as youth unemployment (Elmore, 1982) or small firms' conditions of growth (Hull and Hjern, 1987). In practice it is the researcher himself who in most cases defines the problem and thereby his evaluation standard. This is acceptable if done explicitly, and it can be fruitful if the researcher is able to convince his readers about the appropriateness of his problem definition.

The next task in Hull and Hjern's (1987) *bottom-up* approach is to identify the many actors that are affecting the problem in question and to map relations between them. In these network analyses – using a 'snowball method' – both public and private actors become essential, and the analyses often include several policies that affect the same problem. In this way, the analysis maps the informal, empirical implementation structure around a given problem, while *top-down* research tends to look at the formal implementation structure related to one particular policy program. According to Hull and Hjern, empirical implementation structures tend to be far less hierarchical than formal ones, and they often cross organizational borders in forming collaborative networks at the operational level. The bottom-up analyses by Hjern and associates are important in drawing attention to implementation activities and structures at the local operational level, but the perspective has more the character of guidelines for an inductive research strategy and methodology than a development of theory and hypotheses that can be empirically tested. A recent example of the bottom-up approach is Bogason's (2000) study of local governance. It is inspired by Hull and Hjern but adds elements of institutional and constructivist analyses and points to the fragmented character of the modern state in policy making and implementation.

Suggested Syntheses

The *top-down* and *bottom-up* perspectives were useful in drawing attention to the fact that both top and bottom play important roles in the implementation process, but in the long run the battle between the two approaches was not fruitful. Each tended to ignore the portion of the implementation reality explained by the other (Goggin et al., 1990: 12; Hill and Hupe, 2002). Elmore (1985) actually recommends using both forward mapping – which is essentially a top-down analysis – and backward mapping for policy analysis because each tends to offer valuable insights for policy makers. He claims that policy designers need to consider the policy instruments and the resources they have at their disposal (forward mapping), as well as the incentive structure of the target group and street-level bureaucrats' ability to tip the balance of these incentives in order to affect the problematic situation of the target group (backward mapping).

Other scholars have tried to solve the controversy by specifying the conditions where one approach might be more relevant than the other. Sabatier (1986) claims that the *top-down* perspective is best suited for studying the implementation in policy areas that are dominated by one specific legislation, limited research funds, or where the situation is structured at least moderately well. *Bottom-up* perspectives, on the other hand, would be more relevant in situations where several different policies are directed towards a particular problem, and where one is primarily interested in the dynamics of different local situations.

Attempts were also made to synthesize the two models. Richard E. Matland (1995) suggests that their relative value depends on the degree of ambiguity in goals and means of a policy and the degree of conflict. Traditional *top-down* models, based on the public administration tradition, present an accurate description of the implementation process when a policy is clear and the conflict is low. However, newer *top-down* models, such as the Mazmanian-Sabatier framework, are also relevant when conflict is high and ambiguity is low, which makes the structuring of the implementation particularly important. In contrast, *bottom-up* models provide an accurate description of the implementation process when the policy is ambiguous and the conflict is low. When conflict as well as ambiguity is present, both models have some relevance according to Matland.

Other attempts at synthesizing the two approaches were made by the former main combatants. The *bottom-uppers*, Hull and Hjern (1987), proposed a synthesis – called 'an inductive approach to match outcomes of politics and their intentions,' which calls for systematic interview analysis of relevant actors from the bottom to the very top. The approach would require immense research resources, and I am not aware of any such study performed in practice. In addition, their proposed synthesis suffers from being methodological recommendations rather than theoretically based expectations, which can be tested systematically.

Also Sabatier (1986) has suggested a synthesis – the so-called *Advocacy Coalition Framework* (ACF). However, although making an important contribution to the public policy literature, Sabatier and his later associate,

Jenkins-Smith (Sabatier and Jenkins-Smith, 1993), actually moved the focus of analysis towards policy change and formation and away from implementation.

Another kind of synthesis was suggested by Winter (1990; 1994; 2003a) in his 'Integrated Implementation Model.' Unlike previous attempts, the purpose here is not to make a true synthesis between *top-down* and *bottom-up* perspectives, but rather to integrate a number of the most fruitful theoretical elements from various pieces of implementation research – regardless of their origin – into a joint model. As dependent variable and standard for evaluating the results of the implementation process the model focuses on performance as well as outcome in relation to the official policy objectives. This standard was selected from a democratic point of view, because goals formulated in parliament and in laws have a particular legitimate status and are relevant for holding government accountable.

The first set of factors, which affects implementation results, is the *policy formulation process* and the *policy design*. Too many implementation researchers have erroneously put the whole blame for any lack of goal-achievement on implementation. As noted by Peter May (2003) well designed policies are necessary but not sufficient for improving implementation prospects. Other implementation scholars have ignored or failed to conceptualize the connections between policy formulation, policy design and implementation.

The roots of implementation problems can often be found in the prior policy formulation process. For instance, conflicts in that process often create a policy design that is marked by ambiguous goals as well as an invalid causal theory with a lack of connection between goals and means. Sometimes even symbolic policies are adopted to (appear to) address a problem without actually offering the means that could achieve the stated objectives. And, as mentioned by Bardach (1977), the conflicts in policy formulation often continue in the subsequent implementation process. Not only conflict but also lack of attention among the coalition partners passing a law can lead to implementation failures (Winter, 1986b).

A policy design typically contains a set of goals, a mix of instruments for obtaining these goals, a designation of governmental or non-governmental entities charged with carrying out the goals, and an allocation of resources for the requisite tasks (May, 2003). Policy design and policy instruments have received substantial research interest since the 1980s (Linder and Peters, 1989; Salamon, 2002). The basic claim of this literature is that any policy can be disaggregated to one or a mix of a limited number of generic policy instruments. The research interest, however, has not led to agreement on any typology of instruments (Vedung, 1995). One simple classification consists of mandates, economic incentives, and information, which aim at affecting the behavior of either target groups or intermediaries (implementers).

Policy design affects the implementation process and results in various ways. Different mixes of instruments are not equally effective in obtaining a given policy objective. Policy design is important in affecting the incentives of intermediaries to carry out their requisite tasks, particularly through affecting their commitment and capacity and by signaling desired actions (May, 2003). While the validity of the causal theory linking instruments to objectives certainly is important, however, the research documentation of instrument effects is still meager. One reason is that effects of instruments on implementation are often determined by the context, including the political context. Consequently, designing good policies is not a simple, technocratic process like selecting the best types of materials for building a bridge (May, 2003).

In addition, the chosen instruments may affect the overall implementation structure and process, as certain instruments tend to favor the formation of particular implementation structures. Mandates aimed at regulating the behavior of target groups normally require a staff for inspecting and enforcing the mandate and a set of sanctions. Information strategies and use of economic incentives such as environmental taxes can sometimes be implemented with fewer staff, although there is no one-to-one relationship between instruments and staff requirements. Some taxes are relatively automatic and easy to collect, such as an environmental tax per liter gasoline sold, while others require a substantial staff for inspection and enforcing, for example, taxing diffuse pollution.

It is important to understand that ineffective policy designs are not always due to lack of knowledge on the part of the policy designers. Policy design of instruments and organizational structure is first of all a political process, in which political actors – both policy proponents and opponents – try to maximize their interests, including selecting an organizational structure, which will allow themselves to maximize long-term control of the implementation process (Moe, 1989).

The next set of factors of the model focuses on how the implementation process affects the results. Implementation processes are characterized by *organizational and interorganizational behaviors* representing different degrees of commitment and coordination. Interorganizational implementation settings seem to become ever more important (O'Toole, 2003). As mentioned above, Pressman and Wildavsky (1973) focused on the 'complexity of joint action,' according to which successful implementation is likely to be negatively related to the number of actors and decision and veto points.

However, as shown by O'Toole and Montjoy (1984; O'Toole, 2003) this insight only applies to certain kinds of interorganizational implementation settings. Decision points are not independent of each other, but successful implementation results can be stimulated by an early agreement on basic understandings, which can promote 'bandwagon effects' in later decisions, and decisions can be merged by crafting 'package deals.'

The implementation prospects also depend on the type of resource-dependency among participating organizations. The 'complexity of joint action' best applies to a chain of *sequential* relations, in which one organization depends on outputs from another as input for its own contribution to implementation. However, *reciprocal* relations, in which two organizations depend on each other for inputs can decrease the likelihood of veto points because both have incentives to cooperate. *Pooled* relations, where multiple organizations

can produce and deliver implementation outputs independently of each other, can provide relatively good implementation results, although the coordination may not be optimal. O'Toole (2003) and May (2003) show how interorganizational coordination problems can be reduced by using policy design to increase commitment, build and use a common interest, and facilitate cooperation via exchange.

The behaviors of *street-level bureaucrats* are also crucial for the implementation of most policies, and Lipsky's (1980) insights above on 'street-level bureaucracy' are included in the Integrated Implementation Model. Street-level bureaucrats are making important discretionary decisions in their direct contact with citizens and firms. Because such bureaucrats work in situations characterized by many demands and limited resources, they respond by resorting to coping behaviors. These short-cuts systematically bias the delivery behavior in relation to the policy mandates. While Lipsky's contribution was important for understanding implementation, the theory needs more specifications of the causal mechanisms that can explain variation in coping-behaviors and their consequences (Winter, 2002; Heinesen et al., 2004), cf. below. For a review of the literature on street-level bureaucrats, see Meyers and Vorsanger, 2003).

According to the Integrated Implementation Model also target groups of public policies, that is, citizens or firms, play important roles, not only on the effects of the policy, but also in affecting the performance by street-level bureaucrats through positive or negative actions in co-producing public services and regulation (Hill and Hupe, 2002: 134–36). Finally, socio-economic contexts form important framework conditions for implementation. For example, in employment policies delivery behavior (the types of employment offers) and effects depend heavily on ups and downs in the business cycle.

The Integrated Implementation Model is obviously not a model in the strict sense of a simple causal model. It is rather a framework of analysis presenting key factors and mechanisms that affect implementation outputs and outcomes. For each set of factors a number of more specific hypotheses can be developed (Winter, 1990, 1994, 2003a; Jensen et al., 1991; May, 2003; O'Toole, 2003; Meyers and Vorsanger, 2003).

THIRD GENERATION: QUANTITATIVE RESEARCH DESIGNS

While the first and second generations of implementation studies have been helpful in directing attention to implementation problems and identifying implementation barriers and factors that might ease implementation, the research had not succeeded in sorting out the relative importance of the explanatory variables. A substantial part of the studies could be criticized as merely presenting – often long – checklists of variables that might effect implementation.

Malcolm Goggin (1986) pointed out that, because implementation research had been dominated by single case studies, it was plagued by the problem of 'too few cases and too many variables' or by 'overdetermination,' where two or more variables explain variation in the dependent variable equally well. The fact that the single case-study approach does not allow for any control of third variables had hampered the development of implementation theory, according to Goggin. He therefore called for a third generation of implementation studies that would test theories on the basis of more comparative case-studies and statistical research designs, which could increase the number of observations.

Goggin followed up on these recommendations with his associates (Goggin, Bowman, Lester, and O'Toole, 1990) in a study, which was based mainly on a communications theory perspective on intergovernmental implementation, but also included many variables from previous top-down and bottom-up research. The study focused especially on variation among states in the way and extent they implement federal policies in three different social and regulatory policies. The authors tried to encourage further research involving multiple measures and multiple methods, including quantitative methods.

Later, Lester and Goggin (1998), in making a status for implementation research, called for the development of 'a parsimonious, yet complete, theory of policy implementation.' They suggested that such meta-theory might be developed by combining the insights of communications theory, regime theory, rational choice theory (especially game theory), and contingency theories. As dependent variable for implementation studies they proposed to focus on implementation processes rather than outputs and outcomes.

THE NEED FOR A NEW RESEARCH AGENDA

While agreeing with Goggin's (1986) call for more comparative and statistical research designs based on quantitative methods, I disagree with several of the later methodological and theoretical recommendations made by him and his colleagues. As recognized by one of these authors, O'Toole (2000), to follow the methodological suggestions given by Goggin, Bowman, Lester, and O'Toole (1990) would involve at least outlining a research career's worth of work. This work would require applying research designs that involve numerous variables, across different policy types, across 50 states, over at least 10 years, as well as measuring the relevant variables by a combination of content analyses, expert panels, elite surveys, and expert reassessment of the data from questionnaires and interviews. As such a research strategy is too demanding; less demanding research strategies, which can still secure a sufficient number of observations, would be more realistic.

My suggestions for further development of implementation research can be summarized in six points: (1) providing theoretical diversity, (2) focusing on partial rather than general implementation theories, (3) seeking conceptual clarification, (4) focusing on the implementation output (performance of implementers) as a dependent variable, (5) including studies of outcomes, and (6) using more comparative and statistical research designs (Winter, 1999).

While the last point has been developed above, I will elaborate on the other ones in the following and illustrate them by some of my recent research on implementation of Danish agro-environmental regulation with Peter May and of Danish integration policy towards refugees and immigrants.

Theoretical Diversity and Partial Theories

Given the many exploratory variables, which have already been identified by various implementation scholars, the suggestion by Goggin et al. of developing a 'parsimonious, yet complete implementation theory' by combining theoretical elements from at least four different theories, appear to be a *contradictio in adjecto* and is more likely to lead to theoretical mismatch. Rather than looking for *the* overall and one for all implementation theory, as has been the utopian objective for many implementation scholars, we should welcome diversity in both the theoretical perspectives and methodologies applied. Such diversity will give us new insights. It also strikes me as unrealistic – and probably not very fruitful – that many scholars could agree on applying one common theoretical framework.

Although the general implementation frameworks presented by model builders so far have been helpful in giving an overview of some crucial implementation variables, the generality of such models may in fact be an obstacle for further development of our understanding of implementation. This is due to the fact that generality inhibits precise specification of variables and causal mechanisms (May, 1999). Consequently, it seems more fruitful to use research resources on developing partial theories and hypotheses about different and more limited implementation problems and on putting these to serious empirical tests.

Some of the different implementation perspectives may be integrated into broader analytical frameworks or models (Mazmanian and Sabatier, 1981; Winter, 1990; Goggin, Bowman, Lester and O'Toole, 1990). A new promising research collaboration around a common analytical framework has been initiated by Lynn, Heinrich and Hill (2001; Heinrich and Lynn, 2000). They have proposed a 'Logic of Governance.' They define *governance* as 'regimes of laws, rules, judicial decisions, and administrative practices that constrain, prescribe, and enable the provision of publicly supported goods and services.' The logic can be expressed as a basic 'reduced form' according to which outputs/outcomes are a function of environmental factors, client characteristics, treatments, structures and managerial roles and actions. A more complex form allows for interrelations between the explanatory factors. This framework broadens the scope of traditional implementation research. It focuses on the interrelations and complexities of administrative phenomena, and calls for sound empirical yet theory-driven research. While its main theoretical inspiration is political economy, other theoretical perspectives are welcomed.

The main contribution of the framework is its emphasis on systematic empirical testing of theory driven hypotheses and for generating a framework that allows many studies to talk to each other. The authors claim that both top-down and bottom-up considerations are included, but the top-down control orientation seems to be stronger than bottom-up perspectives. The motivations of street-level bureaucrats have not been conceptualized as part of the framework, which focuses more on managerial behaviors.

A related framework and research program on management and performance has been established by Meier and O'Toole (2004; 2006).

Need for Conceptual Clarification and Focusing on Implementation Outputs as a Dependent Variable

As pointed out by Peter May (1999) most conceptual frameworks in the implementation literature are weakly developed, lacking adequate definitions of concepts and specification of causal mechanisms. The most important issue for the development of implementation research may be to reconsider what constitutes the object of the study. There has been some disagreement in the literature on the term of 'implementation' and on what is the important dependent variable in implementation research.

One problem is that the concept 'implementation' is often used to characterize both the implementation process and the output – and sometimes also the outcome – of the implementation process. Lester and Goggin (1998) view implementation as a '*process*, a series of subnational decisions and actions directed toward putting a prior authoritative federal decision into effect.' Thereby, they reject focusing on the output of the implementation process as 'a dichotomous conceptualization of implementation as simply success or failure.'

Although agreeing that the success/failure dichotomy is problematic, I suggest that the most important focus of implementation research would not be the implementation process but the output of that process in terms of delivery behavior. This would be much more in line with the classic focus of public policy research on the content of policy, its causes, and consequences (Dye, 1976). Implementation output is policy content at a much more operational level than a law. It is policy as it is being delivered to the citizens. However, we should conceptualize output in other ways than the common success/failure dichotomy or interval.

The most common dependent variable in implementation research so far has been the degree of goal-achievement, whether defined in terms of output or outcome. The first problem, however, is that goal-achievement is a fraction. Output in terms of performance of the implementers or outcome in terms of effects on target population is the numerator, and the policy goal is the denominator. Yet, using a fraction as the dependent variable renders theory building problematic when different factors explain variation in the numerator and the denominator. While the policy formation process is likely to account for variation in goals, the implementation process is likely to account for variation in performance, and additional factors are likely to account for variation in outcomes. This renders the construction and accumulation of implementation theory very complex.

Pushing it to extremes, the problem is that any attempt to make generalizations about goal-achievement based on analysis of the behavior or performance of implementers is dependent on the goal variable having a certain value. The generalization may become invalid if the goal changes. Therefore, generalizations about implementation output are extremely relativistic because statements are conditioned by the goals that are formulated. This is problematic when it is recognized that policy makers are often more interested in making decisions on means or instruments than goals; goals are often invented after decisions on the means have been made in order to legitimize the means adopted, and goals are not always expected, or even intended, to be achieved.

The second problem of using goal-achievement as the dependent variable of implementation research is that such goals can be difficult to operationalize. Much has already been written in the implementation and evaluation literatures about the vagueness and ambiguity of policy goals and the difference between official and latent goals. In addition, while most policy statutes state some kind of goal for the outcome of the policy, many fail to specify goals or standards for the behavior of the implementers. This is often the case in regulatory policies that tend to specify the behaviors of regulatees rather than those of the regulators.

Because of the problems of using goal-achievement as a dependent variable, I suggest that we look for behavioral *output* variables to characterize the *performance* of implementers in delivering services or transfer payments to the citizens or enforcing regulations. The first aim of implementation research then should be to explain variation in such performance. This will require substantial effort in conceptualizing and categorizing the performance of implementers at the levels of agency as well as that of the individual street-level bureaucrat. However, as specified below, focusing on implementation output does not mean that outcomes are unimportant.

One very intriguing question is whether we can find behavioral output dimensions and classifications that are universally applicable in all policy areas, or if we should generate concepts and classifications that are different from one policy area to another. In order to stimulate theory building we should avoid concepts that are very policy specific, because generalizations based on these would have a rather narrow sphere of application.

At the other extreme, Lipsky's (1980) street-level bureaucracy theory represents an ambitious attempt to offer a universally applicable set of concepts for describing the coping behavior of street-level bureaucrats in all policy areas. Although Lipsky's coping behaviors might seem to have a better fit for social policies with weak clients, it has been demonstrated that they are also relevant for a regulatory policy with strong clients in a study of Danish agro-environmental and integration policies (Winter, 2002). However, coping focuses on dysfunctional behaviors, and we need more concepts for characterizing agency and front-line staff behaviors adequately.

Other concepts have been developed for classifying the behavior of implementers in almost any kind of social regulation policy (Kagan, 1994). May and Winter (1999; 2000; Winter and May, 2001) have developed concepts for regulatory enforcement at both agency and individual street-level bureaucrat levels. Agency enforcement choices are conceptualized as (1) tools (use of different enforcement measures: sanctions, information, and incentives), (2) priorities (whom to target and what to inspect for), and (3) effort (use and leveraging of enforcement resources). The enforcement style of individual inspectors is defined as the character of the day-to-day interactions of inspectors with the target group. May and Winter expect and verify, in a study of agro-environmental regulation in Denmark, that enforcement style has two dimensions comprised as the degree of formality of interactions and the use of threats and other forms of coercion (May and Winter, 2000; see also May and Burby, 1998; May and Wood, 2003).

In a study of the implementation of Danish integration policy for refugees and immigrants the same two implementation style dimensions have been found relevant for examining a social policy (Winter, 2003b; Heinesen et al.,

2004) However, in addition, the dimension of professional distance (versus close personal involvement with clients) is included, which seems to be particularly relevant in social policy implementation.

One advantage of creating such conceptualization of the behavior of implementers is that it is well suited for testing hypotheses for explaining variation in implementation behavior across time and space. Variables from implementation theory characterizing aspects of the implementation process would be an important basis for the development and test of such hypotheses. However, another advantage of focusing on outputs as a dependent variable in implementation research is that we can integrate the study of implementation much more with theory on bureaucratic politics and organization theory. Implementation research can thereby gain inspiration from these research fields that have a long tradition of studying the behavior of agencies and bureaucrats (see also Lynn, Heinrich and Hill, 2001). In return, these sub-disciplines can benefit from implementation concepts that are much more policy relevant than those behavioral variables applied in most bureaucracy and organization theory.

As an example, Winter (2003b) analyzes the discretion of street-level bureaucrats in implementing agro-environmental regulation and integration policy in Denmark by applying a modified principal-agent perspective and its notion of information asymmetry in examining the extent to which local politicians control their street-level bureaucrats (Moe, 1984; Brehm and Gates, 1999). Regression analyses of 216 local inspectors and 388 social caseworkers show that local politicians' policy preferences have very little direct impact on the behaviors of street-level bureaucrats. However, to some extent the politicians do control relatively visible kinds of performance, such as the number of inspections and the number of timely processed cases, through funding capacity for implementation. On the other hand, when it comes to less transparent front-line behaviors – such as the implementation styles and the strictness front-line staffs apply in reacting to violations of the rules – politicians' policy preferences and their funding of staff resources have little or no influence on these practices. On the contrary, the latter are dominated by the street-level bureaucrats' own values.

The study also examines the impact of various types of attitudes on street-level bureaucrats' behavior. While their abstract and general support for the focal policy does not have much effect, their attitudes on the policy instruments, target population, and their workload have strong impacts. In a study of street-level bureaucratic coping in the implementation of the same two Danish policies, the same types of street-level bureaucrat attitudes have been found to be very important in explaining variation in coping. However, coping is also strongly affected by the number of staff that politicians allocate for implementation (Winter, 2002; Heinesen et al., 2004). Thus, the application of quantitative analysis have confirmed that Lipsky's coping concepts are very useful but also demonstrated that individual attitudes of street-level bureaucrats as well as the level of resources allocated for their work are much more important for explaining the use of coping than Lipsky expected.

Outcome Studies

My suggestion of using implementation output/performance as dependent variable in implementation research does not imply that outcome/impacts are unimportant in public policy analyses. On the contrary, implementation scholars, as well as other political scientists, have paid far too little attention to explaining policy outcomes and to examining the relation between implementation outputs and outcomes (Lynn, Heinrich and Hill, 2001). As mentioned above, some implementation scholars do include outcome in their implementation models or framework (Hull and Hjern, 1987; Elmore, 1982; Mazmanian and Sabatier, 1981; Winter, 1990; Goggin, Bowman, Lester and O'Toole, 1990). It might, however, be fruitful

to make a distinction between explaining implementation outputs and outcomes.

We do not have a complete understanding of the policy process unless we know how target groups respond to public policies. Despite the fact that 'the authoritative allocation of values for a society' (Easton, 1953) and 'who gets what when and how' (Lasswell, 1936) are among the most famous definitions of politics, very few political science studies focus on how citizens respond to public policies. Some would say that this is the province of evaluation research. However, evaluation is characterized by a focus on methods, whereas very little theory development has occurred, especially extremely little political science theory. Some law and society scholars have attempted to explain variation in compliance among citizens and, to lesser degree, firms. So far, very few political scientists and public policy researchers have tried to theorize and test hypotheses about variation in outcome and how implementation behavior affects outcomes. In political science journals the contrast between many studies of citizens' attitudes and behavior at the input side of politics and very few outcome studies is striking. Yet, the study of outcomes is as much, if not more, about policy than are most public opinion studies that relate to the input side of policy.

My suggested redefinition of the dependent variable of implementation research from goal-achievement to a behavioral performance variable has not only the advantage of making it easier to explain variation in implementation outputs and easier to make generalizations. The conceptualization of performance is also likely to make it much easier to study the relation between implementation outputs and outcomes (May and Winter, 1999; Winter and May, 2001; 2002). In such studies delivery level performance/output changes from being a dependent variable to become an independent variable in outcome studies. Most likely, we need different theorizing for explaining implementation outputs and outcomes.

As claimed by Elmore (1982; 1985), to change target groups' problematic behavior requires an understanding of the incentives that are operating on these people as well as of how street-level bureaucrats can influence and build on these incentives. For example, in examining Danish farmers' compliance with environmental regulations, Winter and May (2001) map the regulatees' action model. In multiple regression analyses of survey data of 1,562 farmers, they show that compliance is affected by farmers' (1) calculated motivations based on the costs of complying and the perceived risk of detection of violations (while the risk of sanctions, as in most other studies, had no deterrent effect), (2) normative sense of duty to comply and (3) social motivations based on adaptation to expectations from significant others. Inspectors signal such expectations through their style of interacting with target groups. Inspectors' formalism increases compliance up to a point by providing greater certainty of what is expected of regulatees, while coercive styles with threats of sanctions backfire for regulatees who are not aware of the rules. Willingness to comply is not enough if the ability to comply is not there. Thus, awareness of rules and financial capacity increase farmers' compliance.

An understanding of the motivations and incentives of target groups is essential for specifying causal links between implementation behavior and target group responses. Further research along this line has shown that inspectors not only affect farmers' compliance directly through social motivation. They can also do so indirectly by using deterrence, because frequent inspections increase farmers' perceived risk of being caught if violating the rules – or they can use information provision for increasing regulatees' awareness of rules. Affecting their normative commitment to comply is much trickier. Inspectors try often to do so, but are unlikely to succeed because farmers do not trust them enough. In contrast, advice from credible sources – such as farmers' own professional trade-organizations and consultants – is much more effective in fostering a sense of duty to comply. This demonstrates an important role for third parties – including interest groups and consultants – as intermediaries in affecting policy outcomes through information provision and legitimization (Winter and May, 2002).

By the same token, a study on the implementation of Danish integration policy has found that street-level bureaucrats' use of coping as well as various implementation styles affect the outcome in terms of labor market integration of refugees and immigrants. However, the effects depend on the context (Lynn, Heinrich and Hill, 2001; Hill and Hupe, 2002). In municipalities with a difficult integration task – due to the composition of immigrants and labor market conditions – coping and professional distance increases employment, while in municipalities with an easy integration task formalism decreases employment (Heinesen et al., 2004). As coping is normally assumed to bias the implementation in a dysfunctional way, it is remarkable that it here has positive outcomes, at least in the short run, which may be due to creaming of the most resourceful immigrants. The findings from the two studies illustrate that delivery performance variables can be constructed that are fruitful both as dependent variables in explaining implementation outputs and as independent variables in explaining outcomes.

As the most relevant criterion for evaluating the relevance of a policy is its outcomes, some implementation scholars are tempted to skip focusing on outputs and go directly to examining the relation between implementation processes/ structures and outcomes (Lynn, Heinrich and Hill, 2001; Heinrich and Lynn, 2000; Meier and O'Toole, 2004). However, if implementation is important to outcomes, it is likely to work through outputs, and we will not get a full understanding of the causal links between implementation and outcomes, unless we understand how implementation structures and processes shape outputs, and how outputs shape outcomes. Often a given implementation structure – for example specialization of front-line staffs – affects several front-line practices with opposite effects on outcomes. Outcomes are also often affected by other factors than implementation processes, structures and outputs (Heinesen et al., 2004). Therefore, we need implementation research that seeks to explain variation in outputs as well as in outcomes by focusing on the links between outputs and outcomes.

I have argued for an implementation research agenda that involves theoretical diversity, partial theory and hypothesis building and testing, conceptual clarification, explaining outputs as well as outcomes, and using more comparative and statistical, multivariate research designs. Research by me and Peter May has been used as examples, but fortunately several other scholars have been and are doing research that is similar to all or most of these recommendations (for example Keiser and Soss, 1998; Meyers, Glaser and MacDonald, 1998; Lynn, Heinrich and Hill, 2001; Nielsen, 2002; Bloom, Hill and Ricco, 2003; Gunningham, Kagan and Thornton, 2003; May and Wood, 2003; Norgaard and Pallesen, 2003; Meier and O'Toole, 2004; 2006).

CONCLUSION

Implementation is a relatively young research field in public administration and public policy. The field has made an important contribution in terms of adding a public policy perspective to public administration, with a strong focus on how policies are transformed during the execution process till – and even after – the point of delivery. The research is valuable for our understanding of the complexities of policy implementation. The studies have revealed many important barriers for implementation as well as factors that may make success more likely.

During three decades of implementation research no general implementation theory has emerged, although many implementation scholars have had the development of such a theory as their ultimate, yet far-sighted objective. The implementation sub-discipline has been characterized by many different approaches representing different research strategies, evaluation standards, methodologies, concepts, and focal subject areas for research.

One of the major controversies among implementation analysts has been whether implementation should be studied from the top-down or from the bottom-up. Related to that discussion is whether the proper evaluation standard for implementation studies should be goal achievement or problem solving. In terms of methodology, implementation analyses have been dominated by single case-studies, often with several types of data sources, including both qualitative and quantitative data (Yin, 1982). Other scholars have called for a replacement of single case-studies by comparative and statistical research designs, which can increase the number of observations and control for third variables in order to allow more systematic theory and hypothesis testing and generalization.

Implementation scholars also disagree about the key concepts for implementation research. As their dependent variable some want to focus on the implementation *process*, while others examine implementation performance/output or even outcomes. Somewhat related to the conceptual disagreement are differences in the subjects that implementation researchers study. Many implementation studies present long lists of variables that might explain implementation (e.g. Mazmanian and Sabatier, 1981). However, implementation scholars tend to focus on different explanatory variables and subject matters in their research (Hill and Hupe, 2002).

Implementation research has been one of the fads of political science and its sub-disciplines of public administration and public policy and reached its peak in terms of number of publications in core journals in the mid-eighties. While research published under that explicit label has later decreased (Sætren, 2005; Hill and Hupe, 2002), a substantial amount of research focusing on implementation problems has later been published, albeit often under other labels, such as: public administration, management (Bardach, 2001), regulatory enforcement and compliance (Scholz and Wei, 1986; Kagan, 1994; Winter and May, 2001; 2002), street-level bureaucracy (Lipsky, 1980), principal-agent theory (Brehm and Gates, 1999), new institutionalism, governance (Bogason, 2000; Lynn, Heinrich and Hill, 2001; Heinrich and Lynn, 2000), networks (O'Toole, 2000), policy design and instruments (Linder and Peters, 1989; Salamon, 2002).

However, it is interesting that implementation research has spread extensively to sector specific journals on i.e. education, health, law, economics, and environment. Around the turn of the century, articles in sector journals made up no less than 84 percent of all articles with the word 'implementation' or 'implementing' in their titles, whereas core journals of political science, public administration, and public policy only accounted for 16 percent. The highly fragmented character of implementation research is not very conductive to theory accumulation (Sætren, 2005).

In making a status and reconsideration of implementation research, I suggest that the most promising research program would be dropping the ambition of constructing a general theory of implementation in favor of developing and testing different partial theories and hypotheses; providing more conceptual clarification in specification of causal relations, including focusing on explaining variation in implementation outputs (delivery performance) as well as outcomes; and giving higher priority to comparative and statistical research designs, which can, better than single case-studies, control for third variables and form a better basis for generalizing research findings.

Returning to the classical questions of public policy research (Dye, 1976), implementation outputs is *policy* at its most operational level. Policy design and the implementation processes are important *causes* of policy-outputs, as outcomes are the *consequences*. Consequently, we should seek to explain outputs as well as outcomes.

REFERENCES

Bardach, Eugene (1977) *The Implementation Game.* Cambridge, Mass.: MIT Press.

Bardach, Eugene (2001) 'Implementation, Political,' in N. J. Smelser and P. B. Baltes (eds.), *International Encyclopedia of the Social & Behavioral Sciences.* Amsterdam: Elsevier Science Ltd.

Bloom, Howard, S., Carolyn J. Hill and James A. Riccio (2003) 'Linking Program Implementation and Effectiveness: Lessons from a Pooled Sample of Welfare-to-work Experiments.' *Journal of Policy Analysis and Management* 22(4): 551–576.

Bogason, Peter (2000) *Public Policy and Local Governance: Institutions in Postmodern Society.* Cheltenham: Edward Elgar.

Brehm, John and Scott Gates (1999) *Working, Shirking, and Sabotage: Bureaucratic Response to a Democratic Public.* Ann Arbor: University of Michigan Press.

Dye, T.R. (1976) *What Governments Do, Why They Do It, and What Difference It Makes.* Tuscaloosa, Al.: University of Alabama Press.

Easton, David (1953) *The Political System.* New York: Alfred A. Knopf.

Elmore, Richard F. (1982) 'Backward Mapping: Implementation Research and Policy Decisions,' pp. 18–35 in W. Williams, R. F. Elmore, J. S. Hall et al. (eds.), *Studying Implementation.* Chatham N.J.: Chatham House Publ.

Elmore, Richard F. (1985) 'Forward and Backward Mapping: Reversible Logic in the Analysis of Public Policy,' in K. Hanf and T. A. J. Toonen (eds.), *Policy Implementation in Federal and Unitary Systems.* Dordrecht: Martinus Nijhoff, pp. 33–70.

Elmore, Richard F. (1987) "Instruments and Strategy in Public Policy", *Policy Studies Review* 7(1): 174–86.

Goggin, Malcolm L. (1986) 'The 'Too Few Cases/Too Many Variables' Problems in Implementation Research,' *The Western Political Quarterly,* 39: 328–47.

Goggin, Malcolm L., Ann O'M., Bowman, James P., Lester, and Laurence J., O'Toole, Jr., (1990) *Implementation Theory and Practice: Toward a Third Generation.* New York: HarperCollins.

Gunningham, N., R.A. Kagan and D. Thornton (2003) *Shades of Green: Business, Regulation and Environment.* Stanford: Stanford University Press.

Hargrove, Erwin (1975) *The Missing Link: The Study of the Implementation of Social Policy* Washington, D.C.: The Urban Institute.

Heinesen, E., S. C. Winter, I. R. Bøge and L. Husted (2004) *Kommunernes integrationsindsats og integrationssucces.* Copenhagen: AKF Forlag.

Heinrich, Carolyn and Laurence E. Lynn, Jr. (eds.) (2000) *Governance and Performance: New Perspectives.* Washington D.C.: Georgetown University Press.

Hill, Michael and Peter Hupe (2002) *Implementing Public Policy: Governance in Theory and Practice.* London: Sage Publications.

Hull, Christopher J. with Benny Hjern (1987) *Helping Small Firm Grow: An Implementation Perspective.* London: Croom Helm.

Jensen, T. P., S., Winter, J. Manniche, and P. D. Ørberg, with Thaulow I. (1991) *Indsatsen for langtidsledige – en undersøgelse af administration og effekt af arbejds- og uddannelsestilbud.* Copenhagen: AKF Forlag.

Kagan, Robert A. (1994) 'Regulatory Enforcement,' in David H. Roosenbloom and Richard D. Schwartz (eds.), *Handbook of Regulation and Administrative Law*. New York: Marcel Decker, pp. 383–422.

Keiser, L.R. and Soss, J. (1998) 'With Good Cause: Bureaucratic Discretion and the Politics of Child Support Enforcement.' *American Journal of Political Science*, 42 (4): 1133–56.

Kirst, M. and R. Jung (1982) 'The Utility of a Longitudinal Approach in Assessing Implementation: A Thirteen Year View of Title 1, ESEA,' in W. Williams, R. F. Elmore, J. S. Hall R. Jung, M. Kirst, S.A. MacManus, B.J. Narver, R.P. Nathan and R.K. Yin (eds.), *Studying Implementation*. Chatham N.J.: Chatham House Publ, pp. 119–48.

Lasswell, H.D. (1936) *Politics: Who Gets What, When, How*. New York: McGraw Hill.

Lester, James P. and Malcolm, L. Goggin (1998) 'Back to the Future: the Rediscovery of Implementation Studies,' *Policy Currents – Newsletter of the Public Policy Section of the American Political Science Association*, 8(3): 1–9.

Linder, Stephen H. and B. Guy, Peters (1989) 'Instruments of Government: Perceptions and Contexts,' *International Public Policy*, 9: 35–58.

Lipsky, Michael (1980) *Street-Level Bureaucracy: The Dilemmas of the Individual in Public Services*. New York: Russel Sage Foundation.

Lynn, Laurence E. Jr., Carolyn J. Heinrich and Carolyn J. Hill (2001) *Improving Governance: A New Logic for Empirical Research*. Washington D.C.: Georgetown University Press.

Matland, Richard E. (1995) 'Synthesizing the Implementation Literature: The Ambiguity-Conflict Model of Policy Implementation,' *Journal of Public Administration Research and Theory*, 5(2): 145–74.

May, Peter J. (1999) *Toward A Future Agenda for Implementation Research: A Panelist's Notes*. Prepared for the annual meeting of the Western Political Science Association in Seattle. Department of Political Science, University of Washington.

May, Peter J. (2003) 'Policy Design and Implementation' in B. Guy Peters and Jon Pierre (eds.), *Handbook of Public Administration*. London: Sage Publications, pp. 223–33.

May, Peter J. and Raymond J. Burby (1998) 'Making Sense Out of Regulatory Enforcement,' *Law and Policy*, 20: 157–82.

May, Peter J. and Søren Winter, (1999) 'Regulatory Enforcement and Compliance: Examining Danish Agro-Environmental Policy,' *Journal of Policy Analysis and Management*, 18(4): 625–51.

May, Peter J. and Søren Winter, (2000) 'Reconsidering Styles of Regulatory Enforcement: Patterns in Danish Agro-Environmental Inspection,' *Law & Policy*, 22 (2): 143–73.

May, Peter J. and Robert S. Wood (2003) 'At the Regulatory Frontlines: Inspectors' Enforcement Styles and Regulatory Compliance,' *Journal of Public Administration Research and Theory*, 13: 117–39.

Mazmanian, Daniel A. and Paul Sabatier, (eds.) (1981) *Effective Policy Implementation*. Lexington: Lexington Books.

Meier, Kenneth J. and Laurence J. O'Toole, Jr. (2004) 'Conceptual issues in Modeling and Measuring Management and Its Impact on Performance,' in P. Ingraham and L.E. Lynn, Jr., *The Art of Governance: Analyzing Management and Administration*. Washington DC: Georgetown University Press.

Meier, Kenneth J. and Laurence J. O'Toole, Jr. (2006) *Modeling Public Management: Empirical Analysis of the Management-Performance Nexus*. Paper for delivery at the X International Research Symposium on Public Management (IRSPM) in Glasgow, 10–12 April 2005. Texas A&M University and University of Georgia.

Meyers, Marcia K., Glaser, Bonnie, and MacDonald, Karin (1998) 'On the Front Lines of Welfare Delivery: Are Workers Implementing Policy Reforms?' *Journal of Policy Analysis and Management*, 17(1): 1–22.

Meyers, Marcia K. And Susan Vorsanger (2003) 'Street Level Bureaucrats and the Implementaion of Public Policy' in B. Guy Peters and Jon Pierre (eds.), *Handbook of Public Administration*. London: Sage Publications, pp. 245–55.

Moe, Terry M. (1984) 'The New Economics of Organization,' *American Journal of Political Science*, 28: 739–77.

Moe, Terry M. (1989) 'The Politics of Bureaucratic Structure,' in John E. Chubb and Paul E. Peterson (eds.), *Can the Government Govern?* Washington D.C.: Brookings.

Nielson, Vibeke Lehmann (2002) *Dialogens Pris. Uformelle spilleregler, ressourceasymmetri og forskelsbehandling i offentligt tilsyn*. Aarhus: Politica.

Nørgaard, Asbjørn S. and Thomas Pallesen (2003) 'Governing Structures and Structured Governing: Local Political Control of Public Services in Denmark.' *Journal of Public Administration Research and Theory* 13(4): 543–61.

O'Toole, Laurence J., Jr. (2000) 'Research on Policy Implementation: Assessment and Prospects,'

Journal of Public Administration Research and Theory, 10: 263–88.

O'Toole, Laurence J., Jr. (2003) 'Interorganizational Relations in Implementation' in B. Guy Peters and Jon Pierre (eds.), *Handbook of Public Administration*. London: Sage Publications, pp. 234–44.

O'Toole, Laurence J., Jr. and Robert S. Montjoy (1984) 'Interorganizational Policy Implementation: A Theoretical Perspective,' *Public Administration Review*, 44(6): 491–503.

Pressman, Jeffrey L. and Aron Wildavsky, (1973) *Implementation*. Berkeley: University of California Press.

Rossi, Peter H. and Howard E. Freeman, (1989) *Evaluation*, 4th ed. Newbury Park, London and New Delhi: Sage.

Sabatier, Paul A. (1986) 'Top-Down and Bottom-Up Approaches to Implementation Research: A Critical Analysis and Suggested Synthesis,' *Journal of Public Policy*, 6(1): 21–48.

Sabatier, Paul A. and Hank C. Jenkins-Smith, (eds.) (1993) *Policy Change and Learning: An Advocacy Coalition Approach*. Boulder: Westview Press.

Salamon, Lester M. (ed.) (2002) *The Tools of Government: A Guide to the New Governance*. New York: Oxford University Press.

Sætren, Harald (2005) 'Facts and Myths about Research on Public Policy Implementation: Out of Fashion, Allegedly Dead, But, still very much Alive and Relevant', *The Policy Studies Journal*, 33(4): 559–82.

Scholz, J. T. and Wei, F. H. (1986) 'Regulatory Enforcement in a Regulatory System,' *American Political Science Review*, 80: 1249–70.

Vedung, Evert (1995) 'Policy Instruments: Typologies and Theories,' in M. -L. Bemelmans-Videc, R. Rist and E. Vedung (eds.), *Policy Instruments and Evaluation*. New Brunswick, NJ: Transaction Books, pp. 21–58.

Williams, Walter and Richard F. Elmore, (eds.) (1976) *Social Program Implementation*. New York: Academic Press.

Winter, Søren (1986a) 'Studying the Implementation of Top-Down Policies From the Bottom-Up: Implementation of Danish Youth Employment Policy,' in Ray C. Rist (ed.), *Finding Work: Cross National Perspectives on Employment and Training*. New York: The Falmer Press, pp. 109–38.

Winter, Søren (1986b) 'How Policy-Making Affects Implementation: The Decentralization of the Danish Disablement Pension Administration,' *Scandinavian Political Studies*, 9: 361–85.

Winter, Søren (1990) 'Integrating Implementation Research,' in Dennis J. Palumbo and Donald J. Calista (eds.), *Implementation and the Policy Process*. New York: Greenwood Press, pp. 19–38.

Winter, Søren (1994) *Implementering og effektivitet*. Aarhus: Systime.

Winter, Søren (1999) 'New Directions for Implementation Research,' *Policy Currents – Newsletter of the Public Policy Section of the American Political Science Association*, 8(4): 1–5.

Winter, Søren C. (2002) *Explaining Street-Level Bureaucratic Behavior in Social and Regulatory Policies*. Paper prepared for the Annual Meeting of the American Political Science Association in Boston, 29 August–1 September 2002. Danish National Institute of Social Research Copenhagan.

Winter, Søren C. (2003) 'Implementation' in B. Guy Peters and Jon Pierre (eds.), *Handbook of Public Administration*. London: Sage Publications, pp. 205–11.

Winter, Søren C. (2003) *Political Control, Street-Level Bureaucrats and Information Asymmetry in Regulatory and Social Policies*. Paper prepared for the Annual Meeting of the Association for Policy Analysis and Management held in Washington D.C. 6–8 November 2003. Danish National Institute of Social Research, Copenhagen.

Winter, Søren C. and Peter J.May, (2001) 'Motivations for Compliance with Environmental Regulations,' *Journal of Policy Analysis and Management*, 20(4): 675–98.

Winter, Søren C. and Peter J. May, (2002) 'Information, Interests, and Environmental Regulation,' *Journal of Comparative Policy Analysis*, 4(2): 115–42.

Yin, Robert K. (1982) "Studying the Implementation of Public Programs," in W. Williams, R. F. Elmore, J. S. Hall, R. Jung, M. Kirst, S. A. MacManus, B. J. Narver, R.P. Nathan and R. K. Yin, *Studying Implementation: Methodological and Administrative Issues*. Chatham N.J.: Chatham House Publ., pp. 36–72.

Section Two

Substantive Policy Areas

9

Constitutions and Rights

JOHN UHR

INTRODUCTION

This chapter investigates the place of constitutions and rights in public policy, drawing together three elements of 'constitutions', 'rights' and 'public policy' in ways that might appear unusual to specialists in any one of these three fields. The aim here is to relate the three fields together for a generalist policy audience interested in the policy relevance of constitutions and rights. Predictably, this account will leave unsaid many things that specialist audiences interested in constitutions and rights would expect to find, especially at the level of detail preferred by those searching for scholarly authority on constitutions and rights. Instead, this chapter frames a discussion of the ways that constitutions themselves frame policy discussion of rights. Rights are in the foreground of our analysis because democratic systems of public policy generate much of their most heated and sustained dispute when dealing with rights policies, or the impact on rights-claims on public policy. Focusing then on rights, we present three overlapping stories about constitutions and rights in public policy, arranged to bring together political (rights), policy (constitutions) and personal (policy analysis of constitutions and rights) aspects of democratic governance.

Our first story is about the central value of rights of citizenship in democratic public policy. As a political theory, democracy proclaims the value of equality. But democratic regimes vary in the ways they apply values of equality to political life. Common to all democracies is a formal commitment to equal citizenship rights, yet in practice democracies vary in the range of rights they associate with citizenship. At the conservative end is a preference for equality of opportunity for all citizens, with minimal legal barriers to all the rights (or entitlements) of citizenship, of which the right to political participation is fundamental. At the liberal end is a preference for equality of outcome, one meaning of which is that all citizens share as equally as possible in the rights of citizenship, with each citizen entitled to equal political consideration regardless of other social or economic inequalities.[1] Rights of citizenship not only define *who* participates in the political process but also clarify *how* citizens participate: depending on precisely what range of rights are specified (e.g. rights to vote, rights to public speech, rights to form political parties) citizens can act on their rights or hold all or some of them in reserve for tomorrow's policy causes. Thus, on one hand, democratic policy processes assume some sort of determination of citizenship rights in order to generate a legitimate range of policy participants; and on the other hand, democratic policymaking also reviews, revises and reshapes the rights of citizenship as part of the ongoing struggle of political activity.

The second story is about how constitutions frame policy disputes over rights. Core rights like that of citizenship can be embedded in fundamental laws, such as a constitution, where they are protected against government temptations to tamper with them or reduce their scope. But other rights are creatures of statute, made by the legislature and able to be remade by a subsequent legislature. Many policy rights fit this model, as, for example, laws on social security which define entitlements, or laws on public health insurance which define rights of access to medical facilities and services. Constitutions can protect the rights of legislatures to make laws but they need not protect these legal rights from later alteration or modification by the same legislatures when dominated by different legislators. Still another class of rights derive from discretionary recognition by executive governments which, unless the legislature otherwise provides, can set their own terms and conditions on rights of access to many government programs. But rights extended by one government can be withdrawn by a successor government. A final class of rights are judge-made rights, where courts or tribunals can recognise rights flowing from ordinary laws or constitutions or even from such traditional sources as 'the common law' (meaning other judges, for the most part). How each or any of these rights-determination processes operates will depend on the precise constitutional circumstances of particular policy systems. The important point is that constitutions affect rights-*makers* (among the various branches of government) as well as rights-*takers* (among the citizenry).[2]

Time now to get personal. Our third story is about the story-teller, in this case the practitioner of public policy analysis. The study of public policy is not easily divorced from the private politics of the person undertaking the study. Few policy analysts admit to thoroughgoing neutrality in their work and this personal imprint is probably clearer in the study of rights-policies than other fields. Despite its theoretical ambitions, much of the best policy analysis is applied research, where analysts want to find practical solutions to policy problems. For the purposes of this chapter, we suggest that those telling the story are in some sense part of the story, drawn to the study because of their interest in improving policy processes and outcomes. This situation gives rise to a number of ethical issues about the rights and responsibilities of policy analysts, particularly when dealing with policy debates over equality rights. We can demonstrate that these ethical issues have been with the discipline of public policy analysis since its foundations by reviewing a neglected aspect of the well-known Friedrich-Finer debates from the 1940s over the democratic norms of administrative discretion in the policy process – Friedrich defending the 'inner checks' of public service professionalism against Finer's call for external political accountability.[3]

As we will show, this debate brings together old concerns for democratic rights and new concerns for policy analysis. Friedrich's case is part of a wider justification of the innovation of academic public policy analysis, designed to increase bureaucratic capacities for responsible policy work. For our purposes, Friedrich and Finer mark out two analytical perspectives on the study of rights in the policy process. Friedrich represents an applied and quite personal perspective, aiming for a practical impact through improvements in government capacities to promote citizen rights as beneficiaries of government programs. Finer represents a valuable and equally personal skepticism about the ambitions of public policy analysis, based on his conviction that democratic rights are best protected through political rather than administrative institutions, operating in the political process with its traditional constitutional safeguards against misguided rights enthusiasts, including well-intentioned policy activists within government. The work of most policy analysts falls between these two poles, but it is important to note this foundational debate over the rights and responsibilities of policy analysts in and out of government. Thus, this challenging topic of constitutions and rights impacts on 'our' rights as students of public policy as much as on the rights and wrongs of those policy actors whom we study.

Defining Constitutions and Rights

Constitutions are fundamental laws establishing 'the rules of the game' for the political process. Rights are guarantees about fair treatment: holders of rights expect governments to honour, for example, their obligations to give effect to the rights in question – traditional 'negative' rights such as those against 'unreasonable searches and seizures' (US Constitution, 4th amendment) or more modern 'positive' rights like a 'right to housing' (European Social Charter, act 31). In this sense, negative rights restrain governments; positive rights redirect governments. Rights are often protected in constitutions, sometimes in explicit charters or bills of rights protecting citizens against mistreatment by governments.

In the world of public policy, rights can also refer to entitlements to public services, sometimes claimed as a matter of moral and not simply legal right, as for example in claims by minorities or marginalized groups for special treatment (or more simply 'just deserts') to overcome past injustices. These moral claims become legal disputes over the terms and conditions of citizenship. Thus, the two issues of constitutions and rights come together in policy disputes over *citizenship*, which are amongst the most heated disputes in contemporary public policy.

The argument here is that the discipline of public policy itself arose from debates over relations between constitutions and rights. Over half a century ago, when public policy came together as an analytical endeavour, it promoted a big-government model of a rights-attentive bureaucracy using the new analytical strengths of policy analysis. This sparked considerable constitutional debate over the appropriateness of conferring policy responsibilities on public administrators. We argue that, in the subsequent half century, the original model of a *rights-attentive* policy bureaucracy (a model of welfare paternalism) has been overtaken by models of *rights-responsive* public agencies (models of more open civic activism) dealing more directly with policy activists. The different policy-making frameworks reflect different constitutional perspectives on the protection of rights in the democratic policy process.[4]

Think of constitutions as laws about laws: they are the articles of association for political communities, establishing the rules to determine who governs and how they govern. Constitutions are meant to bring stability to an organisation and are therefore often designed to withstand pressure for easy change by those in power. Constitutions are prior to governments which must work within the limits of their constitutional powers. Typically, constitutions allocate governing powers among the core institutions of state, frequently arranged according to a separation of powers among legislative, executive and judicial branches of government. Constitutions often specify a range of basic rights enjoyed by citizens which governments may not curtail – sometimes even specifying rights to services which governments must honour. Many additional rights are established through the policy process by specific pieces of legislation, such as rights to publicly-funded schooling or rights to subsidised medical services.[5] In many democratic regimes (e.g. the United States), the constitution is a formal written document deriving from a founding period of nation-building. Some democracies however (e.g. the United Kingdom), have a variety of traditional core legal documents, some old (such as the Bill of Rights of 1689) but others quite new (such as the European Convention on Human Rights), that serve constitutional purposes. Rights come in all shapes and sizes. For example, the constitution of the United Nations includes a Universal Declaration of Human Rights which itself articulates into international agreements on five types of rights: civil, political, economic, social and cultural.[6]

At one level, constitutions and rights comprise a basic field of policy attention, and this is clearly evident when new nations debate precisely what sort of constitution and what range of rights are appropriate for their circumstances. Older nations also revisit the policy design of constitutions and rights, often reforming either the explicit legal provisions or the spirit of the laws to bring out new policy possibilities from old legal instruments. Over the last half century we have also seen that nation-states can agree to submit to various international constitutions, either loose arrangements like the United Nations or tighter arrangements like the European Union. At whatever level, constitutions and rights can restrain the policy process when policy participants feel constrained to modify their conduct and their policy ambitions consistent with the legal norms associated with constitutions and rights. In this sense, constitutions and rights are thought to be 'off limits' to the policy process, providing the boundaries of acceptable policy for those engaged in the political contest over policy options. At yet another level, the democratic policy process is never really locked down by unchangeable legal constraints and is best understood as a work in progress, with few limits to the policy implications capable of being derived – by executive, legislative or judicial institutions – from constitutions and rights. Even in the absence of formal change, constitutions and rights are used in new ways to reflect changing community standards by policy actors across the system of government.[7]

This chapter provides an overview of debates over policy implications of constitutions and rights. Our theme is that rights are best considered as claims – particularly claims on government for policy recognition – and that different constitutional arrangements shape the political process for making and determining competing claims.[8] Drawing examples from each of the three levels just outlined, we provide a stylised account of democratic policy arguments, including arguments about the place of constitutions and rights in public policy analysis. We begin by recounting an episode from the foundations of the intellectual history of the modern academic discipline of public policy, revealing a fascinating scholarly debate over the place of constitutions and rights in the practice as well as the theory of public policy. We return to this foundational debate in the conclusion to this chapter, emphasising just how far the discipline has traveled in the days since its foundations, despite the apparently permanent uncertainty over constitutions and rights.

BACK TO THE BEGINNING

In many ways, the intellectual foundations of the academic study of public policy rest on rights or at least a view about how rights can be promoted through public policy. An example of this view is evident in the establishment of the first academic journal to be called *Public Policy*, co-edited by Carl Friedrich of Harvard.[9] This famous journal is the original predecessor of the current *Journal of Policy Analysis and Management*, which contains many international reports on policy debates over rights. The aim of the founding editors of *Public Policy* was to devise an analytical perspective on 'public action' that would overcome traditional barriers of specialisation among the social sciences and that most solid of all analytical barriers: the separation of theoretical studies of 'public action' from the practical applied studies common to the academic study of public administration. Their aim was to bring greater cohesion to 'the analysis of the conditions which determine the success or failure of whatever modern government undertakes'.[10] The decade leading up to this innovation had seen a revolution in 'whatever government undertakes', with social-democracy modifying earlier liberal-democracy. The New Deal in the US had overhauled the regulation of the political economy of the world's most wealthy industrial nation-state, ushering in new forms of state intervention in what had traditionally been unregulated aspects of social life. A welfare state had arisen, with more generous social protection for employees and stricter regulation of the social obligations of private enterprise. Friedrich argued in his own contribution to the first issue of *Public Policy* in 1940 that the new discipline of public policy was an attempt to modernise the study of public administration by bringing a wider range of social sciences to the analysis of public decision-making.[11] The emergence of this new journal marked the arrival of the larger academic enterprise of public policy as a multidisciplinary effort to marshall social science for the purposes of better government, based on more intelligent use of evidence and argument by government officials.

Looking back now and applying contemporary terms, we can see here the beginnings of evidence-based policy-making. What has not been properly appreciated is the debated place of constitutions and rights in this novel public policy orientation. We can take Friedrich as an exemplary exponent of the new discipline. His foundational article in the initial issue of *Public Policy* is something of an intellectual charter for the emerging discipline of public policy. His theme was the importance of 'administrative responsibility', by which he meant the constructive contribution to policy-making made by those holding administrative as distinct from political power. When Friedrich's article is seen against his contribution to the famous Friedrich-Finer debates over the competing forms of democratic accountability,[12] we can see the importance of his reordering of traditional relationships between constitutions and rights. Traditional approaches to the policy process rest on distinctions between a political realm of 'policy' and a non-political realm of 'administration'. In Finer's hands, this older approach is associated with a larger political theory about constitutional government, with elected politicians responsible to voters for public policy and unelected officials responsible – primarily to elected politicians – for public administration. Friedrich distanced himself from this traditional constitutionalism by blurring these distinctions in ways that left unelected public officials with substantial discretionary power over policy as well as administration. This model of social democracy had great potential for official regulation of industry as well as welfare. Friedrich's aim was not to take power away from elected politicians but to recognize the inevitable power of government bureaucrats in modern democratic systems and to try to devise ways in which that power can be increased to serve democratic policy ends – including the protection of economic, social and political rights.

Traditional approaches held that administrative power ideally serves policy ends by confining itself to questions of policy implementation, leaving policy-making in the hands of elected politicians who are directly responsible

to the people. The traditional constitutional arrangement was one where the undoubted power of state officials was held in check by their accountability to elected representatives of the people. With the emergence of the public policy movement, this constitutional arrangement, with its neat divisions between elected and unelected officials, and between policy and administration, is challenged in the name of a more effective and responsible form of democratic government. In Friedrich's orientation, the new discipline of public policy will not only increase the analytical power of state bureaucracy but also increase its capacity to act as a responsive institution of democratic government. Friedrich locates this version of democratic accountability in the professional sense of public service responsibility cultivated by public officials as a condition of their discretionary powers. These powers are partly policy, partly administrative – just as the emerging science of public policy seeks to train officials in the new skills of policy analysis as well as the old skills of administrative competence.

Friedrich's championing of public policy analysis had major implications for the constitution of rights. A state bureaucracy empowered by new forms of public policy analysis could act as a *responsive* instrument of government services by satisfying public *rights* to services in ways not contemplated by traditionally unresponsive state bureaucracies. In Friedrich's formulation, this was a vision of the welfare state, with more than a hint of policy paternalism. The rights-attentive bureaucracy was not envisaged as directly responsive to citizens, as with later developments we will examine below. Instead, in this foundational era of public policy, the welfare bureaucracy was seen as taking responsibility itself for the identification of a rights agenda, and of being responsive to the needs, if not the actual claims, of rights to government services.

As Finer suspected, this new model of responsiveness departed from many of the traditional norms of responsiveness to governing authorities. By contrast, Friedrich's confidence reflected the growing faith in policy analysis: he shared the hope that the innovation of policy analysis would strengthen responsible government by bringing new degrees of responsiveness to administrators by helping them meet and be responsive to the dual standard of what he termed 'technical knowledge and popular sentiment'. Thus, Friedrich argued that 'administrative responsibility' could greatly improve existing forms of responsible government by *supplementing* existing institutions of political responsibility. Finer responded by arguing that in practice these innovations would *displace* rather than supplement existing constitutional safeguards, including the political protection of rights jeopardised by incompetent, however well-meaning, state bureaucracies, armed with Friedrich's misguided 'positive ideal of social service' with its platitudes about 'responsiveness to commonly felt needs and wants'.[13] Finer feared that the 'social service' rights agenda promoted by Friedrich would undermine conventional political rights which were better protected by elected representatives acting openly in the political process – as distinct from the protection of bureaucrats acting bureaucratically.

This debate at the foundations of academic public policy tells a larger tale. The two constitutional orientations illustrate contrasting policies on rights: Friedrich wants government to *promote* rights through the provision of social services; Finer wants government to *protect* rights through the rule of law. The exemplary proponent of public policy is relaxed about traditional constitutional structures (and indeed traditional constitutional strictures) because of the countervailing concern with promoting rights. The traditionalist is wary of a rights-attentive bureaucracy because it might undermine constitutional restraints on the use of political powers by non-political institutions, thereby threatening hard-earned rights of self-government.

But, perhaps most importantly, both orientations are compatible with the constitutional forms of modern democracy, which are quite permissive about acceptable relationships between constitutions and rights. Most of the time, democratic policy-making accepts as given the prevailing constitutional arrangements and operates within inherited policy processes. But occasionally there can be quite significant shifts

in expectations about appropriate policy forms, and the emergence of the public policy movement illustrates one such moment. In his own way, Friedrich is quite a revolutionary, working to reconstitute the role of administrative officials and to rewrite the constitution of public decision-making to confer greater policy responsibility on administrative officials. Despite Finer's protests over the unconstitutional nature of bureaucratic policy discretion, the world has moved in Friedrich's direction. Elected politicians in newly-formed governments typically try to confine this bureaucratic discretion to policy implementation as distinct from policy determination. Yet, even under quite conservative governments, the trend has been to subject more and more rights to the regulatory power of public administrators, in keeping with Friedrich's original hopes for a rights-attentive bureaucracy – now, more than in his era, mixed between core institutions of the state and contracted service providers.

A MODEL OF THE CONSTITUTION OF RIGHTS

Where can we test the utility of our approach to constitutions and rights? We could remain aloft at the level of theory, or we could assemble a mass of comparative data on democratic policy processes, or we could select a case study of democratic polity which illustrates many of the tensions we have identified. Our preference is for the third approach. Canada is a good example of a democratic polity with a policy process increasingly emphasising rights discourse. It is one of the few nations to receive supportive reports from such international rights bodies as Human Rights Watch and Amnesty International. More to our point, Canada shows how even Westminster-derived parliamentary systems, with traditionally slight interest in rights policies, can reshape their public policy processes around rights claims. For our purposes, Canada stands out as a useful case study of a contemporary policy system because of the convergence of so many of the most pressing rights-claimants in modern democratic countries – a range of indigenous peoples, a bicultural social tradition with two settler peoples (French and English), intergovernmental complexity resulting from well over a century of experience of federal government, widely diverse ethnic populations from extensive recent immigration, and multiple perspectives on the national government's internationally pioneering programmes of multiculturalism.

As part of this remarkable mosaic of diverse identities, Canadian political values responded positively to the prospect of a formal bill of rights to lay down some core principles of fair treatment of citizens by governments. What began as a parliamentary 'bill of rights' statute in 1960 gathered institutional strength to emerge as the national *Charter of Rights and Freedoms* in 1982, resulting in an increased policy role for the Canadian courts as a central forum for resolving policy conflicts over competing rights. Some of the rights claims have been traditional civil liberties claims against government interference with the liberties of citizens (e.g. restrictions on police evidence in court proceedings). Others have been more contemporary equality claims against government failures to provide services to discriminated groups (e.g. prisoners' voting rights). These two categories of claims illustrate the broad range of rights preoccupations: at one end, 'negative' rights to protect individual liberties held in common by all citizens and, at the other end, 'positive' rights to promote equality for neglected groups who have been denied access to services necessary for full citizenship. Both ends address *citizenship* claims, but they do so in different ways with different balances of the two core values of liberty and equality.

One particular relevance of the Canadian story is that it shows how the formal provisions of a nation's constitution can be interpreted by different rights-claimants in different ways, sometimes elevating individual liberties over equality for neglected groups and at other times elevating group equality over individual liberties. Constitutions manage the policy process through their allocations of powers and responsibilities among legislative, executive and judicial institutions. The Canadian

policy process has been transformed by the court's growing policy arbitration of interest group conflicts that have become congested in the other two branches of government. The 1982 *Charter of Rights and Freedoms* is not so much the cause of this transformation as the vehicle driven by the real cause – policy activists who have seized on the new policy potential of the courts to settle rights-claims unresolved by legislatures and governments. We acknowledge, of course, that in other nations with no such explicit rights-charter, the judiciary can also get involved in what can be called 'judicial policy-making' by discovering implied if not explicit constitutional rights that governments must respect: the high courts of France, Israel and Australia are all examples.[14] But we see the Canadian policy process as nicely illustrating contemporary democratic policy-making writ-large, with the policy process charged with competing claims against government, at one point demanding the courts to restrain government from undue interference with liberties and at another point demanding the courts to direct governments to interfere to guarantee equality of opportunity for neglected groups. We see the Canadian policy process as containing an armoury of arguments over relationships between constitutions and rights – with a growing case load of public policy dispute over such contemporary challenges over rules relating to disability, discrimination, employment, family status, hate propaganda, race, religious and sex discrimination, and sexual harassment and sexual orientation.

MODELLING RIGHTS DETERMINATION

We will return to the Canadian story below, when trying to identify parallels with the story in other polities. But before we enter the thicket of rights and wrongs, we will try to clarify the general nature of rights resolution in the policy process. Our contention that rights can be usefully understood as claims and analysed by reference to 'claims systems' draws on Peattie and Rein who in turn draw on the clash of rights associated with feminism and the women's movement.[15] Their influential study focuses largely on policy battles in the United States, where so much of public policy is argued out by reference to the right to 'equal protection of the laws' contained in the US Constitution. This constitutional provision is itself a good example of rights as claims, since it is contained in an amendment to the Constitution that arose from the Civil War struggles over slavery. This provision reflects the commitment to equal rights of citizenship for blacks and whites that only came about because of the military victory of the Union over the secessionist South. In this case, tensions within the 'claims system' could only be resolved through a momentous civil war. In extreme cases, might *can* bring right. But extreme cases also illustrate the might that suppresses right: in this case, the might of social groups with vested interests in slavery. The right to 'equal protection of the laws' sounds quite basic but it was denied to substantial racial minorities by established social groups, who benefited economically from slavery. The struggle to right the wrongs of slavery is an awesome example of the war-like potential of the policy process in modernising nations, and of the lengths that democratising systems may have to go to resolve disputed claims about central values of citizenship.

The civil war over equal citizenship rights is a good example because it illustrates a default position not uncommon in democratic societies, where competing social interests have fundamentally opposed views on rights-claims, even to the point that a head of government like President Lincoln understood that his constitutional duty was not simply to erase slavery but to overturn what we might now term judicial policy-making – which had justified slavery by rejecting minority claims to equal rights. Not for nothing does Bernard Crick use the drama of Lincoln's presidency as his primary example of democratic policy-making.[16] To oversimplify: opponents of slavery claimed that the US constitutional order recognised the rights of African–Americans as citizens; proponents of slavery countered that there were no such constitutional rights. Only

in the wake of the military defeat of the slave states did the claims of the opponents of slavery emerge victorious. But, even then, reformers had to institute a formal constitutional amendment to put their preferred policy beyond legal doubt.

Consistent with this, Peattie and Rein acknowledge that their approach to 'claims systems' puts more emphasis on politics than on law. Legal battles emerge as means towards political ends, with rights established only where rights proponents win the political battle over the agenda of public policy. The claims Peattie and Rein deal with are claims on government – articulated by groups demanding provision of government services 'as of right'.[17] Claims tend to develop through a structured process of steadily increasing demand. Claims on government tend to begin as pleas for assistance, turn into requests for closer consideration, before becoming demands for urgent action. We can think of this as a three-fold process involving all three branches of government, beginning with routine requests to the executive government to modify aspects of public administration, followed if necessary by political pressure on legislators to write new laws to authorise preferred practices, and finally followed if necessary by legal challenges against the government to compel compliance with the claimed right.

Claims systems vary, with the constitutional order standing out as the largest domain within modern nation-states. As we argue later, many contemporary rights disputes involve claims on international authorities (such as the human rights committee of the United Nations) to take action against recalcitrant national governments. But within the nation-state, the battle is typically over domestic public policy priorities, which can be won even in the face of determined opposition by executive government. Although victory in this battle has enormous implications for governments, the claimants know that victory can come through the acceptance of their claim by legislative or judicial institutions as much as by the institutions of executive government. Each branch of government has its distinctive claims-system. At the heart of government is the executive administration with its 'realm of interpretation', causing claims advocates to appeal to revised 'interpretations' of the rules and regulations administered by the offending government.[18] As alternatives, claims advocates can pursue their cause through the courts in order to obtain a definitive legal interpretation in favour of their rights; or they can mobilise support so that the political assembly can pass new legislation to superimpose a favourable definition over less sympathetic interpretations from either executive government or the judiciary.

Rights-advocates often present rights as non-negotiable. But even this strategy is part of a larger process of social negotiation over public policy priorities. Established rights might appear to be part of the natural order of social arrangements, but almost every right had at some point to be fought for through a social process of 'requests, bids, bargins or negotiation'. As Peattie and Rein map this out, we see that competing interests engage in political competition to 'demand, extract, request, enforce their bids for resources'. Calling this 'political' might seem to suggest that rights can be reduced to the social and economic interests characteristic of their political advocates. While partly true, such a view misleads us by taking attention away from the important role of ideas and argument in the policy process.

Rights policies are classic expressions of the power of ideas in the public sphere. Peattie and Rein argue that rights policies illustrate the neglected importance of 'a struggle of ideas, a struggle over the extension and application of various principles or claims rationales' in the policy process. They contend that 'one of the basic elements in the claiming process is an intellectual one: a definitional element', usually involving the 'development of a new political language' as illustrated by the deliberately confrontational rhetoric about politics of the personal associated with the women's movement. Finally, it is useful to remember that rights-claims do not necessarily reflect economic or material interests on the pattern of so much traditional interest-group politics. As Peattie and Rein note: 'purposes create interests as well as interests driving purposes'. Many rights-advocates justify their claims in terms of benefits to the general interest in equal citizenship rights rather than to neglected sectoral interests. While it is true that many conventional sectoral interests disguise their specific interests under the rhetorical banner of general interests, it is a distinctive feature of many rights-claimants that they shape the policy process to focus on arguments about citizenship and 'the idea of the public interest' with claims based on 'a rationale of collective purpose'.[19]

RIGHTS AND POLICY-MAKING

We return now to the Canadian story, hoping to identify links to developments in the policy process of other nations. No one nation stands out as exemplifying contemporary practices in public policy. But Canada is relevant because over recent years it has generated a remarkable public dialogue over the competing norms and principles of democratic policy-making. Our interest is not so much in what Canadian policy actors have done as what they have said about what needs to be done, including what needs to be done about aligning constitutions and rights.

The 1982 Canadian *Charter of Rights and Freedoms* begins by declaring that its rights of citizenship are subject to only those 'reasonable limits' which can be 'demonstrably justified in a free and democratic society'.[20] This clearly deals the courts into the policy process as the arbiters of claims to 'reasonable limits' by the two other political branches of government: parliament and the political executive. But, just as importantly, the Charter reinforces the power of the courts by providing a lengthy list of rights with which Canadians may expect governments to comply. The Charter defines a set of so-called 'fundamental freedoms', dealing with free thought, free expression and freedom of assembly. These fundamental freedoms are then followed by an extensive articulation of more specific rights – such as a list of core 'democratic rights' (primarily the right to vote), 'mobility rights' (very relevant to a federal polity with a history of division and separatism), 'legal rights' (eight detailed provisions relating to criminal procedure), 'equality rights' (a combustible combination of anti-discrimination and affirmative action declarations), and finally language and language-of-choice education rights (at least for French and English speakers). The traditional 'treaty rights' of Aboriginal peoples of Canada are separately identified (including new rights to participate in constitutional change processes).

This 1982 change to the Constitution of Canada has given the Supreme Court of Canada a prominent role in arbitrating rights-claims against Canadian governments. Policy activists have used the new rights system to 'constitutionalize policy preferences that could not easily be achieved through the legislative process'.[21] In the first 16 years of Charter jurisdiction, the Court struck down nearly 60 federal and provincial statutes as incompatible with the new Charter. While the Court might not have become a policy-making body, the courtroom has become 'a policy-making arena' because policymaking has become 'judicialized, legalized, and conducted in the vernacular of rights talk…'.[22] We repeat our warning that this new policy-making arena is one that, in principle, can benefit the rights of social establishments as much as the rights of the socially excluded. It all depends on the policy responsibilities and interpretative legal doctrines entertained by the courts themselves. What one generation of judicial officers might favour can be overturned by a succeeding generation. Canadian commentators have noted that contemporary rights-advocates have turned to the courts in ways that are reminiscent of the strategy of earlier 'business elites … (who) used litigation to slow the advent of the emergent welfare state'. This potential variability in judicial policy-making postures has provoked renewed attention in Canada to the policy implications of appointments processes for judges, with hopes that greater public transparency might weaken the power of serving governments to stack courts with policy favourites.[23]

We note two aspects of this new rights-responsive policy process. First, we should not exaggerate the apparent victory of leftish causes in using judicial review to promote their preferred policy agenda. Constitutions can just as easily favour rightist causes, as shown in earlier eras, and not only in Canada, when conservative forces used prevailing legal doctrines of 'judicial restraint' to reinforce a conservative hegemony. To use the old adage: the constitution is what the judges say it is. Therefore, what matters is not so much the internal *text* of the constitution as the external political *context* of judicial interpretation, including the evolution of interpretative doctrines about judicial policy-making. There are always powerful entrenched interests favouring judicial restraint and always vocal outsiders favouring judicial activism. The power of the judiciary is just as crucial to policy outcomes in eras of restraint, when courts decide not to intervene, as in eras of activism, when courts decide to intervene. That is, non-decisions (i.e. decisions *not* to intervene) are decisions too. Second, and building on this, we note that the new rights system in Canada has not established a consensus about preferred policy rights or preferred policy outcomes. Even those policy activists favouring judicial intervention are divided about the policy priorities deserving judicial intervention. For instance, the rights-camps of negative liberty (e.g. civil libertarians) and positive equality (e.g. feminists) continue, as before, to struggle against one another – but now before the courts rather than before the legislature.

An example of the new policy activism comes from the Charter's equality rights (s15), where policy activists opposed to various forms of systemic discrimination – 'women, visible and religious minorities, the mentally and physically disabled, and the elderly', together with gays and non-citizens – have pursued 'judicial revision of legislative decision-making'.[24] Unlike civil libertarian activists, these new social movement activists have sought more rather than less government regulation of social affairs, with governments being called on to resolve inequalities of access to an increasing range of private services (e.g. employment terms and conditions) as well as public services (e.g. employment training).

Where is 'the government' in the larger story of rights struggle? Are governments simply the plaything of judicial arbitration of contested rights? Public policy is often effected by governments who pride themselves on getting ahead of the prevailing political demands. Particularly in the area of citizenship rights, governments can aspire to policy leadership that puts demands on themselves shaping rather than reflecting rights-claims. We conclude this section by noting that governments can shape social movements as much as social movements can shape governments. Again, Canada is a good example. For instance, it was only after the Trudeau government in 1971 proclaimed a national policy on multiculturalism that government bureaucracies actively engaged in programmes of 'social animation' to bring into existence funded bodies representing relevant ethnic groups.[25] This is a case of how the family of identity rights, to take but one prominent example, can be promoted by executive governments exercising a form of policy leadership that owes very little to interest group advocacy. But, once formed, rights groups can take publicly-funded government programmes off in directions unanticipated or even undesired by sponsoring governments – possibly playing off courts against the other branches of government. The larger point is that, despite our focus here on rights policy as determined by the courts, rights-claimants are 'often as much the result of key public policies as the source of those policies'.[26] It is important to remember that governments *can* govern and that a vital part of democratic governing is setting and seeding the policy agenda – if other governing institutions will permit, an issue to which we now turn.

Institutional implications

The Canadian experience has fed into wider international policy debate over the appropriateness of judicial policy-making to norms of democratic governance.[27] We have discussed tensions between political executives and the courts and here we should note a growing international debate over theories and practices of

policy 'dialogue' between governments and courts. This debate reflects widespread uneasiness over the political powers exercised by the courts in the policy process, with various reform options to limit the policy clout of courts to 'dialogue' about, rather than determination of, policy outcomes. An example of this option is the new role of British courts in 'declaring' incompatibility of suspect British legislation with the European Human Rights Convention, thereby calling on government to participate in public 'dialogue' with courts over the necessity for the suspect legislation. In this model, final power rests with executive government to manage the process of resolving instances of 'incompatibility'. This example of course relates to judicial views about incompatible legislative schemes rather than public policies as such. But it is held out as an example of judicial restraint worthy of consideration by policy analysts. Another example is the recently established Bill of Rights in the Australian Capital Territory, which is Australia's first statutory bill of rights: one which allows the legislature to override court 'declarations', but only after a process of deliberate public 'dialogue' between governments and courts over the policy merits of the suspect legislation.[28] These examples illustrate in quite practical ways the potential for courts to operate as mediating rather than determinative institutions, with their policy powers limited to generating greater public accountability (or better, perhaps, 'answerability') in the policy process.

The 'dialogue' metaphor arose from US commentary on judicial review but has now expanded around the globe to inform wider debates about overlaps between the policy process and the judicial process. Concepts of 'dialogue' circulate as ways that supporters of judicial review of government action can describe the ideal form of judicial participation in the policy process. This ideal distinguishes the legal role of courts in exercising judicial power from the more limited role of courts in 'dialoguing' with the political branches of government about the legal form of policy programmes. Critics of judicial review fear that 'dialogue' does not properly describe the considerable policy impacts that disputes about legal form can have on the substance of public policy. There are exaggerated positions at both ends of this debate over constitutions and rights: supporters of the rights of elected representatives to determine policy priorities tend to revive the old policy/administration distinction to limit the policy reach of judicial institutions; and advocates of 'dialogue' claim that judicial power can improve the policy process by drawing governments into public debate over the public merits of suspect policy initiatives. There is no agreed best answer, in part because the range of permissible forms of democratic government is broader than the range of arguments about the relative merits of governments and courts in determining the rights of those affected by public policies.[29]

Three aspects of this growing international debate are of importance here. First, the focus on 'dialogue' highlights the extent to which rights disputes depend for their resolution on extensive public discussion rather than simply decisive action by governments or courts. The effectiveness of most public policies is increased when they have widespread community support, and elected governments in particular have leadership roles in trying to build public support for policy initiatives. Democratic governments rest on the consent of the governed, and one of the important rights of democratic citizens is the right to informed consent. Public authorities have to respect the community's reasonable expectation that their consent should, ideally at least, not be forthcoming until those in authority have convinced them of the merits of policy proposals. Elections are one but not the only means through which informed consent can be tested. Open debate and public argument over policy options are just as important a means of testing informed consent. This rolls into wider consideration of features of deliberative democracy (such as opportunities for oppositions to question and scrutinise governing parties under fair and impartial procedures accepted by both) that might be used to reshape the everyday practices of democratic policy-making to bring about more evenhanded consideration of competing policy perspectives.[30]

Second, the debate over 'dialogue' revives older constitutional debates over separation of powers. There is little scope for serious discussion of policy rights in the absence of discussion of the web of political powers used to manage rights claims. The competing perspectives on the relative balance of governments and courts draw on deeper, more fundamental principles of constitutional design. This is recognised by those participants who acknowledge the place of 'liberal constitutionalism' in conditioning the relationships among different constitutional organs which are not simply autonomous in their choice of public roles.[31] Constitutional doctrines about the separation of powers provide the scholarly backdrop against which the 'dialogue' debate is acted out. But, when trying to locate the rights at issue in this policy debate, much can be gained by an explicit examination of the range of ways that governmental powers can be constitutionally separated and re-arranged. The 'executive government' and the 'courts' are not the only constitutional actors: formally one has to add the 'legislature' and more substantively one has to add 'the people' on whose consent legitimate democratic government ideally rests. Just as the people have rights recognised by democratic constitutions, so too the three branches of government have constitutional rights: the legislature exercising legislative powers, executive governments exercising executive powers and the judiciary exercising judicial powers. As we have seen, rights-claims can be complaints about powers or pleas for more powers. Rights-claims can never be resolved or properly managed without close attention to the constitution of public powers framing them.

Third, the 'dialogue' debate raises questions about which particular institutions are best placed to participate in public argument over contested rights and related policy priorities. We suspect that the legislature is usually honoured in a tokenistic fashion. Opponents of judicial activism advance arguments in defence of the rights of elected political assemblies to determine policy priorities. But, more often than not, they really mean to defend the rights of the political executive to use their party-political influence to manage legislative assemblies along policy pathways determined by the executive. In this scheme, the legislative assembly plays its part by granting formal constitutional approval to policy choices originating in the political executive.[32] This confidence in the ability of executives to mobilise the power of legislative assemblies reflects a very traditional orientation to parliamentary politics that is increasingly at odds with the institutional independence open to parliaments. Our point here is that the 'dialogue' metaphor suggests two players, but this is at odds with the underlying dynamics of the three separated constitutional powers common in modern democratic systems. Our conclusion is that 'dialogue' debates will be unproductive if they persist in ignoring the potential for independent action by legislatures as well as political executives and courts. Or, to put this otherwise: rights at risk in democratic policy systems can be addressed from three rather than two institutional perspectives, as students of presidential systems of government have long appreciated.

RECONSTITUTING RIGHTS

One final issue merits attention. We argued that the public policy movement was originally associated with a *rights-attentive* policy agenda, ideally implemented by a responsible bureaucracy armed with the new skills of policy analysis. Building on the Friedrich formulation, we suggested that this could be seen as a form of policy paternalism, in that the rights agenda in question was one developed by governing officialdom and not, as in the Canadian examples discussed above, frequently by governing bodies in direct response to rights-claims articulated by policy activists. We have termed this later approach a *rights-responsive* model. There is an interesting contrast here between an original public policy model of administrative obligations to keep alive the operational requirements of citizenship, and later public policy models of government obligations to take note of changing citizenship requirements as determined by courts and other adjudicating bodies. Both

seek to develop citizenship but in quite different ways, reflecting contrasting interpretations of democratic rights.

There are also models in between these two alternatives, as this section attempts to show. One of the most prominent is the rise of government-sponsored charters of responsibilities and obligations to balance the rights orientation favoured by so many policy activists. A good example is the framework of 'mutual obligation' introduced by the conservative Howard government elected in Australia in 1996. This framework was devised to modify the notion of welfare rights advocated by many policy activists and adopted by beneficiaries of public services. The concept of mutual obligation was intended to establish a contract of sorts between service providers and service consumers on the basis that consumers had obligations to payback or return some of the investment that 'the community' was investing in them. This payback might be something as simple as the voluntary acceptance of terms and conditions of reporting work-availability while on income assistance; or it might be more onerous acceptance of training programmes to get beneficiaries job-ready and off welfare at the earliest opportunity. The policy framework was not a throwback to earlier eras when welfare was considered a privilege. The innovation was intended to replace the notion of rights to welfare with a more balanced picture of rights and responsibilities – or 'obligations' to use the more formal language of the Howard government.

Mutual obligation is a conservative response to the call for welfare rights. As a policy construct about reciprocity, it is not opposed to welfare as such and draws explicitly on progressive policy analysis of mutual exchange arrangements.[33] This policy construct explicitly addresses 'participation support' rather than 'welfare support'. This reflects the policy aim, which is to get individuals participating actively in society rather than passively as recipients of welfare – and as responsible citizens returning services to the community assisting them. The language of responsibility does not replace that of rights but balances it: 'The right to support should be balanced by a responsibility to the community that provides that support'.[34] The Howard policy framework is flexible enough to justify liberal or conservative experiments in welfare reform: declarations to the effect that 'the whole of society has an obligation to provide assistance to those in most need' can justify the 'leadership role of government' in taxing for welfare; or it can justify government deferring to private forms of welfare assistance. An example of the deferment option flows from the application of mutual obligations to immigrants, who can expect to be 'subject to the two-year waiting period for eligibility for income support'.[35]

The Howard government framework targets the responsibilities of employers as well as employees: businesses must 'look beyond the interests of their shareholders or profit margin'. The stated policy is to ensure that individual and corporate citizens 'behave in ways that are not purely self-centred'. The administrative concept of mutual obligation is 'underpinned by the concept of social obligations' which refers to the 'web of mutual expectations' holding society together. But even a free society requires government leadership. The power of compulsion is often necessary to enforce these mutual obligations, with government working with and, in some cases, on businesses and individuals to participate as full citizens, including honouring obligations to act in socially responsible ways by providing access to jobs (business obligations) and being available for training schemes (individual obligations). Government regulation is required to help some individuals 'achieve their own goals for participation and self-reliance'.[36]

This approach is shared by other conservative governments, such as the Bush administration, and to a not inconsiderable extent by the former Clinton administration. How does this international turn to concepts of responsibility relate to the original 'administrative responsibility' framework of Friedrich? We have suggested that Friedrich's model was one of policy paternalism and there are clearly many elements in common with the responsibility model of mutual obligation. In different ways, both models rests on concepts of citizenship. Friedrich looked to intelligent government, wielding the power of policy analysis, to

bring citizenship to deserving communities. Half a century later, the skills of policy analysis are more generally available, illustrated in the reliance of the conservative Howard government for its rethink of welfare rights on sympathetic elements of the 'not for profit' sector – initially as policy advisors and later as programme providers.

There is a link here between contemporary conservatism and the fears of Finer reported on earlier in our chapter: they are comparable small-government perspectives with a distrust of bureaucracy and of welfare-dependency. We began this chapter with a review of the rise of public policy analysis, noting early fears that increased analytical competence at the disposal of government might harm rather than help the cause of rights.

Taking Finer as our exemplary sceptic, we encountered an explicit constitutional argument against rights-attentive policy analysis performed by unelected public administrators. This was not so much an argument against the emerging discipline of public policy as a restatement of the policy/administration distinction designed to protect the integrity of elective politics against misplaced enthusiasm for bureaucratic rule. Seen in another light, this was an early version of the constitutional case for limited government, with political checks and balances against the regulatory rule of big government.

Finer was understandably wary about rights: his preference for an older constitutionalism with norms of limited government is consistent with much of contemporary public choice theory, which is suspicious of rights that are not embedded in a constitutional framework, with checks and balances against discretionary rights managed by executive government.[37] Rights claims are raised by every politically-ambitious interest group and Finer's scepticism is still valuable in reminding us of the merit of assessing rights-claims against explicit criteria of public choice – constitutionally understood in terms of duly processed popular consent, as distinct from bureaucratically processed government consent. Claims of rights bring with them risks of capture of the political system by rights-advocates in and out of government, and Finer's voice remains relevant when trying to get some distance from government sympathy with rights policies.

CONCLUSION

Recapitulating the main themes in this account of constitutions and rights, we can summarise the three related stories presented here.

(1) Rights are claims on government for policy initiatives to benefit particular classes or groups of individuals. We highlight the importance of one particular set of rights – equality rights – for modern democracy. Most rights claims call for equality of access to policy benefits for traditionally excluded or marginalised classes or groups. We argue that many of the most prominent and enduring policy disputes in democratic systems arise from disagreement over the most fundamental of all of policy applications of equality rights – the rights of citizenship.

(2) We argue that constitutions are important devices for framing the public management of policy disagreement: sometimes by clarifying the meaning of core rights, but more generally by clarifying the procedures for resolving policy disputes, including disputes over rights policies. But even constitutions can become the object of policy disputes, with contest over the appropriate policy roles of executive, legislative and especially judicial institutions.

(3) Finally, we argue that debate over relationships between rights and constitutions can be traced back to the origins of public policy analysis, where Friedrich and Finer mapped out contrasting approaches that help plot the range of analytical possibilities open to contemporary policy analysts interested in the place of constitutions and rights in democratic policy processes. Few policy analysts fit either extreme position; most fall between the two poles; but many move between the two positions, depending on the policies under analysis.

In conclusion, we can identify three main implications of these related stories. First, our argument has been that the policy process in modern democratic regimes involves political contests over the rights of citizenship. All politics involves contests over benefits that governments can confer, and often this is part of a power struggle between competing elites occurring behind the scenes. The secrecy of such power struggles is one indication that they are usually more concerned with *interests* than *rights*. Rights as we present them here derive from norms of citizenship grounded in a set of constitutional principles which are, ideally at least, acknowledged by all citizens. By contrast, interests are inevitably partial, reflecting a narrower range of considerations that cut across the common field of citizenship. This is not to suggest that democratic nations will or should display a social consensus on all or indeed any policies, including rights policies. Democracy involves disagreement, including disagreement about the core value of equality. Interpretations of democratic citizenship are interpretations of equality and of its political and policy implications. At the level of political theory, interpretations differ according to philosophical orientation; and at the level of political practice, interpretations differ from nation to nation and across nations according to political and policy preferences.

Second, we have argued that constitutions are valuable to public policy because they format, or structure or, as the name suggests, 'constitute' the policy process so that rights-claims are considered as fairly as possible. There is no one preferred model of a democratic constitution. Some modern democracies, like the United Kingdom, have no single constitutional text or 'purpose-built' foundational document. Regardless, they manage to generate and regulate a healthy policy process through a variety of other means, attributing privileged status to some historic declarations of public right, such as the Bill of Rights of 1689. Other democratic nations have written constitutions sourced from their nation-building period. In some cases, the text of these documents is unchanged from that founding period, with little or no explicit recognition of equality rights. In other cases, written constitutions are relatively flexible by virtue of amending processes, enabling changing community standards to shape the ongoing development of the original set of constitutional provisions. In still other cases, one or more of the core constitutional institutions can use its power (as in the case of the judiciary) to revise the authorised interpretation of provisions; or (as in the case of executive governments) to reshape administrative practices; or (as in the of legislatures) to fill out the core provisions with supplementary provisions, including legislating for new rights. Rights are thus affected by both original constitutional provisions (with or without explicit declarations of rights) and by later developments by all three branches of government. Democratic policy processes are shaped by the changing institutional relationships among the many clusters of institutions across the three branches of government. Rights-claims vary in the institutions of government they target; and, when most contentious, rights-recognition can involve all three branches of government in the resolution of policy disagreement.

Finally, we note some implications of our story about policy story-telling itself. Just over 50 years ago, the emerging discipline of public policy found itself in the middle of a contest over rights. The polarised positions adopted by Friedrich and Finer left open plenty of room for more practical perspectives, with different analytical approaches to constitutions and rights. We have sketched in some of this middle ground by using a pluralist constitutional model where rights are treated as claims, usually sorted through the policy process as a matter of political contest. Purists might prefer that rights be managed either by a rights-attentive bureaucracy (e.g. human rights commissions inspired by Friedrich's moral mission) or by legislatures with limited legal powers of rights instrusion (e.g. responsible legislatures restrained by Finer's constitutional norms). The world of modern government has developed quite practical policy processes that fall short of the purity of either of these theoretical perspectives. More importantly, the discipline of public policy has escaped the captivity of

institutions of 'the government' and spread out across many institutions of civil society, some with a socialist rights agenda of social justice protected by big government and others with a libertarian rights agenda of individual liberties protected by limited government. Rights are better kept alive by open public dialogue among competing interests than by either the Friedrich tendency towards a government monopoly of 'administrative responsibility' or by the Finer tendency towards the black letters of a constitutional provision. Contemporary democracy has no agreed model of the ideal relationship between constitutions and rights, and one of the enduring strengths of public policy analysis is this open dialogue, over which social interests deserve the attention of policy analysts, within and without government.

NOTES

1. A. Halpin, *Rights and Law: analysis and theory*. Hart Publishing 1997; see also A Phillips, 'Defending Equality of Outcome', *The Journal of Political Philosophy*, 12/1, 2004, 1–19.

2. V. Bogdanor, ed, *Constitutions in Democratic Politics*. Gower 1988; J-E Lane, *Constitutions and Political Theory*. Manchester University Press 1996; L Alexander, *Constitutionalism: philosophical foundations*. Cambridge University Press 2001.

3. Consider T. L. Cooper, *The Responsible Administrator: an approach to ethics for the administrative role*. 4th edition. Jossey-Bass 1998, 132–140, 153–162; M. M. Harmon and R. T. Mayer, *Organization Theory for Public Administration*. Little Brown, 1986, 334–5.

4. M. Bevir, R. A. W. Rhodes and P. Weller, 'Comparative Governance: Prospects and Lessons', *Public Administration*, 81/1, 2003, 191–210.

5. See e.g. J. K. M. Gevers and G. Pinet, *The Rights of Patients in Europe: a comparative study*. Kluwer 1993.

6. J. Cohen, 'Minimalism about Human Rights: the most that we can hope for?', *The Journal of Political Philosophy*, 12/2, 2004, 190–213.

7. Consider E. Giglio, *Rights, Liberties and Public Policy*. Avebury 1995.

8. L. Peattie and M. Rein, *Women's Claims*. Oxford University Press 1983.

9. C. J. Friedrich and E. S. Mason, eds, *Public Policy: Yearbook of the Graduate School of Public Administration, Harvard University, 1940*. Harvard University Press 1940.

10. C. J. Friedrich and E. S. Mason, 'Introduction', *Public Policy: Yearbook of the Graduate School of Public Administration*, xi–xii.

11. C. J. Friedrich, 'Public Policy and the Nature of Administrative Responsibility', *Public Policy: Yearbook of the Graduate School of Public Administration* 3–24.

12. See e.g. the contributions of Friedrich and Finer in P. Woll, ed, *Public Administration and Policy*. Harper Torchbooks 1966, 221–275.

13. Friedrich, 'Public Policy and the Nature of Administrative Responsibility', 19–24.

14. F. L. Morton and R. Knopff, *The Charter Revolution and the Court Party*. Broadview Press 2000, 23–24. See also J. Rohr, *Founding Republics in France and America*. University of Kansas Press 1995; and more generally C. Epp, *The Rights Revolution*. University of Chicago Press 1998; and S. Walker, *The Rights Revolution: rights and community in modern America*. Oxford University Press 1998.

15. Peattie and Rein, *Women's Claims*, particularly 16–36. For more recent accounts, see L. Chappell, 'Feminist Engagements with Federal Institutions', in D. Laycock, ed, *Representation and Democratic Theory*. UBC Press 2004, 65–89.

16. B. Crick, *Democracy: A very short introduction*. Oxford University Press 2002, 69–71. See also B. Crick, *In Defence of Politics*, 2nd edition, Penguin 1982, 151–160.

17. Peattie and Rein, *Women's Claims* 19.

18. Peattie and Rein, *Women's Claims* 88.

19. Peattie and Rein, *Women's Claims* 25, 109, 111, 116, 134.

20. Quoting the text as in R. Knopff and F. L. Morton, *Charter Politics*. Nelson Canada 1992, 385–400.

21. Morton and Knopff, *The Charter Revolution*, 25. Also relevant is M. Glendon, *Rights Talk: the improverishment of political discourse*. Free Press 1991.

22. Morton and Knopff, *The Charter Revolution* 21. Compare P. Hogg and A. Bushell, 'The Charter Dialogue between Courts and legislatures', *Policy Options*, 20/3, 1999, 19–23.

23. Morton and Knopff, *The Charter Revolution* 17, 27, 51. But note M. Mandel, *The Charter of Rights and the Legalization of Politics in Canada*. Thompson Educational, 1994.

24. Morton and Knopff, *The Charter Revolution* 68

25. Morton and Knopff, *The Charter Revolution* 89–90

26. Morton and Knopff, *The Charter Revolution* 92. See also D. Schneiderman and K. Sutherland, eds, *Charting the Consequences*. University of Toronto Press 1997.

27. See e.g. C. P. Manfredi, *Judicial Power and the Charter*. University of Oklahoma Press 1993; C. P. Manfredi and J. B. Kelly, 'Six Degrees of Dialogue', *Osgoode Hall Law Journal*, 37/3, Fall 1999, 513–27; and 'Reply', by P. W. Hogg and A. A.

Thorton, ibid, 529–36. Consider also P. W. Hogg and A. A. Thornton, 'The Charter Dialogue between Courts and Legislatures', and F. L. Morton, 'Dialogue or Monologue?', *Policy Options*, April 1999, 19–26; Compare J. Hiebert, 'A relational approach to constitutional interpretation: shared legislative and judicial responsibilities', *Journal of Canadian Studies*, 35/4, Winter 2001, 161–72. See also J. Rohr, 'Administrative Law and Normative Dialogue' in *Founding Republics in France and America*, 207–251.

28. Consider 'A Dialogue Model' in *Report of the ACT Bill of Rights Consultative Committee*, May 2003, 61–3; and G. Williams, 'Constructing a Community-Based Bill of Rights', in T. Campbell, J. Goldsworthy and A. Stone, eds, *Protecting Human Rights*, Oxford University Press 2003, 247–62.

29. The wider debate is documented in F. L. Morton, ed, *Law, Politics and the Judicial Process in Canada*. University of Calgary Press 2002, Chapter 13, 571–625. cf Waldron, *The Dignity of Legislation*, Cambridge University Press 1999, 63–91.

30. J. Parkinson, 'Why Deliberate?', *Public Administration*, 82/2, 2004, 377–395. See more generally H. S. Richardson, *Democratic Autonomy: public reasoning about the ends of policy*. Oxford University Press 2002, 179–241.

31. See e.g. Manfredi, *Judicial Power and the Charter*.

32. See J. P. Hiebert, *Charter Conflicts: what is Parliament's role?* McGill-Queen's University Press 2002. See more generally Jeffrey Goldsworthy, *The Sovereignty of Parliament: history and philosophy*. Oxford University Press 1999; Waldron, *The Dignity of Legislation*; and Rohr, *Founding Republics in France and America*, 93–137.

33. *Participation Support for a More Equitable Society* (The McClure Report), Final Report July 2000, 4. See also A. Yeatman, 'Mutual Obligations', in S. Shaver and P. Saunders, eds, *Social Policy for the 21st Century*. Sydney: Social Policy Research Centre, 1999.

34. McClure Report, 40. Compare M. Dean, 'Administering Asceticism', in M. Dean and B. Hindess eds, *Governing Australia*. Cambridge University Press 1998, 87–107.

35. McClure Report, 34–5.

36. McClure Report, 32, 40. See also J. Pixley, 'Welfare, Poverty and Social Inequality', in P. Boreham, G. Stokes and R. Hall, eds, *The Politics of Australian Society*. Longman 2000, 286–301.

37. E. C. Page, 'The Civil Servant as Legislator', *Public Administration*, 81/4, 2003, 651–79; and see more generally G. Brennan and A. Hamlin, *Democratic Devices and Desires*. Cambridge University Press 2000.

10

Social Policy: Pensions

HELEN FAWCETT

INTRODUCTION

"In all post-war capitalist democracies, economic responsibility for the maintenance of the elderly has been assumed by the state. Because retirement and receipt of a public pension at or near 65 is now universal, state responsibility for the elderly has become a taken-for-granted part of everyday life in these countries – thus it seems mundane. But the fact that a majority of the population over 65 receive the majority of their income from the state, irrespective of their capacity to work, is both historically novel and not entirely expected in view of the principles of social organisation upon which these soci-eties were founded" (Myles, 1984, 1)

This chapter focuses on the role public pension policy played in welfare state development, and the key theories that relate to this element of public policy. We go on to consider the factors that need to be taken into consideration in pension design. Across the world many countries have developed pension systems, but there are considerable variations in the mechanisms which have been adopted to produce income security in old age. From the point of view of policy analysis, we raise some of the fundamental issues to be taken into consideration. However, from the 1970s, public policy became engaged with the feasibility and desirability of existing pension structures – particularly in the OECD nations. Fears that the modern industrial societies faced a "demographic time bomb" were combined with concerns about the long-term affordability of public pensions. As certain nations attempted to retrench or re-shape their pension systems a new strand of analysis entered the debate. It was argued that retrench-ment was not the obverse of expansion: in fact it was a fundamentally different form of activity. As a result, commentators have dis-cussed the role of policy legacies or inheritance in either constraining or facilitating reform efforts. In addition, as we examine the differen-tial levels of success that countries have experi-enced in re-shaping their pension provision since the 1980s, we also need to consider insti-tutional and political factors that give govern-ments the capability or capacity to influence policy-making. Finally, we explore the recent trend observed in a number of nations in which there has been attempts to encourage private pensions as a way of reducing the burdens on the state. This important development at first seems to be a means of cutting costs. However, as we will show, it adds a whole new range of issues. Reliance on the private sector for security in old age brings the issue of the regu-lation to the fore. How far are governments prepared to regulate the quality of private sector pensions? If regulation is too severe will it act as a disincentive to private pension providers? Most importantly, can the market guarantee to produce good quality pensions for future generations?

THE GROWTH OF THE WELFARE STATE: STRUCTURAL FUNCTIONALIST VS. POLITICAL EXPLANATIONS OF WELFARE STATE DEVELOPMENT

State pension policy has formed one of the key components of the welfare state. Political scientists have been concerned to explain its role in the development of the welfare state. In the nineteenth century retirement did not exist – the old continued to constitute a part of the workforce, and numerous studies found that the elderly were likely to be in poverty. As a result, structural functionalists have argued that pension provision was a product of the processes of modernisation, industrialisation and demographic change (Wilensky, 1975). As family structure evolved with changing patterns of work, supporting and caring for the elderly was no longer a private concern. While the advantage of structural functionalist explanations of welfare state development is their focus on the important pre-condition of state intervention, such as a nation's economic level of development, political explanations tend to highlight the role of strategic choice between competing alternatives. There are significant differences in the timing of government intervention and the manner in which they chose to intervene. However, there are many important political explanations of welfare state development which highlight a wide range of political variables, such as the rise of universal suffrage and how increased democratisation influenced the growth of public pension provision (Uusitalo, 1984). Other commentators have highlighted the role of political learning (Heclo, 1974). Building on explanations of welfare state development, it is important to explain the variations in the level and types of provision provided by the state. After the Second World War most countries amongst the advanced industrial democracies had consolidated pension provision and, as a result, political scientists were concerned to explain variations in character of public pensions amongst these countries. Many commentators have highlighted the importance of left wing parties, trade unions and the role of social democracy (Esping-Andersen, 1990). Much of the comparative research examining

the development of pension policy also confirms the importance of social democracy, and does not support the structural-functionalist hypothesis. Research conducted by Myles questioned the impact of demography on pension development (Myles, 1984). He argued that the effect of increases in the elderly population is the opposite of that predicated by structural functionalist theory. Rather than encouraging the improvement of public pension policy, a large elderly population appears to discourage the development of high quality pensions. In the absence of a political system dominated by the left, it would seem that the characteristic response to a large elderly population is to narrow the entitlements available to the elderly. Using the various indicators of social democratic influence (the size of the vote for the left party, the number of years the left party is in power, union membership, and union centralisation), Myles (1984) found the most convincing correlation between these variables and his index of pension quality. The results suggest that a well-organised and cohesive labour movement that is able to achieve Government office for extended periods of time is the best guarantor of high quality pensions. However, as will be discussed later in this chapter, these results refer to research conducted specifically on the issue of welfare state expansion not retrenchment. In addition, this discussion has focused on the nations that reached a high level of economic development in the late nineteenth and early twentieth century. Provision for the elderly is also an important issue for public policy in countries with fewer resources – those in the medium to low income category (World Bank, 1994) and those transitional democracies of Central and Eastern Europe. All of these countries are, of course, attempting to develop pension systems at a different historical point, and under very different circumstances, in comparison to those which have developed in Western Europe since the nineteenth century.

THE KEY GOALS OF PENSION POLICY

Like any other area of welfare provision, the characteristics of national pension systems are subject to considerable variations. The system design of public pensions is based on a variety of different factors. Despite the contemporary focus on the cost of public pensions, it is important to remember the other key objectives of pension provision in system design. If the arrangements for pension delivery fail, the old may have to rely on means-tested assistance or personal saving. This section explores the key factors that need to be taken into account in system design. Myles (1984) outlines six factors which play a critical role in determining the character of state pension provision.

Pension Level

The first factor that influences the character of a state pension system is the value or level of the retirement pension. Pension level can be evaluated in two ways: firstly, the value of the pension in comparison to the pensioner's earnings during working life; and secondly, the value of the retirement pension in comparison to the standard of living enjoyed by the working population.

Pension Structure

The structure of a pension scheme can range from the provision of flat rate uniform benefits granted to all pensioners on the basis of citizenship, without any reference to their previous earnings or contributions, to the provision of benefits which are strictly related to the contributions which have been paid during working life. As soon as pension arrangements depart from the flat-rate principle and become related to lifetime earnings the wage inequalities which exist among the working population will be extended to the retired.

Income Stability

This is one of the most important features of any pension system because it refers to the mechanisms which ensure the pension will retain its value after the date of retirement. In order to retain its value, the pension must be increased so as to keep pace with inflation.

Furthermore, if wage increases are out-pacing those of prices and the standard of living in society as a whole is rising, a pension which reflected the earnings of the previous decade will appear to have depreciated. If pension increases are linked to wage increases, pensioners will benefit from real growth in the economy. With price indexing, the value of the pension is preserved but the pensioner does not share in economic growth. Whichever option is selected, it is vital to ensure that indexing takes place at regular intervals.

Eligibility

Some societies provide retirement pensions as of right to all citizens. However, most base their arrangements on the insurance principle, which means entitlement is based on the contributions made during working life.

Security

When the individual retires from the labour force s/he will normally experience a reduction in income. In order to maintain the standard of living which is comparable to that enjoyed during working life, the retirement pension must replace 60–80% of pre-retirement earnings. The concept of income security refers to the level of income which allows the pensioners to maintain their pre-retirement living standards. Irrespective of the pension structure, the elderly will not receive inadequate financial support if the value of the pension is low in comparison to the standard of living of society as a whole.

Adequacy

Income security will not protect the poorest members of society from poverty in old age. If the pension system is based on the principle of linking earnings to benefits the poor will not have earned enough during working life to allow their income to be reduced on retirement. To avoid this problem the replacement ratios must be higher for the poor than for the well-paid members of society.

SYSTEM DESIGN OPTIONS

By the mid-1990s the World Bank argued that income security in old age was a world wide problem. However, this crisis has manifested itself in different forms in different parts of the world. Over half the world's old people depend on informal provision. In Africa and some parts of Asia, the old tend to rely on the extended family and personal saving. Both state provision and private pensions tend to be rudimentary. However, the ability of families to support their elderly is under threat from the forces of social and economic change: whether that might be industrialisation or the disruption caused by war and famine. Another cluster of countries face the problem of how to afford the pension systems they already have in place. This is a common feature in Latin America and Central and Eastern Europe. However, the more established social security systems of the advanced industrial countries belonging to the Organisation for Economic Co-operation and Development (OECD) are also facing difficulties, in that it is argued that their pension systems have become too generous and are now unaffordable. By the 1970s talk of a crisis in pension provision became the norm and since that time the proportion of spending as a percentage of GDP has been projected to rise over the next fifty years.

SYSTEM DESIGN AND DELIVERY

According to the World Bank, 40 percent of the world's workers and 30 percent of its old are covered by formal arrangements for old age. In the post-war era this type of state provision followed some basic patterns. First of all, some countries adopted a universal flat-rate state pension aimed at providing basic income security in old age. This was then supplemented by a second tier of earnings-related provision. Other countries instituted a fully earnings-related system. Some countries encouraged the growth of private sector occupational schemes. Other countries had a system design which resulted in the private sector focusing its efforts on the better off or the self employed.

However, government intervention is not limited to the role of pension provider. The state also has a role in regulating private pension, creating a legal framework for financial institutions and pension funds, and offering tax incentives to promote saving for old age. In this sense the state is always involved in pension arrangements whether or not they are a provider.

The types of pension delivery were described above. However, there are many issues of system design that go beyond the basic structure. One of the most important is whether contributions are defined, which is a system under which the contributions are known but not the size of the final pensions. By contrast, defined benefit (otherwise known as final salary) schemes set out the size of the final pension in advance. Equally, there is the issue of how the system should be financed. Some systems operate on a pay-as-you-go basis, in which current pensions are financed by taxes on the current workforce. Other systems operate on a funded basis, in which pensions are financed by accumulated savings. The pay-as-you-go (PAYG) system has tended to be the norm, and has also tended to be mandatory. As the World Bank pointed out, coverage has been "almost universal in high income countries and widespread in middle-income countries. As its name suggests, it places the greatest responsibility on government, which mandates, finances, manages and insures public pensions. It offers defined benefits that are not actuarially tied to contributions and finances them out of a payroll tax (sometimes supplemented from government revenues) on a pay-as-you-go basis. And it redistributes real income, both across and within the generations" (World Bank, 8).

The development of the occupational sector has been an important feature of the post-war period, starting to grow in coverage in the 1950s and 1960s. These are private pensions offered by employers which, in the past, were largely organised around the principle of defined benefit or final salary. Employers and employees both contributed to partially funded schemes, and there are the usual tax advantages attached to the scheme. Employers regarded these schemes as a way of attracting and retaining labour. However, in recent years, as will be discussed later, these schemes have undergone reform, and their generosity has declined. The funding requirements have tightened and many have moved to a less generous defined contribution system. As a result, employees do not know what pension entitlements they will have upon retirement because the final pension depends on contributions and investment. A second common form of private pension saving is Personal Pensions, sometimes known as individual accounts. These plans are fully funded and are based on defined contributions. Again, this form of personnel saving is often aided by tax incentives. The size of the final pension is contingent on stock market performance, so the individual bears the risk. However, in recent years, some countries have made these types of individual pensions mandatory. Sometimes government has managed these mandatory schemes and in others they have been arranged by the private sector.

PENSION REFORM

From the 1980s and throughout the 1990s, public pension systems have undergone a period of transition and reform. In many countries public pensions constitute the largest segment of the social security budget, which has meant there have been powerful economic reasons to either curtail the state's generosity or to privatise elements of provision, thus reducing the state's obligations. However, efforts to reform public pensions have not followed a uniform path, nor have they had uniform consequences. As Bonoli notes, the pension reform trajectory is based on an interaction between the structure of political institutions and the design of the pension schemes operating in each country (Bonoli, 2000). As a result, the impact of retrenchment is subject to marked variations. In the 1990s, the Swedish welfare state offered extensive coverage of the workforce and very generous pensions replacing a high percentage of average male earnings. By

contrast the UK public pension system was far less generous, replacing a far smaller proportion of average male earnings. When the Swedish pension scheme was reformed, the cut backs meant that it was still replacing a significant percentage of average male earnings, and as a result continued to provide good quality provision. In the UK, the base point from which reform took place was already barely providing an adequate pension.

If the design of the pension scheme is important to reform efforts, so too are political institutions, the configuration of societal and political interests and interest groups formation. If welfare reform efforts retrench benefits in such a way that certain individuals lose out, then there will, of course, be political consequences. The issue is how to implement reform measures that avoid blame being attributed to the governing party. In some countries the progress of reform has been relatively easy because the government of the day has not faced effective opposition, or been forced to deal with institutional obstacles. The best example of this was the case of the UK. However, in continental Europe, while reform has taken place, the governments have faced opposition from entrenched interests, which has slowed the progress of reform and also conditioned the character of the reforms that have been attempted. In Germany, attempts to reform the pension system began under Helmut Kohl. The problem with the German pension scheme was that high contributions and high rates of income replacement discouraged growth in employment. High wage costs made employers cautious about expanding their work force and high benefits encouraged early retirement. The public pension scheme was un-funded, which left government responsible for a greater share of the cost (Cox and Fawcett, 2000). However, reform efforts were difficult in Germany because of the contentious nature of the issue: there has been disagreement between the governing parties, opposition from the social partners, and institutional obstacles in the form of the bi-cameral, federal system of government. In addition, there was great public loyalty to the "conservative-corporatist" welfare state, in which citizens had become accustomed to a state which provided income security. This was a marked contrast to a liberal welfare state such as the UK, in which there are strong cross-class divisions in welfare. In the 1970s and 1980s, around half the population were covered by private occupational pensions and were used to market welfare. The state pension had never reached the generous levels of other continental European nations, and therefore was easier to reform.

The German pension reform of 2001 was interesting because it might be termed a "direction-setting or pioneering law" which changed the course of the German pension system set in place in 1957, appearing to introduce minor changes in the first instance (Lamping and Rub: 2004). The law introduced a public private mix in pension provision, with a new private tier of provision, subsidised by the state and based on defined contributions. However, the public PAYG pillar remained the dominant component of provision. The law also introduced a new formula aimed at slowing down or even stopping increases in the contribution rate.[1] Contributing to private pensions is voluntary. The plan had been to make it compulsory in 1999, but now employees are encouraged to contribute via tax incentives.

There are a variety of reforms measures available when attempting to contract expenditure on public pensions, and generally they are associated with attempts to reduce the scope and generosity of the state scheme. First of all, governments can increase the age of retirement. In addition they can reduce the quality of the pension by increasing the eligibility and qualifying criteria. For example, in the past pension levels were often based on something like the "best twenty years" of earnings. This can be extended to the whole of individuals' working life. Equally, the number of qualifying contribution years may be extended. Finally, the proportion of earnings replaced by each year's pension contribution can be made less generous (Fawcett, 1995). Another method of reducing costs is to target benefits. This has generally been applied in countries that had a basic flat-rate state pension, such as Australia and New Zealand. In addition, the indexation of the pension once

it is in payment can also be altered. Some pensions systems have moved from indexation that was based on an annual re-valuation, based on increases in average earnings, to one which increased the pension in line with prices. As a result, the value of the basic state pension fell progressively over the years (Fawcett, 1995).

A further method is to encourage the growth of private sector pensions, by increasing tax incentives or offering other forms of subsidy. Governments attempt to shape individual preferences by reducing the value of the state pension while simultaneously encouraging private sector growth. Increasing private sector coverage overall expands the size of funded pension schemes. In the case of the UK, many of these measures were successfully implemented during the 1980s in combination. The basic state pension was reduced in value by altering the indexation criteria. The State Earnings Related Pension was reduced in generosity and the government encouraged the growth of Personal Pensions with generous incentives.

However, the UK experience also draws our attention to another aspect of how the state is involved in pension provision: the regulation of the private sector. During the 1980s, the government took steps to de-regulate occupation pensions, allowing contracting out of the state scheme if they offered pensions based on defined contributions rather then defined benefit; as a result the number of occupation schemes increased (Fawcett, 1995). In this way, the government re-orientated the UK system, encouraging the growth of private sector pensions in order to reduce the size and the cost of public sector pensions.

REFORMING PENSION SYSTEMS: ISSUES OF PATH DEPENDENCY

From the 1980s, many governments have sought to pursue a welfare reform agenda. However, despite a number of governments committing themselves to change, many commentators observed that the welfare state seemed somewhat impervious to reform attempts, in particular that it appeared difficult to reduce the overall levels of spending on state welfare. This gave rise to a number of theories attempting to explain welfare state retrenchment, one in particular focuses on the notion of path dependency. This appeared highly relevant to the study of pension reform because, of all the component parts of the welfare state, pensions seem highly susceptible to path dependent effects. If we consider the basic characteristics of a pension scheme we can immediately observe certain difficulties in reform measures. The contributory nature of pension schemes means that pension rights are accrued over a long period of time. In addition, there are significant problems in the transition from one pension scheme to another, when pensions are already in payment under one scheme and a high proportion of workers will not have time to contribute to a new scheme. The public pension system of most advanced industrial countries means that governments have made long term pension commitments to large sections of the electorate. In addition, those with a stake in existing programmes and policies have a high level of influence over the reform measures that can be attempted. Since abolition or cuts in provision have significant political risks and may reflect negatively on the government of the day, is it possible to avoid blame?

The most common technique that has been used in pension reform is introducing policies which defer the impact of reform until some future date. Another technique that has been used is to contract or re-shape a pension system by making a variety of small scale reform measures that erode the value of benefits over time. Pension policy is highly complex and it has been shown that consumers have imperfect knowledge of the options available (Mayhew, 2002). As a result, governments can enact highly technical changes that may have a very big impact on the long-term value of these commitments. Often the implications of these changes do not become apparent for some time (Fawcett, 1995).

The path dependency argument, associated with the new institutionalist school of political science, refers to the legacies of past policy: the way in which previous political choices effect the current political agenda and the options open to political parties. Firstly, it is argued that public policies give rise to structures and resources that either encourage or inhibit the formation of interest groups. In this sense, as Schattschneider wrote, "new policies create a new politics" (1935: 288). Policies themselves create a specific constellation of interests and interest groups, and generate incentives which either facilitate or inhibit their expansion. Secondly, existing policies influence the perceptions and agendas of key political actors. Past policy plays an important role in framing political actors' perceptions of policy alternatives.

When we examine the various attempts to reform pension policy since the 1980s we can see that these concepts have some purchase. For example, many continental European countries lacked a well-developed private sector which was ready to take over the burden of public pension provision. Indeed, in some countries, such as Germany and Sweden, the majority of wage earners relied on state provision for all or most of their retirement income. As a result, there was a substantial cross-class coalition in support of public provision which was difficult to de-stabilise.

By the same token, the example of the UK shows how the policy choices of political actors shaped the behaviour of ordinary citizens. 11 million workers joined private sector occupational schemes in the 1960s because the UK lacked a good earnings-related second tier of state pension provision. Future attempts to improve public provision in the late 1960s and 1970s were constrained by these choices. The growth of the private sector created new interests: insurance companies, white collar trade unions, and of course, members of the public who had joined private sector schemes. The design of a state earnings-related scheme in 1975 was based on the notion of partnership rather than competition with the private sector. Equally, any attempt to regulate the quality of pensions offered by the private sector in order to improve quality was likely to provoke opposition from pension providers and resistance from those who had become clients of the private sector. Whereas it had been possible to think of launching an ambitious state scheme in the 1950s and early 1960s, when private pensions accounted for a relatively small sector of the market, and the existing state pension was set at a basic level, there were now severe political costs to be taken into consideration. (Fawcett, 1995, 1996)

As Pierson writes:

> "Policies may create incentives that encourage the emergence of elaborate social and economic networks, greatly increasing the cost of adopting once possible alternative and inhibiting exit from a current policy path. Individuals make important commitments in response to certain types of government action. These commitments in turn may vastly increase the disruption caused by new politics, effectively locking in previous decisions." (Pierson, 1994, 41–3)

However, the importance of path dependency and the feedback effects of previous policy choices should not be exaggerated. Some of the literature in this school has emphasised these factors as a reason why it was difficult to retrench the welfare state during the 1980s. The fundamental problem with this literature is the specification of the dependent variable "welfare state retrenchment". What do we understand by change and how best to measure the degree of change that has taken place? For example, in the mid-1980s, the UK Conservative government under Margaret Thatcher considered abolishing the State Earnings Related Pension Scheme. The fact that the government chose not to pursue all-out abolition has been cited as an example that shows how difficult it was to retrench the welfare state and as proof of the path dependency argument (Pierson, 1996). In fact, the State Earnings Related Pension scheme was not defended by any significant interests. The then Chancellor of the Exchequer, Nigel Lawson, did not see immediate benefit in terms of the administration's priorities and opposed the plan. However, the strategy that was chosen was equally effective but far more politically astute. The government pursued a dual strategy of reducing the generosity of the second tier of earnings-related state pensions, while changing the way in which the basic pension indexed so it rose in line with prices. At the same time, the government de-regulated the occupational

sector and created a new market in private sector defined contribution Personal Pensions. The Personal Pension market was stimulated by generous tax incentives. In the 1970s, about a half of the UK work force was covered by private pensions. By the end of the 1980s, around two-thirds of the workforce was covered by the private sector. The state sector was in long-term decline, and as its benefits became less competitive and the numbers covered less substantial, this paved the way for further retrenchment, eventually leading to the greater reform efforts (Fawcett, 1995).

The fundamental issue here is that a quantitative change can produce a qualitative change. The Conservatives wished to retrench public provision and encourage private provision. The strategy they pursued had a number of component parts which produced the same result in a very short time period. As a result, the state pension system in the UK underwent retrenchment; however, it did so by a rather different route than all-out abolition at one particular time. Hence, the way in which we understand the specification of retrenchment and how we chose to measure it, is the issue here.

In fact, looking back over the history of the 1980s and 1990s, many governments pursued similar courses of action, which we might describe as "path-shaping" (Cox and Fawcett, 2000). The issue of "blame avoidance" is important in devising retrenchment policies, because restructuring can lead to important sectors of the population suffering the negative consequences of retrenchment, which may create electoral losses for politicians. There is some benefit in pursuing a retrenchment strategy that proceeds in a gradual and incremental manner because it assists in a blame avoidance strategy by defusing opposition from groups who feel they will lose out because of reform efforts.

However, the ability to reform public sector pensions varies from country to country. These differences can be explained by the institutional and political veto points which either facilitate or inhibit the progress and the possibility of reform measures. Bonoli points out that the political limits to reform are specific to individual countries, based both on the design of the pension system and the political and institutional structures in place (Bonoli, 2000). His argument is based on new institutionalist focus on the capabilities of government and the fact that the degree of government control over policy-making is subject to significant variation. In any political system there may be institutional structures that have to be managed in order to implement policy change. Equally, there might be coalitions of actors that can obstruct the policy-making process. These "veto points" can act as a major limitation on a government's ability to control policy outcomes. By contrast, the absence of veto points, combined with strong concentrations of power, gives government a much stronger ability to bring about change in policy-making.

The types of factors that impact on government capacities are systems based on a separation of powers; bi-cameralism; proportional representation; referendums; and balanced dual executive. Policy-makers in the UK, a unitary state with a first-past-the-post-electoral system, and a weak second legislative chamber, faced very few institutional obstacles when passing their reform legislation – especially since the governing parties often enjoyed large majorities. Other countries have had to negotiate and frame reform in a far more complex and cautious manner.

ISSUES RELATING TO THE PRIVATISATION OF PENSION POLICY: THE PUBLIC PRIVATE MIX

An important part of the welfare reform efforts that have taken place over the last two decades has been the attempt to introduce increase private pensions coverage. However, some countries have always based their retirement provision on a mix of public and private provision. In many cases, funded private pensions have been small in scale aimed at professional well-paid wage earners. In other countries, private provision was extensive and well-institutionalised after the Second World War. For most of the post-war period, private occupational pension schemes existed as supplements to state pension provision. However, in some countries the pension system was designed from the outset to operate on the basis of a public-private mix of provision. From 1946, the Dutch pension scheme combined public sector pensions with private occupational pensions, and occupational coverage expanded over time so that ninety percent of the population was covered. However, in recent years, we have seen a trend towards increasing the extent of private provision as a way of reducing the state's commitments to public pensions. This has been the case in the German pension reform of 2001, the American debate on social security reform, and the Swedish case.

PRIVATE SECTOR: SOLUTION OR PROBLEM

Does the shift to the private sector mean less adequate income security in retirement? Rein and Schmahl (2004) argue that, to answer this question, we have to examine the overall mix of the state and private sector income package combined. In many countries there seems to be no immediate cause for concern. In two countries in particular, the UK and the USA, there is high-income inequality and high levels of pensioner poverty.

The first point to note in a consideration of the private sector is that the state continues to be involved in a variety of important ways, especially as a public sector employer and as a regulator. There are three principle sources of regulation: trust law, taxation policy, and regulatory authorities. In addition, if the mechanisms for privatisation are based on contracting out of the public sector scheme, the state regulates the conditions of pension quality under which occupational schemes are allowed to contract out. Thus it is still the state's role to stipulate the quality of pension the private sector provides. The increase in private provision may have reduced some of the obligations on the state. However, it raises the issue of whether private pension providers will be able to deliver a high quality of provision for future pensioners. A highly privatised configuration of pension arrangements forces politicians to consider the issue of regulation, and the dilemmas posed in trying to balance risk and regulation. The UK now has one of the least expensive public pension schemes in Europe. However, this has come at the price of de-regulating the private sector, and then being forced to re-regulate to restore public confidence in the aftermath of a variety of scandals (Blake, 1995). These scandals increased public awareness of the degree of risk associated with market provision and a re-evaluation of the regulatory regime. Indeed, since de-regulation, pressure has mounted on this issue, because it was becoming increasingly clear that (for a variety of reasons) funded pensions might not deliver the appropriate level of benefits at the point of retirement. In addition, since 1998, two-thirds of final salary schemes closed to new members and fund deficits are estimated to be £100 billion since the stock market slump of 2000. The government seems caught between the proverbial "rock and a hard place" because increasing regulation is likely to provoke a backlash from the private sector – failing to act is likely to further damage public confidence. However, while it has been important to develop a structure for regulation, as has been done since the 1990s, it is equally important to regulate the quality of pension provision for future pensioners. In this sense, the current crisis in British pensions has been the result of the liberalisation of the quality conditions under which the private sector has been allowed to operate. By moving to defined contribution rather than defined benefit schemes, Blake has shown that the overall level of contributions has fallen (Blake, 2001). Indeed, increased regulation has come at the price of a decline in pension quality. In order to get the private sector to contribute to a Pensions Protection scheme, the government allowed a reduction in inflation proofing, which could have serious implications for future pensioners.

The provision of private pensions is a voluntary activity. If the burden of regulation becomes too onerous, the incentive to provide private provision becomes less attractive. However, the UK's pension arrangements are heavily reliant on the private sector, and both the Labour and Conservative parties have encouraged further increases in private provision. Hence the "regulation/risk" dilemma is acute in the British context. The greater the population covered by the private sector, the more important it is to deliver high quality and reliable benefit systems. However, this reliance on the private sector creates a powerful interest group. The development of regulation is a matter for negotiation rather than imposition. In practical terms, the UK has established a relationship of dependency on the private sector, and, as a result, regulation is viewed in terms of what is perceived as feasible for the private sector to provide. The UK case is an extreme example, perhaps because of a mistaken belief that expanding private pensions is the solution to the problem of financing public pensions. In fact, it may be a cautionary tale, demonstrating what can happen when the state becomes over-reliant on the private sector.

CONCLUSION

During the affluence of the post-war years, pension provision was consolidated and expanded, but by the 1970s pension policy was perceived to be a key part of the "crisis" of the welfare state. In the aftermath of the oil crisis of 1973, stagflation and the pressure to retrench public expenditure, spending on pension policy became of enormous concern in the political and policy debate. At one time, relatively uncontroversial, fears of a demographic crisis – namely a growing number of older citizens living longer – was placing the pension systems under pressure. This was combined with an unfavourable ratio of workers to retired – namely, the size of the working population contributing to the finance of the pension systems – was declining in comparison to the rising number of the elderly.

Since the 1970s, therefore, the succeeding decades of welfare retrenchment and reform have focused heavily on the issue of pension policy. Policy makers have looked for ways to make their pension systems more affordable.

This has usually focused on two aspects of system design: first of all reforming public pensions to make them less generous and to reduce the obligations on the state; secondly, encouraging the privatisation of provision. Reconstituting pension systems in a way in which the private sector became responsible for some proportion of pension provision would seemingly diminish the obligations on the state. However, in the current economic climate, the way in which this has been done can produce lower quality provision. As a result, a new problem may be on the horizon, namely a retirement income package that fails to produce financial security in old age. In addition, the private public mix in pension provision raised other important issues for public policy, namely the regulation of the private sector, as well as their ability to deliver and guarantee high quality pensions.

NOTE

1. According to Lamping and Rub the contribution rate is set so that it should not exceed 20 percent in 2020 and subsequently should remain below 22 percent. The result of the new alteration in the pension formula is that pension level should average 67 percent of average net earnings minus the assumed saving rate for private old age provision.

REFERENCES

Anderson, K. M. and Meyer, T. (2003) 'Social Democracy, Unions and Pension Politics in Germany and Sweden', *Journal of Public Policy*, vol. 23, no. 1, pp. 23–54.

Atkinson, A. B. (1991) The development of state pensions in the UK (Discussion Paper WSP/58: LSE).

Baldwin, P. (1990) *The Politics of Social Solidarity: Class Bases of the European Welfare State 1875–1975*. Cambridge: Cambridge University Press.

Blake, D. (1995) *Pension Schemes and Pension Funds in the United Kingdom*. Oxford: Clarendon.

Blake, D. (2000) Two Decades of Pension Reform in the UK: What are the implications for occupational pension schemes? *Employee Relations*, 22(3): 223–245.

Blake, D. (2001) The United Kingdom Pension System: Key Features, Discussion Paper PI-0107, The Pensions Institute, Birkbeck College, University of London (Revised 2002)

Bonoli, G. (2000) *The Politics of Pension Reform: Institutions and Policy Change in Western Europe*. Cambridge: Cambridge University Press.

Borsch-Supan, A. and Miegel, M. (eds.) (2001) *Pension Reform in Six Countries: What we can learn from each other*. London: Springer.

Clark, G. L. (2000) *Pension Fund Capitalism*. Oxford: Oxford University Press.

Clayton, R. and Ponthusson, J. (1998) 'Welfare State Retrenchment Re-Visited: Entitlement, Cuts, Public Sector Restructuring, and Inegalitarian Trends in Advanced Capitalist Societies', *World Politics*, 51(October), pp. 67–98.

Cooper, D. R. (2000) A Tale of Two Pension Systems, *Employer Relations*, 22(3): 286–292.

Cox, R. H. (1998) 'From Safety Net to Trampoline: Labour Market Activation in the Netherlands and Denmark', *Governance*, 11(4), pp. 397–414.

—— (1997) 'The Consequences of Welfare Retrenchment in Denmark', *Politics and Society*, 25(3), pp. 302–325.

Cox, R. H. and Fawcett, H. (2000) Same Idea, Different Result: Welfare Reform and the Third Way in Britain and Germany, paper presented to the research Committee 27 of the International Political Science Association, Bangalore, India.

Davis, B. (1993) *Better Pensions for All*. London: IPPR.

Davis, E.P. (2000) Regulation of Private Pensions: A case study of the UK, Discussion Paper PI-0009. The Pensions Institute, Birkbeck College, University of London.

Deakin, N. (1994) *The Politics of Welfare: Continuity and Change*. Hemel Hempstead: Harverster Wheatsheaf.

Department of Social Security (1998) *New Ambitions for our Country: A New Contract for Welfare*. Cmnd 3805.

Department of Social Security (1998) *A New Contract for Welfare: Partnership in Pensions*, Cm 4179.

Department of Social Security and HM Treasury (2000) Security for Occupational Pension Schemes: A Consultation Document, London, September.

Department of Social Security and HM Treasury (2001) Security for Occupational Pensions: The Government's Proposal, London, March.

Department of Work and Pensions (2002) *Simplicity, Security and Choice: Working and Saving for Retirement*, Cm 5677.

Department of Work and Pensions (2003) Working and Saving for Retirement: Action on Occupational Pensions, London, June.

DHSS (1969) *National Superannuation and Social Insurance: Proposals for Earnings Related Social Security*, Cmnd. 3883.

DHSS (1974) Better Pensions: Proposals for a New Pension Scheme Fully Protected Against Inflation, Cmnd. 5713.

Emmerson, C. and Tanner, S. (2000) A Note on the Tax Treatment of Private Pensions and Individual Savings Accounts, *Fiscal Studies*, 21(1): 65–74.

Esping-Andersen, G. (1990) *The Three Worlds of Welfare Capitalism*. London: Polity.

Fawcett, H. (1995) The Privatisation of Welfare: The Impact of Parties on the Private/Public Mix in Pension Provision. *West European Politics*: 18(4), 150–69.

Fawcett, H. (1996) The Beveridge-Straight Jacket: Policy Formation and the Problem of Poverty in Old Age. *Contemporary British History*, 10(Spring): 20–42.

Field, F. (2000) *The State of Dependency: Welfare under Labour*. London, Social Market Foundation.

Financial Times (2002) "Unscrambling the Pensions Mess", March 4th, p. 20.

Financial Times (2002) "FRS 17: Little Name, enormous impact" (Michael Peel and Patrick Jenkins), March 3rd.

FT.com, 12 June 2003.

Francis, J. (1993) *The Politics of Regulation: a comparative perspective*. Oxford: Blackwell.

Guardian, 2003, Safety Net Plan for Pension Schemes, 12th June.

Hannah, L. (1986) *Inventing Retirement: the development of occupational pensions in Britain*. Cambridge: CUP.

Heclo, H. (1974) *Modern Social Polices in Britain and Sweden*. New Haven: Yale University Press.

Hills, J. (1998) *Thatcherism, New Labour and the Welfare State*, Centre for the Analysis of Social Exclusion, CASE 13, London, The London School of Economics.

HMSO (1993) *Pension Law Reform, Report of the Pension Law Review Committee* (Goode Committee) Cm 2342, London: HMSO.

Hood, C., James, O., and Scott, C. (2000) Regulation of Government: Has it Increased, Is it Increasing, Should it be Diminished?, *Public Administration*, 78(2): 283–304.

Hood, C., Rothstein, H., and Baldwin, R. (2001) *The Government of Risk: Understanding Risk Regulation Regimes*. Oxford: Oxford University Press.

House of Lords (1995) Hansard, February 7th, col. 109.

Hughes, G. and Stewart, J. (1999) *The Role of the State in Pension Provision: Employer, Regulator, Provider*. London: Kluwer Academic Press.

Johnson, P. (1994) *The Pensions Dilemma*. London: IPPR.

Labour Party (1957) *National Superannuation: Labour's Policy for Security in Old Age*.

Lamping, W. and Rub, F. W. (2004) From the Conservative welfare state to an 'uncertain something else': German pension politics in comparative perspective, *Policy and Politics*, vol. 32, no. 2, pp. 169–91.

Levy, J. (1999) 'Vice into Virtue? Progressive Politics and Welfare Reform in Continental Europe', *Politics and Society*, 27(2), pp. 239–273.

Lynes, T. (1969) Labour's Pension Plan (Fabian Tract 396). London: Fabian Society.

Lynes, T. (1997) The British Case, in Rein, M. and Wadensjo, E. (eds), *Enterprise and the Welfare State*. Cheltenham: Edward Elgar, 309–351.

Mayhew, V. (2002) *Public Attitudes to Pensions*, Department of Work and Pensions.

Minns, R. (2000) *The Cold War in Welfare*. London: Verso.

Myles, J. (1984) Old Age in the Welfare State: The Political Economy of Public Pensions. Kansas: University of Kansas Press.

Myles, J. (1996) When Markets Fail: Social Welfare in Canada and the United States. In *Welfare States in Transition: National Adaptations in Global Economies*, G. Esping-Andersen (ed.). London: Sage.

Myles J. and Quadagno, J. (eds.) (1991) *States, Labour Markets, and the Future of Old-Age Policy*. Philadelphia: Temple University Press.

Myners, P. (2001) *Institutional Investment in the United Kingdom: A Review*. HM Treasury, London, March.

Pickering, A. (2002) *A Simpler Way to Better Pensions*. London: HMSO.

Pierson, P. (1994) Dismantling the Welfare State? Reagan, Thatcher and the Politics of Retrenchment. Cambridge: Cambridge University Press.

Pierson, P. (1996) The New Politics of the Welfare State, *World Politics*, 48: 143–79.

Pierson, P. (ed.) (2001) The New Politics of the Welfare State. Oxford: OUP.

Rake, K., Falkingham J., and Evans, M. (1999) Tightropes and Tripwires: New Labour's Proposals and Means-testing in Old Age, Centre for the Analysis of Social Exclusion, CASE paper 23, London: The London School of Economics.

Rein, M. and Wadensjo, E. (eds.) (1997) *Enterprise and the Welfare State*. Cheltenham: Edward Elgar.

Rein, M. and Schmahl, W. (ed.) (2004) Rethinking the Welfare State: the Political Economy of Pension Reform: Cheltenham: Edward Elgar.

Rose, R. and Davies, P. L. (1994) *Inheritance in Public Policy*. New Haven: Yale University Press.

Ross, F. (2000) Beyond Left and Right: The New Partisan Politics of Welfare, *Governance*, pp. 155–183.

Schattschneider, E. E. (1935) Politics Pressures and the Tariff. New York: Prentice Hall.

Uusitalo, H. (1984) 'Comparative research and the determinants of the Welfare State: the state of the art', *European Journal of Political Research*, 12, pp. 412–13.

Walker, A. (1999) The Third Way in Pensions (by way of Thatcherism and avoiding today's pensioners), *Critical Social Policy*, 9(4): 511–527.

Waine, B. (1999) The Future is Private, *New Economy*, 7–10.

White, S. (ed.) (2001) *New Labour*. Basingstoke: Palgrave.

Wilding, P. (1992) The British Welfare State: Thatcherism's Enduring Legacy, *Policy and Politics*, 20(3): 201–212.

Wilensky, H. L. (1975) The Welfare State and Equality: Structural and Ideological Roots of Public Expenditures, Berkeley, University of California Press.

Wilsford, D. (1994) Path Dependency, or Why History Makes It Difficult but Not Impossible to Reform Health Care Systems in a Big Way, *Journal of Public Policy*, 14(3): 251–283.

World Bank (1994) Averting the Old Age Crisis: Policies to Protect the Old and to Promote Growth. Oxford: OUP.

Internet Sources
http://opra.gov.uk
http://dss.gov.uk
http://dwp.gov.uk

11

Social Policy: Is There A Crisis of the Welfare State?*

HAROLD L. WILENSKY

The essence of the welfare state is government-protected minimum standards of income, nutrition, health and safety, education, and housing assured to every citizen as a social right, not as charity (Wilensky, 1965, p. xii). In the abstract this is an ideal embraced by both political leaders and the mass of people in every affluent country, but in practice, and at high levels of development, it becomes expensive enough and evokes enough ambivalence to become the center of political combat about taxes, spending, and the proper role of government in the economy. In public expenditures, the welfare state is about two-thirds to three quarters of what modern governments do. The core programs of the welfare state, often subsumed under the general heading of "social security," have taken the form of social insurance against the basic risks of modern life: job injury, sickness, unemployment, disability, old age, and income lost due to

illness, shifts in family composition, or other random shocks (wars, depression, recessions). Because the welfare state is about shared risks cross-cutting generations, localities, classes, ethnic and racial groups, and educational levels it is a major source of social integration in modern society. Because it lends a measure of stability to household income, it has also been an important stabilizer of the economy in the downswings of the business cycle, especially since World War II.

The welfare state is at once one of the great structural uniformities of modern society and, paradoxically, one of its most striking diversities. In the past century the worlds 22 richest countries (our 19 rich democracies and three countries that became communist, Czechoslovakia, East Germany, and Russia), although they vary greatly in civil liberties and civil rights, have varied little in their general strategy for constructing a floor below which

*Most of this chapter is excerpted from Harold L. Wilensky, *Rich Democracies: Political Economy, Public Policy, and Performance* (Berkeley: University of California Press, 2002), pp. 211, 221–232. It draws on my remarks at an OECD Conference of Finance Ministers and Social Affairs Ministers (Wilensky, 1981a) and subsequent research. Chapter and table cross-references are to data and evidence in Wilensky, 2002, which also contains a 90-page bibliography. Among those who share my view of the alleged welfare-state "crisis" and provide empirical evidence casting doubt on the idea are Alber (1988), Klein and O'Higgens (1985), Marmor and Mashaw (1988), and Lindert (2004, two vols.). Gene Park assisted in updating the cases.

no one sinks. The richer these countries became, the more likely they were to broaden the coverage of both population and risks. At the level of economic development they achieved in the past 40 years, however, we find sharp contrasts in spending, taxing, and the organization of the welfare state and, of course, in the politics of the welfare state.[1]

CRISIS OF THE WELFARE STATE?

In 1975 I wrote that "the welfare state in its wondrous diversity has proved hard to shoot down;" it marches on through thick and thin (Wilensky, 1975, p. xvii). Since then there's been recurrent talk of a "crisis of the welfare state." Politicians, finance ministers, and even some scholars complain that accelerating social spending accounts for a rising burden of debt and deficits; that public support for the welfare state has eroded, another reason for cutting it down; and that social spending is a drag on economic growth, is inflationary, or contributes to unemployment. We should put these complaints in historical perspective.

Crisis talk has been a feature of welfare-state politics for almost a century. In Germany, when Bismarck's social legislation reached a cost of 1.4 percent of GDP in 1905, it triggered heated debate over its backbreaking economic burden and threat to civic morals. In recent decades crisis-mongering has escalated, aided by the rise of the broadcast media, which amplify extreme views.

If by "crisis" we mean rapidly accelerating social spending among the 19 rich democracies, by any measure social spending as a fraction of GDP has evidenced slower growth since 1975 or 1980, in some cases leveling off. Moreover, the burden of social spending in these countries varies both in level and trend. Thus, if by "crisis" we mean accelerating social spending, there is no crisis common to all.

If the welfare-state crisis means that the social budget is heavy and growing, that the welfare state is the root of public deficits, and deficits are dangerous, then again there is no general crisis. Results are the same whether we consider total

government spending or confine analysis to social spending. A thorough study of gross debt-to-GDP ratios from 1961 to 1990 among 12 EC countries shows that the ratio of government expenditures to GDP is unrelated to the gross debt ratio and that rising deficits are not the result of growing expenditures (von Hagen, 1992, pp. 12–13; cf. Cameron, 1982). For instance, during 1986–90 among welfare-state leaders the average debt ratio ranged from 128 percent of GDP for Belgium and 110 percent for Italy to 44 percent for Germany and 35 percent for France, while among the welfare-state laggards the ratio ranged from 110 percent for Ireland to 50 percent for the United Kingdom (the U.S. ratio in 1994 was 70 percent). Similarly, the annual net government deficit for 1993–94 among big spenders ranged from Sweden's 8.3 percent of GDP (down to 5.2 percent in 1996), Belgium's 3.7 percent, Netherlands's 1.2 percent and Norway's 2.4 percent surplus, while among welfare-state laggards the annual deficits ranged from Japan's 6.0 percent and the United States's 4.1 percent to Ireland's 1.6 percent (OECD National Accounts). Debt ratios depend not upon government spending but upon what else these countries do – whether they tax enough to pay for the services their citizens demand, their economic performance, the structure of their government (e.g., the strategic dominance of the prime minister or finance or treasury minister over the spending ministers), and the structure of the budgetary process. For example, experience with budget norms in the United States shows that they are ineffective in the long run for two reasons: first, the decentralized and divided structure of government means that Congressional spending committees and government agencies can maneuver to increase spending throughout the budgetary process by a principle of reciprocity; second, the states, whether they have spending and taxing limits or not, lavishly issue long-term bonds, resort to creative accounting tricks, and conduct one-time sales of assets to meet legal requirements for a balanced budget (von Hagen, 1992, pp. 38ff.).[2]

In short, there is such great variation in the depth and duration of fiscal stress and debt, and so much evidence that the welfare state is not the culprit causing changes in debt, that it makes no sense to talk about a general welfare-state crisis.

If the meaning of the welfare-state crisis is that there has been a withdrawal of mass support for social programs, there is no evidence of it. The most remarkable and solid finding of public opinion research on taxing and spending – both over time and across countries – is the stability of issue-specific opinion about social programs and the taxes to finance them. Since World War II, pensions and national health insurance remain overwhelmingly popular, most family policies retain a majority, while public assistance to the non-aged, non-working poor remains stably unpopular. Similarly, consumption taxes and social-security payroll taxes evoke no sustained mass hostility, while property taxes and income taxes arouse the most persistent resentment. The rank order of enthusiasm regarding both spending and taxing is similar across countries and over time. Chapter 10 [Backlash, pp. 369–373] reviews the evidence and explains why the relative uniformity of public opinion about the welfare state cannot explain great national differences in the electoral success of tax-welfare backlash movements and parties like those of Mogens Glistrup in Denmark, Ronald Reagan in the United States and Margaret Thatcher in the United Kingdom.

If the "welfare state crisis" is not an inevitably accelerating rate of social spending, not the withdrawal of mass support for social spending, and not the inevitability and dangers of public debt, then surely it means that the burdens of the welfare state universally subvert good economic performance. My Chapter 12 shows that the evidence is overwhelmingly to the contrary. Aggregate social spending up to 1973 was a positive contribution to the combination of low-to-moderate inflation, good real GDP growth per capita, and low unemployment; since the oil shocks of the 1970s it has been on average neutral. In no period and for no measure of performance is social spending a significant drag. Much depends on the mix of social and labor market policies a nation adopts, how it finances and manages the welfare state, and, more important, what economic and industrial relations policies it pursues.

Recent literature on the impact of the welfare state confirms these conclusions. In a careful review of the mixed and weak findings of nine studies, A. B. Atkinson (1995) concludes that none of them shows that the welfare state is bad for economic growth, employment, or productivity. Similarly, recent research by economist Peter Lindert (2004) provides the best overview of growth and retrenchment from the Poor Laws of the 18th century to 2000; he confirms the point. Using measures and econometric methods different from mine he also finds that since 1980 among modern democracies the net impact of social spending on the economy (i.e. GDP/person and growth) is close to zero (2004, vol. 1, ch. 10; vol. 2, chs. 18 and 19).

RETRENCHMENT OF THE WELFARE STATE?

If "crisis" talk, however misleading, is universal; if anti-taxing, anti-social spending, anti-bureaucratic themes have helped candidates to win some elections (see Chapter 10), has the action of governments matched the rhetoric of campaigns? What cutbacks have actually occurred in the period of austerity after 1975 or 1980 when economic growth and productivity growth slowed down? With some exceptions, the core programs of the welfare state – pensions, disability insurance, and national health insurance, programs that have generally outpaced GDP growth – have proved most resistant to real cuts in benefits per capita or even in their GDP shares (on disability insurance see Chapter 16, Environment). Most vulnerable to real cuts or at least spending restraint have been education, family allowances, social assistance, and unemployment compensation. For instance, in the period 1975–1981, ten of the 16 of our rich democracies studied by Jens Alber (1988, pp. 190–191) reduced the GDP share of education. Only Sweden, Italy, and Ireland increased as much as a point or more. In contrast, the GDP share of health spending increased almost everywhere (only Canada, Germany, Denmark and Norway showed either a slowdown in growth or a stagnant share) and the share of pensions climbed everywhere but in Germany, where it leveled off at a high of 12.6 percent.

With few exceptions, there are five main reasons for this pattern of growth and restraint. First, demography, as usual, counts. Declines in education spending reflect declines in school-age populations. The "young" countries with a school-age bulge (measured by schoolagers per prime-age adult) cut education expenditures per child while still raising such spending as a share of GDP, but as the school population declined the GDP share leveled off or declined. The older countries spent more on pensions both per capita and in GDP share, but at a diminishing rate, eventually leveling off (Lindert, 2004, vol. 1, Chs 7 and 9). Aging, as we have seen, also increased health and disability spending, especially as the "old-old" increased their share of the population. Second, after universal coverage is achieved, various measures to control costs or restructure programs had some effect, especially in health care (as in recent German reforms). Third, programs where abuses were obvious and widespread (sick pay, disability insurance) have evoked substantial government reform efforts with varying success; disability cutbacks have encountered especially fierce resistance (see the five-country comparison in 2000, Chapter 15 and Table 15.3). Fourth, the rate of economic growth has an automatic effect on these numbers: below-average growth will automatically increase the expenditure ratio (SS/GDP) as the denominator levels off or decreases while social spending continues upward. Finally, the interaction of three forces – a very large clientele (all pensioners, all the health insured), strong political organization or influence, and great mass popularity – means that welfare-state leaders have already achieved generosity of benefits; their citizens now have entrenched interests and strong sentiments for maintaining the status quo. Conversely, if clientele is small, organization and influence is weak, and majority sentiment is hostile – as with means- tested benefits targeted to the non-aged, non-disabled

poor and to a lesser extent unemployment compensation – real cutbacks are most likely.[3]

To illustrate the patterns of retrenchment of the welfare state since the late 1970s, here are a few examples drawn from a wide range of countries whose economies and polities differ substantially – UK, USA, Netherlands, Germany, Italy, France and Sweden. In all cases, wherever a mass of voters perceives that an incumbent politician is serious about cuts in the core programs of the welfare state and the incumbent has failed to achieve consensus among major power blocs, the next election spells defeat.[4]

USA and UK

Comparing the United States and Britain, Paul Pierson (1994, pp. 142ff.) shows that aggregate real social spending by the national government on employment and training, housing, education, health care (in the U.S. Medicare), personal social services, and social security increased from 1978 to 1992 in both countries. There was, of course, some reallocation among types of spending: in both countries unemployment benefits and means-tested housing benefits were sharply cut back (*Ibid.*, pp. 95–99, 127–128). In housing programs it was a shift from public-sector construction or producer subsidies to cheaper subsidies for housing consumption targeted to the poor, often cutting out the near-poor. Tax-subsidized housing for the middle classes and the affluent, such as tax deductions for interest on mortgages, remained sacrosanct. With the decline of union power in both countries, unemployment benefits were cut, especially for the better-off recipients.

Although President Reagan and Prime Minister Thatcher both launched verbal assaults on the welfare state, they were unable to make more than a marginal dent on aggregate social spending, mostly by expanding means-testing and tightening eligibility rules for the most vulnerable populations – the poor.[5] By changing indexation (cost of living adjustments) of pensions, Thatcher was also able to reduce the rate of growth of this most popular program. In contrast, at the outset of his administration, Reagan proposed to cut the minimum pension benefit for low-earnings workers and to delay a cost-of-living adjustment three months; immediately 96 Senators voted "No," zero "Yes." This episode triggered a big revival of an elderly lobby (the National Committee to Preserve Social Security and Medicare was formed in 1982). Later, in 2005, President Bush II, with dominance in both Executive and Congress, spent a solid year trying to sell the privatization of Social Security with no success.

It is possible that Thatcher could succeed in modest steps where Reagan and Bush II failed, not only because a more centralized parliamentary system with party discipline gives an ideologically-committed prime minister more power than her counterpart in a divided Presidential system, but also because of differences in the degree of consolidation of the pension system. As Pierson (1994, pp. 69–73) suggests, Britain's SERPS (State Earnings-Related Pension Scheme), the target of Thatcher's reform, was a young program first implemented by the Labour government in 1974; America's Social Security law had four additional decades to become institutionalized and therefore more resistant to change. As always, system maturity counts.

That political consenus is esssential for successful reforms is shown by the enactment in the United States in 1983 of the pension-reform recommendations of a bipartisan commission on social security. Rather than cutting benefits they raised payroll taxes slightly, taxed benefits for the first time, brought new federal employees into the system to broaden the payroll tax base, and trimmed future costs by slowly phasing in the higher retirement age from 65 to 67 by the year 2027 – sensible steps, which "fixed" the system for 47 years, hardly a revolution.

Regarding cuts in health-care spending and benefits, Reagan, Thatcher and their successors (Bush, Clinton, and Major) all attempted reforms designed to reduce the rate of growth of government health-care spending; Clinton, in addition, made a failed attempt to overcome American exceptionalism and establish national health insurance. It is a curious paradox

that the United Kingdom, with by far one of the cheapest, most-accessible medical-care systems, made the most radical reforms, while the United States, with by far the most expensive and least accessible system, failed either to control spending or to increase access while it succeeded in increasing the number of families with no medical insurance at all (by 2005 more than 43 million). It is another paradox, which runs through all policy areas (see chapter 8 [Welfare Mess], 15 [Environment], and 16 [Health Care]), that the most ideologically-committed free-marketeers, Prime Minister Thatcher and Presidents Reagan and Bush I, created the most intrusive regulatory regimes. In U.S. health-care reforms it was the Reagan – Bush regulations of hospital and physician payments – rate-setting, prospective payment plans based on diagnostic-related groups, and resource-based relative value scales (Brown, 1991; Ruggie, 1992). The payment reforms did modestly reduce Medicare costs through shifting the burden to private insurers, who then raised premiums and gave employers and providers strong motive to reduce coverage and services, shifting the burden of coverage back to the public sector – a typical cost-shifting game in the uniquely commercialized U.S. public/private system. A second game is risk selection: commerical providers also save money by skimming off the younger, healthier patients while dumping older, sicker, costlier patients onto the public sector. The net effect of all these measures in two decades was to increase administrative complexity and cost (by 2005 more than 15 percent of GDP), reduce medical coverage, enrage doctors, and put the U.S. below the average on a wide range of real health indicators.

Because the recent British restructuring of medical care is so sweeping, a brief account is relevant as we consider "cuts" in welfare-state spending. A popular, universally-accessible, tax-financed, already low-priced health-care system – the National Health Service (costing only 7.1 percent of GDP in 1992 compared to 8.7 percent for Germany and 13.6 percent for the United States) – was radically reformed in 1991 by Margaret Thatcher on both cost-containment and ideological grounds.[6] In 1989 she released

Working for Patients, the product of a closely-held review by her trusted lieutenants plus advisers from neo-liberal think tanks – with no consultation with provider groups (the BMA, the Royal Colleges). Answering critics of her stewardship of the NHS who accused her of over-zealous starving of health care through budget stringency, the report assumed that the NHS as structured subverts the free choice of individuals in the medical market; it claimed that doctors – so dominant in NHS policy-making and implementation – lack the incentives to respond to the patient-consumer; that doctors' monopolistic, self-aggrandizing behavior (e.g., restricting entry to the trade) increases rigidity and inefficiency (e.g., wide variation in patients treated and referrals per doctor) and accounts for long waiting lists for elective surgery and ward closures in hospitals that have used up their NHS budget; and that all of this is a drag on the economy. An underlying ideological theme of all of Thatchers reforms was that the autonomy and monopoly power of professional groups, including doctors, must be checked by creating free markets. The power of physician groups, she felt, threatens not only the sovereignty of the consumer but the proper authority of the state. Although the Thatcher government did not dare to abandon the founding principle of the NHS – to provide a universal, comprehensive, tax-financed health-care service to the entire population – the reforms did introduce an "internal market" into the state system. Purchasers (District Health Authorities) were separated from providers (hospitals and their consultant-specialists); purchasers would no longer manage hospitals but instead buy services for their localities by contracting with NHS hospitals or private hospitals, hopefully the latter. Hospitals could choose to be self-governing trusts. By 1994 "more than 400 providers accounting for about 95 percent of the NHS's activities had become self-governing Trusts" (Klein, 1995, pp. 204–205). A new structure – General Practitioner Fundholders (GPFH) comprised of larger GP practices – was created as another group of presumably cost-conscious purchasers. Fundholders would negotiate contracts with providers to offer care more efficiently without massive extra funds. Instead of capitation payments (originally designed to overcome the overserving tendencies of fee-for-service medicine), fundholders will receive a fixed sum out of which they will buy hospital services; like the self-governing hospitals, they can retain surpluses but must balance deficits from their budgets (Döhler, 1991, pp. 264–265).

Finally, in this war on the autonomy of physicians, the Thatcher reforms increased the powers of managers of the NHS and governing Ministers over practitioners: the trusts specify doctors' job contracts and review them annually; they have increased power to hire and fire hospital personnel. Both professionals and local governments are barred from serving on controlling boards. The Major government continued to implement these 1991–92 reforms.

Britain stands alone in the rapidity, depth, and implementation of reform, although New Zealand recently tried to match the pace of British change. It is too difficult to judge whether this combination of managerialism, statism, and market theory either saves money or improves access, innovation, equity or quality of care, let alone real health (Klein, 1995, pp. 230–237). Besides, some of the Tory reforms have been abandoned. Because there was no consensus on reform or even what problem it was supposed to solve, there is no consensus on criteria of evaluation. There is consensus on four points, however:

1. Reform has not reduced costs. Spending on health care was 6 percent of GDP in 1989; in 1992, after reform, it had gone up to 7.1 percent, a more rapid growth than that of Germany and Netherlands, while Sweden and Denmark actually cut the health-care share of GDP.

2. It inflated both the number and salaries of "bureaucrats." While 50,000 nursing jobs and 60,000 beds have disappeared since 1990, there has been an increase of 20,000 senior managers in the NHS (*New York Times*, August 6, 1996). There is dispute about how much of a managerial explosion there is but no one doubts that there has been a large increase in administrative costs.

3. It has accelerated a 1980s trend toward co-payments in dental, pharmaceutical, and ophthalmic services, with exceptions for the poor.

4. No great change has yet occurred in the behavior of physicians or of health authorities; for instance, they typically refuse to explicitly restrict the menu of services. But the reforms have reduced the power of hospital specialists and secondary-care providers, while enhancing the power and status of general practitioners and primary-care providers, especially the "fund-holders" who now have to pay the bills within a fixed budget. This may be the major achievement of reform. However, even with one of the lowest-cost systems among rich democracies, and in the face of increased demands, the Conservative government of the mid-1990s required annual cuts of three percent at every level. Continued budget stringency put an already lean system under increased strain; many emergency rooms and intensive-care units had to impose long waits before any treatment (New York Times, January 30, 1997.)

When the Labour Party swept to power partly on the promise to reverse the Thatcher/Major health-care ideology, improve service, and spend more on the NHS, Prime Minister Tony Blair increased NHS funding modestly in his first two years (e.g. an extra $2.4 billion in the 1997–98 budget.) He also reversed some of Thatcher's reforms, especially in the "internal market system." In July 2000 Blair promised to accelerate increases. He presented an ambitious 10-year plan to overhaul the NHS and deliver by 2004 an extra 20,000 nurses, 7,500 consultants, 7,500 more specialists and 2,000 more GPs, plus 6,750 more therapists and other professionals. The plan will be funded by an increase in taxes of 5 billion pounds to help pay for both health service and anti-poverty programs, themselves important sources of enhanced health. Substantial increases have, infact, occurred. This is a dramatic reversal characteristic of big party shifts in a polarized, majoritarian political system.

Chapter 16 (2002) assesses the connection between the organization and financing of health-care systems and national health performance.

The Netherlands

The Christian Democratic and Liberal cabinet of 1982 cut social benefits, education, and health care by three percent and froze a number of benefits at that level. In 1986 the link between wage increases in the private sector and social benefits changed so that the Minister of Social Affairs could consider the ratio of workers to beneficiaries in determining benefits each year. Later the generous early retirement benefit was reduced. In 1991 and 1992 sickness and disability benefits were lowered. The social partners, however, rebelled by restoring the benefits through collective bargaining. Despite the unusual Dutch level of abuse of these generous programs (Chapter 15) sickness benefits by 1995 were back to their former level at 80–100 percent of previous wages while most of the disability benefits were back to their former 80 percent level. An uphill effort to reexamine eligibility procedures was begun in 1995–96. The employer is now responsible for paying the first two to six weeks of sick leave before the sickness fund kicks in; employers also have more responsibility for disability benefits, a reform that gives them an incentive to get rid of less-than healthy workers, thereby shifting costs to unemployment compensation or public assistance. (P.K. Keizer, 1996, pp. 4–5, 15–16.) However, the number on partial or full disability did drop from about 985,000 at the end of 1993 (14 percent of the labor force) to 735,000 at the end of 1996 (Wall Street Journal, December 26, 1996). Recent governments have emphasized the need to increase the rate of Dutch labor-force participation and de-emphasize the replacement of income for the unemployed and disabled (Chapter 15).

The Netherlands story is one of many small reductions in a wide array of social benefits that, over 10 or 15 years, add up. These cumulative adjustments and the effort to freeze some spending provoked older voters to form two new parties that won seven seats in May 1994.

Germany

Germany was not only the pioneer of early welfare-state expansion but led in the late 1970s-mid 1990s effort to rein in its growth. Under center-right coalition rule, under the enormous fiscal burden of post-1989 unification (currently DM 170 billion per year), facing great demographic pressure (in 1992, 15 percent of the population was 65 or older, a high rate close to those of Belgium, Denmark, the United Kingdom, and Italy[7]) and in its role as dominant enthusiast for a strong EU and therefore having most incentive to meet the Maastricht economic criteria, the German government has proposed many restraints on social spending and has enacted several. Given these pressures it is surprising how modest the reforms are. Efforts to trim social spending began in 1975 under the Social Democratic government and continued somewhat more intensely under center-right coalitions. Successive cuts have been concentrated on unemployment benefits, health insurance, and means-tested social assistance. Pensions so far have been little affected. Before 1984, successive limits were imposed on eligibility and duration of unemployment benefits; small co-payments and some cost-containment measures were imposed for some health services and drugs; lengthy hospital stays for childbirth were shortened, sick pay was slightly reduced; social assistance to the poor was not increased at the rate of inflation; an increased proportion of college student allowances were transformed into loans; and child allowances were curbed for families above an income limit. (Alber, 1986, pp. 115–116.) Together, these 1975–1983 changes stabilized the social spending share of GDP, making Germany an early exception to the rule of continued expansion among welfare-state leaders before the mid-1980s (Alber, 1988, p. 192; and Brown, 1988, p. 10).

Since the mid-1980s there have been recurrent proposals to reduce pension benefits per recipient by changing the indexing basis but so far they have come to nothing. Although in 1992 Germany increased social assistance benefits for single parents and pregnant women, in 1993 it capped annual increments and cracked down on abuses (Alber, 1996, Table 2). In 1988

and 1992 two medical care cost-containment laws were passed with the help of the Social Democrats. They aimed to stabilize the insurance contributions by restructuring the corporatist bargaining process (Giaimo, 1995). They increased the power of the Krankenkassen (sickness funds) vis à vis the doctors' associations in negotiating guidelines for practice and prescriptions, and broke up the cozy relationship between doctors and pharmaceutical firms.[8] They capped health-care expenditures at the level of wages (and wage increases) of insured persons and froze them at the 1991 level. These reforms also introduced small co-payments on some prescriptions, in-patient stays, and physical therapy and larger co-payments for eyeglasses and dental care, with exceptions for low-income groups. A step in the opposite direction occurred in April 1994, in response to a growing "old-old" population: Germany introduced a new scheme of social insurance to pay for universal and long-term care. Finally, measures introduced by Chancellor Kohl and approved in June 1996 would reduce sick pay by one-fifth, to 80 percent of workers' salaries. Under the new regulations Germans will be entitled to only three weeks of state-subsidized health-spa vacations every four years, compared with the present four weeks every three years. A Kohl proposal to increase by 75 cents the small co-payment per prescription (previously about $1.50 to $5.00) was defeated by the Social Democrats along with bolder proposals for further cost control. While all this might not sound Draconian to American ears, it provoked demonstrations, processions of cars, and brief work stoppages all across Germany. A union-organized pro-welfare state rally in Bonn in June 1996 set a Federal Republic record, with 350,000 participants.

Largely because of the extraordinary burden of extending West Germany's welfare state to impoverished East Germany (still 4% of GDP) combined with a pro-cyclical monetary policy, social spending for unified Germany climbed steadily from just under 29% of GDP in 1990 to nearly 34% in 1999 (Seeleib-Kaiser, 2002, p. 28). In 2001 the entire passive sick pay program for the disabled was scrapped and a more work-oriented substitute adopted.

In the late 1990s through 2003 German governments of both center-right and center-left continued efforts to reform the welfare state with only small results. The SPD (Social Democratic Party) in 2003 accepted Schroeder's "2010 Agenda" aiming to cut non-labor costs by reducing benefits for the long-term unemployed, liberalize the pharmaceutical market and increase co-payments by patients. It also calls for pension reforms. Once more, massive protests greeted the proposals; only cuts in unemployment benefits were adopted. Finally, the German election of 2005 was a standoff between Angela Merkel, a free marketeer, and Gerhard Schroeder, a Social Democrat who defended the "social market" enonomy. What is obvious is that despite three decades of bold talk about big cutbacks of the big welfare-state programs, the action has been severely limited by mass resistance.

Italy

Cutbacks, begun in 1978 under the unity government with Communist support, accelerated in 1981–1983 (e.g., rules on public assistance were tightened, child allowances for children of high income families were reduced). But Italy nevertheless joins Sweden, Denmark, Belgium, and France as the standout cases of welfare-state expansion that substantially exceeds their GDP growth from 1975 to the early 1980s (Alber, 1988, pp. 188–189). Major reforms, driven by cost considerations, were made in the 1980s and especially the early 1990s.[9] A major 1978 reform undertaken by the National Solidarity Coalition changed health-care entitlements from occupation-based funds to all citizens, modeled on the universalism of the British National Health Service – a principle of free and equal benefits to everyone. Severe problems of corruption (parties controlled every component of the system), concomitant cost explosions, and deterioration of services resulted in incremental revisions in the 1980s and 1990s. These reforms include gradual increases in the amount of co-payments and their extension to new areas – e.g., prescriptions, laboratory tests, and out-patient specialist care. A major

structural reform was introduced in 1984 but it took 10 years to be fully implemented, at which point it provoked a storm of protest (Ferrera, 1994). For example, in December 1993 a three-tier system was introduced (users with no charge, users with limited co-payments, users with deductibles). Health-care entitlements for higher-income families were drastically cut back (the only "free" service remaining was hospitalization); for families earning less than the threshold, co-payments were increased; while the poor elderly were exempt, a new voucher system put a ceiling on all services, after which they would bear the full cost. The revolution lasted only a few months. The affluent were incensed at their exclusion; the poor and near-poor complained that the voucher system, like the means-testing that preceded it, was cumbersome and humiliating; and everyone complained about increased out-of-pocket costs. Opposition parties and labor unions gave voice to these complaints. Income-testing and means-testing created a nightmare for administrators, exacerbated by the ineffectiveness of the tax system. Income testing encouraged even more tax evasion as benefit-seekers just above the income threshold rearranged their official labor-force participation to avoid co-payments.

It did not help public acceptance of the 1993 revolution that in the same year the Head of Pharmaceutical Services was arrested for accepting huge bribes from drug companies and the Minister of Health and several of his associates were indicted on corruption charges. In 1994 the new system was abandoned. Income selectivity was replaced by risk selectivity: persons with one of a long list of illnesses (mostly chronic), pregnant women, the disabled, children up to the age of 10 and everyone older than 60 were exempted from cost-sharing, regardless of income. Reforms throughout the decade followed a stop-reverse-go pattern.

Italy has long had one of the most generous paid maternity leave policies. Even hints of possible cutbacks provoke a political uproar; the system remains intact.[10]

Meanwhile the efforts to restructure the state by decentralization of power also shaped the welfare state. New laws of 1991 regulated the financing of non-profit and voluntary agencies in the social services. These reforms accented self-governing municipalities, the merging of small towns and the setting up of consortia for the management and delivery of services; the creation of metropolitan areas for big cities like Rome, Milan, Turin, Naples (they are now accorded the powers of provinces). Municipalities are acknowledged as main actors in all areas of social services, except for the organization and planning of health services. Two laws of 1991 aim to regulate and help finance voluntary associations and social cooperatives to which public administrators may contract out services. Relative to market actors, these cooperatives have a privileged position as contractees. None of this urge to decentralize reduced bureaucratic bloat or total spending but it did enliven the blame game: The central government could point to regional and local governments as the source of trouble and vice versa. In general, however, the structural reforms were a laudable attempt to reduce political clientelism by strengthening the power and responsibilities of administrators and professionals within local agencies and especially within the National Health Service.

Italy is an extreme case, both in acceleration of spending and repeated efforts to cut spending, only a few of which were successful. It uniquely combines political corruption and inefficiency in the administration of both taxation and social spending (even including pensions, health-care and disability insurance), strongly alienated voters, party realignment and dealignment, and very disorderly finances (a uniquely wide gap between revenues and expenditures over long periods). This helps to explain big swings in social policy and the limited modifications in the last 10 years – some shifts toward a more selective universalism in welfare-state design, some actual cuts in benefits, and ultimately a major brake on total social spending. After negotiations between unions and the Dini government, even a broad-pension reform was passed in August 1995. It begins a shift from the old very generous "defined benefit" formula to a new, somewhat less generous "defined contribution" formula to be phased in very gradually.

The vigor and breadth of demonstrations and strikes to protest cuts of benefits in the core programs of the welfare state are greater in France than Italy, largely because Italians are aware of the corruption of major programs and the need for reform. But Italian voters are moving in the direction of the French in their organized resistance to erosion of benefits. For instance, Prime Minister Romano Prodi's center-left majority coalition of 1998 split over $14.5 billion in proposed spending cuts, specifically the $2.9 billion reduction in pensions and health-care programs. Prodi resigned. Renegotiation led to $291 million less in pension cuts but total spending cuts were reduced to almost one-third of those originally proposed and in return the left demand for a 35-hour workweek was accepted.

France

A glimpse of French policy and protest comes from the Spring of 2003 when the conservative Chirac/Raffarin government proposed a broad retrenchment of the welfare state – curbing state spending for pensions and health benefits. An estimated one to three million people demonstrated against these reforms in May 2003. Protests included strikes by about two-thirds of national railway workers, as well as massive street action. In the end, in July, the government got Parliament to approve only a modest pension reform: civil servants would in 2008 be asked to work an additional two and a half years before receiving a full pension after 40 years service so they will be equal to the current system for all private-sector workers. (Wall Street Journal July 24, 2003.)

Again, in late 1995, the conservative Chirac/Juppe government's proposed cuts triggered a strike movement that almost shut down the French economy for three weeks. It had a wider base of public sympathy than les grands événements of 1968. It was presented by the government with almost no consultation or participation, as a non-negotiable policy package to save the French welfare state, restore French competitiveness, and meet requirements for joining the EMU (European Monetary Union).

The changes were sudden and radical. Strikers concentrated on protecting pensions, health care, job security, traditional job rights and working conditions. The government withdrew its proposal to reform public sector pensions (and was subsequently forced to accept a full pay pension for truck divers at age 55); but did not give up its ambition to drastically reform the entire social security system. In July of 1997 Chirac/Juppe were defeated by Lionel Jospin of the center-left. The French rejection of the EU constitution in 2005 was partly inspired not only by high unemployment but also by Chirac's current effort at social cutbacks and the public image of EU policies as imposing an Anglo-American economic model on Europe that would threaten social protections and labor standards.

In 1995, compared to other rich democracies, France had a low "normal" retirement age of 60, a very low labor-force participation rate among men aged 55–64 and a high pension cost/GDP (almost 11%) (Myles and Pierson, 2001, p. 309). In short, its pension problems were severe, so it is not surprising that its government tries to retrench in the face of mass resistance. Neither is it surprising that Napoleonic efforts and style yield so little.

Sweden[11]

Starting in 1980–1982 under a "bourgeois" coalition government, there were minor cuts in already very generous health, housing, and even pension benefits (e.g., reducing compensation for part-time pensions) while unemployment benefits and child allowances were extended (see 2002, Chapter 7). During subsequent years of return to Social Democratic rule, 1982–1991, there were both incremental cutbacks and incremental expansions of social programs. The unprecedented annual deficits run up by a series of center-right coalitions from 1976 to 1982 (13 percent of GDP when the Social Democrats returned) were reduced not mainly by these 1980s spending changes but by currency devaluations, economic growth, and tax reforms.

On the eve of a recession, in the two years leading up to their defeat in the election of 1991, the Social Democratic government increased

the VAT and, in its most unpopular move, changed property tax valuations (see Chapter 10) while it made modest reforms to prevent waste and abuse in social programs, especially in the replacement rate of unemployment insurance and sick pay. For instance, sickness cash benefits were calibrated according to reduced capacity to work, with a doctor's certificate required after the eighth day. In 1992, the Bildt centrist government agreed with the Social Democratic opposition on a "crisis" package: The maximum sickness cash benefit was reduced to 90 percent of lost income. Only 65 percent is paid for the first three days; 80 percent from fourth to 90th day. The cost for the first 14 days of claimed sickness was shifted to the employer instead of the government. Since 1993 no sickness cash benefit has been paid for the first day of illness (Denmark also introduced a waiting period recently) and other minor cuts were made. The result: a sharp decrease in the high rate of absenteeism; Swedes who used to report in sick because of a Monday-morning hangover now show up to work.

Similarly, in reforms of a second program most vulnerable to abuse, job injury insurance, a stricter definition of job injury was adopted in the early 1990s and the insured were required to pay a larger portion of the cost themselves. Deficits in both these programs were turned into surpluses by 1994, although they remain costly. In addition, small downward adjustments were instituted in calculating pension benefits; and unemployment benefits were reduced to 80 percent of previous earnings (still high by any standard).

In January 1996 the present Social Democratic government decided on a second round of austerity – a further tightening of sick pay, reduced child allowances, and a reform of family policy: the parental leave benefit was reduced from 90 percent of income loss to 80 percent (two months of the 12 to 18 months of parental leave will remain at 90 percent, one month for each parent, use it or lose it, then 80 percent); compulsory counseling will be required for the divorced or separated; and child care allowances were cut (in 1994 dollars, to a maximum of about $267 per month up to 3 years of age); families benefiting from municipal subsidies for a daycare center get a reduced child allowance, depending on the hours.

Not all of the 1990s reforms involve reduced benefits and services. The Swedes have long led in rehabilitation programs to reintegrate the physically or mentally disabled into the labor force and promote independent living (for details see 2002, pp. 550ff.). In 1994 this effort to enable the handicapped to live an independent life was extended via a legal right to benefits, including counseling, support for individuals as well as parents with disabled children, escort services, housing with special service, support for minor handicaps, interpreter services for the deaf and blind, and more. At the same time, eligibility standards were tightened.

Finally, after 15 years of debate about pension reform, the 1996 proposals will result in real reductions, especially for middle and upper income earners – e.g., in the pension benefit for married pensioners – and a gradual rise in the retirement age. The accrual rate at retirement will be indexed to the average life expectancy of the retiree's cohort, so more years in the labor force will be required to receive benefits equal to those of earlier cohorts. Two percentage points of the 18.5 percent contribution rate will be allocated to a "premium reserve" account to pay benefits on the basis of return on invested capital – a small step away from pay-as-you-go financing. Sweden leads in a continuing effort to make the pension system flexible by increasing a choice of various combinations of work and pensions. Sweden is also the world's "oldest" country; in 1995 17.4 percent of its population was 65 or older compared to 12.7 percent for the United States.

What about health-care reform? In 1990 the Swedish health-care system spent 8.6 percent of GDP – less expensive than the United States and Canada (despite Sweden's much older population) but more costly than the rest of our 19 rich democracies. It delivers "care of high quality, equity in access and local accountability unrivaled in other countries" and a high level of patient satisfaction (Glennerster and Matsaganis, 1992, pp. 3, 5). (In a recent Swedish national survey 85 percent thought the quality of medical care in Sweden was either very good or good.)

One reason for Sweden's above-average cost of medical care – aside from the strong organizations of provider groups and the unusual percentage of the aged – is that the system is biased toward hospitals; there is no concept of the general practitioner (*Ibid.*, p. 4). Primary care is organized around local health centers staffed with salaried doctors, nurses, and specialists acting as teams. There are significant user charges – co-payments for prescriptions, visits to doctors, and other services (*Ibid.*, p. 5), with no exception but an upper limit of 1600 SEK or $272 per year in 1990 dollars for all publicly-provided health care.

In response to economic austerity and the need for increasing efficiency and consumer responsiveness, parties of left and right agreed in the mid-1980s to replace fee-for-service with capitation payments from the national insurance fund directly to counties, which would decide on reimbursement of practitioners. Most counties are led by Social Democrats. There are "almost as many reform programs as there are [county] councils" (*Ibid.*, p. 8). "Patients still have full freedom of self-referral" (*Ibid.*, p. 6). The net effect of these reforms is that waiting time and lists for non-emergency surgery and out-patient visits have been reduced, especially in the Stockholm district, and the GDP share is down from the 1980 peak of 9.4 percent. In fact, Sweden is the only country among our 19 rich democracies that reduced the share of total domestic expenditure devoted to health care from 1980 to 1991 (OECD, 1993, Vol. 1, Table 1).

With all of these reforms, and despite levels of unemployment and annual deficits unprecedented for Sweden, the contours of the most generous welfare state in the world remain intact; the adjustments may actually make the social-spending share of GDP level off or even move slightly downward. In per capita benefits the Swedes moved in the 1990s from lavish to merely very-generous social expenditures.

Finland: Balancing Equity and Cost

Finland's recent welfare-state reforms are a model of what corporatist bargaining among the social partners (labor, professions, management, and other relevant and inclusive interest groups interacting with government and political parties) can do to forge consensus on major pension and related programs. It is a lesson in how a consensual democracy, especially if it integrates labor and the left into high policy, can reform the core programs of the welfare state to cope with issues of both equity and cost.

Here is a broad outline of a major reform of pension and related programs that was adopted by parliament in 2003 after agreement among the "labor-market parties" and after a thorough government assessment of long-run costs and benefits. Most took effect on Jan 1, 2005.[12]

The major aims: postpone the average effective retirement age by 2–3 years; adapt the pension scheme to an increased average life expectancy and other demographic shifts; achieve unification and simplification of private sector earnings-related pensions. The new system reforms cover three types of pensions: old age, disability, and part-time. (Survivors pensions were left intact.) It changes the pension index (so consumer prices weigh 80%, earnings increases 20%). It establishes specific rights to vocational rehabilitation "if illness, handicap, or injury poses a threat to work capacity within about 5 years" and similar rights within the earnings-related pension system, with appeals procedures. Changes in the disability pension were necessary because some early retirement schemes were abolished (individual early retirement pension and unemployment pension). The tax-financed unemployment insurance program remained. The flat-rate pension was changed to reflect the increased retirement age of the earnings-related mandate.

To further enhance flexible retirement and encourage work, changes in both part time and full pensions are substantial. The part-time pension age is increased from age 56 to 58, with an accrual rate of 1.5% of earnings and 0.75% of the reduction of earnings due to part-time reitirement. Early old-age pensions start at 62. At 63 one can retire on the old-age accrual rate, which begins on earnings after age 18 and climbs in three steps, from 1.5% at age 18–52, to 4.5% at 63–68 – a strong incentive for continued work. Various grandfather clauses are included to prevent transitional shocks to older workers. Finally there will be provision for unpaid periods: periods of earnings-related maternity, paternity, and parental leave; days with earnings-related unemployed allowance, periods of study; caring for a child under 3, and job alternation leave – all with an accrual rate of 1.5%. A wage earner can take a job alternation leave by agreement with the employer – stop working for a defined period, e.g., a year, and receive partial compensation for lost earnings. It is like a publicly financed sabbatical.

Funding will be increased from 2003 on, but savings from the flexible retirement provisions and later retirement are expected to reduce the growth of pension expenditure as a percent of wages from 2005 to about 2030 and thereafter to level off. Combined with real cuts made in the 1990s a product of the same consensual bargaining process among the social partners – the current reforms mean that pension expenditures and premiums will grow much less than they would have without reforms.[13]

All rich democracies have experienced twin trends that pose a serious issue for policy planners: a century-long decline in the age of exit of men from the labor force; and an increase in healthy older populations. At the root of the problem is management and union desire to ease out older workers. Managers prefer younger, cheaper men and women and middle-aged women and, if the state can pick up the tab, they will help older workers into an early retirement; unions go along because they want to reduce unemployment and make way for younger members. In trying to contain exploding costs of pensions while they cope with an oversupply of healthy displaced older workers who prefer to work at least part time, many governments have tried to devise flexible retirement systems. Surely it is good public policy to transform the healthy aged who want to work into taxpayers, part-time workers, and partial pensioners rather than pressuring them to retire fully. But it is extraordinarily difficult both technically and politically to craft social-security systems that would reverse the long-term slide in the age of exit from work. One obstacle is the prevalence of disabilities of various kinds among the aged. The trick is to find the balance between reductions in benefits for very early retirement and generous partial pensions for continued part-time work for those aged, say 60–70, while avoiding pressure on the worn-out workers in the least attractive jobs to postpone retirement. As in the case of the partially-disabled, this necessitates adequate income and medical supports; or, if rehabilitation is the focus, a reallocation of funds toward work-oriented rehabilitation and a tight connection to an active labor market policy.

Both Sweden and Finland, cases of democratic corporatism, have crafted such systems. Their more-or-less centralized systems of national bargaining among the social partners account for the creative compromises they have made. Flexible retirement systems cannot be successful without attention to disability pensions and job-creation, as well as part-time pensions and investment in rehabilitation – an active labor market policy (training and retraining, job placement, counseling, mobility incentives, as well as job creation). Corporatist democracies have evidenced a capacity for the necessary policy linkages.

SUMMARY AND CONCLUSIONS

In short, the cutbacks among rich democracies are concentrated on either the greatest excesses and abuses of the welfare state (sick pay, disability), or on the least politically-organized, marginal groups (single mothers, the unemployed, or the poor), or in sectors where the eligible population is declining (school-age children in the countries with older populations and a declining percentage of youngsters; decreasing unemployment on the upswing of the economy and hence decreasing expenditures on unemployment benefits and vice versa). Health-care reform is prominent everywhere. Benefit formulas for pensions are being modified in most countries; to account for increased longevity, "normal retirement age" is being raised in many. But nowhere have employment-based pension schemes been redesigned according to the American Concord Coalition recommendation for a tax/transfer, needs-based model (Myles and Quadagno, 1996, p. 20). Real cutbacks in benefits are typically small and incremental – trimming around the edges of the welfare state, sometimes making it more efficient. There is an increased use of income-testing and the taxation of benefits. And while the GDP share of social spending is stabilizing, the recent growth of eligible aged, poor, and unemployed has meant some reduction of per-recipient benefits in several countries. But this is a slow process that encounters strong public resistance. Small, incremental reductions in many programs can add up over time; vast majorities of voters whose income and security are threatened sooner or later rebel. (We might call these pro-welfare-state protests "frontlash." See Chapter 10.)

Although both center-left governments committed to egalitarian solutions and center-right governments committed to market solutions have moved toward retrenchment of the welfare state, those divisions have made a difference in who get what and when. In other words, when reforms are necessary, left-labor pressure results in more equality of sacrifice and fairer outcomes; business interests interacting with right-wing parties resist distribution of income and power downward. In my analysis of 19 rich democracies (2002) I show that types of political economy shape both policy clusters and their effects on the well-being of people. By combining mass-based party power over long periods with types of national bargaining arrangements, I show that in descending order, for a great range of real welfare outcomes, these 19 countries rank from top to bottom as follows: (1) left-corporatist (e.g., Sweden, Norway, Finland); (2) left-Catholic corporatist (Austria, Belgium, Netherlands); (3) Catholic corporatist (Italy); (4) Corporatism-without-labor (Japan, France); (5) most fragmented and decentralized (USA, UK, Canada, New Zealand, Australia). All of them are concerned with rising costs, but as we have seen, the more consensual ("Corporatist") democracies have an edge in mobilizing voter support for reforms, in adopting and financing them, and implementing them.

NOTES

1. In 1966 East Germany and Czechoslovakia ranked eighth and ninth of these 22 in social-security spending while the USSR lagged at 16th. They fit a convergence theory because their estimated GNP per capita at factor cost puts the USSR quite a bit below the two more modern Communist regimes, both of which got into the welfare-state business earlier than the former USSR and have older populations (Wilensky, 1975, pp. 121–128). Because so many of the data on these three countries are of dubious comparability, we dropped them from further analysis. The 19 rich democracies were by the mid-1960s, in the upper one-sixth of the world's GNP/capita and remain there. I eliminated democracies with less than 3 million population.

2. Because of variation in what is off-budget, in one-time asset sales, and in other obscurities, measures of debt and deficits are not included in my analysis of economic performance, chapter 12; cf. Pashnik, 2000.

3. Heavy means-testing in these programs creates political resistance to funding them at an adequate level. The distinction between divisive highly-visible means testing and simple quiet income testing is important. By "means-testing" I mean (1) noncategorical benefits targeted to the poor via a stiff income- and/or assets-test, (2) applied by welfare administrators with substantial discretion, (3) with a high probability of stigma. "Income testing" is the opposite. It is categorical as a social right with co-payments graded by income bracket and, because it is private and invisible, has no stigma. Means-testing is characteristic of Britain and other decentralized and fragmented political economies (USA, Canada, Ireland), democratic corpo ratist countries, especially those with cumulative left party power, avoid means testing and rely much more on income testing (Wilensky, 2002, pp. 321–332.)

4. The exception is a country with a Westminster electoral system – first-past-the-post, winner-take-all. That permitted Thatcher to rule for 12 years with about 40% of the popular vote and a steadily rising majority hostile to her social policies (Wilensky, 2002, p. 374).

5. Pierson concludes that Thatcher had more success than Reagan in increasing the share of total social expenditures that are means-tested (Table 6.3, p. 145). But the comparison is misleading. He excludes U.S. state expenditures from the programs he covers (Medicaid, food stamps, public assistance, and Supplemental Security Income). Moreover, the aggregate figure lumps together visible, stigmatized benefits (AFDC and food stamps) with invisible programs targeted to the poor (EITC), which lack stigma and can grow more easily (see Chapter 8); SSI, where the aged population is the target and where stigma is less; and Medicaid, where provider and administrative costs soar and where much of the money comprises the only government support for

long-term care for the aged, a program that enjoys broad popular support. Finally, the measure – percentage of total social spending – yields results different from those of GDP shares or per capita benefits. Cuts in real benefits in means-tested public assistance from 1980 to 1995 were substantial in both countries (see Chapter 6. Cf. Bawden and Palmer, 1984; and Alber, 1996).

6. This account of NHS reforms is based on Klein, 1995; Giaimo, 1995, and Döhler, 1991.

7. One estimate suggests that by 2030, 38 percent of Germans will be over 60, 16 percent under 20, *Economist*, February 1994. Assuming no change in retirement age, a slightly different measure for 1995 and 2025 – the ratio of retirement-age persons to 100 working-age adults – yields similar results: in 1995, 29.6, in 2025, 54.1. That is almost as burdensome as Austria's 36.7 and 61.4. Comparable figures for the United States, where the attack on "entitlements" is most hysterical, are only 22.3 and 35.1.

8. The long established system of tripartite self-governance involves government, patients, and providers, with some input from other groups. Non-profit sickness funds based on occupation or region combine in national associations and must bargain with physicians associations; they are governed by national framework legislation. Since 1977 they must take account of annual recommendations of the Concerted Action in Health Care, a roundtable which includes labor unions, employers, officials at various levels of government, and various provider groups. See Chapter 16.

9. The following account of recent reforms of Italian social programs is based on Maurizio Ferrera, 1994; Chiara Saraceno and Nicola Negri, 1994; MacFarlan and Oxley, 1996 and my interviews.

10. At this writing, mothers are still required to take off two months before and three months after childbirth. For risky pregnancies, they can take off the entire period of pregnancy. (Many women claim "risky" pregnancies from day one, with the acquiescence of their physicians.) Most working women receive full salaries during leave, 80 percent covered by social security, 20 percent by employers. Chapter 7 compares an array of family policies in 19 countries, including parental leave. It shows that corporatist countries with the combination of strong Catholic and left parties score medium on an index of innovative and expansive family policies, reflecting the ambivalence of Catholic parties toward women's place and the offset of both corporatism and left power. But on maternal leave Italy ranks high and remains there.

11. Based on my interviews; publications of the Ministry of Health and Social Affairs and the Swedish National Insurance Board, various years; Niemelä and Salminen, 1994; Huber and Stevens, 1996; Kuhnle, 1996; Palme and Wennemo, 1998.

12. This account is based on documents supplied by the research scholar who directed the calculations and analysis carried out at the Finnish Centre for Pensions, Hannu Uusitalo. I am grateful for his comments.

13. With reform, as % of GDP, pension spending is 11.7% in 2003 and with reform is estimated at 14.5% in 2030 (15.8% if no reform had been made), 13.8% in 2050 (15.7% if no reform).

REFERENCES

Alber, Jens (1988). "Is There a Crisis in the Welfare State? Cross-national Evidence from Europe, North America, and Japan." *European Sociological Review* 4, 3: 181–207.

Alber, Jens (1996) "Selectivity, Universalism, and the Politics of Welfare Retrenchment in Germany and the United States." Paper presented at the 92nd Annual Meeting of the American Political Science Association, San Francisco, August 31.

Atkinson, A.B. (1995) "The Welfare. State and Economic Performance." Discussion Paper WSP/109. Centre for Economics and Related Disciplines, London School of Economics.

Bawden, D. Lee and John L. Palmer (1984). "Social Policy: Challenging the Welfare State." In *The Regan Record: An Assessment of America's Changing Domestic Priorities*, ed. John Palmer and Isabel V. Sawhill, 177–215. Cambridge, MA: Ballinger.

Brown, Lawrence D. (1991) "Knowledge and Power: Health Services Research as a Political Resource." *Health Services Research: Key to Health Policy*, ed. Eli Ginzberg, 20–45. Cambridge: Harvard University Press.

Cameron, David R. (1982) "On the Limits of the Public Economy." *The Annals_*459: 46–62.

Döhler, Marian (1991) "Policy Networks, Opportunity Structures and Neo-Conservative Reform Strategies in Health Policy." In *Policy Networks: Empirical Evidence and Theoretical Consideration*, ed. Bernd Marin and Renate Mayntz, 235–96. Frankfurt/Main: Campus Verlag.

Ferrera, Maurizio (1994) "The Rise and Fall of Democratic Universalism: Health Care Reform in Italy, 1978–1994. "Paper presented at workshop on "The State and the Health System," ECPR Joint Sessions of Workshops, Madrid, April 17–22.

Giaimo, Susan (1995) "Health Care Reform in Britain and Germany: Recasting the Political Bargain with the Medical Profession." *Governance: An International Journal of Policy and Administration* 8, 3: 354–379.

Glennerster, Howard and Manos Matsaganis (1992) *The English and Swedish Health Care Reforms*. Discussion Paper WSP/79. The Welfare State Program, London School of Economics.

Huber, Evelyne and John D. Stephens (1998) "Internationalization and the Social Democratic Model." *Comparative Political Studies*, 31, No. 3: 353–397.

Keizer, P. K. (1996) "A Critical Assessment of Recent Trends in Dutch Industrial Relations." Research Memorandum RM/96/012, University of Limburg, Maastricht, Faculty of Economics and Business Administration.

Klein, Rudolf and Michael O'Higgins (1985). "Introduction: Old Myths–New Challenges." In the *Future of Welfare*, ed. Rudolf Klein and Michael O'Higgins, 1–7, Oxford: Basil Blackwell.

Klein, Rudolf (1995). *The New Politics of the National Health Service*. 3rd ed. London: Longman.

Kuhnle, Stein (1996). "European Integration and the National Welfare State." Paper presented at the Peder Sather symposium on "Challenges to Labor: Integration, Employment, and Bargaining in Scandinavia and the U.S.," Center for Western European Studies, University of California, Berkeley, March 21–22.

Lindert, Peter H. (2004) *Growing Public: Social Spending and Economic Growth Since the Eighteenth Century*. 2 vols. Cambridge: Cambridge University Press.

MacFarlan, Maitland and Howard Oxley (1996). "Reforming Social Transfers." *OECD Observer* No. 199 (April/May): 28–31.

Marmor, Theodore R. and Jerry L. Mashaw (eds.) (1988) *Social Security: Beyond the Rhetoric of Crisis*. Princeton, NJ: Princeton University Press.

Myles, John and Jill Quadagno (1996) "Recent Trends in Public Pension Reform: A Comparative View." Conference on Reform of the Retirement Income System, Queen's University, February 1–2.

Myles, John and Paul Pierson (2001) "The Comparative Political Economy of Pension Reform." In *The New Politics of the Welfare State*, ed. Paul Pierson. New York: Oxford University Press, pp. 25–48.

Niemelä, Heikki and Kari Salminen (1994) "State or Corporations: Trends of Pension Policy in Scandanavia." *Politiikka*, 35, 4 (January).

OECD (1993) *OECD Health Systems, volume 1: Facts and Trends 1960–1991*. Health Policy Studies No. 3. Paris: OECD.

Palme, Joakim and Irene Wennemo (1998) *Swedish Social Security in the 1990s: Reform and Retrenchment*. Stockholm: Valfardsprojektat, Cabinet Office and Ministries.

Patashnik, Eric M. (2000) *Putting Trust in the U. S. Budget*. Cambridge University Press.

Pierson, Paul (1994) *Dismantling the Welfare State? Reagan, Thatcher, and the Politics of Retrenchment*. Cambridge University Press.

Ruggie, Mary (1992) "The Paradox of Liberal Intervention: Health Policy and the American Welfare State." *American Journal of Sociology* 97, 4: 919–944.

Saraceno, Chiara and Nicola Negri (1994). "The Changing Italian Welfare State." *Journal of European Social Policy* 4, 1: 19–34.

Seeleib-Kaiser, Martin (2002). "A Dual Transformation of the German Welfare State." *West European Politics*, 24, 4 (October): 25–48.

Von Hagen, Jürgen (1992). *Budgeting Procedures and Fiscal Performance in the European Communities.* University of California at Berkeley Center for German and European Studies, Political Economy of European Integration Research Group, Working Paper 1.9.

Wilensky, Harold L. (1965) "The Problems and Prospects of the Welfare State." In *Industrial Society and Social Welfare,* by Harold L. Wilensky and Charles N. Lebeaux. v-lii. Enlarged Edition. New York: Free Press-Macmillan.

Wilensky, Harold L. (1975) *The Welfare State and Equality: Structural and Ideological Roots of Public Expenditures.* Berkeley, CA: University of California Press.

Wilensky, Harold L. (1981a) "Democratic Corporatism, Consensus, and Social Policy: Reflections on Changing Values and the 'Crisis' of the Welfare State." In *The Welfare State in Crisis: An Account of the Conference on Social Policies in the 1980s.* Paris: Organization For Economic Cooperation and Development, 185–195.

Wilensky, Harold L. (1981b) "Leftism, Catholicism, and Democratic Corporatism: The Role of Political Parties in Welfare State Development." In *The Development of Welfare States in Europe and America,* ed. Peter Flora and Arnold J. Heidenheimer, 345–382. New Brunswick, NJ: Transaction Books.

Wilensky, Harold L. (2002) *Rich Democracies: Political Economy, Public Policy, and Performance.* Berkeley: University of California Press.

12

Health Policy

MICHAEL MORAN

PUBLIC POLICY AND HEALTH POLICY

Public policy is a notoriously balkanised field of study. It has, true, acquired some independent institutional identity, principally in the United States, in the form of university teaching departments and some think tanks avowedly devoted to researching public policy. It has nevertheless never acquired the same level of intellectual identity as adjacent fields, such as economics and political science. By the second half of the twentieth century the latter were institutionalised in well organised disciplines, with their own university departments, professional networks, and a fair level of consensus about core curricula for undergraduate and even graduate study.

The most obvious feature of the study of public policy, by contrast, is the extent to which there has developed an intellectual division of labour based largely on the substantively different areas of study. In these separate fields – whether we speak of health or pensions policy, defence or transport policy – there exist distinct intellectual agendas, dense professional networks and, often, well organised university departments and research institutes. The weight of resources, and the power of intellectual identity, has overwhelmingly concentrated in these substantive domains,

rather than in the study of 'public policy' as a distinct vocation. Health policy illustrates this kind of specialisation to perfection, with all the attendant strengths and weaknesses.

These contrasting intellectual histories do not arise from features inscribed in the intellectual content of different fields of study. Political science, for instance, has all the potential for balkanisation which the study of public policy has realised. As a field of study with something as wide as the state as its main focus, it could easily have fragmented into numerous specialisms. Indeed, the modern proliferation of sub-fields in an increasingly professionalised academic world often threatens to do exactly that. There seem to be two main reasons for the comparative failure of public policy to match adjacent fields in intellectual and institutional integration, and both again apply with perfection to the study of health policy. Both in essence have to do with the timing of intellectual and institutional developments. Economics, and to a lesser extent political science, enjoyed 'first mover' advantages: they already occupied intellectual and institutional terrains before there emerged the conscious development of the study of public policy. By the time policy studies emerged as a self-conscious academic field ready to compete for student business in the university teaching market, economics and political science were already entrenched in faculties and degree programmes. The result has been that individuals interested in policy studies have tended to find a home within the pre-existing institutional shelters – established social science departments – or, as we shall see in a moment, have tried for differentiation by stressing distinct, substantive policy domains. (It is of course interesting to ponder why policy studies was not able to achieve what was accomplished by other new quasi-disciplines, like cultural studies, which was to use the independent power of student demand to acquire a secure, independent institutional base.)

Part of the history of the field of policy studies is therefore shaped by the timing of its emergence as an activity in higher education. A second critical aspect of the timing of intellectual development is particularly relevant to health policy. The study of health policy on any systematic scale is closely associated with, and, as we shall see, has in part been prompted by the rise of health as a significant policy sector in the state. The most obvious indicator of that rise is money. In the three decades or so after 1945 – the period roughly corresponding to the 'long boom' which was the most important feature of the leading capitalist economies in the middle decades of the twentieth century – societal spending on health care rose substantially, and public spending more or less matched this rise. (For a summary of policy history, Moran 1999: 2–3; and OECD, various dates, for the underlying data collection.) The observation holds virtually right across the advanced capitalist world. And the three decades since the end of the long boom have been dominated by attempts to cope with the consequences of that first great historic rise in spending: if the thirty years after the Second World War were the age of health-care expansion, the next thirty were the age of (attempted) cost containment (for examples: Levit et al., 1994; Saltman and Von Otter, 1995; Altenstetter and Björkman, 1997; Freeman, 2000). The study of health policy has been shaped by this extraordinary history: by the attempt to make sense of those early boom decades; by the attempt to make sense of what has happened since the end of the long boom;

and by the need to make some practitioner relevant sense of how to allocate this huge flow of resources. The result, unsurprisingly, is a field of study which is dominated by substantive issues to do with the health field itself.

The reader might respond that it is hardly surprising that students of health policy are focused on substantive issues to do with health. But this apparently obvious feature, replicated across substantive policy domains, is exactly what helps explain so much of the fragmented nature of policy studies as a field. And, as we shall see in a moment, the historical conjuncture between the rise of health policy as a specialised field of study and the rise of health as a major consumer of societal resources has had important consequences for the way health policy is framed as a field of study. As in all framing exercises, the results privilege particular approaches, questions, and even answers, over others.

FRAMING HEALTH-CARE POLICY: THREE DOMAINS OF HEALTH CARE

Policy domains are not 'given'; they are constructed. The practical meaning of 'health policy' famously varies from jurisdiction to jurisdiction. These variations are the product of entirely unsurprising considerations: of cultural understandings of what constitutes the concept of health; of administrative and historical conventions; of bureaucratic politics which in virtually all jurisdictions constantly reshape the 'turf' of state institutions. (For some illustrations, Kelman, 1975; Wildavsky, 1977; Evans and Stoddart, 1990.) A simple example of this point at work in practice can be provided by the nightmare of trying to construct accurate comparative cross-national estimates of health-care spending, where the results are hugely sensitive to the classification conventions allocating particular programmes to particular domains. For instance, Swedish health-care spending has looked consistently high, viewed comparatively, because, unlike many other nations, care of the aged in Sweden has been allocated to the health care, rather than the social security, budgets. Beneath this administrative variation in classification lies a conceptual jungle, notably the tangled issues of what constitutes 'health' itself.

This does not mean that our understanding of health or of health policy is an arbitrary matter. On the contrary: it has been shaped intensely by national cultural patterns, by the workings of economic interests, by the manoeuvrings of bureaucratic politics – and by recent historical experience. The last of these takes us to the heart of the way health policy has been framed by both policy makers and researchers in the last generation. It is a simplification, but a serviceable simplification, to say that health policy can be framed in one of three ways: as a species of social policy; as a species of labour market policy; and as a species of industrial policy. The three are not mutually exclusive. On the contrary, they arise out of historically embedded linkages between different parts of health-care systems. Converted into influences over how we can think about health policy, however, they truly represent (mostly unselfconscious) framing exercises: that is, the different ways of framing put different parts of health-care systems at the centre or the margins of the policy picture.

Some modes of framing are more popular than others, which is where the policy experience of health care in recent decades becomes relevant. The boom in health-care spending in the decades of the long boom, and the turn to efforts at cost containment in the decades since the mid-1970s, plainly mirrors a wider policy history: that tracking the golden age of the welfare state, and the decades of structural reform and comparative austerity that have followed the end of the golden age. (Definitively anatomised in Esping-Andersen, 1996). Framed thus, health policy is a sub-set of welfare policy. The way to tell health policy stories is in the vocabulary, and the dramaturgy, of stories about the achievements and problems of welfare states. When the health arena is framed in these 'welfarist' terms, the dominant vocabulary is a vocabulary of consumption and of social citizenship. It focuses on entitlements to health care, on the conditions under which those entitlements can be exercised, and

the policy problems arising from the exercise of those entitlements. The shape of the health policy arena is thus largely determined by the wider welfare state arena. This conceptualisation of health policy as health-*care* policy then feeds into the definition of both policy problems and policy issues. Thus, the account of the last three decades or so is seen largely as an age of retrenchment, parallel to the wider pressures experienced by the welfare state (for instance, Ferrera and Rhodes, 2000). This approach, we shall see later in the chapter, has also helped frame the definition of the most famous and most intensely studied puzzle in health policy: the puzzle of what is commonly called American exceptionalism, to which I later return. As I shall show, American 'exceptionalism' is indeed only 'exceptional' when health policy is framed in these 'welfarist' terms. And when health policy is framed in alternative ways – notably as a form of industrial policy – the United States, far from looking like a deformation, looks state of the art.

Approaching health-care policy through the recent historical experience of the welfare state, and through the vocabulary of social policy, has some clear advantages. It reflects an obvious, important facet of the historical experience of the last sixty years, since plainly the 'golden age of the welfare state' and the golden age of health-care provision did indeed closely coincide. It also helps counter one of the key features of the study of public policy generally identified at the start of this chapter – the tendency towards balkanisation – since it links themes in health policy to important sets of wider themes in welfare policy.

But this particular framing device, like any other mode of framing, has its costs. It focuses attention overwhelmingly on issues of health-care consumption: crudely, in the era of the long boom on how it could be extended, and in the era since the end of the long boom on how it can be constrained. Health-care policy gains from being linked to a wider policy domain – that of welfare policy – but is heavily shaped by the consumption concerns of that wider domain. If we push our historical vision backwards, beyond the beginning of the golden age of the welfare state, we can immediately see other framing possibilities. In the half century or so before the beginning of the First World War, in both North America and Western Europe two critical features of modern health-care systems were established. Both concerned the *delivery* rather than the consumption of care, and both have left huge imprints on modern health-care systems: in summary, they help explain why the delivery of modern health-care is a labour intensive process, in which the labour is highly professionalised, and why for over a century it has involved the mobilisation of an elaborate apparatus of high technology.

These two features of health-care delivery immediately introduce us to our two alternative ways of framing health policy. In the second half of the nineteenth century doctors emerged as the dominant actors in health-care systems, separating themselves from a long historical association with lesser occupations. In the United States, for example, the process involved the suppression of a wide range of 'folk' medicine with its roots in a democratic culture (Starr, 1982). In the United Kingdom, and in other European countries, it involved the separation of doctors from a long trail of more 'artisan' occupations, like barbering, and a process of social closure involving all the classic forms of professionalisation: suppression of price competition, control of entry, regulation of both clinical and ethical practices (Freidson, 1970; Berlant, 1975; Waddington, 1984). These developments gave to the organisation of medical care a highly distinctive imprint, of which two are particularly important: the almost universal domination of health-care delivery, at least in the advanced capitalist world, by doctors; and the long term emergence of a wide range of specialised professions attempting to emulate the success of doctors in establishing their occupational autonomy.

An important consequence of these developments – labour intensive service delivery, an elaborate division of labour based on professionalisation, the historical dominance of one particular profession, doctors – is to alter the 'frame' of health policy. Viewed in this light, much of health policy is an aspect, not simply of the consumption of welfare type services, but of

labour market policy. That in turn ties health-care policy to the wider imperatives of labour market policy: to issues such as labour supply, training and the discipline of the labour force. One very important connection with these wider economic policy issues is provided by the need to manage medical labour forces which are increasingly globalised, or at least internationalised: issues of the circulation of medical labour forces across national boundaries, of the supply and training of labour, and of the place of medical labour in the international political economy of labour are all central (Moran and Wood, 1996; Alsop and Saks, 2002).

Framed thus, the appropriate vocabulary of health policy becomes subtly, but importantly, different from the vocabulary offered by a 'welfarist' framing. For now, health policy is tied to the political economy of labour markets, and the stories about policy that need to be told involve in particular one part of labour markets – that marked by competition for professional power and privilege. In terms of research agendas, too, the study of health policy framed thus becomes linked to the kinds of issues of occupational control central to the classic literatures on professionalism (Johnson, 1972).

Framing health policy as a process involving service delivery through highly organised and competing institutions of professionalism already ties health care to the international political economy of the advanced capitalist world. Our second historical 'take' on delivery produces a way of framing policy that makes the link to a global political economy even more direct. In the decades before the First World War, when the medical profession was establishing its ascendancy in health-care delivery, there also occurred a great change in the technology of medicine. Hitherto a species of 'bodging', or the domain of the low level artisan, medical technology was subjected to the full power of laboratory science (Reiser, 1978). In the half century or so from about 1870 there emerged two linked industries which became, and remain, central to health-care delivery: the pharmaceutical industry, based on laboratory developments in immunology; and the medical devices industry, which at its most highly capital intensive was spurred by, first, developments in electronics, and latterly by IT related innovations in digitalisation (Brown, 1979; Pickstone, 1992; Foote, 1992). These developments have by the twenty first century created a large, globalised industrial economy of health care. The technologically based health-care industries are central to the industrial economies of many of the most advanced capitalist economies. They are also often symbiotically connected to other industrial sectors – a striking example being the link between digitalised health technology and the wider IT sector (for example Trajtenberg, 1990). An equally striking link existing historically is between innovation in the technology of war and innovations applied in the health-care sector. Much of the highly sophisticated imaging technology used in medical care, for example, has its origins in innovations like ultrasound used for hunting and detection in sea warfare; many modern developments in fields like surgery are traceable back to innovations in battlefield surgery designed to cope with the horrific injuries of the great total wars of the twentieth century; and the development of penicillin was greatly assisted by innovation under the demand of war (for examples, Foote, 1992; Temin, 1980).

The three domains of health policy identified here obviously overlap in important ways. For instance, health care as a form of welfare consumption intimately involves the professionalised world of health-care labour markets; and the twin roles of the health-care technology industries as suppliers of goods central to the consumption of modern health care and as key sectors of the modern industrial economy hugely complicates the management of both health-care consumption and the management of national economies. But 'framing' is a particularly appropriate image to describe how we think about three domains of health policy. When we frame in one way – whether in 'welfare policy' or 'industrial policy' terms – we decide what is put into the centre of the picture and what is pushed to the margins, even when we do not acknowledge, or are perhaps even not aware, of what is going on.

Health care policy, like other policy domains, does not 'frame itself'. How it is framed is not an arbitrary business, but it is an uncertain business. The purpose of sketching the three frames above is to show that how the meaning of health policy is conceived depends heavily on which route we approach health domains through. Is it the world of the health-care consumer, in which case we instinctively frame health policy as a facet of welfare policy? Is it the world of professionalised medical delivery systems, in which case we instinctively see health policy 'framed' inside labour market policy, especially policy about professionalised labour markets? Or is it the world of medical technology, in which case we frame health policy as part of the wider management of the modern industrial state?

The way policy is framed is plainly important for how we study it, but in the case of health policy it is important also for a more substantive reason. The way 'framing' happens depends crucially on the role of states. States are key actors in all three domains of health-care policy sketched here – consumption of care, delivery of that care as a personal service, application of technology to care. But, as we will shortly see, they are actors in very different ways. The state's role in the three domains in effect helps us identify what kind of health-care system we are looking at. All states are in different ways 'health-care states', in the sense that all health-care institutions are embedded in the surrounding state system. That innocent image of 'embeddedness' is suggesting two distinct, complex processes, The first is obvious: that states have a shaping and continuing influence over the character of health-care institutions – over consumption, over professionalised labour markets, and over medical technology. Indeed, in many cases they have been historically responsible for constituting these markets, and everywhere remain critical to their functioning. But a second facet of embeddedness is less obvious: health-care institutions also have a shaping influence on their surrounding environment. They amount to large scale concentrations of interests, economic activity and, often, electoral muscle, and in these guises intervene in the wider shaping of policy.

To try to make these sweeping generalisations clearer I next show, by some examples from real existing states, how and why 'health-care states' do indeed exhibit different policy patterns, and encounter different policy problems. Space imposes drastic selection in this exercise, but the highly selective approach is justified because of the point of the exercise. My purpose is not to offer a systematic classification of health-care systems, but to use some critical examples to show how the varying roles of states help constitute the character of some of the most important kinds of health systems. In this way, we will see how the manipulation of the framing exercise critically determines how we compare systems and how we view policy problems and patterns.

STATES, HEALTH-CARE STATES AND POLICY PATTERNS

States are central to the practice of health policy, and how states 'frame' health policy is the product of a complex mix of historical factors and institutional constraints. And the most immediately observable feature of states are the striking variations in the way states behave in health-care systems. Even if we confine our observations to the advanced capitalist nations, we soon see very striking variations.

In this section I try to make these points concrete by taking three examples of national health-care systems: the United States, the United Kingdom and Germany. These systems have a powerful substantive importance. Simply: by most measures they are big, with the United States by any measure the largest national health system on Earth, and Germany by most measures the largest in Europe. But their choice does not depend on these substantive measures. They stand as critical cases. In part – in the case of the United Kingdom and Germany – they exemplify larger families of health-care systems, and the justification for focusing on them alone is that, in the space available, this is the most economical way of illustrating with convincing detail the traits of these larger families. The case for focusing on

the United States, we shall see in a moment, is rather different: in a nutshell, the United States is *sui generis*, but a unique case of overwhelming importance for the global system of health-care policy.

Narrowing the focus on these cases plainly has intellectual costs. Two should be highlighted. First, the cases focus us mostly on health care in the advanced capitalist world. My defence for this is simply pragmatic: that, beyond noting some of the global characteristics of the political economy of health care, space just does not allow analysis of health policy in the impoverished nations of the world. Second, though the United Kingdom and Germany are here to do work on behalf of wider groups of health-care systems, the implicit classifications which they represent are not exhaustive. In particular, we should note the exclusion of Mediterranean members of the European Union, with their own distinctive histories of clientelist politics, which have played an important part in shaping patterns of health policy in those countries; and the health systems of the rising economies of East Asia which, like those economies, exhibit highly distinctive patterns of both state intervention and policy development (for examples of the former, Ferrera, 1996; Guillén and Cabada, 1997).

If the case for focusing on the United States is its uniqueness, in what does that uniqueness consist? In a nutshell, the uniqueness is three-fold: it is analytically unique; it is unique in its scale; and it is unique in its impact on the wider global political economy of health.

Of these three species of uniqueness, the first has dominated the comparative health policy literature. Every comparative observer of health-care policy very quickly notices a striking American anomaly, which has been well expressed by Rothman as follows:

> There are some questions that historians return to so often that they become classics in the field, to be explored and reexplored, considered and reconsidered. No inquiry better qualifies for this designation than the question of why the United States has never enacted a national health insurance program. Why, with the exception of South Africa, does it remain the only industrialized country that has not implemented so fundamental a social welfare policy? (1994: 11).

Over a period of nearly eighty years to the 1990s there were six major attempts to create some system of comprehensive health insurance in the United States: they spanned the Progressive campaign for compulsory insurance that originated before the First World War, to the failed Clinton reforms of the 1990s. All failed.

The particulars of failure have been extensively trawled over in a rich series of policy histories (for an anthology of failure, Morone and Belkin, 1994; for the most recent comprehensive failure, of the Clinton reforms, Skocpol, 1996). Not surprisingly, these individual policy histories all stress their own special contingencies. Behind all these contingencies lies broad structural features of the relations between the state and health care in the United States. The most important of these relate to the historical timing of the development of the system. The American federal state emerged late – or at least emerged onto the health-care scene as a significant actor after the rise of other powerful interests in health-care policy. Of the latter, two were especially important. First, there were the interests embodied in the medical profession, who by the early twentieth century had organised into a powerful regulatory group, and a powerful, well organised national lobby in the form of the American Medical Association. The second was a nascent 'medical industrial complex': the creation of a high quality, well organised research based complex linked to important corporate interests, and united in the pursuit of advances in high technology medicine. The upshot was that, from the beginning the shape of health policy in the United States has been dominated by private corporate interests, and particularly by well organised suppliers of medical care (Wohl, 1984, on the origins of the 'complex').

This history also helps explain the second unique feature of the US system. The country almost unique in not offering some kind of comprehensive health coverage is also the country with by far the highest level of spending on health care. A word should be said about this correlation. Health spending has many of the characteristics of a 'luxury' good, not least that, across nations, spending rises with wealth. One of the best predictors – perhaps the best

single predictor – of the level of health-care spending is some standard measure of national wealth, such as per capita income. But any examination of the trend line of the distribution points on a graph mapping the health spending/wealth correlation soon makes clear that the United States is well above the trend: in short, it spends far more on health-care than we should 'expect' given its wealth. The best summary of why this state of affairs obtains links it to the historical development sketched above, and helps explain the twin anomalies of the failure to develop comprehensive health insurance and the unusually high levels of spending on health care. It has been offered by Jacobs:

> the general sequence and form of health policy in the United States diverge from those of all other industrialized nations. The U.S. government's first and most generous involvement in health care focused on expanding the supply of hospital-centered, technologically sophisticated health care … . In contrast to the United States, however, other Western countries have made the expansion of access their first and primary priority; governments have accelerated the expansion of supply in response to widening access and growing demand for care. (1995: 144–5).

This quotation catches exactly the important feature. The state in the U.S. has been by no means an unimportant actor in the health-care system. But in terms of the 'three worlds' sketched earlier in this chapter the contents of its interventions have been most heavily shaped by the interests represented by the two linked worlds of health-care suppliers – suppliers of professionalised medical care and suppliers of high technology medical care. It has, in summary, been a *supply state*. That is, it has been dominated by actors in the second and third domains identified in our preceding section, the organised corporate suppliers of care.

The mixture of sheer scale and the importance of suppliers of care – notably suppliers of high technology medicine – also lies at the base of the third unique feature of the American system noted earlier: its unique global impact. Two remarkable signs of this should be highlighted. First, some of the most important innovations in care, many stimulated by the search for cost containment, have been diffused from the United States. One reason for this is the character of American policy networks, which are uniquely well organised and profession-alised. The sheer size of the American system also supports the best health policy analysis and health economics on Earth (for examples, Brown, 1998). A second, more easily measurable sign, is provided by the case of medical technol-ogy. The medical technology industries amount to a powerfully organised system of innovation which is constantly creating new health-care ossibilities – with all that implies for resource commitments. This system of innovation, organ-ised in markets on a global scale, is American dominated: whether we look at the demand side – where the biggest markets lie – or the sup-ply side – who the biggest firms are – the domi-nance of the United States is remarkable (see Weisbrod, 1991: 526, and Moran, 1999: 138).

I have spent some time on the single case of the United States because its importance tran-scends American conditions. Some of this becomes plainer when we turn to sketch our other cases. Evidently the kind of patterns we can observe in the practice of health-care policy are highly sensitive to how the different domains interact. That hunch is reinforced by the case of a very different historical policy configuration, that represented by the case of the United Kingdom. We can start with one particularly remarkable contrast in policy out-comes. If the United States has historically been a high spender on health care, notably in the last generation, the United Kingdom has been until very recently a low spender. If we do the parallel exercise tracking health spending and measures of national wealth, in other words, we find that levels of spending in the UK have been lower than we would 'expect' given the UK's level of measured wealth. In short, if the US health-care system seems to be uniquely weak at controlling health spend-ing, the UK seems to be particularly good at that job.

To understand why this is so, we need to look at the configuration of our 'three domains' of policy: of professionalised deliv-ery, of medical technology, and of consump-tion. The critical moment in the modern history of the British health-care system was the foundation of the National Health

Service in 1948 because it consolidated a highly distinctive kind of health-care system, one that Saltman and von Otter (1992) charac-terise as 'command and control'. 'Consolidated' is used here because the elements of the system that emerged in the National Health Service already existed in substantial outline before 1948, and in particular had developed from reforms introduced by the Liberal Government before the First World War. (For the standard history, Webster, 1988). The system that emerged out of the NHS reforms nevertheless marked the emergence of the UK as an exem-plary member of a family of 'command and control' health-care states. This family was once widespread. It described the creaking and ineffective systems of Eastern Europe under Communism, and in a more limited way it existed across swathes of north western Europe – encompassing the United Kingdom and the institutionalised welfare states of Scandinavia. (Saltman and von Otter, 1992). 'More limited' for an obvious reason: command and control health-care policy in western Europe amounted to an island of socialist controls within the environment of democratic capital-ism. This set very particular restraints on the way 'command and control' operated. In essence, the state owned the physical 'plant' for health-care delivery; it also trained and employed the most important health-care deliverers. Most important of all, it combined a system of entitlements to health care as virtual rights of citizenship with tight state constraints over the global levels of spending. In short, like any system of command and con-trol allocation it depended on some method of rationing other than by price.

It is plain that what is described here largely concerns what we have been calling the first domain of health-care policy – that concerned with the delivery of health care as a personal service. And it is the intersection with the second and third domains which reveal critical points of weakness. The need to practise some form of administrative rationing immediately put those delivering health care in a key role. In the case of the United Kingdom, for instance, rationing depended heavily on the main deliv-erers of primary care, general practitioners who provided primary care from 'high street' surgeries. The general practitioners were key 'gatekeepers' to the wider health-care system. In a famous summary, Klein characterised the British system as 'the politics of the double bed':

> On the one hand the state became a monopoly employer: effectively members of the medical profession became dependent on it not for only for their own incomes but also for the resources at their command. On the other hand the state became dependent on the medical profession to run the NHS and to cope with the problems of rationing scarce resources in patient care (Klein, 1990.)

There was also a critical intersection with the 'third world' of health-care policy: with that created by the medical technology industries. Although the 'command and control' system in health care mimicked some of the features of a command and control economy, it is this point of intersection that reminds us that it was an island of socialism embedded in a large market economy. For over a century the market economy has been a powerful driver of medical technology – and a driver increasingly organised on a global scale. Not only is this system of innovation largely out of the control of the state – and in particular out of the control of any 'command and control' arrangement. It is a global economy with a particular bias: it is dominated, both as far as production and markets are concerned, with the 'supply driven' American health-care system that we described earlier. The British medical technology industries are locked into this global system, and, especially in the case of the pharmaceutical industries, are comparatively successful parts of the competitive economy. The effect of this intersection between the two domains of health care – the domain of consumption, and the domain of technology production – was to produce a fatal contradiction at the heart of the health policy governing system: governments simultaneously needed to inhibit the medical technology industries in order to keep the lid on costs, and to promote this vital part of the economy as part of the management of industrial policy.

The intersections between the different domains of health care in the command and control systems have, we shall see later, shaped some key problems in health-care policy.

The United Kingdom's command and control system shared one important characteristic with the greatest of all the corporatist systems, that developed in Germany: they were based on an attempt to suppress market forces. And, as in the UK case, we shall see, this attempt at suppression has been a source of immense policy problems. At the core of these corporatist arrangements lay two features: the institutional arrangements for financing health care; and the institutional arrangements for its delivery. Financing of health care is extensively 'franchised' to independent health-care insurance funds, typically occupationally based. The delivery of health care, both primary care and hospital based care, is likewise extensively franchised to associations of doctors, who typically control entry to, and management of, the profession. The financing of health-care delivery is largely dependent on independent negotiations between the insurers and the health-care deliverers (for overviews, Alber, 1992; Burau, 2001). A systematic attempt is thus made to lock together two of our three domains of health-care policy: the domain of consumption and the domain of service delivery. One persistent theme of health-care policy in corporatist systems such as this is the struggle for power and resources between the key actors in the two domains: the various insurance funds who pay for consumption, and the key dominant interest, doctors, in the domain of delivery.

Two sets of interests do not have an obvious, settled place in this corporatist system. First, the key actors in the third domain of medical technology – the big corporatist interests who dominate the production and marketing of medical innovation – are in effect external to this system. In the particular case of Germany, for well over a century, since the great German inspired breakthroughs in laboratory based medical research in fields like immunology, the German medical technology industries have been world leaders, both in the sphere of pharmaceuticals and in 'big ticket' technologies based on innovations in electronics. Second, the role of the state in these arrangements was potentially problematic: it was a 'steerer' of the system, but this left open what steering amounted to (Döhler, 1995; Burau, 2001.) As we shall see, in recent decades this has proved a critical difficulty for corporatist health-care systems.

ISSUES IN HEALTH-CARE POLICY

I have argued throughout that health policy is essentially a 'constructed' concept, and that the way we understand it depends heavily on which domain we view it from: from the domain of consumption, from the domain of service delivery, or from the domain of technology. This thought also shapes our understanding of issues and problems in health-care policy. The simple typology of health-care states that informed discussion in the preceding section amounts to a kind of classification of 'families' of health-care states: the supply, the command and control and the corporatist. Health-care families, like human families, tend to be functional in their own special ways, and dysfunctional in their own special ways. To put it slightly more formally: there is no unique set of health-care issues 'out there'. Each state formation has great achievements, and each has weaknesses, and the achievements and weaknesses are inscribed in their natures.

The American supply state has huge achievements to its credit. For the section of the population that has comprehensive health insurance – and that amounts to the majority of Americans – it delivers care that is highly sensitive to the demands of payers, and that makes accessible the very latest innovations from a hugely creative system of high technology innovation. Its problems are also well documented. As we have already seen, there is one task beyond the system which has been accomplished by a wide range of much less affluent nations: universal coverage. A large and growing number of Americans have no, or inadequate, health insurance cover, and because the most effective systems of health insurance are occupationally based, this also largely means Americans who are already either excluded from work or are in sections of the labour market where employment is precarious.

In a nutshell: the system excludes millions from health insurance coverage, and those millions tend to be among the most vulnerable of Americans. At the same time, in the last generation, the American system has been disastrous at cost containment. The wider political system has proved incapable of producing systemic reform capable of addressing either of the issues of coverage and costs. One result of the latter failure is that policy struggles in the United States now involve a constant, complex battle of attrition between providers and third party payers, both in the public sector and in the commercial insurance industry.

The achievements of command and control systems are well summed up in the British experience. They have succeeded in integrating health *care* into the domain of the welfare state, and thus of extending free, or nearly free, care to whole populations as a right, or virtual right, of citizenship. In the British case the system also proved highly successful at the containment of global costs. But these achievements depended fundamentally on systems of administrative rationing. Virtually all the command and control systems have tried, with varying success, to replace administrative rationing with some systems that at least mimic markets in recent decades. The problems of administrative rationing have been threefold. First, the fact that the third domain of health policy – the technology innovation system – has been external to the command system has meant that a constant stream of innovations has flooded onto markets, widening the range and effectiveness of health care, and widening also the cost base of systems. Second, the actual administration of rationing has depended heavily on the medical profession acting as 'gatekeepers' – and doctors' willingness in turn to perform this role has depended on a fragile political compact with the state. Finally, command and control in health care has had to survive in an increasingly alien environment: one where consumption is organised predominantly according to demands expressed through markets, rather than through queues. The political sensitivity of health-care queuing – expressed, for example, in the high political salience of health-care waiting lists – is a sign of this difficulty.

Though corporatist systems have typically based their health insurance arrangements in the workplace, and therefore have to some degree replicated inequalities of the labour market, they have nevertheless proved remarkably successfully in creating universal systems of coverage and, in the case of the leading system, Germany, in delivering health care that matches the American in its ability to give access to the most technologically sophisticated health care. But at the heart of corporatist states lies a steering deficit. The system works by franchising responsibility to autonomous public law institutions. The outcome of policy in these circumstances depends heavily on the bargaining power of different actors, notably third party payers and medical professionals. In the years of the boom in health-care spending, medical professionals were in the saddle. The problematic institution in all this has been the state. The history of attempts at health reform in recent decades, therefore, has consisted of attempts to create, or restore, for the state some effective steering capacity, notably in pushing through reforms of the system. In this authority lacuna corporatist systems resemble, though for different institutional reasons, the semi-paralysed character of the American health-care state's attempts at systemic reform.

CONCLUSION: REFRAMING HEALTH POLICY

The domains of health policy are hardly fictions but they are, I have argued here, constructions. How we view health policy depends heavily on the domain from which we do the viewing. The dominant tradition in the study of health policy has involved a stress on health *care*. Out of this has come the assumption that health policy is best viewed as a sub-set of welfare policy. That is indeed an important part of health policy, but only one part. Perhaps the most neglected of the three domains has been the domain of medical technology – or, rather, it is a domain which has itself been segregated off from the mainstream of the study of health policy. Yet an important

implication of my argument in this chapter is that the medical technology innovation system is a key to the understanding of health policy. It is the link that joins most effectively the domain of care with the wider world of industrial policy, and thus the global political economy. It is the source both of huge opportunities and huge problems: opportunities because for over a century it has been a near miraculous source of hugely effective health therapies; problems, because it is a virtually uncontrollable source of innovations that have huge consequences for costs and rationing. We thus need to reframe health policy to put the domain of health technology nearer the centre of the picture than has hitherto been the case.

REFERENCES

Alber, J. (1992). *Das Gesundheitswesen der Bundesrepublik Deutschland*. Frankfurt: Campus Verlag.

Alsop, J. and Saks, M. (eds.) (2002). *Regulating the health professions*. London: Sage.

Altenstetter, C. and Björkman, J. (eds.) (1997) *Health Policy reform: national variations and globalization*. Basingstoke: Macmillan.

Berlant, J. (1975). *Profession and monopoly: a study of medicine in the United States and Great Britain*. Berkeley: University of California Press.

Brown, A. (1998). 'Exceptionalism as the rule? U.S. health policy innovation and cross-national learning', *Journal of Health Politics, Policy and Law*, 10:5, 35–51.

Brown, E. (1979). *Rockefeller medicine men: medicine and capitalism in America*. Berkeley: University of California Press.

Burau, V. (2001). 'Medical reform in Germany: the 1993 health care legislation as an impromptu success', in M. Bovens, P. t'Hart and B. Guy Peters (eds), *Success and failure in public governance: a comparative analysis*. Cheltenham: Elgar, 199–218.

Döhler, M. (1995). 'The state as architect of political order: policy dynamics in German health care', *Governance*, 8:3, 380–404.

Esping-Andersen, G. (1996). *Welfare states in transition: national adaptations in global economies*. London: Sage.

Evans, R. and Stoddart, G. (1990). 'Producing health, consuming health care.' *Social Science and Medicine*, 31:12, 1347–63.

Ferrera, M. (1996). 'The "southern model" of welfare in Europe', *Journal of European Social Policy*, 6: 17–37.

Ferrera, M. and Rhodes, M. (eds) (2000). *Recasting European Welfare States*. London: Cass.

Foote, S. (1992). *Managing the medical arms race: public policy and medical device innovation*. Berkeley: University of California Press.

Freeman, R. 2000. *The politics of Health in Europe*. Manchester: Manchester University Press.

Freidson, E. 1970. *Profession of Medicine: a study in the sociology of applied knowledge*. New York: Harper and Row.

Guillén, A. and Cabada, L. (1997). 'Towards a National Health Service in Spain: the search for equity and efficiency'. *Journal of European Social Policy*, 7: 319–36.

Jacobs, L. (1995). 'Politics of America's supply state: health reform and technology.' *Health Affairs*, 14:2, 143–57.

Johnson, T. (1972). *Professions and power*. London: Macmillan.

Kelman, S. (1975). 'The social nature of the definition problem in health.' *International Journal of Health Services*, 5:4, 625–42.

Klein, R. (1990). 'The state and the profession: the politics of the double bed'. *British Medical Journal*, 301: 700–02.

Levit, K., Cowan, C., Lazenby, H., McDonnell, P., Sensenig, A., Stiller, J., Won, D. (1994). 'National health spending trends, 1960–93', *Health Affairs*, 13:5, 14–31.

Moran, M. (1999). *Governing the Health Care State: a comparative study of the United Kingdom, the United States and Germany*. Manchester: Manchester University Press.

Moran, M. and Wood, B. (1996). 'The globalisation of health care policy', in P. Gummett, ed., *Globalisation and public policy*. Cheltenham: Elgar.

Morone, J. and Belkin, G. eds., (1994), *The politics of health care reform: lessons from the past, prospects*

for the future. Durham, NC.: Duke University Press.

OECD (various dates). *Health Data*, cd rom. OECD: Paris.

Pickstone, J. (ed.) (1992). *Medical innovations in historical perspective*. London: Macmillan.

Reiser, S. (1978). *Medicine and the reign of technology*. Cambridge: Cambridge University Press.

Rothman, D. (1994). 'A century of failure: class barriers to reform', in J. Morone and G. Belkin, eds., *The politics of health care reform: lessons from the past, prospects for the future*. Durham, NC: Duke University Press, pp. 11–25.

Saltman, R. and von Otter, C. (1995). *Planned markets and public competition: strategic reform in Northern European Health Systems*. Buckingham: Open University Press.

Skocpol, T. (1996). *Boomerang: Clinton's health security effort*. New York: Norton.

Starr, P. (1982). *The social transformation of American medicine*. New York: Basic Books.

Temin, P. (1980). *Taking your medicine: drug regulation in the United States*. Cambridge, Mass.: Harvard University Press.

Trajtenberg, M. (1990). *Economic analysis and product innovation: the case of CT scanners*. Cambridge, MA.: Harvard University Press.

Waddington, I. (1984). *The medical profession and the Industrial Revolution*. Dublin: Gill and Macmillan.

Webster, C. (1988). *The health services since the war. Vvolume 1, problems of health-care: the National Health Service before 1957*. London: HMSO.

Weisbrod, B. (1991). 'The health care quadrilemma: an essay on technological change, insurance, quality of care, and cost containment'. *Journal of Economic Literature*, 29:1, 523–52.

Wildavsky, A. (1977). 'Doing better and feeling worse: the political pathology of health policy' *Daedalus*, 106:1, 1–5–23.

Wohl, S. (1984). *The medical industrial complex*. New York: Harmony Books.

13

Education Policy

SUSAN MARTON

INTRODUCTION

It is hard to ignore today that the role of education in our societies is taking on increased importance. The term "knowledge society" has become a common phrase for most citizens, heard almost daily in the media, in the school corridors and promulgated by our politicians. Education is now viewed as the key component to economic competitiveness in an increasingly global world (Brown & Lauder, 1997; Mok & Tan, 2004) and thus educational achievements and success are increasingly seen as a way to better handle the economic challenges facing today's societies.

This chapter will discuss the challenges which education policy is facing in the 21st century. Questions to be investigated include: How is the role of the state changing as education delivery is restructured? What happens to the modes of involvement by the state in education policy as 'government' changes to 'governance'? What social justice issues arise as the state restructures education policy? Are similar trends evident in higher education policy? Finally, the chapter will conclude by identifying some policy issues for the future and reflecting upon possible solutions.

First, it is appropriate to briefly review the current debate on globalization and its effects on the restructuring of national education systems. Defining precisely what globalization means has been at the forefront of academic discussions and generally includes such components as the new patterns of communication between people and nations, which is evidenced through new information technologies, the culture of consumerism, the demands for increased flexibility in almost all aspects of social life, increased competition in economic life, and the rise of new social movements (Held et al., 1999). Globalization effects that are most often underscored in education are marketization, privatization, corporatization and decentralization. The effects of globalization on nation states' policy autonomy has been one of the hottest topics for academic review during the 1980s and 1990s, with the role and capacity of the state in providing public services being put in question against the backdrop of these effects (Castles, 1998). Those who see this capacity as limited by globalization have been referred to by Weiss as the "constraints school" (Hirst & Thompson, 1996; Strange, 1996), versus those in the "enabling school" who want to investigate the potential of the global economy in enabling governments to pursue their policy goals (Swank, 2002; Weiss, 2003). The basic argument of the "enabling school" is that the institutional structure of the polity and the welfare system itself shapes the domestic policy response to globalization. In order to study such responses, one must focus on the importance of institutions as organizational structures and as the embodiment of normative orientations.

Recent policy studies in education restructuring also reflect this dichotomy between globalization as primarily constraining versus globalization as enabling. It is beyond the scope of this chapter to address this debate in length, but let it suffice to say that demands for restructuring state education in order to meet these globalization pressures are evident across the industrialized, and even the developing nations, albeit with different timing patterns. The advanced industrial nations went through restructurings primarily in the 1980s, whereas the Asian and Arab countries changed more in the 1990s. A new language has appeared in the sphere of education policy across the globe, incorporating terms such as: excellence, competitiveness, efficiency, accountability and devolution. Nonetheless, it is important to point out that "the considerable convergence at the policy rhetoric and general policy objectives may not satisfactorily explain the complicated processes of changes and the dynamic interactions between global-regional-local forces that shape education policy-making in individual countries" (Mok & Welch, 2003: 25; see also Dale, 1999; and Green, 1999). Educational restructuring may not only be a response to global competition and human capital needs, but also to a state's particular financial situation and management capabilities, as well as communitarian and post-modernist demands (Daun, 2002). The forms that these restructuring demands acquire are not unilateral, but rather are embedded in the specific political circumstances and structures (such as the relationship between church and state), and the cultures and histories of the particular nations. Thus, there is no "monolithic strategy" at the state level, but rather a complex interweaving of internal and external dynamics that contribute to the specific context for restructuring education policies (Mok & Welch, 2003).

THE IMPORTANCE AND UNIQUENESS OF EDUCATION POLICY

John Dewey's declaration from 1958 reminds us that education is "essentially about the development of democratic communities in which everyone can feel free and capable of participating" (Taylor et al., 1997:19). Education obviously has an individual role (increasing one's knowledge levels) but education also has a societal role where schools function as a mechanism to transfer 'values into future citizens' and to socialize them in preparation for their future voting rights (Heidenheimer et al., 1983). It is the nature of this societal role that is often misunderstood in education policy. Citing Bernstein (1971), Whitty emphasizes that, "How a society selects, classifies, distributes, transmits and evaluates the educational knowledge it considers to be public, reflects both the distribution of power and the principles of social contract" (2002: 9). Educational reforms depict widespread social changes, and are therefore not just a matter of pedagogy or didactics, but rather social reforms that should be analyzed as such (Husén, 1998; Kogan, 1973).

Certainly, one of the most significant social reforms has been the transformation of schooling as a private activity for the few (often religiously organized and charity-based), to that of education as a right to be provided based on public expense for the masses. As the modern nation-state developed, two goals for the education system were delineated: first, to create a common culture and, second, to educate the future generations of civil servants (Heidenheimer et al., 1983). A common culture was seen as a necessity in promoting social solidarity. The state was to treat its citizens based on ability; not on class, gender or race. The notion of equality of opportunity was an important component of this common culture, with the bureaucracy playing a key role in promoting and implementing the idea of meritocracy. Given the second goal of an educated administrative corp, the state could ensure its ability to steer effectively and to attract the loyalty of its citizens (Castles, 1998).

As the role of the state in providing education grew, education as a national policy concern augmented in importance. Policy issues such as the extent of professional autonomy versus bureaucratic control, and the proper form of financing (local versus state-wide) have characterized the uniqueness of this policy area since the 1950s. The role of the teaching profession in carrying out the goals of public education has become even more complex given the advance of globalization. In comparison to other policy areas, the study of education policy includes the need to review the profession's claims for autonomy in the implementing process. As Hargreaves has pointed out, there is a difference between restructuring as bureaucratic control "where teachers are controlled and regulated to implement the mandate of others" versus restructuring based on professional empowerment "where teachers are supported, encouraged, and provided with newly structured opportunities to make improvements on their own" (cited in Brown et al., 1997: 23). Today it appears that some restructuring policies threaten teachers' collective professional autonomy and responsibility. One can also question whether rewards based on individual performance, merit pay and school performance are legitimate when student achievement is the result of collective efforts over many years, and can not be seen as the product of one teacher (see Torrance, 1997).

Furthermore, new forms of decentralization threaten teacher autonomy (Brown et al., 1997). New financing systems have ended the previous system of zoning principles and legislated "catchment areas", where teachers had a "guaranteed" supply of students to teach, and a "guaranteed" job regardless of their classroom performance. These new decentralized financing systems, along with decentralized employment arrangements, can be used as a way to weaken the power of organized teacher trade unions on the central level. National, or statewide, employment conditions may no longer be relevant with decentralization of employment policies down to the local school level.

A further aspect requiring consideration in education policy is the relationship between the bureaucrat and the politician. Today the role of the education bureaucrat is being challenged, given an uneasiness regarding the Weberian

principles of equality and meritocracy. Mok & Welch (2003) argue that Weber's classic ideal type of bureaucracy is being deconstructed as control of the public service is being handed over to non-state actors. The nature of government has changed from service providers to regulators – with the regulation of quality as a high priority. Politicians, in the name of decentralization and choice policies, have delegated management of schools to parental and/or community control. One can ponder to what extent this impacts upon the role of the bureaucratic experts – can they maintain their influence in the face of what may be unreasonable state/central policies?

Returning to John Dewey's statement, we need to ask how education policies are contributing to the development of democratic communities. The democratic view of education emphasizes the "collective, common and community purposes, and it recognizes that the political values of freedom and equality are interdependent rather than antithetical" (Reid, 2002: 573). Castles (1998) argues that it is doubtful whether the state will retreat from its responsibility for public education given that the state is not willing to surrender its role in the development of human capital and political socialization. However, in analyzing the recent educational reforms in New Zealand, Peters (2003) describes a situation where education as a social good has disappeared, replaced by an ideology where education is an economic good for which one must pay. Reid (2002) reports similar findings for the case of Australia, where the collective community purposes of public education are at risk in the face of neo-liberal ideas of individualism and competition. Reid argues that the classic view of the public good must be revised to meet the challenges related to globalization. We will return to Reid's suggestion for a deeper problematization of the concept of the "public good" at the end of this chapter.

Using state theory, Carnoy (1992: 159) has outlined the two extreme positions for the state regarding its role in providing education. The first position argues that the state is independent from civil society, and thus the state can be seen as "interfering" in the workings of a "social welfare maximizing free market". The second position views the state as reflecting and reinforcing "the power relations that derive from those free market economic relations". Using an institutionalist view of the state for the second position, the state can potentially act as a "good cop", using democratically represented interests to ensure equal opportunities and outcomes.

Between these two extreme positions, one can place various ideologies regarding education. Focusing first on the neo-liberal ideology, there is an emphasis on individual motivation, competition, decentralization, fiscal restraint, freedom of choice, and private consumption (Griffin, 2002; Wells, 2002). Forcing public sector institutions to act more like private sector businesses with the initiation of "quasi-markets", the neo-liberals believe that quality is produced through competition (Lauder, 1997). In this light, families should be encouraged to see choices regarding schooling in a similar way as decisions regarding private consumption. It is argued by the neo-liberals that the time has come for consumer interests to lead the way, and that "producer-capture" in education should end (Brown et al., 1997; Demaine, 1999). More reliance on market forces, voluntary services and individual demands are seen as the way to achieve social goals.

On the other side of the ideological spectrum, the social-democratic ideologies regard these neo-liberal policies as privileging individual rights at the expense of social justice and do not contribute to a more equal society, but rather to one that is more "acceptably unequal" (Whitty, 2002 citing Connell, 1993). Social justice concerns have unfortunately been put to the side, the social democrats would argue, since there is no longer any aspiration towards equality of outcome between social classes or ethnic groups. Yet the counter argument from the neo-liberals would be that diversity in the provision of schools is actually a way of opening a democratic society, so that it can be more responsive to the needs of special communities with multiple identities. It is believed that such diversity is more attractive to these communities than the previously one-dimensional notions of comprehensive schooling and citizenship. In the final section of this chapter, possible solutions to bridge this gap will be reviewed.

RESTRUCTURING STATE EDUCATION – GENERAL TRENDS AFTER 1950

The post-war period can be described as an "era of optimism" in terms of the ability of the state to implement social reform. Provision of and access to education expanded in the 1960s and 1970s in all industrialized countries as part of the state-driven modernization process. National education policy at that time was "an important site of struggle over class formation and social distribution" within the nation-state (Marginson, 1999: 27). Human capital theory combined with pressures for the democratization of the education system in order to spur the expansion of the system. Political debates focused on spending levels, types of facilities and structural barriers to equality, but the guiding principle was "collective provision by elected bodies with a mandate to cater for the needs of the whole population" (Whitty, 2002: 85).

Yet, in the 1980s, doubts about the states' ability to maintain welfare provisions, in combination with challenges to Keynesian economic policy, have led to a restructuring of the state. The provision of state services is now more dependent on individual behavior and institutions of civil society than previously. New steering mechanisms are in place, such as new regulations, incentive programs and sanctions for "autonomous individuals and autonomous quasi-governmental and non-governmental institutions", which Marginson refers to as "steering from a distance" (1999: 25); a concept developed in the work of Kickert (1995) on governance in the Netherlands.

In the old system, the publicly managed education system provided for a scientific form of competition with curricula, pedagogy and modes of assessment that were "monocultural in process and culturally homogenizing in effect" (Marginson, 1999: 28). Today, contemporary governments emphasize a welfare-ethic based on "self-responsibility" and the "work-ethic", and the teacher-student relationship is more individualized (Tomlinson, 2001). Diversity, both ethnically and religiously, is now one of the major policy challenges, with questions of access focusing on the needs of various cultural groups and the cultural dimensions of curricula and achievement. The relationship between the state and its political constituencies (including teacher organizations, school boards and parental groups) is further complicated by these "politics of difference and shifting identities" (Taylor et al., 1997: 80).

FROM GOVERNMENT TO GOVERNANCE IN EDUCATION POLICY

The new forms of governance in education policy are putting the following issues at the forefront of policy debates: centralization versus decentralization, public versus private, autonomy versus accountability, and equality versus quality. Before reviewing these issues in more detail, the work of Dale (1997) will help in clarifying how governance in education policy can be understood. First, we can identify three separate governance activities regarding education: funding, provision and regulation. Second, we can identify three coordinating institutions which may carry out these activities: state, market, and/or community. Public education exists when all three of the activities are provided by the state. Dale argues that we should be more aware of the complexities involved in the shift from state control to other governance forms and that the distinction between "public" and "private" is sometimes inadequate.

Carrying the discussion further, various models of education governance have been outlined in the literature. A recent OECD report presented four ideal-type models for education governance: (1) "competitive market", (2) "school empowerment", (3) "local empowerment", and (4) "quality control" (OECD, 2003). Below we will combine the discussion of the models outlined in the OECD report with those reported in Cordingley and

Kogan (1993). This will allow for some degree of synthesis as well as further specification. These models will later be used to analyze the case studies of England and Sweden in the later section of this chapter "Policy change in National Contexts".

First, in the "competitive market model", the school is viewed primarily as a business operating in a commercial market place with a high degree of autonomy from government structures. The school competes for both pupils and funding within a "competitive area" with nearby schools. Cordingley and Kogan referred to this as the "individualistic model" where the individual client acts as purchaser of a product.

In the second model, that of "school empowerment", the focus instead is on the school itself and how freedom and choice, often along with managerial ideas on allocating decision making to the shop-floor, can empower the school. Ideas regarding participation are also different from the "competitive market" model due to the emphasis here on ideas of partnership and community.

Model three, the "local empowerment" model, is quite different from the "school empowerment" model, given that the focus is instead on the devolution of previously central government powers to a local authority, rather than to the schools. The school is envisioned as part of a local educational system, where there are reciprocal rights and obligations to be carried out. The distinguishing point of this model is that more power is given to the local authorities than to the schools. Yet, in the work of Cordingley and Kogan, the school empowerment and local empowerment models may be mixed, allowing for a "professional-electoral model", where power is to be shared between the principles and teachers in the school and a locally based intermediary body. In addition, the role of government in relating to the "individual school boards" may vary, with one type based on a stronger role for the central government in relating to the school board, whereas in another type, there is more anchorage in the local community through a mixture of locally appointed and elected members.

In the fourth model, that of "quality control", the government aims for control over both school processes and products, relying heavily on bureaucratic procedures of rules and requirements. This is in line with the Cordingley and Kogan model of "funding councils" which would provide funds to institutions (i.e. schools and/or school districts) that meet their contractual demands for quality levels, costs and volume.

The four main models outlined above will naturally imply different usages for concepts such as school autonomy and accountability. Starting with school autonomy, one can ask: "Autonomy for whom, and autonomy over what?" As Bullock and Thomas (1997) point out, autonomy is a relative concept, depending on if it is viewed from the position of the individual learner, the educator or the institution (cited in OECD, 2003). Viewing autonomy from the point of the institution to the higher authority on a continuum ranging from "full autonomy; decisions made after consultation with another authority at an adjoining level; and those made within guidelines set by another authority, generally at the top", the OECD report related the governance models to the types of autonomy. The "competitive market" model depicted "substantial" autonomy; the "school empowerment" model entailed "devolved" autonomy since the school is still part of an overall system; the "local empowerment" model emphasized "consultative" autonomy since the school is a member of a network of institutions; and the "quality control" model described "guided" autonomy since there is a pronounced role for an authority at a higher level.

Using terminology developed from Halstead (1994), the OECD 2003 study also evaluated accountability in the models based on "contractual" versus "responsive" accountability. Contractual accountability deals with fulfilling the expectations of particular audiences by providing them with standards and outcomes. Responsive accountability is based on decision making by educators, after listening to the desires of relevant stakeholders. Clearly the "competitive market" model relates to a contractual, "consumerist" view of accountability, since this is analogous to commercial behavior. The "school empowerment" and the "local education" models are both demonstrating responsive

accountability through their responsibilities to stakeholders, and here one could say that the "local empowerment" model is very responsive, like a "community forum", whereas the "school empowerment" model has dual accountability to both professionals and non-professionals. The "quality control" model also represents a contractual type of accountability, which can be characterized as "hierarchical", since a higher-level power decides over the definitions in the contract.

Working from these various governance models, efforts have been made to study the linkages between the models and school efficiency and student learning, but the relationship certainly is complex and is not automatic (Cohen & Spillane, 1992). Positive school reform has been found in models where the leaders and teachers involved are empowered and share decision making through a supportive structure and where the professional community has a shared normative base (OECD 2003, citing Silins and Mulford, 2002; Goddard et al., 2000; and Heck, 2000). But others have reported that many managers are following the principle of "do things right rather than doing the right thing" (Sizer, 1984 cited in OECD, 2003: 78). Regarding school-based management, both Hannaway (1993) and Elmore (1993) have found little effect on student achievement (cited in Daun, 2002).

Decentralization, Multi-Level Governance and Democracy

As the section above described, there are various models for governing education policy, and the ramifications of some of these on decentralization and democracy will now be discussed. McGinn (1992: 163) poses two major questions regarding the effect of decentralization policies on democracy: "Do they reflect a genuine shift in power toward those who believe in popular democracy? Would decentralization improve education in an equitable fashion?" Three types of decentralization are outlined: deconcentration, decentralization and devolution. Deconcentration entails a territorial sense of decentralization, with government authority shifting from central level to local level by moving the offices of government officials. Decentralization involves the "delegation of authority for the control and governance aspects of education to another organization, generally at a lower level in the hierarchy of size" whereas devolution means "the more central authority turns over all responsibility, including that of funding, to a more local organization" (McGinn, 1992: 164).

Karlsen (2000), in his study of Norway and British Columbia, introduces the concept of "decentralized centralism". This term allows him to discuss the dynamic interactions in the decentralization process when a strategy of bottom-up innovation is present. He found that decentralization of tasks and administration responsibility did not necessarily mean a shift of power from a higher to a lower level and that the decentralization of authority could have a legitimating role for the central level. Bache (2003) found similar results in his analysis of the local education authorities in England. Although much of the deregulation seemed to be in line with New Public Management ideas, the decentralizing could be viewed as part of the state's strategy to retain policy control (Pierre, 2000). Using a multi-level governance and policy networks perspective, Bache found that the state retained its power to control policy and to achieve its policy goals more effectively. This leaves us, however, with the important question of the role of local authorities as institutions of local democratic accountability when such central-level control is exercised.

McGinn (1992) highlights two forms of decentralization that reduce the vitality of mechanisms for democratic participation in the education system; professionalization and privatization. First, professionalization refers to the professional management of schools by education administration specialists. There is a risk that this type of development could alienate participation by parents, or even by teacher groups, if they are challenging the "expert" solutions put down by the professionals. Second, privatization can also limit possibilities for democratic participation by reducing the input from existing political organizations that were created to express the popular will and by weakening the voice of members of society who may have a disproportionate share of resources, both economically and socially. Privatization, however, is a very complex concept, and "is not necessarily driven by market forces nor does it necessarily follow market principles and practices" (Daun, 2002: 95). Many different factors may be involved in the usage of the term "private school", with various "combinations of ownership, governance, management, degree of subsidization, type of control and type of students" (Daun, 2002: 95; see also Boyd and Cibulka, 1989). Nonetheless, as diversity is encouraged by market solutions, the role of the education system to form shared political values may put collective action at risk.

The debate on these issues is certainly not settled. Moe (1994) and Pollard (1995) argue instead that the introduction of quasi-markets has given deprived children a chance for better educational opportunities. Tooley (1995) argues that the positive effects of deregulation and school choice have not yet fully materialized because the policies have not gone far enough. Yet Henig discusses the "sad irony of the current education/reform movement" in that the heavy emphasis on market-based ideas overshadows "the healthy impulse to consider radical reforms to address social problems" and instead may bring about "initiatives that further erode the potential for collective deliberation and collective response" (Henig, 1994: 222, cited in Whitty, 2002: 21). Given recent changes in the governance of education, Dale argues that Western governments must face two major issues in the future: first, "the question of how equality of resources and outcomes can be achieved under a complex system of governance in which particularism rather than universalism is an important guiding factor in the provision of education" and second, "the question of how effective democratic accountability can be introduced into the system" (Dale, 1997: 281).

SOCIAL JUSTICE ISSUES

The predominant role of government after the post-war period had been to ensure access to education – the expansion of the school system and compulsory education for all were key components of this policy. When these levels of participation were achieved, it was believed that governments had accomplished as much as was in their power. During the 1960s this view was challenged by broad-based popular movements such as the civil rights movement in the US and the feminist movement that was gaining strength world-wide. The role of government was increasingly understood to include more than just access policies, and thus the causes of educational disadvantage came to the forefront of policy discussions (Taylor et al., 1997).

Four main approaches to improving social justice have been tried in the past, and some continue to be used today. These include: (1) meritocracy, the idea that social advancement will take place based on individual merits and an educational system that is able to recognize such merits; (2) compensatory mechanisms, such as free meals in school for low-income families; (3) specific intervention programs, such as the Head Start pre-school programs for children from disadvantaged families; and (4) school improvement projects, which allow the teachers, staff and school administrators to decide how to improve their institutions (Whitty, 2002: 108–109). However, although there are individual success stories (Maden and Hillman, 1996), the problem remains that the long-term "patterning of educational inequality has been strikingly consistent throughout the history of public education" (Whitty, 2002: 110; see also Wilson, 1997 and Ogbu, 1997).

It may, however, be necessary to admit that the demands placed on the educational system at times have been much broader than the system's capacity to handle such problems. The negative correlation between most forms of social disadvantage and school achievement is a multi-faceted problem that is not easily fixed. Social disadvantage impacts on schooling both directly and indirectly, for example through poor health conditions and housing arrangements. As Halsey pointed out over twenty years ago, "the teacher cannot reconstruct the community unaided" (cited in Whitty, 2002: 116). But, as policies are encouraging individuals'

rights to education over citizens' rights, a vacuum exists as to who has responsibility for the whole. Important issues regarding the need to build social capital versus the need to meet the demands for diversity come to the forefront, especially in terms of faith-based schools that may be culturally and religiously exclusive. Relating the education system to the societal sphere can bring about contradictory demands in regards to culture and linguistic sensitivity.

Research on the topic of school choice and deregulation discusses the risks of horizontal diversity in schooling, meaning that no greater diversity in the provision of educational services is achieved. Instead, the previously existing hierarchy of schools can be strengthened based on academic test results and social class (Glatter et al., 1997). Difficulties arise in the way schools are judged, as evaluations may be based on social grounds or narrow academic criteria that ignore the overall performance of the school. Furthermore, the funding system can make it extremely difficult for schools in disadvantaged neighborhoods to break out of the cycle of decline (Goldhaber, 1999).

Certainly, when discussing equity in education systems, the gender aspect is also relevant. Most studies of gender politics and school reform concentrate on (a) the gendered nature of teaching as a profession, (b) the divergence of career opportunities among men and women teachers, and (c) the "counter-hegemonic, anti-sexist efforts of feminist teachers" (Datnow, 2000: 133). In addition, studies on parental choice and market forces in education (David, 1999) are focusing on the role of families, and in particular mothers, in a child's schooling decision (an issue which is increasingly important as politicians place more responsibility on the family for schooling).

POLICY CHANGE IN NATIONAL CONTEXTS

In the brief review below of national policy changes in England and Sweden, the interconnectedness of governing models and ideologies of education is evident. However, the cases represent policy movements in nearly opposite directions, raising interesting questions about the significance and consequences of decentralization and centralization. The English case represents a movement from a highly local, decentralized system to one where significant powers over provision and regulation have been centralized. The Swedish case on the other hand reflects a transformation of a highly centralized system, where education was a core element of the Swedish welfare state, to a largely decentralized, fragmented system.

England

The provision of education prior to the 1988 Education Reform Act was primarily conducted in state schools under the political and bureaucratic control of a local education authority (LEA) which was democratically elected. When the Conservatives came to power, the LEA represented a monopoly over state schooling that was subsequently to be broken through various Education Acts passed throughout the 1980s and early 1990s. School self-management became a primary concern, with the leading idea that "the proper management of schools is best achieved through partnership and the co-operative participation of parents, teachers, local politicians and community representatives, within the context of national policy" (Demaine, 1999: 17).

The marketization of the public schools was largely conducted through two initiatives. The first is known as "grant-maintained schools" which allowed existing LEA schools to opt-out from the LEA structure if a parental ballot voted in favor (these were later renamed "foundation schools" by the New Labour government). Funding was provided directly from the central government, thus bypassing the LEA. The second initiative was the establishment of the City Technology Schools, which were a new type of secondary school with a focus on science and technology studies for the inner cities. Cooperation was to be attained from business sponsors and the school would be run by independent trusts. For those schools that remained under LEA provision, the Local Management of Schools (LMS)

policy gave individual schools much more power over budgets and daily management issues. Funds were distributed based on the number of students a school could attract, which helped to create a "quasi-market" for education. Sexton (1987) refers to this as the "virtual voucher" system (cited in Whitty, 2002). Thus parents were defined as the main consumers, the customers of education, and seen as most able to decide what is best for their children.

Ideologically, the movement in England to allow for local school empowerment was not only a right-wing movement, but the new left was also attracted by the potential of the LMS for turning around negative bureaucratic effects and poor professional practice. It was believed that this framework also could allow for social justice and increased stakeholding – with new co-operative efforts for the local and national agencies (Demaine, 1999).

In addition to the focus on the management of the schools, the reform policies also heavily emphasized quality and assessment in the school system. In a detailed account of these assessment policies, James (2000) describes the process from the *Task Group of Assessment and Testing* appointed under the Conservative government in 1987, to the latest policy from the Department for Education and Employment. Every year, the Office for Standards in Education (OFSTED) provides national summary results and national benchmark data to all schools, with detailed accounts of how schools rank against each other. Furthermore, the quality of the teaching staff has been under debate, and recently a General Teaching Council, somewhat like a professional honor society, has been arranged to help raise standards for teachers.

Although their assessment strategies have been similar, James (2000) argues that the Conservative and Labour governments originally had different goals with their assessment policies. The Conservative governments under Thatcher and Major were primarily concerned in fostering economic growth, with increased competition in the "market of education" contributing to this. The Labour government was also concerned with the competitiveness of the economy, but their emphasis was more on transforming the old manual-skills labor supply to a labor force ready to compete in the knowledge economy. Issues of broader access were important to Labour, but raising the quality of education and training was more pronounced. Although meritocracy as a way of selecting the best and the brightest is still actively promoted, James concludes that Labour recognizes that all social classes should have an equal opportunity.

Thus, the Assisted Places Scheme (started under the Thatcher government to provide public funding for academically talented but economically disadvantaged students to attend elite private schools) was later cancelled by the Labour government, which argued that it was better to benefit the many and not the few. Instead Labour introduced "Education Action Zones" (EAZs), based on the idea of business, schools and local education authorities and parents working together to modernize schools in deprived areas. As Whitty (2002) explains, the policy seemed to entail both a private market, managerial feature (with the input from the business leaders) plus a community emphasis that equates with collective responsibility for education. Studies analyzing the results of EAZs show so far mixed success (see Dickson et al., 2001).

Sweden

In the late 1980s, the Social Democrats decentralized the state controlled education system, and transferred significant powers to the municipalities. Although the overall funding responsibility remained with the central state, the usage of funds was significantly more flexible for the municipalities after the reform. The policy was now one of "lump-sum funding" provided directly to the municipalities rather than the specified, earmarked funding of the past. When the Conservative-coalition government came to power in 1991, they introduced subsidies for what were to be called the "free schools" – basically a similar idea to that of the "charter" schools in the US. Any group could apply for

their school to have the status of "free", with funding following the pupil to the "free school" from the municipality (like a system of "vouchers") and thus a quasi-market in education was introduced, now enrolling approximately four percent of the student population. (A private education company operates a very small amount of these "free schools" – but the law prohibits the charging of tuition fees.) The Conservatives also increased autonomy for the schools in relation to the national curriculum, making the curriculum more flexible and less-regulated by the national authorities (Daun and Benincasa, 1998). The state however did impose some new forms of control, through national tests and a new national grading system, as well as the introduction of a system of quality audits in 1997.

The reforms were put in place by both Social Democratic and Conservative-coalition parties, without any major swings in policy in relation to government changes. (The "free-school" reform remains in some ways ideologically difficult for the Social Democrats to accept, but there has been no successful overturn of the policy.) In trying to explain this policy consensus, Lundahl states that the politicians in Sweden (on both the Left and the Right) had the same view on the necessity of change. The following three justifications were provided for the policy changes: (1) it was no longer possible for the state to steer over education and regulate the schools in detail given the pace and complexity of change in today's society; (2) the variance between regional needs and municipalities' needs was too broad to handle with detailed state steering; and (3) schools had lost their authority over the years as the parents' own level of education rose, thus making it necessary for the schools and teachers "to earn their legitimacy" (Lundahl, 2002: 691).

Recent Social Democratic reforms have included the adding of a third year of education to the vocational training programs, thus encouraging a stronger academic emphasis. The main purpose of this reform was to increase individual flexibility and broaden students' possibilities to enter the university from the upper-secondary education programs. These reforms have been motivated by both a goal of broader access to higher education as well as economic concerns regarding the changing conditions in the labor market. However, Lundahl questions to what extent equality was a goal in the reforms of the 1990s and concludes that, for Swedish Social Democrats, "the belief that education could play a significant role in reducing class and other social differences had become seriously weakened" (Lundahl, 2002: 696).

Comparing Sweden and England: Governance Models and Institutional Explanations

Although we see similar "global" trends in the two cases above, in order to understand what shapes the domestic policy response and choice of governance models in each country, we need to look at institutions as both organizational structures and as the embodiment of normative orientations.

In the English case, we find elements of both a "school-empowerment" model and a "competitive market" model. The "school-empowerment" model is evident in such policies as the Education Action Zones and the City Technology Schools, emphasizing both the role of the school in its community along with the role of businesses to participate, even at the funding level. With these policies, the role of the local community is very important, yet the role of the local politicians seems to be sidelined. Such a policy emphasis may very well be explained by a desired break in the institutional legacy of the LEAs (a very favorable development in the view of central-level policy-makers after the many years of undesirable local political control). There is also an explanation to be found in the normative orientations, which in the English case can be said to reflect a belief in the ability of business in helping to solve societal problems. The Thatcher ideological legacy is also found in the policies that relate to the "competitive market" model; such as the running of schools by independent trusts (sometimes in co-operation with business) and the "virtual" voucher system. In reviewing the

significant, hierarchical follow-up of quality through control and assessment programs, and the contractual accountability which the system entails, one can also find an explanation based on normative orientations of the English polity – a strong public discourse regarding the failure of the schools and an acute awareness for the need for increased competition to solve the problem. Thus a strong, central-level authority for quality control could be established where one previously did not exist.

In the Swedish case, we see similar "global" trends as those in the English case, yet rather different governance models are adopted because of different institutional conditions. It is important to note that the "school-empowerment" model was not adopted in Sweden. Instead, local empowerment in the Swedish case meant power to the local politicians, not to the school boards, or to the professionals, or to the parents. And even if we see some elements of the "competitive market" model in the Swedish case (given the policy initiatives of "vouchers" and the "free" schools), it is important to note that these schools are not able to "opt-out" from local government control as in the English case. By studying historical institutional structures, this difference in the Swedish case can be more thoroughly explained. For example, in Sweden there continues to be a strong Social Democratic consensus, which combines with strong teacher trade unions to prevent parental influence (Lindbom, 1995). In addition, the recent establishment of parental advisory boards has not been enacted in the name of increasing parental influence over school policy, but rather in the name of furthering democratic education and participation (Jarl, 2004). And although Sweden has adopted some aspects of the "competitive market" model, only very limited business interests are allowed. This can be partly explained by the dominant normative orientations that are quite critical to business interests in the provision of public goods (seen also in the cases of health care and higher education provision). Regarding quality control and assessment, the situation is more mixed in Sweden than in England. Elements of both "contractual" and "responsive" accountability are present. The "contractual" elements relate to the standards that are still set by the national government through the national curriculum (albeit a much less detailed version than previously given reforms in the late 1980s), which teachers are required by law to follow. However, the assessment of quality and the interpretation of outcomes is more a local responsibility, tending to reflect more "responsive" accountability. Thus, this mixed system could be seen as reflecting both the many years of traditional, central-level bureaucratic steering from Stockholm (which continues somewhat in the maintenance of a milder, revised national curriculum) as well as the new normative orientations that prefer steering by local communities rather than central government.

HIGHER EDUCATION POLICY: SIMILAR DEVELOPMENTS?

The ideological, social and economic movements that influenced education policy during the 1980s and 1990s certainly reached the sphere of higher education as well. Although the timing of the reforms and the extent of the reform policies vary across nations, the general trends are without a doubt similar. New public management techniques for example emerged strongly in the modes and practices of higher education. Public universities have been opened to influences from various interest groups, marketization has brought a new consumerism (particularly to European higher education systems), and evaluation has come to the forefront as a guarantee for quality (Henkel and Little, 1999).

As higher education systems have moved from an "elite" system of enrolment to a mass system of enrolment, the growing importance of higher education to the political system and the economy can not be denied. The university graduates' role in the knowledge economy has intensified and the need for the success of research results to be transformed into commercial products are reflected in new theories of knowledge production. Nowotny et al.,

(2001) discuss knowledge production in terms of the "context of application", and the "societal contextualization" of science. Etzkowitz and Leydesdorff (1997) have introduced the concept of the "triple helix" to describe the new type of institutional arrangements among universities, industries and governments. Certainly the economic role of higher education, and governments' interest in it, cannot be denied. With this increased societal role for universities, the universities are confronted with new challenges. University profiling and identity searches are crucial for success in a diverse market (Clark, 1998; Sporn, 1999).

These recent changes in the socio-economic foundations of higher education require us to call into question previous models of governance of the system and to reflect upon what this entails for university autonomy. Governance by regulation has been replaced by a model where universities are expected to have a more active role and are allowed increased levels of authority. van Vught (1989) labels this the shift from "State Control" to "Self-Regulation" for the universities, with a "Supervising State" as a consequence. But what are the forces behind such changes, and how do they impact governance? Clark's triangle of the forces pressuring the higher education system for change identifies the state authority, the academic oligarchy and the market forces (Clark, 1983). Becher and Kogan (1992) added a welfare state force, which today could also be referred to as the civil society force, accommodating the community's need for higher education. Combining these forces with levels of university autonomy, Marton (2000) describes four models of university governance: (1) a "security guard" model built upon the ideas of the Humboldtian tradition, with the nation-state safeguarding university autonomy but retaining state control; (2) a "honor society" model based on the British autonomous model with little state control, and autonomy which emphasizes cultural values in the pursuit of knowledge; (3) a "social goals" model with strong state control and utilitarian values which steer over higher education (thus autonomy is weak); and (4) an "invisible hand" model where state authority is decentralized and higher education institutions operate in an open market to provide services to clients (thus autonomy is at risk).

Comparing higher education reforms over time and across nations, these models help to depict the changes taking place. Empirically applied to cases in England, Norway and Sweden it has been shown that, although all countries started at a different position in the 1960s, they all matched the "invisible hand/ market model" in the 1990s (Kogan et al., 2000). In a separate study, Musselin (1999) described the governance changes in France in the 1990s as one of "negotiated contract". The state maintained primary control over the system, but the provision of higher education services were "contractualized" which placed the state in the role of "consumer".

Given the increased marketization of higher education, evaluation as a tool for state monitoring and control was a dominant policy reform in the 1980s and 1990s. Neave and van Vught (1991) have labelled this as a change from "process control" to "product control". The previous bureaucratic and uniform-across-system regulations are being replaced by more diverse and discretionary quality audits and assessment exercises. In studying evaluation systems in Europe, Brennan found that "much quality assessment within individual institutions appears to be unrelated to external quality assessment requirements of national agencies" (1999: 231). Although no exact explanation for this finding is given, references are made to the potential conflicts of interest that arise with evaluation procedures. In a study of the fifty American states, Nettles and Cole (2001: 216) also found tension between the actors involved in the assessment exercises, since the states and the public institutions did not necessarily "share the goal of accountability".

POLICY CHALLENGES FOR THE FUTURE

As discussed previously, globalization pressures have contributed to the framing of education policy in terms of economic competitiveness. Given this background, it is worthwhile to pose the question of whether another type of "framing" of education policy is needed. What would happen if "education is conceptualized as part of the cultural rather than the economic domain?" (Taylor et al., 1997: 77). This is not to say that the important role of education in producing talent for the labor market should be neglected, but rather that the more humanizing effects of education could also come to the forefront of policy discussions (Apple, 1994; Cox, 1995). Critical questions about citizenship and identity in multicultural societies could be addressed.

Therefore, we need to contemplate to what extent the democratic ideals and notions of the education system as an important democratic institution can be upheld. As test scores, curriculum content, and assessment exercises dominant the scene, some would argue we have reached the point of an "educational war of all against all" (Hargreaves & Fullan, 1998). How are we going to maintain a healthy democracy if our state school system is not serving the "public good"? As society becomes more ethnically and religiously diverse, transforming values to future citizens becomes more complex.

Thus, we should investigate what type of institutional structures in the education system could enable citizens to engage in civic life. Hargreaves & Fullan (1988) argue that what is needed are "democratic communities" which value participation, equality, inclusiveness and social justice (citing Mertz & Furman (1997)). Whitty (2002) suggests new forms of "collective association" which would exist between the state and the "marketized" civil society and would be based on a new concept of citizenship, focusing on citizen rights instead of consumer rights. Such a form of association could reassert a collective responsibility for education policy, but without returning to the bureaucratic machinery that contributed to previous shortcomings in the system. Reid argues, "there is a need to reclaim the public sphere and reinvest community discourse with notions of social capital. Places are needed where people can share and understand differences, and where they can demonstrate a collective concern for all members of society"

(Reid, 2002: 578). But in advocating an exchange of "collective concerns", Reid is careful to point out that this is not the same as a "search for consensus". The notion that groups need to share some "common ground" in order to talk with one another is not incompatible with diversity, but rather is crucial to it.

Hargreaves and Fullan (1998) believe that these types of communities can start in the classroom where pupils would share responsibility for their own learning and pupils and parents would be involved in decision making on an array of topics from teaching and learning to assessment of achievement. Whitty (2002) and Reid (2002) argue, however, that the association should be democratically accountable, not just accountable to the school or the classroom. Given that the power of market forces can benefit those with resources already, a more democratic forum to counterbalance structural inequalities is required. Referring to Apple and Beane (1996), Whitty concludes that "if we want students to learn democratic citizenship we need to put in place structures that embody those principles" (2002: 104).

Thus a major issue for the future of educational systems is what type of democratic structures can be representative and legitimate? Reid urges us to "retheorize the role of public schools in building and sustaining a pluralist moral democracy" (2002: 581). This is based on the view that a democratic society needs a democratic education system, and vice versa. Reid outlines at least four policy implications which can be derived from this retheorizing of the role of public schools: (1) policy should not be designed at the "top" by a level of experts, but rather with a range of participants at all levels; (2) the notion of the "nation-building" role of education should be revised to incorporate the more relevant global elements as well as the local (see also Lödén, 2002); (3) the notion of "choice" needs to be re-positioned from the emphasis on individual choice to pursue self-interest to a more collective notion which emphasizes the privilege to make choices for the future of society; and (4) the concept of "public good" needs to be understood in broader terms, allowing for

diversity and pluralism. Such a reform could take place if the polity agreed and supported a new set of principles for education that would apply to both public and private schools and a funding system that would be dependent on whether the schools operated according to these principles. Principles viewed as particularly important include: (1) a school curriculum emphasizing skills important for a pluralist moral democracy, (2) a democratic school management system with a pedagogy reflecting democratic principles, (3) an emphasis on diversity, which includes promoting inclusiveness – not based on homogenous communities or notions of assimilation – but based on a sense of shared community; and (4) the non-discrimination of the students in acceptance procedures. Reid admits that further discussion is needed regarding the political structure to carry out these tasks as well as the details for the funding mechanisms; however the principles are needed in order to begin to rethink the relationship between democracy and public education in a global world.

In other works discussing the new politics of education, there is a similar effort to identify new institutional principles along with a questioning of whether the traditional "school system" is the adequate structure for learning today. Halpin, citing the work of Bentley (1998), writes "that education should strive, not so much for equality of educational opportunity, but the provision of opportunities for learning that foster autonomy, responsibility and creativity" (1999: 358). Halpin argues that this may best take place in "contexts where knowledge is actually used and valued" and thus structures such as "overlapping networks of learning" may be better suited for the task. Such networks would include not just the schools, but a "public knowledge infrastructure" based on "homes, libraries, firms, universities, community centers and voluntary organizations as well" (Halpin, 1999:358). New ideas are also coming to the table in New Zealand and England regarding "Community Education Forums". The exact role and institutional powers such forums will possess is still unclear, but certainly worthy of further investigation.

However, one issue does seem to have been resolved: a common school system for all students will not meet the demands for diversity in today's modern society. Other arrangements still need to be encouraged.

ACKNOWLEDGMENTS

The author would like to acknowledge financial support provided for this project from STINT (The Swedish Foundation for International Cooperation in Research and Higher Education). In addition, many thanks are extended to the Political Economy Research Centre (PERC) at Sheffield University and the Center for Public Sector Research (CEFOS) at Göteborg University for providing a generous research environment during the completion of this project.

REFERENCES

Apple, M. (1994). *Official Knowledge*. New York: Routledge.

Apple, M., & Beane, J. (eds.). (1996). *Democratic Schools*. Buckingham: Open University Press.

Bache, I. (2003). Governing through Governance: Education Policy Control under New Labour. *Political Studies, 51*(2), 300–315.

Becher, T., & Kogan, M. (1992). *Process and Structure in Higher Education*. London: Routledge.

Bentley, T. (1998). *Learning Beyond the Classroom*. London: Routledge.

Bernstein, B. (1971). On the classification and framing of educational knowledge. In M. F. D. Young (ed.), *Knowledge and Control*. London: Collier Macmillan.

Boyd, W. L., & Cibulka, J. G. (eds.) (1989). *Private Schools and Public Policy. International Perspectives*. London: Falmer.

Brennan, J. (1999). Evaluation of Higher Education in Europe. In M. Henkel & B. Little (eds.), *Changing Relationships between Higher Education and the State*. London: Jessica Kingsley.

Brown, P. (1997). The 'Third Wave': Education and the Ideology of Parentocracy. In A. H. Halsey, H. Lauder, P. Brown & A. Wells (eds.), *Education, Culture, Economy, Society*. Oxford: Oxford University.

Brown, P., Halsey, A. H., Lauder, H., & Wells, A. (1997). The Transformation of Education and Society: An Introduction. In A. H. Halsey, H. Lauder, P. Brown & A. Wells (eds.), *Education: Culture, Economy and Society*. Oxford: Oxford University.

Brown, P., & Lauder, H. (1997). Education, Globalization, and Economic Development. In A. H. Halsey, H. Lauder, P. Brown & A. Wells (eds.), *Education, Culture, Economy, Society*. Oxford: Oxford University.

Bullock, A., & Thomas, H. (1997). *Schools at the Centre? a study of decentralisation*. London: Routledge.

Carnoy, M. (1992). Education and the State: From Adam Smith to Perestroika. In R. F. Arnove (ed.), *Emergent Issues in Education*. Ithaca: State University of New York.

Castles, F. (1998). *Comparative Public Policy. Patterns of Post-war Transformations*. Cheltenham: Edward Elgar.

Clark, B. (1983). *The Higher Education System: Academic Organization in Cross-National Perspective*. Berkeley: University of California.

Clark, B. (1998). *Creating Entrepreneurial Universities. Organizational Pathways of Transformation*. New York: Pergamon.

Cohen, D., & Spillane, J. P. (1992). Policy and Practice: The Relation Between Governance and Instruction. *Review of Educational Research, 18*.

Connell, R. W. (1993). *Schools and Social Justice*. Toronto: Our Schools/Our Selves Education Foundation.

Cordingley, P., & Kogan, M. (1993). *In Support of Education: Governing the Reformed System*. London: Jessica Kingsley.

Cox, E. (1995). *A Truly Civil Society*. Sydney: ABC Books.

Dale, R. (1997). The State and the Governance of Education: An Analysis of the Restructuring of the State-Education Relationship. In A. H. Halsey, H. Lauder, P. Brown & A. Wells (eds.), *Education: Culture, Economy and Society*. Oxford: Oxford University.

Dale, R. (1999). Specifying globalization effects on national policy: a focus on the mechanisms. *Journal of Education Policy, 14*(1), 1–17.

Datnow, A. (2000). Gender Politics in School Reform. In N. Bascia & A. Hargreaves (eds.), *The Sharp Edge of Educational Change*. London: Routledge Falmer.

Daun, H. (ed.) (2002). *Educational Restructuring in the Context of Globalization and National Policy*. New York: Routledge Falmer.

Daun, H., & Benincasa, L. (1998). *Restructuring Education in Europe. Four Country Studies*. Stockholm: Stockholm University, Institute of International Education.

David, M. (1999). Educational Reforms, Gender and Families. In J. Demaine (ed.) *Education Policy and Contemporary Politics*. Basingstoke: Palgrave.

Demaine, J. (ed.) (1999). *Education Policy and Contemporary Politics*. Basingstoke: Palgrave.

Dickson, M., Halpin, D., Power, S., Telford, D., & Whitty, G. (2001). Education Action Zones and Democratic Participation. *School Leadership and Management, 21*(2), 169–181.

Elmore, R. F. (1993). School Decentralization: Who Gains? Who Looses? In J. Hannaway & M. Carnoy (eds.), *Decentralization and School Improvement. Can We Fulfill the Promise?* San Fransisco: The Jossey-Bass Publications.

Etzkowitz, H., & Leydesdorff, L. (eds.) (1997). *Universities and the Global Knowledge Economy: A Triple Helix of University-Industry-Government Relations*. London: Pinter.

Glatter, R., Woods, P. A., & Bagley, C. (eds.) (1997). *Choice and Diversity in Schooling: Perspectives and Prospects*. London: Routledge.

Goddard, R., Hoy, W., & Hoy, A. (2000). Collective teacher efficacy: its meaning, measure, and impact on student achievement". *American Educational Research Journal, 37*(2), 479–507.

Goldhaber, D. D. (1999). School choice: an examination of the empirical evidence on achievement, parental decision-making, and equity. *Educational Researcher, 28*(9), 16–25.

Green, A. (1999). Education and globalization in Europe and East Asia: convergent and divergent trends. *Journal of Education Policy, 14*(1), 55–71.

Griffin, R. (2002). *Education in Transition: International Perspectives on the Politics and Processes of Change*. Oxford: Symposium Books.

Halpin, D. (1999). Utopian realism and a new politics of education: developing a critical theory without guarantees. *Journal of Education Policy, 14*(4), 345–361.

Halsey, A. H., Lauder, H., Brown, P., & Wells, A. S. (eds.) (1997). *Education, Culture, Economy, Society*. Oxford: Oxford University.

Halstead, M. (1994). Accountability and values. In D. Scott (ed.), *Accountability and Control in Educational Settings*. London: Cassell.

Hannaway, J. (1993). Decentralization in Two School Districts: Challenging the Standard Paradigm. In J. Hannaway & M. Carnoy (eds.), *Decentralization and School Improvement. Can We*

Fulfill the Promise? San Fransisco: The Jossey-Bass Publications.

Hargreaves, A., & Fullan, M. (1998). *What's Worth Fighting for in Education?* Buckingham: Open University.

Heck, R. (2000). Examining the impact of school quality on school outcomes and improvement: A value-added approach. *Educational Administration Quarterly, 36*(4), 513–552.

Heidenheimer, A. J., Heclo, H., & Adams, C. T. (1983). *Comparative Public Policy: the politics of social choice in Europe and America* (2nd ed.) New York: St. Martin's.

Held, D., McGrew, A., Goldblatt, D., & Perraton, J. (1999). *Global Transformations: Politics, Economics and Culture*. Cambridge: Polity.

Henkel, M., & Little, B. (eds.) (1999). *Changing Relationships between Higher Education and the State*. London: Jessica Kingsley.

Henig, J. R. (1994). *Rethinking School Choice: Limits of the Market Metaphor*. Princeton: Princeton University Press.

Hirst, P., & Thompson, G. (1996). *Globalisation in Question: The International Economy and the Possibilities of Governance*. Cambridge: Polity.

Husén, T. (1998). The Swedish School Reforms: Trends and Issues. In A. Tjeldvoll (ed.), *Education and the Scandinavian Welfare State in the Year 2000*. New York: Garland.

James, M. (2000). Measured lives: the rise of assessment as the engine of change in English schools. *The Curriculum Journal, 11*(3), 343–364.

Jarl, M. (2004). *En skola i demokrati? Föräldrarna, kommunen och dialogen (A school in democracy? Parents, municipalities and dialogue)*. Göteborg: Department of Political Science, Göteborg University.

Karlsen, G. E. (2000). Decentralized Centralism: Framework for a Better Understanding of Governance in the Field of Education. *Journal of Education Policy, 15*(5), 545–538.

Kickert, W. (1995). Steering at a Distance: A New Paradigm of Public Governance in Dutch Higher Education. *Governance, 8*(1), 135–157.

Kogan, M. (1973). *The Politics of Education*. London: Penguin.

Kogan, M., Bauer, M., Bleiklie, I., & Henkel, M. (2000). *Transforming Higher Education : A Comparative Study*. London, Philadelphia: J. Kingsley Publishers.

Lauder, H. (1997). Education, Democracy and the Economy. In A. H. Halsey, H. Lauder, P. Brown & A. Wells (eds.), *Education: Culture, Economy and Society*. Oxford: Oxford University Press.

Lindbom, A. (1995). *Medborgarskapet i välfärdsstaten: Föräldrainflytande i skandinavisk grundskola (Citizenship in the Welfare State: Parental influence in the Scandinavian compulsory school)*. Stockholm: Almqvist & Wiksell.

Lundahl, L. (2002). Sweden: decentralization, deregulation, quasi-markets – and then what? *Journal of Education Policy*, 17(6), 687–697.

Lödén, H. (2002). Skilda världar? Om nationell och global identitet (Separate worlds? On national and global identity. *Utbildning & Demokrati (Education & Democracy)*, 11(1), 37–55.

Maden, M., & Hillman, J. (1996). Lessons in Success. In National Commission on Education (ed.), *Success Against the Odds*. London: Routledge.

Marginson, S. (1999). After Globalization: The Emerging Politics of Education. *Journal of Education Policy*, 14(1), 19–31.

Marton, S. (2000). *The Mind of the State: The Politics of University Autonomy in Sweden 1968–1998*. Göteborg: BAS.

Mertz, C., & Furman, G. (1997). *Community Schools: Promise & Paradox*. New York: Teacher's College Press.

McGinn, N. (1992). Reforming Educational Governance: Centralization / Decentralization. In R. F. Arnove (ed.), *Emergent Issues in Education*. Ithaca: State University of New York Press.

Moe, T. (1994). The British battle for choice. In K. L. Billingsley (ed.), *Voices on Choice: The Education Reform Debate*. San Francisco: Pacific Institute for Public Policy.

Mok, K., & Tan, J. (2004). *Globalization and Marketization in Education: A Comparative Analysis of Hong Kong and Singapore*. Cheltenham: Edward Elgar.

Mok, K., & Welch, A. (eds.) (2003). *Globalization and Educational Restructuring in the Asia Pacific Region*. Basingstoke: Palgrave Macmillan.

Musselin, C. (1999). State/University Relations and How to Change Them: The Case of France and Germany. In M. Henkel & B. Little (eds.), *Changing Relationships between Higher Education and the State*. London: Jessica Kingsley.

Neave, G., & van Vught, F. (eds.) (1991). *Prometheus Bound. The Changing Relationship Between Government and Higher Education in Western Europe*. Oxford: Pergamon Press.

Nettles, M., & Cole, J. (2001). A Study in Tension: State Assessment and Public Colleges and Universities. In D. Heller (ed.), *The States and Public Higher Education Policy*. Baltimore: Johns Hopkins University.

Nowotny, H., Scott, P., & Gibbons, M. (eds.) (2001). *Re-Thinking Science: Knowledge and the Pubic in an Age of Uncertainty*. Cambridge: Polity.

Ogbu, J. (1997). Racial Stratification and Education in the United States: Why Inequity Persists. In A. H. Halsey, H. Lauder, P. Brown & A. Wells (eds.), *Education: Culture, Economy and Society*. Oxford: Oxford University.

Organisation for Economic Co-Operation and Development (OECD). (2003). *Networks of Innovation: Towards New Models for Managing Schools and Systems*. Paris: OECD.

Peters, M. (2003). The New Zealand Education Experiment: From Democratic Participation to Self-Management, and From Universal Welfare Entitlement of Private Investment. In K. Mok & A. Welch (eds.), *Globalization and Education Restructuring in the Asia Pacific Region*. Basingstoke: Palgrave.

Pierre, J. (ed.) (2000). *Debating Governance: Authority, Steering and Democracy*. Oxford: Oxford University Press.

Pollard, S. (1995). *Schools, Selection and the Left*. London: Social Market Foundation.

Reid, A. (2002). Public education and democracy: a changing relationship in a globalizing world. *Journal of Education Policy*, 17(5), 571–585.

Sexton, S. (1987). *Our Schools – a Radical Policy*. Warlingham: IEA Education Unit.

Silins, H., & Mulford, B. (2002). Leadership and school results. In K. Leithwood & P. Hallinger (eds.), *Second International Handbook of Educational Leadership and Administration*. Dordrecht: Kluwer.

Sizer, T. (1984). *Horace's Compromise*. Boston: Houghton-Mifflin.

Sporn, B. (1999). *Adaptive University Structures*. London: Jessica Kingsley Publishers.

Strange, S. (1996). *The Retreat of the State: The Diffusion of Power in the World Economy*. Cambridge: Cambridge University.

Swank, D. (2002). *Global Capital, Political Institutions, and Policy Change in Developed Welfare States*. Cambridge: Cambridge University.

Taylor, S., Rizvi, F., Lingard, B., & Henry, M. (1997). *Educational Policy and the Politics of Change*. London: Routledge.

Tomlinson, S. (2001). *Education in a Post-Welfare Society*. Buckingham: Open University.

Tooley, J. (1995). Markets or democracy? A reply to Stewart Ranson. *British Journal of Educational Studies*, 43(1), 21–34.

Torrance, H. (1997). Assessment, Accountability, and Standards. Using Assessment to Control the Reform of Schooling. In A. H. Halsey, H. Lauder, P. Brown & A. Wells (eds.), *Education, Culture, Economy, Society*. Oxford: Oxford University.

van Vught, F. (1989). *Governmental Strategies and Innovation in Higher Education*. London: Jessica Kingsley.

Weiss, L. (ed.) (2003). *States in the Global Economy: Bringing Domestic Institutions Back In*. Cambridge: Cambridge University.

Wells, A. S. (2002). *Where charter school policy fails: the problems of accountability and equity*. New York: Teachers College Press.

Whitty, G. (2002). *Making sense of education policy: studies in the sociology and politics of education*. London: Paul Chapman.

Wilson, W. (1997). Studying Inner-City Social Dislocations: The Challenge of Public Agenda Research. In A. H. Halsey, H. Lauder, P. Brown & A. Wells (eds.), *Education: Culture, Economy, and Society*. Oxford: Oxford University.

14

Environmental Policy

CHRISTOPH KNILL

INTRODUCTION

Compared to many other areas, environmental policy is a rather new policy field. Although important political activities to curb air pollution or to improve water quality in many countries date back to the 19th century, it was not before the late 1960s that environmental policy emerged as a central area of governmental activities. This development can mainly be traced to an increasing public awareness of problems of environmental pollution and the excessive use of natural resources. The perception of far-reaching environmental problems which, in many instances, exceeded the boundaries of the nation state (such as acid rain), as well as alarming scientific publications on the environmental consequences of economic growth, contributed to a strong politicization of environmental issues both at the national and international level. As a consequence, since the late 1960s encompassing programs and new administrative agencies for environmental protection were established by most industrialized countries (Weale 1992). At the same time, nation states increasingly tried to tackle transnational problems of environmental pollution through international cooperation on the level of the United Nations, the Organization for Economic Cooperation and Development (OECD) or the European Union (EU) (Bungarten 1978; Rehbinder/Stewart 1985).

Since that time, the environmental field developed into a highly differentiated policy sector which is characterized by a broad range of subfields and governance approaches. Activities concentrate not only on specific areas (air and water pollution, noise, control of chemicals or waste management), but often cut across different environmental media and explicitly seek to address potential interaction effects of media-specific approaches. Examples are policies on environmental impact assessment or integrated pollution control.

In terms of governance patterns, environmental regulations typically followed interventionist 'command and control' approaches. Policies were characterized by often detailed, legally binding requirements, to be followed by the private and public actors addressed. In recent years, interventionist approaches are increasingly combined with new forms of bottom-up regulation. The latter are characterized by softer and more flexible patterns of regulation (such as voluntary agreements, private self-regulation) or the emphasis of economic incentives to reduce environmental pollution (e.g. energy taxes or emission licenses) (Knill and Lenschow 2000; Tews, Busch and Jörgens 2003).

Recent comparative studies emphasize striking parallels in the development and regulatory patterns characterizing national policies of environmental protection across OECD countries, often beyond the borders of the Western industrialized world. For instance, both OECD and Central and Eastern European countries have progressively adopted similar policies and administrative structures in the areas of air and water protection, as well as waste management from the 1950s onwards (Kern, Jörgens and Jänicke 2000). However, these developments are not restricted to the initial establishment of basic legislation and specific institutions in this relatively new policy area. A more recent parallelism refers to the shift from sectorally fragmented media-specific approaches to integrated policies which seek to tackle environmental problems from a cross-media perspective (Lenschow 1999). Moreover, we observe a general trend towards the introduction of new policy instruments which emphasize economic incentives, public participation and information, as well as voluntary agreements and private self-regulation (Héritier 2002; Holzinger, Knill and Schäfer 2003).[1]

With regard to these developments it is the central objective of this article to investigate potential causes for this parallelism in national environmental policies. How can the broad convergence of regulatory patterns be explained? To be sure, one plausible explanation could be that governments throughout the world are reacting independently, but similarly to similar environmental problem pressures. As Simmons and Elkins put it: 'Just as individuals open their umbrellas simultaneously during a rainstorm, governments may decide to change their policies in recession, in the presence of capital flight, or in the presence of high world interest rates' (2003, 275). Such a constellation implies that there is 'one best solution' to a problem that is common to all countries. This scenario, however, will hardly apply for the comprehensive area of environmental protection in general, as different geographical, biological, economic and social conditions will lead to highly varying pressures on national policy-makers. Although parallel problem pressures might indeed constitute an important factor to account for similar policy developments in certain cases, this approach is hardly sufficient to explain the broad convergence patterns that are observed empirically.

As a consequence, we have to look for alternative explanations. In the literature, a variety of potential sources of cross-national policy convergence is discussed. Notwithstanding this diversity, three analytically distinct factors can be identified, namely regulatory competition, international cooperation and transnational communication (Hoberg 2001; Bennett 1991; Holzinger and Knill 2004). In the following sections I will investigate the relevance of each of these factors with respect to environmental policy. The central conclusion which can be drawn from this analysis is that none of the three factors alone, but only the investigation of their combined effects, provides a satisfactory explanation for the striking parallelism in national regulatory patterns.

REGULATORY COMPETITION: THE EFFECTS OF INTERNATIONAL ECONOMIC INTEGRATION

A first factor that might explain the observed pattern of increasingly similar environmental policy arrangements across countries refers to the effects of regulatory competition. With the increasing integration of European and global markets and the abolition of national trade barriers, there is a certain potential that the international mobility of goods, workers and capital, puts pressure on the nation states to redesign domestic market regulations in order to avoid regulatory burdens restricting the competitiveness of domestic industries (Goodman and Pauly 1993; Keohane and Nye 2000).

As a consequence, national governments compete over the optimal design of domestic regulations in order to attract foreign capital and to improve the competitive position of their economy. The presence of mobile capital can induce governments to attract capital from elsewhere by lowering environmental standards on the one hand, and, on the other, domestic capital can threaten to exit and this way exert pressure on the governments to lower the level of environmental regulation, hence implying cross-national policy convergence (Hoberg 2001, 127; Simmons and Elkins 2003; Drezner 2001, 57–59).

The central and already classical research question in the public policy literature refers to the consequences of this development on the level of environmental standards. Can we expect a race to the bottom, implying the gradual weakening of environmental regulations? Or is it even conceivable that regulatory competition coincides with the opposite scenario of a mutual strengthening of national standards (race to the top) (Holzinger 2002, 62–63)? Theoretical work suggests that there are a number of conditions, which may drive policy in both directions (Vogel 1995; Scharpf 1996, 1997; Kern, Jörgens and Jänicke 2000; Drezner 2001; Holzinger 2002, 2003). In this context, particular emphasis is placed on the distinction of different types of environmental regulation, namely product standards and process standards.

Product versus Process Standards

Product standards define regulatory requirements for the quality and specific characteristics of traded goods. Process standards, by contrast, refer to the conditions under which certain goods are produced. While for product standards several factors might inhibit a race to the bottom and even trigger a race to the top, we find a widely shared expectation that policy convergence will occur at the lowest common denominator in the case of process standards (Drezner 2001; Holzinger 2002, 2003). Typical examples of process standards are sulfur dioxide or nitrogen oxide emission standards for large combustion plants. Strict standards demand filters, which raise production costs. Then the domestic steel industry, for example, suffers from a competitive disadvantage against the steel producers abroad, if the latter need not apply the same strict standards. In order to avoid such a disadvantage governments may want to decrease their standards to the level of other countries.

In the case of product regulation, two conditions can avoid downward dynamics of national standards. First, competition between products might not only be based on their price, but also on their quality. If quality aspects dominate, stricter standards will constitute a competitive advantage, hence implying a race to the top (Scharpf 1997, 523). Second, downward pressures can be avoided if trade rules allow individual countries to erect exceptional trade barriers for products which do not comply with national environmental standards. Such measures are, for instance, possible within the trade regimes of the World Trade Organization (WTO) and the EU.

David Vogel (1995) shows that the erection of trade barriers might not only avoid a race to the bottom, but can even induce an upward dynamic between national regulations. He observed this development for the regulation of car emission standards in the United States (US). When California raised its emission standards, most US states followed quickly for two reasons. First, California was permitted to apply its standards to foreign car producers. Second, since licensing procedures for cars are very expensive, car producers wanted to avoid multiple arrangements and hence demanded harmonized requirements throughout the US.

The described mechanisms are less relevant, however, when it comes to process standards. First, competition over product quality has no effects on the conditions under which the goods of similar quality are produced. For instance, for consumers of energy it makes no difference whether the producing company had to cope with strict environmental standards or not. Second, in the case of process standards, governments are not allowed to erect exceptional trade barriers. No member state of the EU or WTO can restrict the import of foreign products, claiming that the foreign process regulations applying to these goods were below their domestic standards. In the case of process standards, there is thus a higher probability that regulatory competition between countries implies a race to the bottom (Scharpf 1999, 92).

Other Factors

Notwithstanding these rather clear theoretical expectations, the empirical literature generally finds 'lack of empirical support' (Drezner 2001, 75) for the hypothesis that regulatory competition leads to convergence 'at the bottom'. There is case study evidence for races to the top but no systematic confirmation of a race to the bottom (Tobey 1990; Vogel 1997; Jänicke 1998; Beers and van der Bergh 1999; Kern 2000). These findings suggest that the extent and level of environmental policy convergence is affected by a number of additional factors.

First, it has to be emphasized that the distinction of product and process standards covers only parts of environmental policy, namely those regulations which affect competition among national industries. By contrast, no convergence can be expected for environmental policies that are not directly related to products or production processes, such as ambient quality standards or the protection of nature. Second, pressures to adjust national standards can be low, even if trade-related policies are concerned. This is the case, for instance, if the level of environmental regulation has no significant impact on production costs (Vogel 1995; Jänicke 1998). The same holds true if the relative market shares of the countries involved in competition are rather small. Third, the extent and direction of national adjustment is affected by the political and social context in which regulatory decisions are made. In this respect, the political strength and presence of other interests than business in national politics, such as environmental groups or green parties, plays a central role. Depending on the power and political support of these actors, the opportunities for regulatory adjustments to strengthen the competitiveness of national industries might thus be quite restricted (Holzinger 2002).

However, even if we accept that these factors play a role in avoiding an overall pattern of a constant downgrading of environmental standards, we are still left with two unresolved questions. First, it is unclear from the theoretical considerations presented so far why there should be convergence, even for those environmental policies that neither refer to product nor to process standards. Second, it is puzzling that there is only clear empirical support for races to the top but not for the opposite scenario of races to the bottom. Although the factors mentioned above can account for this pattern in some cases, they hardly constitute a

sufficient explanation for this general tendency. In the following sections, the focus is therefore on additional factors which might fill this explanatory gap.

INTERNATIONAL COOPERATION

Environmental policy convergence might not only be the result of competitive pressures related to economic integration. It can also emerge from deliberate activities of national governments to reduce such pressures through regulatory cooperation at the supranational or international level (Holzinger and Knill 2004). This pattern of 'obligated transfer' (Dolowitz and Marsh 2000, 15) or 'convergence through harmonization' (Bennett 1991, 225) refers to constellations, in which national governments are legally required to adopt policies and programs as part of their obligations as members of international institutions. In other words, national policies converge because of corresponding legal obligations defined in international or supranational law.[2]

International cooperation as a source of environmental policy convergence is generally traced to the existence of interdependencies or externalities which push governments to resolve common problems through cooperation within international institutions, hence sacrificing some independence for the good of the community (Drezner 2001, 60; Hoberg 2001, 127). Once established, institutional arrangements will constrain and shape the domestic policy choices, even as they are constantly challenged and reformed by their member states. This way, international institutions are not only the object of state choice, but at the same time consequential for subsequent governmental activities (Martin and Simmons 1998, 743). However, as member states voluntarily engage in international cooperation and actively influence corresponding decisions and arrangements, the impact of international legal obligations on national policies constitutes no hierarchical process; it can rather be interpreted as 'negotiated transfer' (Dolowitz and Marsh 2000, 15).

The impact of legal obligation on cross-national policy convergence was analyzed in particular for the EU. Studies emphasized the strong institutionalized forces for harmonization at the Community level superseding national tendencies for divergence (Hurwitz 1983; Brickman, Jasanoff and Ilgen 1985). More recent studies focusing on the Europeanization of domestic policies, processes and institutions, arrive at a more differentiated picture, indicating both the influence of national institutions and interest constellations, as well as peculiarities of the European legislation in question (Caporaso, Cowles and Risse 2001; Héritier, Knill and Mingers 1996; Héritier et al. 2001; Knill 2001).

Regardless of the specific impact of international cooperation on national policies and regulatory structures, there is strong empirical evidence that the level of international harmonization of environmental standards generally reflects the levels of high-regulating rather than low-regulating states. In other words, international harmonization typically occurs at the top rather than at the bottom level of existing domestic regulations (Jänicke 2003; Kern, Jörgens and Jänicke 2000; Holzinger 1994). The impact of international cooperation thus reflects an important factor in order to explain why downward pressures on national environmental standards, as they are expected by theories of regulatory competition, are hardly observed empirically.

This argument, however, still leaves us with the question of why international harmonization of environmental policies actually occurs at comparatively high regulatory levels. This is even more surprising, as from the perspective of theories of regulatory competition, international cooperation, in many instances, is very difficult to achieve in the first place.

To resolve this puzzle, the following argument is based on two analytical steps. First, I will summarize the (skeptical) expectations on the occurrence and level of international cooperation, as they can be derived from theories of regulatory competition. In a second step, I present theoretical insights which help to explain that regulatory developments at the international level are more dynamic as predicted by this initial perspective of regulatory competition theories. In so doing, I concentrate on environmental policy-making in the EU, although these dynamics have also been observed in other contexts of international cooperation (Jänicke 2003).

Regulatory Competition and International Cooperation – I

Both the establishment and the level of harmonization at the international or European level are crucially affected by the underlying constellation of the national interests. In the regulatory competition literature, it is generally argued that this constellation varies with the underlying type of regulation. In the case of product standards, national interests favor the adoption of strict international regulation. For process standards, by contrast, the failure of international negotiations is very likely; i.e., agreements on any standards level are difficult to achieve.

In analyses of EU environmental policy-making, these expectations are typically based on a distinction between poor and rich member states (Rehbinder and Stewart 1985; Holzinger 1991, 2002; Scharpf 1996, 1997). Rich countries are characterized by high economic development. The protection of the natural environment as a societal objective is deeply rooted in the public mind. Those in positions of political responsibility are therefore under high pressure to take action in the environmental field, even if this comes at higher economic costs. In economically less-developed, poor countries, by contrast, environmental protection is of lower importance on the political agenda. The public is to a lesser extent prepared to bear the economic costs associated with higher environmental standards. As a consequence, the level of environmental regulation in poor countries is generally much lower than it is the case for the richer, high-regulating countries.

This general conflict of interests, however, constitutes no major problem for international cooperation on product standards. In this case, both rich and poor countries benefit from harmonization advantages, as different national requirements for the quality and market access of products would complicate international trade and hence imply economic disadvantages for the industries in all countries. As a consequence, all member states share a common interest in international or European harmonization; i.e., all states prefer an international agreement to the status quo of different national regulations (Holzinger 2002, 69). Interests differ, however, with respect to the level of harmonization, with poor countries preferring lower standards than rich countries.

In this context, however, member states interested in higher standards are generally in a more powerful bargaining position in order to realize their objectives. This can be traced to two aspects. First, they have the opportunity to erect exceptional trade barriers, denying market access to products which do not comply with the domestic regulatory requirements. For the EU, this option is specified in article 30 of the European Treaty. Second, article 95 of the Treaty allows member states under certain conditions to keep or introduce stricter domestic regulations, even if corresponding harmonization at the European level has already been agreed (Stewart 1993). Although the erection of exceptional trade barriers based on articles 30 or 95 is confined to specific conditions, these rules nevertheless allow rich member states to unilaterally push through their strict standards at the European level (Scharpf 1996, 118). As a consequence, there is a high probability that harmonization for environmental product standards occurs at the top rather than bottom level of national standards.

The conditions for international cooperation are less favorable, by contrast, for the harmonization of process standards. From the perspective of rich countries, their high level of regulation implies economic disadvantages, because they cannot restrict market access for products from countries with lower process standards. Rich countries, therefore, have a strong interest to establish their strict regulations as international standard. If this objective cannot be achieved, the second-best solution would be harmonization at a lower level in order to avoid economic disadvantages for the domestic industry. This solution, however,

hardly constitutes a feasible alternative. In view of the high political priority attached to environmental protection in rich countries, any attempt to downgrade regulations will meet strong political opposition and hence be difficult to achieve. As a consequence, rich countries will generally prefer the status quo of different national regulations to international harmonization at the level of the low-regulating countries (Scharpf 1996, 119–120).

The same constellation applies, albeit for different reasons, also to poor countries. On the one hand, strict international standards would imply massive problems for their less developed industrial sectors. On the other hand, even harmonization at a lower level would imply high economic disadvantages, as domestic industries would face strong competition from their more productive counterparts in rich countries. Similar to rich countries, poorer states therefore prefer the status quo of different national standards to international or European harmonization (ibid.). Figure 1 summarizes the different interest constellations of rich and poor countries for product and process regulation.

In sum, this theoretical perspective suggests that international agreements on strict process standards are rather unlikely. In view of the underlying constellations of interests, the establishment of strict international regulations can only be expected if rich states are able and prepared to financially compensate the poor countries for potential economic disadvantages emerging from a high level of international regulation. By contrast, the chances for international cooperation look much better for product regulation, given the harmonization advantages for both rich and poor countries.

As mentioned earlier, however, empirical evidence does not confirm the pessimistic expectations on the occurrence and level of international harmonization of process standards. The EU, for instance, in many areas (regulation of chemicals, air and water pollution) adopted process standards that are far beyond the 'lowest common denominator' of national regulations (Jachtenfuchs 1996; Knill 1998). Moreover, member states often accept European

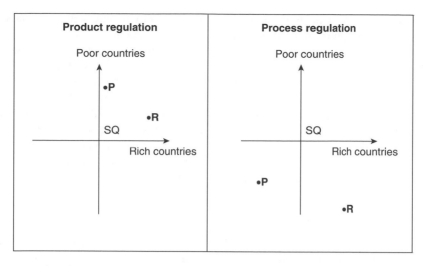

Figure 14.1 *Benefits of possible agreements compared to the status quo (SQ) of different national standards for product and process regulation (P = regulation at the level of the poor countries, R = regulation at the level of the rich countries). Agreements above SQ improve the position of poor countries; agreements on the right of SQ improve the position of the rich countries (compared to the status quo)*

(Source: Scharpf 1996, 121).

policies, although their implementation entails high costs of economic and institutional adaptation (Héritier, Knill and Mingers 1996; Holzinger 1994; Jordan 1999). As will be shown in the following, the theoretical considerations presented so far require further differentiation in order to better account for the empirical developments. In particular, it has to be considered that the level of international regulation is not only affected by economic factors, but also by the objective of national governments and administrations to avoid costs of institutional adaptation.

Regulatory Competition and International Cooperation – II

How can we explain the rather progressive development and level of international cooperation in the environmental field, which is rather surprising, from the perspective of regulatory competition in integrated markets? Research on the formulation of EU environmental policy shows that this form of competition is not the only factor determining the interest position of the member states in negotiations at the European level. Rather regulatory competition, in the sense of systems competition between member states, is overlapped by a second pattern of regulatory competition which is characterized by a highly different logic. Central to this argument is the empirical observation that member states pursue their interests not only through the adjustment of national standards (as suggested by classical theories of regulatory competition). At the same time, they strive to make the regulatory design of European policies as much as possible consistent with their domestic arrangements; i.e., they want to establish their approach as the respective European policy.

As a consequence, member states permanently compete for influence in European policy-making. They engage in a regulatory contest to shape European policy, to champion their interests and push through their policy concepts. All member states are interested to a greater or lesser degree in putting their stamp on Community policy. As shown by Héritier, Knill and Mingers (1996), the big three member states Britain, France, and Germany, have been the major protagonists in a regulatory contest to introduce their philosophies and practices in combating industrial emissions at the European level, whilst other countries in the Union have acted as coalition partners, negotiating specific exchange deals for their concessions. Similar patterns were also observed in other fields of environmental policy both at the European (Andersen and Liefferink 1997) and international level (Jänicke 2003).

What are the reasons for this phenomenon? Why should member states be interested in influencing European policy-making in line with their regulatory approaches and instruments? In this context, two factors are of importance: institutional and economic interests of the member states (1) as well as the specific advantages for those member states relying on the strategy of the first move (2).

The interests of the member states in the context of EU policy-making refer to two basic aspects. First, member states concentrate on strengthening the competitive position of their industries. In so doing, their focus is not only on the protection of domestic markets against foreign competition, but also on the opening-up of new markets for domestic producers of environmental protection technology. While this orientation is basically in line with the underlying assumptions of classical theories of regulatory competition, this no longer holds true for a second issue that is of crucial relevance for member states in European negotiations, namely, the objective to minimize costs of institutional adjustment emerging from potential incompatibilities between EU requirements and domestic regulatory arrangements.

The particular importance of this latter aspect can be traced to the fact that, in many instances, European policy content and institutional requirements for the effective implementation of these policies are closely related. While being aware of the fact that the degree to which policy contents and institutional implications are coupled may vary from policy to policy and from sector to sector, it cannot be ignored that the growing importance of European policies leaves its mark on domestic administrations and institutions. Accordingly, it is well conceivable that European policies

that are not in line with existing regulatory traditions and approaches require fundamental institutional changes at the level of the member states (Knill and Lenschow 1998; Knill 2001). The attention of member states is therefore not so much directed at the level of environmental standards to be decided at the European level, but at the extent to which the underlying approaches and instruments of the respective policy can be integrated into the domestic regulatory framework without triggering major institutional changes.

The fact that this problem is far from trivial is demonstrated by the widespread implementation deficit of EU environmental policy. A large part of these implementation problems are the result of a lack of fit European policies with national regulatory institutions (Knill and Lenschow 2000). In many member states, for instance, the state tradition with a strong emphasis on the rule of law pre-structures the administration's behavior in the environmental field; European policies implying administrative discretion or a transparent relationship with the public are perceived as misfits in this regulatory framework and hence resisted (Kimber 2000).

To be sure, it could still be argued that national interests to avoid institutional adjustment must not necessarily imply a constellation where member states compete over influencing the design and content of European policy proposals. Why do national governments not just simply rely on the option to block policies which are not in line with their interests? How can we explain the proactive strategies of many countries to influence the development of European policies already at very early stages?

The central factor accounting for this development refers to strategic advantages of the first move. Environmental leader or pioneer states have better chances to successfully influence European policy decisions in line with their interests as it is the case for states that rely on more passive strategies. This holds true, especially for the case of the EU, as the possibilities to veto environmental policy decisions have been subsequently reduced through the introduction of qualified majority voting as a decision rule in the Council (Andersen and

Liefferink 1997; Héritier, Knill and Mingers 1996; Jänicke and Weidner 1997).

First mover advantages can be observed in particular during the stages of problem definition and agenda-setting at the European level. The strategy of the 'first move' gives the initiator the opportunity to participate in determining which problems require action from the European perspective, and thus to influence the European decision-making agenda. However, it succeeds only with the support of the European Commission, which is the 'gatekeeper' in this process, given its formal monopoly to initiate European policies. The policy concepts advanced by the first mover therefore have to be in line with the ideas and interests of the Commission.

If in this regulative contest the first mover is able to win the support of the Commission for its proposal, it gains the opportunity to add an item to the European agenda for which it has a relatively precise concept. If the proposal is compatible with the Commission views on the issue and how to tackle it, the initiator country has a good chance of seeing its national approach become the received view of the issue for the ensuing drafting phase. The strong interest in the policy proposal generally goes hand in hand with a higher degree of national expertise in the area to be regulated. Both aspects enhance the first mover influence. Once an actor has formulated a proposal and – in cooperation with the Commission – has occupied the problem-solving terrain in a specific manner, and has moreover collaborated in drawing up the agenda (profiting from the inactivity of those concerned) the others are necessarily in less favorable starting positions. Initially, where it is a matter of developing this specific proposal, other member states can only react to the initiator's project. In other words, whoever takes the initiative and makes the proposal calls the tune in this phase of defining the problem and setting the agenda (Héritier, Knill and Mingers 1996, 13).

However, if and to what extent the advantage of the first move actually results in corresponding policy decisions, crucially depends on the negotiations in the Council. Member states which were not successful in puting

through their interests in earlier stages of the policy process now have a final chance to achieve their objectives. In general, the extent to which the final decision deviates from the initial proposal is strongly affected by the underlying constellation of national interests in the Council.

Empirical evidence indicates four possible patterns in this context, systematized from the perspective of the first mover in the question. In making the first move, what success does the initiator country have in shaping the measure concerned? First, the first mover succeeds in pushing through its regulatory proposal in all phases up to policy formation with respect to both the basic regulatory approach and substantive provisions. This was the case, for instance, for the development of the directive on free access to environmental information which was strongly influenced by corresponding policies in Britain (Kimber 2000). The second path is taken where the initiator's proposal is complemented and expanded by additional requirements. Here, too, the first mover attains its regulatory goal, which is, however, amplified and augmented by the Commission and other member states until a comprehensive piece of legislation on the issue is adopted. In a third scenario, opposition from other member states implies that the initial proposal is scaled down so that countries opposed to the measure can see their way to giving their approval. A fourth pattern includes constellations in which the initiator comes up against the decided opposition of other countries and might have to accept far-reaching changes that call into question the fundamental regulatory approach. The reason may be that either another high-regulating country prefers a different approach and wants to see it receive equal consideration, which results in the typical policy mix or leads to a new, third solution being worked out jointly (Héritier, Knill and Mingers 1996, 332–334; Eichener 1997, 604). In some cases, this constellation implies that individual policies are characterized by different, partially contradictory regulatory traditions of different member states. A case in point is the directive on integrated pollution and prevention control which combines both the German orientation on best available technologies and the British emphasis on balancing environmental quality and economic costs of pollution control (Weale et al., 2000).

In sum, it becomes apparent that it is only in the fourth scenario that the advantage of the first move is completely lost during the decision-making stage. In all other cases that can be observed empirically, pioneer countries more or less succeed in influencing the final policy decision in line with their interests. The strategy of the first move thus consists of a rather promising way to effectively influence the output of international and European cooperation (Kern, Jörgens and Jänicke 2000, 512; Andersen and Liefferink 1997). What are the effects of this type of regulatory competition for influencing European cooperation on policy design and levels of environmental standards?

First, diverging interests of the member states play an important role in promoting the regulatory variety of EU environmental policy. As regulatory and institutional arrangements differ from member state to member state, the regulatory contest favors the emergence of EU environmental policy as a regulatory patchwork. Not only within a single policy area but sometimes within one and the same directive, divergent approaches can be on parallel offer if it has proved impossible to negotiate a consensus (Héritier, Knill and Mingers 1996, 21–22). On the other hand, the regulatory contest favors an equal distribution of adaptational requirements between different member states, given that regulatory competition is unlikely to always favor the same 'winner' (Knill 1997). As a consequence, member states are generally more prepared to accept adaptations in one area as long as their interests are sufficiently taken into account when other measures are decided.

The patchwork character of EU environmental policy can be illustrated with respect to several dimensions. First, there is a variance in regulatory principles, including both reactive and preventative approaches to environmental protection. Second, we find a multitude of regulatory instruments, including (1) numerical standards concerning the state of the environment (quality standards), the maximum emission of pollutants at point sources (emission standards), the control or construction of products (product standards), limits for all emission irrespective of origin (emission 'bubbles'), the application of control technologies (technological standards); (2) procedural requirements concerning the authorization of industrial processes or other projects as well as public participation, and (3) voluntary agreements and industrial self-regulation (Haigh 1996; Knill 2003, 39–72).

This general picture holds true, although one can distinguish different stages of EU environmental policy, with certain approaches and instruments playing a more or less dominant role. Initial attempts of the Community to control environmental pollution were largely based on a reactive approach relying on quality-based instruments and were directed at single environmental media. During the 1980s, the Commission – strongly inspired by the first mover role of Germany – abandoned this strategy in favor of emission-based instruments and placed greater emphasis on the preventative character of EU environmental policy. From the late 1980s onwards, a further stage of EU environmental regulation can be observed. Strongly influenced by the pioneering role of Britain, the focus is on so-called 'new instruments', emphasizing regulatory transparency, participation, self-regulation and voluntary agreements, as opposed to classical forms of hierarchical top-down regulation (Knill and Lenschow 2000a). However, the emergence of new regulatory stages characterized by the dominance of certain approaches increased rather than reduced the regulatory variety of EU environmental policy, as new regulatory concepts were generally added to existing approaches rather than replacing the latter. Moreover, the dominance of certain approaches only implied the reduction rather than exclusion of concepts that were still associated with approaches dominant during earlier regulatory stages.

Second, the regulatory contest for influence in international cooperation activities generally helps to avoid the often expected scenario of an environmental dumping or race to the bottom. At the European level, this can be traced to the fact that member states striving to set the agenda in line with their interests have to win the support of the Commission. Since the Commission has a strong institutional self-interest in increasing its regulatory competencies towards the member states, it will promote only such proposals which fit with these objectives. From this constellation, we thus can expect the gradual expansion and upgrading of EU environmental policy over time (Eichener 1997). Although this general tendency does not exclude potential failures of negotiations on individual policy issues, or the possibility that in some cases European standards will remain below the level of the highest-regulating member state, the long-term dynamics of the regulatory contest increase the scope and level of environmental protection within the EU (Knill 2003, 135). Similar dynamics have also been reported for environmental cooperation at the international level (Jänicke 2003; Kern, Jörgens and Jänicke 2000).

TRANSNATIONAL COMMUNICATION

The interplay of economic pressures emerging from global market integration and the specific dynamics underlying international cooperation can thus be seen as important factors which explain not only the broad convergence of national environmental policies, but also the fact that convergence does not automatically coincide with a downgrading of levels of environmental protection. As empirical evidence shows, in many instances, quite the opposite pattern is the case. Notwithstanding the relevance of the explanatory factors investigated so far, however, we are still left with some unresolved questions. This holds true in particular for those constellations in which national environmental policies converge even in the absence of either economic pressures or corresponding legal obligations emerging from international agreements. Empirical studies indeed reveal many cases for which this scenario applies, including, for instance, the establishment of environmental ministries and agencies, the introduction of energy or carbon taxes, national environmental plans or strategies

for sustainable development, as well as regulatory measures opening up the access to environmental information for the general public (Tews, Busch and Jörgens 2003, 571). For all of these measures, a still increasing number of OECD countries has progressively adopted similar legislation and created similar administrative structures, although neither market forces nor international agreements would have suggested such a broad pattern of cross-national convergence.

To account for this development, the literature emphasizes varying convergence mechanisms which are based on transnational communication networks. The first scenario of policy emulation implies the simple copying of policy decisions taken elsewhere. This pattern is generally explained by a broad variety of factors, including the number of countries which have already adopted a certain policy (Meyer and Rowan 1977), the striving for legitimacy in constellations of high uncertainty (DiMaggio and Powell 1991, 70), the desire of actors 'not to be left behind' (Meyer et al. 1997), the existence of time-pressures (Bennett 1991, 223), or the striving to avoid high costs of information which are probably much less with simple imitation than with more demanding forms of learning (Tews 2002, 180).

Second, policy convergence can be the result of learning processes, understood as the rational utilization of available experience elsewhere (Rose 1991). Learning through transnational communication, however, is not restricted to bilateral policy transfer (Dolowitz and Marsh 2000), but can also result from the development of common problem perceptions and corresponding solutions within transnational elite networks or epistemic communities (Haas 1992). Convergence in this sense results from the development of shared ideas and beliefs amongst a relatively coherent and enduring network of elites engaging in regular interaction at the transnational level (Bennett 1991, 224).

A third convergence factor linked to transnational communication is the promotion of policy models by international institutions. They often play a highly active role, promoting the spread of distinctive policy approaches by learning through performance comparisons (Tews 2002, 174). For instance, with regard to sustainable development, the United Nations Commission on Sustainable Development regularly publishes status reports on the national implementation of Agenda 21 – the latest of which was on the occasion of the 2002 World Summit of Johannesburg (Tews, Busch and Jörgens 2003). In a similar vein, think tanks, consultancy firms or foundations regularly disseminate information on best practice and new policies at the national and international levels.

Cross-national policy transfer is stimulated by international agreements on broad goals and standards that national policies should aim to achieve, institutionalized peer review and identification of best practice (benchmarking) as well as the construction of league tables ranking national policies in terms of performance to previously agreed criteria (Bomberg and Peterson 2000; Humphreys 2002, 54). In constantly searching for new policy ideas, disseminating best practice and evaluating domestic policy performance, international institutions function as mediators of cross-national policy transfer, driving national governments to adopt successful policy models (Kern, Jörgens and Jänicke 2000, 10).

In general, the impact of transnational communication on the development of national environmental policies is expected to increase with the density of information exchange within transnational networks (Simmons and Elkins 2003). This includes not only the frequency of interaction, but also the breadth of interaction; i.e., the functional differentiation of transnational networks. It is well-acknowledged in the literature that interaction density between states increases with their membership in international institutions which strongly facilitate and intensify transnational information exchange (Kern 2000, 267). Moreover, geographical proximity and cultural ties between states were identified as important factors increasing cross-national interaction density (Rose 1991).

The embeddedness of national bureaucrats and policy-makers in transnational expert networks implies not only that these actors can observe developments in other countries represented in the network, but also that they are at the same time 'observed' by their counterparts; i.e., they have to demonstrate the quality and legitimacy of their concepts in the transnational discourse. National representatives have to legitimize and justify national developments in light of 'transnational scrutiny'. In this context, difficulties to legitimize distinctive national approaches will increase, the more other countries have already moved to another model which is perceived as the most promising approach within the transnational setting (Meyer and Rowan 1977; Meyer et al., 1997).

The competition of ideas, as it emerges in particular from the dissemination and evaluation of best practice, can generally be expected to result in an overall strengthening of regulatory concepts; hence, inducing an upward shift of environmental standards, as international organization will generally promote the most innovative national approach (Holzinger and Knill 2004). For instance Jörgens (2003) shows that the worldwide proliferation of green plans and sustainable development strategies was to a large extent based on the effects of transnational communication and benchmarking activities by different public and private institutions and networks.

CONCLUSION

This article started from two general empirical observations on the development of national environmental policies. First, we observe an increasing similarity of domestic policies and regulatory frameworks in many issue areas. Second, this pattern of convergence does not coincide with an often feared scenario of a race to the bottom in levels of environmental protection. Several explanatory factors were presented in order to explain these patterns, including regulatory competition, international cooperation and transnational communication.

On the one hand, the analysis of these factors indicates that the observed patterns and developments of national environmental policies, in many instances, can hardly be fully understood by focusing on the isolated effects of individual factors. Rather, we need to apply a broader perspective, taking into account that several causal factors might operate in parallel. In this context it is well conceivable that the different factors interact. It is thus an important area of future research to develop hypotheses on the interaction effects of all causal factors of convergence.

On the other hand, the consideration of the three convergence mechanisms reveals that fundamental shifts in the level of intervention, in the sense of races to the bottom, can only be expected in rather specific constellations. More specifically, such scenarios are restricted to situations in which regulatory competition is the only or dominant mechanism to be effective. In all other constellations, upward shifts are a more likely scenario.

These findings, together with the fact that different causal factors are often operating in parallel, indicate that an environmental dumping is indeed a highly unlikely scenario. This does not automatically imply that we should be overoptimistic about environmental problem-solving at both the national and international level. But we should be aware that global market integration, international cooperation and transnational communication, offer promising ways to effectively address the problem of environmental pollution.

NOTES

1. Notwithstanding this general discussion over new instruments, interventionist patterns still constitute the dominant form of environmental regulation both at the domestic and international level (cf. Héritier 2002; Holzinger, Knill and Schäfer 2003).

2. I use the term international cooperation here in its strictest meaning, as being equivalent with international legal obligation. In a wider understanding, international cooperation might also include non-binding agreements and all kinds of voluntary activities of international organizations. However, as the effects of non-binding policies are even more difficult to predict than the effects of legal obligation and of regulatory competition, the inclusion of non-binding international policies would strongly increase the complexity of the argument. I therefore stick

to the narrow meaning of international cooperation. The meaning of 'cooperation' is thus equivalent to its meaning in cooperative game theory.

REFERENCES

Andersen, M. S. and Liefferink, D. (1997). European Environmental Policy. The Pioneers. MUP: Manchester.

Beers, C. and van der Bergh, J. C. J. M. (1999). An Empirical Multi-Country Analysis of the Impact of Environmental Regulations on Foreign Trade Flows. In: *Kyklos* 50, 29–46.

Bennett, C. (1991). What Is Policy Convergence and What Causes It? In: *British Journal of Political Science*, 21, 215–233.

Bomberg, E. and Peterson, J. (2000). Policy Transfer and Europeanization. Passing the Heinecken Test? Queens Papers on Europeanization 2, at http://www.qub.ac.uk/ies/ accessed in May 2001.

Brickman, R. and Jasanoff, S. and Ilgen, T. (1985). Controlling Chemicals. The Politics of Regulation in Europe and the United States. Ithaca, New York: Cornell University Press.

Bungarten, H. H. (1978). Umweltpolitik in Westeuropa. EG, internationale Organisationen und nationale Umweltpolitiken. Bonn: Europa Union.

Cowles, M. and Carporaso, J. and Risse, T. (2001). Transforming Europe. Europeanization and Domestic Change. Ithaca, London: Cornell University Press.

DiMaggio, P. J. and Powell, W. W. (1991). The Iron Cage Revisited. Institutionalised Isomorphism and Collective Rationality in Organizational Fields. In: Powell, W. W. and DiMaggio, P. J. (eds.), The New Institutionalism in Organizational Analysis. Chicago: Chicago University Press, 63–82.

Dolowitz, D. P. and Marsh, D. (1996). Who Learns What From Whom. A Review of the Policy Transfer Literature. In: *Political Studies*, 44, 343–357.

Dolowitz, D. P. and Marsh, D. (2000). Learning from Abroad: The Role of Policy Transfer in Contemporary Policy Making. In: *Governance*, 13, 5–24.

Drezner, D. W. (2001). Globalization and Policy Convergence. In: *The International Studies Review*, 3, 53–78.

Eichener, V. (1997). Effective European problem-solving. Lessons from the regulation of occupational safety and environmental protection. In: *Journal of European Public Policy* 4(4), 591–608.

Goodman, J. and Pauly, L. (1993). The Obsolescence of Capital Control. In: *World Politics*, 46, 50–82.

Haas, P. M. (1992). Introduction: Epistemic Communities and International Policy Coordination. In: *International Organization*, 46, 1–36.

Haigh, Nigel (1996). The Manual of Environmental Policy: the EC and Britain. London: Catermill Publishing.

Héritier, A. (2002). New Modes of Governance in Europe: Policy making Without Legislating? In: Héritier, A. (ed.), The Provision of Common Goods. Governance across Multiple Arenas. Boulder: Rowman & Littlefield.

Héritier, A., Knill, C. and Mingers, S. (1996). Ringing the Changes in Europe. Regulatory Competition and the Transformation of the State, Berlin: de Gruyter.

Héritier, A., Knill, C., Kerwer, D., Lehmkuhl, D., Teutsch M. and Douillet, A. C. (2001). Differential Europe. New Opportunities and Restrictions for Member-State Policies. Lanham: Rowman and Littlefield

Hoberg, G. (2001). Globalization and Policy Convergence: Symposium Overview. In: *Journal of Comparative Policy Analysis: Research and Practice*, 3, 127–132.

Holzinger, K. (1991). Does Legal Harmonization Really 'Harmonize' the Quality of the Environment in the European Community? In: Pal, L. A. and Olfa-Schultze, R. (eds.), The Nation State versus Continental Integration. Bochum: Brockmeyer, 297–313.

Holzinger, K. (1994). Politik des kleinsten gemeinsamen Nenners. Umweltpolitische Entscheidungsprozesse in der EG am Beispiel des Katalysatorautos. Berlin: Edition Sigma.

Holzinger, K. (2002). The Provision of Transnational Common Goods: Regulatory Competition for Environmental Standards. In: Héritier, A. (ed.), Common Goods: Reinventing European and International Governance. Lanham: Rowman and Littlefield, pp. 59–82.

Holzinger, K. (2003). Common Goods, Matrix Games, and Institutional Solutions. In: *European Journal of International Relations*, 9, 173–212.

Holzinger, K.; Knill, C. and Schäfer A. (2003). Steuerungswandel in der europäischen umweltpolitik? In: K. Holzinger, C. Knil and D. Lehmkuhl (eds.), *Bedingungen und Muster politischer Steuerung im historischen Vergleich*. Opladen: Leske + Budrich, 57–85.

Holzinger, K. and Knill, C. (2004). Regulatory Competition and Regulatory Cooperation in Environmental Policy: Individual and Interaction Effects. In: *Journal of Public Policy* 24 (1) (forthcoming).

Humphreys, P. (2002). Europeanisation, Globalisation and Telecommunications Governance: A Neo-Gramscian Analysis. In: *Convergence: The Journal of Research into New Media Technologies*, 8, 52–79.

Hurwitz, L. (1983). The Harmonization of European Public Policy. Regional Responses to Transnational Challenges. Westport: Greenwood Press.

Jachtenfuchs, M. (1996). Umweltpolitik. In: Kohler-Koch, B. and Woyke, W. (eds.), Lexikon der Politik, Band 5: Die Europäische Union. München: C.H. Beck, 254–258.

Jänicke, M. (1998). Umweltpolitik. Global am Ende oder am Ende global? In: Beck, U. (ed.), Perspektiven der Weltgesellschaft. Frankfurt a. Main: Suhrkamp, 332–344.

Jänicke, M. (2003). Die Rolle des Nationalstaats in der globalen Umweltpolitik. In: *Aus Politik und Zeitgeschichte* B 27/2003, 9–17.

Jänicke, M. and Weidner, H. (1997). Summary: Global Environmental Policy Learning. In: Jänicke, M. and Weidner (eds.), National Environmental Policies. A Comparative Study of Capacity-Building. Berlin: Springer, 299–313.

Jordan, A. (1999). Editorial Introduction: The Construction of a Multilevel Environmental Governance System. In: *Environment and Planning C: Government and Policy*, 17(1), 1–17.

Jörgens, H. (2003). Governance by Diffusion-Implementing Global Norms Through Cross-National Imitation and Learning. In *Governance for Sustainable Development. The Challenge of Adapting from to Function*, edited by W. M. Lafferty. Cheltenhan: Edward Elgar.

Keohane, R. and Nye, J. (2000). Globalization: What's New? And What's Not? (And So What?) In: *Foreign Policy*, 118, 104–112.

Kern, K. (2000). Die Diffusion von Politikinnovationen. Umweltpolitische Innovationen im Mehrebenensystem der USA. Opladen: Leske + Budrich.

Kern, K., Jörgens, H. and Jänicke, M. (2000). Die Diffusion umweltpolitischer Innovationen. Ein Beitrag zur Globalisierung von Umweltpolitik. *Zeitschrift für Umweltpolitik* 23, 507–546.

Kimber, C. (2000). Implementing European Environmental Policy and the Directive on Access to Environmental Information. In: Knill, Ch. and Lenschow, A. (eds.), Implementing EU Environmental Policy: New Directions and Old Problems. Manchester: Manchester University Press, 168–196.

Knill, C. (1997). The Implementation of EU Environmental Policy in the UK. In: Knill, Ch. (ed.), The Impact of National Administrative

Traditions on the Implementation of EU Environmental Policy. Florence: European University Institute.

Knill, C. (1998). European Policies: The Impact of National Administrative Traditions on European Policy-Making. In: *Journal of Public Policy*, 18(1), 1–28.

Knill, C. (2001). The Europeanisation of National Administrations. Cambridge University Press: Cambridge.

Knill, C. (2003). Europäische Umweltpolitik. Steuerungsprobleme und Regulierungsmuster im Mehrebenensystem. Opladen: Leske und Budrich.

Knill, C. and Lenschow, A. (1998), Coping with Europe: The Implementation of EU Environmental Policy and Administrative Traditions in Britain and Germany. In: *Journal of European Public Policy*, 5(4), 595–614.

Knill, C. and Lenschow, A. (2000a). On Deficient Implementation and Deficient Theories: The Need for an Institutional Perspective in Implementation Research. In: Knill, C. and Lenschow, A. (eds.), Implementing EU Environmental Policy: New Directions and Old Problems. Manchester: Manchester University Press, 9–38.

Knill, C. and Lenschow, A. (ed.) (2000). Implementing EU Environmental Policy: New Directions and Old Problems. Manchester: Manchester University Press.

Lenschow, A. (1999). The Greening of the EU: The Common Agricultural Policy and the Structural Funds. In: *Environment and Planning C: Government and Policy*, 17(1), 91–108.

Martin, L. and Simmons, B. (1998), Theories and Empirical Studies of International Institutions. In: *International Organization*, 52, 729–757.

Meyer, J. W. and Rowan, B. (1977). Institutionalized Organizations. Formal Structure as Myth and Ceremony. In: *American Journal of Sociology*, 83, 340–363.

Meyer, John W., David John Frank, Ann Hironaka, Even Schofer, and Nancy Brandon Tuma. (1997). The Structuring of a World Environmental Regime, 1870–1990. *International Organisation*, 51(4), 623–51.

Rehbinder, E. and Stewart, R. (1985). Environmental Protection Policy. Integration Through Law. Berlin: de Gruyter.

Rose, R. (1991). What is Lesson-Drawing? In: *Journal of Public Policy* 11, 3–30.

Scharpf, F. W. (1996). Politische Optionen im vollendeten Binnenmarkt. In: Jachtenfuchs, M. and Kohler-Koch, B. (eds.), Europäische Integration. Opladen: Leske und Budrich, 109–140.

Scharpf, F. W. (1997). Introduction. The problem-solving capacity of multi-level governance. In: *Journal of European Public Policy*, 4, 520–538.

Scharpf, F. W. (1999). Regieren in Europa. Effektiv und Demokratisch? Frankfurt/M.: Campus.

Simmons, B. A. and Elkins, Z. (2003). Competition, Communication or Culture? Explaining Three Decades of Foreign Economic Policy Diffusion, mimeo, University of California, Berkeley.

Stewart, R. B. (1993). Environmental Regulation and International Competitiveness. In: *Yale Law Journal*, 102, 2039–2106.

Tews, K. (2002). Politiktransfer: Phänomen zwischen Policy Lernen und Oktroi. Überlegungen zu unfreiwilligen Umweltpolitikimporten am Beispiel der EU-Osterweiterung. In: *Zeitschrift für Umweltpolitik und Umweltrecht*, 2, 173–201.

Tews, K. and Busch, P.-O. and Jörgens, H. (2003). The Diffusion of New Environmental Policy Instruments. In: *European Journal of Political Research*, 42(4), 569–600.

Tobey, J. (1990). The Impact of Domestic Environmental Policies on Patterns of World Trade. An Empirical Test In: *Kyklos*, 43, 191–209.

Vogel, D. (1995). Trading Up. Consumer and Environmental Regulation in the Global Economy. Cambridge: Harvard University Press.

Vogel, D. (1997). Trading up and governing across. Transnational governance and environmental protection. In: *Journal of European Public Policy*, 4, 556–571.

Weale, A. (1992). The New Politics of Pollution. Manchester: Manchester University Press.

Weale, A. et al. (2000). Environmental Governance in Europe. An Ever Closer Ecological Union. Oxford: Oxford University Press.

15

Cultural Policy

KEVIN V. MULCAHY

This essay has four major goals. First, it attempts to operationalize the elusive notion of culture and the broad outlines of what is entailed in a cultural policy. Second, there is an overview of what is entailed in public culture as a public policy. Third, the objectives and justifications of public culture are surveyed. Fourth, the relationship between political cultures and the particular expressions of public cultures is specified. Finally, the future trends in cultural policy are briefly evaluated.

WHAT IS CULTURAL POLICY?

Culture, according to literary critic Raymond Williams, is one of the two or three most complicated words in the English language (Williams, 1977: 76).

It is worth noting that the root of the word is from the Latin *colere*, to till. There is the cultivation of a field as there is the cultivation of intellectual and esthetic sensibilities; the process of becoming educated, polished, refined; that is, cultured: the state of being civilized. In sum, culture suggests a process for the deliberate and systematic acquisition of an intellectual sensibility.

The *Oxford English Dictionary* first defines culture with reference to tillage. Secondly, it is the cultivation and refinement of the mind; "the artistic and intellectual side of civilization;" finally, "the distinctive customs, achievements, production, outlooks, etc., of a society or group; the way of life of a society or group." The latter can be characterized as the "anthropological" sense of culture.

The *American Heritage Dictionary* first defines culture as: 'the totality of socially transmitted behavior patterns, arts, beliefs, institutions, and all other products of work and thought; the predominant attitudes and behavior that characterize the functioning of a group or organization.' Secondly, culture is "intellectual and artistic activity and the works produced by it;" a high degree of taste and refinement formed by esthetic and intellectual training.

Typically, culture is used in political discourse as the "arts." A Ministry of Culture is an administrative agency responsible for public support of these artistic activities and often the humanities and scholarship as well (Williams, 1977: 80).

In its broadest sense, "public policy is whatever governments choose to do or not to do" (Dye, 2005: 1). Similarly, public policy can be seen as a purposive decision "followed by an action or set of actions in dealing with a problem or matter of concern" (Anderson, 1975: 3). "Stated most simply, public policy is the sum of government activities, whether pursued directly or through agents, as those activities have influence on the lives of citizens" (Peters, 1996: 4).

These various definitions, gleaned from standard textbooks on public policy, suggest two general notions: first, that governmental actions (or inactions) constitute value choices, that these choices are policies, and the policies are politically determined; second, that the decisions of public officials are implemented by the production of goods and services that produce discernable societal outcomes. However, as a policy, public culture differs substantially from these criteria if only because the programs funded are often markedly atypical and the societal impacts difficult (if not impossible) to assess (Bennett, 2004).

For example, what is a cultured society? Moreover, is there a role for a public policy in promoting such a goal? Does culture denote exclusively the "high arts?" If so, is the programmatic issue its quality or accessibility; or is the goal the promotion of "cultural populism" with programs to support artistic representativeness? Are cultural programs a matter of taste preferences and better left to market forces? (Gans, 1999). Or, are there esthetic expressions that for reasons of national heritage, social cohesion, and intellectual value have a claim on public attention?

Finally, there is a conception of cultural policy that sees public involvement in the cultural domain through the prism of "governmentality;" that is, the process by which the state comes to manage individuals (Foucault, 1991: 87–90). In this sense, cultural policies are a form of "hegemony," which is secured when "the dominant culture uses education, philosophy, religion, esthetics and art to make its dominance appear normal and natural to the heterogeneous groups that constitute society" (Miller and Yudice, 2002: 9). This emphasis on the "social" definitions of culture, which has characterized the cultural studies field (for example, in the writings of Tony Bennett, Stuart Cunningham, Stuart Hall, among others), has manifested a deep "skepticism toward traditional values," which "has resulted in an almost exclusively anthropological or sociological emphasis on the products and meanings of popular culture" (Stanbridge, 2002: 125).

The general difficulty of determining an agreed upon definition of culture, the susceptibility of public culture to ideological coloration, and the politically sensitive nature of cultural programs, has been the cause for arguments that cultural policy should be formulated and implemented "at arms-length" (Chartrand and McCaughey, 1989). Arms-length administration has the overall cultural budget determined by the government with decisions about specific allocations being made by a quasi-autonomous council. These arts councils are typically appointed by the government for fixed, staggered, limited terms to insure political independence. The members are usually artists, cultural administrators, and philanthropists (Mulcahy, 2002).

To further insulate cultural bureaucracies from political interference, panels of "experts" are frequently used to advise on the quality of the cultural activities to be supported. Also, this expert advice was designed to deflect criticism of public culture on the grounds that there had been a professional, disinterested, vetting process. However, the panel system has not been without difficulties. First, panel advice has not exempted cultural agencies from criticism when the grant awards have been controversial. Second, panels have often been accused of "cronyism;" that is, being a network of insiders who serve as a "mutual admiration society." Third, panels composed of members of the same disciplines often share uniform assumptions about what constitutes "good art." Fourth, the panels arguably act as an official academy and become the arbiters of public culture. Fifth, an over reliance on outside panelists' advice may be less accountable and responsive to the public interest than a cultural plan that must be explained and defended by a public official (Galligan, 1993; Mulcahy, 1991; Cummings and Katz, 1987: 6, 361–362).

PUBLIC CULTURE AS PUBLIC POLICY

As a practical matter, cultural policy can be most usefully considered as the sum of a government's activities "with respect to the arts (including the for-profit cultural industries), the humanities, and the heritage" (Schuster, 2003: 1). Cultural policy, then, involves governmental strategies and activities that promote "the production, dissemination, marketing, and consumption of the arts" (Rentschler, 2002: 17). Yet, if policy is the "intentionality" of programs that seek to achieve certain outcomes in a field of activity, there are also goals that are "implicit" in a policy and its programs (Schuster, 2003: 1).

Using the metaphor of "mapping," Mark Schuster argues that understanding a policy requires viewing programmatic activities as a "terrain of intentions." The actions that a state and its many operational entities take that affect the cultural life of its citizens, whether directly or indirectly, whether intentionally or unintentionally, collectively constitute the cultural policy of the state. In sum, a state's cultural policy "can best be understood once one has an atlas of such maps"(Schuster, 2003: 3).

A cultural policy encompasses a much broader array of activities than what was traditionally associated with an arts policy. The latter typically involved public support for museums, the visual arts (painting, sculpture, and pottery), the performing arts (symphonic, chamber and choral music, jazz, modern dance, opera and musical theatre, "serious" theatre), historic preservation, and humanities programs (such as creative writing and poetry). A cultural policy would involve support for all the aforementioned activities, but also other publicly-supported institutions such as libraries and archives; battlefield sites, zoos, botanical gardens, arboretums, aquariums, parks; as well as community celebrations, fairs and festival; folklore activities such as quilting, "country" music, folk dancing, crafts; perhaps certain varieties of circus performances, rodeos and marching bands.

Television and radio, although considered separately as broadcasting policy, have long functioned as "major supporters of the arts by purchasing the work of performing artists on a massive scale, by developing audiences for live performances, and sometimes even by making direct grants to artistic organizations. Moreover, television and radio have become major vehicles for delivery of the arts" (Cummings and Katz, 1987: 359). With the prominent exception of the United States, where the Broadcasting Act of 1920 essentially licensed the airwaves to commercial networks, broadcasting was from its earliest days a public responsibility. Official control, however, is often delimited by the creation of some sort of autonomous governing board. Governments often saw broadcasting as a means of fostering national bonds (for example, the Canadian Broadcasting Corporation with both French and English programming) and sponsoring shared national rituals (such as the sovereign's Christmas address on the British Broadcasting Corporation).

It should be noted, however, that "public" broadcasting in the Unites States is provided programmatically by the Public Broadcasting System (PBS) and National Public Radio (NPR). These are both 501(C)(3)s, that is, private, not-for-profit organizations. The Corporation for Public Broadcasting (CPB) is a quasi-autonomous, government corporation that provides limited funding to local stations for technical assistance and program acquisitions; however, CPB is forbidden by law from producing programming. Public radio and television in the U.S. is essentially a confederation of independent entities, which are free to schedule such programming as they deem appropriate. Moreover, each station is responsible for its own financial support. In essence, American public broadcasting rests on a "bedrock of localism" in both administration and funding (Katz, 1982; Mulcahy and Widoff, 1986; Mulcahy and Widoff, 1988).

Another important example of the broader net cast by the concept of cultural policy is the role of the education community. There is a natural affinity between education and culture. In countries with well-established and widely recognized cultural traditions, cultural offerings are core components of the educational curricula. The U.S. is an exception again with arts and cultural courses being the most frequently cut offerings. Moreover, there are decided benefits from an alliance between the cultural and educational communities (Cummings and Katz, 1987: 358). First, it is an example of coalition-building to broaden the constituency in support of the arts and culture. Second, exposure to cultural activities at any level of the educational system increases dramatically the likelihood of future participation and, consequently, broader support for a public cultural policy.

Finally, it should be noted that many countries support what is known as "cultural industries," or what would be known in the United States as the "entertainment business," whether because of an old cultural heritage to be preserved or a nascent culture to be developed. In sum, there is frequently an association between culture and civic identity. Consequently, the subvention of film, books, music, and audiovisual production is an important political issue (Perret and Saez, 1996; Rouet and Dupin, 1991). In France, the Ministry of Culture has become "a sort of ministry of cultural industry in which the cultural policy is integrated into a total strategy of the French government" (Saez, 1996: 135).

The juxtaposition of the terms cultural industries and entertainment business speaks loudly about the valuational differences between a worldview that exults in its popular-cultural hegemony and that of nations which feel threatened by the diminution, or outright annexation, of their cultural identity. Some nations (notably Canada and France) have claimed a "cultural exemption" predicated on the absence of a correspondence of artistic products with goods and services. Indeed, the issue of "American cultural imperialism" is an important aspect of much of the discourse on international cultural policy (Mulcahy, 2000a). What can be noted without much debate is that culture is at the heart of much of the concern about the condition of public life and civil society in many countries (Pratt, 2005).

OBJECTIVES AND JUSTIFICATIONS OF PUBLIC CULTURE

Cultural policy, while a small part of the budgets of even the most generous of public patrons, is a sector of immense complexity. It entails "a large, heterogeneous set of individuals and organizations engaged in the creation, production, presentation, distribution, and preservations of and education about esthetic heritage, and entertainment activities, products and artifacts" (Wyszomirski, 2002: 187). Although this is specifically a description of the American cultural landscape, its details are generally universalizable. In a study of cultural policy at the subnational level in the United States, the following characteristics were observed that are also generally applicable. First, there are many more agencies involved in cultural policy than is conventionally understood. Second, it is not common that one would think of the aggregation of these agencies and their activities as constituting a conceptual whole. Third, much of cultural policy is the result "of actions and decisions taken without expressed policy intention." Fourth, much of cultural policy is not just the result of direct financial support, but a wide variety of interventions (Schuster, 2003: 8–9).

Given the ecological complexity of cultural policy, it should not be surprising that there are a number of justifications for a variety of programs imbued with distinct objectives. There are certain broad emphases that have informed cultural policy. While it is the policies of the post-World War II era that are of concern herein, it is important to recognize the historical antecedents of contemporary cultural policy.

Culture as Glorification

From the period of the Renaissance until well into the twentieth century, cultural patronage was the manifestation of the taste and connoisseurship of great potentates. These might be kings, aristocrats, ecclesiastics, or merchant princes. While the motivations of personal patronage varied in this reputed golden age, there is no doubt that self-glorification and/or national glorification played a role (Cummings and Katz, 1987: 6). Louis XIV's Versailles reflected both the personal grandeur of the Sun King himself and the power of the state that he had created. As a royal residence,

Versailles symbolized the king's personal rule and was widely imitated by European monarchs and princelings.

For the great mercantile princes of the nineteenth and early twentieth century, cultural patronage also represented a form of glorification. Admittedly, the question of motivation is complex, but great palaces of culture, in the form of museums open to the public, signified a grandness of philanthropic spirit and created an edifice that visually bespoke the donor's personal grandeur. Of course, support for the arts could also serve to legitimize these "robber-barons" and confirm the social status of the *nouveaux riches*. As with royal patronage, the art forms subsidized were a matter of personal taste preferences.

By contrast, a democratic state cannot be seen as simply indulging the esthetic preferences of a few, however enlightened. Consequently, a democratic cultural policy must articulate its purposes in ways that demonstrate how the public interest is being served.

Democratization of Culture

Since culture is a "good," and one that is "good for you," governments have pursued programs to promote greater accessibility. In this conceptualization, significant esthetic works should be made broadly available to the public. In other words, "high culture" should not be the exclusive preserve of a particular social class or of a metropolitan location. Rather, the benefits of the highest reaches of cultural excellence should be made available broadly and widely. In sum, national cultural treasures should be accessible without regard to the impediments of class circumstances, educational attainment or place of habitation.

Typically, the cultural programs following this policy formulation have been vertical in nature; that is, top-down, center-periphery. For example, Norway is a large, sparsely populated country, with its cultural institutions concentrated in Oslo, the capital and largest city. With public subsidies, these national institutions have extensive touring programs to bring symphonic music, opera, ballet, and

theatre to the remotest regions of the country and to culturally underserved areas within cities (Bakke, 1994: 115). Under Charles DeGaulle, the first modern Minister of Culture, Andre Malraux established a network of *maisons de la culture* throughout the French provinces. As "beacons of hope" in the provincial darkness, these cultural agencies would serve as venues for Parisian and international offerings, as well as showcases for high-quality local productions (Lebovics, 1999).

The objective of cultural democratization is the esthetic enlightenment, enhanced dignity, and educational development of the general citizenry. "Dissemination was the key concept with the aim of establishing equal opportunity for all citizens to participate in publicly organized and financed cultural activities" (Dueland, 2001: 41). To further this goal, performances and exhibitions are low cost; public art education promotes equality of esthetic opportunity; national institutions tour and perform in work places, retirement homes and housing complexes.

Cultural Democracy

As indicated earlier, the "democratization of culture" is a top-down approach that essentially privileges certain forms of cultural programming that are deemed to be a public good. Clearly, such an objective is open to criticism for what is termed cultural elitism; that is, the assumption that some esthetic expressions are inherently superior – at least as determined by a *cognoscenti* concerned with the acquisition of cultural capital (Bourdieu, 1984). "The problem with this policy was that, fundamentally, it intended to create larger audiences for performances whose content was based on the experience of society's privileged groups. In sum, it has been taken for granted that the cultural needs of all society's members were alike" (Langsted, 1990: 17). The objective of cultural democracy, on the other hand, is to provide for a more participatory (or populist) approach in the definition and provision of cultural opportunities.

In essence, there is a shift from a top-down to a bottom-up policy; that is, the government's responsibility is to provide equal opportunities for citizens to be culturally active on their own terms. This shift involves a broad interpretation of cultural activities that comprises popular entertainment, folk festival, amateur sports, choral societies and dancing schools. As an alternative, or complement, to a strategy of fine-arts dissemination, cultural democracy provides a stronger legitimization of the principle of state subsidy, with the concept of culture as a "process in which we are all participatory" (Dueland, 2001: 22). The programmatic emphases recognize the diversity of cultural differences among regions, between the capital and the provinces, between urban and rural areas, among social groups. Emphasizing a strategy of cultural decentralization, cultural democracy substitutes a pluralistic for a monocultural concept.

It should also be noted that the coupling of cultural democracy to the democratization of culture has a pragmatic as well as a philosophical component. Cultural patronage in democratic governments is markedly different from patronage by individuals. Private patrons are responsible only to themselves and are free to indulge in their taste preferences. Democratic governments, on the other hand, are responsible to the electorate and are held accountable for their policy decisions. There is no political immunity for cultural policy – despite what its advocates often claim. Given the fact that the fine-arts audience is a small percent of the population, and by the nature of its esthetic demands will likely remain so even if its demographic characteristics could be rendered more representative (DiMaggio and Ostrower, 1992; Robinson, 1993), cultural policy is an easy (and often attractive) target for ideological and budgetary attack (Wyszomirski, 1995a). "An important lesson the advocates of support for 'high culture' had to learn was that it is politically advantageous to expand the definition of culture to include more popular art forms and activities" (Cummings and Katz, 1987: 357). In sum, the "high brow" cultural activities are often able to expand their base of support when coupled with cultural pursuits with a more "low brow" orientation.

Populism versus Elitism

The two objectives just discussed – dissemination of high culture and participation in a broader range of cultural activities – evoke a related debate about the content of public culture: "elitist" or "populist." Proponents of the elitist position argue that cultural policy should emphasize esthetic quality as the determining criterion for public subvention. This view is typically supported by the major cultural organizations, creative artists in the traditionally-defined field of the fine arts, cultural critics, and the well-educated, well-to-do audiences for these art forms. Ronald Dworkin terms this the "lofty approach," which "insists that art and culture must reach a certain degree of sophistication, richness, and excellence in order for human nature to flourish, and that the state must provide this excellence if the people will not or cannot provide it for themselves" (Dworkin, 1985: 221).

By contrast, the populist position advocates defining culture broadly and making this culture broadly available. The populist approach emphasizes a less traditional and more pluralist notion of artistic merit and consciously seeks to create a policy of cultural diversity. With a focus on personal enhancement, the populist's position posits very limited boundaries between amateur and professional arts activities. Indeed, the goal is to provide opportunities for those outside the professional mainstream.

"Proponents of populism are frequently advocates of minority arts, folk arts, ethnic arts, or counter-cultural activities" (Wyszomirski in Mulcahy and Swaim, 1982: 13–14). Cultural "elitists," on the other hand, argue in support of excellence over amateurism and favor an emphasis on esthetic discipline over "culture as everything." There are "two key tensions for national cultural policy between the goals of excellence versus access, and between government roles as facilitator versus architect" (Craik et al., 2003: 29).

In effect, elitism is to democratization as populism is to cultural democracy. Unfortunately, there has been a tendency to see these positions as mutually exclusive, rather than complementary. "Elitists" are denounced as "high brow snobs" advocating an esoteric culture; populists are dismissed as "pandering philistines" promoting a trivialized and commercialized culture. However, these mutual stereotypes belie complementariness between two bookends of an artistically autonomous and politically accountable cultural policy. There is a synthesis that can be termed a "latitudinarian approach" to public culture; that is, one that is esthetically inclusive and broadly accessible (Mulcahy, 1995b: 180–181; Mulcahy, 1995c: 223–224).

Such a public-cultural policy would remain faithful to the highest standards of excellence from a broad range of esthetic expressions, while providing the widest possible access to people from different geographic locales, socio-economic strata, and educational background (Mulcahy, 1991: 22–24). In conceiving of public policy as an opportunity to provide alternatives not readily available in the marketplace, public cultural agencies would be better positioned to complement the efforts of the private sector rather than duplicate their activities. Similarly, cultural agencies can promote community development by supporting artistic heritages that are at a competitive disadvantage in a cultural world that is increasingly profit-driven. In sum, excellence should be viewed as the achievements of greatness from a horizontal, rather than a vertical, perspective and a cultural policy as supporting the totality of these varieties of excellence.

Cultural Utilitarianism

Given the demands in a democratic system that public policies show a return to the taxpayer, cultural policy has frequently argued for support on the basis of utility. Governments have certainly supported the arts and culture "for their intrinsic value to the fulfillment of the human potential of their citizens. Art and culture are, from this perspective, essential elements to a life that is worth living…" (Cummings and Katz, 1987: 351). It can be

argued that there is a parity between the state's responsibility for its citizens' social-economic-physical needs and their access to culture and opportunities for artistic self-expression. However, the esthetic dimension of public policy has never been widely perceived as intuitively obvious or politically imperative. Accordingly, the cultural sector has often argued its case from the secondary, ancillary benefits that result from public support for programs that are seemingly only esthetic in nature. Cultural policy is not justified on the grounds that it is a good-in-itself, but rather that it yields other good results; culture is good because of its utilitarian value, not because of its inherent value.

The most commonly invoked argument from utility is the "economic impact of the arts." As a staple of political advocacy, the data from a veritable cottage industry of commissioned studies document the contributions of arts organizations to the local economy and serve to dispel any notions that cultural subsidies are a "handout." A quantitative justification is provided, demonstrating that every expenditure on arts activities produces a multiplier that ripples through the local economy, with increased spending on hotels, restaurants, taxis/car parks; also, arts organizations buy supplies from local vendors and employ people who pay taxes and consume goods and services (Cohen et al., 2003; Myerscough, 1988) There is no doubt that there is an important economic contribution that culture can make. On the other hand, the methodology of these economic-impact studies, as well as the self-serving, exaggerated and uncritical nature of their findings, has come under strong attack by professional economists (Sterngold, 2004; Bianchini and Parkinson, 1993).

However, the methodological fallacies that flaw the validity of economic-impact studies may constitute a secondary objection (Caust, 2003). Arguably, the limits of utilitarianism have been reached. Arguments from economic utility may tell us how valuable the arts are as goods, but not why they are good things. Economic-impact studies are understandably valued given the controversies over the arts and culture as merit goods (Netzer, 1978; Cwi, 1982). Consequently, the politically expedient justification for a cultural policy is an appeal to the numbers, not to its values. Yet, questions of value "remain at the heart of cultural policy even when they have been strangely silenced by the relativizing language of economics and markets" (McGuigan, 1996: 71). What an ideology of cultural utilitarianism does not articulate is an understanding of the role that a cultural policy can play in preserving, transmitting, and expanding a community's cultural heritage. An alternative ideology of merit good would argue that culture, "like parks, libraries and schools, provide benefits all out of proportion to the amount of their subsidies and merit support because of their contributions to the general welfare" (Mulcahy, 1986: 46).

Culture and Creative Cities

Much research has argued that the true significance of the arts may not be in their direct or indirect economic effects as much as in their more induced and qualitative effects (Mulcahy, 1982b). In the case of cities, culture adds a dimension of attractiveness that, while difficult to quantify, is very real.

First, cultural organizations are important to a city's self-worth – enhancing its attractiveness to residents, visitors and businesses. Cities are particularly desirable for firms that have highly educated and well-paid personnel. Other things being equal, a culturally vibrant city is likely to improve its economic health because businesses are attracted to locations with strong cultural amenities. Second, certain industries such as publishing, advertising, broadcasting and fashion depend on the concentration of cultural workers found in many urban centers. Third, cities are also venues for fashion and cuisine. Given their education, income and lifestyle, cultural consumers are attracted to the goods and services provided in urban markets. Fourth, culturally vibrant cities often attract "urban homesteaders" who are committed to community improvement.

These research findings were established in the 1980s. Interestingly, one of the most

provocative, if controversial, recent works in urban studies and cultural economics, Richard Florida's *The Rise of the Creative Class*, offers conclusions that are remarkably similar. Following are some of the major findings concerning the attractiveness of localities for the admittedly amorphous, and relatively privileged, "creative class:" (1) these are places that offer stimulating cultural environments; (2) there is a "street-level culture – a teeming blend of cafes, sidewalk musicians, and small galleries and bistros;" (3) various "hybrid spaces" and "small venues" exist like coffee shops, restaurants and bars, art galleries, bookstores, alternative theaters for film and live performances; (4) there is an authenticity that comes from "historic buildings, established neighborhoods, a unique culture scene" (Florida, 2002: 95, 166, 183, 226).

Understandably, Florida's findings have been celebrated in the cultural sector in the support that they offer for investments in a variety of "lifestyle amenities" that include comprehensively developed recreational, educational, entertainment, and artistic infrastructures. It would appear that the "creative class" is attracted to cities with a cultural (not simply an arts) policy that emphasizes spheres for public interaction rather than institutional edifices.

PUBLIC CULTURE AND POLITICAL CULTURE

At the risk of stating a self-evident truth, a nation's public policies reflect the historical experience and value systems that have characterized its societal development. This orientation toward politics involving "general attitudes about the system and specific attitudes about the role of the self in the system" is termed a nation's political culture (Almond and Verba, 1965: 13). "To understand the cultural politics of a country, one must first understand its political culture. State policies toward the arts are shaped by wider beliefs about how government ought to be conducted and what it should try to do" (Ridley, 1987: 225). Depending on their political cultures, governments vary in the way that their cultural policies are conceptualized. "This variety reflects not only differing national traditions in the organization of public functions and the delivery of public services, but differing philosophies and objectives regarding the whole area of culture and the arts" (Cummings and Katz, 1987: 4). Cultural policies, then, need to be understood not simply as administrative matters, but as reflecting a societal *Weltanschauung*; that is, a world view that defines the character of a society and how its citizenry define themselves.

With regard to the variety of institutions and programs that have been created to implement a cultural policy, their esthetic values reflect deeper popular cognitions. In this sense, cultural policies represent a microcosm of social and political world views. At the risk of oversimplification, certain Weberian "ideal types" of cultural patronage rooted in different socio-historical traditions can be identified (Mulcahy, 2000b; Zimmer and Toepler, 1996). These ideal types arc useful for understanding why nations attach an importance to supporting cultural activities through public intervention (or choose not to do so). However, it is important to remember that any ideal type is a generalized construction that may not reflect particularized exceptions.

With these caveats in mind, four cultural value-systems are posited: patrimony (cultural preservation); identity (cultural sovereignty); social welfare (cultural entitlements); libertarian (cultural laissez-faire). Frequent reference is made to four representative nations: France, Canada, Norway and the United States, respectively.

Patrimony

The hegemonic status of French culture; that is, the claim of its language, literature, philosophy and fine arts as universal accomplishments worthy of preservation and emulation, is a widely accepted principle of French political discourse. Whether Andre Malraux (1959–1969) in DeGaulle's government, or the Socialist Jack Lang (1981–1986 and 1988–1993), ministers of culture have often employed aggressive policies to promote these hegemonic claims. "Ostensibly,

Lang challenged Malraux, substantially rewriting the department's initial mission statement in order to place creativity and creation above democratisation, though in practice there was a good deal of continuity between the two pioneers" (Looseley, 2003: 228; Looseley, 1995).

French intellectuals frequently position themselves as the last exponents of high culture and esthetic discernment in the face of the onslaught of mass-entertainment culture appealing to the lowest common denominator of taste. In particular, it is American popular culture that is identified as the enemy of esthetic excellence and French cultural traditions (Ahearne, 2002). For many French intellectuals, Euro-Disney was not just a theme park, but a "cultural Chernobyl." However, it should be noted that resistance to Americanization and the more excessive assertions of France's status as an alternative cultural hegemon has not been without criticism (Fumaroli, 1999).

Despite much rhetorical hyperbole, what is important to note is that the French see culture as an essential part of the *sens civique*; that is, a sense of civic solidarity that has traditionally been regarded as a distinguishing characteristic of French society, especially when compared to the Anglo-Saxon alternative (Konig, 1995: 95–106). Although there is constant debate about the content of French cultural policy, "at least there are cultural policies, at least there is public patronage of the arts, both national and local, at least the French remain self-conscious about their creative genius" (Gildea, 1996; 232).

France may be the preeminent patron state in the preservation and promotion of its cultural heritage; in sum, France is *l'Etat Culturel*. However, Austria could be described as a "*Kulturstaat*" and Vienna as a "*Kulturstadt*." Also, Italy is endowed with so rich a cultural heritage that its preservation absorbs almost all of the resources available. Each of these nations, characterized in many ways by their cultural heritages, pursues a cultural policy in which its patrimony is a central concern. This is realized through a highly developed system of subsidies for the arts throughout the country and direct management of national cultural institutions.

Identity

What is most notable about Canada's cultural policy is the importance in political discourse of the relationship between cultural identity and political sovereignty. For the Royal Commission on National Development in the Arts, Letters and Sciences, chaired by Vincent Massey from 1949 to 1951, it was an article of faith that there was an identifiable Canadian identity. In particular, opposition to American mass culture was the basis of its cultural identity (Meisel, 1989: 22–23). Indeed, many Canadians mobilized to fight the North American Free Trade Association as a threat to national cultural values.

This cultural "crisis-mentality" is understandable in a nation of 27 million adjacent to one of 270 million whose popular culture dominates the world's entertainment venues. The fear of "cultural annexation" can best be understood when one realizes that 95 percent of their movies, 75 percent of their prime-time television, 70 percent of radio airtime (despite the latter two media having Canadian-content quotas), 80 percent of the magazines, 70 percent of the books are American products (Acheson and Maule, 1999: 16).

The issues of Canadian cultural identity, with a vertical cleavage of asymmetry with the U.S., is compounded by a horizontal cleavage with Quebec and its 7 million francophones. It may be that an unanticipated consequence of the Massey Commission's efforts to create a distinct Canadian culture was to encourage artists and intellectuals in Quebec to achieve a "*societé distincte*;" that is, to assert the distinctiveness of their francophone culture and separate identity. Since the "quiet revolution" of the 1960s, the Quebecois developed an outward-looking cultural awareness along with strong cultural institutions. Quebec's Ministere des Affaires Culturelles has actively supported the *epanouissement* (blossoming) of its arts and literature (Mulcahy, 1995d; Mulcahy, 1995e). Canada is effectively a "consociational society" that must adjust its national policies to accommodate the special status of a large, historically recognized cultural region (Lijphart, 1977).

Social Welfare

The four nations surrounding the Baltic Sea, as well as Iceland, represent a distinctive economic and political unity in their shared commitment to social-democratic principles and the welfare state. Each is a small nation; each has a huge measure of ethnic and religious homogeneity; their militaries are small; their foreign relations are pacific and are distinguished by high per-capita levels of humanitarian assistance to the international community. Most notably, there is a common commitment to equality, egalitarianism, and equity that is realized through long-standing public policies. Cultural policy is part of a much broader array of governmental efforts to provide a high-level quality of life that is accessible, sustainable, and representative. In sum, the Nordic cultural model reflects this ideological superstructure; cultural democracy is an analog of social democracy (Dueland, 2003).

For example, Norway is a social-democratic state with a well-articulated policy of cultural democratization and a strong emphasis on promoting maximum feasible accessibility to its national cultural heritage. Funding for culture in Norway is rooted in a social-democratic ideology that views government as the primary actor for providing social goods. "The welfare state's task is to make sure that the good are present, meaning that they are created or made, and that the goods are distributed equally among the population" (Bakke, 1994: 124).

Norwegian governments in the post-World War II era have accepted responsibility for public culture as a logical extension of the welfare state. "The welfare ideology implied that 'cultural goods' should be fairly distributed throughout the country, and that the population should have extended influence upon decisions affecting the cultural life of its own community" (Mangset, 1995: 68). The welfare principle also applies to the artists' right to economic security and recognizes that cultural activities – the crafts as well as the fine arts – are "a national resource for social and economic development" (Kangas and Onsér-Franzén, 1996: 19).

Overall, the social-democratic model views culture as one of those rights to which all citizens are "entitled;" that is, having a defined right, in the same sense that they are to other benefits of the welfare state. As a cultural-policy commitment, the state intervenes to correct free-market inequalities in the distribution of cultural products and opportunities through subsidies to national cultural institutions, through sinecures to guarantee the status of artists, and through support for local cultural heritage as well as for opportunities for individual self-expression.

Libertarian

There is no "ministry of culture" in the United States; that is, a Cabinet-level department responsible for comprehensive cultural policy-making and for administering a wide range of artistic activities. The cultural programs of the federal government are highly fragmented, located in a variety of administrative agencies, overseen by different congressional committees, supported by and responsive to a variety of interests and articulating the policy perspectives of discrete segments of the cultural constituency (Cherbo, 1992). This institutional fragmentation reflects both the diffuse nature of artistic activity in the United States and a fear of the effects that a unified cultural bureaucracy might have on artistic expression (Shattuck, 2005).

The symbolic importance of the NEA in the cultural world is decidedly greater than its monetary resources (Mulcahy, 1995b). Overall, government is a minority stockholder in the business of culture (Mulcahy, 1992). Public subsidy from all levels of government accounts for about 6 percent of the resources of performing arts organizations and 30 percent of museums. The American cultural organization is typically a private, not-for-profit entity, supported by earned income, individual philanthropy, corporate sponsorships and (mostly local) government grants; it is neither a public agency nor one that is largely supported by public funds. The indirect public support provided by tax-exempt charitable deductions is the crucial element in sustaining America's 8,000 museums, 2,000 local arts councils, 351 public television stations, 548 public radio stations, 7,300 community theaters,

and 1,899 symphony orchestras among other components of its cultural infrastructure (President's Committee on the Arts and the Humanities, 1997).

The U.S. government promotes culture through philanthropy; that is support for non-profit arts organizations through special preferences in its tax code (Heilbrun and Gray, 1993). For example, like all nonprofit 501(c)(3)s, cultural organizations benefit from provisions allowing corporations, foundations, and individuals to deduct the full amount of their charitable contributions when filing taxes. Also, nonprofit arts organizations generally do not pay income tax, local property taxes, or local sales taxes on revenue that is related to their mission. Nonprofits also receive substantial subsidies through preferential postal rates (Cummings, 1991: 39–41).

What makes American public policy unique is the extent to which the indirect mechanisms of tax exemptions are a means by which the government empowers private institutions and individuals to address public purposes, including culture. As indicated earlier, a public policy can be whatever a government chooses to do, or chooses not to do. In this sense, the American government takes a *laissez-faire* approach, where culture is indirectly supported by allowing individuals through tax incentives to shape the nature of cultural activities. Whether such a privatized culture best serves the public's interest is a matter of political values.

THE FUTURE OF CULTURAL POLICY

The conventional wisdom of cultural policy has traditionally compared the reputedly deplorable condition of public support for cultural activities in the United States with an idealized conception of European public culture (Schuster, 1989). Like most observations about comparative public policies, however, broad generalizations often disguise substantial exceptions. Four examples will suffice.

First, while it is certainly true that European governments substantially support a broad array of cultural endeavors, these subsidies have declined in recent years.

Moreover, if the esthetic dimension of public policy-making is more apparent in many European nations, this aspect of public policy is not totally absent in the United States.

Second, the universe of funded culture is very different outside of the United States, as this includes support for what is primarily commercial in the U.S. such as film, books and audio-visual products. On the other hand, many European nations are considering the reputed virtues of privatization and searching for alternative sources of support for cultural activities.

Third, the role of the not-for-profit sector distinguishes the American case from that of other nations. To an extent unknown elsewhere, the American government through its tax code has delegated broad policy-making powers to private institutions in the pursuit of various eleemosynary goals. The American system of cultural patronage is, in effect, much broader and stronger than would appear from considering just the NEA's budget or even that of all cultural agencies collectively.

Fourth, generally public culture is associated positively with identity and heritage, with how people define their communities and see themselves in the world and in history. A cultural policy that would appear to offer the best opportunity for public support is one that positions itself as part of broad public culture that includes the humanities, historic preservation, public broadcasting and arts education. This ideal cultural policy would promote a sense of communal continuity and definition while continuing to support esthetic discourse and artistic creativity.

The future of cultural policy would seem to predict an increasingly inexorable demand that the arts "carry their own weight" rather than rely on a public subsidy to pursue "art for art's sake" (Wyszomirski, 1995a). This "cultural Darwinism" is most pronounced in the United States, where public subsidy is limited and publicly-supported esthetic activities are expected to demonstrate a direct public benefit (Mulcahy, 2003). Non-American cultural institutions are less constrained by the need to maintain diversified revenue streams that demand high levels of earned income and individual and corporate donations to compensate for limited government appropriations. On the other hand, cultural institutions everywhere are increasingly market-driven in their need for supplementary funds and as a justification for continued public support. The American model of an essentially privatized culture is increasingly attractive to governments seeking to curtail their cultural subsidies.

In a system of mixed funding, public culture can nurture the arts groups and cultural activities that contribute to individual self-worth and community definition, even if counting for less in the economic bottom-line. At root, a cultural policy is about creating public spheres that are not dependent upon profit motives nor validated by commercial values. As political democracy is dependent upon the existence of civil society and socio-economic pluralism, cultural policy stands as an essential public commitment in realizing these fundamental preconditions.

REFERENCES

Acheson, Keith and Christopher Maule. 1999. *Much Ado about Culture: North American Trade Disputes.* Ann Arbor: University of Michigan.

Ahearne, Jeremy. 2002. *French Cultural Policy Debates: A Reader.* New York: Routledge.

Almond, Gabriel A. and Sidney Verba. 1965. *The Civic Culture: Political Attitudes and Democracy in Five Nations.* Boston: Little, Brown.

Anderson, James E. 1975. *Public Policy-Making.* New York: Praeger.

Bakke, Marit. 1994. "Centralized Decentralization in Norwegian Cultural Policy." *The Journal of Arts Management, Law, and Society,* 24: 111–127.

Bennett, Oliver. 2004. "The Torn Halves of Cultural Policy Research." *The International Journal of Cultural Policy,* 10: 237–248.

Bianchini, Franco and Michael Parkinson, eds. 1993. *Cultural Policy and Urban Regeneration: The West European Experience.* Manchester: Manchester University Press.

Bourdieu, Pierre. 1984. *Distinction: A Social Critique of the Judgment of Taste.* Cambridge: Harvard University Press.

Caust, Jo. 2003. "Putting the "Art" back into Arts Policy Making: How Arts Policy has been "Captured" by the Economists and the Marketers." *The International Journal of Cultural Policy,* 9: 51–59.

Craik, Jennifer, Libby McAllister and Glyn Davis. 2003. "Paradoxes and Contradictions in Government Approaches to Contemporary Cultural Policy: An Australian Perspective." *The International Journal of Cultural Policy,* 9: 17–34.

President's Committee on the Arts and the Humanities. 1997. "Creative America." Washington, D.C.

Chartrand, Harry Hillman and Claire McCaughey. 1989. "The Arm's Length Principle and the Arts: An International Perspective – Past, Present, and Future." *Who's to Pay for the Arts?: The International Search for Models of Arts Support*, eds. Milton C. Cummings Jr. and J. Mark Davidson Schuster.

Cherbo, Joni M. and Margaret J. Wyszomirski. 2000. *The Public Life of the Arts in America.* New Jersey: Rutgers University Press.

Cherbo, Joni M. 1992. "A Department of Cultural Resources: A Perspective on the Arts." *Journal of Arts Management, Law, and Society*, 22: 44–62.

Cohen, Randy, William Schaffer and Benjamin Davidson. 2003. "Arts and Economic Prosperity: The Economic Impact of Nonprofit Arts Organizations and theirAudiences." *Journal of Arts Management, Law and Society*, 33(1): 17–31.

Cummings, Jr., Milton C. 1991. "Government and the Arts: An Overview", in *Public Money and the Muse*, ed. Stephen Benedict. New York: W.W. Norton.

Cummings, Jr., Milton C. and Richard S. Katz. 1987. *The Patron State.* New York: Oxford University Press.

Cummings, Jr., Milton C. 1982. "To Change a Nation's Cultural Policy," in *Public Policy and the Arts*, eds. Kevin V. Mulcahy and C. Richard Swaim. Boulder: Westview Press.

Cwi, David. 1982. "Merit Good or Market Failure: Justifying and Analyzing Public Support for the Arts," in Kevin V. Mulcahy and C. Richard Swaim, *Public Policy and the Arts.* Boulder: Westview Press.

DiMaggio, Paul J., and Francie Ostrower. 1992. *Race, Ethnicity, and Participation in the Arts.* Washington, D.C.: National Endowment for the Arts and Seven Locks Press.

Dorian, Frederick. 1964. *Commitment to Culture.* Pittsburgh: University of Pittsburgh Press.

Dorn, Charles M. 1995. "Privatization of the Arts and the Public Interest: An Issue for Local Arts for Local Arts Agencies." *The Journal of Arts Management, Law and Society*, 25: 182–91.

Dueland, Peter. 2003. *Nordic Cultural Model.* Nordic Cultural Institute, Copenhagen.

Dueland, Peter. 2001. "Cultural Policy in Denmark." *The Journal of Arts Management, Law, and Society*, 31: 34–57.

Dworkin, Ronald. 1985. "Can a Liberal State Support Art?" in Ronald Dworkin, *A Matter of Principle.* Cambridge: Harvard University Press, 221–233.

Dye, Thomas R. 2005. *Understanding Public Policy, Eleventh Edition.* New Jersey: Pearson Prentice Hall.

Florida, Richard. 2002. *The Rise of the Creative Class.* New York: Basic Books.

Foucault, Michel. 1991. "Governmentality." *The Foucault Effect: Studies in Governmentality.* Graham Burchell, Colin Gordon, and Peter Miller. London: Harvester Wheatsheaf.

Fumaroli, Marc. 1999. *L'Etat Culturel: Une Religion Moderne.* Paris: Fallois.

Galligan, Ann. 1993. "The Politicization of Peer Review Panels", in Judith H. Balfe, ed., *Paying the Piper: Causes and Consequences of Arts Patronage.* Chicago: University of Illinois Press.

Gans, Herbert J. 1999. *Popular Culture and High Culture: An Analysis and Evaluation of Taste, Revised and Updated Edition.* New York: Basic Books.

Gildea, Robert. 1996. *France Since 1945.* New York: University of Oxford Press.

Heilbrun, James and Charles Gray. 1993. *The Economics of Art and Culture: An American Perspective.* New York: Cambridge University Press.

Kangas, Anita and Jill Onsér-Franzén. 1996. "Is There a Need for a New Cultural Policy Strategy in the Nordic Welfare State?" *The International Journal of Cultural Policy*, 3: 15–26.

Katz, Richard S. 1982. "Public Broadcasting and the Arts in Britain and the United States", in Kevin V. Mulcahy and C. Richard Swaim, *Public Policy and the Arts.* Boulder: Westview Press.

Konig, Hans. 1995. "A French Mirror." *Atlantic Monthly*, December.

Langsted, Jorn, ed. 1990. *Strategies. Studies in modern cultural policy.* Aarhus: Aarhus University Press.

Lebovics, Herman. 1999. *Mona Lisa's Escort: André Malraux and the Reinvention of French Culture.* Ithaca: Cornell University Press.

Lijphart, Arend. 1977. *Democracy in Plural Societies.* New Haven: Yale University Press.

Litt, Paul. 1992. *The Muses, the Masses, and the Massey Commission.* Toronto: University of Toronto Press.

Looseley, David. 2003. "Back to the Future: Rethinking French Cultural Policy, 1997–2002." *The International Journal of Cultural Policy*, 9: 227–234.

Looseley, David. 1995. *The Politics of Fun: Cultural Policy and Debate in Contemporary France.* Washington D.C.: Berg.

Mangset, Per. 1995. "Risks and Benefits of Decentralisation: The Development of Local Cultural Administration in Norway." *International Journal of Cultural Policy*, 2: 67–86.

McGuigan, Jim. 1996. *Culture and the Public Sphere.* New York: Routledge.

Meisel, John. 1989. "Government and the Arts in Canada", in *Who's to Pay For the Arts*, eds. Milton

C. Cummimgs, Jr. and J. Mark Davidson Schuster. New York: American Council for the Arts.

Miller, Toby and George Yudice. 2002. *Cultural Policy.* Thousand Oaks: SAGE Publications.

Mulcahy, Kevin V. "Entrepreneurship or Cultural Darwinism: Perspectives on the American System of Cultural Patronage," *Journal of Arts Management, Law and Society,* (Fall 2003): 165–184.

Mulcahy, Kevin V. 2002. "The State Arts Agency: An Overview of Cultural Federalism in the United States." *Journal of Arts Management, Law and Society,* 32: 67–80.

Mulcahy, Kevin V. 2000a. "Cultural Imperialism and Cultural Sovereignty: U.S.–Canadian Cultural Relations." *The American Review of Canadian Studies,* 30: 181–206.

Mulcahy, Kevin V. 2000b. "The Government and Cultural Patronage: A Comparative Analysis of Cultural Patronage in the United States, France, Norway, and Canada," in Joni M. Cherbo and Margaret J. Wyszomirski, *The Public Life of the Arts in America.* New Jersey: Rutgers University Press.

Mulcahy, Kevin V. and Margaret Jane Wyszomirski. 1995a. *America's Commitment to Culture.* Boulder: Westview Press.

Mulcahy, Kevin V. 1995b. "The NEA and the Reauthorization Process: Congress and Arts Policy Issues," in Mulcahy and Wyszomirski, *America's Commitment to Culture.* Boulder: Westview Press.

Mulcahy, Kevin V. 1995c. "The Public Interest and Arts Policy," in Mulcahy and Wyszomirski, *America's Commitment to Culture.* Boulder: Westview Press.

Mulcahy, Kevin V. 1995d. "Public Culture and Political Culture," in *Quebec Under Free Trade: Making Public Policy in America,* ed. Guy Lachapelle. Quebec: Presses de l'Universite du Quebec.

Mulchay, Kevin V. 1995e. "Public Culture and Political Culture: La Politique Culturelle du Quebec." *Journal of Arts Management, Law and Society,* 25: 25–49.

Mulcahy, Kevin V. 1992. "Government and the Arts in the United States," in *Public Policy and the Esthetic Interest,* eds. Ralph A. Smith and Ronald Berman.

Mulcahy, Kevin V. 1991. "The Public Interest in Public Culture." *Journal of Arts Management, Law and Society,* 21: 5–25.

Mulcahy, Kevin V. 1986. "The Arts and Their Economic Impact: The Values of Utility." *Journal of Arts Management, Law and Society,* 16: 33–39.

Mulcahy, Kevin V. 1985. "The NEA as Public Patron of the Arts," in *Art, Ideology, and Politics,* eds.

Judith H. Balfe and Margaret Jane Wyszomirski. New York:Praeger.

Mulcahy, Kevin V. and C. Richard Swaim. 1982a. *Public Policy and the Arts.* Boulder: Westview Press.

Mulcahy, Kevin V. 1982b. "Culture and the Cities," in Kevin V. Mulcahy and C. Richard Swaim, *Public Policy and the Arts.* Boulder: Westview Press.

Myerscough, John. 1988. *The Economic Impact of the Arts in Britain.* London: Policy Studies Institute.

Netzer, Dick. 1978. *The Subsidized Muse: Public Support for the Arts in the United States.* Cambridge University Press, Cambridge and New York.

President's Committee on the Arts and Humanities. 1997. *Creative America: A Report to the President.* Washington, D.C.

Perret, Jacques and Guy Saez. 1996. *Institutions et vie culturelles.* Paris: La Documentation Francaise.

Peters, B. Guy. 1996. *American Public Policy: Promise and Performance, Fourth Edition.* New Jersey: Chatham House.

Pratt, Andy C. 2005. "Cultural Industries and Public Policy: An Oxymoron?" *The International Journal of Cultural Policy,* 11: 31–44.

Public Law 89–209. 1965. *Congressional Declaration of Purpose Establishing the National Endowment for the Humanities and the National Endowment for the Arts; National Foundation on the Arts and Humanities Act of 1965.* Washington, D.C.: U.S. Government Printing Office.

Rafool, Mandy and Laura Loyacono. 1995 *Creative Solutions for Funding the Arts.* National Conference of State Legislatures.

Rentschler, Ruth. 2002. *The Entrepreneurial Arts Leader: Cultural Policy, Change and Reinvention.* Brisbane: University of Queensland Press.

Ridley, F.F. 1987. "Tradition, Change, and Crisis in Great Britain." in Milton C. Cummings, Jr. and Richard S. Katz, *The Patron State.* Oxford: Oxford University Press.

Robinson, P. John. 1993. *Arts Participation in America, 1982–1992: A Report of the National Endowment for the Arts.* NEA Report no. 27. Prepared by Jack Faucett Associates.

Rouet, Francois and Xavier Dupin. 1991. *Le Soutien Aux Industries Culturelles.* Paris: Department des Etudes et de la Prospective.

Saez, Guy. 1996. "Les politiques culturelles des villes," in *Institutions et vie culturelles,* eds. Jacques Perret and Guy Saez. Paris: La documentation Francaise.

Schuster, J. Mark. 2003. *Mapping State Cultural Policy: The State of Washington.* Chicago: The University of Chicago, Cultural Policy Center.

Schuster, J. Mark Davidson. 1989. "The Search for International Models: Results from Recent Comparative Research in Arts Policy," in *Who's to Pay for the Arts?*, eds. Milton C. Cummings, Jr. and J. Mark Davidson Schuster. New York: American Council for the Arts.

Shattuck, Roger. 2005. "In the Thick of Things." *New York Review of Books*. May 26: 19–22.

Stanbridge, Alan. 2002. "Detour or Dead-End? Contemporary Cultural Theory and the Search for New Cultural Policy Models." *The International Journal of Cultural Policy*, 8: 121–134.

Sterngold, Arthur R. 2004. "Do Economic Impact Studies Misrepresent the Benefits of Arts and Cultural Organizations?" *Journal of Arts Management, Law and Society*, 34: 166–188.

Williams, Raymond. 1977. *Keywords: A Vocabulary of Culture and Society*. New York: Oxford University Press.

Wyszomirski, Margaret J. 2004. "From Public Support for the Arts to Cultural Policy." *Review of Policy Research*, 21: 469–484.

Wyszomirski, Margaret J. 2002. "Arts and Culture," in *The State of Nonprofit America*, ed. Lester M. Salamon. Washington D.C.: Brookings University Press.

Wyszomirski, Margaret J. 1995a. "Federal Cultural Support: Toward a New Paradigm?" *Journal of Arts Management, Law, and Society*, 25: 69–83.

Wyszomirski, Margaret J. 1995b. "From Accord to Discord: Arts Policy During and After the Culture Wars," in *America's Commitment to Culture*, eds. Kevin V. Mulcahy and Margaret Jane Wyszomirski. Boulder: Westview Press.

Wyszomirski, Margaret J. 1982. "Controversies in Arts Policymaking," in *Public Policy and the Arts*, eds. Kevin V. Mulcahy and C. Richard Swaim. Boulder: Westview Press.

Zimmer, Annette and Stefan Toepler. 1996. "Cultural Policies and the Welfare State: The Cases of Sweden, Germany, and the United States," *Journal of Arts Management, Law, and Society*, 26: 167–193.

16

Tax Policy

B. GUY PETERS

Taxation is one of the oldest and most important activities of government. Governments have always needed money in order to pay for the services they provide, and that has meant that they needed to tax. Despite its necessity, taxation has never been popular with the public and therefore governments have had to find ways of raising the money with the minimum political opposition.[1] As governments have undertaken more functions, growing from the Nightwatchman State to the contemporary Mixed Economy Welfare State, the need for tax revenue has grown, and with that the need to find politically acceptable means of taxing has also become more important for governments. Citizens have become somewhat more resistant to taxation, even in high-tax, high service political systems such as the Nordic countries, so government also consider more carefully other forms of revenue collection, such as fees for services that do tend to be more palatable to the public.

Although the primary purpose of taxation is to raise revenue for government, tax policy also can be used to achieve a number of substantive policy goals. Governments can advantage some products and activities in the private sector by taxing them more lightly than other types of income (capital gains), or by allowing the taxpayer to deduct expenditures from taxable income (mortgage interest payments in many countries). Governments may effectively ban some products and actions by taxing them heavily, or attempt to reduce consumption by high taxes (tobacco, for example). Taxation can also be an important tool for managing the economy, with lower taxes presumed (especially by analysts and political parties on the right) to stimulate economic growth, and higher taxes being useful for controlling inflation. In short, taxation is a powerful instrument for the public sector that can be used in a number of ways to move resources, both from the private sector to government and from various segments of the private sector to others.

Politically, tax policy is often a more convenient mechanism for coping with complex issues than are public expeditures, or many other forms of implementing public policy, such as regulation (see Peters, 2001). Citizens talk a great deal about taxes but the process through which taxes are made is often more technical, and less visible to the public, than are expenditure politics (see Steinmo and Tolbert, 1998). Benefits created for individuals or businesses through taxes tend not to involve creating service programs, hiring employees or all the other trappings of "big government", but rather can be created through complex changes in the rules used to collect taxes. These complexities also create difficulties in the international environment as organizations such as the World Trade Organization attempt to maintain fair competition in the world economy.

MAKING TAX CHOICES

Making tax policy, as is true for any policy, involves a number of choices. For taxation these choices include the total amount of tax to be raised, the type of taxes to be used, the rates at which those taxes will be charged, and the specific exclusions from taxation that will be used to benefit particular groups in the economy. These choices have a wide range of consequences, so that making the choices involves balancing a number of considerations, and the different views of a wide range of actors. Taxation is usually considered primarily from an economic perspective (see Salanie, 2003; James and Nobes, 1996) but there are also crucial political, legal, and even ethical considerations that must be considered when making tax policy choices. Many citizens would not consider any tax a good tax, but some choices may be better than others. The virtues of particular taxes may, however, be contingent and what is a good tax in some settings will be a less wise choice in others. Those contingencies are, in turn, both economic and political, and a tax that may be a good technical instrument for achieving certain economic goals may be politically unacceptable, and in this game politics is generally trumps.

TAX HANDLES

When governments tax they have a wide range of possible targets for their actions, but these targets are basically three: income, expenditure and accumulated wealth. Less developed economies, in which a good deal of production is not monetized, e.g. the importance of subsistence agriculture, may have fewer options to tax and hence may have to focus on imports and exports (Radian, 1980), but more modern economies will have a very wide range of options. As already noted, the choice of any one of these, or more commonly the choice of the mixture among the three, will influence the success of government in raising revenue, the political acceptablity of the choices, and the economic impacts of the tax system.

Income is the principal tax handle for modern governments. In addition to the income tax (personal and corporate) *per se,* the other major tax relying on income as a tax handle are social insurance contributions used to fund social programs in many countries, especially in Europe. The logic undergirding taxes based on income is that individuals and firms earning incomes have the ability to pay, and therefore income taxes are a relatively fair form of revenue collection. Likewise, the income tax is generally at least somewhat progressive, with higher rates charged on higher incomes; with the logic being that for the more affluent the marginal value for each additional unit of income is less, and therefore again the tax can be considered fair, and fairer than imposing average rates across the whole income spectrum.[2] Not only would this facilitate collection, but it would also mean (it is argued) that each member of the society is funding government at an equal level.

As implied, income taxation of various sorts has been central in financing the welfare state in the affluent democracies. There have been, however, marked differences in the tax choices made by governments in financing similar service programs, and those differences have real consequences for the impacts of social programs on the distribution of income in society through public action. Some countries fund social security from general income taxation, thus producing the most redistributive possible outcomes. Other countries have used dedicated social insurance contributions for these purposes, but impose more of the burden on employers than on the employees,[3] while many tax systems split the total social insurance contribution more or less evenly between workers and employers.

Although perhaps the most fair, income taxation also may be the easiest form of tax to evade. The average person earning most or all of his income from an employer required to keep records and report that income to government may not be able to evade taxes, but independent workers, such as plumbers or gardeners or taxi drivers, may receive a good deal of their income in cash and simply not report part of that income. More highly paid professionals, such as dentists or lawyers, may have the same opportunities for evasion, having a good deal of their income in cash. Some countries have established themselves as tax havens for corporations, with very low taxes and strict laws preventing corporate or individual income information to tax authorities as a means of assisting individuals who want to evade taxes to do so.

The second major alternative source for tax revenue is consumption. The Value Added Tax, for example, is paid by consumers in European countries whenever they purchase an item in the stores, although they may not notice because the tax is included in the price. Consumers in North America and Australia pay sales taxes and goods and services taxes that are added to the costs of the product on the shelf, and hence are more visible to the consumers or taxpayers. Tariffs levied on imports are also consumption taxes because, in the end, they will be passed on by the importer and paid by the final consumer of the products. Excise taxes – the famous sin taxes on products such as alcohol, tobacco and gambling, and simple necessity taxes on products such as gasoline and phone service – also come out of the pockets of the consumers of these products. Most citizens find that they are helping to fund government every time they go to the shops.

In most instances[4] consumption taxes fall more heavily on the less affluent, but may be considered fair politically because everyone in society should be obliged to pay at least something for the maintenance of the society. The actual incidence of consumption taxes can be altered somewhat by careful design of the taxes, e.g. not charging VAT on food or medicines, but the impact still tends to fall more heavily on those less capable of paying. Consumption taxes also are generally more difficult to evade than are income taxes, and have the additional advantage that government can use stores (or casinos, or wherever) that sell the products to collect the taxes. Given that the incidence of consumption taxes is general rather than on industry, many countries have been shifting their tax burdens somewhat in this direction in the face of pressures from globalization and tax competition.

For the less developed countries of the world consumption taxation tends to be the principal form of revenue collection. If the economy is highly decentralized and has a number of segments that are not conducted in cash, then counting money incomes may be difficult. Further, to the extent that incomes are in money they may well be in cash that is difficult to trace, as compared to salaries paid by larger firms. Therefore, these countries may find it easier to collect excises and customs rather than attempt to tax incomes, or even attempt to impose consumption taxes on personal consumption, such as sales taxes.

Finally, governments can also tax accumulated wealth. One of the most common forms of tax using this "handle" is the property tax, a mainstay for local taxation in Anglo-American countries. This tax also is justified on the ability to pay, with ownership of a house, or other assets, being evidence of that ability, although it is also assumed that homeowners benefit more from services such as fire protection and public utilities than do other citizens. Inheritance taxes also use wealth as a basis for collecting revenues as that wealth is passed between generations. While these taxes do appear fair, given the possession of the assets, some people (especially the elderly) find that their incomes do not match their assets, and have to sell their homes simply because of the taxes imposed. Further, heavy taxes on accumulated wealth may discourage investment and savings, and hence have negative long-term economic consequences.

Again, governments can fine tune a tax instrument in order to produce the type of outcomes desired. For example, if there is a desire to keep the elderly in their homes, governments can provide a "homestead exemption" up to a modest amount to protect those homeowners from tax. Likewise, property may be passed on to spouses without tax, and to children with limited tax, but other forms of transfer may be taxed more heavily. These tax instruments may appear to be rather blunt when first considered, but governments can make them into very sensitive tools for altering the distribution of income and providing incentives for certain types of economic and social behavior.

To this point I have been speaking about taxes *per se*, but governments have other important revenue sources as well. In particular, governments provide a number of goods and services for which they can charge their "customers". Governments have been raising an increased amount of revenue from fees and charges over the past several decades. This shift in revenue patterns has come about for several reasons. First, this form of revenue collection tends to be more acceptable politically than does taxation, given that there is a direct exchange of money for the service rather than the perception that tax money goes into some vague general fund. Secondly, governments also use fees as a means of rationing consumption of certain types of services that might otherwise be overused by the public. Finally, the ideology of the New Public Management and of the political right has emphasized the capacity to use more business-like mechanisms within the public sector.

The choices among these tax handles, as well as among individual forms of taxation within those broader categories of taxes, involve economic, political, administrative and ethical criteria. One of the most important strategies that governments have adopted in attempting to be able to raise adequate revenue without creating large-scale resistance among taxpayers is to spread their tax net as widely as possible. Most governments take at least some revenues from as many sources as possible. This broad-based approach to taxation may help reduce political opposition, but it may also make achieving other policy goals through taxation more difficult. If all aspects of the economy are being taxed, or being given tax relief, then there is little that any one type of economic action is likely to gain from government. Thus, taxation, perhaps more than policy areas, involves a set of complex trade-offs among a number of competing values and critieria for assessment.

CRITERIA FOR ASSESSING TAXES

The above discussion has implied the application of criteria for assessing taxes, but I should present those somewhat more systematically. As noted, tax policy tends to involve very large-trade-offs of these criteria. Economists have tended to dominate policy-making for taxation, and hence the economic criteria discussed below tend to be the dominant values. That having been said, in the public sector politics is usually trumps, so, even though there may be good economic arguments for a tax policy if that policy produces political difficulties, it may well be rejected for a program that economists might consider inferior. Economists do vote, but there are fewer of them than of many other groups in society and politicians in democratic systems have to appeal to majorities.

Many of these criteria for taxes are distributive, and are concerned with the economic, political and ethical consequences of who pays taxes. That assessment is, however, somewhat incomplete without a simultaneous assessment of where the money is being spent. A tax, such as the Social Security "contribution" in the United States, that is negatively redistributive because it is not charged on earned incomes above $90,000 (2005) and not charged on incomes from investments, is used to fund a program that is slightly progressive. The net effect, therefore, may be roughly proportional among economic classes. In general tax systems have become less progressive in most of the industrialized democracies, but spending continues to go to the programs of the Welfare State, and perhaps in larger proportions, because of the aging of the populations, so that the net effects may not be altered as much as expected.

Economic Concerns

Economic values tend to be considered first when assessing taxes, and the political criteria discussed below are often seen by economists as introducing distortions into the more efficient solutions that might be produced by focussing more single-mindedly on the economics of taxes. Indeed, to some analysts any tax may be considered a distortion in what might otherwise be a more efficient economy, but, given the needs for contemporary governments to raise money in large amounts, these distortions must be minimized rather than eliminated. The tax distortions of markets may be especially apparent when tax systems favor one use of money over others. For example, tax expenditures[5] for housing favor personal homes over other forms of investment, even though housing may be less productive than many other potential uses of capital. Politically, however, houses are widely held in many economies so that a tax advantage for this use of capital is very good politics indeed.

The desire to eliminate distortions arising from taxation does not, however, necessarily imply removing all special treatments of income and expenditures. Indeed, creating a tax system that is free of distortions might involve introducing a large number of special treatments and the creation of a very complex tax code. For example, although depletion allowances for oil and gas producers have been written into tax codes in part because of the political influence of those industries, they also reflect a real economic consideration about the short lifetime of returns from what can be significant investments. Given this and numerous other needs to fine tune taxes, the resultant tax code may have to be extremely complex if the goal is eliminating distortions in the tax system.

Economists are also concerned with the incidence of taxation. That is, who finally pays the tax? While for the personal income tax it is clear that the individual is the payer, for the corporate tax there continues to be a debate about who pays, and under what conditions. Do consumers pay corporate taxes through higher prices, or do stockholders pay through lower dividends, or do employees through lower wages, or is it a combination? The answer is that it is probably a combination, but that the mixture will differ under different conditions, e.g. the elasticity of demand for the products of the firm.[6] The incidence of taxes is important for more than technical reasons. If taxes are being used to attempt to affect the behavior of firms, or to alter the distribution of income, then it is important to understand who really pays.

Economic analysis of taxation focuses some of its attention on the incidence of taxes. Levying a tax on a business or on an individual is one thing, but the question of incidence is who actually bears the burden on that tax. For example, the corporation tax is apparently a tax on businesses, but in reality that tax is paid by employees, by customers, and/or by investors. The actual incidence of the tax will depend upon factors such as the elasticity of demand for the product and therefore the ability to pass along the tax in higher prices. Determining the true incidence of a tax is important because it allows determining just where the burden of the tax falls within the economy. For example, if corporations can pass along their taxes they may be less interested in opposing those taxes politically, and indeed may be more than willing to publicize the amount that they pay as "good corporate citizens".

Political Criteria

The economic criteria above may appear scientific and rationalist, while the political criteria discussed here are more difficult to quantify or link to specific analytic justifications. That having been said, however, these criteria are often crucial to the success of the policy. The most important political criterion for taxation is fairness, and most citizens are willing to pay their taxes if they believe they are fair. People do not like paying taxes, and, unfortunately for governments, a significant propotion of the populations in many countries do not believe that the tax system to which they are a party is fair. Most people believe that they and people like them pay too much, and other people (whether the rich or the poor, or whoever) do not pay enough. Likewise, many citizens believe that other people in the society are evading taxes, although the respondents to surveys often lump together illegal evastion with legal avoidance of taxes through tax expenditures (Seldon, 1979).

Perhaps the most fundamental political criterion for taxation is that an old tax is a good tax. This statement reflects not only public resistance to new taxes but also indicates the strong path dependence in tax policy (Kato, 2003). For example, the property tax, especially as a means of funding local governments, is a traditional form of revenue collection in Anglo-American countries and, despite a number of serious problems in administration and equity, remains in place. The political traditions of countries in taxation persist and make some taxes appear quite normal and acceptable to citizens, while introducing others might be politically infeasible. This cultural impact on taxes may even affect the level at which a tax can be used. Citizens in the United States are accustomed to consumption taxes levied at the state and local level, but the idea of a national consumption tax is considered innovative, and perhaps too innovative.

As already noted, one of the most important political criteria is minimizing the visibility of the tax to the public. Taxes are not popular, so if the money can be raised without the public understanding the exact impact of the tax on their own resources, then political resistance can be reduced. Therefore, although economists might prefer direct taxation, e.g. taxes on income, politicians might prefer indirect taxes that are included in the price of a product rather than charged directly to the citizen. Another means of reducing visibility is to use the full range of taxes available, charging each at a small rate, but have the total add up to the needed revenue. Citizens may see that their disposable income is lessened, but not have a clear target as they might with a few large taxes.

Although most politicians in government may like the idea of less visible taxes, some politicians on the political right have been opposed to reducing tax visibility. They argue that if citizens really understood how much they were paying in taxes they would mobilize politically (presumably on behalf of those conservative politicians) and oppose the expansion of the public sector. Constitutional rules, such as requiring referenda for tax increases in some American states, and in Switzerland, have been devised to ensure that citizens are indeed aware of the level of taxation, and have the opportunity to oppose any new taxes or increases in rates.

Earmarking is another of the political strategies that can be utilized to enhance political support for taxes, or at least minimize adverse political reactions. A good deal of survey evidence indicates that citizens are more likely to accept a tax if they can be sure that it is being used in a particular way. For example, gasoline taxes in a number of countries have been dedicated to highways and other transportation purposes. In the United States and Switzerland, even in periods in which there is strong public resistance to taxation in general, citizens have voted for taxes so long as they could identify the actual use of the revenues. So-called "sin taxes" may be a particular form of earmarked taxes. Although governments do derive some general revenues from taxes on alcohol, tobacco and gambling, increasingly some or all of that revenue is dedicated to particular purposes, and often to dealing with the problems created by the substance or activity being taxed. Revenues from taxes are often used to pay for advertising against smoking, and some revenue from alcohol is used to fund rehabiliation and advertising.

To this point I have been talking about taxation, but it is important to remember that this is but one of the possible revenue sources for government. Governments have a number of other ways to raise revenues, notably through charging fees for services. For example, when taxation may be politically impossible, governments can charge for services such as garbage collection, recreation facilities, passports, and a host of other activities. This source of revenue has the obvious advantage of being directly related to services, and, further, are paid only by the people who actually avail themselves of the services.

Public lotteries are a special case of "user fees" to finance public services. These gambling programs have been successful in providing a great deal of money for the public sector where they have been used. For example, in the American states in which they are used, lotteries provide an percent of public revenues. Likewise, in the United Kingdom the lottery has been used to fund a number of major public works. In most instances lotteries are in essence an earmarked tax, paying for services such as education and the support of the elderly. Although lotteries are often critisized as being negatively redistributive, and as government sponsored gambling (see below), they are too dependable a source of income for governments that have the option to use them to ignore.

As well as minimizing the resistance to taxation, redistribution is a major political concern when making tax policy. While economists may want to ensure the neutrality of taxes, politicians generally want to use the tax system to move money around among social groups, especicially social classes (for a somewhat polemical view of this debate, see Shugart, 1997). Thus, the income tax – the principal source of income for industrialized democracies – tends to be at least moderately progressive. Taxpayers pay a higher marginal rate after certain levels of income, although the strength of conservative politics in recent decades has tended to reduce the level of progression. The Bush tax cuts in the United States, for example, have gone primarily to the most affluent members of the society, with the economic justification that their investments will produce economic growth.

ADMINISTRATIVE CRITERIA

A good tax (although some people might argue there is no such thing) must be fair, it must not distort economic activity more than is absolutely necessary, and it must also be collectible without imposing excessive administrative costs. There is little use in having a tax in the law books if it cannot be collected, or if it imposes so many costs on government to collect that it is not worth the effort. While the fortunes of government in collecting taxes are to some extent a function of the laws and policies themselves, they are also to some extent a function of the social and economic environment in which the taxation is being conducted. Some countries have a long tradition of ignoring tax laws, and reducing evasion in these cases may present a major challenge for government. Likewise, in societies in which a good

deal of the economic activity is not traded in the market for money, attempting to collect taxes from most of the population may be rather pointless.[7]

One common strategy for coping with the problem of collecting taxes is for government to have private sector actors bear a major part of the burden. This practice goes back to "tax farming" in Roman times, in which tax collectors were private individuals given the right to collect taxes in return for the option of keeping a part of the take. In more recent times governments have come to depend upon firms to do a major part of the record-keeping and administration. Most employers have to withdraw a portion of their employees' incomes as tax and turn that over to government. Likewise, firms and individual proprietors are responsible for collecting the Value-Added Tax (VAT) and other consumption taxes for government. In the case of the VAT, this can impose a substantial administrative burden on the private sector actor, given the often complex questions involved in this tax.

Ordinary citizens also do a good deal of work for government in collecting taxes. Many countries now use self-assessment of taxes, requiring citizens to retain records and then file annual tax forms detailing income and deductions. Government will still have to review these returns and audit a percentage to prevent fraud, but much of the work is done by the citizens. The Internal Revenue Service in the United States estimates that the average filler of the principal tax form (1040) spends nn hours per year keeping records and another mm hours filling out the form. More complex tax issues require the citizen to engage lawyers and accountants, again imposing a good deal of the cost of administration on the private sector.[8]

The necessity of actually administering the tax code and collecting money from the public may conflict with several of the economic and political criteria already advanced. For example, if governments attempt to fine tune taxes in order to prevent significant distortions in the economy, they increase the administrative problems of government (and citizens) in complying with that code. Governments in a number of countries have been attempting to simplify their tax codes in order to facilitate administration, as well as to respond to political claims that the complexity of the codes actually hides numerous benefits for more affluent citizens. Simplification of tax systems has not been as easy as the political advocates have made it appear, and many of the provisions written into law appear to have some justification.

ETHICAL CRITERIA

Finally, taxes, like all public policies, also have an ethical dimension (see Hughes and Moizer, 2005). The ethical dimension of analysis centers on the issue of the fairness of taxes, and the need to balance the other criteria. On the one hand, it can be argued that all members of the society should bear some of the cost of maintaining basic public services, so that tax programs that spread these costs broadly and find ways of extracting at least some revenue, even from the poorest segments of society, are indeed fair. On the other hand, fairness may imply that those most capable of paying should pay the largest share of taxes, and that the operations of government (taxing and spending togcthcr) should make the distribution of income more equitable.

Raising revenues from lotteries and from sin taxes raise some of the more vexing ethical problems for government. While these taxes are paid by everyone who smokes, drinks or gambles, it is well known that lower income citizens engage in these activities at higher rates, especially in relationship to their income. Thus, especially lotteries and the tobacco tax have a negative redistributive effect, and take a substantial amount of money out of the pockets of the less affluent. Part of the logic of having high alcohol and tobacco taxes is to deter consumption, but it is not clear that this is effective, and the continued use of these substances, especially by poorer people, has those taxpayers who are less able to do so funding many important public services.

CURRENT ISSUES IN TAX POLICY

Although tax policy is indeed a very old activity of government, there are some recent developments in the use of this instrument that demonstrate the continuing development of this policy area. The majority of these issues concern the use of tax policy as a means of achieving other policy goals, and therefore are in some ways merely extensions of a logic that has been in place for some time. That having been said, however, several of these uses of tax policy are more extensive and innovative, and demonstrate the limits of using tax policy as an instrument of policy.

The Carbon Tax

The carbon tax is a mechanism for addressing the issue of climate change and global warming, as well as the more general question of the continuing use of scarce, non-renewable resources in a profligate manner in contemporary economies. The basic idea of the carbon tax is simple. Given that increasing levels of carbon-dioxide is a major cause of global warming, a tax should be levied by each country on the amount of carbon in fuels. This tax should create an increased cost for inefficient use of energy and drive firms to find better ways of producing, and create incentives for individuals to use less energy at home and in transportation. The tax could be fine-tuned to advantage renewable sources of energy, such as ethanol, even if carbon-based.

Although the basic idea of the carbon tax is simple, there are a number of technical and political issues that are raised about the implementation of the idea. One of the most important of the objections arises around issues of equity. On the one hand, raising carbon taxes from all countries will disadvantage the less-developed countries, while raising it only from the more affluent countries will disadvantage those countries that already feel that they are losing industrial jobs because of globalization. While some sense of equity might argue for facilitating the development of the poorer countries, an unemployed textile worker in Lancashire might not find the argument compelling.

The Tobin Tax

Another variant of using taxes on an international level in order to alter behavior is called the Tobin Tax, after James Tobin (1978) the Nobel-laureate economist who first proposed this means of dealing with the problems of globalization. The idea of the Tobin Tax is to impose a tax on foreign exchange as a means of imposing some restraint on the global movement of capital. This tax would, it is argued, first help to reduce distortions in the international capital markets because of the herd behavior of currency traders who tend to exaggerate runs on currencies (as in the Asian currency crisis in 1997). Further, borrowing and lending might be considered more carefully were there some additional costs involved.

While this tax may be able to produce some real benefits for the world economy, it poses several interesting implementation problems for governments and international organizations. How could the tax be collected, and by whom, in an already decentralized and complex market in foreign exhange, and would not such a tax drive exchange operations into less stable instruments such as derivatives? Further, how would the revenues from the tax be used? The usual assumption is that the revenue from this tax would be used by the International Monetary Fund (IMF) to ameliorate some of the consquences of speculation for poorer countries. This tax is hardly the solution for all the problems of globalization, but it does illustrate the possibilities of using tax instruments even in the international environment.

Taxing the Internet

Coping with globalization is one of the issues for contemporary taxation, but the increasing importance of internet commerce represents another interesting challenge to traditional forms of managing tax programs.

The magnitude of commerce conducted on-line is difficult to estimate, but is certainly substantial in most of the wealthy democracies, and is also certainly increasing in importance in the international marketplace. This form of commerce is, however, extremely decentralized and some aspects can be anonymous, and it therefore can pose difficulties for governments attempting to monitor the flow of funds and extract the revenue that it believes is appropriate from these transactions.

For tax authorities there is little doubt that the transactions on the Internet are in principle subject to tax, just as if they had taken place in any shop in the center of town. Money is changing hands – or perhaps goods are being bartered – but this is market activity. For citizens, however, shopping, selling or bartering on the internet is perceived as a means of escaping from the long arm of tax authorities. Governments are encountering a number of legal and administrative difficulties in coping with the growth of e-commerce, and have been generally effective at tapping the tax revenue that might be derived from these activities (Lymer, 2005). The amorphous nature of e-commerce makes basic issues like the locus of the activity, and hence the responsible taxing authority, difficult to determine.

Tax Competition

Tax competition is hardly a new concept, or a new concern for governments, but globalization and increasing levels of international trade have brought it forward as a significant concern in the contemporary economy. Countries, as well as sub-national units within countries, compete with one another to have businesses locate within their territory so that there will be more jobs and greater wealth in that territory. Offering lower levels of taxation is one of the many incentives that can be manipulated by governments to encourage firms to select one area over another. Part of the critique of globalization of economies is that destructive tax competition has reduced the capacity of governments to raise revenues in the manner, and in the amounts, that they would like and, therefore, the overall quality of government programs have been declining.[9]

It is important to note that taxes are but one of many factors involved in making decisions about industrial location, and perhaps not the most important. Some research indicates that taxes, in fact, fall rather far down the list of the factors that are crucial for location decisions, although firms may still act as if receiving tax breaks will be the central factor in the decision. Indeed, for some types of industries requiring highly skilled workforces, low levels of public revenue, usually associated with a poor education system, may in reality be an impediment to persuading a firm to locate in an area. Further, the range of possibilities available to governments in raising revenues means that sacrifices in some types of taxation may be made up in other forms of taxation, or in fees levied for services.

Tax Cuts

Although they have been most evident in the United States, many of the industrialized democracies have been reducing some of their taxes, especially taxes on personal and corporate income. The assumption is that this reduction in government revenue will result in more spending by the public, which will, in turn, increase economic growth. This strategy is a variation on the familiar Keynsian logic of enhancing effective demand as the means of coping with a slow-down in the economy. The difference is, in part, that many of these tax reductions (again, especially those in the United States (Pollack, 2003)) have benefitted the more affluent rather than the less affluent, who are most likely to spend any additional income they may receive. On the other hand, the advocates of the contemporary tax cutting strategies for the top of the economy argue that these are the people who are most likely to invest in the economy and produce long-term economic growth.[10] For some countries the important issues are, however, cutting corporate income taxes and other business taxes as a means of promoting investment and economic growth.

The pressures for reducing taxation are obviously related to the issue of tax competition mentioned just above. The competition over taxation is often discussed in terms of corporate taxation, or perhaps individual income taxation, but some of the important contemporary issues concerning cutting are about the social costs of employment. When firms are deciding whether to add new employees, in addition to the actual wage being paid to the individual, the firm must consider the tax costs – especially for social security taxes – that are involved with the job. Especially in countries where collecting direct taxes is difficult,[11] there has been a tendency to impose high rates of social insurance contributions on both individuals and firms, so that the marginal cost of the additional employee can be very high.

The logical question then becomes whether tax cuts are indeed an important tool for economic management, or simply an ideologically driven device to aid the more affluent to reduce their contributions to the public purse. The answer to that question may depend in large part upon the political persuasion of the individual answering. The answer may also depend upon the nature of the economy at the time, and the need for stimulus from more cash in the hands of citizens – even the more affluent. What is clear, however, is that many, if not most governments, now face increasing pressures to justify any taxes they may impose, or even those they choose to retain. At the same time that governments may want to reduce levels of taxation, many are constrained by their involvement in institutions such as the European Union that constrain their economic actions. Even in those constrained situations, however, there are increasing pressures in some countries to reduce taxes to address continuing unemployment, even in countries, such as Germany, with a significant social welfare system.

Tax Expenditures

At the same time that there are some political pressures to reduce taxation there are other changes in tax systems that are having the effect of increasing taxes. In particular, many countries (see Brixi, Valenduc and Swift, 2004) have been eliminating tax expenditures, or "loopholes" that had advantaged certain types of activity. Even some of the more popular tax expenditures, such as supports for home ownership, have been reduced or eliminated to simplify tax systems. The logic of tax expenditures has been that the tax system can be as efficient, or even more efficient, a mechanism for moving resources about in the economy as is public expenditure. Allowing citizens to escape taxation on certain types of activity, or to receive tax credits for others, have had something of the same effects as spending, but did not require governments to go through the political pain of taxation to fund the program, nor the economic costs of managing a program.[12]

While there is certainly some evidence of abuse of tax expenditures, providing tax relief for some activities can also constitute an important policy tool for governments. In addition to the political advantage of lessened visibility of the programs that are developed, using tax expenditures also displaces much of the administrative burden for programs on to the individual taxpayers and can save the public sector itself a good deal of money. If we use the familiar example of deductibility of mortgage interest as a tax expenditure, then a major housing program is being administered through the individual actions of taxpayers, who retain their own information about their costs, file the forms, and do all the work that would normally have to be done in the public sector.

Tax expenditures do, however, tend to have negative redistributive consequences. Tax relief from these exemptions and deductions is more significant the higher the individual's tax rates are. Therefore, most tax expenditures tend to benefit the more affluent differentially (Howard, 1997; Greve, 1994). These benefits available through the tax system, therefore, tend to reflect the political power of the middle and upper classes. That having been said, however, there are notable examples of tax expenditures being used to produce benefits for the poor, notably the Earned Income Credit in the United States, and the Integrated Child Credit in the United Kingdom. These mechanisms

have used the tax system as a means of providing something approaching a guaranteed income to the working poor. Again, these benefits might not have survived the more visible politics involved in adopting expenditure programs.

SUMMARY AND CONCLUSIONS

Taxation is one of the oldest areas of government policy, and many of the questions raised by the first attempts to raise revenue continue to be important today. Although primarily designed to raise the money governments need to fund their spending activities, taxes can also be used for a variety of other purposes, advantaging some activities and disadvantaging others. Even the simple choice of what type of tax to impose in order to raise the revenue will have consequences other than simply collecting money. Therefore, taxation involves a number of complex decisions that involve political, economic, administrative and ethical concerns. Different political forces will stress one or another of these criteria as the most important for any decision, but there will have to be some trading-off of values.

In the end, however, governments have to raise revenue, and their first priority must be to find the money they need. Even when faced with an international environment that poses substantial economic competition for industrial location, governments have to find a way of getting enough money to fund their expenditure commitments. This ever increasing need for public revenue now means that a greater proportion of the burden of government finance is falling on average citizens and perhaps even the less affluent in society. On the one hand, that change in revenue collection patterns makes funding government very democratic, and everyone is contributing to maintaining the public sector. On the other hand, however, the process may now be less fair than in the past, given that the more affluent are in many societies now bearing a smaller proportion of the total costs of governing.

NOTES

1. As Richard Rose has written, the golden goose must be relieved of the maximum feathers with the minimum of squawking.

2. This logic is contested by the advocates of the "flat tax", who argue that it is in fact fairer for everyone to pay the same rate (usually with few if any deductions permitted).

3. This may appear more distributive but employees may actually pay the tax through lower wages or the unemployed may pay it because they will not be hired when the marginal costs of hiring an additional worker are high.

4. A major exception would be higher taxes on luxury items such as jewelry.

5. A tax expenditure (see Howard, 1997; Also see Wildavsky, 1985) is government assistance given to a particular industry or use of resources through the tax system rather than through an expenditure. Politically, these may be more palatable given that it keeps the public budget smaller than pursuing the same ends through a subsidy. Further, providing the support through the tax system tends to be less visible than doing it through the expenditure budget.

6. The ability to pass taxes along is one explanation for why corporation income taxes have been relatively high in countries such as Switzerland and the United States that might have been expected to have their tax systems influenced heavily by business interests.

7. In a good deal of sub-Saharan Africa and South Asia a significant part of the population are in subsistence agriculture and have little money income to be subject to an income tax.

8. Although a cost home by the taxpayer, the principal reason for taxpayers engaging these professionals is to reduce tax, hence producing a net reduction of tax costs.

9. Reduced tax revenue has contributed to the reduced quality of some programs, but there have been more conscious choices to reduce levels of regulation so that again firms may find it more attractive to locate.

10. This is a variant of the "supply side economics" of Ronald Reagan, based on the assumption that, if, money is placed in the hands of the most affluent members of society, they will invest that money and that will, in turn, create economic growth.

11. In particular, countries that have high levels of tax evasion tend to rely more heavily on indirect forms of taxation. Individual employees have an incentive to see that the social taxes are collected, since their pensions and health insurance coverage are dependent directly upon the taxes.

12. Some loopholes, such as the deductibility of keeping racehorses (usually by the very affluent) might not have stood scrutiny if they had been considered as subsidies for the same activities as a part of the expenditure process.

REFERENCES

Brannland, R. and I.-M.Gren (1999) *Green Taxes: Economic Theory and Empirical Evidence From Scandinavia* (Cheltenham: Edward Elgar).

Brixi, P., C. M. A. Valenduc and Z. L. Swift (2004) *Tax Expenditures: Shedding Light on Government Spending Through the Tax System* (Washington, DC: World Bank).

Greve, B. (1994) The Hidden Welfare State, Tax Expenditures and Welfare Policy, *Scandinavian Journal of Social Welfare*, 3, 203–11.

Howard, C. (1997) *The Hidden Welfare State: Tax Expenditures and Social Policy in the United States* (Princeton, NJ: Princeton University Press).

Hughes, J. F. and P. Moizer (2005) Taxation and Ethics, in M. Lamb, A. Lymer, J. Freedman, and S. James, eds, *Taxation: An Interdisciplinary Approach to Research* (Oxford: Oxford University Press).

James, S. R. and C. Nobes (1996) *The Economics of Taxation* (New York: Prentice-Hall).

Kato, J. (2003) *Regressive Taxation and the Welfare State: Path Dependence and Policy Diffusion* (Cambridge: Cambridge University Press).

Lymer, A. (2005) Taxation in an Electronic World, in M. Lamb, A. Lymer, J. Freedman, and S. James, eds, *Taxation: An Interdisciplinary Approach to Research* (Oxford: Oxford University Press).

Peters, B. G. (2001) The Politics of Policy Instruments, in L. M. Salamon, ed., *Handbook of Policy Instruments* (New York: Oxford University Press).

Pollack, S. D. (2003) *Refinancing America: The Republican Anti-Tax Agenda* (Albany: State University of New York Press).

Radian, A. (1980) *Resource Mobilization in Poor Countries: Implementing Tax Policy* (New Brunswick, NJ: Transaction Books).

Salanie, B. (2003) *The Economics of Taxation* (Cambridge, MA: MIT Press).

Seldon, A. (1979) *Tax Avoision* (London: Institute of Economic Affairs).

Shugart, W. F. (1997) *Taxing Choice: The Predatory Politics of Fiscal Discrimination* (New Brunswick, NJ: Transaction Publishers).

Steinmo, S. and C. J. Tolbert (1998) Do Institutions Really Matter?: Taxation in Industrialized Democracies, *Comparative Political Studies*, 31, 165–87.

Tobin, J. (1978) Proposal for International Monetary Reform, *Eastern Economic Journal* 4, 153–9.

Wildavsky, A. (1985) Keeping Kosher: The Epistemology of Tax Expenditures, *Journal of Public Policy* 5, 413–31.

17

Industrial Policy in Developed Nations

RICHARD D. BINGHAM

Industrial policy is a generally misunderstood concept. When most people think of industrial policy, if they think of it at all, they think of development banks to aid manufacturing, or government policies to stimulate exports. They think of the central bank lowering interest rates to stimulate economic growth and productivity, or extending the North American Free Trade Agreement (NAFTA) to South America. Yet none of these actions would be part of a nation's industrial policy; because industrial policy is sector specific. Sector specific means that the policy is applied to a specific industry, like steel production.

In 2002, U.S. President George W. Bush placed tariffs on a variety of steel products being imported into the United States. This is a sector specific policy – applying only to the steel industry. Thus, steel tariffs became a part of America's national industrial policy.

INDUSTRIAL POLICY DEFINED

Industrial policy is *a nation's official total effort to influence sectoral development and thus, the national industrial portfolio* (Bingham, 1998: p. 6). But a policy or a set of policies for a specific industry (e.g., steel) is not, in and of itself, industrial policy – it is an *industry policy* because it pertains to one specific industry.

A nation's industrial policy is the sum total of its sector specific industry policies.

The above definition is a modification of one formulated by historian Otis Graham, Jr. in his book *Losing Time: The Industrial Policy Debate* (1992, p. 6). Graham defined industrial policy as *a nation's declared, official, total effort to influence sectoral development and thus, national industrial portfolio* (1992, p.6). But the United States (and other developed nations as well) can never have a "declared, official" industrial policy because to do so would require industrial planning, something the modern American government is unlikely to do – because the American political economy is a *Broker State* (term coined by Chamberlain, 1941). In a Broker State:

> government did not look ahead, aiming at coherent strategic objectives. Instead, the Broker State orchestrated the conflict of organized interest groups. Washington was not the site of a government with its own purposes, but of a sort of modified marketplace, a "parallelogram of pressures," or place of political exchange where groups within the economy and society brought their special problems and bargained for state-conferred benefits. The economy aimed itself; the government's role was to ensure that it did not slow down, too much, for too long. The style of policymaking was incremental and piecemeal, the government's time horizon close in, timed to the electoral cycle. It displayed a weak sense of an overriding public interest and a deferential reliance upon the electorate's and in particular large corporations' private agendas. It was a reactive system, flexible and responsive to its admirers, aimless and without vision to its detractors (Graham, 1992: p. 280).

A broker state can never have a "declared, official" industrial policy – it can only have a de facto one. And that is what the United States has – "an unacknowledged melange of all federal, state, and local government policies affecting goods producing sectors" (ibid., p. 3). So, to identify industrial policy in a Broker State it is not possible to focus on what government says about industrial policy, for it says nothing. Instead, it is necessary to focus on what government does in order to be able to identify industrial policy. This is what will be done here.

WHY INDUSTRIAL POLICIES?

Nations adopt industrial policies for a variety of reasons. For example, industrial policies are sometimes developed to provide the home nation with the presence of an industry which it deems vital to its economic future. Back in the late 1950s this was the case with Japan's successful development of the semiconductor industry (Prestowitz, 1988: pp. 33–36; Lodge, 1990: pp. 76–78). It was also the reason for the United States' attempt to develop a flat panel display industry during the 1990s (Bingham, 1998: pp. 120–126).

Market failure is an oft-cited reason for national industrial policies. In many nations, most utilities are publicly licensed monopolies. Thus there is little incentive for these utilities to be particularly innovative, or for that matter efficient. Industrial policies might thus be necessary to move one of these protected industries in a direction it might have taken itself in a more competitive environment. In industrialized nations this would be one reason for government support for the development and commercialization of high-temperature superconductivity initiatives. There is every reason for governments to want to move in this direction but there are few incentives for public utilities to be directly involved in these efforts.

Industrial policies are often adopted to correct negative externalities and/or to promote the national interest. These were certainly reasons why the Clinton administration (in the United States) initiated the Partnership for a New Generation of Vehicles in 1993 (to be discussed later). It was in the nation's best interest to develop a fuel-efficient, nonpolluting automobile, but this was not in the best interests of the big-three auto makers.

Also, there is a belief among some that technology-intensive industries make special contributions to the long-term health of national economies. Laura Tyson, President Clinton's Chair of the Council of Economic Advisors, believes that success in high-technology industries bestows national benefits in productivity, technology development, and job creation and that nations must devise industry policies that promote high-technology industries (Tyson, 1993: pp. 2–3):

> A dollar's worth of shoes may have the same effect on the trade balance as a dollar's worth of computers. But … the two do not have the same effect on employment, wages, labor skills, productivity, and research – all major determinants of our long-term economic health (Tyson, 1993: p. 12)

But, while the above suggest that industrial policies are adopted by nations for rational, and even laudable purposes, many are not. Most common is old-fashioned protectionism. Many countries go to great lengths to protect inefficient and even corrupt industries – often for political purposes. This has historically been the case with Japan, where the government goes to great lengths to protect the inefficient agriculture, distribution, and construction industries. Diet (Japanese legislature) members have close ties to all three industries (Nester, 1991: pp. 44–76).

THE DIMENSIONS OF A NATIONAL INDUSTRIAL POLICY

Observation shows that there are regularities in the ways developed nations support specific industries. These regularities, or dimensions, are a useful way to view the various policies toward industries that advanced nations have adopted. One of the editors of this volume, Professor Jon Pierre, suggested that one potentially useful way of viewing or classifying industrial policies was to make the distinction between "offensive, strategic elements of industrial policy, on the one hand, and defensive, 'bail-out' types of policy on the other." An excellent suggestion and one which will be followed here.

Both offensive and defensive policies are common to most industrialized nations. By offensive policies we mean policies which are designed to develop or enhance an industry's position in the international economy. These industries are often, but not always, in the high-technology arena. Defensive policies are less elegant and less justifiable in today's era of free(er) trade. They are policies designed to protect or revive existing industries and even specific enterprises. They are often the result of intense political pressure to "do something" to preserve jobs.

It is suggested here that there are seven dimensions to the industrial policies of developed nations – three which can be classified as defensive policies and four as offensive.

Defensive policies	Offensive policies
Protectionism	Urban development/
Too Big to Fail	redevelopment
Subsidies	Aggressive unilateralism
	National defense
	High technology

DEFENSIVE POLICIES

Protectionism

Protectionism broadly defined is simply the erection of some form of barrier to free trade. These barriers come in many forms, including protective tariffs, import restrictions, voluntary export restrictions, and other similar obstacles. One clear example of old-fashioned protectionism is George W. Bush's tariffs on imported steel, designed to prop-up America's steel industry.

Too Big to Fail

Too Big to Fail is a policy dimension in response to significant industries, or even firms, whose failure is unacceptable because it would create havoc in the country or in the industry, as the case may be. The most commonly used tool in response to Too Big to Fail is the bailout. Bailout can be in the form of some favored treatment (e.g., special government contract), loan guarantee, or direct cash transfer. Two examples from the United States come immediately to mind: First is America's bailout of the airline industry immediately following the tragedy of 9–11. The second is George H.W. Bush's bailout of the American savings and loan industry.

Subsidies

This dimension of industrial policy was difficult to isolate because subsidies are often tools to achieve other defensive or offensive industrial policy dimensions, and thus are not dimensions themselves (a government subsidy simply directs resources to preferred industries). For example, subsidies were used to support and develop Airbus Industries. But the development of Airbus Industries and its series of Airbus aircraft was an offensive industrial policy designed to bring a new technology (aviation) to the nations supporting Airbus, with the eventual goal of competing with Boeing and the United States.

In the United States, subsidies were originally used as bailout strategies for American agriculture first in 1933 in response to the Great Depression and again in 2002. But these bailouts became permanent industry policies. And this is the distinction. Traditional subsidies are a tool (with a discrete time limit) while subsidies, *in the industrial policy sense*, are essentially permanent.

OFFENSIVE POLICIES

Urban Development/Redevelopment

Policies designed to support and aid the real estate and construction industries are common components of the industrial policies of nations throughout the world. But what is unique about this dimension is that in many cases real estate and construction industries are the (industrial policy) beneficiaries of policies implemented for other purposes. In other words, they are unintended consequences. This has been the case in the United States with President Jimmy Carter's urban policy, Urban Development Action Grants (UDAG), and with Ronald Reagan's economic recovery package, the Economic Recovery and Tax Act of 1981 (ERTA). It may also be the case in Korea (dating back to the 1970s) with the various measures to limit the growth of Seoul and promote balanced regional development.

Aggressive Unilateralism

Aggressive unilateralism represents an assertive trade stance for a home nation in demanding that trading partners reduce barriers to the home country's exports and foreign investments. A classic example of aggressive unilateralism is U.S. President Bill Clinton's 1995 attempt to open the Japanese market to U.S. autos and automotive products. A more recent example is the European Union's efforts to force the United States to remove its steel tariffs and repeal long-standing export subsidies.

Industrial Policy through National Defense

In the United States particularly (although in other nations as well), industrial policy has been a product of defense research and development for decades. Historically, spin-offs into the civilian market from military products has produced these impacts. The aircraft industry is an obvious example. Jet engines were developed by the military during World War II (WWII) and were significantly improved over the next 20 years. The C5A transport project provided the technological breakthrough for the high-bypass-ratio engine used in commercial wide-bodied jets. And, with the KC-135 tanker aircraft, military R&D and procurement reduced the cost of commercial development and tooling for the Boeing 707 (Pascall and Lamson, 1991: pp. 65–73).

While evidence today suggests that the rate of civilian spillover from military spending is less than in the past, it is still significant. Dual use technologies funded by the Defense Advanced Research Projects Agency (DARPA) provide such benefits.

Promoting High Technology Industries

Industrial policy through the development of high technology is the final dimension of industrial policy. The rationale was stated earlier. Technology-intensive industries make special contributions to the long-term health of national economies. In the United States, developing a new generation of automotive vehicles met this criterion. The same is true of the impending development of the mag-lev train.

DEFENSIVE INDUSTRIAL POLICIES

Protectionism as a Dimension of Industrial Policy

Developed nations adopt protectionism as a dimension of their industrial policies when the impacted industries are able to apply sufficient pressure to the political system to potentially affect future electoral outcomes.

Old-fashioned protectionism appears to be creeping back into American and European industrial policies after years of liberal trade actions (multi-lateral free trade agreements). Protectionism here is called old-fashioned because it brings to memory the impacts of the protectionist Tariff Act of 1930 (commonly known as "Smoot-Hawley") in the United States, establishing the highest general tariff rate structure the country has ever experienced. By one estimate, the tariff on dutiable imports, on average, reached 60 percent. Country after country retaliated, driving American exports down from $5.2 billion in 1929 to $1.7 billion in 1933. The Great Depression deepened and became global. Smoot-Hawley is generally acknowledged to be one of the major causes of the Depression (Bingham, 1998: p. 70). The Smoot-Hawley attitude is back with the Democratic (party) candidate for president making serious protectionist noises during the 2004 campaign.

Example. In late 2002, the price of a ton of hot-rolled steel fell below $200; low steel prices, in part, causing massive lay-offs in the American steel industry and culminating in the bankruptcy of 15 steel makers. Steel company executives and union officials claimed they needed trade protection to upgrade their mills and become competitive again.

On Tuesday March 5, 2002, President George W. Bush responded to this pressure and imposed "temporary safeguards" (the administration's term for Tariffs), effective on March 20th, on key steel products to provide relief to those parts of the U.S. steel industry that had been most damaged by import surges. These tariffs ranged from 8 to 30 percent on 10 separate steel products for a period of three years – presumably enough time for the U.S. steel industry to get back on its feet (Rust never sleeps, 2002). While the move was expected, it was somewhat unusual in that, according to a White House news release (www.whitehouse.gov), "Free trade is a cornerstone of President George W. Bush's agenda to help generate jobs for American workers, open markets to American products and services, and spur economic growth" (p. 1).

The tariffs were particularly beneficial to steel companies and workers in three states – Ohio, Pennsylvania, and West Virginia – all of which were closely contested in both the 2000 and 2004 presidential elections. While steel has only about 160,000 workers, its extraordinary political clout comes from its concentration in these three key political states.

The move infuriated the Europeans, as more than one-third of their $4 billion of steel exports to America were hit by the tariffs, prompting a swift complaint to the World Trade Organization (WTO) (the WTO eventually ruled against the tariffs).

In late September 2003, about half way through the tariffs' planned three-year duration, the U.S. International Trade Commission (ITC) issued an assessment of the tariffs' impact. The report concluded that the tariffs had cost the U.S. economy about $30.4 million a year, with steel users facing sharply higher steel prices in the early months of the tariffs.

These steel consuming industries saw their earnings decline by $601 million, while the earnings of steel producers, mining companies, etc., rose by $67.4 million, Thus, the overall economic impact of the tariffs was trivial – costing the economy 0.0003 percent of output (Weisman, "Tariffs Help Lift," 2003).

However, the conclusions were subject to some debate. A study backed by steel-using companies concluded that, through the end of 2000, higher steel prices had cost the country about 200,000 manufacturing jobs.

But the steel producers had their own numbers. A report by University of Maryland business professor, Peter Morici, commissioned by the steel industry, claimed that 16,000 steel jobs were resurrected, more than 30,000 when steel suppliers were included (Allen and Weisman, 2003).

But, in the scheme of things, the studies were virtually irrelevant. In November 2003 the WTO issued its final ruling against the steep steel tariffs President Bush had imposed (ruling them illegal). European Union (EU) Trade Commissioner Pascal Lamy threatened to impose $4 billion in retaliatory tariffs on 1,866 U.S. products if the tariffs were not ended, with $2.2 billion in tariffs to be imposed immediately. The U.S. exports were selected for their own political resonance and included products such as Harley-Davidson motorcycles, Southeastern textiles and Florida citrus fruit (Weisman, EU Trade Negotiator, 2003).

President Bush gave in. On December 4, 2003, Bush revoked the tariffs he had imposed on imported steel, averting a potential trade war with Europe. In a prepared statement, read by his press secretary, the president said "These safeguard measures have now achieved their purpose, and, as a result of changed economic circumstances, it is time to lift them … U.S. steel companies are now once again well-positioned to compete both at home and globally." Minutes after the statement, the European Union cancelled plans to launch the retaliatory $2.2 billion in sanctions (Entous and Palmer, 2003).

But, of course, the steel tariffs were never an economic issue – they were a political issue. From the beginning, Bush's economic advisors had advised against the tariffs, but his political advisors (recognizing the centrality of Ohio, Pennsylvania, and West Virginia to the 2004 presidential election) convinced him to impose the tariffs. By the fall of 2003, however, there was near consensus in the White House that the tariffs should go. The revocation marked a rare about-face for the Bush Administration and the action, although expected, brought angry reactions from labor unions, steel executives, and politicians in the steel-producing states. On the other hand, executives from steel-consuming industries, who had lobbied hard for the tariffs' lifting, praised the action (Weisman, "Bush Rescinds Tariffs," 2003).

Too Big to Fail

The doctrine known as "Too Big to Fail" is an industrial policy dimension adopted by industrialized nations that protects the largest corporations and industries from failure – typically with bailouts.

Too Big to Fail is a policy in response to firms or industries whose dominant position is so large that their failure would create havoc in the industry or the country, as the case may be. This was the case with the 1983 failure of the Continental Illinois Bank. It was such an important part of the banking industry, particularly in the Midwest, that failure was never a possibility.

Too Big to Fail also concerns matters of public convenience. Penn Central Railroad, with all of its commuter trains, was Too Big to Fail because of the millions of commuter passengers on the East Coast. Events like the failure of Penn Central would have created not only economic havoc but political havoc as well. The same can be said of the airline bailout in the United States following 9–11.

Similarly, Chrysler was Too Big to Fail for political reasons. It could not have been allowed to fail because Chrysler parts suppliers, banks, and dealerships were spread throughout the country – virtually in every House and Senate district in America. The pressure on Congress was simply too great to allow failure to occur.

Finally, Too Big to Fail is also a policy response to failing industries whose position in life is so important that failure is unthinkable. This is exactly what happened with the U.S. savings and loan industry.

Example. Examples of Too Big to Fail abound. The case selected here is far from the latest incidence of Too Big to Fail, but was selected because of its enormous proportion. The savings and loan bailout in the United States cost the American taxpayers over $200 billion – an amount equal to about 3 percent of gross domestic product. The savings and loan fiasco forced the closing of about one-third of the S&Ls in the United States.

From the 1930s through the 1960s, savings and loans in the United States grew like weeds, although their functions were limited to lending for home mortgage loans and liabilities restricted almost entirely to savings deposits. Passbook savings accounts were a stable and low-cost source of funds. During this lengthy period it was profitable to "borrow short and lend long." That is, to use short-term savings accounts to fund long-term, fixed interest rate mortgage loans. But, as it turned out, "borrow short and lend long" was a formula for disaster. There were a number of reasons for this (see Bingham, 1998: pp. 55–56), but chief among them was the period of high and volatile interest rates during the late 1970s and early 1980s. This was a period of superinflation. To combat this inflation, the Federal Reserve forced interest rates to unprecedented levels, severely affecting the financial condition of the savings and loan industry. When interest rates skyrocketed, S&L net operating income plummeted. It was here that "borrow short and lend long" came unglued.

The federal government tried to cope with the situation by giving the S&Ls new powers. The Carter administration began, and the Reagan administration accelerated, reductions in regulations in the industry patterned after reductions in government regulations of the airlines, trucking, railroads, and communications. The policy was a disaster.

Throughout most of the 1980s, S&L problems were like the proverbial hot potato – no one wanted to touch it; not the Federal Home Loan Bank Board, not the Reagan administration, not Congress. They all hoped that by buying time the problem would go away. They were counting on deregulation, lower interest rates, and an improved economy, to solve the problem. The Reagan administration stuck its head in the sand and refused to recognize or deal with the extent of the problem. Its only concern was to keep any possible solution off budget.

So the S&L debacle became George (HW) Bush's problem. The election of George Bush to the presidency in November 1988 brought about a change in policy toward the S&Ls and with it a recognition that the problem would not go away. Immediately after Bush was inaugurated in January 1989, his rescue plan, the Financial Institutions Reform, Recovery and Enforcement Act (FIRREA), was passed by Congress and signed into law. The law corrected the mistakes of the president's predecessors.

FIRREA also created the Resolution Trust Corporation (RTC), which would "take over, dissect, bury, and dispense with the sick and dying S&Ls" (Seidman, 1993: p. 195). The RTC took its name from the financial term "resolve," which means to dispose of a firm's assets and reach a final solution for the firm.

Over its lifetime, the RTC resolved all 747 institutions for which it was appointed conservator or receiver. From its inception in August 1989 through the end of 1995, it disposed of assets with a book value of more than $455 billion, or approximately 98 percent, of the assets under its control. Its work essentially complete, the RTC went out of business on January 1, 1996. Its affairs were taken over by the Federal Deposit Insurance Corporation.

William L. Seidman, first head of the RTC, summarizes the debacle:

> The S&L crisis was born in the economic climate of the times. It was nurtured, however, in the fertile ground of politics as usual and the political mentality of "not on my watch." The system may have given rise to the crisis, but human beings, with all their faults, ultimately determined the scope of the debacle. The S&L mistakes resulted in the closing down of one-third of the industry, destroying the agency charged with promoting and insuring it, and costing the American taxpayers around $200 billion, plus interest on that amount, probably forever! No larger financial error appears to be recorded in history (Seidman, 1993: pp. 196–197).

Subsidies as a Dimension of Industrial Policy

Developed nations often have a long history of subsidizing favored industries. This is particularly true when the industry is politically powerful due to its prevalence in society and/or because it has a disproportionate influence in the political system.

One industry that has historically been subsidized in the industrial policy sense (permanently) by a large number of nations is agriculture. Whether it be rice in Asia, beef in Europe, or grain in the United States, agricultural products frequently have permanent subsidies. While this may be partially attributed to the unique structure of the producers (hundreds of thousands of individual decision makers) and the markets, politics always plays the dominant role. Examples shown here are from two very different societies and government structures, but the outcomes are similar. The examples are Japan and the United States.

Examples. **Japan.** Conservative political parties (particularly the Liberal Democratic Party (LDP)) ruled Japan for all but nine months between 1945 and 1993. And, while in 1993 the LDP "lost" its majority and had to form a coalition government, that coalition and the "new" LDP that emerged, have been traditionally conservative.

The LDP dominance is no accident. About 90 percent of all Japanese live in urban areas. But, because of gerrymandering, rural electoral districts, until fairly recently, had been politically weighted as much as three times greater than urban areas, making the farmers and their families and constituents an important LDP voting block (about 70 percent generally vote LDP). They support and follow an iron triangle of agricultural industrial policy composed of the Ministry of Agriculture, Forestry, and Fisheries (MAFF), the National Federation of Farmers, and the LDP Farm Policy Research Group. They are supported by a range of other groups of which the LDP Farm Policy Group is among the most influential.

Given farm support for the LDP, the farming sector is probably the most heavily protected industry in Japan. And it is the Japanese consumers who take the hit. In many cases, food goods of the store shelves in Japan cost five or six times the world market prices.

Permanent agricultural subsidies are a significant component of Japanese farm industry policy. Agricultural price supports account for about one-fourth of MAFF's annual budget, with about 60 or 70 percent of all agricultural products receiving price supports. For the individual farm families these price supports have been a blessing indeed. Largely through income received from supports, farm income has risen from about 70 percent of nonfarm income in 1950, to 90 percent in 1970, 100 percent in 1975, and is about 115 percent today.

A second major component of Japan's agricultural industry policy is protectionism. Nowhere is this more obvious than with rice. The rice market is monopolized by the powerful nokyo (Central Union of Agricultural Cooperatives), which sells about 95 percent of the crop at fixed price – a price about five times the international market level. Rice is heavily protected by both tariffs and import quotas. In fact, Japan justifies its protectionist policies toward rice by claiming it is a central aspect of Japanese national culture (Bingham, 1998: pp. 182–183). Political scientist William Nester concludes that:

> By neoclassical economic measures, Tokyo's farm policies have been an immense failure since protection annually adds $65 billion to Japan's food bill … By neomercantilist measures they have been highly successful, the political trade-off of protectionism for votes has allowed the LDP to remain in office and continue the industrial policies that helped transform Japan from a developing country into the world's manufacturing, financial, and technological powerhouse (Nester, 1991: p. 207).

The United States In the United States, the national government's policy toward the agricultural industry is a product of the industry's historical dominance in society and its present disproportionate influence in the American political system.

Modern American agricultural policy was a product of the Depression and the recovery measures of President Franklin Roosevelt's New Deal. At the time, farmers were a political force to be reckoned with. There were over 6 million farmers in the United States, one-quarter

of the nation's population. The average farm size was 155 acres and farming income was often the only source of household wealth.

In contrast, today there are only 2.2 million American farmers, making up just two percent of the population. Average farm size is now 435 acres, but most commodity production comes from large, mass-producing firms. Farm household income is now about 115 percent of nonfarm income (Allen, 2002).

Yet American farm policy has remained *relatively* unchanged, and very expensive, over the years in spite of a drastically reduced farm population. It is easy to understand farm influence in the 1930s when farmers had such a dominant role in society, but it is not as easy to understand their influence today.

It is because of the peculiarity of America's bicameral legislature that farm influence has remained strong. The 435 members of the U.S. House of Representatives are apportioned based on the states' population. Thus, populous California has 53 representatives while rural North Dakota has 1; New York has 29 while Vermont has 1. But in the upper chamber, the Senate, each state has equal representation – two senators. Thus the most rural state has the same numerical influence as the most populous. So numbers do not always count. In addition, many of the largest states have significant farm areas and thus sympathetic senators – California, Texas, Florida, Illinois, and Ohio, to name a few. Thus farm influence has remained strong.

America's contemporary farm policy tool – price supports – is rooted in the events associated with the end of World War I, but actually began a few years later with the Great Depression. During the decade 1910–1920, American farms prospered, with an increased demand for food from a growing American urban population and from the world demand for food created by the war. But, after the war, food prices plummeted as European producers recovered. American farm leaders then called for a national program to support farm prices.

The Depression gave the farmers what they wanted with the Agricultural Adjustment Act of 1933. The solution to rapidly falling farm incomes was primarily price supports, achieved through dramatic reductions in supply. Supply controls for staple commodities included payments for reduced planting and government storage of market-depressing surpluses when prices fell below a predetermined level. This combination of price supports and supply management, with several modifications, was the essence of federal farm policy through 1996 (Effland, 2000: 23–24).

The Federal Agricultural Improvement and Reform Act (FAIR) of 1996 legislated a dramatic shift in federal assistance to farmers. The Act was in response to both budget-cutting measures in Congress and a desire by farmers for more production flexibility. The hope was to move farmers into a free market system. FAIR removed the link between money income support payments and farm prices by providing for seven annual fixed, but declining "production flexibility contract payments", whereby participating producers would receive government payments largely independent of farm prices. Farmers had much greater flexibility to make planting decisions, with the elimination of acreage idling programs and given the freedom to plant any crop on contract acres. As a result, producers were forced to rely more heavily on the market as a guide for production decisions. Farmers also bore a greater risk because payments to them were fixed and unrelated to market prices.

But the economic situation for farmers changed in the late 1900s and it became clear that American farmers could not succeed in a free market. Thus, in 2002, Congress passed the Farm Security and Rural Investment Act of 2002 which moved farm policy back to where it had historically been. The key features of the Act were a return of direct payment supports for farm products and a series of countercyclical payments to covered commodities whenever the effective price was less than the target price (The 2002 Farm Bill).

OFFENSIVE INDUSTRIAL POLICIES

Aggressive Unilateralism

Developed nations, particularly those with substantial trade deficits, are taking more aggressive action against perceived trade barriers in order to enhance their export markets and slow the movement of jobs offshore.

Aggressive unilateralism is a power play by developed nations to force trading partners to make trade concessions that they do not wish to make. The trade stance is aggressive because it is backed by threats of retaliation. It is unilateral because (1) the home nation unilaterally decides that the actions of a trading partner are unfair, and (2) it requires that its partner unilaterally liberalize without any reciprocal concessions from the home nation (Bayard and Elliott, 1994: p. 1).

Example. One of the most highly publicized *attempts* (more discussion on this later) at aggressive unilateralism over the past several decades was U.S. President Bill Clinton's 1995 actions designed to open Japanese markets to U.S. autos and auto parts, and to convince the Japanese to purchase more U.S. parts for their transplant assembly operations in the United States. The June 1995 agreement was the culmination of almost two years of on-again-off again negotiations in which, ultimately, the threat of retaliation by the United States seems to have played a role in the final reaching of an agreement.

The conflict began on May 6, 1995, when President Clinton's economic advisor recommended that he impose significant sanctions against Japanese imports in retaliation for Tokyo's refusal to open up its auto markets to the United States. The recommendation came the day after negotiations between U.S. Trade Representative (USTR) Mickey Kantor and the MITI (Ministry of International Trade and Industry) Minister Ryutaro Hashimoto broke down. Several days later President Clinton ordered an unfair trade complaint to be filed with the World Trade Organization (WTO). The United States then formally notified the WTO that it would file its case within the next 45 days.

In late May the United States announced that its sanctions for failing to reach an agreement by the end of June would be a 100 percent punitive tariff on 13 Japanese luxury car models. The tariffs, worth about $5.9 billion, would be retroactive to May 20. The U.S. imposed deadline was June 28, 1995.

As has been typical with so many of the U.S.–Japanese negotiations in the past, agreement was not reached until the very last minute – the day before sanctions were to go into effect. The agreement came after three days of intensive talks between Kantor and Hashimoto. With the new agreement in hand, the United States did not impose the threatened sanctions.

In the agreement, the major Japanese car makers, with MITI guidance, announced plans to open up their dealerships to American cars. All five major automakers said that they would reassure their dealers that they are totally free to deal in products of other companies, both at home and abroad. This is a far cry from past practices, where only seven percent of Japanese dealers handle foreign cars.

With regard to autos and parts, Toyota agreed to increase North American production by 200,000 units from 1994 to 1998. Nissan agreed to consider producing transmissions in Tennessee at a future date and will establish a forklift engine plant in the United States with an annual production of 20,000 units. Honda will start up a parts development division for the purchase of after-market parts. Mazda will expand the number of vehicles produced by Ford plants in the United States, and Mitsubishi will invest an additional $300 million in U.S. production facilities (the Japanese companies, in announcing these plans, were quick to claim that these moves were already in the works and were not in response to U.S. pressures).

What were the outcomes that the Clinton Administration expected? Washington estimated that by 1998 Japanese transplants would have increased their auto production in the United States by 550,000 units, increased purchase of U.S. parts by $6.75 billion, and raised the local content of transplant-assembled vehicles to 56 percent. Washington also expected Tokyo to import $6 billion worth of parts for assembly operations in Japan. USTR Kantor was also optimistic about Japan opening its markets to Big Three autos. He said that the number of Japanese dealerships handling

foreign cars should increase by about 200 during the first year of the agreement and should reach 1,000 by the year 2000 (Bingham, 1998: pp. 92–83).

But, of course, very little of this ever occurred, as is often the case with negotiations between the U.S. and Japan. The Japanese market is difficult to crack. Reaching agreements like this U.S.–Japanese Auto Accord of 1995 literally takes years. Then it takes several more years before measurable results can occur. In this there were no significant results, and when the Clinton administration pushed for an explanation, the Japanese reply was that the severe economic downturn in Japan was responsible and not Japanese policy. President Clinton was not willing to push the issue further in the final years of his administration. Nor was George W. Bush – especially after his unhappy experience with the steel industry.

Urban Development/Redevelopment

Industrial policies which ultimately aid in renewal and development of cities are common to industrialized nations. Unlike most other industry policies, however, many of the policies which promote cities, or spur renewal, are the unintended consequences of other policies.

The development of world-class cities has been a crowning achievement of industrialized societies during the 20th century. One only has to visit London, New York, Tokyo, Paris, Berlin, or Seoul to recognize this. Much of the vitality of these and other urban areas is due to government policies promoting cities. This is true not only for world-class cities, but for smaller urban places as well.

Back in 1991, *Washington Post* journalist Joe Garreau examined the development of new urban places in the United States – places he called "Edge Cities." He reported that there were more than 200 new (less than 30 years old) Edge Cities in the United States. But the incredible statistic is: "two thirds of all American office facilities are in Edge Cities, and 80 percent of them have materialized in only the last two decades" (Garreau, 1991:

p. 5). And much of this development has been fostered by the federal government, both through direct subsides for real estate construction and through tax benefits stimulating this development.

It is easy enough to see why governments single out real estate and its related industries for favored treatment. In the United States, real estate employs about 7.6 million people if one includes all of the related activities like finance, construction, building supplies, brick, lumber and the like. And these workers are well represented in all congressional districts.

Example. The example discussed here is different from the other examples in this chapter in that the policy outcome – urban development – was an unintended consequence.

In 1981, the United States was suffering from both high inflation and high interest rates and Ronald Reagan had just been elected president. The Economic Recovery and Tax Act of 1981 (ERTA) was one of the new administration's first legislative initiatives and an example of its supply-side policies. It was designed to reduce tax rates and thus stimulate the economy to recover from a serious recession. Both inflation and interest rates were very high and the unemployment rate had been rising. Productivity and savings were stagnant.

The objective of ERTA was to upgrade the nation's industrial base, stimulate productivity and new business, lower personal taxes, and restrain the growth of the federal government. As a result of ERTA's focus on investment, the real estate sector of the economy was a major beneficiary of the law. ERTA included provisions that provided incentives for real estate investors by reducing their tax liabilities. The Act also reduced the marginal rate on long-term capital gains.

It turned real estate into a true "tax shelter." A tax shelter in real estate is property with the following characteristics: (1) it can be depreciated over a shorter period of time than its useful life, (2) when sold, the profit will be taxed as a capital gain, and (3) the tax loss deducted (probably over several years) is greater than the amount of cash that the investor has in the deal.[1]

These changes significantly enhanced the tax incentives for investing in real estate and,

consequently, the real estate sector of the economy boomed. The result was an astonishing boom in urban development. Unfortunately, it also resulted in significant overbuilding in the real estate sector, resulting in high vacancy rates, foreclosures, and the savings and loan crisis discussed earlier. For example, in terms of commercial space, from 1983 to 1986 there were 937 million square feet in new construction starts but the market could absorb only 575 million square feet. In the residential market the apartment vacancy rate went from 5.5 percent in the second quarter of 1984 to 6.9 percent in the first quarter of 1986. Five years after ERTA, Congress would conclude that the ERTA tax incentives had contributed to the overbuilding of office space, high vacancy rates, and distorted business decisions at all levels (Veres, 1986: 62–63).

What ERTA did was give several million wealthy people the opportunity to invest in real estate that actually produced a large cash return, but, once depreciation was taken, produced a paper loss that individuals then used to reduce their reported ordinary income and thus their taxes. These tax shelters led to unfairness and inefficiencies in the tax structure. Although these tax shelters could be employed through a number of different legal entities, limited partnerships became the main vehicle. They were attractive mainly because of the limited liability of the partners (the number of limited partners reporting losses on their tax returns went from 2.55 million in 1981 to 5.11 million in 1986 (with $35.5 billion in losses). One thing about wealthy Americans – they are quick learners).

But limited partnerships and high-income individuals were not alone in skimming the Treasury; corporations were also able to take advantage of these tax preferences to reduce their tax liabilities. Major U.S. corporations were significantly reducing their tax liabilities, paying little or no federal income taxes, while their financial reports to stockholders showed strong earnings.

As time progressed, Congress, and even the Reagan administration, began to find politically unacceptable inequities in ERTA. The generally accepted view was that ERTA had created a situation whereby middle-income Americans were carrying an unfair share of the tax burden and were unable to take advantage of the ERTA tax shelters. By the mid-1980s, the Reagan administration and congressional leaders believed that broad-based tax reform was necessary to restore fairness to the tax system. The result was the Tax Reform Act of 1986 (TRA), called "the most significant change in the Federal income tax system since broad-based taxation was introduced during World War II (California Department of Real Estate, 1991: p. 19).

This all leads to one unmistakable conclusion, ERTA was an industry policy initiated by the Reagan administration. It was successful in moving investment into activities that, without ERTA, would not have occurred – a clear example of industrial policy, perhaps unintended, but industrial policy nevertheless. The unfortunate thing was that ERTA produced a boom in real estate development, in which many S&Ls, along with banks and insurance companies, experienced enormous losses when the inevitable bust occurred.

Industrial Policy through National Defense

Those developed nations with a strong defense industry use that industry to commercialize new and innovative high-technology products for eventual use in the civilian economy.

There is no question but that defense research, at least in the past, has provided a technological benefit to the nations engaged in it. And yet it creates its own controversies. The impact of government funding of military R&D has long been of concern to policymakers. Military R&D is thought to distort national research capacity in ways that damage national economic competitiveness. In terms of spending alone, for example, in the United States the military controls about 12 percent of basic research, 15 percent of applied research, and 45 percent of development. Historically, the most active aspect of this debate is the rate of spin-offs into the civilian market from military

products. Because of the national impact of spin-offs, one United States Department of Defense Agency, the Defense Advanced Research Projects Agency (DARPA), has had an important role in America's industrial policy.

Example. In a building located a few miles from the Pentagon, a few hundred scientists and engineers are in the industrial policy business. DARPA project managers essentially hire private companies and academics to do research. Spending about $100 million a year on basic research makes DARPA America's premier venture capital company. DARPA searches the nation for new technologies with military potential. When it identifies a promising new concept or product, DARPA contracts out research in the area to universities, government labs, and private corporations. The private firms provide research to fulfill DARPA's military needs, but are free to fully exploit commercial applications of any unclassified research results.

The results of the majority of the agency's projects fall into the "dual use" category – whereby innovations have both important defense and civilian technologies. The Internet and global positioning systems (GPS) are both examples.

During the early and mid-1990s, flat panel displays were one of the technologies of interest to DARPA. As we all now know, flat panel displays (FPDs) are thin electronic devices that present images without the bulk of a picture tube. Flat panel displays have allowed the development of devices such as digital wristwatches, video cameras, the laptop and notebook computers, and of course, high-definition television (HDTV) – televisions that are so light and thin that they can be hung on a wall. FPDs are also critical to the military. They are used in displays in aircraft, ships, and vehicles. While there are over 50 firms worldwide producing flat panel displays, the U.S. industry remains quite small. No U.S. firm produces FPDs for the commercial market.

In 1989, DARPA initiated the High-Definition Systems (HDS) program. The HDS program was designed to develop a domestic capability to manufacture FPDs by bringing together firms from three levels of the industry;

materials and equipment, display manufacturers, and end users. The first phase (from 1990 to 1992) focused on developing the materials and equipment sector of the industry and also supported research into advanced displays technologies. Phase two of the program began in 1993 with the objective of adding manufacturing testbeds to the ongoing R&D programs. These awards were made in 1993 and 1994.

Then the big push began – the National Flat Panel Display Initiative (NFPDI), announced in April 1994. The government would spend $587 million over the next five years to promote U.S. *manufacturing* of flat panel displays. NFPDI was ostensibly initiated to meet defense needs by developing a high-volume commercial flat panel display industry. While the justification related to national security, the initiative came under the administration's dual use policy. This policy called for DoD to use commercial capabilities wherever possible and to focus on capabilities that would support both defense and the commercial technology base. The thrust of NFPDI was threefold: continuation of the DARPA R&D and testbed programs, awarding grants to firms planning to manufacture flat panel displays, and applying DoD funding to procurement programs if they use domestic flat panel displays. The goal of the initiative was to develop a flat panel display industry in the United States equaling 15 percent of world production by the end of the decade (from about 5 percent). The key, of course, was manufacturing. The innovation in the initiative was an explicit plan to encourage new production facilities rather than just new R&D efforts.

The U.S. was quite late with its initiative. Dr. Lance Glasser, head of DARPAs Electronic Systems Technology Office, the office responsible for the initiative, called the initiative "a long shot. It's a hedge. We should have started in 1983 but we missed it. Now we are trying to repatriate a technology. We have to learn how to do that, because each year there are more candidates for repatriation. The problem now is to get the big users on board" (Lodge and Novak, 1995: p. 14). Unfortunately the initiative failed and there is no high-volume commercial flat panel display manufacturer in the United States.

Developing High-Technology Industries

Developing high-technology industries is an industrial policy of most developed nations because of the special benefits high-technology brings to society.

High-technology industries bring special benefits to their host nations. They lead to well-paid workforces, increased educational levels of the population, promote exports, and a host of other benefits. As Laura Tyson states:

> ... because technology-intensive industries finance a disproportionate share of the nation's R&D spending, there is a strong presumption ... that they generate positive externalities for the rest of the economy (Tyson, 1993: p. 12).

Example. In September, 1993, President Bill Clinton initiated the *Partnership for a New Generation of Vehicles* (PNGV) program, a cooperative research and development (R&D) program between the U.S. government and a consortium of the big-three auto manufacturers, the United States Council for Automotive Research (USCAR). The auto industry was a good place to start an industrial initiative for the new Clinton/Gore administration. For one thing, the industry accounted for almost 5 percent of U.S. gross domestic product, with more than 13 million Americans employed in motor vehicle-related industries (PNGV, 1994: p. 2). For another, the program was designed to promote the national interest and correct the industry's negative externalities. That is, it was in America's best interest to have a fuel-efficient, non-polluting automobile, but this was not necessarily in the best interests of the auto companies. Thus these objectives would not be realized through the marketplace alone. Also, success in this endeavor would vault U.S. autos over their international competitors and significantly increase American exports.

The PNGV effort created a unique government and industry partnership, with the goal of strengthening U.S. competitiveness by developing technologies for a new generation of vehicles (PNGV, 1995). The vehicles were conceived of as using new technologies (not improved existing technologies) to reduce national gasoline consumption and carbon dioxide emissions. To have this substantial impact the vehicles must be sold in high volume. This required that:

> they meet all emission and safety requirements and include all of the characteristics that result in strong customer appeal. In addition to product redesign the program embraced research aimed at improving the effectiveness of the broad manufacturing enterprise, including everything from the development of new analytical tools to the use of new materials and manufacturing processes (NRC, 2001: p. 13).

The specific objectives of the program were:

Goal 1. Significantly improve national competitiveness in manufacturing for future generations of vehicles. Improve the productivity of the U.S. manufacturing base by significantly upgrading U.S. manufacturing technology, including the adoption of agile and flexible manufacturing and reduction of costs and lead times, while reducing the environmental impact and improving quality.

Goal 2. Implement commercially viable innovations from ongoing research on conventional vehicles. Pursue technology advances that can lead to improvement s in fuel efficiency and reductions in the emissions of standard vehicle designs, while pursuing advances to maintain safety performance. Research will focus on technologies that reduce the demand for energy from the engine and drivetrain. Throughout the research program the industry has pledged to apply those commercially viable technologies resulting from this research that would be expected to increase significantly vehicle fuel efficiency and improve emissions.

Goal 3. Develop vehicles to achieve up to three times the fuel efficiency of comparable 1994 family sedans. Increase vehicle fuel efficiency up to three times that of the average 1994 Concorde/Taurus/Lumina automobiles, with equivalent cost of ownership adjusted for economics (NRC, 2001: p. 14).

At program inception, three milestones were established: (1) a technology selection in 1997, (2) concept vehicles in 2000, and (3) production/prototype vehicles in 2004. At the end of 1997, PNGV made its technology selections. The year 2000 concept vehicle goal was met when the three manufacturers each introduced concept cars – the Daimler/Chrysler ESX3, the Ford Prodigy, and the General Motors Precept. Each company adopted a different approach to their vehicles, although there were some significant PNGV-related commonalities. All three concept vehicles utilized hybrid-electric power trains designed around small, turbo charged, compression-ignition direct-injection (CIDI)

engines, using diesel fuel. All three incorporated significant technical advances developed in the PNGV program to reduce the energy used to propel the vehicle (NRC, 2001: pp. 1–19).

But, by 2001, in spite of its successes, the program was in trouble. It became clear that all of the elements of Goal 3 (the heart of the program) would not be met in production/prototype vehicles in 2004. First, were problems with the engine. From the beginning, the power train with the highest probability of achieving the 80 mpg fuel target was the CIDI engine. But, in 1999, about midway through the program, the Environmental Protection Agency (EPA) promulgated new admission standards substantially more stringent than those at the start of the program, requiring a radically better emission control technology. The required after-treatment devices would significantly degrade the efficiency of the CIDI engine and increase its cost.

Second, the automotive market changed substantially during the program. Light trucks and SUVs now account for about 50 percent of the automotive market and these vehicles are heavier and bigger than automobiles and have lower fuel economy. Why produce a fuel efficient sedan if no one wants to buy it?

Finally, the National Research Council committee charged with evaluating the program reports that the cost premium of a PNGV-type vehicle with a fuel economy close to 80 mpg would be several thousand dollars more than a competing conventional vehicle. The new vehicles would simply not be cost-competitive (ibid.).

But, on the bright side, Toyota and Honda have already introduced hybrid-electric vehicles; the Toyota Prius and the Honda Insight. And Ford, General Motors, and Chrysler all planned to introduce some form of hybrid-electric vehicle in 2004 (although it had not occurred as of this writing).

In late 2002, following critical interpretations of the NRC reports, President George W. Bush announced that his FY 2003 budget proposal directed that PNGV be terminated and that research be transferred from the Department of Commerce to the Department of Energy in a new Freedom Cooperative

Automotive Research Program (Freedom CAR) with a focus on fuel cells (U.S. Department of Energy, December 2002) (fuel cells were already a significant part of PNGV). This meant a move from high mileage automotive technologies with a short-term payoff to a program which uses hydrogen as a fuel and will take years, or even decades, to bring to market.

CONCLUSIONS

In an earlier work on industrial policy in the United States, the author wrote:

> George [HW] Bush announced to the world that he did not have an industrial policy. Presumably Jimmy Carter and Ronald Reagan would have said the same thing of themselves. Even Bill Clinton, who is consistently more active in promoting specific industries than any of his three predecessors, would presumably also deny that he has an industrial policy. And all four would be correct to some degree. As presidents, they never articulated a coherent and comprehensive industrial policy.
>
> And yet, while these presidents may not have had an industrial policy, the country they have governed certainly does, and it is actually coherent and reasonable.
>
> But the presidents would not be alone in thinking that the United States lacked an industrial policy. Much of the policy community has been vocal in its criticism of any government efforts at industrial development. Mainstream economists are critical because these proposals usually violate some of their theories. Conservatives are critical because they see industrial policy as nothing more than meddling with the free enterprise system – the only "perfect" system known to humankind. Liberals are not much happier. They see industrial policy efforts as disconnected and uncoordinated, sometimes working at cross purposes (Bingham, 1998: p. 151).

And, while the author has limited knowledge of industrial policy systems beyond the United States, the above is undoubtedly true in many industrialized societies.

This chapter has sought to identify the dimensions of industrial policies in developed nations. Three defensive dimensions and four offensive dimensions have been identified. While most of these have been discovered while examining United States industry policies, they undoubtedly hold elsewhere in the developed world. This is not to suggest that the seven dimensions are the totality of industrial policy dimensions. There are probably others which the author has not discovered.

But there are some conclusions which can be reached through the dimensions and case studies presented here. First, industrial policies are pragmatic, not ideological. Conservative American presidents were equally at home using the policy dimensions as liberals. While they spoke one way and acted in another, the actions they took had very practical hoped-for outcomes.

Advanced industrial societies will adopt defensive industrial policies to protect their globally inefficient/ineffective industries for political and not economic reasons. This was very clear in the discussion of President George W. Bush's decision to protect the U.S. steel industry in 2002. The three large steel-producing states of Pennsylvania, Ohio, and West Virginia were critical to his election in 2000 and were also critical in 2004 (Bush won Ohio and West Virginial). His political advisors recommend for the tariffs while his economic advisors recommended against. And when he removed the tariffs two years later it was because of the political pressure from the steel-using states (e.g., Ohio), also critical to Bush's 2004 reelection effort.

Finally, it appears that economic logic, and less so political considerations, are the driving forces behind the adoption of offensive industrial policy dimensions. Offensive policies really seem to be good for the host nation. There was compelling economic logic behind Bill Clinton's PNGV program. A fuel efficient car is good for the United States, although it did nothing for the auto makers. There was also compelling logic in George Bush's replacement of PNGV with the FreedomCAR program – at least at the time it was adopted.

Yet one must be careful not to read too much into industrial policies. They do not impact on all industries in a nation – just a few. And those few industries, while important, are hardly at the heart of economic growth or decline. Industrial policies may be economically or politically necessary, but they are used sparingly as components of a nation's total economic policy. As such, they have a small but vital place in developed nations' economic arsenals.

NOTE

1. Details are shown in Bingham, 1998: pp. 97–105.

REFERENCES

Entous, Adam and Doug Palmer, "Bush Ends Steel Tariffs, Averting Trade War," (December, 2003) www.dailynews.att.net.

Allen, Mark "Bush Gets Up Early to Sign Farm Bill," *Washington Post* (May 13, 2002), pp. D1, D3.

Allen, Mike and Jonathan Weisman, "Steel Tariffs Appear to Have Backfired on Bush," *Washington Post* (September 19, 2003), pp. A1, A16.

Effland, Anne B. W. "U.S. Farm Policy: The First 200 Years," *Agricultural Outlook* (March, 2000) 21–25.

Bingham, Richard D. *Industrial Policy American Style: From Hamilton to HDTV* (Armonk, NY: M.E. Sharpe, 1998).

Bayard, Thomas O. and Kimberly Ann Elliott, *Reciprocity and Retaliation in U.S. Trade Policy* (Washington, DC: Institute for International Economics, 1994).

California Department of Real Estate, *The Impacts of Tax Reform on Real Estate Investment in California* (Sacramento, CA: California Department of Real Estate, December 1991).

Chamberlain, John *The American States* (New York: Carrick and Evans, 1941).

Prestowitz, Clyde V. Jr., *Trading Places: How We Allowed Japan to Take the Lead* (New York: Basic Books, 1988).

Orden, David Robert Paarlberg, and Terry Roe, *Policy Reform in American Agriculture: Analysis and Prognosis* (Chicago, IL: University of Chicago Press, 1999).

Garreau, Joel *Edge City: Life on the New Frontier* (New York: Doubleday/Anchor Books, 1991).

Graham, Otis Jr., *Losing Time: The Industrial Policy Debate* (Cambridge, MA: Harvard University Press, 1992).

Lodge, George C. *Perestroika for America: Restructuring U.S. Business-Government Relations for Competitiveness in the World Economy* (Boston, MA: Harvard Business School Press, 1990).

Lodge, George C. and Sharon Novak, "The Flat Panel Display Initiative," (Boston, MS: Harvard Business School, April 27, 1995).

Pascall, Glenn R. and Richard D. Lamson, *Beyond Guns and Butter: Recapturing America's Economic Momentum after a Military Decade* (Washington, DC: Brasser's, 1991).

Weisman, Jonathan "Bush Rescinds Tariffs on Steel," *Washington Post* (December 5, 2003), pp. A1, A10.

Weisman, Jonathan "EU Trade negotiator Unyielding on Subsidies," *Washington Post* (November 5, 2003), pp. E1, E10.

Weisman, Jonathan "Tariffs Help Lift U.S. Steel Industry, Trade Panel Reports," *Washington Post* (September 21, 2003), pp. A12–A13.

Tyson, Laura D'Andrea *Who's Bashing Whom? Trade Conflict in High-Technology Industries* (Washington, DC: Institute for International Economics, 1993).

Nester, William R. *Japanese Industrial Targeting: The Neomercantilist Path to Economic Superpower* (New York: St. Martin's Press, 1991).

NRC (National Research Council), *Review of the Research Program of the Partnership for a New Generation of Vehicles, Seventh Report* (Washington, DC: National Academy Press, 2001).

PNGV (Partnership for a New Generation of Vehicles) *Program Plan* (Washington, DC: U.S. Department of Commerce, July, 1994).

PNGV *Program Plan* (Washington, DC: U.S. Department of Commerce, November 29, 1995).

"Rust never sleeps," *The Economist* (March 7, 2002). www.economist.com/displaystory.cfm?story.

Veres, Robert "The Sunset Hour," *Financial Planning* 15 (July, 1986) 56–65.

Standing Committee to Review the Research Program of the Partnership for a New Generation of Vehicles, Transportation Research Board, National Research Council, *Review of the Research Program of the Partnership for a New Generation of Vehicles: Seventh Report* (Washington, DC: National Academy Press, 2001).

U.S. Department of Energy, Office of Transportation Technology, "FreedomCAR: Restructuring the Partnership for a New Generation of Vehicles," www.ott.doe.gov/freedom_car_ fact_sheet.shtml, December, 2002. www.whitehouse.gov/infocus/steel/index.html.

Seidman, William L. *Full Faith and Credit: The Great S&L Debacle and Other Washington Sagas* (New York: Times Books, 1993).

18

Agriculture and Food

WYN GRANT

Agriculture and food policy is characterized by its simultaneous exceptionality and centrality. Exceptionality is to be found in the persistence of high levels of subsidy of agricultural production in many countries of the world, ranging, from Japan to the United States. It is also to be found in the high sensitivity of consumers to any perceived risk associated with food, even if the actual level of risk is much lower than that encountered in many everyday activities. 'You are what you eat' is a frequently repeated mantra and citizens expect wholesome and affordable food to be readily available. 'Unlike other commodities ... food isn't viewed, read, played or worn. It enters the body and becomes part of the consumer' (Schlosser, 2002: 10). As new issues such as obesity, originating in health policy, enter into discussions of food policy, the centrality of the policy domain is enhanced. The controversy about genetically modified (GM) crops has also enhanced the visibility of discussions of agriculture and food policy. However, although agriculture and food policy has a number of special features, it is not so distinctive that it cannot be used to illustrate more general points about the policy-making process. It is evident that many of the processes of internationalization and globalization observable in many other policy sectors can also be found in agriculture and food, even if there is considerable uncertainty and much

contestation about the nature and extent of the changes taking place (Coleman, Josling and Grant, 2004).

THE POLITICS OF PRODUCTION

Agriculture and food was for a long time the prototypical example of the politics of production and it should be emphasized that many of these features of the policy-making process have not disappeared, even if they have been increasingly eroded and challenged. A politics of production is concerned with the organization of the production process and the battle about who should benefit from the surplus value that is generated. In many sectors, it was a battle between employers and employees, but agricultural workers have generally been a weakly organized group, a few exceptions aside. Moreover, production in farming has often been dominated by the 'family farm', although this as much an ideological and rhetorical label as it is a clearly defined analytical construct. Many family farms, particularly in countries where large-scale farming is common, such as Australia and the United States, have developed into family controlled corporations that have moved upwards into various forms of food processing. 'Traditional' family farms still exist, especially in Europe, but they are often able to survive because family labor is not fully costed or because the farmer has diversified into on or off farm businesses, or the farmer's partner (still most usually a woman) works off the farm.

The politics of production in agriculture was usually characterized by tightly knit policy communities in which farming interests were the policy makers and consumers and other actors were the policy takers. They were typically organized around an agriculture department in government which had a close and clientilistic relationship with a farmers' organization or organizations, usually dominated by larger-scale farmers. The pattern in the United States was somewhat different because of the importance of commodity rather than general farmers' organizations and the significance of committees and sub-committees in the legislature in the policy-making process. However, the key point was that the complexity and distinctiveness of the policy-making process made it very difficult for outsiders to have an effective impact on the decisions that were taken. This was exemplified by the Common Agricultural Policy (CAP) of the European Union (EU), where decisions are processed through a Special Committee on Agriculture and a tightly knit club-like Council of Agriculture Ministers, with the details of the policy being handled by Management Committees accessible to special interests.

This politics of production has by no means disappeared. Evidence of its continuation is to be found in the high level of producer subsidies still provided to agriculture in most developed countries (see Table 1) and the way in which the United States backed away from a more market oriented approach to agriculture embodied in the 1996 Federal Agriculture Improvement and Reform Act when the sector encountered a period of crisis. Nevertheless, the traditional politics of production has been challenged on a number of fronts. The budgetary burden of the CAP became so great in the 1980s that it threatened to bankrupt the EU and a number of significant adjustments were made to policy. The accession of ten new member states to the EU in 2004 promised a new set of budgetary challenges to the CAP,

Table 18.1 *Producer support estimates as a percentage of farm income by selected countries (2002 provisional)*

Australia	5%
Canada	20%
European Union	36%
Japan	59%
New Zealand	1%
Norway	71%
Switzerland	75%
United States	19%
OECD average	31%

Source: Organization for Economic Cooperation and Development

although these were ameliorated in the medium term by the phasing in of subsidies in the accession states. Budgetary pressures, however, rarely provide a sustained form of pressure for change in farm policies. Other actors soon lose interest in the complexities of farm policy and it is often possible to come up with a policy 'fudge' that delivers less than it promises and is misunderstood by those outside the agricultural policy community.

Trade policy brings a new set of actors into consideration of agricultural policy issues. Industrial and other business interests are ultimately unwilling to see trade policy negotiations wrecked by agricultural policy issues and urge national heads of government to become involved in bringing about a solution. Before the Uruguay Round of trade negotiations, agriculture was effectively excluded from the General Agreement on Tariffs and Trade (GATT), largely at the behest of the two leading agricultural powers, the United States and the EU. The negotiations in the Uruguay Round systematically addressed agricultural issues for the first time. Although some changes were made in tariffs and agricultural subsidies, what was important was the conclusion of an Agreement on Agriculture which embedded agricultural trade issues as an agenda item for the new World Trade Organization (WTO). The agricultural negotiations in the Uruguay Round were effectively concluded by a series of private deals between the US and the EU with France playing a key role. This power duopoly was viewed less tolerantly by other WTO members in the Doha Round negotiations, which finally got under way after the collapse of the 1999 Seattle ministerials. The Cairns Group of agricultural exporting countries led by Australia continued to seek to shape policy. They were joined by a new group of emerging countries led by Brazil, India and China, known as G-20 or G-21 (the membership varied). The long run outcome is likely to be continued pressure from the Global South on the EU, Japan, the US and Canada to lower the protectionist barriers and generous subsidies they provide for their domestic agricultures. This in turn would further undermine the traditional politics of production.

Evidence of the erosion of the traditional politics of production is to be found in the weakening of the traditional domestic politics duopoly of an agriculture department in government closely linked to a national farm organization. Most countries still retain an agriculture department (and the EU DG Agri), a situation that gives agriculture a privileged position in relation to other sectors of industry. It means that agriculture has its own voice within government and the agriculture department usually also has a key role in the farm related aspects of international trade negotiations. However, there is an emergent trend for traditional agriculture departments to be replaced by ministries with a much broader mandate. Thus, in Britain the Ministry of Agriculture, Fisheries and Food was replaced by a Department of Environment, Food and Rural Affairs (Defra), sometimes referred to by farmers as the Department for the Extinction of Farming and Rural Activity. A similar development has taken place in Germany, with the formation of a new ministry giving a greater emphasis to food quality and safety and consumer concerns. There has also been a trend in Europe, in part influenced by the model of the US Food and Drug Administration, to create new food safety agencies separate from the agriculture ministry, such as the Food Standards Agency in Britain. These are matched by a new EU level food safety agency, the European Food Safety Authority, although its role is confined to risk assessment.

The traditional farm organizations persist and, given that farm ministries survive in most countries and that the generous provision of subsidies continues, might seem to be as influential as ever. However, there is some evidence of a process of 'hollowing out' of these organizations. As the number of farmers decline, it is sometimes difficult to maintain the levels of resources necessary to sustain an effective role in the policy-making process. Staff numbers may not appear to decline that much, but often experienced staff members may be replaced by inexperienced recent graduates hired on low salaries. One survival strategy might be to transform farm organizations into more broadly based bodies looking after rural interests, recruiting the growing numbers of 'hobby farmers' and other countryside dwellers. However, that can set up new tensions within the organization over policy that then hampers its effectiveness.

More moderate farm organizations that based their strategy on a dialog with government often find themselves increasingly challenged by more militant movements, led by farmers who have particularly suffered from processes of change, often smaller scale farmers. This has long been a feature of farm politics in France, but the more militant bodies seemed to have gained even more ground, bolstered by the use of popular anti-globalization discourses. In Britain, the National Farmers' Union (the NFU) offered the classic example of an 'insider' group locked in a close relationship with government. However, the emergence of Defra, and the hard financial times experienced by some farmers, led to an increase in questioning of this strategy and the emergence of a direct action group based on the French model, Farmers for Action. The NFU decided to move its headquarters out of London and signalled that it would move away from its traditional 'insider' strategy.

The traditional production oriented policy community has increasingly been challenged by groups emerging from a politics of collective consumption. Their agendas come from outside farming: the environment; health; global social justice. Because they do not share the assumptions that have underpinned agriculture and food policy for so long, they are able to challenge the way in which issues have been framed and to penetrate and disrupt issue networks based on production based paradigms of policy. Later in the chapter, three sets of issues that have been raised by these new actors are considered: food safety; obesity; and environmental issues. It is first necessary to place public policy in the area of agriculture and food in the context of the other influences on policy outcomes and the efficacy of policy itself.

THE DRIVERS OF POLICY

What happens in the area of agriculture and food is influenced by four main drivers of policy:

- Technology
- Market structure
- Consumer preferences
- Public policy

Technology

Let us consider each of these drivers in turn. Technology has had a major impact on the ways in which food is grown, processed and delivered to the consumer. The mechanization of agriculture, involving the replacement of human, horse and oxen power by tractors and combine harvesters, a process not complete in all parts of the world, had a major effect on levels of agricultural productivity. It can also have a profound effect on the nature of the product that the consumer is offered, as the shape, texture and content of a natural product may have to be changed to make it amenable to mechanical harvesting and transportation to distant markets. Technology, however, extends far beyond the use of mechanical power to sow and harvest crops. It embraces the shift from hand to automated forms of milking; the development of new seeds and new varieties of livestock; and the deployment of new veterinary drugs to combat animal diseases. There was also an important 'chemical revolution' in agriculture involving the widespread use of fertilizers and various types of agrochemical to deal with plant diseases, insect pests, etc. Most controversially, it involves the use of genetic

modification technologies to create new crops, new drugs and potentially new breeds of animal. There have also been important transformations in the technology of food processing, starting with canning and bottling and moving on through the development of frozen foods that met the growing need of consumers for convenience foods. More recent technologies such as irradiation have proved too controversial to deploy. In many ways, however, food processing represents a relatively mature set of technologies and the technological frontier is to be found in seeds, crops and livestock.

Under the politics of production, technology was seen as a benefactor from a public policy perspective. Considerable investments were made by national governments in demonstration farms and teams of field agents to ensure that new innovations were disseminated to farmers as quickly and as effectively as possible. The development of a more technologically intensive agriculture also had a transformative effect on its politics. Commentators are often puzzled why a sector as economically small as agriculture in advanced countries should nevertheless exert considerable political influence. There are a number of reasons why this is the case, but one that is often overlooked is the extent to which the suppliers of agriculture are linked to its economic fate. These include the multinational firms who manufacture various farms of farm machinery, agrochemicals and veterinary drugs, as well as the increasingly concentrated group of firms who provide seeds. At a national and international level, these firms and their representative organizations can supplement the lobbying activities of farmers' associations. At a local level, their representatives, along with other service providers to agriculture such as accountants, auctioneers and lawyers, may well identify with the agriculture community to the extent that they effectively form part of the 'farm vote'.

Market Structure

Changes in market structure have seen power flow down the food chain from farmers to processors and retailers. Although there are some very large scale farmers who are able to engage in vertical integration, the typical farmer is not large enough to shape the market and is essentially a price taker rather than a price maker. Even for a large scale farmer, very small fluctuations in price can have a big effect on profitability. For most farmers, farming is a high volume, low margin business. Despite technological advances, farming is very susceptible to variations in the weather, and if global warming leads to more volatile weather patterns, these effects could be enhanced. Weather variations can lead to production cycles. In one year, favorable weather conditions increase output and the price falls. In the following year, farmers plant less of the crop in response and the price rises, and so the cycle continues. It was the need to dampen down these cycles that was one of the factors initially prompting government intervention in agriculture, although the policies then created went far beyond simple 'safety nets' which, in any case, could in principle be provided by insurance markets.

Another reason for government intervention in agriculture was to protect potentially vulnerable farmers against oligopolistic processors, particularly in dairying. The deregulation of dairy markets, after an initial competition for contracts, has often left dairy farmers in a much less strong market position. More generally, the trend towards multinational organization of food processing has continued to exploit economies of scale and the exploitation of brands, a key investment in food processing and retailing. These Fordist forms of standardized production are, however, complemented by post-Fordist production of high quality, high value added products occupying market niches and often with a strong regional identification. 'In terms of global market concentration, food and agricultural industries are less dominated by internationally coordinated production systems linked through mechanisms such as common ownership or strategic alliances, compared with industries such as electronics, automobiles, energy production and chemicals' (Pritchard and Burch, 2003: 254). As Pritchard and Burch point out, Nestlé is the largest food

company in the world but ranked only 59th in terms of sales in the year 2000. Of course, any account of market structure would have to also take account of the role of major trading companies such as Cargill that play a key role in grain markets. Processors themselves have to be to some extent eclipsed by retailers, most notably in Britain which has a highly concentrated food retailing sector. Retailers are then able to drive down profit margins, impose conditions for access to shelf space and keep deliveries waiting until they are ready for them. There are also incipient trends towards globalization in food retailing, although the opportunities are constrained by differences in consumer preferences and the significance of local land use and other laws, some of which are designed to protect smaller-scale, domestic retailers.

An important development has been the increasing importance of global supply chains which can tie, say, apple producers in South Africa to supermarkets in Britain where consumers are reassured that products are air freighted for freshness. These supply chains ensure that consumer demands for the availability of fresh products out of season is met. The tomato is a good lens for these developments, given its ubiquity both as a fresh product used extensively in salads and increasingly seen as having health giving properties. It is also used as the basis for tomato soup, juice and ketchup converted into tomato paste, a highly tradeable product, which is used extensively in a number of popular food products such as pizza. Nevertheless, the analysis of the industry by Pritchard and Burch (2003: 260) leads them to the conclusion that 'Whereas the dimensions and importance of global restructuring in this industry are profound, changes are occurring within the contexts of production–consumption complexes that remain organized at national or regional scales'. They argue (2003: xi) that 'Global agri-food restructuring needs to be understood as an intricate set of processes operating at many scales, and on many levels, rather than as a unilateral shift towards a single global marketplace'. Globalization in agriculture and food is an emergent and contested paradigm with a number of outcomes possible (Coleman, Grant and Josling, 2004).

Consumer Preferences

Consumer preferences are not shaped in a vacuum. Considerable sums of money are spent on market research and advertising in an effort to convince consumers of the merits of a particular product. Nevertheless, consumer preferences are shaped by long term shifts in the structure of society. Although the 'traditional' American family model of the 1950s may have been as much image as reality, clearly a different pattern of demand for food is generated when the family sits down together for a meal carefully prepared by a woman for whom cooking is viewed as a key component of her role as a 'housewife' and mother. Gender roles have changed, as have family structures, and, despite the promise of automation, people's lives in developed countries have become more subject to time pressures. Meals are less likely to be taken by a family together and 'grazing' and 'snacking' is a more common practice. Ease of preparation of foods becomes a key consideration, while snacking habits create demands for different types of foods. The proportion of foods that is 'catered' has also generally increased, not so much through traditional restaurant sit down meals, but through fast food outlets, 'takeaways' or the delivery of products such as pizzas. As consumers have travelled more, their tastes have become more cosmopolitan and regional cuisines have been introduced in other parts of the world, although usually in a high moderated form. 'Chinese' restaurants are ubiquitous in northern countries, but what they generally are is a moderated version of a particular regional (usually Cantonese) cuisine which is a very different experience from eating a meal in, say, Kunming (although one could use the local Kentucky fried chicken outlet there).

Even popular diets can have an effect on consumption patterns, with the Atkins diet having a significant depressing effect on demand for bread and potatoes in North America and northern Europe. Concerns about food safety, in the wake of the BSE episode and other incidents, have led to a rapidly growing demand for organic products, although there is no evidence that they are healthier than conventional foods.

Nevertheless, consumers were effectively mobilized against foods containing GM products in northern Europe, although all the available evidence suggested that the main disadvantages of GM crops lay in environmental risks than any threat to human health.

Pages and supplements in the print media, and cooking programs on television, as well as internet sites, constitute a growth industry of their own and generally emphasize food that is 'healthy' as well as enjoyable and attractively presented. This media output is produced by prosperous, well educated people for other prosperous, well educated people and it is well to remember that, for those living in the Global South, as well as the many poorer people in advanced countries, price remains an important determinant of consumer choices. A further complication for poorer citizens in advanced countries is the phenomenon of 'food deserts'. Retail outlets in socially excluded areas may not have adequate, fresh or competitively priced supplies of nutritious products such as fruit and vegetables. In the Global South and for poorer citizens in the north, being able to regularly enjoy products such as chickens and eggs represents an important step forward in living standards. Paradoxically, if standards are not maintained in their processing, or if they are poorly prepared and cooked, these very products present a threat to human health through salmonella, an increasing problem in many countries. Even wealthier consumers will make some of their purchases on the basis of price, with large retailers insisting that it is difficult to maintain substantial premiums for organic products.

The continuing importance of price in relation to consumer purchases and the structure of the agri-food industries can be effectively illustrated by the example of wine. Wine has become less of a luxury good as consumer incomes have grown and prices have fallen as new producers have entered the market to challenge the traditional wine producing countries. Per capita consumption has increased in many countries. Australia has captured a significant slice of market share through producing everyday drinking wines at competitive prices. Nevertheless, the Australian wine industry has encountered increasing difficulties. Other countries such as Chile and South Africa have penetrated the lucrative mid-market with increasing success. On price Australia finds it difficult to compete with large-scale producers in, for example, California. One Australian producer told the author that a Californian competitor had produced a two dollar bottle of wine with which Australian producers simply could not compete given transportation costs. The answer might seem to be for Australia, as well as exploiting new markets in Asia, to move up market through producing more expensive, high quality wines for niche markets. Australia already produces such wines, but they are generally only available at wineries, in restaurants or perhaps within the region. Australia's image is not that of a high quality wine producer and such an image can only be established with difficulty and at some expense. In the meantime, the industry faced a grape glut, price wars, a sustained drop in profit, mergers, takeovers and forced sales.

Public Policy

What, then, is the role of public policy in managing all these developments? The question of what public policy ought to be in this area is highly contested. What is evident is that public policy has often failed to take sufficient account of developments in technology, market structure and consumer preferences that should help to shape decisions about public policy. A classic example is the EU's CAP. In pursuing security of supply objectives set out in the Treaty of Rome, policy-makers encouraged the production of surpluses because intervention buying, as well as creating a floor to the market, also stimulated the market by creating a risk free outlet for surplus produce. Yet, even without any government intervention, technological improvements in grain production would have pushed up output, without any change in the area of land farmed, by about two per cent a year.

There is no doubt that public policy has an effect on decisions made by the farmer. For example, the growth in popularity of oilseed rape (canola) as a crop in the EU was partly influenced by considerations of agronomy (it is a good break crop) and the availability of oilseed crushing plants. However, it was also driven by a favorable subsidy regime. When that regime became less favorable, farmers had to consider whether growing the crop still represented a good commercial decision. More generally, subsidy policies have unintended consequences by forcing up land prices. This makes it more difficult for new entrants to come into the industry with succession occurring largely by inheritance. This in turn can produce an aging farm population which is less amenable to innovation and new methods of farming. In the longer run, there could be a problem about the availability of the combination of the wide range of skills, both knowledge-based and practical, that are required to run a modern farm.

Public policy on agriculture and food is often highly reactive in character rather than being proactive. It often has to react to very difficult policy dilemmas caused by earlier policy decisions or to crises in animal health or food safety. In part, the problem has been the closed nature of agriculture and food policy communities that have not been receptive to new ways of thinking. That has started to change, but the availability of relevant expertise can be a problem in crisis situations, e.g., the lack of sufficient large animal veterinary practitioners during the foot-and-mouth crisis in the UK. Compared to other policy areas being considered in this book, it can be argued that agriculture and food policy is an area where there have been some spectacular policy failures and a general inability to achieve policy goals, albeit that those goals are often poorly specified and contradictory.

OLD AND NEW NARRATIVES IN AGRICULTURE AND FOOD POLICY

Agriculture and food policy is characterized by some recurrent debates which often seem only to edge forward, e.g., how can subsidies be reduced and delivered more effectively? Other debates are longer standing ones, but assume new forms, e.g., about food safety. Yet other debates introduce issues that are new to the policy arena, e.g., about obesity. Environmental narratives have slowly inserted themselves into debates about agricultural policy and have influenced the development of a new paradigm, that of multifunctionality.

Food Safety

Food safety has been a long standing issue in debates about agriculture and food policy and a justification for government intervention. In large part this is because it involves narratives that extend beyond agriculture and food policy, e.g., about public and environmental health and fair treatment for consumers. Early food safety legislation was particularly concerned with the issue of adulteration of food and drink products, e.g., the watering down of milk or the introduction of foreign substances to bulk out bread. Adulteration activities were common as early as the eighteenth century 'when pepper was adulterated with glove dust, or mustard, butter and coffee were mixed up with flour, grass, radish seeds or lard' (de Vroom, 1987: 181). It was relatively easy for campaigners to portray consumers as the innocent victims of scams that might, at worst, be dangerous to them, but at least involved a form of cheating and to induce state intervention. However, one consequence was that food safety regulation became treated as a relatively technical and depoliticized matter. 'The law appeared comparatively early in response to food adulteration scandals, but implementation was dispersed, was low key, and involved the familiar construction of regulatory offences as technical and economic, rather than criminal, in character' (Moran, 2003: 149). Although the British system had its own special features, much of Moran's comment would apply elsewhere for much of the twentieth century. Not just in Britain, mid-twentieth century 'health thinking was based on the assumption that the main health problems of the UK population were and would continue to be caused by the insufficiency and unaffordability of food' (Lang and Rayner, 2003: 67). This in turn underpinned

production oriented agricultural policies that emphasized security of supply, secured if necessary by generous subsidies to farmers. Nevertheless, food policy in the Second World War and the immediate post-war period, at least in those countries that experienced food rationing, was able to use the insufficiency of food to push policies that emphasized a nutritious and balanced diet. Thus, while less food was available to consumers, their consumption of it may have been healthier.

Food safety policy is a complex area, with many dimensions to it, but the central story to be told is one of politicization and institutional reform, particularly in Europe, at the end of the twentieth century. Indeed, it has almost received an attention that is out of proportion to its importance relative to other illnesses. Barling and Lang (2003: 5) point out that 'heart disease, which fells 1.5 million Europeans prematurely each year, receives next to no attention while food safety, which kills barely a thousand, dominates legislatures'. Nevertheless, there is a certain compelling force in statements such as that 'Every day in the United States, roughly 200,000 people are sickened by a foodborne disease, 900 are hospitalized, and fourteen die' (Schlosser, 2002: 195). The United States has a long record of effort on food safety issues. Nevertheless, 'The long-established US Food and Drug Administration and Center for Disease Control, after all, have not been able to prevent 5,000 deaths from food poisoning every year' (Lang and Rayner, 2003: 68).

An underlying problem is that regulatory arrangements in many countries have had a strong local focus, for understandable reasons. The food industry is necessarily a dispersed one at the point of supply because individual consumers are being served, notably in the catering sector, where some of the most serious food safety incidents have occurred. There is therefore a logic in having localized systems of enforcement, even if they produce inequities that result from discrepancies in resources and different regulatory styles. However, modern food supply chains are often highly elongated, so the problem may not be simply one of a caterer with poor hygiene standards. Flynn, Marsden and Smith's comments (2003: 40–41) apply to Europe, but could apply equally to North America or China:

> Within Europe the speed and distance at which foods move along supply chains can make it very difficult for regulators to confine a food safety problem geographically. By the time regulators are aware of a problem in one place, the product may have moved to another location or locations elsewhere. The result is that regulators firefight along a supply chain of whose start and end points they may not even be aware.

The politicization of food safety issues, particularly in Europe, at the end of the twentieth century may be presented in terms of a series of 'food scares' fuelled by intense media interest. A stylized account could, however, probably focus on two scares, salmonella and BSE (or 'mad cow disease' as it popularly became known), although an American account would have to give a great emphasis to E. Coli. These food scares were not accidents or simply the result of inadequate enforcement, but were seen as having a systematic relationship with more intensive and industrialized forms of agriculture. Animals kept at high densities, often among their own feces, mean that bacteria could spread more widely. The extensive use of antibiotics to keep animals healthy can lead to resistant strains of bacteria entering the human food chain. Schlosser argues (2002: 195), on the basis of a review of E. Coli. episodes in the US, that 'the nation's industrialized and centralized system of food processing has created a whole new sort of outbreak, one that can potentially sicken millions of people'.

The salmonella in eggs crisis in Britain in 1988–9 prompted a new Food Safety Act and changes to institutional arrangements for food safety. Salmonella in chickens was not a new problem, but it became evident that a new strain had emerged that did not make birds ill and therefore did not have economic implications for a highly concentrated and industrialized segment of the food industry. 'The recycling of infected birds in poultry feed was thought to have created the conditions in which a new dominant strand of salmonella emerged' (Orbach, 2001: 70). An attempt was made to shift the blame for the outbreak on to poor hygiene standards lower down the food chain. Food safety became a prominent media issue, a

junior minister was forced to resign and the Government was forced to abandon its preference for secrecy:

> It is clear that with the politicization of food and new entrants into the policy network, food policy-making is not what it was. The salmonella affair reveals the extent to which food has become a key political issue and how the consensual food policy community has been more divided and more conflictual and much more open to new interests (Smith, 1991: 251).

The impact of the salmonella affair, or of E. Coli outbreaks, in both Europe and the US, was relatively limited compared with the impact of the emergence of BSE (Bovine Spongiform Encephalopathy), first recognized as a novel brain disease of cattle in 1986. The UK had experienced 180,000 confirmed BSE cases by the end of 2003, although as many as 750,000 animals may have entered the British food chain before the disease was recognized and proper precautions put in place. Diseases that cross species are relatively rare, but BSE became linked with a new variant of Creutzfeld-Jakob Disease (CJD), an invariably fatal disease in which the brain effectively deteriorates into a sponge-like substance. The pathology of the disease is still imperfectly understood, involving as it does prions, which are essentially distorted proteins. It would appear that not everyone who consumes offal from an affected animal is necessarily infected, although younger people seem to be particularly vulnerable, whereas classical CJD is characteristically a disease of older people. Probably the quantity of meat consumed and genetic considerations are intervening factors.

However, the key point as far as public policy is concerned is that a number of people (138 in the UK by the end of 2003) have suffered an avoidable and particularly unpleasant death as a result of consuming unsafe food which was initially said by those in positions of responsibility, worried about the implications for the industry, to be safe to eat. The financial costs to the public purse were also considerable, estimated at £4 billion in the UK. What was undoubtedly a major policy failure was not the result of negligence or poor judgement by individuals, but was more systemic in character. 'It failed, first, because it subordinated consumer protection and public health to an economic and political agenda'. The state's task was seen as being 'actively to support the commercial and industrial objectives of farmers and the food industries, and to give that goal a very high priority within its overall portfolio' (Van Zwannenberg and Milstone, 2003: 28).

The problem was initially seen as a purely British one, but later developed in continental Europe. In 2003, an infected animal was found in the US, albeit one that originated in Canada. BSE called into question intensive forms of agriculture that had moved away from traditional methods of raising cattle on grass and had used feeding methods that had made carnivores out of ruminants.

The BSE episode, reinforced by the experience of government mishandling of an animal health crisis in the form of the outbreak of foot-and-mouth disease, undermined public confidence in the handling of food safety policy, initially in Britain and then elsewhere in Europe. It led to the dissolution of the agriculture ministry in the UK, the creation of an independent Food Standards Agency, the creation of similar agencies in other EU states and institutional changes at the EU level. Above all, the food safety arena, formerly a low key and highly technical area of policy, became highly politicized, a development that in turn affected public attitudes towards GM crops and foods. Given the media's intense interest in any hint of a food scare, and the way in which the new institutional arrangements have involved a much wider range of actors, there is unlikely to be a reversion to old style food safety politics in Europe. The position in the US is somewhat different because of longer established regulatory arrangements that seem to have retained public trust and different attitudes towards the use of technology in food production, even different cultural attitudes towards the 'countryside' and to food, although one has to be cautious about speculative claims about difference that are not backed by sufficient evidence. What is clear is that the divergent politics of food safety and consumption in the EU and the US has spilled into the arena of international trade politics, with a dispute about whether EU policies on the regulation of GM

crops, their traceability and their labelling, are compatible with international trade rules.

Obesity

The issue of obesity is a relatively new one in debates about food policy, but it has profound implications for the future of the sector. It is a powerful narrative because it has close links with health policy and is an increasing focus of activity for the World Health Organization (WHO). 'Obesity has reached epidemic proportions globally, with more than 1 billion adults overweight – at least 300 million of them clinically obese – and is a major contributor to the global burden of chronic disease and disability' (World Health Organization, 2003: 1). Obesity poses a major risk for serious diet-related chronic diseases, among them type 2 diabetes, cardiovascular disease and certain forms of cancer, especially the hormonally-related and large bowel cancers. Chronic obesity can also contribute to osteoarthritis, a major cause of disability in adults. Obesity rates increased three times or more since 1980 in some parts of North America and Europe and notably in the Pacific Islands, with an obesity rate of over 75 per cent in urban Samoa. The attention given to a health issue is enhanced if a link can be demonstrated with the health of children. 'Childhood obesity is already epidemic in some areas and on the rise in others. An estimated 17.6 million children under five are estimated to be overweight worldwide' (World Heath Organization, 2003: 2). Some popular representations of the issue in the media also seem sometimes to draw on narratives critical of the US, given the high proportions of overweight and obese individuals in the American population.

Genetic factors can help to explain the susceptibility of a particular individual to obesity, but they cannot explain away the overall upward trend. This has been caused by a combination of reduced physical activity combined with increased consumption of more energy-dense, nutrient-poor foods with high levels of sugar and saturated fats. The chair of the House of Commons health committee in Britain has claimed that a McDonald's cheeseburger with fries and milkshake would take a nine mile walk to burn off (*Financial Times*, 28 November, 2003). Using an analogy with tobacco, political pressures are increasing to use taxes to discourage people from eating too much sugar, salt and saturated fat. It has also been argued that food advertising aimed at children should be banned and that restaurant menus should list calorie levels in the items listed. The food industry has responded by arguing that the problem is not junk food, but junk diets. There are certainly some interesting issues here about the relative part to be played by individual responsibility and government intervention. What foods an individual eats is very much a personal choice, but it can also have wider social consequences, with obesity estimated to account for at least seven per cent of health care costs in developed countries. This new food policy agenda item is likely to gain momentum.

Environmental Policy and Multifunctionality

A range of environmental issues arise from modern forms of farming. Productivity oriented agricultural policies encouraged forms of farming that were environmentally damaging. Hedgerows were ripped up to create larger fields that were easier for modern equipment to plough and harvest. This in turn had an impact on biodiversity, particularly in terms of bird populations. Chemical intensive farming was encouraged and this led to problems of water pollution in streams and rivers from the run off from fertilizers. Modern forms of pig and dairy farming also produced serious problems of water pollution. Soil erosion is a serious problem in drier climates and increased salinity in the soil is a significant problem in many countries. Agriculture is a major user of increasingly scarce water resources, with modern forms of agriculture often relying heavily on irrigation. In Australia, irrigation has permitted intensive agriculture in areas that would otherwise be barren but may ultimately threaten the fragile ecology of the Murray-Darling river basin. Elsewhere, wetlands, which often support distinctive and endangered bird and other populations, have been allowed to dry out or have been deliberately drained. Coastal marshes have been reclaimed, destroying distinctive natural habitats. Agriculture is a significant source of greenhouse gases, including carbon dioxide and methane.

The accession of central and east European countries to the EU poses a number of threats to valuable natural habitats. Many of these countries are rich in biodiversity, ranging from plants to mammals. However, much of this biodiversity has depended on the maintenance of relatively unproductive forms of farming. The additional funds made available under the CAP may encourage the ploughing up of grassland that has sustained particular forms of biodiversity. More marginal farmers may feel that the funds they receive are insufficient to encourage them to continue farming, particularly given that the adoption and implementation rate of agri-environmental schemes in these countries is often slow. Land abandonment is often harmful to biodiversity as the scrubland that develops is not supportive of a number of species. In southern European countries, traditionally cultivated olive groves can support rich insect and bird populations, but these are not sustained if the land reverts to scrub.

Inserting environmental considerations into agricultural policy is not easy. Production oriented approaches to agriculture have not been concerned with the negative externalities generated. Traditional policy communities have not been greatly concerned with environmental issues and when they have responded to them have often relied on arguments that 'the countryside' is best looked after by its traditional 'stewards', the landowners and farmers. As far as the environment is concerned, governments are faced with a wide variety of problems and often a wide range of approaches to dealing with them. The 'environmental' lobby is fragmented between a wide range of interests and perspectives. Some groups are concerned with the preservation of traditional landscapes and the aesthetic value of the countryside's appearance. Others are concerned with the way that farming impacts on the marine environment through water pollution. Yet others are concerned with the well being of farm animals. The group that can ensure that issues are framed in terms of its own particular approach can have a substantial impact on the way in which policy is developed. Groups concerned with birds are particularly strong in northern Europe, with the Royal Society for the Protection of Birds in Britain having more members than all the political parties combined. It has been successful in getting farmland bird populations widely adopted as a measure of environmental stress, although it may not necessarily be the best indicator.

The EU has tried to respond to these diverse demands and issues by developing a new paradigm of agricultural policy, that of multifunctionality, sometimes known as 'the European Model of Agriculture'. The development of this new paradigm is in part a response to the exhaustion of the old production oriented paradigm. It forms part of a long run effort by the European Commission to convert the CAP into a more broadly based rural development policy, with a greater emphasis on funding through the so-called 'Second Pillar' that covers such policies as agri-environmental schemes. The EU is still at the beginning of its move down the multifunctionality path and Second Pillar funding is likely to still be in the low teens as a share of total agricultural spending by the end of the first decade of the twenty-first century. The policy is also very contentious internationally. Within the WTO it is supported as a policy approach by a loosely knit group of 'Friends of Multifunctionality' that includes Japan, Norway and Switzerland. However, the United States and the Cairns Group see it as a means of perpetuating agricultural subsidies in the EU and elsewhere by qualifying them for placement in the 'green box' that covers subsidies that are not judged to be trade distorting. It also sees multifunctionality as a means of erecting new trade barriers around so-called 'Non Trade Concerns' such as animal welfare.

'While precise definition is difficult, there would none the less seem to be a general consensus that key elements of multifunctional agriculture are the joint production of commodity and non-commodity outputs and the fact that some of these non-commodity outputs may be characterized as externalities or public goods' (Rodgers and Cardwell, 2003: 11). The

public goods that are seen to be provided include the rural landscape, the protection of the environment, the maintenance of viable rural communities as part of a cultural heritage and high standards of plant, animal, occupational and public health. This is a diverse list and it is not easy to devise appropriate policy instruments. Agri-environmental initiatives face the problem that they may end up paying farmers for doing something they would have done anyway so that there is no value added from the expenditure of public funds. The EU has placed some faith in cross-compliance, which means that farmers would not receive their other subsidies if they did not meet certain environmental and other standards. However, such an approach can require intrusive and expensive monitoring at the farm level, replicating the concern about the CAP that it involved high transaction costs both for government agencies and for farmers. Cross-compliance is 'arguably an inappropriate tool with which to address some of the priorities for the reform of agri-enviromental measures highlighted by the Commission … cross-compliance measures apply across whole market sectors within the CAP in an unfocused and non-targeted manner' (Rodgers, 2003: 287). Agri-environmental policy faces the problem often encountered in agriculture and food policy of deciding what the policy goals and their priorities are, seeking to resolve any contradictions and then devising appropriate policy instruments.

CONCLUSIONS

One theme that has emerged from this chapter is the increasing intersection of agriculture and food policy with other areas of policy, notably health policy, environmental policy and trade policy. These phenomena are both a cause and effect of the breakdown of traditional agricultural policy community. More space is created for the entry of new actors, which in turn accelerate the breakdown of traditional policy assumptions and modes of policy-making.

However, it is also important to be aware of the limits of this process. Agriculture remains highly subsidized and protected at a time when these protections have been removed from manufacturing industry. The traditional institutions and decision-making processes of agricultural policy retain much of their strength and the impact of environmental arguments has so far been at the margin rather than the core of policy. Paradoxically, relatively little of the large amount paid out in subsidies reaches farmers, and much of what does goes to large scale farmers in rich countries who should be able to survive commercially. Much of the benefit is absorbed by those who store surplus commodities, by traders and by processors. The transaction costs of running complex agricultural policies are high and they are open to fraud both by individual farmers and criminal organizations. The CAP has paid out arable aid for a farm in the watery wastes of the North Atlantic and for cows allegedly housed on the fifth floor of an office block in Rome.

Nevertheless, in the longer run the conversion of CAP subsidies into aids not linked to production may increase public pressure for further reform. The Global South will increase its pressure in the WTO for greater access to the markets of developed countries. Protectionist barriers and export subsidies are likely to be dismantled in the longer run as the costs of failing to reach agreement on agricultural trade for other trade issues are too high. New discourses about food policy are likely to continue to have a major impact. This has already been seen in relation to food safety issues, defined in the minds of many consumers to include GM crops, and obesity will become a major item on the policy agenda. Agricultural and food policy in the twentieth century was known for its stability, exceptionality and insularity. In the twenty-first century it will be characterized more by its contentious character and its integration into the mainstream of policy-making. A more central emphasis will be given to providing citizens with safe and nutritious food and ensuring that producers in the Global South are not exploited rather than subsidizing prosperous farmers in the north.

REFERENCES

Barling, D. and Lang, T. (2003) 'The Politics of UK Food Policy: an Overview', *Political Quarterly,* 74: 1, 4–7.

Coleman, W., Grant, W. and Josling T. (2004) *Agriculture in the New Global Economy.* Cheltenham: Edward Elgar.

Flynn, A., Marsden, T. and Smith, E. (2003) 'Food Regulation and Retailing in a New Institutional Context', *Political Quarterly,* 74: 1, 38–46.

Lang, T. and Rayner, J. (2003) 'Food and Health Strategy in the UK: a Policy Impact Analysis', *Political Quarterly,* 74: 1, 66–75.

Moran, M. (2003) *The British Regulatory State.* Oxford: Oxford University Press.

Orbach, M. (2001) 'A Modern History of British Eggs', *Petits Propos Culinaires,* 68: 49–76.

Pritchard, B. and Burch, D. (2003) *Agri-Food Globalization in Perspective: International Restructuring in the Processing Tomato Industry.* Aldershot: Ashgate.

Rodgers, C. (2003) 'Environmental Policy and the Reform of European Agriculture Law' in M. N. Cardwell, M. R. Grossman and C. P. Rodgers (eds.), *Agriculture and International Trade: Law, Policy and the WTO.* Wallingford: CABI Publishing.

Rodgers, C. and Cardwell, M. (2003) 'The WTO, International Trade and Agricultural Policy Reform' in M. N. Cardwell, M. R. Grossman and C. P. Rodgers (eds.), *Agriculture and International Trade: Law, Policy and the WTO.* Wallingford: CABI Publishing.

Schlosser, E. (2002) *Fast Food Nation.* New York: Perennial.

Smith, M.J. (1991) 'From policy community to issue network: *Salmonella* in eggs and the new politics of food', *Public Administration,* 69: 235–55.

Van Zwannenberg, P. and Millstone, E. (2003) 'BSE: a Paradigm of Policy Failure', *Political Quarterly,* 74: 1, 27–37.

de Vroom, B. (1987) 'The Food Industry and Quality Regulation' in W. Grant (ed.) *Business Interests, Organizational Development and Private Interest Government: An international comparative study of the food processing industry.* Berlin: de Gruyter.

World Health Organization (2003) 'Fact Sheet on Obesity and Overweight'.

19

Transportation and Infrastructure

KENNETH BUTTON

INTRODUCTION

Transportation is a classic case of a network industry. It traditionally involves the movement of goods and people between various locations, and more recently in the 'Communications Age' (Andersson et al., 1990) has become concerned with the movement of information between various points. It is also a very visible activity, requiring significant amounts of both link (roads, railways, etc.) and node (stations, airports, etc.) infrastructure. Since there seems to be a natural proclivity for people to want to move around, and for efficient production to require the combining and distributions of diverse inputs, transportation is a regular topic of public debate. The fact that much of the necessary infrastructure used to provide transportation is expensive and generally unsightly often adds to the intensity of the discourse.

The transportation infrastructure networks of the 21st century are extensive in the industrial world and skimpy in the rest. Western Europe[1] has some 50,000 kilometers of motorway (freeway), 156,000 kilometers of railways lines, and over 300 commercial airports and nearly 11,000 seaports. The network of North America is even larger, although in many parts less dense because large parts of the region are sparsely populated. Adding in systems that transport liquids, spacecraft, or information expands these networks considerably. In contrast, Africa in general, and parts of South America and Asia, have very limited networks that are often of poor quality.

It is not just the amount of transportation infrastructure that is imposing, it is its diversity, the ways in which it is used, and public attitudes towards it. Looking back, transportation has not only been at the forefront of public policy because of its current social and economic roles that are now often the main preoccupations of policy makers. Over 4,000 years ago paths existed across the Alps in Europe that seem to have emerged with no pre-planning. By Roman, times, however, military logistics largely determined what transport infrastructure was provided and maintained, and this element of policy has certainly remained. The Romans, for example, had over 320,000 of paved highway in Central Europe (the first international transportation system) and could march their troops from Rome to Northern Spain in 27 days. This military focus continues, and, more recently, the rationale behind the US Interstate Highway System, for example, was almost entirely logistical in nature; President Eisenhower wanted to ensure the US army could swiftly be moved around the country.

Transportation has also been an integral part of policies designed for political integration (sometimes after conquest); the Canadian rail network was constructed largely on this premise, and the Trans-European Networks initiative of the European Union (EU) has motivations of political cohesion underpinning it. Indeed, the very concept of the 'King's highway' that in various languages can be found throughout Europe from the Middle Ages, harks back to this idea of the role of roads as a tool in governance. From the 11th to the 13th century the road networks in Europe were largely within political boundaries and designed to secure local political integrity.

Economic analysis of transportation infrastructure as we understand it is relatively new and can be traced back to the sea changes in economic thinking of the late 18th century. Adam Smith (1776) talks of its importance, and indeed one function that he concedes government should perform is to invest in major infrastructure, because private concerns are unlikely to be able to muster the necessary resources. Techniques for appraising the social benefits of devoting resources to transportation infrastructure investment, and also for defining appropriate pricing for the use of such facilities, provoked much of the early development of modern microeconomics policy. French engineers seeking to help move the national economy forward into the industrial age were much concerned with the efficiency of the transportation system as well as its technical features. Dupuit (1844), and his innovative work on cost-benefit analysis, is often cited in this context, but there was an entire body of analysis conducted by these engineers during the 1840s and 1850s.

As the railroads came on-line in the mid-19th century new commercial appraisal techniques (e.g., involving discounting costs over time) were developed, with the subsequent move to mechanized road transport using public infrastructure being accompanied by innovative social and economic assessment tools. Technically, however, these variants on cost-benefits analysis are a partial equilibrium methodology, whereas the large infrastructure projects of the later 20th century (such as the Channel Tunnel or 'Big Dig' in Boston) can only truly be analyzed within a larger general equilibrium framework. Methods of strategic network planning and decision-making have been made possible to do this as computer technology has developed; this has led to better informed decisions although not always better decisions.

Underlying all this is the fact that transportation, and its associated infrastructure, is not sought as an end in itself but rather there is a derived demand for the services that it offers to fulfill some other end. It is an input into industrial and social processes rather than being an output – it facilitates trade and allows individuals to access final goods and services. This makes policy formulation, and the public administration of transportation, particularly challenging. In policy terms it has often meant that transportation has been treated institutionally alongside other intermediate inputs (such as energy policy or land use planning) to exploit synergies, or within a larger setting (such as part of an environmental ministry or department) to minimize institutional distortions. It has also led to wide variations in the way responsibility for transport infrastructure is allocated, with more or less devolution to lower levels of government.

This contribution is largely angled from the perspective of the now often unfashionable political economy. It seeks to look at the ways in which transportation infrastructure is viewed, both as a part of transport policy and in its larger role in public policy, but in doing so the focus is on the economic issues. It is not about the more technical engineering debates or the strict political trade-offs that are made.

WHAT CONSTITUTES TRANSPORTATION INFRASTRUCTURE?

If is often, although not always, useful to have a good idea of what one is talking about. There is, however, no agreed definition of what constitutes transportation infrastructure. Indeed, infrastructure in the general sense is often highly contextual. Whilst a politician or planner may think in terms of ports or roads as infrastructure, a logistics company may view its infrastructure to embrace its vehicles and buildings.

In many cases infrastructure is limited to physical facilities, but, in the age of computers, information bases constitute infrastructure for many companies. Infrastructure would also seem to have contextual temporal characteristics; something considered infrastructure now may be seen as operating capital if viewed over a week. Of course, one could resort to the neoclassical economic use of long- and short-run when defining infrastructure, with it only being variable in the long-run, but this begs the immediate question of what is long- and what is short-run.

Many macroeconomists often argue that the provision of adequate infrastructure per se is a necessary prerequisite for economic advancement but, while economists are generally rather particular in the ways in which specific goods are categorized, the definition of infrastructure even here tends to be vague and imprecise. Indeed, the underlying concept is sometimes equally opaquely referred to as 'social overhead capital'. Lakshmanan (1989) talks of the term as 'often employed in a loose impressionistic manner'.

Where there have been efforts, for practical and administrative reasons, at delineation, the tendency is frequently to look for particular physical features and to offer lists of such characteristics as indicating 'infrastructure'. Nurske (1953), for instance, lists features such as: 'provide services basic to any production capacity'; 'cannot be imported from abroad' and 'large and costly installations'. Hirschman (1958) lists sectors, *viz.*, 'In its widest sense it includes all public services, from law and order through education and public health to transportation, communications, power and water supply, as well as such agricultural overhead capital as irrigation and drainage systems. The hard core of the concept can probably be restricted to transportation and power'.

More recently, these characteristics of infrastructure have tended to be outlined in rather more technical terms and, in particular, the possible relevance of notions such as information flows in defining infrastructure (Youngson, 1967) or the treatment of infrastructure as a specific case of externalities, of public goods, etc. But this literature often moves from a foundation in an intellectual concept to seeking illustrations of its relevance, rather than trying to define and delineate particular types of capital.

No effort is made here to offer any better definitions than those that have gone before. Basically, we have an idea of what we understand by infrastructure but do not have the ability to articulate exactly what we mean.

THE POLICY CONCERNS OF THE 21ST CENTURY

Modern policy has emerged from a succession of waves in public and private attitudes towards infrastructure. As with virtually all aspects of transport, the demand for transportation hardware is derived from final demands for other goods and services. In the context of infrastructure, the link is one step removed because the demand for infrastructure is determined by the more general demands for mobility and access that transportation in general meets. Consequently, policy attitudes and implementation regarding the role and forms of transport infrastructure is inevitably entwined with much broader swings in social attitudes, technology, economic growth, and knowledge. It also varies considerably between countries and regions within them as societal priories differ in general.

Putting aside matters of military logistics, the link between transportation policy and economic prosperity is a key one and one that is dealt with in some depth later. It underpins, and often dominates, public attitudes towards infrastructure provision and use. Growth per se, however, is seldom the dominant short-term goal of policy makers. There is ample evidence (e.g., Frey, 1985) that policy makers, especially in democratic society, take cognizance of the distribution of this growth. Transportation infrastructure, because of its role in facilitating spatial interaction, is frequently seen as a way of spreading economic growth and as a means of pulling peripheral regions into the core. The extent to which this holds true may be debated (after all, transportation allows movement in two directions and there are certainly cases of major investments sucking out the limited income and jobs from depressed areas to relocate them in the prosperous regions – the 'Appalachians Effect'). Nevertheless, it often seems to have a hold in the political psyche.

Much of the immediate post-Second World War policy debate, especially in Europe and Asia, was understandably focused on infrastructure reconstruction. This led to a heavy engineering input into policy-making and, as time passed and reconstruction moved into development and renewal, this engineering focus remained; the ethos was very much one of providing infrastructure capacity to meet demand. The increasing difficulty in many cases was that users of the infrastructure did not pay, or did not pay directly, for its use. While resources are abundant, and the true opportunity costs of these actions are effectively hidden as part of a larger growth trend, this poses few political problems, although potentially economically wasteful. As time passed, however, projects became more costly for what they achieved (simply following the law of diminishing efficiency of capital). The result was a shift towards management of infrastructure – which is dealt with in more detail later.

But there was also another important trend at work. As incomes in Western Europe, North America and parts of Asia rose, so did environmental awareness. First, local issues came to the fore (e.g., lead in petrol and traffic noise), followed by wider geographical impacts (acid rain) and then the whole question of environmental sustainability as evidence on global warming began to emerge. This has led to policy debates, not only about the extent to which transportation as a whole should grow, but also, if it does, whether specific 'environmental friendly' modes should be given preference. This, for example, is the underlying ethos of the European Commission's (2001) medium-term approach to infrastructure policy and its emphasis on trying to move more freight to rail and urban passenger traffic to transit.

The increased globalization of activities has added new dimensions to policy. In almost a return to the days of the Roman Empire there is a focus on linking international infrastructure networks and allowing easier global movements of goods and people. Freight movement

has been facilitated by the development of containerization (unitization) since the late 1960s and this has led to technical standardization of infrastructure in many areas – tunnel heights, port facilities, loading/unloading bays, etc. The European Union has pushed measures to increase interoperability, intermodality, and interconnectivity in terms of the creation of Trans European networks (European Commission (1989) and in financing individual investments. The World Trade Organization, by reducing tariffs and non-tariffs barriers, acts to facilitate trade, with implications for the overall, global demands on transportation infrastructure.

TRANSPORT INFRASTRUCTURE AND ECONOMIC DEVELOPMENT

One of the main, if not the dominant, ongoing public policy concerns with transportation infrastructure involves the ties that it seems to have with economic development. Over the years the creation of international agencies such as the World Bank, and regional bodies such as the European Union, have sought to expand, up-grade, and maintain transportation infrastructure as a driver or facilitator, dependent on the details of the prevailing philosophy of the day, of economic growth. The planned economies of Central and Eastern Europe expended considerable resources on transport infrastructure, but perhaps should ultimately be seen as prime examples of quantity not being a good substitute for quality.

This attitude is not a new one. In practice it goes back to the earliest states and empires, but its intellectual rationale is perhaps more modern. Adam Smith (1776), for example, devoted considerable attention to the role of infrastructure and its pricing. In many ways his views fit with the thinking of institutions such as the World Bank, the European Bank for Economic Reconstruction, and the European Union. For instance, 'Good roads, canals and navigable rivers, by diminishing the expense of carriage, put the remote parts of the country more nearly upon a level with those in the neighbourhood of the town. They are upon that account the greatest of all improvements. They encourage the cultivation of the remote, which must always be most extensive circle of the country. They are advantageous to the town, by breaking down the monopoly of the country in its neighbourhood.'

But the issues involved are not perhaps as simple as Smith and others believed, and the empirical evidence that has emerged on the success of pump-priming economic development with transportation infrastructure hardware has not always been compelling.

Over-riding Philosophies

There are two broad approaches to economic policy-making. These apply as much to transport as anything else. First, there is the Anglo-Saxon approach, whereby the onus is on leaving things to the market unless it is clear that interventions would reduce the distortions of market failure – more is said on this in the transportation infrastructure context latter. Second, there is the continental approach, where government plans, in a general sense, supply to meet its objectives and only uses markets when these result in outcomes coincidental with these objectives. In fact, the reality is somewhere between these extremes and de facto debates focus on the degree of market orientation rather than any absolute.

In terms of transportation infrastructure policy, the tradition has largely been one more akin to the continental philosophy. Government has exercised a heavy hand. Even in countries such as the US, while private companies have built facilities such as railroads, there has been immense political involvement and, of course, airports, seaports, and roads have largely been public sector activities. The activities of the authorities in the former Soviet economies and of the socialist governments that remain in many developing countries have been ones of direction rather than facilitation.

Over time there have been shifts in emphasis with a more recent movement toward approaches closer to the Anglo-Saxon approach. This is most clearly manifest in the encouragement of the private sector to invest in traditional transport infrastructure, and the privatization of some existing facilities. But it is also evident in the willingness of governments to allow the private development of new forms of infrastructure, and especially the communications infrastructure that transports information.

Theories of Transport Infrastructure and Macro-economic Growth

The exact importance of infrastructure as an element in the economic development process has long been disputed. Much seems to depend upon the degree to which supply considerations are thought important. The Keynesian economic approach, epitomized by the Harrod–Domar framework, indicates that causality runs from economic exploitation to income and infrastructure generation. In contrast, neo-classical economics is essentially supply-driven and transportation and other infrastructure are generally seen as important elements in the production function.

Much of the recent work follows the neo-classical mode in looking at the links between infrastructure provision and economic development through some form of aggregate production function analysis. It has sought to see how well it, and its individual elements, explains economic performance. The usual approach has been to take a production function of the standard form, with public capital (which is largely transportation infrastructure) being one of the variables used to explain variation in output or productivity.[2] These types of model were used to estimate the output elasticities of public infrastructure investments but the results generated have not been highly robust, as can be seen in the summary of some of the main studies set out in Table 19.1.

Many of the early studies, especially from the US, at the national and state levels, provided statistically significant and apparently robust evidence that well designed and operated infrastructure can expand the economic productivity of an area. Aschauer (1989), for example, looking at data covering the period

Table 19.1   *Selection of estimated output elasticities of public infrastructure investments*

Author	Aggregation	Output elasticity of public capital
Aschauer (1990)	National	0.39
Holtz-Eakin (1992)	National	0.39
Munnell (1990)	National	0.34
Costa et al. (1987)	States	0.20
Eiser (1991)	States	0.17
Munnell (1990)	State	0.15
Mera (1973)	Regions	0.20
Duffy-Deno and Eberts (1991)	Urban areas	0.08
Eberts and Fogarty (1987)	Urban areas	0.03

1949 to 1985, concluded that a 1% increase in the public capital stock could raise total factor productivity by 0.39%, while Munnell (1990) tabulates output elasticities of public capital derived from US studies in the 0.03 to 0.39 range, although with a preponderance of results toward the upper end of the range. Biehl (1991) regarding the European Union (EU) records similar positive findings.

More recently, these studies have been subjected to a variety of criticisms. Gramlich (1994) and Button (1998) offer summaries but, very briefly, the key points include:

- First, while econometric studies may throw up positive correlation between economic performance and the state of infrastructure, the direction of causation is not immediately clear. Wealthier areas may simply have more resources for infrastructure provision. The efforts at testing for causality are, as yet, minimal.
- Second, as seen above, the term infrastructure is a flexible one with no agreed definition, and simply taking official accountancy data may disguise important measurement, qualitative and definition factors. In US work, for instance, while Aschauer and Munnell used a 4-category 'core' sub-set of the nine US Bureau of Labor Statistics infrastructure categories, others have employed the full set.
- Third, the way in which infrastructure is managed and priced may be as important as the provision of infrastructure *per se* (Winston, 1991). In terms of policy, therefore, account must be taken of the short-term

levels of utilization, maintenance and so on, in addition to the stock of, and investment in, infrastructure.

- Fourth, even within the very vague notion we have regarding what constitutes infrastructure, there are numerous sectors and elements. From a policy perspective it is, therefore, important to isolate the roles of, say, transport, energy and softer infrastructure such as law, education, business services and defense in influencing macroeconomic performance.
- Fifth, there are similar issues on the output side and Nadiri and Manuenias (1996) have pointed to closer links between infrastructure investment and particular industrial sectors.
- Sixth, as more studies emerge they are producing much wider ranges of results; as Morrison (1993) puts it, 'A clear consensus about the impacts of infrastructure investment has as yet been elusive, at least partly because different methodologies generate varying results and implications'. A study by Sturm and de Haan (1995), deploying US and Netherlands data, for instance, points to the fact that the data series in most studies looking at the economic effects of public capital are neither stationary nor co-integrated and, thus, conclusions that public capital has a positive effect on private sector productivity are not well founded. Equally, Jorgensen (1991) has questioned the basic premise underlying the use of a production function approach. This sensitivity may, of course, go beyond simple matters of technique if there is, in fact, no underlying relationship.

- The studies that have been completed frequently indicate rates of returns on public capital investments – Aschauer's (1989) calculations give returns of 38% to 56% – in excess either of levels outside the range of any *a priori* expectation or of those found in individual micro-project appraisals.

Local Development Effects of Transportation Infrastructure Investments

While the debates over the macro significance of transportation infrastructure still need final resolution, the local geographical implications for locations adjacent to new facilities is less murky. This is important because many policy questions ride at least as much on who benefits from an action as on the overall net effect of that action. Distributional considerations are seldom insignificant.

One of the most immediate ways of gaining an insight into the local importance of adequate transportation infrastructure is to consider economic impact studies. These are often mandatory when investments are made in transportation infrastructure and essentially seek to assess the income and employment of the action. Techniques vary, and do influence the results, but, quantitatively, the economic impacts of an investment in transportation infrastructure depend primarily both on the time frame examined and on the geographical space under review. In broad terms, infrastructure enhancements have four potential economic impacts of varying duration and spatial coverage.

- *Primary effects.* These are the benefits to a region derived from the construction or expansion of the transportation infrastructure – the design of the facility, its construction, the installation of supplementary hard- and software and so on. These effects represent once-for-all injections of expenditure into the local economy, with associated employment in industries involved in infrastructure planning, construction and development. These types of effect are, however, transient, lasting no longer than the construction itself, and should be seen to act more as Keynesian stimuli than as development factors.

- *Secondary effects.* These are on-going local economic benefits of running and operating the transportation infrastructure – employment in maintaining and repairing the facility, in handling traffic, in policing and so on. These secondary effects can be extremely important to some local economies in terms of employment, income and, for local government, they can add to taxation revenue. While important, and accepting that they can generate important multiplier effects, they are not the main development rationale for infrastructure investments.

- *Tertiary effects.* These stem from the stimulus to a local economy resulting from firms and individuals having improved transportation services at their disposal. A large part of modern industry relies on good quality transportation to support just-in-time supply chain production. The importance of the mode varies according to location and the type of production involved, but access to high-quality and appropriate transportation infrastructure can act as catalysts to attract mobile industry and to nurture the growth of local firms. Technically, it can push output up the local production function and, through resultant economies of scale and scope, create centers of employment.

- *Perpetuity effects.* These reflect the fact that new forms of economic growth, once started in a region, becomes self-sustaining and may accelerate. Availability of good transportation links can change the entire economic structure of a region – technically it can shift its aggregate production function rather than just bring about a movement along it as with tertiary effects. The change from Florida being primarily an agricultural based economy to one with a large and profitable tourist sector is an example, as are some of the mega high-technology clusters that emerged. These changes would have been very unlikely without good road and air transportation infrastructure.

Whilst it is interesting to isolate these beneficial effects, there remains the practical questions of how large they are, and whether they justify major market interventions by policy makers. It is also often challenging to isolate the individual components that may be important when looking at specific sectors of the economy. There are basically three ways of getting a handle on these issues:

- It can be done through questioning those involved in the provision of the transportation services in the area or who are involved in local industry – so-called expert opinion analysis, or stated quantitative analysis. This method does, however, pose the problem of ensuring appropriate views are elicited and that there is objectivity in the responses obtained. It can become a basis for lobbying rather than for analysis.
- It can be done using local Keynesian multipliers or input-output analysis. Basically tracing through either in aggregate (multipliers) or by sectors (input-output analysis) the implications of local expenditure on transportation. It is a technique often deployed in transportation impact assessments. But there are issues of the geographical coverage of the analysis and the time frame to consider (e.g., which type of effect is actually being captured).
- Finally, there are econometric methods that make use of statistical techniques. These can be highly complex and can be structured to determine the specific implications of, say, an airport for an economy when a variety of other developments are taking place in parallel. But, while offering the ability to isolate transportation effects on local development, they do pose problems of ensuring an appropriate model specification and in using correct estimation procedures. They can also be heavily data intensive.

But, irrespective of the method used, the body of evidence on the potential scale of local secondary and tertiary effects of most transportation provision on economic growth is compelling. Pulling all the information that we have of standard impacts is not practically possible, but some general impressions can be gleaned on the importance of air transport infrastructure from the selection of results seen in Table 19.2. The studies cited are in no way atypical. The details of their findings differ, as might be expected given the geographical coverage they embrace, the variety of techniques used, and differences in the forms of infrastructure investments being considered. They all, however, offer fairly strong support for the notion that infrastructure investment can generate significant local economic benefits.

INTERNATIONAL, NATIONAL, REGION AND LOCAL INTERESTS

The Interested Parties

Transportation infrastructure, because of the diversity and intensity of its implications, inevitably results in divergent views, and the creation of various forms of coalitions. Some of these can exercise considerable lobbying power outside of normal democratic processes, and have what is often called 'voice' in debates. There has traditionally been a strong road construction coalition in many developing countries, made up of not only those who plan, build, and maintain the infrastructure, but also those that make use of it – the automobile and trucking associations – and those that provide the vehicles – the car manufacturers. There are also well organized, and frequently very vocal, labor interests that seek to further develop the transportation activities that they engage in.

These traditional types of structure, that have really focused on the type of infrastructure rather than its amount, have been confronted in more recent times with groups that have been more concerned about excessive investment in transportation hardware. Environmentalists have been the most obvious of these new lobby groups, as they have sought to highlight the local and global ecological damage that motorized transportation and its

Table 19.2   *Benefits of enhanced air services*

Survey techniques

- The Atlanta Chamber of Commerce found, from a survey 264 foreign-based firms, that availability of direct international services was the third most important factor in location decisions. Subsequent study showed that the number of foreign firms locating in the region from a particular country grew significantly after the introduction of a non-stop service.
- Ernst and Young, looking at location decisions of 57 companies in Europe making decisions regarding the location of a manufacturing plant, found that the air transportation network was the third most important factor in the decision process. Air services were much more important for service sector companies.
- The Amsterdam Chamber of Commerce found that the availability of an airport was one of five key factors considered in company relocation decisions.
- A survey of firms around Zurich found that 34% considered the airport as 'very important' and 38% as important as a location factor.
- Loudoun Chamber of Commerce (Virginia) found that airport/freeway access was important to 68% of firms.
- A study of small business firms in the Washington area that were engaged in export activities found the availability of easy access to international air transportation one of the six most important factors in their success.

Multipliers

- An academic study by Rietveld estimated that Schiphol Airport (Netherlands) generates about 85,000 jobs for the country.
- A study of Vienna International Airport by Industriewissenschaftliches Institute in 1998 indicated that, on a turnover of ATS25 billion in 1996, there was an impact of ATS11.2 billion on the local economy.
- The Institute of Social and Economic Research found that the total annual economic importance of the air transportation services offered from Anchorage International Airport on local payrolls was $130 million above the $316 million for on-site activities.

Econometric

- Analysis by George Mason University, taking variations in high-technology employment across all US Metropolitan Standard Areas, found that an airline hub in a region increases that region's new economy employment by over 12,000.
- Brueckner, looking at the possible expansion of Chicago O'Hare airport, found that an increase of airline passenger traffic of 50% would increase service related employment in the region by 185,000 jobs.
- An econometric study by Science Applications International of the implications of the Open Skies agreement between Germany and the US on the regional economy around Hamburg Airport found annual gains for the regional economy of $783,318 in 1994 prices.
- Button and Taylor examined the impact on US cities of having European services and found that employment was systematically positively related to both the scale of services offered by the supplying airlines and the range of destinations served.

Source: Button (2004)

associated infrastructure causes. Combined with these groups have been others with a stronger social orientation that have questioned the equity of many infrastructure investment decisions that they see as largely benefiting higher income car owning groups in society. These types of groups question traditional views about links between welfare, in its broadest sense, and the amount of mechanized transportation that is invested in. Over the past thirty years the 'voice' of these environmental and socially concerned groups have grown as

they have organized and more scientific evidence that emerges about the wider impacts of transportation. Whist many of the resultant technical changes have been to vehicles (cars, planes, ships, etc.) there have also been new approaches to infrastructure design and management (e.g., traffic calming on street, sound barriers, and tunneling) as well as more extension consultation procedures.

While many of these new pressure groups started at the local level, there are now often parallel national and international groups that act as a counterweight to the international automobile, aircraft, and other manufacturing conglomerates and to the global consulting and construction multinationals. These pressure groups effectively lobby for more social awareness in infrastructure decision-making, as opposed to the more financially motivated transportation interests.

Levels of Responsibility

The network nature of transportation infrastructure irrespective of the mode being considered raises issues of coordination. Links must tie in with nodes in any interconnected system for it to provide useful services for potential users. From the policy perspective, the transportation infrastructure network poses a series of challenges, not least of which is who is responsible for ensuring optimal coordination is achieved. Indeed, in Europe, when the European Economic Community (the forerunner of the EU) came into existence in 1957, a Common Transport Policy was one of only two major common policies in the Treaty of Rome.[3]

In practice, jurisdiction and forms of authority differ between countries. Sometimes this is a reflection of variations in the larger institutional structure of the country – federal USA has a different structure to centralized France – but geography may play a role – Switzerland is a federal state, Austria is not, but both have similar polices on major infrastructure decisions because of the large amount of international traffic that passes through them. There are issues of the geographical extent to which network effects exhaust themselves. These are often a function of technology and management limitations as much as any overriding policy consideration. Local transportation infrastructure (local roads, transit, and terminals for long distance modes) are generally treated as urban matters, although seldom financed on that basis, and come under local jurisdiction, whereas inter-urban infrastructure is generally the responsibility of state, national, or international agencies. In larger units, such as the European Union, the notion of subsidiarity become relevant, with

institutional responsibilities being devolved down to what is considered the appropriate level of administration. But, whatever structure is adopted, it is not uncommon for the detailed planning and implementation of policy to be separate from its funding. This is often a pragmatic matter of being the only way to bring sufficient resources together for larger projects, but also can reflect macroeconomic policies of placing financial stimuli in economically depressed regions.

Areas of Conflict

The inherent interconnectivity of transportation infrastructure networks makes the practical development of virtually any type of jurisdiction responsibility difficult and trade-offs are needed. In a federal system each state or province engages in what is often called 'pork-barrel politics' with political trade-offs emerging over the dispensation of the national tax income. Each state seeks to extract as much of the national budget for transportation facilities in its area as it can, but it also often does this within a larger context. The nature of federal financing frequently means that transportation decisions are decided in a broader political framework that extends across all areas of public finance. At the macro-macro level this is clearly seen in the budgetary allocation decisions of the European Union, where horse-trading of investment priorities between sectors is as common as that within any particular sector such as transportation.

Since transportation is often viewed as an aid to local economic development, beggar-thy-neighbor policies are not uncommon, with cities vying for private sector investment by providing economically inefficient large amounts of transport infrastructure. This is most directly seen in the case of the strategy and routing regarding interurban investments, including ports and airports, where every city seeks to have maximum access to the network, but also extends to local infrastructure. At the very much more micro-level, however, the perspective can be very different when it comes to deciding exactly where an airport or road should be located. Transportation is effective industry on wings or wheels and, as such, while most people like to have access to it, there are often vocal objections to having the infrastructure in one's 'back-yard'. To this end most countries have devised various forms of local participation in the decision-making process that seek to facilitate at least a degree of conflict resolution. To help structure such debates techniques such as cost-benefit analysis and planning balance sheet analysis have been developed and are now widely used in many countries.

There are also larger interface problems at the macro level. In the federal system, whilst roads of national importance are often the domains of the central government, there is often little coordination of links between states. Indeed, it is not uncommon for one state to favor expanding capacity at the same time as adjacent states seek to limit traffic growth, with the result that infrastructure links vary in quality and capacity along their length. Each country has its own approach to these types of problem, generally closely related to other policies covering such things as agriculture, land-use planning, regional development, environmental protection, and industrial policy.

Internationally, this problem is compounded and it is not uncommon for different technical standards (e.g., road pavement thickness, railway track standards, and air traffic control equipment) to exist on different sides of national borders. Sometimes this is a historical legacy (the UK driving on the left and the French on the right) but it has also been used as part of non-tariff trade barrier policy. Some regional national groupings, notably the EU, seek to reduce them, as do some global organizations such as the UNs International Civil Aviation Organisation and the International Maritime Organisation, but, other than allowing access on the terms of the host country, these arrangements are the exceptions.

THE ROLE OF THE PUBLIC SECTOR

Transportation infrastructure, because of its strategic economic importance, either real or perceived, has long been the subject of regulations and frequently of state ownership. Whether regulation or ownership has dominated public policy depends to some extent on the philosophical view taken, Anglo-Saxon or Continental. But infrastructure also serves a variety of non-economic purposes. Over the centuries roads and ports have often been seen primarily as logistic tools to wage war, with economic considerations coming a poor second. The Roman road network had a commercial value but was primarily seen as a way of maintaining an empire. In some cases transportation infrastructure that would have been of economic benefit has been neglected to serve another end. It was no accident, for example, that the French road network along the Belgium border was poor in 1914; it could not sustain the advance of the German Imperial Army and directly led to the French victory at the Battle of the Marne.

Combining economic, military, and social considerations in assessing transportation infrastructure investment and control is complex. Normally a nation or super-national entity has a strategic plan for the network as a whole. This emerges through consultation and discussion of relevant parties, and the outcome depends upon the strength of the various coalitions of interest that exist. In the case of the current effort to develop a trans-European transport network, concerns about economic, political, and social integration dominate. But the US Federal Highway System was the product of a military need to move the US military rapidly across the country, with any consideration of macro economic benefits being a poor second.

This still leaves the question of who provides the facility. There are wide variations across countries even for a single mode. In the US, for example, the private railway companies own both the track and the rolling stock, in the UK the track is state owned (after a short period of privatization) but private railway companies supply the rolling stock. In most of Continental Europe both track and operating capital is state owned.[4]

Setting aside any military or similar reasons, the issue of who owns and operates transport infrastructure often rests on political and economic arguments. In some cases it involves practical considerations; the private sector, for example, may not be sufficiently coordinated to raise the funds and construct the hardware. These are perhaps most pronounced in less industrial countries that do not have sophisticated governance structures to allow private finance markets to operate with confidence. In other cases, most notably when transportation is seen as a way of attaining larger national objectives, it is sometimes thought that government control offers the most likely course to success. The idea that prevailed post-Second World War UK of the government needing to control the 'towering heights of industry' to steer the national economy forward is a case in point.

In other cases the rationale has been more towards state provision being the most effective means of circumventing market failures that were feared if the private sector were the suppliers. These failures include a potential lack of coordination of network based infrastructure, exploitation of market power where the infrastructure involves a degree of monopoly, and the potential for excessive external costs (embracing such things as environmental damage and inadequate safety concerns). Of course, this begs the question, if indeed market failures are likely to be excessive, whether ownership or regulation is the best way of combating them.

In recent years there has been a shift, as in many other sectors, away from public ownership to more private sector involvement. The first private tolled road of recent times, for example, has opened in the UK, but before then many countries such as New Zealand had privatized air traffic control, airports and seaports in many countries have been taken out of state control, and outsourcing of many activities such as maintenance had become commonplace. In some cases, as with some build and operate schemes, the structure has been one more akin to leasing than freehold ownership, with the infrastructure reverting to the state after a predetermined period. In other cases, state ownership has remained but the control of decision-making has been depoliticized. The Crown Corporation owning air traffic control in Canada (NAV Canada) is an example of this.

The changing ownership (or management structure in the case of Crown Corporations) does not necessarily mean less government control over transportation infrastructure, but rather the use of other regulatory controls. In the case of monopolies this can entail price capping, as with BAA that owns the three London airports and other provincial UK airports. This allows flexibility in pricing of individual services but under a fixed, inflation adjusted annual increase for average charges. To limit environmental damage there are planning regulations for most forms of transportation infrastructure that involve some form of cost-benefit assessment, embracing a wide of external considerations as well as narrow financial effects (Jansson, 2000). Engineering, design, and operating standards are set to meet safety requirements.

This move away from public ownership and the greater participation of private investors and contractors stems from changes, both in public attitudes, fostered by intellectual shifts, regarding the effectiveness of state industries in meeting social and economic goals generally, and in the financial underpinning of public investments. The traditional public interest concepts of state ownership, whereby the controlling body seeks only to fulfill social objectives began to be questioned intellectually in the 1960s by economists of the Public Choice persuasion, who argued that state managers themselves have personal motivations. The tendency, which is seen as a normal part of human nature, is for bureaucrats to have their own agendas that include their career advancement, job security, and other factors that can conflict with their seeking to meet social criteria. The result is inefficiency that manifested itself most clearly in the state owned transportation systems in Central and Eastern Europe before 1989.

Even where state owned entities were more efficiently managed, and social objectives still came near the forefront of activities, developments outside of the transportation have forged change. In particular, the traditional view that state ownership is needed to finance large infrastructure investments, a position even Adam

Smith took, has been dented as private sector financial markets have become more sophisticated and international. Macroeconomic policy has also moved away from the idea that the state can steer the economy through its public sector investments. Added to this has been the shift in thinking towards economic efficiency per se. This has raised questions about access to transportation infrastructure and making sure that priority is with those who actually gain most from it. User charges have become common, and technological advances in areas of Intelligent Transport Systems (ITS) have help in the facilitation of this.

But issues of ensuring that the private sector meet larger social goals as well as narrower financial ones still remains a concern of policy makers. Essentially, the approach has shifted from always owning the infrastructure to one where the authorities set objectives or characteristics (that may be in design standards, quality of service, capacity, etc.) but then devising mechanisms whereby facilitating provision by the private sector at minimum cost. The result has been the creation of a variety of bidding and tendering systems that seek to produce competition for the provision of these predefined packages of infrastructure characteristics. Overlaying this are regulatory structures governing things like prices (often involving price-caps) to prevent exploitation as markets change over time.

PUBLIC POLICY ON TRANSPORTATION INFRASTRUCTURE ACCESS

Whilst many of the traditional debates on infrastructure policy, or at least the economic debates, have centered on ways of assessing of alternatives (e.g., the development of various forms of cost-benefit analysis techniques) and on means of finance, there has been a recent upsurge of interest in access issues; basically making better use of existing transportation facilities. One contributing factor to the long-standing focus on investment and capacity was that much transportation infrastructure was fallaciously viewed as being a public good.[5]

Access is not an issue if this were the case because, by definition, public goods are non-excludable. While things like national defense may be seen as a public good, essentially it is impossible for the nation's army not to protect me if it is protecting everyone else, this is manifestly not the case with transportation infrastructure. A simple barrier can thwart assesses to a road. Equally, there is no problem with efficient use of a public good because, by definition it is non-rival; there is no congestion. But this is hardly a characteristic that pertains to transportation infrastructure. To put it simply, generically transportation infrastructure has all the features of a private good.

The general lack of appreciation of the intrinsic economic nature of transportation over the years has resulted in a continued display of policy gymnastics to try to make the best use of it. Some of these have entailed simple physical command and control rationing devices; e.g., the allocation of airport runway take-off slots. Others have relied, rather perversely, when infrastructure is taken as public good, on congestion to deter use by deteriorating the quality of service offered; generally slower and less reliable movement. In some cases where privately provided infrastructure is regulated, or provided publicly without subsidies, and costs require to be recovered, revenues are collected from users. The normal basis for this, however, is aimed at cost recovery without distorting excessively the pattern of use from what it would be with no charges; technically, Ramsey pricing is advocated for this. What this does not do, however, is ration the overall use of the transportation infrastructure to the economically efficient level.

What is noticeable is that where transportation suppliers, either of services or infrastructure, are left to their own devices is that they seek to levy fares or charges that both give priority to those most willing to pay and act to make the overall optimal use of the facilities.

Most roads, for example, can either be used without any direct payment[6] or by paying a fixed toll designed to cover the capital and maintenance costs of roads. Excessive traffic congestions of roads, in particular in cities but now often spreading to inter-urban highways, is now generally agreed to be rife. Public policy has, over the years tried to deal with this by expanding capacity, redesigning cities so that less travel is needed, encouraging use of less congestive buses and transit systems, usually by giving massive subsidies, regulating complements to car use (notably parking policies), physically managing traffic flows (e.g., through computerized traffic signals, informational signs, unidirectional streets and other 'intelligent transportation systems' measures), or by trying to encourage people to use cars more efficiently (e.g., high occupancy lanes). Singularly these have failed in anything but the short-term. The basic problem is that these measures ignore the fact that they may initially speed traffic but that this in itself, by reducing generalized costs, simply attracts more traffic; a phenomena often referred to as 'Down's Law' but pretty well know to economists for 150 years or so.

All may have merit and, by their very adoption, presumably do not significantly offend any important coalition of interests, but most would agree that they have not in any way met primary criteria with regard to making the best use of the infrastructure. The only major urban areas where traffic congestion has come down are Singapore and Central London. In each case there has been an attempt to price road use at the point of consumption and to set that price at a level that would achieve a defined traffic flow. This is not quite the same as privatization, where market forces would determine both the charge and the traffic flow, but, given the continued political stability of the government in Singapore and the subsequent reelection of the mayor in London, it would seem to meet current social criteria.

In fact similar policies are being developed across a range of modes and embrace international, as well as domestic, use of infrastructure. The EU rules on rail infrastructure are indifferent to the form of ownership but do concern themselves with open access to operators from all EU nations at rates that do not favor national rail concerns. This also holds for airports, although here the overriding policy comes from the United Nations' International Civil Aviation Organization.

CONCLUSIONS

There is really no clear definition of what constitutes transportation infrastructure but everyone has a pretty good idea of what is meant by the term. The perception has, however, widened in recent years as the information society has developed, and now many elements of infrastructure, including those important for transport, are less physically identifiable than in the past. But, while these changes have nuanced policy, many of the same basic challenges remain; the nature of responsible institutions, mechanisms for funding, deciding between alternatives, making best use of the hard- and software and so on. In many ways, perhaps, the biggest change in recent years is that globalization, internationalization, and the creation of regional blocks such as the EU has forced countries to coordinate more in their infrastructure policies and plans.

Whatever the details of the definition or statistics measure adopted, transportation infrastructure forms a major part of the capital stock of virtually all countries, and much of it has traditionally been in the hands of the state, or strongly controlled by the state. This is gradually changing, and where state ownership remains, the way infrastructure is viewed and managed is going through something of a transformation. To put it simply, the public sector now often finds it difficult to husband the resources needed for large investments and its ability to manage existing systems effectively has come under question.

NOTES

1. The 15 European Union countries before enlargement in 2004.

2. The relevant parameters are often employing a Cobb-Douglas specification – using either time series data for a particular area or by cross-sectional analysis across regions.

3. Agriculture was the other.

4. Although, in the case of EU countries, track has to be open to any user from another country at a reasonable fee.

5. There is also the political factor that much more kudos comes from adding capacity than from either its maintenance or making good use of it. The large number

of pieces of transportation infrastructure, some of dubious merit, bearing the name of some defunct politician or dignitary, hints at the legacy effects of getting involved in supporting investments.

6. Where there are dedicated 'road funds' financed by fuel or vehicle taxation, these sources of payment are remote from the actual use of a road for any particular trip. As such they have very little impact on peoples' decisions whether to drive or not.

REFERENCES

Andersson, Å. E., Anderstig, C. and Hårsman, B. (1990) Knowledge and communications infrastructure and regional economic change, *Regional Science and Urban Economics*, 20: 359–376.

Aschauer, D. A. (1989) Is public expenditure productive?, *Journal of Monetary Economics*, 23: 177–200.

Biehl, D. (1991) The role of infrastructure in regional development, in R.W. Vickerman (ed), *Infrastructure and Regional Development*, London, Pion.

Button, K. J. (1998) Infrastructure investment, endogenous growth and economic convergence, *Annals of Regional Science*, 32: 145–162.

Button, K. J. (2002) High-technology employment and hub airports: infrastructure's contribution to regional development, in Y. Higano, P. Nijkamp, J. Poot and J. J. van Wijk (eds), *The Region in the New Economy: An International Perspective on Spatial Dynamics in the 21st Century*, Ashgate, Aldershot.

Button, K. J. (2004) *Wings Across Europe: Towards an Efficient European Air Transport System*, Ashgate, Aldershot.

Button, K. J. and Rietveld, P. (2000) A meta-analysis of the impact of infrastructure policy on regional development, in H. Kohno, P. Nijkamp and J. Poot (eds), *Regional Cohesion and Competition in the Process of Globalisation*, Edward Elgar, Cheltenham.

Costa, J., da Silva Ellson, R. W. and Martin, R. C. (1987) Public capital, regional output and development: some empirical evidence, *Journal of Regional Science*, 27: 419–37.

Dupuit, J. A. (1844) De la mesure de l' utilité des travaux publics, *Annuales des Ponts et Chaussés*, 8.

Duffy-Deno, K. and Eberts, R. W. (1991) Public infrastructure and regional economic development: a simultaneous approach, *Journal of Urban Economics*, 30: 329–43.

Eisner, R. W. (1991) Infrastructure and regional economic performance, *New England Economic Review*, September/October: 47–58.

European Commission (1989) *Council Resolution in Trans-European Networks*, COM(89)643/FIN, Brussels.

European Commission (2001) European Transport Policy for 2010: Time to Decide, White Paper, Brussels.

Eberts, R. W. and Fogarty, M. S. (1987) Estimating the relationship between local public and private investment, *Federal Reserve Bank of Cleveland Working Paper* 8703.

Frey, B. S. (1985) *Democratic Economic Policy*, Martin Roberson, Oxford.

Gramlich, E. M. (1994) Infrastructure investment: a review essay, *Journal of Economic Literature*, 32: 1176–96.

Holtz-Eakin, D. (1992) Public sector capital and productivity puzzle, *National Bureau of Economic Research Working Paper* 4122.

Hirschman, O. A. (1958) *The Strategy of Economic Development*, New Haven: Yale University Press.

Jansson, J. O. (2000) Transport infrastructure: the investment problem, in J. B. Polak and A. Heertje (eds), *Analytical Transport Economics: An International Perspective*, Edward Elgar, Cheltenham.

Jorgensen, D. (1991) Fragile statistical foundations: the macroeconomics of public infrastructure investment, comment on Hulten and Schwab, presented at the American Enterprise Institute Conference on Infrastructure Needs and Public policy Options for the 1990s, Washington.

Lakshmanan, T. R. (1989) Infrastructure and economic transformation, in A. E. Andersson, D. F. Batten, B. Johansson and P. Nijkamp (eds), *Advances in Spatial Theory and Dynamics*, Amsterdam: North-Holland.

Leitham, S. (1993) Predicting the economic development effects of transportation projects, Proceedings of the 25th Annual Conference of the Universities Transport Research Group, Southampton.

Mera, K. (1973) Regional production functions and social overhead capital: an analysis of the Japanese case, *Regional and Urban Economics*, 3: 157–86.

Morrison, C. J. (1993) Macroeconomic relationships between public spending on infrastructure and private sector productivity in the United States, in J. M. Mintz and R. S. Preston (eds), *Infrastructure and Competitiveness*, John Deutsch Institute for the Study of Economic Policy, Ottawa.

Munnell, A. H. (1990) Is there a shortfall in public capital investment? *New England Economic Review*, September/October, 11–32.

Nadiri, I. and Manuenias, T. (1996) *Contribution of Highway Capital to Industry and National Productivity Growth*, Federal Highway Administration Office of Policy Development, Washington.

Nurske, R. (1953) *Problems of Capital Formation in Developing Countries*, Oxford: Basil Blackwell.

Smith, A. (1776) *An Enquiry into the Nature and Causes of the Wealth of Nations*. 2000 edition published by The Modern Library, New Work.

Stough, R., Vickerman, R., Button, K. J. and Nijkamp, P. (eds) (2002) *Transport Infrastructure*, Edward Elgar, Cheltenham.

Sturm, J. E. and de Haan, J. (1995) Is public expenditure really productive? New evidence from the USA and the Netherlands, *Economic Modelling*, 12: 60–72.

Winston, C. (1991) Efficient transportation infrastructure policy, *Journal of Economic Literature*, 5: 113–27.

Youngson, A. J. (1967) *Overhead Capital. A Study in Development Economics*, Edinburgh: Edinburgh University Press.

20

Foreign Policy

WALTER CARLSNAES

Taking the broad historical perspective is often a suggestive strategy for gauging the current state of a field of study. The chapter on 'Foreign Policy' in the magisterial eight-volume *Handbook of Political Science*, published in 1975, is in this regard insightful for at least two reasons. The first is its tone, which is guardedly optimistic about the future of foreign policy analysis, despite deep-rooted disagreements within the field regarding both its conceptual boundaries and the most appropriate manner to analyze its substance. There is, the two authors write, a 'sense of movement at last, akin to one's first responses as a traffic jam unlocks and cars begin, hesitantly and tentatively, to pick up forward speed' (Cohen and Harris, 1975: 381). The second reason is the unquestioned assumption that the subject matter of foreign policy belongs naturally to the empirical domain of public policy rather than of international relations – so much so that Cohen and Harris' chapter was published in the volume on 'Policies and Policymaking' rather than that on 'International Politics'. To most readers today, a quarter of a century later, both of these characterizations will undoubtedly raise more than a few puzzled eyebrows. The first due to its misplaced (if admittedly guarded) optimism about the future disciplinary development of the field; and the second because, if there is anything which all foreign

policy analysts today can and do agree on (and there is not much else), it is that they belong squarely to the scholarly domain of International Relations (IR) rather than to any of the policy sciences.

This is not to say, however, that the study of foreign policy currently enjoys an undisputed professional domicile within IR. This uneasy state of affairs is due, at least in part, to the failure of foreign policy researchers, during the past twenty-five years, to consolidate their field in the manner once envisioned. Instead, their practice has to a considerable degree become one of eclecticism and defensiveness within a larger scholarly milieu which, on the whole, is not especially engaged with the issues at the head of the agenda of foreign policy analysis. A quick perusal of the table of contents of the major IR journals published during the past decade or so is quite clear on this score: very few contain titles in which the concept of 'foreign policy analysis' plays a prominent role. At the same time interest in the development of IR theory itself has grown exponentially, but for the most part with little or no reference to 'foreign policy', either as an integral part of such theory or as a separate but important approach in its own right. On the contrary, most of the time it is simply ignored in these debates and discussions, or politely dismissed, with reference to the distinction between system level and unit level theories, the former pertaining to international politics proper, the latter 'merely' to the behaviour of individual states. 'Theory development at this level', a recent review of theories of foreign policy thus states laconically, 'has received comparatively little attention' (Rose, 1998: 145). Alexander Wendt's declaration of (a lack of) interest is equally symptomatic: 'Theories of international politics are distinguished from those that have as their object explaining the behaviour of individual states, or "theories of foreign policy" … Like Waltz, I am interested in international politics, not foreign policy' (Wendt, 1999: 11). Perhaps of equal significance, foreign policy analysts themselves seem to have lost heart. Hence, as a British scholar noted in 1999, 'These are testing times for foreign policy analysts. At issue is whether their area of study remains a major sub-field of International Relations or whether it has become anachronistic, either subsumed or replaced by other approaches to understanding and explaining state behaviour' (White, 1999: 37). Similarly, a German colleague has noted that, despite a plethora of publications on the topic in his home country, the study of foreign policy itself is currently in the throes of a conceptual crisis and theoretically at a standstill (Schneider, 1997). However, let me already at this point signal that, although there is some justification for the bleak picture of the sub-field of foreign policy analysis adumbrated above, it by no means represents the whole picture. It reflects a disciplinary development during the past two to three decades which has put a strong structuralist-systemic stamp on IR, and hence also an effective damper on approaches – such as foreign policy analysis – premised not primarily on the international system as the generator of behaviour but on the importance of unit-level factors and actors for understanding and explaining state behaviour. But this structuralist-systemic perspective has never been totally hegemonic, even in North America, and in Europe it has failed to achieve the same grip on the scholarly imaginations of its mostly small, eclectic and not equally 'scientistic' or 'rationalistic' IR communities. More importantly, since at least the end of the Cold War – and

perhaps to a considerable extent as a result of it – this dominant perspective has increasingly had to provide space for a view of the substance of interstate interactions which is more in tune with some of the basic premises of foreign policy approaches. In other words, a case can be made for why a focus on foreign policy is once again regaining ground within IR, and why it should indeed do so.

The way I intend to proceed is as follows. In the next section an intellectual history of foreign policy analysis will be presented, primarily covering developments during the past half-century. After that a conceptual and analytical overview of the field itself will be provided, in which I will first very briefly discuss fundamental definitional issues and present four rock-bottom types of explanatory frameworks defined, not in terms of 'schools', 'grand debates' or 'contending approaches', but with reference to two fundamental meta-theoretical dimensions within the philosophy of social science. On the basis of these four generic perspectives, my intention in the subsequent and core part of the chapter is to highlight and briefly discuss some of the more prominent contemporary attempts to structure and to pursue analysis within the field. After this the question will be raised – and a brief answer suggested – whether a synthetic or integrated approach to foreign policy analysis is at all feasible. The concluding section will pinpoint a few current and contentious issues straddling the various approaches discussed, indicating some areas of potential development within the field.

INTERNATIONAL RELATIONS AND FOREIGN POLICY ANALYSIS: A SHORT INTELLECTUAL HISTORY

As is the case with IR itself, most historical accounts of foreign policy analysis – and there are not many available – tend to suffer from a Whig interpretation of this history, or from what Brian C. Schmidt has called the problem of 'presentism': 'the practice of writing a history of the field for the purpose of making a point about its present character' (Schmidt, 2002: 5). These accounts are also to a considerable degree infused with parochialisms of various shades, both of a geographic, scholarly and subdisciplinary nature. The combination of these two characteristics makes for interesting reading but hardly for a fully illuminating overview of this historical development. In other words, they have on the whole contributed to conventional images of the progression, and hence identity of the field, that need to be challenged and corrected.

As suggested above, the conception of foreign policy as an academic subject matter has had strong roots in the broader domain of public policy, especially in the United States. However, this is not where the field originated but is, rather, a reaction to the earlier tradition – primarily of a European provenance, with origins in the seventeenth century and the rise of the modern state thereafter – of viewing foreign policy as a distinct domain differing in fundamental respects from all other spheres of public policy. 'The leading assumption', Bernard C. Cohen thus noted some years ago, 'is that foreign policy is "more important" than other policy areas because it concerns national interests, rather than special interests, and more fundamental values' (Cohen, 1968: 530). A further consequence of this doctrine of the 'primacy of foreign policy' was, of course that, being distinct in this manner, political elites demanded that it be treated differently from all other areas of public policy, that is, beyond democratic control and public scrutiny. However, the experiences leading up to, and the consequences of, the First World War convinced some influential statesmen – in particular Woodrow Wilson – that an end should be put to the traditional secretive practices of statecraft and diplomacy.

Despite the subsequent failure of the Wilsonian project, the study of foreign policy was deeply affected – especially in the United States – by this liberal and democratic ideology, with the result that much of its activities subsequent to the Second World War, when foreign policy analysis first came to be firmly established academically, was concerned with the study of two major implications of these

beliefs (Cohen, 1968). The first was to focus on how the governmental institutions responsible for the formulation and implementation of foreign policy could be made more efficient in the pursuit of their tasks. The second had a more ideological thrust, essentially involving a plea for the democratization of foreign policy – of why and how public values and interests should be introduced to every stage in the formulation and execution of such policy.

However, concomitant with this institutionally focused and policy-oriented tradition in the academic study of foreign policy, which enjoyed its American heyday during the two decades following the Second World War, we also find a second major tradition, and one which has left a much stronger and seemingly indelible imprint on the subsequent development of the field. I here have in mind the induction into American thinking of a powerful European influence, and one that stands in marked contrast to the indigenous strands of the liberal Wilsonian project. Realism is its name, and Hans Morgenthau was for decades its undisputed high priest (Morgenthau, 1948). As argued by Stefano Guzzini in his comprehensive sociological analysis of the history of realism, Morgenthau's main concern, as that of realists more generally, was to resuscitate an older tradition by translating 'the maxims of [the] nineteenth century's European diplomatic practice into more general laws of an American social science' (Guzzini, 1998: 1; see also Dunne, 1998; Kahler, 1997). To summarize a complex argument, he did this by claiming 'that the inherent and immutable self-interested nature of human beings, when faced with a structure of international anarchy, results in states maximizing one thing, power' (Smith, 1986: 15). By linking this view of power to the concept of the national interest, he believed that he could provide a universal explanation for the behaviour of particular states.

The behaviouralist turn in American social science in the 1950s and 1960s had a decisive effect on both of these approaches to the study of foreign policy. Its impact on the institutionally oriented research tradition was perhaps the more deep-going, in the sense that it changed its character altogether from being an essentially idiographic and normative enterprise – analyzing particular forms of policy or prescribing better means for its formulation and implementation – to one which now aspired to generate and to test hypotheses in order to develop a cumulative body of empirical generalizations. The main outgrowth of this fundamental theoretical and methodological reorientation was a movement, starting in the late 1960s, which became known as the comparative study of foreign policy, or CFP for short. Its strong behaviouralist character is manifested in its focus on explaining foreign policy in terms of discrete acts of 'behaviour' rather than in the form of 'purposive' state actions in the realist mode; and taking its cue from how American behavioural political science focused on the 'vote' as its fundamental unit of analysis, it posited the 'event' as its dependent variable. In this view foreign policy is seen as the exercise of influence in international relations, with 'events' specifying 'who does what to whom, and how' (Hudson and Vore, 1995: 215). As a consequence, the task of collecting data on and analyzing such events, with the aim of generating and accumulating empirical generalizations about foreign policy behaviour, became a major industry within CFP (Brecher, 1972; East, 1978; McGowan and Shapiro, 1973; Rummel, 1972; Wilkenfeld et al., 1980). It was also an activity generously funded by a federal government fully in tune with these ambitions (Andriole and Hopple, 1984).

However, it is generally acknowledged by friend and foe alike that this programme of establishing a truly 'scientific' approach to the analysis of foreign policy was, on the whole, a significant if commendable failure. The empirical results of the major research programmes which had been launched during these years turned out to be disappointing (Hudson and Vore, 1995: 215–16), and it became increasingly evident that the aim of a unified theory and a methodology based on aggregate analysis had to be rejected as empirically impracticable and analytically unfruitful (Caporaso et al., 1987; East, 1978; Kegley, 1980; Munton, 1976; Smith, 1987).

The CFP programme did not, however, eclipse the type of foreign policy analysis which all along had focused mainly on the processes involved in foreign policy decision-making, or on contextual or sociopsychological factors influencing such behaviour (Hudson and Vore, 1995: 216–19). The former, with roots going back the pioneering work on decision-making by Snyder, Bruck and Sapin (1954), developed into extensive research exemplified by, for example, studies focusing on small group dynamics (C. Hermann, 1978; Janis, 1982; Tetlock, 1979), the 'bureaucratic politics' approach made famous by the publication in 1971 of Graham Allison's study of the Cuban crisis, as well as Steinbruner's attempt to present foreign policy-making as analogous to cybernetic processes (Steinbruner, 1974). The latter type of research focus, concentrating on more particular aspects of the decision-making process, produced a number of distinguished studies, ranging from Michael Brecher's (1972) work on Israel, Robert Jervis's (1976) book on perceptions and misperceptions, and a long series of studies – continuing to the present time, as we shall see below – on the role of cognitive and psychological factors in the explanation of foreign policy actions (Axelrod, 1976; Cottam, 1977; M. Hermann, 1974, 1980a, 1980b; Holsti et al., 1968).

What can be said generally about this broad tradition is that, whereas there was perhaps a brief moment in time when it could be asserted that foreign policy analysis was self-consciously in the process of achieving an identity of its own ('all the evidence', James N. Rosenau thus proclaimed in 1974, in a statement that was soon and forever after to cause him considerable chagrin, 'points to the conclusion that the comparative study of foreign policy has now emerged as a *normal* science'), this is certainly not the case at the beginning of the new millennium (quoted in Smith, 1986: 20). Instead, if anything is typical of its practitioners at present, it is the almost total lack of such a sub-disciplinary identity. In the words of one of its contemporary chroniclers, the attitude today is instead one of allowing 'a hundred flowers to bloom' (Hudson and Vore, 1995: 22); or, as another reviewer has put it (in a slightly more upbeat locution), of opening 'conversational space' to the multiple perspectives and 'new vistas' of foreign policy analysis (Neack et al., 1995: 12).

Turning to the development of realism in the face of the behaviouralist challenge, we are presented with an intriguing paradox in the history of foreign policy analysis. On the one hand, it was believed by many that, given the centrality in Morgenthau's approach of power defined in terms of the innate, unobservable but crucial notion of a fixed human nature, it would not be able to withstand this confrontation. Yet, this is precisely what it did, insofar as the behaviouralists never really challenged the underlying assumptions of realism, only its methodology (Vasquez, 1983). Nevertheless, while continuing to be the major intellectual force defining IR itself (Guzzini, 1998; Hollis and Smith, 1990), realism became methodologically divided as a consequence of the debate on its scientific status, and suffered a setback – by no means permanent – with the publication of Allison's in-depth penetration of the Cuba crisis in terms primarily of an analysis of unit-level rather than systemic factors (Allison, 1971). Since the celebrated appearance of Kenneth Waltz's *Theory of International Politics* (1979), an even clearer bifurcation within realism has occurred, particularly in response to the strong stand against all forms of reductionist approaches – typified by most theories of foreign policy – which lies at the core of his structuralist reformulation of realism.

In summation of half a century of foreign policy analysis one can thus say that two broad traditions have played a major role in it, and that they continue to do so. The first is the more difficult to label, insofar as it contains a host of different and disparate approaches, including work on cognitive and psychological factors, bureaucratic and neoinstitutional politics, crisis behaviour, policy implementation, group decision-making processes, and transnational relations, to name some of the most important (see Hudson and Vore, 1995: 222–8). If only for lack of a better term, we can refer to this tradition in terms of the primacy allocated within it to the role of *Innenpolitik* – of domestic factors – in the explanation of foreign policy. As recently noted, although there 'are many variants of this approach, each favouring a different specific

domestic independent variable … they all share a common assumption – that foreign policy is best understood as the product of a country's internal dynamics' (Rose, 1998: 148). Juxtaposed against its explanatory logic we find realism broadly conceived, and for the sake of simplicity (and linguistic consistency) we can refer to this tradition as that of *Realpolitik*. Although not averse to allowing for the play of domestic factors in the pursuit of foreign policy, the major explanatory weight is here given to material systemic-level factors in one form or another.

However, although this characterization in terms of the classical divide between domestic and international politics has a long historical pedigree, it does have at least one major drawback as a criterion for classifying contemporary foreign policy analysis. For, while many scholars continue to think of this analytical boundary as the major line of division within the field, and one that continues to be conceptually fruitful in analysis, it is nevertheless based on an assumption which is highly questionable as both an empirical and a theoretical proposition: that it is indeed feasible to determine the nature and function of such a boundary, and to do so without begging a fundamental question in the study of international relations. Thus, while it can be argued that this characterization of the field in terms of these two broad traditions continues to reflect a sub-disciplinary selfunderstanding of its development, it will not be used below when discussing the current state of affairs in foreign policy analysis. Instead of a criterion based specifically on the *substantive* nature of foreign policy (and one of dubious value), the discussion will proceed from two *meta-theoretical* dimensions – one ontological, the other epistemological – which are entirely neutral with regard to the substance of foreign policy itself.

CONCEPTUALIZING THE DOMAIN

'There is a certain discomfort in writing about foreign policy,' we are forewarned in the first lines of the *Handbook of Political Science* chapter on foreign policy, 'for no two people seem to define it in the same way, disagreements in approach often seem to be deep-seated, and we do not yet know enough about it to be able to say with confidence whether it may be differentiated from all other areas of public policy' (Cohen and Harris, 1975: 318). What its two authors point to here is a twin *problematique* which has occupied a central place in the history of foreign policy analysis, and which needs to be addressed as much today as in the past. The first of these concerns the crucial issue of what constitutes the particular explanandum of the study of foreign policy: what it is that is to be explained. For while this definitional issue may on first sight seem trivial, it in fact goes to the core of what distinguishes this field of study from that of both domestic and international politics, and hence lies at the heart of the long-standing issue of where and how to draw the analytical boundary between a sub-field that willy-nilly straddles these two major disciplinary foci of political science. Secondly, this issue is also crucial to the choice of theoretically feasible instruments of analysis, since the nature of a given explanandum has obvious and fundamental implications for the types of explanans, that is, explanatory factors, which in principle are appropriate and in practice fruitful. Although there is today (in contrast to a generation ago) a relatively stable consensus with regard to the explanandum, which therefore need not detain us for long, this is not the case with respect to the considerably more contentious meta-theoretical issue.

This consensus boils down to a specification of the *unit of analysis* that emphasizes the purposive nature of foreign policy actions, a focus on policy and the crucial role of state boundaries. The following stipulation is intended to capture these definitional aspects: foreign policies consist of those actions which, expressed in the form of explicitly stated goals, commitments and/or directives, and pursued by governmental representatives acting on behalf of their sovereign communities, are directed toward objectives, conditions and actors – both governmental and non-governmental – which they want to affect and which lie beyond their territorial legitimacy.

As a starting point for discussing the types of *explanatory factors* that have characterized foreign policy analysis, it is necessary to consider two fundamental issues that have dominated current meta-theoretical debate within social theory (and IR). The first concerns the ontological foundation of social systems: the type of issue exemplified by the claim, reputedly made by Margaret Thatcher, that there is 'no such thing as a society', but 'only individuals'. Essentially, it revolves around the question of where the dynamic foundations of social systems are located. This dynamism either has its origin in 'the effects, intended or not, of individual action; or from the slowly evolving rules of the self-reproducing structure' (Guzzini, 1998: 197). This classic distinction in social theory is usually expressed in terms of the dichotomy between 'individualism' and 'holism', the former holding 'that social scientific explanations should be reducible to the properties or interactions of independently existing individuals', while holism stands for the view 'that the effects of social structures cannot be reduced to independently existing agents and their interactions' (Wendt, 1999: 26).

This ontological polarity between individualism and holism should be clearly distinguished from the epistemological issue of whether social agency is to be viewed through an 'objectivistic' or an 'interpretative' lens. Using a different metaphor, two choices are available here: to focus on human agents and their actions, either from the 'outside' or from the 'inside', corresponding to the classical Weberian distinction between *Erklären* (explaining) and *Verstehen* (understanding). As argued by Martin Hollis and Steve Smith, these two approaches tell two different types of 'stories' about international relations, each with its own view of human nature and a concomitant range of 'appropriate' theories (Hollis and Smith, 1990). The choice is thus between an approach that models itself on the natural sciences, and one premised on the independent existence of a social realm constituted by social rules and intersubjective meanings. Whereas the former is based on a 'naturalistic' epistemology self-consciously replicated on that of the natural sciences, the latter – and the epistemological notion of *Verstehen* – is based on Weber's claim that 'The science of society attempts the interpretative understanding of social action' (quoted in Hollis and Smith, 1990: 71). This means that 'action must always be understood from within', and this in a double sense: the investigator must both get to 'know the rules, conventions, and context governing the action', and 'to know what the agent intended by and in performing the action' (Hollis and Smith, 1990: 72). Although not uncontroversial and hence in need of further discussion (which cannot be provided here), this epistemological distinction will in the present context concern us only by virtue of its implications when combined with the two ontological choices presented above.

The individualistic answer to the ontological question reduces the epistemological issue to a choice between either treating actors from the 'outside' as rational or cognitive agents in social systems, or from the 'inside' as interpretative or reflexive actors in an intersubjective world of meaning. In either case, the individual is viewed as the primary source of social order, and hence all conceptions of the link between agents and social structures are ultimately reduced to explanations in terms of individual action. Explanations proceeding from a holistic approach to social order treat action either as a function of structural determination in some sense or other, or with reference to processes of socialization broadly defined. In both cases the relationship between actors and social structures is tendered in terms of some form of structural determination in which individual action is conceived as a function of a pre-established social order.

On the basis of these two dimensions we can now summarize their implications for foreign policy approaches in the following fourfold matrix (Figure 20.1) (see also Dunne, 1995: 370–2; Guzzini, 1998: 190–210; Hollis, 1994: 183–260; Hollis and Smith, 1990: 155–9, 214–16; Wendt, 1999: 22–40). I shall now proceed to discuss prominent examples of each of the four types of rock-bottom perspectives in the study of foreign policy identified in

Ontology	Epistemology	
	Objectivism	Interpretativism
Holism	Structural perspective	Social-institutional perspective
Individualism	Agency-based perspective	Interpretative actor perspective

Figure 20.1 *Four types of rock-bottom perspectives in the study of foreign policy*

Figure 20.1. Given the space available, the ambition here is to be illustrative rather than comprehensive or exhaustive.

CURRENT APPROACHES IN FOREIGN POLICY ANALYSIS

Approaches Based on a Structural Perspective

Realism Although, as we shall see below, there are other structurally oriented approaches to foreign policy analysis as well, there is no doubt that most contemporary forms of realism fit this bill best. It is also the case that, despite the massive attacks which neorealism has experienced as a consequence of its reputed inability either to predict or to explain the end of the Cold War, it continues not only to be alive and well (especially in North America), but also to contribute to the contemporary analysis of foreign policy. For, although Waltz has repeatedly claimed that neorealism is a theory of international politics and hence not a theory of foreign policy (Waltz, 1996), strong counter-arguments have been made that this is essentially an untenable position, and hence that nothing prevents neorealists from formulating a theory of foreign policy of their own (Elman, 1996a, 1996b). It has also been noted that, despite such denials, neorealists in actual fact frequently engage in the analyses of foreign policy (Baumann et al., 2001: 37–67).

However, there are different variants of (neo)realism, of which at least the following play important roles in the contemporary debate. First of all, a distinction should be made between 'aggressive' and 'defensive' types (Snyder, 1991: 11–12; see also Lynn-Jones and Miller, 1995: xi–xii; Rose, 1998). During the past decade *aggressive neorealism* has been pre-eminently represented by John Mearsheimer, who has argued that, whereas the Cold War, based on bipolarity, military balance and nuclear weapons, produced peace in Europe for 45 years, its demise will – contrary to the conventional wisdom – perforce have deleterious effects in the long run. This pessimistic scenario follows from a strict application of neorealist tenets, especially of the view that, insofar as the international system invariably fosters conflict and aggression, rational states are compelled to pursue offensive strategies in their search for security (Mearsheimer, 1995: 79–129; see also Layne, 1995: 130–76). It also emphazises the role of the polarity of the international system – bipolarity being more conducive to peace than multipolarity – as well as the effects of changes in the relative power of states.

Defensive neorealists, on the other hand, do not share this pessimistic and essentially Hobbesian view of the international system, instead arguing that, although systemic factors do have causal effects on state behaviour, they cannot account for all state actions. Instead of emphasizing the role played by the distribution of power in the international system, scholars such as Stephen Walt and Charles L. Glaser thus instead pointed to the importance of the source, level and direction of *threats*, defined primarily in terms of technological factors, geographic proximity, offensive capabilities and perceived intentions (Glaser, 1995; Walt, 1995; see also the references in Rose, 1998: 146, fn. 4). The picture presented here is that states pursuing security in a rational manner can on the whole afford to be relatively relaxed, except in rare instances; and that security can generally be achieved by balancing against threats in a timely way, a policy that will effectively hinder most forms of actual conflict. 'Foreign policy activity', Rose thus explains, 'is the record of rational states reacting properly to clear systemic incentives, coming into conflict only in those circumstances when the security dilemma is heightened to fever pitch' (Rose, 1998: 150; see also Glaser, 1995;

Lynn-Jones and Miller, 1995: xi; Snyder, 1991; Van Evera, 1990/91: 11–17; Walt, 1995; Zakaria, 1995: 475–81).

Neoclassical realists should be distinguished from both offensive and defensive neorealists. They share with neorealists the view that a country's foreign policy is primarily formed by its place in the international system and in particular by its relative material power capabilities. However, and here the classical roots of this approach come to the fore, they also argue that the impact of systemic factors on a given country's foreign policy will be indirect and more complex than neorealists have assumed, since such factors can effect policy only through intervening variables at the unit level (Rose, 1998: 146). This view is clearly contrary to the whole tenor of offensive neorealism, but neoclassical realists also fault defensive neorealists, mainly because it is claimed that their systemic argument fails to explain much of actual foreign policy behaviour and hence needs to be augmented by the *ad hoc* introduction of unit-level variables (see, e.g., Schweller, 1996: 114–15; Zakaria, 1995). As a consequence of the stress on the role of both independent (systemic) and intervening (domestic) variables, research within neoclassical realism is generally conducted in the form of theoretically informed narratives – ideally supplemented by counterfactual analysis – that trace how different factors combine to forge the particular foreign policies of states (Rose, 1998: 153). More specifically, this has yielded extensive narrative case studies of how twentieth-century great powers – especially the United States, the Soviet Union and China – have reacted to the material rise or decline of their relative power in the international system (Christensen, 1996; Schweller, 1998; Wohlforth, 1993; Zakaria, 1998).

Neoliberal institutionialism Although not generally touted as an approach to the analysis of foreign policy, it is obvious that the type of focus that usually goes under the name of neoliberal institutionalism is as relevant to the study of foreign policy as are realism and neorealism in their various configurations. Indeed, insofar as this school of thought is posited as an alternative to realism (and, the view of some, as the only one), it also *pari passu* entails an alternative approach to foreign policy analysis (see Baldwin, 1993).

Neoliberal institutionalism is a structural, systemic and 'top-down' view for some of the same reasons that realism constitutes such an approach. It assumes that states are the primary actors in the international system; that they behave like egoist value maximizers; and that the international system is essentially anarchic (Baldwin, 1993: 8–14; Grieco, 1993). It is also for this reason that Andrew Moravcsik has claimed that 'neoliberal institutionalism' is a misnomer insofar as it essentially constitutes a variant of realism (Moravcsik, 1997: 537).

What then is distinctive about the neoliberal institutionalist approach to foreign policy analysis? Very briefly, the following: whereas both realists and neoliberals view foreign policy-making as a process of constrained choice by purposive states, the latter understand this constraint not primarily in terms of the configurations of power capabilities facing policy-makers, but in terms of an anarchic system which, while it fosters uncertainty and hence security concerns, can nevertheless be positively affected by the institutional provision of information and common rules in the form of functional regimes. The result is that international cooperation under anarchy *is* possible in the pursuit of given state preferences (Oye, 1985); and hence certain specific features of an international setting can explain state outcomes in the form of cooperative foreign policies (Axelrod and Keohane, 1993; Keohane, 1993).

Organizational process approaches While both realism and neoliberal institutionalism are structural approaches of a systemic kind, foreign policy analysis can be pursued 'structurally' on a lower level of analysis as well, in which the structural factor driving foreign policy behaviour is not external but internal to the state. As argued by Hollis and Smith, a 'top-down' approach on the sub-systemic level either focuses on the causal relationship between the state and its agencies – how the

latter conform to the demands of the former – or between agencies and individuals; on this level a structural view would imply that individual decision-makers do not act independently but generally in conformity with the dictates of the agencies employing them (Hollis and Smith, 1990: 8–9, 196–202).

The latter type of claim has become known as the organizational process approach ever since the celebrated publication of Allison's *Essence of Decision* in 1971. With roots in organizational theory, it focuses on decisions not in terms of instrumental rationality but as *outputs* of large organizations functioning according to regular patterns of behaviour, usually referred to as standard operating procedures. The most prominent recent research in which organizational theory has been used in foreign policy analysis has focused on decision-making in general, and on the role of decision-making units – particularly small groups – in this process. This has been the case, for example, in recent work reconsidering and going beyond Irving Janis's notion of 'groupthink', focusing on the interplay between group dynamics and the role of broader organizational cultures and socialization in foreign policy decision-making (Beasley, 1998; 't Hart et al., 1997; Ripley, 1995). This type of research points to the applicability of recent organizational theory (see, e.g., March and Olsen, 1998), in particular the celebrated (if not entirely transparent) distinction between the logic of 'consequences', defining the type of action appropriate within both realist and neoliberal thinking, and the logic of 'appropriateness', which – as Allison and Zelikow have claimed in their recent and substantial updating of the organizational model – is very much at the heart of the organizational process approach to decision-making (Allison and Zelikow, 1999: 146).

Approaches from an Agency-Based Perspective

Cognitive and psychological approaches Although research on the cognitive and psychological characteristics of individual decision-makers has been viewed with considerable scepticism in some quarters, this has in fact been one of the growth areas within foreign policy analysis over the past quarter of a century (see, e.g., Hudson, 1997; Renshon and Larson, 2001; Rosati, 2000; Singer and Hudson, 1992; Sylvan and Voss, 1998). As against the rational choice assumption – common to both realism and neoliberal institutionalism – that individuals are in principle open-minded and adaptable to the dictates of structural change and constraints, it is based on the contrary assumption that they are to a considerable degree impervious to such effects due to their underlying beliefs, the way they process information, as well as a number of other personality and cognitive traits. From having in its earliest years focused essentially on the study of attitudes and attitudinal change, and more specifically on theories of cognitive consistency, including cognitive dissonance, congruity and balance theory (Rosati, 1995: 52), psychological analysis underwent a 'cognitive revolution' in the 1970s. Instead of the conception of the passive actor underlying previous work, a new view emerged stressing the individual as problem-solver rather than malleable agent (Rosati, 1995: 52–4; Young and Shafer, 1998). The most significant of these have been the application of 'operational codes' (George, 1979; Walker, 1990, 1995; Walker et al., 1998), 'cognitive mapping' (Axelrod, 1976; Bonham et al., 1997; Young, 1996), 'attribution theory' (Heradstveit and Bonham, 1986) and 'image theory' (Herrmann and Fischerkeller, 1995).

Important book-length work done during the 1980s and onwards includes Deborah Larson's study of changes in the attitude of major American decision-makers between 1944 and 1947 (Larson, 1985), her more recent analysis of Cold War mistrust between the two superpowers (Larson, 1997), Richard Herrmann's (1985) study of perceptions and behaviour in Soviet foreign policy, Jerel A. Rosati's (1987) cognitive study of the Carter administration, Yuen Foong Khong's (1992) study of the role of historical analogies in foreign policy decision-making, and Martha Cottam's (1994) work on Latin America. In this context mention must also be made of Yaacov Y.I. Vertzberger's magisterial *The World in their Minds* (Vertzberger, 1990), which not only provides a very useful summary of much of the work done within this genre by the end of the 1980s, but also propounds a comprehensive and multicausal framework for analysing information processing, cognition and perception in foreign policy decision-making. This was also a period when studies of how the characteristics of leadership – beliefs, motivations, decisional and interpersonal styles – affected the pursuit of foreign policies first received serious attention, a focus which has continued to this day (M. Hermann, 1993; Hermann and Preston, 1998).

To this list one must also add prospect theory, not least because it reputedly 'has evoked the most interest among students of foreign policy-making' (Kahler, 1998: 927). This approach, pioneered by Kahneman and Tversky more than twenty years ago (Kahneman and Tversky, 1979), holds that decision-makers frame – that is, identify – their choices, not in terms of maximizing their expected utility (as assumed in rational choice models) but, rather, with regard to a so-called reference point (often the status quo), in terms of which they are risk-averse with respect to gains, and risk-acceptant with respect to losses (Farkas, 1996: 345; Kahler, 1998; Levy, 1997; McDermott, 1998). In other words, it claims that people are more sensitive to gains and losses from a given reference point than to changes in net asset levels; and that they tend to overvalue losses relative to gains (Levy, 1997: 89). Finally, a review of cognitive and psychological approaches to foreign policy analysis would be incomplete without touching upon the issue of learning in foreign policy. The literature here is substantial and growing, and to some extent overlapping with some of the cognitive approaches mentioned above (although some of these have a holistic rather than individualist thrust). Fortunately, Jack S. Levy has written an excellent overview of this field, and hence – taking heed also of his characterization of it as a minefield – I will not elaborate on this theme here; he has already swept much of it for us (Levy, 1994).

Bureaucratic politics approach Although the so-called bureaucratic politics – or governmental – approach to the analysis of foreign policy, first popularized by Allison in his study of the Cuban crisis, is often assumed to be closely similar to the organizational process model discussed above (and sometimes conflated with it), it is premised on an agency-oriented rather than a structural view of the field (Allison, 1971). Insofar as it focuses on interaction among organizational players involved in bargaining games and competing preferences, it does not aim to explain in terms of organizational outputs but on the basis of the actual 'pulling and hauling that is politics' (Allison and Zelikow, 1999: 255). At the same time, although in a certain sense akin to rational choice thinking insofar as its main rationale is to explain why decisions often take the form of 'resultants', as distinct from what any person or group intended, it does this, not in terms of given preferences and strategic moves, but 'according to the power and performance of proponents and opponents of the action in question' (Allison and Zelikow, 1999: 256). The power in question is not in the first hand personal but bureaucratic, insofar as the actors involved in these bargaining games represent sectional or factional rather than individual interests. Hence the famous apothegm (reputedly minted by Don Price, but also known as Miles's law) which encapsulates this bureaucratic link between individual actors and their organizational anchorage: where you stand depends on where you sit (Hollis, 1994; Stern and Verbeek, 1998: 206).

Although explicitly theorized on the basis of the empirical realities of how governments actually work (at least in the United States), this view of foreign policy decision-making has over the years received considerable criticism, both with reference to conceptual confusion and poor empirical performance (see, e.g. Bendor and Hammond, 1992; Bernstein, 2000; Rhodes, 1994; Welch, 1998). Nevertheless, it continues to stimulate research on foreign policy, and, although earlier claimed to be excessively US-centred in its empirical applicability, it is slowly finding its way to Europe as well (see, e.g., the contributions in Stern and Verbeek, 1998). Allison (with his coauthor) has also upgraded the chapter on governmental politics in the second edition of his study, including in it a host of empirical examples postdating the Cuban crisis (Allison and Zelikow, 1999: 255–378; see also Karbo, 1998).

Liberal approach Although it has roots going back to the early Rosenau (Rosenau, 1969) and prominent European scholars of foreign policy (Czempiel, 1981; Hanrieder, 1967), as well as to research on the role of domestic structures in foreign policy analysis pioneered by Peter Katzenstein (Katzenstein, 1976, 1978) and subsequently developed by Matthew Evangelista, Thomas Risse-Kappen and others (Evangelista, 1988, 1995; Risse-Kappen, 1991; Snyder, 1991), Andrew Moravcsik must nevertheless be given primary credit for having put the liberal approach squarely on the contemporary IR agenda (Moravcsik, 1997; but see also Doyle, 1997). In his view, three core assumptions underlie this challenge to neorealism and neoliberalism: the primacy of societal actors over political institutions, the implication of which is that being based on a 'bottom-up' view of the political system, individual and social groups are treated as prior to politics, insofar as they define their interests independently of politics and then pursue these through political exchange and collective action; state preferences represent the interests of a subset of society, in the sense that state officials define state preferences and act purposively in world politics in terms of these interests; and state behaviour in the international system is determined by the configuration within it of interdependent state preferences, that is, by the constraints imposed on a given state by the preferences of other states (Moravcsik, 1997: 520). Each of these core assumptions, Moravcsik argues, supports a specific variant of liberal theory, that is, ideational, commercial and republican liberalism, respectively. The first pertains to the generation of domestic social demands, the second to the causal mechanisms by means of which these are transformed into state preferences, and the third to the resulting patterns of national preferences in international settings (Moravcsik, 1997: 524–33).

Approaches Based on a Social-Institutional Perspective

Social constructivism   Although 'social constructivism' (or simply 'constructivism'), like 'rational choice', is essentially a meta-theoretical standpoint in the study of social phenomena, and hence is foundational to political analysis rather than being a specific analytical or 'theoretical' approach within IR, it will here – following most constructivist scholars (Adler, 1997; Dunne, 1995; Guzzini, 2000; Hopf, 1998; Ruggie, 1998; Wendt, 1999: 31) – be used to designate a more or less coherent and emerging body of thought in IR, including foreign policy analysis. Although it has roots going back to Grotius, Kant and Hegel, and was embedded already in some of the classic contributions by Karl Deutsch, Ernst Haas and in particular the English School (Bull, 1977; Deutsch, 1954; Haas, 1964, 1990; see also Dunne, 1995), it is nevertheless regarded by most IR scholars today as a relative newcomer to the sub-discipline; the term itself was first introduced to IR by Nicholas Onuf as recently as 1989 (Onuf, 1989). At the same time, however, it has quickly established itself as perhaps the main contender to a mainstream perspective in IR usually designated as 'rationalist' (see Katzenstein, 1996; Fearon and Wendt, 2002).

Although this is not the place to go into the details of social constructivism (for these, see, e.g., Adler, 2002; Guzzini, 2000), it is fruitful to distinguish between essentially 'thinner' and 'thicker' versions, since constructivism incorporates – rather uneasily – an increasingly broad spectrum of views. The former is quintessentially represented by Wendt in his recent treatise on international politics (Wendt, 1999), but also by other 'modernist' constructivists, including Emanuel Adler and

Michael Barnett (1998), Jeff Checkel (1999), John Ruggie (1998), Peter Katzenstein (1996), Thomas Risse-Kappen (1995b) and Martha Finnemore (1996b). Followers of 'thicker' versions range from what Adler terms 'modernist linguistic' (or 'rule-oriented') constructivists such as Friedrich Kratochwil (1989) and Nicholas Onuf (1989), the 'discursive' group to be discussed below, to the 'postmodernists' such as Richard Ashley (1984) and Rob Walker (1993), in addition to a number of feminist scholars, particularly Spike Peterson (1992), J. Ann Tickner (1993; 2002) and Christine Sylvester (1994). Since Wendt's type of constructivism is explicitly not designed for the analysis of foreign policy (Wendt, 1999: 11), I will not discuss it further here. Similarly, insofar as postmodernist versions are difficult to incorporate within a foreign policy framework as defined here, these too will be left aside. The specifically discursive approach will, however, be discussed below.

This leaves us here with contributions to the study of foreign policy from within the 'modernist' type of constructivism. This stream can be said to consist, first of all, of a normative and ideational strand, which emphasizes that the world of international relations does not exist independently of human action and cognition but, rather, that it is an intersubjective and meaningful world whose rules and practices are made and reproduced by human interactions. A second strand, often intertwined with the first, emphasizes the role of identities in international relations, and does this by pointing to the 'constitutive' role that norms and ideas play in defining identities and hence prescribing proper behaviour on the part of given types of actors.

Both these strands are exemplified in the various chapters of the influential volume on *The Culture of National Security* (1996), edited by Peter J. Katzenstein. Although it by no means cuts its roots to mainstream social science (see Ruggie, 1998: 38), it takes issue with the rationalism of both neorealism and neoliberalism with regard to the role of both norms and identities in world politics. In particular, it 'makes problematic the state interests that predominant explanations of national security often take for granted', as Katzenstein writes in his introduction (1996: 1). In this volume two studies in particular exemplify a constructivist analysis of foreign policy. The first, by Richard Price and Nina Tannenwald, shows that, while a rationalist analysis of the non-use of both nuclear and chemical weapons cannot account for such policies, a constructivist view, emphasizing the socially constructed nature of deterrence and deterrence weapons, shows that the non-use of these weapons can only be understood if one takes 'into account the development of prohibitionary norms that shaped these weapons as unacceptable "weapons of mass destruction"' (Price and Tannenwald, 1996: 115). Similarly, Martha Finnemore has focused on another form of foreign policy behaviour which cannot be adequately explained by either realist or liberal theories: humanitarian interventions which have no geostrategic and/or economic importance to the interveners in question (Finnemore, 1996a; see also Finnemore, 1996b). Instead, she argues, this type of behaviour, and the manner in which it has changed and developed since the nineteenth century, cannot be understood apart from the changing normative context in which it occurs, insofar as 'international normative context shapes the interests of international actors and does so in both systematic and systemic ways' (Finnemore, 1996a: 154). A third study which also exemplifies a constructivist analysis of foreign policy along these lines is Audie Klotz's analysis of the role of international norms in the international embargo against the *apartheid* regime in South Africa (Klotz, 1995). She argues that the emergence of an international norm of racial equality led states – such as the United States – to redefine their foreign policy interests despite a lack of material incentives for so doing.

Discursive approaches Following the so-called linguistic turn in philosophy and social theory, a second holistic-interpretative approach, focusing on the role of language in social inquiry, is slowly but determinedly making inroads into foreign policy analysis. One strand of this movement – belonging to the so-called Copenhagen School (see, e.g., Buzan

et al., 1998) – has as its starting point a critique of the use of psychological and cognitive factors in the explanation of the role of belief systems in foreign policy, in particular a tendency to focus exclusively on individual decision-makers, viewing and analysing beliefs in positivists terms, and an assumption that language is a transparent medium without an inner dynamic of its own (Larsen, 1997: 1–10). Instead of analysing the belief systems of individual decision-makers in this conventional manner, the emphasis is here put on viewing the discourse characterizing the foreign policy domain as a powerful structural constraint, on a high level of generality, shaping the foreign policy of the state in question. More specifically, drawing on social constructivist premises, Henrik Larsen has argued that 'the framework of meaning within which foreign policy takes place is seen as the basis of the way in which interests and goals are constructed' (Larsen, 1999: 453). However, contrary to 'thinner' constructivists, the assumption in this type of discursive approach is that intersubjective meaning cannot be apprehended in or by itself but, rather, that it is constituted by language. As a consequence, discourses 'provide the basis on which policy preferences, interests and goals are constructed' (Larsen, 1999: 453; Waever, 1998). Along similar lines, Ole Waever has argued for a conceptualization of security – as 'securitization' – based not on the 'objective' measures of traditional security studies but on speech act theory and its emphasis on language as a privileged vehicle for gaining and exercising social power. In this view, he writes, 'security is not of interest as a sign that refers to something more real; the utterance *itself* is the act', and hence 'something is a security problem when elites declare it to be so' (Waever, 1995: 55, 54).

A second, different and broader strand has recently been presented and discussed by Jennifer Milliken (Milliken, 1999: 225, 228–30; see also 2001). She characterizes discourse theorists as crossing over and mixing 'divisions between poststructuralists, postmodernists and some feminists and social constructivists', sharing at least the following three commitments: viewing discourses as systems of signification that construct social realities (see, e.g., Milliken,

1996; Mutimer, 1999; Weldes and Saco, 1996); the claim that discourses are productive of the things defined by the discourse, such as common sense and policy practices (see, e.g., Campbell, 1993; Doty, 1996; Huysmans, 1998; Waever, 1995; Weber, 1995; Weldes, 1999; Weldes and Saco, 1996); and 'studying dominating or hegemonic discourses, and their structuring of meaning as connected to implementing practices and ways of making these intelligible and legitimate' (see, e.g., Bartelson, 1995; Fierke, 1998; Neumann, 1998; Sylvester, 1994). Discourse analysts thus focus on significative practices and the knowledge systems underlying them, and are as such not only concerned with meta-theoretical critique but also with critical theorizing about the knowledge/power nexus (on the latter, see also Guzzini, 2000; Neufeld, 1993).

Approaches Based on an Interpretative Actor Perspective

In their book-length discussion of core metatheoretical issues in IR, Martin Hollis and Steve Smith have described individualist interpretative approaches to foreign policy as follows:

> Understanding proceeds by reconstructing at an individual level. This Weberian line has been much used in International Relations, especially in the sub-field known as Foreign Policy Analysis. Here the concern is to understand decisions from the standpoint of the decision-makers by reconstructing their reasons. The foreign policy behaviour of states depends on how individuals with power perceive and analyse situations. Collective action is a sum or combination of individual actions. (Hollis and Smith, 1990: 74)

In addition, they make the distinction within hermeneutics – which the above approach exemplifies – between understanding individual actions through social rules and collective meanings (a top-down procedure), and understanding collective policy through their individual elements (bottom-up). Inasmuch as the top-down view is quintessentially the one discussed above in terms of social-institutional approaches, we are here left with the latter type of focus, which also happens to be the least utilized today in the study of foreign policy.

The historical antecedents of this approach go back to the pioneering work of Richard C. Snyder and his associates, focusing on a systematic empirical analysis of the actual deliberations of foreign policy decision-makers (Snyder et al., 1962; see also Paige, 1968). Insofar as the focal point in studies of this kind are the *reasoned* – rather than rational – choices made by decision-makers, certain aspects of role theory also exemplify this approach, at least insofar as the analysis of particular role conceptions puts the focus on the reasoning of individual national foreign policy-makers and their understanding of the international system and the perceived role of their own states within this larger system (see, e.g., Holsti, 1987; Hyde-Price, 2000: 42–7; and the discussion of 'role-players' in Hollis and Smith, 1990: 155–9, 214–16). The same goes for more classical understandings of the role of the 'national interest' in foreign policy decision-making, based on individual interpretations of this much maligned but exceedingly flexible concept, as well as to the study of the role of crucial decision-makers during crises (see, e.g., Bernstein, 2000: 161–4).

However, a more illustrative and contemporary exemplar of this type of analysis is Philip Zelikow and Condoleezza Rice's detailed study of German reunification (Zelikow and Rice, 1995). It offers an insider's view of the innermost workings of the top elites of the United States, the Soviet Union, West Germany, East Germany, Britain and France in the creation of a united Germany. The logic of explanation is to determine the thinking of these elites – the reasoning behind their choices – and then to proffer it in explanation of the immense changes that occurred during the year following the collapse of the Berlin Wall. This is 'thick description' at its best; and although they have been chided for eschewing theory altogether in following this strategy (see, e.g., Risse, 1997), it should at the same time be emphasized that, although no causal analysis (or theorizing) in the conventional sense is provided, the focus is most certainly not simply on 'what' occurred, but also on the 'why' and 'how' aspects of this process. The assumption underlying this type of analysis is the counter-factual argument that, had not the main actors in this historical process reasoned and made choices the way they actually did, the history of this period would have been different. In any case, insofar as 'why' issues can have both a 'because of' and an 'in order to' implication, and since there are strong philosophical arguments in favour of imputing some form of causality also to purposive behaviour (see Carlsnaes, 1986: 32–8), there is no justification for off-hand denigrating this type of an approach for being 'descriptive' rather than 'explanatory'. In this connection it should also be noted that, despite a deep concern with its lack of theoretical anchorage, Risse has been able to utilize this descriptive-analytic study to illustrate the role of 'communicative action' and 'friendly persuasion' in international relations (Risse, 2000). Indeed, insofar as the 'logic of arguing' – as distinct from the logics of 'consequentialism' and 'appropriateness' – aims at achieving a reasoned consensus on the part of real life decision-makers (such as Kohl and Gorbachev), this approach seems to be ideally suited for analysis from within the interpretative actor perspective.

IS A SYNTHETIC APPROACH TO FOREIGN POLICY ANALYSIS FEASIBLE?

This rich flora – indeed, surfeit – of alternative approaches to foreign policy analysis raises the question whether it is possible to synthesize or integrate at least some of these, or if we are willy-nilly obliged to choose between them. Hollis and Smith, for example, have claimed that there are always two stories to tell – that of 'explanation' versus 'understanding', corresponding to the distinction above between 'objectivism' and 'interpretativism' – and that they cannot be combined into one type of narrative (Hollis and Smith, 1990). Similarly, 'holism' and 'individualism' have most often been assumed to be in principle mutually exclusive categories, forcing us into either a 'top-down' or 'bottom-up' mode of analysis. However, other scholars – often with a less pronounced meta-theoretical bent – have argued for the feasibility of such analytical

integration, usually combining this with empirical research that has lent strong support for such an integrative view of foreign policy analysis.

Perhaps the most notable recent example of such an ambition is provided by a number of studies that have focused on the link between domestic structures and foreign policy actions. Peter Katzenstein's early work (1976, 1978) has played a pioneering role in paving the way for studies of this kind, which have often had the added advantage of being comparative and hence reaching back – albeit without the same 'scientist' ambitions – to earlier work within CFP. Significant research stimulated by this approach has included studies by Matthew Evangelista (1988, 1995), Risse-Kappen (1991, 1994, 1995a) and Jack Snyder (1991; see also the discussion in Evangelista, 1997). Some of this work has also taken its cue from Peter Gourevitch's notion of the 'second-image reversed', focusing on how international institutions affect foreign policy change via its effects on domestic publics and hence on state actions (Gourevitch, 1978; Checkel, 1999; Keck and Sikkink, 1998; Risse et al., 1999).

However, the main problem with 'domestic structure' as an integrative bridge is that it assumes and hence reinforces the divide between domestic and international politics, which, as I have suggested above, is highly questionable as a feasible foundational baseline for a sub-discipline that needs to problematize this boundary rather than positing it by assumption. Furthermore, this argument has various strands that are not necessarily mutually compatible as explanations. Thus, it can refer to an essentially holistic structural view, as in Katzenstein's work on the role of weak versus strong societies (Katzenstein, 1976), or in the 'democratic peace' argument (Russett, 1993); to an agency-based view in terms of which domestic structures act as intervening factors between societal actors and state action (Checkel, 1997; Risse-Kappen, 1991); or to more recent constructivist approaches emphasizing the impact of ideas and norms – either domestic or international – as sources of foreign policy change (Checkel, 1997; Finnemore and Sikkink, 1998; Reus-Smit, 1999). Given these contending uses to which the domestic structure argument has been put, as well as the more fundamental criticism raised above, it is difficult to see how it can sustain a central role as a 'theoretical bridge' (Evangelista, 1997: 204) in foreign policy analysis.

My own view is that a synthetic framework for analysing foreign policy is indeed possible, but that it has to be on a level of abstraction that does not substantively prejudge explanation in favour of any particular type or combination of empirical factors (such as 'domestic structure'). Since I have elaborated on it elsewhere, I will here simply give a skeletal outline of the explanatory logic of such a suggested synthetic framework of analysis (Carlsnaes, 1986, 1992, 1993, 1994). The starting point is the claim that, while the meta-theoretical matrix used above is specifically designed for the purpose of classifying approaches to foreign policy analysis in terms of their most fundamental ontological and epistemological presuppositions, it is less suitable for *empirical* analysis itself as distinguished from *meta-theoretical* dissection. Arguably, in the 'games real actors play' (Scharpf, 1997) action is always a combination of purposive behaviour, cognitive-psychological factors and the various structural phenomena characterizing societies and their environments, and hence explanations of actual foreign policy actions must perforce be able to give accounts that do not by definition exclude or privilege any of these types of *explanans*. Insofar as the matrix used above does have such implications (albeit for good analytical-cum-pedagogical reasons), it simply will not be able to deliver the goods in this respect. Indeed, an ironic implication of this way of conceptualizing and understanding the foundational issues underlying foreign policy analysis is that it is only when we succeed in *overriding* the logic exemplified in this chapter – the four generic perspectives, which by definition are mutually exclusive – that there will be a real chance of achieving this ambition.

Thus, rather than thinking in terms of a logic of mutual exclusion, I suggest that we instead conceptualize such an analytic framework in terms of a tripartite approach, consisting of an *intentional*, a *dispositional* and a *structural* dimension of explanation, as follows:

Foreign Policy Actions

(1)

↑

intentional dimension

(2)

↑

dispositional dimension

(3)

↑

structural dimension

Although analytically autonomous, these three dimensions are conceived as closely linked, in the sense that they can be conjoined in a logical, step-by-step manner to render increasingly exhaustive explanations of foreign policy actions qua explanandum, as defined earlier. This means, first of all, that a teleological explanation (1) in terms solely of the intentional dimension is fully feasible, based either on strict rationality assumptions or on more traditional modes of intentional analysis. It also means, however, that one can choose to 'deepen' the analysis by providing a causal determination (2) of policy – as opposed to an explanation wholly in terms of given goals and preferences – in which the factors characterizing the intentional dimension are themselves explained in terms of underlying psychological-cognitive factors which have disposed a given actor to have this and not that preference or intention. The distinction between these two levels can also be described in terms of an 'in order to' and a 'because of' dimension, the former referring to the intentional sphere, the latter constituting the link between this intention and the having of it: how a particular intention has become a particular actor's intention. Finally, the third layer is based on the assumption that, in so far as intentional behaviour is never pursued outside the crucible of structural determination, factors of the latter kind must always be able to figure causally (3) in our accounts of the former. As conceived here, this link between structure and agency can be conceived as both of a constraining and of an enabling kind, causally affecting policy actions via its effects on the dispositional characteristics of the agents of policy. (Although not indicated in the figure, foreign policy actions can in turn affect – either by intention or unintentionally in the form of outcomes – both the structural and dispositional dimensions, providing for the dynamic interaction over time between agential and structural factors, thus invoking the agency–structure issue, to be discussed briefly below.)

Although this type of an integrative framework eschews the dichotomization of approaches discussed above, it does not as such negate the applicability of any of these – as long as they are used when and if analytically appropriate. Indeed, approaches from all the four types of rock-bottom perspectives discussed above can be fully utilized: the 'structural' and 'social-institutional' when analysing causal links between the structural and dispositional dimensions; 'agency-based' perspectives when tracing causal patterns between the dispositional and the intentional dimension; and the 'interpretative actor' perspective when the purpose is to penetrate the teleological links between intentions and foreign policy actions.

CONCLUDING REMARKS

To round up this overview I would like to conclude by briefly pointing to three theoretical issues that cut across the perspectives discussed above and which, in my opinion, will continue to remain topical and controversial in the study of foreign policy (as in the social sciences in general).

The first of these pertains to explaining the dynamics of foreign policy *change*, both in terms of actor and policy characteristics. Except for a short burst of interest in the early 1980s (Buzan and Jones, 1981; Gilpin, 1981; Goldmann, 1982; Holsti, 1982; Holsti et al., 1980; see also Goldmann, 1988), this was not a topic that attracted much attention until the profound transformations occurring at the end of that decade. These developments

revealed the embarrassing fact that, not only were many of these changes unanticipated, but also that the events in question were difficult to explain even *ex post facto* in terms of existing theories, models or analytic approaches. Although this theoretical dearth led to a renewed interest in the analysis of foreign policy change (Carlsnaes, 1993; Gustavsson, 1998, 1999; Hermann, 1990; Rosati et al., 1994; see also Koslowski and Kratochwil, 1995), there is little consensus on the best way of doing so. Given the eclectic nature of the field as such, as well as the fundamental differences between the types of perspectives presented above, some of which are inherently more amenable to the study of change than others, this should of course not come as a surprise. At the same time, this issue is seminal to the future of the field as a whole, given the increased globalization of international relations – a process arguably undermining the relative *autonomy* of the state qua foreign policy actor – as well as the emergence of new types of foreign policy actors, such as the EU, claiming not only foreign policy competencies of their own but also as representing their member states, hence eroding the *sovereignty* of the latter (see, e.g., White, 2001).

A second contentious and topical concern within the field pertains to the role of *ideas* in the explanation of foreign policy. For long banished from mainstream social science explanations, the ideational factor finally gained full admission in the early 1990s with the publication of the edited volume on *Ideas and Foreign Policy* (Goldstein and Keohane, 1993). Underlying this introduction lay the realization that explanations based solely on rational actors maximizing a utility function rooted in material interests were often inadequate to account fully for the foreign policy behaviour of states. Instead, it was suggested, ideas too can have an independent causal effect on foreign policy 'even when human beings behave rationally to achieve their ends' (Goldstein and Keohane, 1993: 5; see also Checkel, 1997; Jacobsen, 1995; Risse-Kappen, 1994; Yee, 1996). Although welcomed by scholars on the interpretative side of the epistemological fence, this admission of the causal efficacy of ideas has nevertheless led to considerable controversy within the field (see, e.g., Koslowski and Kratochwil, 1995; Laffey and Weldes, 1997). The basic criticism is that 'rationalists' continue to think in terms of 'naturalistic' factors, even when conceptualizing ideas (viewing them as cognitively and individually held 'beliefs' with causal effects, as well as being distinct from 'interests'), whereas the social constructivist view is that 'ideational factors relate to social action in the form of constitutive rules', as Ruggie notes (Ruggie, 1998: 38). In the light of this view, to speak of 'ideational variables' is tantamount to perpetrating an oxymoron – a begging of the whole question of what ideas are and are not, and hence how they are affected by and affect social interaction. Clearly, this debate is only at its beginning and will continue to be a focal point for critical discussion.

Finally, a third issue, and one that has received considerable theoretical attention during the past decade, and continues to do so today, is the *agency-structure problematique* in foreign policy analysis. For all practical purposes Wendt put it on the agenda in a much-quoted article published in 1987, and since then it has been hotly debated but hardly resolved to the satisfaction of all concerned (Bieler and Morton, 2001; Carlsnaes, 1992, 1994; Dessler, 1989; Doty, 1997; Friedman and Starr, 1997; Guzzini, 1993; Hollis and Smith, 1991, 1992, 1994; Patomäki, 1996; Suganami, 1999; Wight, 1999). At the heart of this problem lies the increasingly widespread recognition that, instead of being antagonistic partners in a zerosum relationship, human agents and social structures are in a fundamental sense dynamically interrelated entities, and hence that we cannot account fully for the one without invoking the other. The 'problem' is that, although such views of reciprocal implication suggest that the properties of both agents and social structures are relevant to a proper understanding of social behaviour (including the study of change), we nevertheless (as Wendt noted in his original article) 'lack a self-evident way to conceptualize these entities and their relationship' (Wendt, 1987: 338).

This is also, perhaps, an appropriate issue and tone of voice with which to put an end to this overview of the vicissitudes and current condition of foreign policy analysis, since it touches on the central core of the field itself: the fact that foreign policy actions are located at the very centre of the international relations of states, incorporating a multitude of influences – structural and agential, as well as international, societal and individual – that continually impinge on them and on their decision-makers. To capture these complex and reciprocal processes, and to do so well, is the challenge that will persist in energizing this field of study as long as states continue to remain viable actors within the international system.

NOTE

This is an emended version of a chapter first published in Carlsnaes et al. (2002). The author would like to thank the following colleagues (as well as an anonymous reviewer) for commenting on earlier versions of the chapter: Stefano Guzzini, Valerie Hudson, Jennifer Milliken, Thomas Risse, Jerel Rosati, Beth Simmons and Colin Wight. The author also thanks participants at various seminars in Uppsala, Oslo and Gothenburg.

REFERENCES

Adler, Emanuel (1997) 'Seizing the Middle Ground: Constructivism in World Politics', *European Journal of International Relations*, 3: 319–63.

Adler, Emanuel (2002) 'Constructivism and International Relations' in Walter Carlsnaes, Thomas Risse and Beth A. Simmons (eds), *Handbook of International Relations*. London: Sage.

Adler, Imanuel and Barnett, Michael (eds) (1998) *Security Communities*. Cambridge: Cambridge University Press.

Allison, Graham T. (1971) *Essence of Decision: Explaining the Cuban Missile Crisis*. Boston: Little, Brown.

Allison, Graham and Zelikow, Philip (1999) *Essence of Decision: Explaining the Cuban Missile Crisis*. New York: Longman.

Andriole, Stephen J. and Hopple, Gerald W. (1984) 'The Rise and Fall of Events Data: From Basic Research to Applied Use in the US Department of Defense', *International Interactions*, 11: 293–309.

Ashley, Richard (1984) 'The Poverty of Neorealism', *International Organization*, 38: 225–86.

Axelrod, Robert (ed.) (1976) *Structure of Decision: The Cognitive Maps of Political Elites*. Princeton: Princeton University Press.

Axelrod, Robert and Keohane, Robert O. (1993) 'Achieving Cooperation Under Anarchy: Strategies and Institutions', in David A. Baldwin (ed.), *Neorealism and Neoliberalism: The Contemporary Debate*. New York: Columbia University Press.

Baldwin, David A. (1993) 'Neoliberalism, Neorealism, and World Politics', in David A. Baldwin (ed.), *Neorealism and Neoliberalism: The Contemporary Debate*. New York: Columbia University Press.

Bartelson, Jens (1995) *A Genealogy of Sovereignty*. Cambridge: Cambridge University Press.

Baumann, Rainer, Rittberger, Volker and Wagner, Wolfgang (2001) 'Neorealist Foreign Policy Theory', in Volker Rittberger (ed.), *German Foreign Policy Since Unification: Theories and Case Studies*. Manchester: Manchester University Press.

Beasley, Ryan (1998) 'Collective Interpretations: How Problem Representations Aggregate in Foreign Policy Groups', in Donald A. Sylvan and James F. Voss (eds), *Problem Representation in Foreign Policy Decision Making*. Cambridge: Cambridge University Press.

Bendor, Jonathan and Hammond, Thomas H. (1992) 'Rethinking Allison's Models', *American Political Science Review*, 86: 301–22.

Bernstein, Barton J. (2000) 'Understanding Decision making, U.S. Foreign Policy, and the Cuban Missile Crisis', *International Security*, 25: 134–64.

Bieler, Andreas and Morton, Adam David (2001) 'The Gordian Knot of Agency–Structure in International Relations', *European Journal of International Relations*, 7: 5–35.

Bonham, G. Matthew, Sergeev, Victor M. and Parshin, Pavel (1997) 'The Limited Test-Ban Agreement: Emergence of New Knowledge Structures in International Negotiation', *International Studies Quarterly*, 41: 215–40.

Brecher, Michael (1972) *The Foreign Policy System of Israel: Setting, Images, Process*. London: Oxford University Press.

Bull, Hedley (1977) *The Anarchic Society*. New York: Columbia University Press.

Buzan, Barry and Jones, J. Barry (1981) *Change and the Study of International Relations*. London: Pinter.

Buzan, Barry, Waever, Ole and Wilde, Jaap de (1998) *Security: A New Framework for Analysis*. Boulder: Lynne Rienner.

Campbell, David (1993) *Politics without Principle: Sovereignty, Ethics, and the Narratives of the Gulf War*. Boulder: Lynne Rienner.

Caporaso, James A., Hermann, Charles F. and Kegley, Charles W., Jr (1987) 'The Comparative Study of Foreign Policy: Perspectives on the Future', *International Studies Notes*, 13: 32–46.

Carlsnaes, Walter (1986) *Ideology and Foreign Policy: Problems of Comparative Conceptualization*. Oxford: Blackwell.

Carlsnaes, Walter (1992) 'The Agency–Structure Problem in Foreign Policy Analysis', *International Studies Quarterly*, 36: 245–70.

Carlsnaes, Walter (1993) 'On Analysing the Dynamics of Foreign Policy Change: A Critique and Reconceptualization', *Cooperation and Conflict*, 28: 5–30.

Carlsnaes, Walter (1994) 'In Lieu of a Conclusion: Compatibility and the Agency–Structure Issue in Foreign Policy Analysis', in Walter Carlsnaes and Steve Smith (eds), *European Foreign Policy: The EC and Changing Perspectives in Europe*. London: Sage.

Carlsnaes, Walter, Risse, Thomas and Simmons, Beth A. (eds), (2002) 'Handbook of International Relations'. London: Sage.

Checkel, Jeffrey T. (1997) *Ideas and International Political Change: Soviet/Russian Behavior at the End of the Cold War*. New Haven: Yale University Press.

Checkel, Jeffrey T. (1999) 'Norms, Institutions, and National Identity in Contemporary Europe', *International Studies Quarterly*, 43: 83–114.

Christensen, Thomas J. (1996) *Useful Adversaries: Grand Strategy, Domestic Mobilization, and Sino-American Conflict, 1947–1958*. Princeton: Princeton University Press.

Cohen, Bernard C. (1968) 'Foreign Policy', in David L. Sills (ed.), *International Encyclopedia of the Social Sciences*. New York: Macmillan and The Free Press.

Cohen, Bernard C. and Harris, Scott A. (1975) 'Foreign Policy', in Fred I. Greenstein and Nelson W. Polsby (eds), *Handbook of Political Science*, vol. 6: *Policies and Policymaking*. Reading, MA: Addison–Wesley.

Cottam, Martha (1994) *Images and Intervention: US Policies in Latin America*. Pittsburgh: University of Pittsburgh Press.

Cottam, Richard (1977) *Foreign Policy Motivation: A General Theory and a Case Study*. Pittsburgh: University of Pittsburgh Press.

Czempiel, Ernst-Otto (1981) *Internationale Beziehungen: Ein Konfliktmodell*. Munich: UTB.

Dessler, David (1989) 'What's at Stake in the Agency–Structure Debate?', *International Organization*, 43: 441–73.

Deutsch, Karl (1954) *Political Community at the International Level*. Garden City, NY: Doubleday.

Doty, Roxanne Lynn (1996) *Imperial Encounters*. Minneapolis: University of Minnesota Press.

Doty, Roxanne Lynn (1997) 'Aporia: A Critical Examination of the Agent–Structure Problematique in International Relations Theory', *European Journal of International Relations*, 3: 365–92.

Doyle, Michael (1997) *Ways of War and Peace: Realism, Liberalism, and Socialism*. New York: W.W. Norton.

Dunne, Timothy (1995) 'The Social Construction of International Society', *European Journal of International Relations*, 1: 367–89.

Dunne, Timothy (1998) 'International Theory and the Mirror of History', *European Journal of International Relations*, 4: 347–62.

East, Maurice A. (1978) 'National Attributes and Foreign Policy', in Maurice A. East, Stephen A. Salmore and Charles F. Hermann (eds), *Why Nations Act*. Beverly Hills: Sage.

Elman, Colin (1996a) 'Horses for Courses: Why No Realist Theories of Foreign Policy?', *Security Studies*, 6: 7–53.

Elman, Colin (1996b) 'Cause, Effect, and Consistency: A Response to Kenneth Waltz', *Security Studies*, 6: 58–61.

Evangelista, Matthew (1988) *Innovation and the Arms Race: How the United States and the Soviet Union Develop New Military Technologies*. Ithaca: Cornell University Press.

Evangelista, Matthew (1995) 'The Paradox of State Strength: Transnational Relations, Domestic Structures, and Security Policy in Russia and the Soviet Union', *International Organization*, 49: 1–38.

Evangelista, Matthew (1997) 'Domestic Structure and International Change', in Michael W. Doyle and G. John Ikenberry (eds), *The New Thinking in International Relations Theory*. Boulder: Westview.

Farkas, Andrew (1996) 'Evolutionary Models in Foreign Policy Analysis', *International Studies Quarterly*, 40: 343–61.

Fearon, James and Wendt, Alexander (2002) 'Rationalism v. Constructivism: A Skeptical View', in Walter Carlsnaes, Thomas Risse and Beth A. Simmons (eds), Handbook of International Relations. London: Sage.

Fierke, Karin (1998) *Changing Games, Changing Strategies: Critical Investigations in Security*. Manchester: Manchester University Press.

Finnemore, Martha (1996a) 'Constructing Norms of Humanitarian Intervention', in Peter J. Katzenstein (ed.), *The Culture of National Security: Norms and Identity in World Politics*. New York: Columbia University Press.

Finnemore, Martha (1996b) *National Interests in International Society*. Ithaca: Cornell University Press.

Finnemore, Martha and Sikkink, Kathryn (1998) 'International Norm Dynamics and Political Change', *International Organization*, 52: 887–917.

Friedman, Gil and Starr, Harvey (1997) *Agency, Structure, and International Politics: From Ontology to Empirical Inquiry*. London: Routledge.

George, Alexander L. (1979) 'The Causal Nexus Between Cognitive Beliefs and Decision Making Behavior: The "Operational Code" Belief System', in L.S. Falkowski (ed.), *Psychological Models in International Politics*. Boulder: Westview.

Gilpin, Robert (1981) *War and Change in World Politics*. Cambridge: Cambridge University Press.

Glaser, Charles L. (1995) 'Realists as Optimists: Co-operation as Self-Help', in Michael E. Brown, Sean M. Lynn-Jones and Steven E. Miller (eds), *The Perils of Anarchy: Contemporary Realism and International Security*. Cambridge, MA: MIT Press.

Goldmann, Kjell (1982) 'Change and Stability in Foreign Policy: Détente as a Problem of Stabilisation', *World Politics*, 34: 230–66.

Goldmann, Kjell (1988) *Change and Stability in Foreign Policy: The Problems and Possibilities of Détente*. New York: Harvester Wheatsheaf.

Goldstein, Judith and Keohane, Robert O. (eds) (1993) *Ideas and Foreign Policy: Beliefs, Institutions, and Political Change*. Ithaca: Cornell University Press.

Gourevitch, Peter (1978) 'The Second Image Reversed: The International Sources of Domestic Politics', *International Organization*, 32: 881–912.

Grieco, Joseph M. (1993) 'Anarchy and the Limits of Cooperation: A Realist Critique of the Newest Liberal Institutionalism', in David A. Baldwin (ed.), *Neorealism and Neoliberalism: The Contemporary Debate*. New York: Columbia University Press.

Gustavsson, Jakob (1998) *The Politics of Foreign Policy Change*. Lund: Lund University Press.

Gustavsson, Jakob (1999) 'How Should We Study Foreign Policy Change?', *Cooperation and Conflict*, 34: 73–95.

Guzzini, Stefano (1993) 'Structural Power: The Limits of Neorealist Power Analysis', *International Organization*, 47: 443–78.

Guzzini, Stefano (1998) *Realism in International Relations and International Political Economy*. London: Routledge.

Guzzini, Stefano (2000) 'A Reconstruction of Constructivism in International Relations', *European Journal of International Relations*, 6: 147–82.

Haas, Ernst (1964) *Beyond the Nation-State.* Stanford: Stanford University Press.

Haas, Ernst (1990) *Knowledge is Power.* Berkeley: University of California Press.

Hanrieder, Wolfram F. (1967) 'Compatibility and Consensus: A Proposal for the Conceptual Linkage of External and Internal Dimensions of Foreign Policy', *American Political Science Review,* 61: 971–82.

Hart, Paul 't, Stern, Eric K. and Sundelius, Bengt (eds) (1997) *Beyond Groupthink: Political Dynamics and Foreign Policy-Making.* Ann Arbor: University of Michigan Press.

Heradstveit, Daniel and Bonham, G. Matthew (1986) 'Decision-Making in the Face of Uncertainty: Attributions of Norwegian and American Officials', *Journal of Peace Research,* 23: 339–56.

Hermann, Charles F. (1978) 'Decision Structure and Process Influences on Foreign Policy', in Maurice A. East, Stephen A. Salmore and Charles F. Hermann (eds), *Why Nations Act.* Beverly Hills: Sage.

Hermann, Charles F. (1990) 'Changing Course: When Governments Choose to Redirect Foreign Policy', *International Studies Quarterly,* 34: 3–21.

Hermann, Margaret G. (1974) 'Leader Personality and Foreign Policy Behavior', in James N. Rosenau (ed.), *Comparing Foreign Policies: Theories, Findings, and Methods.* New York: Sage–Halsted.

Hermann, Margaret G. (1980a) 'Assessing the Personalities of Members of the Soviet Politburo', *Personality and Social Psychology Bulletin,* 6: 332–52.

Hermann, Margaret G. (1980b) 'Explaining Foreign Policy Behavior Using Personal Characteristics of Political Leaders', *International Studies Quarterly,* 24: 7–46.

Hermann, Margaret G. (1993) 'Leaders and Foreign Policy Decision Making', in Dan Caldwell and Timothy McKeown (eds), *Diplomacy, Force, and Leadership: Essays in Honor of Alexander George.* Boulder: Westview.

Hermann, Margaret G. and Preston, Thomas (1998) 'Presidents, Leadership Style, and the Advisory Process', in Eugene R. Wittkopf and James M. McCormick (eds), *Domestic Sources of American Foreign Policy.* New York: Rowman and Littlefield.

Herrmann, Richard K. (1985) *Perceptions and Behavior in Soviet Foreign Policy.* Pittsburgh: University of Pittsburgh Press.

Herrmann, Richard K. and Fischerkeller, Michael (1995) 'Beyond the Enemy Image Spiral Model: Cognitive- Strategic Research After the Cold War', *International Organization,* 49: 415–50.

Hollis, Martin (1994) *The Philosophy of Social Science.* Cambridge: Cambridge University Press.

Hollis, Martin and Smith, Steve (1990) *Explaining and Understanding International Relations.* Oxford: Clarendon Press.

Hollis, Martin and Smith, Steve (1991) 'Beware of Gurus: Structure and Action in International Relations', *Review of International Studies,* 14: 393–410.

Hollis, Martin and Smith, Steve (1992) 'Structure and Action: Further Comments', *Review of International Studies,* 18: 187–8.

Hollis, Martin and Smith, Steve (1994) 'Two Stories about Structure and Agency', *Review of International Studies,* 20: 241–51.

Holsti, K.J. (1982) *Why Nations Realign: Foreign Policy Restructuring in the Postwar World.* London: Allen & Unwin.

Holsti, K.J. (1987) 'National Role Conceptions in the Study of Foreign Policy', in Stephen Walker (ed.), *Role Theory and Foreign Policy Analysis.* Durham, NC: Duke University Press.

Holsti, Ole R., North, Robert and Brody, Richard (1968) 'Perception and Action in the 1914 Crisis', in J. David Singer (ed.), *Quantitative International Politics: Insights and Evidence.* New York: The Free Press.

Holsti, Ole R., Siverson, Randolph M. and George, Alexander L. (1980) *Change in the International System.* Boulder: Westview.

Hopf, Ted (1998) 'The Promise of Constructivism in International Relations Theory', *International Security,* 23: 171–200.

Hudson, Valerie M. (ed.) (1997) *Culture and Foreign Policy.* Boulder: Lynne Rienner.

Hudson, Valerie M. and Vore, Christopher S. (1995) 'Foreign Policy Analysis Yesterday, Today, and Tomorrow', *Mershon International Studies Review,* 39: 209–38.

Huysmans, Jef (1998) 'Security! What Do You Mean? From Concept to Thick Signifier', *European Journal of International Relations,* 4: 226–55.

Hyde-Price, Adrian (2000) *Germany and European Order: Enlarging NATO and the EU.* Manchester: Manchester University Press.

Jacobsen, John Kurt (1995) 'Much Ado about Ideas: The Cognitive Factor in Economic Policy', *World Politics,* 47: 283–310.

Janis, Irving J. (1982) *Groupthink: Psychological Studies of Policy Decisions and Fiascoes.* Boston: Houghton Mifflin.

Jervis, Robert (1976) *Perception and Misperception in International Politics.* Princeton: Princeton University Press.

Kahler, Miles (1997) 'Inventing International Relations: International Relations Theory After 1945', in Michael W. Doyle and G. John Ikenberry (eds), *The New Thinking in International Relations Theory*. Boulder: Westview.

Kahler, Miles (1998) 'Rationality in International Relations', *International Organization*, 52: 919–41.

Kahneman, D. and Tversky, A. (1979) 'Prospect Theory: An Analysis of Decision Under Risk', *Econometrica*, 47: 263–91.

Karbo, Juliet (1998) 'Power Politics in Foreign Policy: The Influence of Bureaucratic Minorities', *European Journal of International Relations*, 4: 67–97.

Katzenstein, Peter J. (1976) 'International Relations and Domestic Structures: Foreign Economic Policies of Advanced Industrial States', *International Organization*, 30: 1–45.

Katzenstein, Peter J. (1978) *Between Power and Plenty: Foreign Economic Policies of Advanced Industrial States*. Madison: University of Wisconsin Press.

Katzenstein, Peter J. (1996) 'Introduction: Alternative Perspectives on National Security', in Peter J. Katzenstein (ed.), *The Culture of National Security: Norms and Identity in World Politics*. New York: Columbia University Press.

Keck, Margaret E. and Sikkink, Kathryn (1998) *Activists Beyond Borders: Advocacy Networks in International Politics*. Ithaca: Cornell University Press.

Kegley, Charles W., Jr (1980) 'The Comparative Study of Foreign Policy: Paradigm Lost?', published by Institute of International Studies, University of South Carolina, Essay Series No. 10.

Keohane, Robert O. (1993) 'Institutional Theory and the Realist Challenge After the Cold War', in David A. Baldwin (ed.), *Neorealism and Neoliberalism: The Contemporary Debate*. New York: Columbia University Press.

Khong, Yuen Foong (1992) *Analogies at War: Korea, Munich, Dien Bien Phu, and the Vietnam Decisions of 1965*. Princeton: Princeton University Press.

Klotz, Audie J. (1995) *Protesting Prejudice: Apartheid and the Politics of Norms in International Relations*. Ithaca: Cornell University Press.

Koslowski, Rey and Kratochwil, Friedrich V. (1995) 'Understanding Change in International Politics: The Soviet Empire's Demise and the International System', in Richard Ned Lebow and Thomas Risse-Kappen (eds), *International Relations Theory and the End of the Cold War*. New York: Columbia University Press.

Kratochwil, Friedrich (1989) *Rules, Norms, and Decisions*. Cambridge: Cambridge University Press.

Laffey, Mark and Weldes, Jutta (1997) 'Beyond Belief: Ideas and Symbolic Technologies in the Study of International Relations', *European Journal of International Relations*, 3: 193–237.

Larsen, Henrik (1997) *Foreign Policy and Discourse Analysis: France, Britain and Europe*. London: Routledge.

Larsen, Henrik (1999) 'British and Danish European Policies in the 1990s: A Discourse Approach', *European Journal of International Relations*, 5: 451–83.

Larson, Deborah W. (1985) *Origins of Containment: A Psychological Explanation*. Princeton: Princeton University Press.

Larson, Deborah W. (1997) *Anatomy of Mistrust: U.S.–Soviet Relations during the Cold War*. Ithaca: Cornell University Press.

Layne, Christopher (1995) 'Kant or Cant: The Myth of the Democratic Peace', in Michael E. Brown, Sean M. Lynn-Jones and Steven E. Miller (eds), *The Perils of Anarchy: Contemporary Realism and International Security*. Cambridge, MA: MIT Press.

Levy, Jack S. (1994) 'Learning and Foreign Policy: Sweeping a Conceptual Minefield', *International Organization*, 48: 279–312.

Levy, Jack S. (1997) 'Prospect Theory, Rational Choice, and International Relations', *International Studies Quarterly*, 41: 87–1121.

Lynn–Jones, Sean M. and Miller, Steven E. (1995) 'Preface', in Michael E. Brown, Sean M. Lynn-Jones and Steven E. Miller (eds), *The Perils of Anarchy: Contemporary Realism and International Security*. Cambridge, MA: MIT Press.

March, James G. and Olsen, Johan P. (1998) 'The Institutional Dynamics of International Political Orders', *International Organization*, 52: 943–69.

McDermott, Ross (1998) *Risk-Taking in International Politics: Prospect Theory in American Foreign Policy*. Ann Arbor: University of Michigan Press.

McGowan, Patrick J. and Shapiro, Howard B. (1973) *The Comparative Study of Foreign Policy: A Survey of Scientific Findings*. Beverly Hills: Sage.

Mearsheimer, John J. (1995) 'Back to the Future: Instability in Europe After the Cold War', in Michael E. Brown, Sean M. Lynn-Jones and Steven E. Miller (eds), *The Perils of Anarchy: Contemporary Realism and International Security*. Cambridge, MA: MIT Press.

Milliken, Jennifer (1996) 'Prestige and Reputation in American Foreign Policy and American Realism', in Francis Beer and Robert Hariman (eds), *Post-Realism: The Rhetorical Turn in International Relations*. East Lansing: Michigan State University Press.

Milliken, Jennifer (1999) 'The Study of Discourse in International Relations: A Critique of Research and Methods', *European Journal of International Relations*, 5: 225–54.

Milliken, Jennifer (2001) *Conflict Possibilities: The Social Construction of the Korean War*. Manchester: Manchester University Press.

Moravcsik, Andrew (1997) 'Taking Preferences Seriously: A Liberal Theory of International Politics', *International Organization*, 51: 513–53.

Morgenthau, Hans J. (1948) *Politics Among Nations: The Struggle for Power and Peace*. New York: Alfred A. Knopf.

Munton, Don (1976) 'Comparative Foreign Policy: Fads, Fantasies, Orthodoxies, and Perversities', in James N. Rosenau (ed.), *In Search of Global Patterns*. New York: The Free Press.

Mutimer, David (1999) *The Weapons State: Proliferation and the Imagination of Security*. Boulder: Lynne Rienner.

Neack, Laura, Hey, Jeanne A.K. and Haney, Patrick J. (1995) 'Generational Change in Foreign Policy Analysis', in Laura Neack, Jeanne A.K. Hey and Patrick J. Haney (eds), *Foreign Policy Analysis: Continuity and Change in Its Second Generation*. Englewood Cliffs: Prentice Hall.

Neufeld, Mark (1993) 'Reflexivity and International Theory', *Millennium: Journal of International Studies*, 22: 53–76.

Neumann, Iver (1998) *Uses of the Other: The 'East' in European Identity Formation*. Minneapolis: University of Minnesota Press.

Onuf, Nicholas (1989) *World of Our Making*. Columbia. University of South Carolina Press.

Oye, Kenneth (ed.) (1985) *Cooperation Under Anarchy*. Princeton: Princeton University Press.

Paige, Glenn D. (1968) *The Korean Decision*. New York: The Free Press.

Patomäki, Heikki (1996) 'How to Tell Better Stories about World Politics', *European Journal of International Relations*, 2: 105–33.

Peterson, V. Spike (ed.) (1992) *Gendered States*. Boulder: Lynne Rienner.

Price, Richard and Tannenwald, Nina (1996) 'Norms and Deterrence: The Nuclear and Chemical Weapons Taboo', in Peter J. Katzenstein (ed.), *The Culture of National Security: Norms and Identity in World Politics*. New York: Columbia University Press.

Renshon, S.A. and Larson, Deborah W. (eds) (2001) *Good Judgement in Foreign Policy*. Lanham, MD: Rowman and Littlefield.

Reus-Smit, Christian (1999) *The Moral Purpose of the State: Culture, Social Identity, and Institutional Rationality in International Relations Theory*. Princeton: Princeton University Press.

Rhodes, Edward (1994) 'Do Bureaucratic Politics Matter? Some Disconfirming Findings from the Case of the US Navy', *World Politics*, 47: 1–41.

Ripley, Brian (1995) 'Cognition, Culture, and Bureaucratic Politics', in Laura Neack, Jeanne A.K. Hey and Patrick J. Haney (eds), *Foreign Policy Analysis: Continuity and Change in Its Second Generation*. Englewood Cliffs: Prentice Hall.

Risse, Thomas (1997) 'The Cold War's Endgame and German Unification', *International Security*, 21: 159–85.

Risse, Thomas (2000) '"Let's Argue!": Communicative Action in World Politics', *International Organization*, 54: 1–39.

Risse, Thomas, Ropp, Steven and Sikkink, Kathryn (eds) (1999) *The Power of Principles: International Human Rights Norms and Domestic Change*. Cambridge: Cambridge University Press.

Risse-Kappen, Thomas (1991) 'Public Opinion, Domestic Structures, and Foreign Policy in Liberal Democracies', *World Politics*, 43: 479–512.

Risse-Kappen, Thomas (1994) 'Ideas Do Not Float Freely: Transnational Coalitions, Domestic Structures, and the End of the Cold War', *International Organization*, 48: 185–214.

Risse-Kappen, Thomas (ed.) (1995a) *Bringing Transnational Relations Back In: Non-State Actors, Domestic Structures, and International Institutions*. Cambridge: Cambridge University Press.

Risse-Kappen, Thomas (1995b) *Cooperation among Democracies. The European Influence on US Foreign Policy*. Princeton: Princeton University Press.

Rosati, Jerel (1987) *The Carter Administration's Quest for Global Community: Beliefs and Their Impact on Behavior*. Columbia: University of South Carolina Press.

Rosati, Jerel A. (1995) 'A Cognitive Approach to the Study of Foreign Policy', in Laura Neack, Jeanne A.K. Hey and Patrick J. Haney (eds), *Foreign Policy Analysis: Continuity and Change in Its Second Generation*. Englewood Cliffs: Prentice Hall.

Rosati, Jerel A. (2000) 'The Power of Human Cognition in the Study of World Politics', *International Studies Review*, 2: 45–75.

Rosati, Jerel, Hagan, Joe D. and Sampson, Martin W. (eds) (1994) *Foreign Policy Restructuring: How Governments Respond to Global Change*. Columbia, SC: University of South Carolina Press.

Rose, Gideon (1998) 'Neoclassical Realism and Theories of Foreign Policy', *World Politics*, 51: 144–72.

Rosenau, James N. (ed.) (1969) *Linkage Politics: Essays on the Convergence of National and International Politics*. New York: Free Press.

Ruggie, John Gerard (1998) *Constructing the World Polity*. London: Routledge.

Rummel, Rudolph J. (1972) *The Dimensions of Nations*. Beverly Hills: Sage.

Russett, Bruce (1993) *Grasping the Democratic Peace: Principles for a Post-Post-Cold War World*. Princeton: Princeton University Press.

Scharpf, Fritz W. (1997) *Games Real Actors Play: Actor-Centered Institutionalism in Policy Research*. Boulder: Westview.

Schmidt, Brian C. (2002) 'On the History and Historiography of International Relations', in Walter Carlsnaes, Thomas Risse and Beth A. Simmons (eds), Handbook of International Relations. London: Sage.

Schneider, Gerald (1997) 'Die bürokratische Politik der Aussenpolitikanalyse: Das Erbe Allisons im Licht der gegenwärtigen Forschungspraxis', *Zeitschrift für Internationale Beziehungen*, 4: 107–23.

Schweller, Randall L. (1996) 'Neorealism's Status Quo Bias: What Security Dilemma?', *Security Studies*, 5: 90–121.

Schweller, Randall L. (1998) *Deadly Imbalance: Tripolarity and Hitler's Strategy of World Conquest*. New York: Columbia University Press.

Singer, Eric G. and Hudson, Valerie M. (eds) (1992) *Political Psychology and Foreign Policy*. Boulder: Westview Press.

Smith, Steve (1986) 'Theories of Foreign Policy: An Historical Overview', *Review of International Studies*, 12: 13–29.

Smith, Steve (1987) 'CFP: A Theoretical Critique', *International Studies Notes*, 13: 47–8.

Snyder, Jack (1991) *Myths of Empire: Domestic Politics and International Ambition*. Ithaca: Cornell University Press.

Snyder, Richard C., Bruck, H.W. and Sapin, B. (1954) 'Decision-Making as an Approach to the Study of International Politics', *Foreign Policy Analysis Project Series No. 3*. Princeton: Princeton University Press.

Snyder, Richard C., Bruck, H.W. and Sapin, B. (eds) (1962) *Foreign Policy Decision Making: An Approach to the Study of International Politics*. New York: Free Press.

Steinbruner, John D. (1974) *The Cybernetic Theory of Decision*. Princeton: Princeton University Press.

Stern, Eric and Verbeek, Bertjan (1998) 'Whither the Study of Governmental Politics in Foreign Policymaking? A Symposium', *Mershon International Studies Review*, 42: 205–55.

Suganami, Hidemi (1999) 'Agents, Structures, Narratives', *European Journal of International Relations*, 5: 365–86.

Sylvan, Donald A. and Voss, James F. (eds) (1998) *Problem Representation in Foreign Policy Decision Making*. Cambridge: Cambridge University Press.

Sylvester, Christine (1994) *Feminist Theory and International Relations in a Postmodern Era*. Cambridge: Cambridge University Press.

Tetlock, Philip E. (1979) 'Identifying Victims of Groupthink from Public Statements of Decision Makers', *Journal of Personality and Social Psychology*, 37: 1314–24.

Tickner, J. Ann (1993) *Gender in International Relations*. New York: Columbia University Press.

Tickner, J. Ann (2002) 'Feminist Perspectives on International Relations', in Walter Carlsnaes, Thomas Risse and Beth A. Simmons (eds), Handbook of International Relations. London: Sage.

Van Evera, Stephen (1990/91) 'Primed for Peace: Europe After the Cold War', *International Security*, 15: 7–57.

Vasquez, John (1983) *The Power of Power Politics: A Critique*. New Brunswick: Rutgers University Press.

Vertzberger, Yaacov Y.I. (1990) *The World in Their Minds: Information Processing, Cognition, and Perception in Foreign Policy Decisionmaking*. Stanford: Stanford University Press.

Waever, Ole (1995) 'Securitization and Desecuritization', in Ronnie Lipschutz (ed.), *On Security*. New York: Columbia University Press.

Waever, Ole (1998) 'Explaining Europe by Decoding Discourses', in Anders Wivel (ed.), *Explaining European Integration*. Copenhagen: Copenhagen Political Studies Press.

Walker, R.B.J. (1993) *Inside/Outside: International Relations as Political Theory*. Cambridge: Cambridge University Press.

Walker, Stephen G. (1990) 'The Evolution of Operational Code Analysis', *Political Psychology*, 11: 403–17.

Walker, Stephen G. (1995) 'Psychodynamic Processes and Framing Effects in Foreign Policy Decision-Making: Woodrow Wilson's Operational Code', *Political Psychology*, 16: 697–717.

Walker, Stephen G., Schafer, Mark and Young, Michael D. (1998) 'Operational Codes and Role Identities: Measuring and Modeling Jimmy Carter's Operational Code', *International Studies Quarterly*, 42: 173–88.

Walt, Stephen M. (1995) 'Alliance Formation and the Balance of World Power', in Michael E.

Brown, Sean M. Lynn-Jones and Steven E. Miller (eds), *The Perils of Anarchy: Contemporary Realism and International Security*.

Waltz, Kenneth (1979) *Theory of International Politics*. Reading, MA: Addison–Wesley. Waltz, Kenneth N. (1996) 'International Politics is not Foreign Policy', *Security Studies*, 6: 54–7.

Weber, Cynthia (1995) *Simulating Sovereignty: Intervention, the State and Symbolic Exchange*. Cambridge: Cambridge University Press.

Welch, David A. (1998) 'A Positive Science of Bureaucratic Politics?', *Mershon International Studies Review*, 42: 210–16.

Weldes, Jutta (1999) *Constructing International Interests*. Minneapolis: University of Minnesota Press.

Weldes, Jutta and Saco, Diana (1996) 'Making State Action Possible: The United States and the Discursive Construction of "The Cuban Problem", 1960–1994', *Millennium*, 25: 361–98.

Wendt, Alexander (1987) 'The Agency–Structure Problem in International Relations', *International Organization*, 41: 335–70.

Wendt, Alexander (1999) *Social Theory of International Politics*. Cambridge: Cambridge University Press.

White, Brian (1999) 'The European Challenge to Foreign Policy Analysis', *European Journal of International Relations*, 5: 37–66.

White, Brian (2001) *Understanding European Foreign Policy*. London: Palgrave.

Wight, Colin (1999) 'They Shoot Horses Don't They? Locating Agency in the Agent–Structure Problematique', *European Journal of International Relations*, 5: 109–42.

Wilkenfeld, Jonathan, Hopple, Gerald W., Rossa, Paul J. and Andriole, Stephen J. (1980) *Foreign Policy Behavior: The Interstate Behavior Analysis Model*. Beverly Hills: Sage.

Wohlforth, William (1993) *The Elusive Balance: Power and Perceptions during the Cold War*. Ithaca: Cornell University Press.

Yee, Albert S. (1996) 'The Causal Effect of Ideas on Politics', *International Organization*, 50: 69–108.

Young, Michael D. (1996) 'Cognitive Mapping Meets Semantic Networks', *Journal of Conflict Resolution*, 40: 395–414.

Young, Michael D. and Shafer, Mark (1998) 'Is There Method in Our Madness? Ways of Assessing Cognition in International Relations', *Mershon International Studies Review*, 42: 63–96.

Zakaria, Fareed (1995) 'Realism and Domestic Politics: A Review Essay', in Michael E. Brown, Sean M. Lynn- Jones and Steven E. Miller (eds), *The Perils of Anarchy: Contemporary Realism and International Security*. Cambridge, MA: MIT Press.

Zakaria, Faheed (1998) *From Wealth to Power: The Unusual Origins of America's World Role*. Princeton: Princeton University Press.

Zelikow, Philip and Rice, Condoleezza (1995) *Germany Unified and Europe Transformed*. Cambridge, MA: Harvard University Press.

21

Criminal Justice Policy

TIM NEWBURN[1]

It is clear enough that criminal conduct does not determine the kind of penal action a society adopts ... [I]t is not 'crime' or even criminological knowledge about crime which most affects policy decisions, but rather the ways in which 'the crime problem' is officially perceived and the political positions to which these perceptions give rise. (Garland, 1990: 20)

Intriguingly, in the main, scholars of social and public policy have tended to ignore the area of criminal justice. Compared with, say, health, education, welfare, and culture, criminal justice has been relatively invisible. And, yet, the creation and maintenance of systems for protecting against the breakdown of internal social order is generally thought to be among the key characteristics and functions that define the modern nation state (Weber, 1978). Interestingly, just as it appears that the ability of modern states to lay claim to 'sovereignty' in the area of security and order is in decline, so criminal justice and penal policy are drawing greater attention from scholars beyond the immediate confines of criminology. Indeed, it is arguably the case that those self-same social transformations that are reconfiguring our responses to criminality also help to account for the degree of attention such matters now enjoy.

The last two centuries or so have seen the progressive rationalisation and bureaucratisation of criminal justice and penal processes. From localised, community-based systems of policing and punishment there have developed huge state-managed apparatuses, and vast bodies of laws, rules and regulations, aimed at controlling crime. What I want to do in this short overview is examine this shifting landscape, looking at the developing functions, purposes (avowed and implied) and techniques that have developed in response to changing perceptions of the problem of crime and social order. My focus will be primarily upon the USA and the UK, partly because these are the jurisdictions I am most familiar with, and whose histories of crime and control have been most extensively documented, but also because it is argued that they are, in different ways perhaps, at the forefront of the changes sweeping the penal systems of a great number of late modern societies (Wacquant, 1999).

I begin by briefly looking at historical trends in crime before moving on to look at the emergence of the modern criminal justice state. As the penal system has developed and changed so the aims of criminal justice policy have altered and the third section of the chapter looks at these changing rationales and philosophies and how they are related to broader structural processes. In recent times, in particular, it appears those broad social, cultural, political and economic processes that are often encapsulated within the term 'late modernity' have been accompanied by a set of often quite radical shifts in the organisation and deployment of punishment and other strategies for the control of crime. In this connection, the final two sections of the chapter explore the emergence of what has been characterised as a new and harshly punitive 'culture of control' (Garland, 2001a) in America and Britain, as well as briefly looking at some of the slightly divergent trends evident in other jurisdictions.

TRENDS IN CRIME

Before looking at what has happened to levels of crime it is important to pause momentarily to consider the basis upon which we 'know' and judge levels of crime. Broadly speaking there are two main methods used for measuring and tracking trends in crime. One is taken from data collected routinely by law enforcement agencies concerning crimes reported by the public or otherwise coming to the attention of the authorities. In the United States these are referred to as the Uniform Crime Reports (UCR) and are collected and collated by the FBI. In England such data are collected by the police and are generally referred to as *recorded crime statistics*. Similar methods of tracking crime via police records are used in most jurisdictions. The second main method uses survey methods to elicit information from a representative sample of the population about their experiences of crime – primarily as victims wherever this is the case – usually over the previous 12 months. The US National Crime Victimization Survey (NCVS) was established in 1972 and has been undertaken twice a year since then. In the UK, a similar approach underpins the British Crime Survey (BCS). This was first undertaken in 1981 and has run intermittently since then – though it too is now undertaken annually. For a number of reasons it is now generally assumed by most commentators that victimisation surveys are a more accurate measure of crime levels and trends than data collected by law enforcement agencies (Farrington and Langan, 2004). As a consequence such surveys are becoming increasingly common in other jurisdictions

and, indeed, there are now regular comparative surveys, such as the International Crime Victims Survey (Nieuwbeerta, 2002).

It is widely believed that we live in times of unprecedented levels of crime. Whether such beliefs are accurate rather depends on the timeframe being utilised. It is certainly the case compared with, say, the 1940s, 1950s or 1960s that current levels of crime are very high. However, if we take a longer historical perspective then there is rather reliable evidence to suggest that previous eras were characterised by very high levels of crime and disorder, even by contemporary standards (Gurr, 1989). In public policy terms, of course, political timeframes tend to be very much shorter. It is here that we confront an interesting irony. It is that, although the public tend to believe that crime is rising, it is, in fact, falling and has been doing so for some time. Figures 21.1 and 22.2, based on NCVS data, show trends in the two main categories of crime in the past 30 years in America. The former indicates that property crime – which accounts of the bulk of crime – has been in fairly consistent decline since around 1975. Although the trend in violent crime is somewhat different, again it hardly indicates a particular 'crisis' in most recent times. Thus, although there were some rises and falls, violent crime remained relatively stable between the mid-1970s and the mid-1990s. Since 1995 violent crime has been declining significantly in the USA. In neither case does this sit easily with popular representations.

Similarly, if we turn to crime trends in the UK we see a similar pattern. Figs 21.3 and 21.4 are based on official crime statistics and the BCS respectively. The former appears to show something of a rise in crime over the past decade. However, the bulk of this change is accounted for by changes in the rules by which crime is counted. By contrast, crime trends, as measured by the BCS – generally considered to be more accurate – indicate that crime overall is likely to have diminished since the mid-1990s.

As the quote from Garland at the top of this chapter indicates, in recent times at least it has not been trends in crime that have been the dominant feature in determining the shape

Figure 21.1   *Property crime USA 1973–2003*
Source: Bureau of Justice Statistics http://www.ojp.usdoj.gov/bjs/glance/tables/proptrdtab.htm)

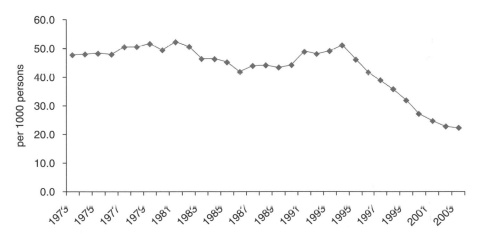

Figure 21.2   *Violent crime USA 1973–2003*
Source: Bureau of Justice Statistics (http://www.ojp.usdoj.gov/bjs/glance/tables/viortrdtab.htm)

and nature of criminal justice policy in many developed societies (the USA and UK in particular perhaps). As we have seen for much of the past 30 years crime in the USA has either been stable or in decline. During the same period the prison population in the USA has been expanding at an unparalleled rate. In some resects it is possible to argue that America is something of an exception in this regard; it is certainly the case, for example, that its incarceration rate is incomparably higher than that in any other developed liberal democracy. Nevertheless, as we will see in greater detail below, the dislocation between crime levels and crime policy is evident elsewhere. In the UK, for example, the period since the early 1990s has seen a rapidly expanding prison population – at almost precisely the point at which crime started to reduce. Given that it appears that criminal justice policy appears not to be some direct response to immediate trends in crime, we are required to look elsewhere in order to understand how penal policies come to take the form they do. We begin by looking at the origins and development of the modern criminal justice system.

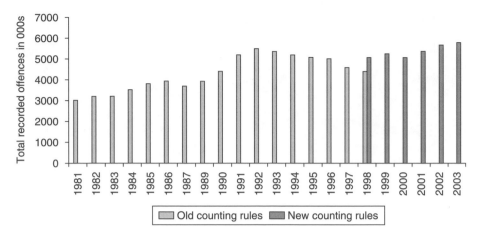

Figure 21.3   *Trends in recorded crime (England & Wales) 1981–2003*
Source: Dodd et al., 2004

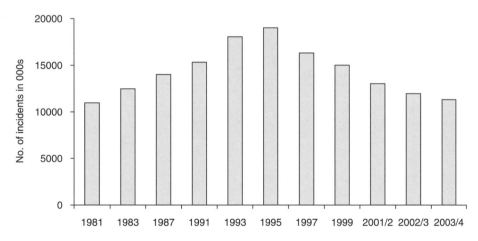

Figure 21.4   *Trends in all BCS crime, 1981–2003/4*
Source: Dodd et al., 2004

THE EMERGENCE OF THE MODERN CRIMINAL JUSTICE SYSTEM

Walker (1998) divides his history of American criminal justice into three eras: the colonial era, which lasted roughly 150 years from the late 1600s until the 1820s prior to the establishment of a formal criminal justice system; an era from the 1820s to the 1920s in which all the main institutions of criminal justice were established; and the modern era, in which dual processes of consolidation and reform have shaped and reshaped the criminal justice

system. Though the criminal justice systems of the US and the UK have been shaped by different historical pressures and circumstances, there is nevertheless considerable commonality between the two jurisdictions, especially over the past 200 years.

In the colonial era in the USA, and prior to the industrial revolution in the UK, crime control was relatively informal and community-based. Communities were small and enforcing moral codes was relatively straightforward. As one legal historian puts it, they 'had both the will and the ability to enforce laws against fornication, sins of the flesh, minor vices, and bad behaviour. They punished these offences the way autocratic fathers or mothers punish children; they made heavy use of shame and shaming' (Friedman, 1993: 37). Confession and repentance were key parts of the system, and public identification and humiliation through branding and letter-wearing ('A' for adulterer for example) were not uncommon. The stocks, the ducking stool and, for more serious offences, bodily mutilation or banishment, were also invoked. Then, finally, there was the death penalty, though, according to Friedman (1993: 41), 'on the whole, English law was more liberal with capital punishment than colonial law. In England, men and women swung from the gallows for theft, robbery, burglary; in the colonies, this was exceptionally rare'. Where it was used, the death penalty was much more common in the southern United States than in the north, and was used most frequently on slaves.

In Britain Radzinowicz (1948: 231) notes that according to 'one line of contemporary thought on penal matters eighteenth century criminal law was insufficiently severe to afford adequate protection against crime. Death, which … was then the appointed penalty for a large – and growing – number of offences, was considered too mild a punishment for a great many of them'. Though the death penalty was the focus of the penal system in medieval times, and levels of capital punishment were high, it underwent something of a brief boom from about the mid-seventeenth century through to the early eighteenth. The so-called 'bloody code', under which a large number of new capital offences were placed on the statute book from 1688, came under increasing attack and much of the century was characterised by a search for viable secondary punishments (Sharpe, 1990). Transportation was the other major form of judicial punishment in Britain in the latter half of the seventeenth century, but by the turn of the century a number of British colonies were beginning to refuse to receive any further convicts. Nevertheless, by the 1760s transportation to the American colonies accounted for at least 70% of all sentences at the central criminal court in London.

From this point on, however, transportation declined and the use of imprisonment began to grow.

The system of punishment in Victorian Britain differed quite significantly from that of the late eighteenth century. The use of the death penalty declined markedly throughout the 1800s, public ceremonies of execution ceased in 1868 and corporal punishment of adults was rare by the second half of the century. Similarly, whereas in the Colonial era in America punishment was conducted publicly, the Revolution had a major impact on criminal justice, bringing formal criminal codes and, from the late eighteenth century, the creation of the modern prison. As Garland (1985) and others have noted, the steady decline in the infliction of pain upon the body was paralleled by increasing use of incarceration as the main form of punishment of adult offenders. According to Ignatieff (1978: 90) this shift indicated 'a loss of confidence in the morality and efficacy of ritual punishments, a growing resistance to the idea that the state should share the infliction of the punishment with the community'.

Put crudely, imprisonment moved from being merely a repository for those awaiting trial, sentence or death in the sixteenth and seventeenth centuries, to a site where punishment was inflicted on an increasingly wide range of offenders during the course of the eighteenth and nineteenth centuries. Although in Victorian Britain and late nineteenth century America the formal priority of the prison system remained 'the repression of crime' through deterrence (Garland, 1985) nevertheless a growing emphasis on the reform and rehabilitation of offenders was emerging. From the mid-twentieth century, for approximately three decades, the notion of 'treatment and training' became the explicit guiding principle of the prison system.

Like the prison, so a body of uniformed police agents organised bureaucratically, functioning to maintain order and detect and investigate crime, is similarly a product of the modern industrial nation state. In the pre-industrial era, 'policing' was a community-based, less formal set of activities. In eighteenth century America, for example, a system of 'brotherly watch' existed in which community members were expected to monitor each others' behaviour and to report drunkenness, sexual promiscuity, heretical views and failure to attend Church, among other activities. In the UK the establishment of formal policing was preceded by community-based systems, such as the 'hue and cry', in which local citizens took responsibility for raising the alarm and for chasing down the offender. On both sides of the Atlantic at this time the maintenance of order was essentially a civic duty shared, at least in principle, by all.

Eighteenth-century England was characterised by increasing concerns about crime. By the mid- to late eighteenth century, crime and disorder was perceived to pose a threat to social stability. It was around this time that what we now understand as 'the police' emerged on both sides of the Atlantic – in 1829 in London, in Boston in 1838 and New York City in 1845 (Miller, 1975). The nineteenth and early twentieth centuries saw the creation of all the fundamental institutions of the modern criminal justice system: the prison, the police, the courts and related systems of criminal prosecution, probation and, in due course, an increasingly complex array of non-custodial penalties. Toward the end of the nineteenth century separate systems for dealing with juvenile offenders also emerged in both the US and the UK. The first half of the twentieth century, dominated of course by two world wars, saw the consolidation and reform of modern criminal justice systems. Policing provides a good example. Kelling and Moore (1988) argue that the period between the introduction of formal police departments in the early to mid-1800s and the turn of the twentieth century can be characterised as a 'political era', characterised by the struggles between various groups to control the police. The 'reform era' emerged in the early twentieth century, had its high point in the 1950s and 1960s and eroded through the 1970s, eventually to be replaced by a community problem-solving era.

The reform era involved the progressive professionalisation of policing and saw, toward the end of the period, the high point of police

legitimacy. Declining police legitimacy coincided broadly with, and in part signalled, the ending of the 'modern' period in criminal justice and penal policy. This was the period in which the 'solidarity project' (Garland, 1996) – the post-Enlightenment aim in which the state was the guarantor of full citizenship and security for all – was increasingly eclipsed by market forces. Recent decades have seen the emergence of a rapidly expanding mixed economy in policing and in other areas of criminal justice. Crucially, this period has also seen what to many appears to be a decisive shift in what are believed to be the purposes and ambitions of our criminal justice and penal policies, and it is to these that we turn next.

THE CHANGING GOALS OF CRIMINAL JUSTICE AND PENAL POLICY

In pre-industrial/colonial times much punishment was public in character and, as such, was designed to shame, to bring forth expressions of guilt, remorse and repentance. Loss of freedom – through imprisonment – was far from a common response to criminal infractions and was not assumed, as yet, to be an effective method for stimulating reform. By the nineteenth century this had all changed.

The post-colonial era in America saw the operation of two distinct approaches to imprisonment. One, most notably at the Eastern State penitentiary, opened in 1829, subjected inmates to total solitary confinement with only one hour of exercise allowed and no contact permitted with other prisoners. By contrast, the Auburn system in New York permitted communal work and eating, though in silence, otherwise confining inmates to individual cells. Both systems reflected the view that crime was the product of corrupting external influences (Walker, 1998) and reflected a shift from the earlier era when crime was viewed as an individual failing or simply as the product of sin. In 1779 in the UK the Penitentiary Act was passed with the intention of building two establishments to house convicts who otherwise would have been sentenced to transportation. In custody they would be made to undertake hard and servile labour during the day and kept in solitary confinement at night. A regime of total silence was established at the Coldbath Fields House of Correction in the 1830s, and the new austere period in British penal history was completed with the opening of Pentonville in 1842, with a regime based explicitly on the Philadephia model in the USA in which inmates were kept separate. Such a regime was believed to be 'not only morally beneficial, by preventing contamination and providing an opportunity for reflection and self-examination, but greatly facilitated the task of security and control' (Home Office, 1979, para 2.6).

By the end of the nineteenth century in the UK a major public debate about the prison system was under way. The system, it was suggested, was failing in its objective of deterring criminals whilst simultaneously being too harsh (similarly in the US prisons had begun to relax the rule of silence by the 1860s). Thus emerged, in due course, a new system of penality of which 'the great object of reclaiming the criminal' was the avowed cornerstone. The range of sanctions available to criminal courts expanded markedly, probation and other forms of training became established, and a range of new institutions were established or consolidated, many of which were conceived as direct alternatives to imprisonment. There emerged 'a calibrated, hierarchical structure' of penalties (Garland, 1985), including indeterminate prison sentences, into which offenders were placed according not only to the nature and severity of their offence, but partly in response to the diagnosis of their condition and the treatment considered necessary in consequence. Whilst *deterrence* remained an important goal of criminal justice policy, reform and *rehabilitation* lay at the heart of this new penal complex. The flexibility required for such a system to operate opened the door to considerably different 'treatments' (sentences) for offenders convicted of ostensibly similar offences, and eventually became one of the sources of its eventual demise.

The move from penal modernism to its 'post' or 'late' modern successor has occurred in a relatively short space of time. If the penal-welfare strategies that developed in the late nineteenth century reached their high point a little after the mid-twentieth century, the criminal justice and penal systems to which they gave rise are now radically restructured and reoriented. At the heart of this shift has been a decline of faith in the welfare and rehabilitative functions of criminal justice and the gradual rise to dominance of a set of discourses and practices that are more punitive, politicised and populist. Moreover, these emergent discourses are indicative of a declining interest in, and possibly even belief in the importance of, the social and environmental causes of crime. By the late 1970s there was a clear loss of faith in the power of the state to reform and, through reform, to reduce crime.

Much of the criticism of contemporary criminal justice was focused on discretion. Advocates of the so-called 'justice' model sought to redress what was perceived to be the inequity and unfairness built into current practices. In fact there was a threefold attack on the extant philosophy of rehabilitation and the associated practice of indeterminate sentencing. In addition to what might be thought a liberal critique, there was also a more specifically conservative critique of rehabilitation, most closely associated with commentators such as James Q. Wilson and John DiIulio. Much of this critique centred on what was perceived to be the tendency in penal modernism to excuse offending behaviour through the focus on issues beyond individual responsibility, such as poverty and inequality. Nothing perhaps captures the spirit of the new punitiveness better than James Q. Wilson's (1975: 209) observation that: 'Wicked people exist. Nothing avails except to set them apart from innocent people'. The punitive turn in recent decades has seen the re-emergence of a neoclassical model of criminals as self-determining, usually rational, individuals exploiting the increasing opportunities and declining controls argued to be characteristic of contemporary society.

It was not only conservatives that were critical of the modernist penological project, but liberals or progressives too. Hugely influential in this regard was an article written by Robert Martinson (1974) exploring existing academic evidence on the impact of correctional interventions. Though Martinson's article was entitled 'What Works?', and his conclusions were mixed – limited impact was found in something under half of all interventions – the interpretation generally drawn from his work was that 'nothing works'. Though Martinson quickly distanced himself from such a conclusion (Martinson, 1979) penal pessimism was deeply embedded by this time and was anyway being overtaken by broader social processes associated with neoliberalism that were undermining penal-welfarism. The last 30 years have seen the emergence of a qualitatively different model of penal trends, in which the systems of punishment and control have been reconfigured and which are punitive and populist in intent (Sparks, 2003).

The most obvious signal of this change was the rapidly increasing use of imprisonment in many jurisdictions, most spectacularly the USA, where its 'imprisonment orgy' (Walker, 1998) resulted in a fivefold increase in the prison population between 1970 and 2003 (Tonry, 2004). The outcome of the 'crisis of penal modernism' (Garland, 1995) has seen the discretion of judges and other sentencers considerably limited, indeterminate sentencing progressively replaced by determinate alternatives as a result of legislative restriction and sentencing guidelines. Indeed, in many jurisdictions mandatory forms of sentencing – the most infamous being California's 'Three strikes and You're Out' laws – became increasingly popular, particularly as a result of the 'war on drugs'. Perhaps the other most obvious indicator that the tenor of the times has changed markedly, within the US at least, has been the return of the death penalty. By 1967, when arguably the modern rehabilitative ideal was at its height, an effective moratorium on executions was established in America. It lasted 10 years and ended, in Utah, with the execution of Gary Gilmore. Though the rate of executions rose only relatively slowly, and even at its current (2005) level of 60, remains considerably below the levels reached earlier in the century, it is now the case that the United States uses the death penalty more frequently than all nations other than China, Iran and Vietnam (Amnesty International, 2005).

Criminal justice policy has been caught up in the battle between two competing versions of the role of the state. The first emphasises welfare and civil rights, and the reduction of social inequalities. The other rails against 'big government' and seeks to limit state intervention in citizens' lives in most areas, with the exception of criminal justice. In this second model the state has a much diminished role in managing and protecting social welfare, something increasingly left to the market, but has an increasingly enhanced role in the management of social order. Indeed, for commentators such as Charles Murray, rising crime and disorder are precisely a product of welfare dependency. In this clash of ideologies, the vision espoused by the moral conservatives won out despite the fact that such calls for tighter control should have clashed with the deregulatory trends set in train by neoliberalism in the economic sphere (Garland, 2001a). That they did not illustrates the extent to which the neo-conservative argument successfully portrayed the problems of crime, disorder – and immorality – as specifically problems of particular social groups: the unemployed, those on welfare, offenders and drug-users. As a consequence effective criminal justice and penal policy 'came to be viewed as a matter of imposing more controls, increasing disincentives, and, if necessary, segregating the dangerous sector of the population' (Garland, 2001a: 102). Over the course of the past 20 years such punitiveness has become the standard political position on crime and order and, indeed, 'is a stance that no serious politician can safely disavow' (Sparks, 2003: 170).

A NEW POLITICS OF CRIME?

The starting gun in penal policy's equivalent of the arms race was fired in 1964 by US Republican presidential candidate Barry Goldwater. In his acceptance speech he argued, 'History shows us that nothing prepares the way for tyranny more than the failure of public officials to keep the streets safe from bullies and marauders. We Republicans seek a government that attends to its fiscal climate, encouraging a free and a competitive economy and enforcing law and order' (quoted in Chambliss, 1999). Though his position was controversial, and ultimately unsuccessful, the tough on crime message he sought to use has become a staple of national politics in recent times. The 'war on poverty' fought through the Great Society programs, which Lyndon Johnson also believed to be anti-crime programs, were eventually to be replaced by the conservative view, expressed by Richard Nixon, that the 'solution to the crime problem is not the quadrupling of funds for any governmental war on poverty but more convictions' (quoted in Beckett, 1997: 38). As Beckett astutely observes, however, at that time the President had relatively little leverage over street crime outside of the confines of Washington DC. The initial reaction was to take refuge in tough sounding rhetoric and largely symbolic legislation. Successive administrations have sought both to increase federal aid to, and federal leverage over, local and state law enforcement in order to mitigate this problem, not least through successive *wars* on drugs (Zimring and Hawkins, 1992).

Although criminal justice policy took something of a backseat under both Presidents Ford and Carter, it re-emerged with a vengeance from 1980 onward under Reagan and not just his Republican but also his Democrat successors. According to Reagan, 'the war on crime will only be won when an attitude of mind and a change of heart takes place in America – when certain truths take hold again ... truths like: right and wrong matters; individuals are responsible for their actions; retribution should be swift and sure for those who prey on the innocent' (quoted in Beckett, 1997: 47). The wars on crime and drugs adopted by the Reagan and Bush administrations involved tougher sentencing laws, a profound shift back toward determinate sentencing, increased use of preventive detention, vastly upgraded interdiction arrangements, and increased street-level enforcement.

The rising prison population in the United States is quite simply one of the most staggering phenomena in criminal justice in the last half century. The bare facts are startling. There were approximately 200,000 people in state and federal prisons in 1972. Twenty five years later the number was well over 1.1 million. Similarly, in 1972 there were 130,000 in local jails; by 1997 it was 567,000. In two and half decades – a period, let us remind ourselves, in which crime was falling – the number of Americans incarcerated increased fivefold. The overall numbers incarcerated exceeded two million in 2002. The sheer scale of this imprisonment *orgy* now means that commentators routinely refer to this aspect of penal policy in the US as 'mass incarceration' (see Garland, 2001b).

Of course, we focus on imprisonment because it somehow represents the symbolic heart of criminal justice policy, the apex of our contemporary, hierarchical system of punishments. However, prison numbers only convey part of what has happened in the US. The reach of the criminal justice system is much broader than just the incarcerated population. If one includes in the calculations those also under criminal justice supervision via probation or parole then the numbers are even more startling. As Fig. 21.5 illustrates, the numbers subject to parole and probation have also increased and the total under correctional supervision reached almost seven million by 2003.

Again, however, staggering as they are, the bare facts of mass imprisonment and mass correctional supervision actually hide some important features of what has occurred in the US in the last 30 years. As Garland (2001b) notes, mass imprisonment has an important feature beyond the fact of the sheer numbers incarcerated. Its second important feature is that it involves the systematic imprisonment of whole groups of the population. In the USA this is young black urban males. As Mauer (1999: 118–119) observes, 'A walk through nearly any courtroom or prison in the United States reveals a sea of black and brown faces at the defendant's table and in the prison yard. Half of all prison inmates are now African-American, and another 17% are Hispanic'. The lifetime likelihood of imprisonment for African-Americans is 32% compared with 17% for Hispanics and 6% for Whites. Approximately one in eight black

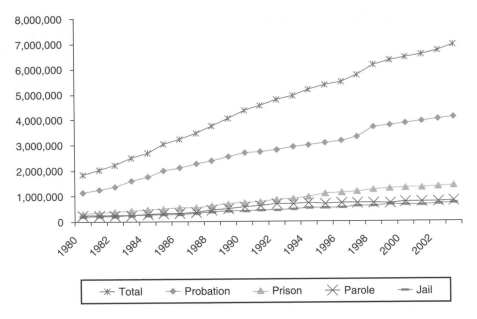

Figure 21.5   *Correctional population USA 1980–2003*

males aged 25–29 was in prison at midyear 2003 compared with 1 in 27 Hispanic males and 1 in 63 white males of the same age (Sentencing Project, 2004).

What makes for such unprecedented growth in the prison population? In part the war on crime and, more particularly, the war on drugs have had a dramatic on the supply side – providing 'an almost limitless supply of arrestable and imprisonable offenders' (Simon, 2001). Second, there are features of the 'macho penal economy' itself (Downes, 2001), not least the expanding private corrections sector, which tend toward expansionism (Christie, 1993). The third, and possibly most important, factor is the general transformation of political culture that has occurred in America and elsewhere.

Crime is now a staple of political discourse and of electoral politics. Whilst this may not feel surprising it is, in fact, a relatively new political phenomenon. Until the early 1960s in the USA and the early 1970s in the UK, for example, criminal justice policy barely featured in major elections and certainly was far from the 'wedge issue' it has often been since. As we have seen, the 1964 presidential election campaign signalled an important shift in American politics, making crime a salient issue in national politics. 'Conservatives blamed the increase in crime on liberal social policies, arguing that the courts had "handcuffed" the police, that bail reform and rehabilitation programs turned predatory criminals loose on society, and that the moratorium on executions removed the deterrent effect of the death penalty' (Walker, 1998: 201). Similarly, it was not until the mid-1970s in the UK that 'law and order' became an important feature of national, electoral politics (Downes and Morgan, 1997).

In the criminal justice arena, politicians' concern with how they are likely to be perceived has had a profound effect on policymaking in recent times. Crucially, as numerous commentators have noted, by the 1990s the old divisions between 'conservative' and 'liberal' political positions on crime had disappeared, and had been replaced by what appeared to be a straightforward 'tough on crime' message. The past two decades have seen a progressively intensifying battle by the major political parties to be seen as the party of law and order. Initially in the USA, and subsequently in the UK and other jurisdictions, a 'tough on crime' stance has come to be associated with electoral success and its opposite, being 'soft on crime', with electoral failure.

Crucial in this regard was Michael Dukakis' defeat in the 1988 presidential election in the US. In the aftermath of the defeat the Democratic Party sought to reinvent and reposition itself on a number of core public policy issues, not least crime. The 'New Democrats' sought to break free from what they perceived as the failed 'liberalism' of the Party, regaining the 'mainstream' voters that had been alienated over the course of the 1980s. In the aftermath of the Dukakis defeat, Bill Clinton, then an active member of the reformist Democratic Leadership Council observed that: 'No matter how popular your programs may be, you must be considered in the mainstream on the shared values of the American people, the ability to defend the nation and the strength to enforce its laws' (quoted in Baer, 2000: 126). Subsequently, he became a 'tough on crime' Democratic president, supportive of the death penalty, introducing federal 'three strikes' sentencing and, though supportive of drug treatment programs and community policing, by 1994 was overseeing 'a repressive criminal justice climate rivalling that of any time during the preceding twenty years' (Mauer, 1999: 71).

The parallels between the politics of criminal justice in America and Britain at this time are strong. The lengthy political dominance of Conservatism during the 1980s in the UK led to vociferous debates within the British Labour Party over the possible sources of electoral success in what were clearly changed times. Paralleling the remodelling of the Democratic Party in the aftermath of the 1988 presidential election, the Labour Party sought to dump its various 'hostages to fortune' (Downes and Morgan, 1997) not least of which was its previously more liberal policies on crime control. 'New Labour' in the UK embraced so-called 'third way' politics. In the criminal justice arena this meant attempting to modify the old-fashioned liberal penal-welfarism that the party had largely clung to throughout the 1980s and into the 1990s by adding into the mix what was by now considered the *sine qua non* of successful electoral politics: a healthy dose of punitive rhetoric – much of which was drawn from the

Clinton administration (Newburn and Jones, 2005) and the promise of similarly punitive policies. The amalgam has never been more successfully captured than in Tony Blair's 1993 soundbite, 'tough on crime and tough on the causes of crime'. Here, in only 10 words, the relegation of traditional liberal concerns with poverty and social inequality as the generators of criminality was successfully conveyed whilst also using the new symbolic keywords (Fairclough, 2000) 'tough' and 'crime' twice each. Though the rise is by no means as spectacular as in America, nevertheless the consequence of the emergence in the early to mid-1990s in Britain of a punitive bipartisan consensus on crime is a rapid and substantial increase in the prison population. In 1994 the prison population in England and Wales stood at a little over 44,000. A decade later it had reached 75,000, with the Labour government looking to institute measures to cap the population at 80,000. Again, the bulk of this prison expansion took place during a period of declining crime. With the main political parties seemingly wedded to tough on crime rhetoric, on the surface there seems little prospect of breaking out of the 'new iron cage' (Garland, 2001a) of punitive justice.

The 'culture of control' in America and Britain that Garland so vividly describes is by no means confined to those nations. Elements of this new configuration are visible elsewhere. Prison populations are rising sharply in many jurisdictions, including hitherto quintessentially liberal societies such as the Netherlands and punitive rhetoric, often originating in the US, has spread through much of northern and southern Europe (Wacquant, 1999) and beyond. Just as there are global pressures transforming and seemingly homogenising many aspects of national political cultures, the structural changes accompanying the shift to late modernity appear to be creating the conditions across the developed economies in which a newly punitive culture of control can flourish. These developments are so pervasive that they frequently appear irresistible. And, yet, it would be a mistake not to acknowledge the continued existence of considerable variations in the localised cultures of control that are visible internationally, for, not only are they important illustrations of some of the limits of current trends, but potentially also help identify the sources of resistance to the new iron cage.

INTERNATIONAL VARIATIONS

As an increasing body of scholars have noted (*inter alia,* Tonry, 2004; Newburn and Sparks, 2004; Melossi, 2004) that beneath what appears a general trend in the direction of increased punitiveness and exclusionary practices in crime control, there remain some considerable and apparently quite deeply embedded national differences in criminal justice and penal policies. Indeed, there exist considerable variations within some jurisdictions. Thus, the USA is made up of many criminal justice systems and that there exist considerable variations between these. As one example, taking incarceration rates in the 30 years 1970–2000, Hinds (2005) has shown that custody rates were consistently higher in this period in the Southern States and lower in the Northeast and Midwest compared with other regions. In 2000 the custody rate in the Southern States, at 8.34, was twice that of the Northeastern States (at 4.09). Similarly, by no means all the states in the Union still have the death penalty, let alone still use it. Mandatory sentencing varies hugely by state (Jones and Newburn, forthcoming) as does the nature of policing. Whilst identifying general trends continues to be important, it is equally vital not to lose sight of the nature and sources of continuing variation.

Thus, in Scandinavia for example, despite generally rising crime rates over the past 40–50 years, prison populations have remained relatively stable (Denmark, Norway and Sweden) or reduced from a previously enormously high level to something akin to other Scandinavian countries (Finland). It is important to note, however, that there appear to have been some increases in incarceration rates in recent years (von Hofer, 2004), possibly related to extended sentence lengths, particularly for drug-related crimes (Bondeson, 2005). How might one explain the existence of generally milder penal policy in Scandinavia? Bondeson suggests that there is some evidence, though far from unequivocal, that attitudes to punishment are less punitive in Scandinavia and that fear of crime is also lower. Moreover, it seems possible the media are also more constrained, and thoughtful, in their treatment of crime and justice issues. A number of broader socio-cultural explanations also seem plausible. On a general level it appears to be the case that there remains greater support for a broadly welfarist approach to public policy, including penal policy, in Scandinavia than in some other parts of Europe and certainly than in the US. The Nordic countries have more homogenous populations than, say, the UK and the US, and higher levels of functional democratisation, both of which, arguably, have served to protect against the emergence of those forms of populist punitiveness that are increasingly visible elsewhere.

The number of people in prison in Italy has been rising slowly, but the incarceration rate remains close to the European average of 100 per 100,000 population (Solivetti, 2004). Italy does differ somewhat from much of the rest of Europe, however, in the way it reaches its average. The prison population in Italy has both a higher proportion of very long prison sentences compared with, say, the Scandinavian countries, and also a significant proportion of those in prison are detained awaiting final sentence (Nelken, 2005). In explaining the relatively lenient criminal justice responses found in Italy, particularly in relation to dealing with youthful criminality, Nelken (2005) points to a number of important socio-cultural factors, including the relative absence of ghetto housing estates, the strength and surveillance capacities of the family, and the lack of a youthful drinking culture (at least when compared with Northern Europe).

One of the most interesting and intriguing contrasts with the USA is Canada. Mulroney's Progressive Conservative government of the late 1980s largely continued the approaches established by its Liberal predecessor (Hatt et al., 1992) and during the 1990s the new Liberal federal government set about establishing a distinct 'Canadian way' for dealing with social problems, including crime (Meyer and O'Malley, 2005). This distinctive way was explicitly designed to differ from the example being set by the nation's nearest neighbour: [W]e have two choices – go the way of the US and build more prisons, or develop meaningful, lasting alternatives to incarceration for low-risk offenders who can be better managed in the community. (Canada, 2001, quoted in Meyer and O'Malley, 2005). In sum, such an approach to criminal justice policy has led to a federal prison system with a comprehensive pro-gramme of health, educational and training programmes for inmates, incarceration rates that are both low and declining, together with the removal of the death penalty. That said, as Moore and Hannah-Moffatt (2005: 97) con-clude in their recent review, '[A]ppearances can be deceiving. The liberalism of Canadian punishment is a veil underneath which remains an extremely punitive system' albeit of a dis-tinctive form in which therapeutic initiatives are central to the system of punishment.

The varied cultures of control in contempo-rary advanced economies clearly have many commonalities. Moreover, such shared charac-teristics are undoubtedly the product of broad social, cultural, political and economic pres-sures. However, it is also clear that particular socioeconomic, cultural and political contexts frame and shape *local* cultures of control in quite different ways. As Lacey (2003: 86) observes, 'it is crucial for us to recognise that the salience and politicisation of criminal justice vary from country to country' and that our understanding of this variation remains very far from developed. Understanding similarities and differences in the pattern of contemporary systems of crime control is arguably, therefore, one of the most pressing tasks facing us.

CONCLUSION

I opened this chapter with a quote from David Garland's magisterial study of punishment and modern society in which he observes that criminal justice and penal policy have less to do with trends in crime than with the political

and cultural frames through which crime is understood. That the whole area of penal policy has become intensely and minutely politicised is one of the central changes of recent times. Crime and criminal justice is now accepted as being a major political issue – if not yet a major area of scholarly study among political scientists. Not only do we expect politicians to spend much of their time talking about crime and criminal justice, but we expect them to disagree. It was not always thus. As many commentators have noted (Beckett, 1997; Chambliss, 1999; Downes and Morgan, 1997) for much of the twentieth century there existed something close to a bipartisan consen-sus about how best to respond to crime, both in the US (certainly at a Federal level) and the UK. Broadly speaking, the consensus view was that a set of strategies aimed simultaneously at punishing and reforming – characterised by Garland as 'penal-welfarism' – was the most appropriate and efficacious means by which the modern state could maintain order and reduce crime.

Though there remain jurisdictions in which an attachment to penal-welfarism persists, the general trend appears to be away from such approaches and toward a set of highly puni-tive and exclusionary strategies. Indeed, it is arguably the case that a new political consen-sus has emerged around precisely such 'tough on crime' rhetoric and practice. At the heart of the emergent punitive strategies lies the language of risk. The shift away from concerns with causes and toward the management and administration of crime problems has led some commentators to argue that we are witnessing the emergence of a distinctive form of criminal justice policy that they characterise as a 'new penology' (Feeley and Simon, 1992). Such strategies are risk-oriented and based on actuarial calculations rather than individual diagnoses, and future preventive-orientation rather than the imposition of sanctions *ex poste ante*. Such strategies are clearly compati-ble with the broader neo-liberal political pro-ject, which seeks to roll-back the welfare state, both resting on a view of those caught in poverty, offending and drug dependence as straightfor-wardly feckless and morally culpable. The result in the crime control arena is policies dominated by rational choice models, the racheting up of penalties and hazards attendant on behaviour deemed to fall short of required standards, together with vast increases in the technologies of surveillance available to monitor populations of risk.

In discussing the politics of crime control, Simon (1997) has described the strategy of 'governing through crime'. Simon's central argument is that advanced industrial societies are experiencing a crisis of governance (rather than a crisis of crime) and that the response to this has been to prioritise crime and punishment as the preferred contexts for governance. Though the argument may be overstated in some respects, he is undoubtedly right in arguing that crime currently casts a 'disproportionate shadow over what we primarily identify with governance, i.e. politicians and the electoral process of democracy' (1997: 174). This has been true for well over a decade in the USA, for a similar period in the UK, most evidently under the New Labour administrations of the past eight years, and appears to be a growing force in other jurisdictions besides.

One possible explanation for the rise up the political agenda of crime policy generally, and punitive policies particularly, is what Beckett (1997) calls the 'democracy-at-work' thesis. This thesis has it that the significant increases in crime that have occurred have led to increases in public fear of crime. Heightened fears put crime on the political agenda, in turn this leads to demands for harsher punishments for offenders and eventually to a significant growth in the number of people incarcerated. She quotes James Q. Wilson (1975), arguing along these lines that 'public opinion was well ahead of political opinion in calling attention to the rising problem of crime'. In fact, using public opinion data during the US war on crime period (1964–1974) and the war on drugs era, (1985–1992), she is able to show that, in practice, it was political initiatives in relation to crime and drugs that was a significant factor in shaping public concerns rather than the other way around. Moreover, the assumption that there is a close link between levels of public concern and the reported rate

of crime and drug use is also shown to be much more complex than the 'democracy-at-work' thesis would allow. This, of course, is not to deny any link between public opinion and political initiative in this area – it is highly likely that they are mutually reinforcing in many respects – merely to reiterate the point that the 'punitive turn' in contemporary criminal justice policy can neither be explained by reference to trends in crime nor as a simple extension of public concerns and fears about crime. Rather, as in so much else in public policy, it is the broader restructuring of social relations and political cultures associated with late modernity that is central to the explanation of contemporary developments. The particular irony here is that, as the 'limits of the sovereign state' become more visible, so part of the response appears to have been to engage 'in a more expressive and more intensive mode of punishment that purports to convey public sentiment and the full force of state authority' (Garland, 2000: 349). The result is a set of arrangements for dealing with criminality that pay precious little regard to root causes, and have little interest in punishment beyond its utility as a means of reducing threats and managing risks. Churchill's observation that 'The mood and temper of the public in regard to the treatment of crime and criminals is one of the most unfailing tests of the civilisation of any country' (quoted in Radzinowicz and Hood, 1990: 774) is often cited – particularly now that the mood and temper so often seems so illiberal. Less often quoted are the sentences that followed this most famous of observations. I conclude with them as it is they perhaps that best capture the general philosophy that underpinned criminal justice policy until as recently as 30 years ago and so clearly demonstrate how far, in what direction, we have travelled since:

> A calm and dispassionate recognition of the rights of the accused against the State, and even of convicted criminals against the State, a constant heart-searching by all charged with the duty of punishment, a desire and eagerness to rehabilitate in the world of industry all those who have paid their dues in the hard coinage of punishment, tireless efforts towards the discovery of curative and regenerating processes, and an unfaltering faith that there is a treasure, if you can only find it, in the

heart of every man – these are the symbols which in the treatment of crime and criminals mark and measure the stored-up strength of a nation, and are the sign and proof of the living virtue in it.

NOTE

1. Professor of Criminology and Social Policy and Director, Mannheim Centre for Criminology, London School of Economics. Contact details: Dept of Social Policy, LSE, Houghton St, London WC2A 2AE, UK; t.newburn@lse.ac.uk

REFERENCES

Amnesty International (2005) *The Death Penalty Worldwide: Developments in 2004,* http://web.amnesty.org/library/Index/ENGACT500012005.

Baer, K. (2000) *Reinventing Democrats: The politics of liberalism from Reagan to Clinton,* Kansas: University Press of Kansas.

Beckett, K. (1997) *Making Crime Pay: Law and Order in Contemporary American Politics,* New York: Oxford University Press.

Bondeson, U. V. (2005) Levels of punitiveness in Scandinavia: description and explanations, in Pratt, J. Brown, D. Brown, M. Hallsworth S. and Morrison W. (eds), *The New Punitiveness: Trends, theories, perspectives,* Cullompton: Willan Publishing.

Chambliss, W. J. (1999) *Power, Politics and Crime,* Boulder, Co: Westview Press.

Christie, N. (1993) *Crime Control as Industry,* London: Routledge.

Dodd, T., Nicholas, S., Povey, D. and Walker, A. (2004) *Crime in England and Wales 2003/2004,* London: Home Office.

Downes, D. (2001) The macho penal economy, in Garland, D. (ed.), Special Issue on Mass Imprisonment in the USA, *Punishment and Society,* vol. 3, no. 1.

Downes, D. and Morgan, R. (1997) Dumping the 'Hostages to Fortune'? The politics of law and order in post-war Britain, in Maguire, M., Morgan, R. and Reiner, R. (eds), *The Oxford Handbook of Criminology,* Second Edition, Oxford: Clarendon Press.

Emsley, C. (1991) *The English Police: A Political and Social History,* Hemel Hempstead: Harvester Wheatsheaf.

Fairclough, N. (2000) *New Labour, New Language?,* London: Routledge.

Farrington, D. P. and Langan, P. (2004) England and Wales, in Farrington, D. P., Langan, P. and Tonry, M. (eds), *Cross-National Studies in Crime and Justice,* Washington DC: U.S. Department of Justice.

Feeley, M. and Simon, J. (1992) The new penology: Notes on the emerging strategy of corrections and its implications, *Criminology,* 30, 4, 449–474.

Friedman, L. (1993) *Crime and Punishment in American History,* New York: Basic Books.

Garland, D. (1985) *Punishment and Welfare: A history of penal strategies,* Aldershot: Gower.

Garland, D. (1990) *Punishment and Modern Society,* Oxford: Clarendon Press.

Garland, D. (1995) Penal modernism and postmodernism, in Cohen, S. and Blomberg, T. G. (eds), *Punishment and Social Control: Essays in Honor of Sheldon L. Messinger,* New York: Aldine de Gruyter

Garland, D. (1996) The limits of the sovereign state, *British Journal of Criminology,* 36, 4, 445–471.

Garland, D. (2000) 'The culture of high crime societies: Some precondition of recent 'law and order' policies', British Journal of Criminology, 40, 347–375.

Garland, D. (2001a) *The Culture of Control: Crime and social order in contemporary society,* Oxford: Oxford University Press.

Garland, D. (2001b) 'The meaning of mass imprisonment', in Garland, D. (ed.), Special Issue on Mass Imprisonment in the USA, *Punishment and Society,* vol. 3, no. 1.

Gurr, T.R. (1989) *Violence in America,* Thousand Oaks, CA: Sage.

Hatt, K., Caputo, T. and Perry, B. (1992) Criminal justice policy under Mulroney, 1984–90: Neoconservatism, eh?, *Canadian Public Policy,* 18: 245–260.

Hinds, L. (2005) Crime control in Western countries, 1970–2000, in Pratt, J. Brown, D. Brown, M. Hallsworth S. and Morrison W. (eds), *The New Punitiveness: Trends, theories, perspectives,* Cullompton: Willan Publishing.

Hofer, H. von (2004) 'Crime and the reaction to crime in Scandinavia', Journal of Scandinavian Studies in Criminology and Crime Prevention, 5, 2, 148–166.

Home Office (1979) *Committee of Inquiry into the United Kingdom Prison Services* (The May Inquiry), Cmnd 7673, London: Home Office.

Ignatieff, M. (1978) *A Just Measure of Pain: The penitentiary in the industrial revolution 1750–1850,* Harmondsworth: Penguin.

Jones, T. and Newburn, T. (forthcoming) Three Strikes and You're Out: Exploring Symbol and Substance in American and British Crime Control Politics. *British Journal of Criminology.*

Kelling, G. L. and Moore, M. H. (1988) The evolving strategy of policing, reprinted in Newburn, T. (ed.), *Policing: Key Readings*, Cullompton: Willan Publishing.

Lacey, N. (2003) Principles, politics and criminal justice, in Zedner, L. and Ashworth, A. (eds), *The Criminological Foundations of Penal Policy: Essays in Honour of Roger Hood*, Oxford: Clarendon Press.

Martinson, R. (1974) What Works?, *The Public Interest*, March, 22–54.

Martinson, R. (1979) New Findings, New Views: A note of caution regarding sentencing reform, *Hofstra Law Review*, 7, 243–258.

Mauer, M. (1999) *The Race to Incarcerate*, New York: The New Press.

Melossi, D. (2004) The Cultural Embeddedness of Social Control: Reflections on the Comparison of Italian and North-American Cultures Concerning Punishment, in Newburn, T. and Sparks, R. (eds), *Criminal Justice and Political Cultures*, Cullompton: Willan.

Meyer, J. and O'Malley, P. (2005) Missing the punitive turn? Canadian criminal justice, 'balance' and penal modernism, in Pratt J., Brown D., Brown M., Hallsworth S. and Morrison W. (eds), *The New Punitiveness: Trends, theories, perspectives*, Cullompton: Willan Publishing.

Miller, W. (1975) Cops and Bobbies 1830–1870, *Journal of Social History*, vol. IX, 73–88.

Moore, D. and Hannah-Moffat, K. (2005) The liberal veil: revisiting Canadian penality, in Pratt, J., Brown, D., Brown M., Hallsworth S. and Morrison W. (eds), *The New Punitiveness: Trends, theories, perspectives*, Cullompton: Willan Publishing.

Nelken, D. (2005) When is a society non-punitive? The Italian case, in Pratt, J. Brown, D. Brown, M., Hallsworth S. and Morrison W. (eds), *The New Punitiveness: Trends, theories, perspectives*, Cullompton: Willan Publishing.

Nieuwbeerta, P. (2002) Introduction, in Nieuwbeerta, P. (ed.), *Crime Victimisation in Comparative Perspective: Results from the ICVS, 1989–2000*, Den Haag: Boom Juridische uitgevers.

Newburn, T. and Jones, T. (2005) Symbolic politics and penal populism: the long shadow of Willie Horton, *Crime, Media, Culture*, 1(1), 72–87.

Newburn, T. and Sparks, R. (eds) (2004) *Criminal Justice and Political Cultures: National and International Dimensions of Crime Control*, Cullompton: Willan.

Radzinowicz, L. (1948) *A History of English Criminal Law and its Administration*, Vol. 1, *The Movement for Reform*, London: Steven and Stevens.

Radzinowicz, L. and Hood, R. (1990) *The Emergence of Penal Policy in Victorian and Edwardian England*, Oxford: Clarendon Press.

Sentencing Project (2004) *Facts about prisons and prisoners*, Washington DC: The Sentencing Project.

Sharpe, J.A. (1990) *Judicial Punishment in England*, London: Faber and Faber.

Simon, J. (1997) 'Governing through crime', in L.M. Friedman and G. Fisher (eds), The Crime Conundrum: Essays on Criminal Justice, Boulder, CO: Westview Press.

Simon, J. (2001) Fear and loathing in late modernity, in Garland, D. (ed.), Special Issue on Mass Imprisonment in the USA, *Punishment and Society*, vol. 3, no. 1.

Solivetti, L. (2004) *Italian Prison Statistics*, Department of Statistics, La Sapienza, Rome, 21.

Sparks, R. (2003) States of insecurity: punishment, populism and contemporary political culture, in McConville, S. (ed.), *The Use of Punishment*, Cullompton: Willan Publishing.

Tonry, M. (2004) *Thinking About Crime: Sense and sensibility in American penal culture*, New York: Oxford University Press.

Wacquant, L. (1999) How Penal Common Sense Comes to Europeans: Notes on the transatlantic diffusion of the neoliberal doxa, *European Societies*, 1(3), 319–352.

Walker, S. (1998) *Popular Justice: A history of American criminal justice*, New York: Oxford University Press.

Weber, M. (1978) *Economy and Society*, Roth, G. and Wittich, C. (eds), 2 vols, Berkeley, CA: University of California Press.

Wilson, J. Q. (1975) *Thinking About Crime*, New York: Basic Books.

Zimring, F. and Hawkins, G. (1992) *The Search for a Rational Drug Control Policy*, Camb, MA: Cambridge University Press.

22

Privatisation by Divestment

IAN THYNNE

INTRODUCTION

Privatisation came of age as both a word and a reality in the last two decades of the 20th century. In many respects, it became a world-wide phenomenon, with significant questions being asked about the nature and extent of state activity and market potential, and with equally significant questions needing to be asked about the social, economic and political consequences of the array of initiatives taken in its name. Thus, by the mid-late 1990s, few if any countries had been untouched by extensive privatising action in one or more of its discernible forms (Farazmand 2001; OECD 2003; Wettenhall and Thynne 2002a; World Bank 1995).

For academics and practitioners alike, "privatisation" was soon to become an umbrella word covering numerous developments. It tended to be all things to all people, though with a common thread being that something, whatever that thing might be, was being moved from the public sector to the private sector. This thread was significant, but it obscured the various forms of change which could be adopted. Each of the forms needed to be identified more specifically for analytical and practical purposes. Accordingly, the relevant literature soon became replete with a host of refining terms such as "divestment", "asset sales", "load-shedding", "contracting-out", "outsourcing", "franchising",
"user-charges", "liberalisation", "deregulation", "de-monopolisation", and so on, along with acronyms like "BOOs" (build, own and operate schemes) and "BOOTs" (build, own, operate and transfer schemes) (Coopers and Lybrand 1988; Steel and Heald 1984; Thynne 1995; Wiltshire 1987).

These terms and acronyms, in turn, became household names for the raft of changes introduced by states in the developed, transitional and developing world (Farazmand 2001; Hodge 2000; OECD 2003). The ownership of organisations and other assets in government was divested by various methods of sale, such as public flotations on the stock exchange, direct trade sales, and management and employee buy-outs. The performance of particular functions or roles was transferred to private operators, while still being at least partly funded out of state revenue and with no accompanying changes in ownership. The financing of other roles was altered in line with the idea that users should pay for certain public services, again normally with no changes in ownership. The performance of these and other roles was opened to competition by decisions to deregulate or de-monopolise selected roles and the organisations responsible for them. Public infrastructure was built and operated by the private sector, but according to state plans and often with provision for future state ownership.

In all cases, there was a distinct move away from politics and administration to money and management. A central concern was to ensure a results-oriented response to market forces and demands, while often retaining varying degrees of state involvement through joint ownership, regulatory and funding arrangements, and other mixes of public and private activity.

Privatising action in its different forms continues to be taken throughout the world, but in many instances it is now being complemented or tempered by important initiatives involving civil society organisations as well as market firms. Competition often gives way to collaboration, with synergies being sought through partnerships, networks and other alliances which adopt a more cooperative, integrative approach to the management of public affairs. The flow of market forces and related exchange relationships based on contracts are being contained or softened by associational arrangements which can enhance the collaborative bases of collective endeavours in pursuit of public goals (Evans 1997; Flynn 2002, ch 7; Huxham 2000; Lowndes and Skelcher 1998; Wettenhall 2003).

The focus hereafter is on privatisation by divestment, which has enabled states to withdraw from the ownership of selected public/ state/government enterprises ("public enterprises") and associated assets, without necessarily giving up all interest in and responsibility for the work involved, be it in the domestic or international arena (OECD 2003; Lane 2002; Thynne 1995; Wettenhall 1993; World Bank 1995). Often, the withdrawal has only been partial, resulting in joint or mixed public and private ownership. Often, too, the ownership, production and provision roles of a state have been replaced by those of regulation and facilitation, such that state involvement in certain sectors has become less direct and less active, but remains significant. Meanwhile, many enterprises and assets have not actually become the targets of divestment, and some new ones have been established or acquired which could well become future targets. So, at one and the same time, states have often been both "rolled back" and "rolled over", while also being "rolled on" (Ariff, Asher and Thynne 1995; Steel and Heald 1984).

SOME FACTS AND FIGURES

Public enterprises around the world have been constituted in a variety of forms (Thynne and Wettenhall 2001). They have ranged from departments subject to direct government control, through to statutory bodies, companies, trusts and so on, with varying degrees of legal and operational autonomy. They have usually had a capacity to enter into contracts, to buy and sell property, and to sue and be sued in their own corporate names. But only those in company form have been open to immediate divestment. All of the others have needed first to be reconstituted as companies, which are the only organisations capable of having a divisible share capital that can be offered for sale and subsequently traded.

Beyond the form of organisation, governments have had considerable choice concerning the objectives, targets and methods of divestment, as well as the means and extent of any ongoing control over the companies involved. Not all choices and related decisions have been rational in the usual sense of the word, either at the time or with hindsight. But most have been strategic, with a focus on aims and purposes of present and future significance, including the development of political, economic and social capital in various guises. The choices made can be addressed here quite briefly, with reference to objectives, targets, etc. as identified in a few surveys and other pertinent discussions.

Objectives

A questionnaire-based analysis of the divestment experience of numerous countries in Europe, Africa, Asia, the Pacific and Latin America in the mid-1990s considered, among other things, the rating of six likely objectives of divestment, namely to improve business efficiency, to reduce state activity, to reduce state debt and/or cut budget deficits, to obtain funds, to enlarge the capacity of a stock exchange, and to build a share-owning democracy (Gonzalo, Pina and Torres 2003). While the findings are of a decade ago, they apply to

Table 22.1   *Objectives of divestment (with percentage ratings as one of the top three)*

	Improve business efficiency	Reduce state activity	Reduce state debt/ cut deficit	Obtain funds	Enlarge stock exchange capacity	Build share-owning democracy
19 developed countries	79%	47%	63%	37%	16%	21%
9 Eastern European countries	100%	90%	0%	80%	0%	40%
17 developing countries	88%	76%	61%	33%	28%	22%

The developed countries: Australia, Austria, Canada, Denmark, Finland, France, Germany, Greece, Iceland, Ireland, Italy, Japan, Netherlands, New Zealand, Norway, Portugal, Sweden, Switzerland, United Kingdom

The Eastern European countries: Albania, Bielorusia, Czech Republic, Estonia, Hungary, Latvia, Lithuania, Poland, Yugoslavia

The developing countries: Algeria, Bahamas, Bahrain, Barbados, Brazil, Chile, Costa Rica, India, Indonesia, Israel, Korea, Maldives, Mexico, Morocco, Nigeria, St Kitts & Nevis, Turkey

Source: adapted from Gonzalo, Pina and Torres 2003: 181–182.

a time when there was considerable divestment activity in many countries, with keen attention being given to aims, processes and achievements. Accordingly, they are a valuable basis on which some relevant lessons and conclusions can be drawn.

The findings are summarised in Table 22.1 They are clear enough from the table, but at least three are worth highlighting. The first is that more than 60 percent of the countries beyond Eastern Europe rated the reduction of state debt and budget deficits as one of their top three divestment objectives, whereas none of the countries in Eastern Europe did so. The second is that 100 percent of the latter countries rated the improvement of business efficiency as one of their top three objectives, and 90 percent of them also rated the reduction of state activity in the top three; while the percentages for the other countries were lower in both cases. The third is that only 40 percent or less of all of the countries rated the building of a share-owning democracy as one of their top three objectives.

None of these findings is at all surprising. Over the last two decades, many governments have had to cope with substantial public debts and budget deficits, and the former communist states have needed to recast their public management systems and affairs substantially in response to the demands of a market economy. Also, while for some governments the idea of a

share-owning democracy has had a particular appeal or ring to it, its likely benefits have been less tangible than those attainable through the pursuit of more concrete objectives and thus not necessarily a matter of central concern. It has remained a good idea without frequently being reflected in specific divestment decisions.

Overall, the objectives of divestment have inevitably varied from one sector to another. This has been the case both within countries and internationally, as affected by the particular production or provision roles being performed in each sector.

Targets

Within and across sectors, the actual targets of divestment have also varied significantly. Numerous enterprises have been subject to some degree of divestment as a means of meeting one or more of the objectives to which governments have been committed.

A survey of OECD countries covering the 11-year period 1991–2001 considered five sectors (plus a catch all "other") in terms of the annual revenue generated by the divestment of companies and related assets in each sector (Mahboobi 2002). The five were financial intermediation, manufacturing, public utilities (including electricity, gas and

Table 22.2   *Methods of divestment (with number ratings as most commonly used)*

	Stock market	Direct sale	MBO	Gift	Auction	Combination	Others
17 developed countries	4	5	2	1	1	3	1
7 Eastern European countries	0	1	2	1	2	1	0
15 developing countries	6	6	3	1	4	2	0

The developed countries: Australia, Austria, Canada, Denmark, Finland, France, Germany, Greece, Iceland, Ireland, Japan, Netherlands, New Zealand, Norway, Portugal, Sweden, United Kingdom

The Eastern European countries: Albania, Bielorusia, Czech Republic, Estonia, Hungary, Lithuania, Poland

The developing countries: Algeria, Bahrain, Barbados, Brazil, Chile, Costa Rica, Indonesia, Israel, Korea, Maldives, Mexico, Morocco, Nigeria, St Kitts & Nevis, Turkey

Source: adapted from Gonzalo, Pina and Torres 2003: 185.

water), telecommunications and transportation. Telecommunications stood out as a key target, especially in the period 1997–2000. It was followed by banking and associated work, as well as public utilities, with manufacturing and transportation also being significant, but less so than the other sectors.

Targets obviously changed over time, as the divestment of companies in the banking and manufacturing sectors gave way to initiatives in telecommunications, public utilities and transportation. Various factors affected the selection of targets and the sequencing of their divestment. Included were the urgency with which particular objectives needed to be met, the degree of competition already present in the relevant sectors, the extent to which the targets had to be restructured in preparation for divestment, the need or otherwise for appropriate regulatory arrangements to be made to govern post-divestment work by the companies concerned, and the capacity of the capital markets and related institutions to cope with the financial and other demands of divestment (Mahboobi 2002).

On occasions, targets have been enterprises with objectives that are more social than commercial, as in the case, for example, of hospitals and educational establishments. Where such enterprises have been subject to some degree of divestment, governments have often introduced legislation to protect the public interest via appropriate monitoring and regulatory mechanisms. Sometimes the organisations concerned have ended up looking or operating rather like incorporated associations, cooperatives or mutuals (Curtis 1991; McKinlay 1999; Sawyer and O'Donnell 1999; Thynne 1994).

Methods and Proceeds

The objectives pursed and the targets selected have both influenced and been influenced by the possible methods of divestment. The methods, in turn, have had implications for the revenue generated by each sale.

The multi-country analysis of divestment objectives, as addressed in Table 22.1, also considered the methods of divestment, as outlined in Table 22.2, with reference to a slightly smaller number of countries (Gonzalo, Pina and Torres 2003). Again, the findings are clear from the table. Significantly, and not surprisingly, public floats on the stock market, as well as direct sales, have been prominent in both developed and developing countries, but not in countries in Eastern Europe. The use of the stock market in many countries, especially in the developed world, has had the affect of broadening the investor base of divested companies and deepening the stock markets concerned, just as direct sales have been possible in cases where private firms in the relevant sectors have been ready and willing to invest in public enterprises. In countries of Eastern Europe, stock markets have usually developed after various divestment initiatives have been taken rather than being established in advance. Also, private firms in other countries have often been a little slow in buying companies in that part of the world, at least partly because such companies understandably have been quite difficult to value in terms of their likely productivity and profitability.

The earlier-mentioned survey of OECD countries found that, over the 12-year period 1990–2001, public flotations were clearly the most favoured method of divestment (Mahboobi 2002). This was followed by the direct sale of companies as trade sales, and then by other methods such as management or employee buyouts and the sale of non-organisational assets.

Over the period, more than US$670 billion was generated by the divestment of companies and related assets in the OECD countries. The high peak was 1997–99, during which some US$290 billion was raised. The big sales were in the telecommunications, financial and public utility sectors.

Ongoing Control

The objectives pursued, targets selected, methods chosen and proceeds expected as integral components of divestment have all had a bearing on the means and extent, if any, by and to which governments have continued to exercise control over divested companies. Broadly, there have been two means, one internal and the other external, with both taking one or other of two forms and being open to varying degrees of involvement (Thynne 1994, 1995).

The internal means of control have been based on two forms of ownership. One has seen governments in many countries often retaining a sufficiently significant ordinary tradeable shareholding in divested companies to enable them to continue to control the whole range of company affairs (Thynne 1995, 1998). The other has been in the form of a special non-tradeable "golden share" by which governments, notably in the United Kingdom

and New Zealand, have been able to preserve control over such matters as the appointment of company boards and the making of changes to company constitutions, including any provisions limiting foreign ownership (Graham and Prosser 1988; Taggart 1990). The latter type of share has been criticised in the United Kingdom as giving the government an opportunity to determine relevant policy "by stealth" (Graham and Prosser 1988). Its use, both in the United Kingdom and in Spain, has also been condemned by the European Court of Justice as unjustifiably restricting the flow of capital between or among countries in the European Union (BBC News 2003).

The external means of government control over company activities has comprised the establishment of appropriate regulatory arrangements. In the United Kingdom, for example, various sector-based regulatory bodies have been created, such as the Offices of Electricity, Gas, Telecommunications and Water Services (Maloney and Richardson 1992; Vass 1992; Veljanovski 1987). These specialist bodies stand in contrast to the broadly-focused, generalist Commerce Commission which serves to regulate divested and other companies in New Zealand (Taggart 1990).

The various regulatory arrangements have also included anti-trust schemes which have long existed in the United States and have more recently become a feature of initiatives in the European Union (Lane 2002). In addition, a range of specialist, international regulatory bodies now exist in non-government form, with power which is often more extensive and more effective in protecting public interests than the power of government bodies (Scott 2003).

SOME THEORIES AND MODELS

The facts, figures and associated material just addressed have been underpinned by various theories and models on why and how choices are or could be made within and beyond a state. Individually or in clusters, the latter have served to stimulate, justify and/or describe what governments have done with regard to divestment and other reforms involving significant structural and operational change.

The Why-type

Why-type theories and models have been grounds-based, with much of the emphasis being on actual or assumed weaknesses of the state and strengths of the market. They have combined state failure ideas with thoughts about likely market successes, along with some reflections on political manoeuvring. They have focused on the relationships between form and function and also function and space in the state and market. Those of public choice, agency and transaction costs have been particularly prominent (Boston, Martin, Pallot and Walsh 1996, ch 2; Hood 1994; Self 1993, 2000; Williamson 1985).

Public choice theory has cast individuals as rational utility maximisers who will use the organisations in which they work as avenues to advance their self-interests. This idea has been translated to mean that in state organisations officials will pursue goals and objectives which are often at odds with what the organisations are expected to be achieving in terms of government policy. Thus, it has been thought that, where such organisations are public enterprises which need not be state-owned, then divestment will serve to bring their top management to heel by subjecting them to the disciplines of the market and the active scrutiny of shareholders. Thereafter, if need be, politicians can pursue relevant policy goals and protect the public interest by using external regulatory means rather than by internal means based on ownership. In essence, for the performance of commercial roles, companies in private ownership and subject to market forces, but possibly operating within a state regulatory framework, have been the favoured form of organisation over any continuation of direct state involvement through various forms of public enterprise.

Notwithstanding the perceived need to limit or counter managerial self-interest, politicians themselves have often been motivated by a degree of self-interest in their support for divestment. They have seen it as a possible vote-winning initiative by generating resources which could be used for electorally popular purposes, including the off-setting of timely tax-cuts. This has often been buttressed by a practice, if not a policy, of governments' under-pricing the shares in companies to be divested as a means of ensuring widespread investor interest and commitment. In the process, members of the public have essentially been hoodwinked into becoming individual owners of enterprises of which they were already owners in their collective capacity as citizens and taxpayers. The result is that divestment in such circumstances has reaffirmed the publicness of the enterprises involved, but in individual rather than collective terms.

The rational self-interest basis of public choice theory has been given a specific focus by agency theory. The latter concentrates directly on the relationship between principals and agents and on means by which principals can seek to have agents act in accordance with their expectations and objectives rather than the agents' own interests. This too has been related to public enterprises in terms of the difficulties faced by politicians as principals in exercising meaningful, goal-oriented control over their agents as the top management in such enterprises. Again, supported by the same line of thought as in public choice theory, divestment has been seen as a necessary step towards containing the assumed self-interested propensities of top managers, with any ongoing government policy and public interest concerns similarly being responded to by appropriate regulatory means.

Ironically, this solution to the principal-agent problem was actually an arena in which the problem was first identified, namely in the relationship between the owners as principals and the managers as agents in large private firms, especially publicly listed ones with a wide shareholder base. Thus, in assuming the problem was now one confronting state organisations and particularly public enterprises, the advocates of divestment have simply or conveniently overlooked its origins and proposed a solution that was already known to be flawed.

The basis of public choice theory and the focus of agency theory have been broadened by transaction costs theory, which addresses factors affecting the relative costs of responding to market circumstances through different governance arrangements, including means by which principals can cope with agents. The factors include market size and certainty, the availability of required skills, the extent of opportunistic behaviour on the part of key individuals, and the physical and cognitive capacity of individuals to collect and use information. These factors have been relevant to public enterprises, as they have to private firms, but their implications in terms of divestment have been mixed. For example, the divestment of a monopoly with no change in its monopoly status will not have altered its basic mode of operation and associated transactions in any appreciable way. This contrasts with the breaking up and divestment of a monopoly, say, in the electricity industry into generation, transmission and supply. Such action will have served to decrease intra-company transaction costs and also to foreclose on any internal cross-subsidisation, while increasing external costs because of there now being more companies involved and possibly a degree of competition, particularly with regard to supply. Thus, overall, while transaction considerations have been used to support divestment, resulting in companies in private ownership, specific features of the market from one sector to another have obviously impacted on company performance.

Another body of theory – or, perhaps, theory in the making – concerns elements of globalisation which have stimulated divestment (Farazmand 2002; Hood 1994; Ikenberry 1990; Lane and Ersson 2002). At least three interrelated elements are worth noting. All three have been significant, but not necessarily applicable to the experience in all countries.

One element is the global spread of ideas and practices. Thus, one country after another has seemingly felt compelled to get on the divestment "bandwagon". This has often been by choice, with governments consciously seeking to reap the financial benefits of enterprise and other asset sales. But it has often also been because of considerable pressure from the World Bank, International Monetary Fund, and other international or regional lending agencies.

A second element has to do with market globalisation involving international competition and investment. Governments have frequently seen the need to divest enterprises, notably in the airline, banking and telecommunications sectors, as a means of opening them up directly to international market forces and equity with the aim of expanding their scope of influence, enhancing their performance, and increasing their financial resources.

A third element concerns both ideas and market forces. Governments have often rethought what constitutes an asset of strategic significance. In doing so, they have realised, for example, that utilities such as electricity, gas and water can be managed effectively by private firms with either a domestic or an international base, though subject to some form of state regulation.

A further line of argument addresses the cases where governments have only partially divested selected enterprises, resulting in mixed public and private ownership (Thynne 1995, 1998; Thynne and Ariff 1989; Wettenhall and Thynne 2002a). The impetus has often been for governments to seek to enjoy the best of both worlds. They have been able to acquire needed resources from the sales involved, while still retaining a degree of internal control through the ongoing exercise of ownership rights. This has enabled them to influence the operation and direction of the enterprises at the same time as facilitating the injection of private funds and some market control.

The retention of state ownership, partially for some enterprises and fully for others, has raised questions about the way in which governments have actually perceived and approached their ownership and control responsibilities. In this regard, there are two broad models (Wettenhall and Thynne 2002b). One is "public" in the sense that it emphasises the centrality of the state and the public at large. The other is essentially "private" to the government of the day.

The public model suggests that a government can create and hold shares in a company only where it has an explicit, legally prescribed right to do so. The company in question is best described as being "publicly-owned" or "state-owned". The government acts on behalf of the public as a delegate or proxy, with the public being the real owners in their collective capacity as members of the state. The activities of the company are rightly subject to parliamentary and judicial review as a matter of public law.

The private model, by contrast, implies that a government can create and hold shares in a company largely by reason of its prerogative. The company concerned is best described as being "government-owned". It essentially exists and operates at the behest of the government, within the bounds of private law.

Companies functioning partially or fully in state hands have tended to be in line with the private model. This has meant that governments have often been able to interact and deal with them, including organising their divestment, almost as though they were personal possessions. They have thus proved to be valuable instruments of government action, with policy goals, party influences and individual political commitments all potentially coming into play without necessarily impeding company efficiency and profitability. Indeed, given their status as free-standing legal persons, they will sometimes have been used by governments to achieve purposes that the governments themselves have actually lacked the constitutional or statutory power to achieve (Seddon and Bottomley 1998).

The internationalisation of company affairs involving mixed ownership arrangements across state borders has opened the possibility of governments directly influencing specific commercial developments beyond their constitutional and political spheres of responsibility. This has created an incentive for them to support company mergers, share-swapping agreements and other kinds of business alliances in the international arena, but unfortunately with little thought being given to the implications for public control, accountability and legitimacy (Lane 2002; Thynne 2003a; Wettenhall 1993).

The theories, models and related ideas addressed here have all had some bearing on the development of capital, be it economic, political or social (Fukuyama 2001; Hodge 2000; Schuurman 2003; Self 2000). Various relationships have been assumed or actually forged by the choices and decisions made on divestment and other reforms. Some have been based on an identifiable cause and effect. Others have been less certain in this regard, but still important.

Capital can be an elusive thing which is hard to pin down and define, especially when applied not just to economic affairs but also to political and social life. In political, economic and social terms, it broadly comprises two interrelated elements, respectively. First, there is the support, wealth and trust which are generated by some kind of promise or action, exchange and association. Second, the support, wealth and trust so generated could well be essential to the achievement of desired goals within a state, market and society. Thus, in political, economic and social analyses, capital is potentially both a dependent and an independent variable.

Public choice, agency and transaction costs theories, along with ideas on globalisation, have had implications particularly for economic capital formation through increases in company productivity, business competition, investor interest, and so on. These have all been aims and possible consequences of divestment in individual cases or sectors and more generally within an economy. They can be assessed with reference to actual results, which in turn need to be causally linked to economic growth and increased levels of economic development as wider policy goals. Thus, a two-stage analysis is required for any convincing or compelling conclusions to be reached.

Such an analysis is also necessary in relation to political and social capital. These are more subjective forms of capital than the economic and, accordingly, are much less amenable to quantification. But this is not to say anything about their relative importance to the operational dynamics of a state, market and society.

For the enhancement of political capital, governments have needed to play-up the expected advantages of divestment in terms of debt and deficit reductions, caps on tax rises, and investment opportunities, all as a counter to public concerns about likely price hikes, staff lay-offs, inflated salaries for top management, and so on following divestment. Any support that they have been able to garner by stressing the possible benefits of divestment will have had little political significance unless it was manifest in an increased vote for them, coupled with an ability on their part to use the increase to meet important policy commitments and objectives. Thus, it is necessary to consider the relationship between expressed support and voting percentages, followed by the impact of the percentages on policy capacity and action.

Similarly, of relevance to social capital, it has been expected that, where members of the public, management and employees become shareholders in divested companies, they will develop a particular affinity with those companies and possibly also have some beneficial associational opportunities. But, in practice, to what extent, if any, have these factors had a positive affect on their willingness to trust one another, the companies, and other organisations? In turn, has this led to any increase in social togetherness, cohesion and well-being within the companies and the community? These are empirical questions which ideally need to be addressed, but no doubt with some difficulty.

Aspects of economic, political and social capital potentially have been intertwined when employees of divested companies have invested in those companies and, as a result, have contributed more actively to company productivity, profitability and growth, have become politically disposed towards the government which provided them with the opportunity to invest, and have felt much more part of the social life of the companies and the immediate environment thereof. A broadly similar result could possibly also have flowed from customer investment, with positive contributions being made to profitability through increased purchases, along with a change in political dispositions and in feelings towards the companies concerned.

These are matters that governments could well have played on in taking various divestment decisions. In doing so, however, they will have needed to recognise that the principal-agent relationships involved have inevitably become more complex. Employees will have become principals through share-ownership, while still being agents through their employee positions. Customers, too, will have become principals, as well as being recipients and beneficiaries of the goods and services being produced or provided by the companies. Also, where the companies have remained partly state-owned, both groups will have continued to be principals collectively as members of the public within a state. In all cases, there will have been significant implications for company control and accountability.

The How-type

Why-type theories and models such as those just considered have been complemented by various process-based, how-type theories and models about the scope, direction and style of policy-making in government, including the existence of reform drivers and supporters. These theories, etc. can be used to throw light on how divestment and associated initiatives have been approached, with politicians, administrators and others coming together in differing ways to bring about or limit reform. Notable are theories concerning rational-comprehensiveness, mixed-scanning, incrementalism, opportunities and rummaging in the policy process (Cohen, March and Olsen 1972; Etzioni 1967; Howlett and Ramesh 1995, chs 5, 7; Kingdon 1984; Lindblom 1959, 1979).

The comprehensiveness of the rational-comprehensive theory has had some descriptive value, especially where there has been a fundamental re-assessment of the nature and extent of state activity, leading to widespread divestment as, for example, in the United Kingdom and New Zealand in the 1980s and early 1990s, as well as in countries in Eastern Europe. The detailed analyses of values, goals, problems, options and possible consequences have resulted in considerable structural and operational movement along a continuum of different approaches to the management of public affairs. Thus, at one extreme, a state can be directly engaged in the production and provision of a wide range of goods and services, with state ownership serving to regulate and facilitate the economic and social life of a country, such that the market and civil society are constrained by and subordinated to the state. At the other extreme, the market and civil society are extensively involved in the production and provision of goods and services, subject to a sparing degree of state regulation and facilitation. State ownership is minimal and thus of little significance in terms of production, provision, regulation and facilitation. There is a limited, non-interventionist state, with an established and largely self-regulating market and a freely formed and active civil society. The movement achieved through divestment decisions and related reforms has been in the direction of this latter extreme, though over the last few years the arrangements have tended to become clustered around the centre of the continuum.

The mixed-scanning theory, which highlights the significance of general scoping over a wide range, followed by detailed probing with a narrow focus, has been relevant to the way in which possible targets of divestment have been identified and assessed by governments. It would seem that most governments have surveyed their public enterprise systems both broadly and quite quickly and then, having done so, zoomed in on those enterprises which have most readily caught their eyes as being ripe for divestment. At that point, the analyses have become more specific and concentrated. The objectives of divestment have been addressed on a case-by-case basis, and the various legal, financial and other requirements have been dealt with in a manner suited to the particular needs and circumstances of the governments, companies and other stakeholders involved.

Once a few enterprises had been divested, with experience gained and lessons learnt, the theory of incrementalism has increasingly become an apt depiction of divestment action and events. It has been applicable within governments, and often also between or among governments, with successful divestments providing a basis and stimulus to pursue similar initiatives, just as failures have served as a caution or dissuasion. Thus, an incrementalist approach will have included a degree of rummaging through relevant policy files, if not "garbage cans", both at home and abroad, with "windows of opportunity" having been opened or closed as pertinent problems, policies and politics either coalesced or diverged domestically and internationally.

Whatever the approach or mixes thereof, the contributions of politicians and administrators have been particularly important as drivers and supporters in the reform equation. In this regard, three broad models of reform can be mentioned concerning senior politicians and administrators in terms of policy roles, electoral politics and government-legislature alignments (Thynne 2003b).

The first model is "politically-driven reform, with administrative support", as represented by developments particularly in the United Kingdom and in New Zealand (largely until the mid-1990s), but also in Australia to a lesser extent. The second model is "administratively-driven reform, with political support", as illustrated by developments in Continental Europe and Scandinavia, most notably in Germany and Norway. The third model is "politically/administratively-driven reform, with mutual support", as informed by developments especially in Singapore and Malaysia.

The first two models have a much more firmly established democratic foundation than the third one, with essentially a two-party arrangement in the first, a multi-party arrangement in the second, and a single or very dominant party in the third. In the first model, ruling politicians, with the keen professional support of administrators, are seen to have been the drivers by articulating and pushing the reform agenda forward in public and through the legislature, without necessarily being the prime advocates. In the second model, administrators have been the drivers, albeit quite low-key ones, as affected by party mixes and their own relative autonomy, though with the backing of politicians in and beyond the legislature. In the third model, the bonds between politicians and administrators, producing a quite tightly integrated elite, have resulted in the two groups being joint drivers, with little need to manage the legislature.

The first model has covered situations in which divestment and related reforms have been extensive, with the roles, organisations and management practices of the state being reshaped and transformed quite substantially. The state has been "rolled back" as an active owner, producer and provider, while also being equipped, or re-equipped, with a facilitatory and regulatory capacity to determine national agendas and to protect matters of public interest.

The second model has applied to reform that has been relatively modest, with an emphasis more on changing organisations and management practices than on reshaping the state through significant divestment and associated initiatives. The state has largely being "rolled on" in its existing roles, while having its organisational and management capability upgraded.

The third model has seen considerable reform, but less than in the first model, with some reshaping of the state involving strategic divestment, along with other changes to organisations and management practices. The reshaping has led to the state's being "rolled over" into some new areas of activity, while also being both "rolled on" and re-equipped, with a concomitant transformation of organisations and management.

Obviously, numerous other drivers and supporters have also contributed to divestment and related reforms, including personal advisers to politicians, hired consultants, merchant bankers and associated financial experts, the World Bank and IMF, the media, interest groups, and the voting public. All have had some form of influence and impact, positively or negatively, on the political, economic and social affairs of communities through their reform activities.

CONCLUDING COMMENT

While the strategic choice aspects of divestment as a significant reform policy are now well understood in the case of many countries, the capital development and associated features have not been studied and highlighted to any appreciable extent. They clearly remain an important item of unfinished business in research and analysis. The theories and models considered here serve generally to identify areas of future inquiry in which questions about capital and reform impacts in their various forms need to be addressed. Such inquiry ought ideally to refine and extend the theories and models, with detailed reference to ongoing practical experience in a wide range of countries and with a keen eye on the ways in which choices and related developments are, or can become, closely intertwined in the social, economic and political life of societies in various parts of the world. Only then will it be possible to reach some very meaningful conclusions about whether privatisation by divestment is something largely to be heralded or to be scorned.

REFERENCES

Ariff, M. Asher, M. and Thynne, I. (1995) "Singapore" in I. Thynne (ed.), *Corporatization, Divestment and the Public-Private Mix: Selected Country Studies*, Hong Kong: AJPA in collaboration with IASIA.

BBC News (2003) "BAA 'Golden Share' Ruled Illegal", http://news.bbc.co.uk/2/hi/business/3022809.stm 8 August.

Boston, J. Martin, J. Pallot, J. and Walsh, P. (1996) *Public Management: The New Zealand Model*, Auckland: Oxford University Press.

Cohen, M. March, J. and Olsen, J. (1972) "A Garbage Can Model of Organisational Choice", *Administrative Science Quarterly*, 17(1): 1–25.

Coopers and Lybrand (1988) *Privatisation: Its Place in Public Enterprise Reform*, London: Coopers and Lybrand.

Curtis, D. (1991) *Beyond Government: Organisations for Common Benefit*, London: Macmillan.

Etzioni, A. (1967) "Mixed Scanning: A 'Third' Approach to Decision-Making", *Public Administration Review*, 27(5): 385–392.

Evans, P. (1997) "Government Action, Social Capital, and Development: Reviewing the Evidence on Synergy", in P. Evans (ed.), *State-Society Synergy: Government and Social Capital in Development*,

Berkeley: University of California at Berkeley (International and Area Studies).

Farazmand, A. (ed.) (2001) *Privatization or Public Enterprise Reform? International Case Studies with Implications for Public Management*, Westport, Connecticut: Greenwood Press.

Farazmand, A. (2002) "Globalization, Privatization and the Future of Modern Governance: A Critical Assessment", *Public Finance and Management*, 2(1): 125–153.

Flynn, N. (2002) *Public Sector Management*, 4th ed, Harlow, UK: Pearson Education.

Fukuyama, F. (2001) "Social Capital, Civil Society and Development", *Third World Quarterly*, 22(1): 7–20.

Gonzalo, J. A., Pina, V. and Torres, L. (2003) "Objectives, Techniques and Valuation of State-Owned Companies in Privatization Processes, *Public Management Review*, 5(2): 177–196.

Graham, C. and Prosser, T. (1988) "Golden Shares: Industrial Policy by Stealth", *Public Law*, 33: 413–431.

Hodge, G. A. (2000) *Privatisation: An International Review of Performance*, Boulder, Colorado: Westview Press.

Hood, C. (1994) *Explaining Economic Policy Reversals*, Buckingham: Open University Press.

Howlett, M. and Ramesh, M. (1995) *Studying Public Policy: Policy Cycles and Policy Subsystems*, Toronto: Oxford University Press.

Huxham, C. (2000) "The Challenge of Collaborative Governance", *Public Management*, 2(3): 337–57.

Ikenberry, G. J. (1990) "The International Spread of Privatization Policies: Inducements, Learning, and 'Policy Bandwagoning'", in E. N. Suleiman and J. Waterbury (eds), *The Political Economy of Public Sector Reform and Privatisation*, Boulder, Colorado: Westview Press.

Kingdon, J. W. (1984) *Agendas, Alternatives and Public Policies*, Boston: Little, Brown and Company.

Lane, J.-E. (2002) "Transformation and Future of Public Enterprises in Continental Western Europe", *Public Finance and Management*, 2(1): 47–66.

Lane, J.-E. and Ersson, S. (2002) *Government and the Economy: A Global Perspective*, London: Continuum.

Lindblom C. E. (1959) "The Science of Muddling Through", *Public Administration Review*, 19(2): 79–88.

Lindblom, C. E. (1979) "Still Muddling, Not Yet Through", *Public Administration Review*, 39(6): 517–526.

Lowndes, V. and Skelcher, C. (1998) "The Dynamics of Multi-Organisational Partnerships: An Analysis

of Changing Modes of Governance", *Public Administration*, 76(2): 313–333.

Mahboobi, L. (2002) "Recent Privatisation Trends in OECD Countries", *Financial Market Trends* (OECD), 82: 43–55.

Maloney, W. A. and Richardson, J. J. (1992) "Post-Privatisation Regulation in Britain", *Politics*, 12: 14–20.

McKinlay, P. (1999) *Public Ownership and the Community*, Wellington: Institute of Policy Studies, Victoria University of Wellington.

OECD (2003) *Privatising State-Owned Enterprises: An Overview of Policies and Practices in OECD Countries*, Paris: OECD.

Sawyer, M. and O'Donnell, K. (1999) *A Future for Public Ownership*, London: Lawrence and Wishart.

Schuurman, F. J. (2003) "Social Capital: The Politico-Emancipatory Potential of a Disputed Concept", *Third World Quarterly*, 24(6): 991–1010.

Scott, C. (2003) "Organizational Variety in Regulatory Governance: An Agenda for a Comparative Investigation of OECD Countries", *Public Organization Review*, 3(3): 301–316.

Seddon, N. and Bottomley, S. (1998) "Commonwealth Companies and the Constitution", *Federal Law Review*, 26(2): 271–307.

Self, P. (1993) *Government by the Market? The Politics of Public Choice*, London: Macmillan.

Self, P. (2000) *Rolling Back the Market: Economic Dogma and Political Choice*, London: Macmillan.

Steel, D. and Heald, D. (1984) "The New Agenda" in D. Steel and D. Heald (eds), *Privatizing Public Enterprises: Options and Dilemmas*, London: Royal Institute of Public Administration.

Taggart, M. (1990) "Corporatisation, Privatisation and Public Law", An Inaugural Lecture presented at the University of Auckland, New Zealand.

Thynne, I. (1994) "The Incorporated Company as an Instrument of Government: A Quest for a Comparative Understanding", *Governance*, 7(1): 59–82.

Thynne, I. (ed.) (1995) *Corporatization, Privatization and the Public-Private Mix: Selected Country Studies*, Hong Kong: AJPA in collaboration with IASIA.

Thynne, I. (guest ed.) (1998) "Symposium on Government Ownership and Enterprise Management", *Public Administration and Development*, 18(3): 217–305.

Thynne, I. (2003a) "Making Sense of Organizations in Public Management: A Back-to-Basics Approach", *Public Organization Review*, 3(3): 317–332.

Thynne, I. (2003b) "Making Sense of Public Management Reform: 'Drivers' and 'Supporters' in Comparative Perspective", *Public Management Review*, 5(3): 449–459.

Thynne, I. and Ariff, M. (eds) (1989) *Privatisation: Singapore's Experience in Perspective*, Singapore: Longman.

Thynne, I. and Wettenhall, R. (2001) "Public Enterprises: Many Faces, Much Questioning, New Challenges", *International Review of Public Administration*, 6(1): 1–9.

Vass, P. (1992) "Regulated Public Service Industries", in F. Terry and P. Jackson (eds), *The Public Domain: The Public Services Year-Book*, London: Chapman and Hall.

Veljanovski, C. (1987) *Selling the State: Privatisation in Britain*, London: Weidenfeld and Nicolson.

Wettenhall, R. (1993) "The Globalization of Public Enterprises", *International Review of Administrative Sciences*, 59(3): 387–408.

Wettenhall, R. (2003) "The Rhetoric and Reality of Public-Private Partnerships", *Public Organization Review*, 3(1): 77–107.

Wettenhall, R. and Thynne, I. (guest eds) (2002a) "Symposium on Turn-of-the-Century Trends and Future Prospects in Public Enterprise and Privatization: Contexts, Structures and Dynamics", *Public Finance and Management*, 2(1): 1–153.

Wettenhall, R. and Thynne, I. (2002b) "Public Enterprise and Privatization in a New Century: Evolving Patterns of Governance and Public Management", *Public Finance and Management*, 2(1): 1–24.

Williamson, O. (1985) *The Economic Institutions of Capitalism: Firms, Markets, Relational Contracting*, New York: Free Press.

Wiltshire, K. W. (1987) *Privatisation: The British Experience – An Australian Perspective*, Melbourne: Committee for Economic Development of Australia and Longman Cheshire.

World Bank (1995) *Bureaucrats in Business: The Economics and Politics of Government Ownership*, New York: Oxford University Press.

Section Three

Evaluating Policy

23

Evaluation Research

EVERT VEDUNG

Evaluation in its everyday sense refers to the general process of determining the merit, worth, and value of something – or the product of that process. It implies distinguishing the worthwhile from the pointless, the precious from the worthless. In present-day public sector management, however, evaluation has acquired more specific and narrow meanings. Here, evaluation is a mechanism for monitoring, systematizing, and grading ongoing or just finished government interventions (policies, programs, projects, activities, their effects, and the processes preceding these effects, perceptions of the content of the intervention included) so that public officials and stakeholders in their future-oriented work will be able to act as responsibly, creatively, equitably and economically as possible. In the present article, the following minimal definition of evaluation will be adopted:

> Evaluation = careful assessment of the merit, worth, and value of content, administration, output, and effects of ongoing or finished government interventions, which is intended to play a role in future, practical action situations.

Evaluation is data-gathering and data-analysis but also the application of value criteria to the data gathered and analyzed.

THE SYSTEM VIEW

Evaluators tend to view the public sector as a system. A system is a whole, the component parts of which are dependent upon each other. In its simplest form, a system consists of input, conversion, and output.

When the simple system model is used in public sector evaluation, more functions are added and the terminology is changed. The *conversion* stage is renamed administration, and an effects phase is tacked to the output stage. By *output* is meant phenomena that leave government bodies such as prohibitions, grants, subsidies, taxes, exhortation, moral suasion, services, and goods. Outcome are what happens on the addressee side, the actions of the addressees included, but also what occurs beyond the addressees in the chain of influence. We may distinguish between immediate, intermediate, and ultimate outcome. *Effects* are a subgroup of outcome, i.e. that portion of the outcome that is at least to some minimal extent produced by the intervention and the intervention activities. Another term for effects is *impacts. Results* is used as a summarizing term for either outputs or effects or outcomes or all

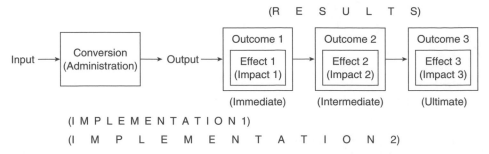

Figure 23.1   *The general system model adapted to government intervention evaluation*

Source: Adapted from Vedung 1997: 5.

three of them. The term *implementation* usually covers administration and output. The reasoning is summarized in Figure 23.1.

THE EIGHT PROBLEMS APPROACH TO EVALUATION

The problems to be attacked in evaluation can be phrased as eight questions. I shall call this the *Eight Problems Approach to Public Policy Evaluation.*

1. The comprehensive purpose problem: For what overall aims is the evaluation launched?
2. The organization (evaluator) problem: Who should exercise the evaluation and how should it be organized?
3. The value criteria problem: By what value criteria can and should the merits of the intervention be assessed? By what standards of performance on the value criteria can and should success or failure or satisfactory performance be judged? And what are the actual merits and demerits of the intervention?
4. The intervention analysis problem: How is the evaluand, that is, the government intervention, e.g. the policy, the program, the components of policies and programs, the project, the provision of services and goods, or the management strategy, to be characterized and described?

5. The implementation problem: Are there any obstacles or malfunctionings in the execution phase between the formal instigation of the intervention through the final outputs? How can such problems be mitigated?
6. The outcomes problem: What are the possibly relevant outcomes – immediate, intermediate and ultimate, intended, unintended – of the intervention?
7. The impact (effect) problem: To what extent is the outcome effects of the intervention? Besides the intervention, what other contingencies (operating causal forces) or factors (mechanisms) contributed to the outcome?
8. The utilization problem: How is the evaluation to be utilized? How is it actually used? How can utilization be improved?

Source: Adapted from Vedung 1997: 93 f.

COMPREHENSIVE PURPOSES OF EVALUATION

The overall rationale of evaluation is to create repositories of descriptive and judgmental insights for reasoned practical thought and action. Under this practice-servicing umbrella, evaluation is performed for either accountability, improvement or basic insights. In addition, evaluation is laced with strategic aims to gain time, or to show up a front of rationality to the world.

The key rationale of *accountability* evaluation is to find out how agents have exercised their delegated powers so that principals can judge their work and take appropriate action. The first dimension of accountability is reporting in which descriptions are provided. A second function is a justifying analysis or explanation. In instances where a justifying analysis recognizes deficiencies, true accountability requires answerability – that is those in charge must be held responsible.

In the *improvement* perspective, evaluation aspires to guide amelioration of the intervention in its implementation. It is felt that the intervention will continue its operations in the foreseeable future and that it must function as smoothly as possible. Sub-aims in this category include effectiveness, cost-efficiency, sustainability, equitability, and being adapted to client concerns and needs.

The primary intended user of improvement evaluation is staff and management immediately responsible for or involved with the intervention. Accountability evaluation, on the other hand, is a tool for superiors to check their subordinates and keep them and the intervention responsible for their actions.

Intervention improvement, or "learning", "lesson-learning", "formative evaluation", "promotion", is a worthy aspiration of evaluation. Several experts, particularly in education, maintain that learning must be the major comprehensive purpose of evaluation.

In the third comprehensive purpose, *basic insights*, evaluation is seen as a kind of fundamental research that seeks to increase the general understanding of actions and events in the public sector. This is probably the major aim of evaluative investigations initiated, carried out, and funded by academics. In evaluations commissioned by public sector agents to be swiftly reported, the basic insights purpose is secondary to accountability and improvement, and best regarded as a by-product consideration in the pursuance of the other two. In metaevaluation or synthesis analysis, the basic insights ambition seems adamant.

Since public intervention evaluation takes place in action settings, it is always permeated with *strategic* purposes, often hidden. Agents scheme to use evaluation to gain time, hide shortcomings from their principals, display attractive images of programs and projects, and in general provide appearances more flattering than reality. Evaluations are launched to become Potemkin villages.

THE ORGANIZATION (EVALUATOR) PROBLEM

Who should exercise evaluation and how should it be organized? Internal versus external evaluation is one option.

Internal evaluation is the use by an organization of evaluators who are employees of that organization to assess the organization's own interventions. An internal evaluation is arranged and financed by the organization, carried out by people from the organization, focused on the organization's own activities and intended to be used primarily by people in the organization.

If activities of an organization are evaluated by employees of an outside body, the *evaluation* is *external.* External evaluations can be arranged and used by insiders, but must by definition be produced by outsiders. When a subordinate agency is commissioned by its principal to do an accountability report, and the subordinate contracts with some consulting firm to produce the study, the assessment will be external.

External evaluations may be contracted out to for-profit consultants and non-profit institutions. The latter include public investigatory commissions, government auditing agencies, universities and other institutions of higher learning, government-funded public policy institutes, and non-profit think tanks and foundations. Mass media, think tanks and universities may also carry out evaluations on their own initiative and financing.

CRITERIA OF MERIT

A key process in evaluation is to determine the merit, worth or quality of the public intervention under appraisal. The quandary is: what constitutes a valuable public intervention and how

```
I   Substance-only Merit Criteria

    1   Goals (Effectiveness Evaluation)
    2   Goals plus criteria for assessing side-effects
    3   Client criteria
    4   Stakeholder concerns and issues
    5   Professional criteria: Peer criteria, Self-criteria
    6   Underlying problem

II  Economic Merit Criteria

    1   Economy (Cost-only)
    2   Productivity
    3   Efficiency: Cost-effectiveness, Cost-benefit

III Process Merit Criteria

    1   Legality
    2   Equity (Rule of Law)
    3   Publicity
    4   Representativity
    5   Participatory democracy (Public participation in final decision-making)
    6   Deliberative democracy
```

Figure 23.2   *Substantive, economic, and process merit criteria in evaluation*

can it be appraised? This is captured by four exercises:

- Identification of appropriate criteria of merit to be used in the assessment.
- On the chosen criteria, selection of performance standards that constitute success or failure.
- Ascertaining the actual performance of the evaluand on each criterion and comparing it to each standard.
- Decision whether or not to integrate the judgments into a single, overall appraisal of worth of the intervention.

Criteria may be determined at the beginning of the evaluation (ex ante), during the process of doing the evaluation (ex nunc) or after the evaluation is finished (ex post).

Furthermore, criteria can be descriptive or prescriptive. In *descriptive valuing*, the evaluator chooses the values of others as criteria and standards. In *prescriptive valuing*, the evaluator herself advocates the primacy of particular values, such as justice, equality and client needs, regardless of whether these values are adopted by any decision-making body or held by some stakeholding constituency.

Aside from the general orientations to be adopted (ex ante – ex nunc – ex post, descriptive – prescriptive) the particular values preferred in each orientation must be justified. The most commonly used substance criteria, economic criteria and process criteria are listed in Figure 23.2.

Substance-only criteria primarily address substantive intervention content, outputs and effects (and, secondarily, the processes preceding and connecting them). Economic merit criteria attend to either intervention costs only or to the relationship between intervention costs and substantive output and impact. Process criteria, finally, check for legality, equity, publicity, representativeness, participatory democracy, deliberative democracy, and other qualities of the procedures according to which the interventions are supposed to be handled by ministries and agencies.

GOALS

The use of the institutionalized goals and objectives of the intervention is a classic in evaluation. Earlier literature took it for granted that evaluators should use prefixed intervention goals as value criteria. Nowadays, many more criteria are actually applied.

There are, however, several worthwhile *reasons in favor of goal-attainment* assessment in the public sector. Fundamental is the argument from representative democracy.

In a democracy, all power belongs to the people. Yet, the people cannot make every decision concerning citizens and nature due to lack of competence and lack of time. The people doesn't have the necessary time and competence to participate in millions of decisions on, for instance, placement of patients in line for surgery, or day-to-day care for ailing senior citizens in public-sector homes for the elderly. For these reasons the citizenry must elect political representatives to make the decisions for them. But representatives in political assemblies don't have time and competence to make all decisions. They must delegate their power to governments to make decisions for them. But governments don't have time and crucial knowledge, so they in turn have to delegate to civil servants and professionals to take decisions, etc. etc. The public sector is made up of long chains of principal-agent relationships.

To safeguard that agents won't cheat their principals, public-sector goal-setting is circumscribed by formal rule systems. Goal-setters are obligated to honor the rules of the constitution and more specific rules of procedure. Once a decision on goals comes out of the system, it has a special institutional status.

This is the case with all entities in the public sector. If an agency adopts a program in order to reach some goals, these stated goals get their legitimacy from the fact that the agency's decision-making authority has been delegated to it by the government and that the government, in turn, has received its authority to do so from parliament, and the parliament, in turn, from the people. It is a merit of the goal-attainment approach that it recognizes this democratic aspect of public-sector goals.

On the other hand, the goal-attainment approach also suffers from weaknesses. The *haziness argument* maintains that predetermined intervention goals are deficient as criteria of merit due to their obscurity. Occasionally, programs are based on *indeterminate goals*.

Particular goals may be *ambiguous* and carry two or more simultaneous meanings. Yet ambiguity in this sense of dual meanings is exceptional in political and bureaucratic language, and barely bothers evaluators. More uncertainty is caused by *vagueness*. The outer border delimiting the extension of a vague word is so fuzzy that within a certain range it is impossible to know what is included in the extension and what is not.

Yet, the real problem with haziness is produced by *goal catalog*. Most large social reforms contain impressive directories of diverse goals. While a single goal may be hailed as the major one, it is often also maintained that this one must be balanced against all the others, maybe including potentially conflicting ones. But the necessary trade-offs between the several goals are not indicated, which makes it impossible to elicit from such lists of goals one distinct, transparent, expected outcome. Thus, an array of program goals of this type are not lucid enough to be usable as value criteria against which to measure intervention successes and failures.

The gist of the *inflationary argument* is that goals are exaggerated. They are set not only to be achieved but to garner support from various audiences. Therefore goals are not good value criteria for performance and achievement.

The most compelling rebuttal of the predetermined goals approach emanates from its blindness to *unintended side-effects*. Public sector interventions invariably lead to consequences which were not foreseen in the original decision situation. Since nobody can state in advance any reasonable goals for something unknown, the evaluator guided by premeditated stated goals only won't be able to trace any unforeseen spillovers. And if she discovers such things, there will be no prestated goals which can work as value criteria for judging them. The prestated goals approach is obviously deficient on this account.

CRITERIA FOR SIDE-EFFECTS

It is a compelling duty of evaluation to map and assess serendipitous results and unanticipated side-effects outside goal areas. The term "side-effects" refers to at least partial consequences of the intervention occurring outside its target areas. Taking this into consideration, evaluators should always search for side-effects while not ignoring main effects, of course. In these enterprises, preset intervention goals are retained as the fundamental value yardsticks for the main effects. But for the unanticipated side-effects, value criteria must be developed either in the evaluation process or ex post when the evaluation is finished.

CLIENT-ORIENTED CRITERIA

Responsiveness to *intervention client concerns* has been suggested as an alternative or supplement to intervention goals and merit criteria for side-effects. Cases of such concerns are the desires, values, objectives, and expectations of the intervention addressees. At the heart of the full-blown client-oriented approach is the question whether the intervention, its implementation, outputs, and effects satisfy client desires, values, and interests, or are in accord with client expectations, assumptions, and needs. Client criteria can be weakly, moderately and strongly included in the evaluation. In the weakly-included case, participants respond to data-gathering instruments and provide information but nothing more. Studies of client satisfaction with public-sector services belong to this category.

Strongly-included means that the evaluation is initiated, funded, designed, carried out and reported by the clients themselves. Let me reason from the moderately-included case where the evaluation (i) is commissioned by the administrators but (ii) charted to involve the service-users in important decisions regarding its planning and execution. Once an evaluation team is appointed and its terms of reference agreed upon, intervention clients are located and sampled. Now clients are asked to select intervention dimensions to be judged and value criteria to be used. For instance, clients are asked to judge program output, service availability, service quality, or even

service process and service administration. Is the core service tailored to the demands of the clients? Do the service employees encounter the clients with respect and correctness? These are two questions that might be answered by the service-users in their self-reports.

The clients may also choose to raise the effects issue, that is, estimate service impacts on themselves or on the client community in general. In such effects-on-clients evaluation, targets try to determine the relative change in themselves or in the overall client body as a result of their participation in specific treatment modalities.

In data assembly, advocates of client-criteria prefer client self-observation and sustained interviewing to questionnaires, documentary methods, and evaluator observation. In-depth interviewing of individual targets is one favored technique, distribution of self-report instruments that clients and their network can easily complete themselves another. In some cases, client-oriented evaluators endorse *focus-group interviewing* which allows for *group deliberations* among the participants and between the participants and the evaluator. Such forums of debate will support the development of new ideas, service concepts, solutions and technologies. It might also, as a side-effect, educate participants to become better citizens in the future.

Today, client-based value criteria are employed in numerous evaluative contexts, particularly those concerning public service provision such as child care, nursing homes for the elderly, public housing, mental health, urban transit, public utilities, parks and recreation, and physical health services, where clientele participation is crucial to program operation. Client-based criteria are used to evaluate library services, museums, national parks, swimming pools, soccer fields, tennis halls, trash hauling, street cleaning, snow removal, traffic noise, traffic congestion, and urban transit. It is a favorite with educators. At universities, students are routinely requested to share their opinions of courses, reading lists and lectures. They are asked to rate their teachers' abilities to organize the course contents, to stimulate and promote altercation and discussion, to stir student interest, foster critical thinking, and to show concern and enthusiasm for the students. In some contexts, these evaluations are occasionally used to rank faculty and courses so that prospective future students can make better-informed choices.

The use of client concerns as value criteria will adjust public interventions to serve the clients. It is based on the notion that public administration produces goods and services for customers in the market place. In buying a commodity in the store, the consumer pays no attention to producer goals. Her own assessment of the value of the good is what counts. Public services should also be regarded in this way and geared toward consumer tastes. The main rationale of public services is actually to serve the public. Therefore, the customer's own assessment of the value of the good is what counts. In situations where recipients are moderately to strongly involved in the evaluation, an additional *participatory-democracy* and *deliberative-democracy* case is made for the use of client-based criteria. According to this justification, the customer parallel cannot be pushed too far, since the client notion includes a participatory as well as a deliberative aspect, which is absent from the customer concept. The participatory feature suggests that clients are also citizens who may voice their complaints and desires to the evaluators and service providers, and to some extent influence and take responsibility for service content. The deliberative feature engenders a discursive, reasoning, discussing, learning-through-dialog countenance, which may educate clients to become better citizens in general: the customer as citizen rather than the customer as consumer. Still, the major idea is to get the services more geared toward consumer desires. The better-citizens aspect is best regarded as a side-effect.

Adoption of client criteria may also increase the *legitimacy* of the intervention. If clients are allowed to participate and exert some influence on the intervention, their approval of the intervention will probably increase.

In addition, application of client criteria may foster *effectiveness* and *efficiency* because concentration on clients will force service-providers and managers to do away with many

other things they are preoccupied with besides providing good services.

But evaluators must be aware of the tendency of the clientele to exaggerate complaints in order to get more service. Clients may also nurture fiscal illusions. Greater client involvement in evaluation may surrender power to groups with vested and narrow interests.

All in all, application of client criteria may supplement the previously presented merit criteria, since they pose other problems for consideration. They can make important contributions to evaluation, but must be balanced against other criteria like goal-attainment and professional norms for service excellence.

PROFESSIONAL MODELS: SELF-EVALUATION PLUS PEER REVIEW

Another set of value criteria are *professional conceptions of merit*. Members of a profession are entrusted to evaluate their own and their colleagues' performances with respect to the profession's own criteria of merit and standards of quality.

In some areas of public life, quality criteria are so complex and the subject-matter so intricate that political officials have found it wise to leave the shaping and debating of them to well-educated professionals. Architects, judges, university professors, doctors, nurses, veterinarians and engineers would be cases in point. Hence, it is also considered natural to delegate ex nunc and ex post evaluation to the professions.

Evaluation of research in an economics department of a European university may be used as a case. The professional evaluation usually starts with *self-evaluation* by the evaluatees. The professionals to be evaluated carry out an appraisal of their own performance. What are the *s*trengths and *w*eaknesses of our department? What *o*pportunities do we have? What *t*hreats are confronting us now or in the near future? In sum, they perform a *SWOT analysis*.

Then comes a *peer review*. Highly renowned scientists of the particular field, but from some other universities, are assigned to appraise the scholarly quality and relevance. Beside the written self-evaluation, these peers base their assessment on additional documentary evidence and site visits with face-to-face evaluator–evaluatee dialogs. The evaluators pass their preliminary judgments in a draft report, often organized according to the SWOT-scheme. Then the evaluatees are given the opportunity to comment on the draft report before it is finalized. The final peer review report is particularly aimed at performing an overall quality judgment of the evaluand.

Usually, evaluation based on professional merit criteria is interactive. The evaluators meet and listen to the evaluatees and the evaluatees learn from the evaluators. Dialog, deliberation and interaction among the evaluatees themselves and between evaluatees and evaluators are important.

Self-evaluations and peer reviews frequently produce questionable results. Studies with matched panels show that peers use widely different merit criteria and performance standards and reach miscellaneous conclusions. However, in complex fields, interactive collegial evaluation is probably the finest method available to judge the quality of what is produced.

STAKEHOLDER CONCERNS AND ISSUES

Finally, the concerns and issues of all actors who have an interest in or are affected by the intervention can be employed as evaluative yardsticks.

The stakeholders may constitute themselves as the evaluation team and carry out the evaluation. In the sequel I shall reason from another case where the evaluation is conducted by particular evaluators, who elicit the views of the stakeholders.

The stakeholder approach starts by evaluator mapping of the major groups who are involved or thought to have an interest in the intervention. The evaluator identifies the people who initiated, hammered out, funded, and adopted the intervention. She identifies those who are charged with its implementation: managers, staff, and front-line operators.

She singles out the intervention's primary target group, the clients, and the clients' associations. She identifies relatives and relatives' associations. She may also include lay people. And she searches for those who are unaware of the stake they hold.

Advocates of stakeholder criteria nurture a strong penchant for qualitative, interactive, hands-on methodology. The evaluator must talk to the stakeholders to elicit their narrative histories and observational data. The evaluator must be responsive and let the issues and concerns of the affected people govern the next step in the investigatory enterprise. After a while, she might discover what issues various stakeholders are occupied with and what concerns they nurture regarding these issues. The evaluation design will be gradually determined. Stakeholder evaluation is *responsive evaluation.*

To gather final data on stakeholder issues and concerns, stakeholder self-observation and sustained dialogical methods are preferred to surveys, questionnaires and statistics. In-depth interviewing of individual targets is one favored technique. Self-report instruments that clients, parents, relatives and other stakeholding networks can easily complete is used. In some cases, stakeholder evaluators endorse *focus-group interviewing,* which allows for *group deliberations* among the participants and between the participants and the evaluator. After data are amassed and processed, the reporting of findings, which might vary from one stakeholder to another, will commence. The key word seems to be "*portrayals*", that is, information-rich characterizations using pictures, anecdotes, thick descriptions, and quotes.

The use of stakeholder criteria have *several advantages.* The *democratic arguments* depart from participative and deliberative points of view. True, democracy means that citizens in general elections vote for competing elites that are supposed to make decisions on their behalf (*representative democracy*). Yet, the citizenry should also be able to partake in final public decision-making between elections (*participative democracy*). Furthermore, discussion, dialog and debate are also important democratic values because they help people to form and refine their beliefs and preferences (*deliberative democracy*).

Stakeholder models satisfy these participative and deliberative values somewhat more than the goal-achievement and the side-effects approaches. It might also, as a positive spillover, educate participants to become better citizens in the future.

According to the *knowledge argument*, stakeholders nurture convictions about inadvertent side-effects, sophisticated implementation barriers, and outright cheating which may furnish the evaluator with ideas about topics for further investigation. Since stakeholder-orientation will bring up more aspects of the subject-matter for discussion, the quality of the evaluation findings will increase.

There is also a *utilization argument* in support of stakeholder evaluation. The stakeholder approach increases the chances that issues of genuine interest to concerned parties will be addressed. It brings to light information that meets the real requirements of the different stakeholders, thereby enhancing the probability that the findings actually will be put to use.

A last rationale for stakeholder models is that they might promote *compromises*, and forestall bitter political struggle. Stakeholder assemblies are vehicles for shaping agreement on the results of earlier efforts and, most importantly, proposals for future action. Consensus-building and the rendition of legitimacy to fundamental decisions are considered great advantages of stakeholder evaluation.

There are also *drawbacks* with stakeholder criteria. Stakeholder evaluations are *inordinately impractical and resource-demanding*, since every stakeholding constituency must be contacted and nurtured. Stakeholder models are *fuzzy*. They provide no clear-cut answer to the question of who the stakeholders are. Furthermore, all the stakeholding audiences, however selected, are treated as equals. But, in a representative democracy, elected politicians must carry more weight than administrators or experts on the substantive matters under consideration. The stakeholder model embodies *no priorities among the stakeholders*. There is a risk that small, well-organized and very committed stakeholders are consulted and listened

to more than vaguely concerned groups and the majority of citizens.

This raises a problem with stakeholder evaluation, or, more properly, collective decision-making on the insights base brought forward by stakeholder evaluations. Since representative democracy is the dominant form of democratic government in most developed societies, decisions on various sectoral policies cannot be left to the stakeholders. The power belongs to the people, its representatives and their delegates. Stakeholder evaluation must work within the frames fixed by representative democracy.

Another objection involves the risk that the stakeholder approach will embrace a *pragmatic theory of truth*. Truth may turn into a matter of usefulness, utility or acceptability to stakeholders. Stakeholders often entertain politicized views of program effects. Supporters ascribe everything positive occurring after the program as caused by the program and everything negative as caused by something else. Detractors hold the opposite view. Facts are essentially contested. In these situations the various parties will accept only those findings that fit into their preformed opinions.

COST CRITERIA OF MERIT

Substance-only criteria pay no heed to costs. To remedy this omission, economists have devised three cost criteria: economy, productivity and efficiency. *Economy* is a cost-only criterion. Is the intervention carried out in a reasonably cheap fashion? Have cheaper options been preferred to more expensive ones? Is implementation carried out in the cheapest way possible?

Productivity is the ratio of outputs to costs, i.e. outputs:inputs. Productivity is operationalized differently due to type of output and type of cost. A study of productivity in municipal libraries can use cost productivity as a measure: number of books borrowed: costs in euros (or dollars) to have these books borrowed. As an alternative to cost productivity, work productivity can be used. It can be illustrated by the expression: number of books borrowed: number of hours worked.

In both cases, output is indicated in physical terms, for example, number of books charged out. The difference is that costs in the former case are indicated in monetary terms, in the latter case in number of hours worked, that is, in physical entities. It should be emphasized, perhaps, that costs can be computed in both ways in productivity measurement.

Productivity as an output yardstick is not an ideal measurement rod for assessing the merit of public sector activities. The public institution may do wrong things, i.e. the outputs may not produce the desired effects. Therefore, efficiency, as a yardstick for effects, is a better metric.

Ideally, efficiency presupposes two things. The evaluator must know that the effects are produced, at least partly, by the intervention and not by something else. Secondly, the value of these intervention effects must be calculated by using some value criterion such as intervention goals. If efficiency is measured in cost-benefit analysis, it can be expressed as the ratio of the monetarized value of the intervention effects to the monetarized costs, i.e. value of intervention effects (in euros): costs (in euros).

PROCESS CRITERIA

All of the criteria of public intervention evaluation expounded so far provide partial perspectives. They overlook or treat as givens other requirements normally demanded from public sector activities in contemporary democracies, such as process goals. Achievement of goals, client hopes, professional standards, and efficiency must be balanced against *legal equity*, legitimacy, procedural fairness, and openness to public scrutiny. Substantive and economic effects goals must also be balanced against *democratic values*, such as client involvement, and deliberative processes.

The task of combining, for instance, goal-achievement with economy, procedural fairness, representativeness, and client involvement into one overall value cannot, at least for the moment, be fulfilled by scientific means. Such global scoring necessitates political judgment.

INTERVENTION ANALYSIS PROBLEM

What can be evaluated? The answer is: anything. This article is about public intervention evaluation. A public intervention could be a policy, a reform, a program, a plank in a program, a project. It could also be an activity, like child care service provision. It could be administrative strategies like results-oriented management.

Public interventions vary widely. Some are broad, others exceedingly narrow. Some may last indefinitely; others will continue for a few hours only. Some are regular programs that have been going on for decades, others are projects expected to be finished at a set date. Some are very local in their scope; others intraregional, national, interregional (EU) or even global. Yet, however wide or narrow, long lasting or short lived, permanent or provisional, when evaluated they need to be described— the fourth item in the Eight Problems Approach. It is essential that these portrayals do not render the interventions too idiosyncratic and situation bound.

One possibility is to represent the evaluand in terms of its policy instruments. Public policy instruments are a set of techniques by which public sector authorities wield their power in attempting to effect social change or eliciting support. There are three, and only three, basic instruments that governments have recourse to: carrots, sticks, and sermons. Governments can either reward us or charge us materially for doing what they want (carrots or economic means), force us to do it (sticks or regulations), or preach to us that we should do it (the sermon or information). In characterizing interventions in this general or more elaborated terminology, evaluations will be more relevant and their findings more attended to and used.

QUALIFIED MONITORING

Qualified monitoring and impact assessment are two major forms of evaluation. *Qualified monitoring* keys in on implementation, outputs, and outcomes (but not effects)—the fifth and the sixth problem in the Eight Problems Approach.

Qualified monitoring, commonly called formative evaluation, checks the various stages in the implementation chain through the outputs and outcomes in search for malfunctions and hindrances. The monitor searches for problems, discovers problems, verifies problems, disentangles causes of problems, extricates mechanisms releasing problems, suggests solutions to problems. Is the intervention being delivered to the clients in ways envisioned in the formal intervention decision? Is the intervention as delivered reaching all the prospective participants? In addition, qualified monitoring also focuses on processes preceding delivery. Qualified monitoring is actually a process evaluation, in the sense that the complete implementation process from formal intervention adoption to eventual addressee participation in delivery is scrutinized for possible problems. The point is to examine whether, for instance, an intervention decision is carried out according to plan at lower levels of authority in order to correct mistakes and omissions during execution and delivery.

Simple monitoring, as opposed to qualified monitoring, engenders data assembly only on some variable without marrying this activity to interventions, value criteria or problem search. True, data gathered through simple monitoring may be used for qualified monitoring and impact assessment. But, in itself, simple monitoring is not evaluation.

IMPACT ASSESSMENT

Impact assessment probes the issue of intervention effects upon outcomes, whether immediate, intermediate, or ultimate. Impact assessment attempts to determine to what extent outcomes are produced by the intervention or by something else operating besides the intervention. Impact assessment addresses the seventh problem in the Eight Problems Approach to Evaluation. Are the outcomes, inside or outside the targeted areas, at least indirectly and to some extent triggered and shaped by the

intervention or are they brought about by something else?

Types of Effects

To capture effects the evaluation community has developed an analytical language. *Main effect* is defined as the central substantive impact that the intervention instigators *by intention* wanted to achieve. Main effects are associated with the substantive objectives of the intervention-makers and with what the intervention was capable of achieving. Aside from transpiring in the target area, main effects are by definition anticipated as well as positively valued by the intervention adopters. In a similar vein, a *side-effect* is defined as a consequence outside the main target area(s) of the intervention. Side-effects can be anticipated and unanticipated, negative or positive. *Perverse effects* run exactly counter to the purposes stated in the intervention. These impacts may occur in the target area(s) of the public intervention. Yet, they may also arise outside the target areas and be side-effects. Perverse effects may ensue far down in the purported chain of control, i.e. in the second, third, or even fourth outcome stage. In addition, they often crop up after many years. Perverse effects are different from *null effects*. Null effects means that interventions generate no impacts at all inside or outside their targeted areas.

The effects tree in Figure 23.3 shows which aspects of effects that might be studied in evaluation research.

The importance of noticing main effects, perverse effects, and null effects should be obvious to every evaluator. But why is paying attention to side-effects vital? Because by-products, whether detrimental or beneficial, are crucial factors in every inclusive judgment of the operation of an intervention.

Designs for Impact Assessment

There is no widely recognized solution to the impact problem in evaluation. A number of different designs are available. Sometimes, it is maintained that the approaches can be

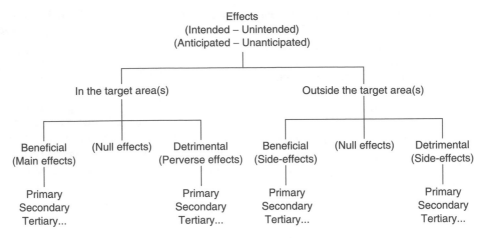

Figure 23.3   *Main effects, side-effects, perverse effects, and null effects*

Source: Adapted from Vedung 1997: 54.

rank-ordered according to their capacity of resolving the intervention impact issue in public sector evaluation. Figure 23.4 shows a condensed and expanded variant of this assumed ranking order, expanded because explanatory process evaluation has been added to the list.

Radical experimentalists argue that designs with randomized and matched controls constitute the best methodology available for solving the effects issue.

Yet, to allow for such sound two-group experimentation on a grander scale, public sector decision-making must be pursued in two discernible steps. Decisions on installing full-scale interventions must be preceded by preliminary pilot tests, designed as randomized or matched experiments. And, equally important, decision-makers must pay heed to the strict evaluative knowledge coming out from these experiments when, in the second stage, they frame the permanent interventions. In this way, public policy would become more scientific and evidence-based and less anecdotal and muddling-through-like.

These are harsh demands on policy formation processes. The preconditions—that the target group must be randomly divided into one experimental group and one control group before the intervention is inaugurated across the board and that the experimental group but not the control group must be exposed to the intervention— often cannot be fulfilled in public policy.

In addition, both laboratory experiments and field trials are *time consuming*, while political bodies sometimes must react promptly. Experiments also produce *narrow knowledge*. Processes between intervention adoption and intervention effects are rarely adumbrated in experiments; the finer mechanisms of implementation and addressee responses are treated as black boxes. To public officials, this is a disadvantage, since information on implementation and addressee reactions is of substantial interest to them.

Although having strong internal validity, experimental findings have weak *external validity*. Experimental findings are context-independent but in real life contexts play decisive roles. An intervention tried out under small-scale experimental conditions may produce entirely different effects when transferred to large field settings in the real world.

Evaluators should carry out their studies in close contact with evaluatees and stakeholders, for instance by using dialog, interviewing and deliberative methods. Experimentation, on the other hand, treats participants as guinea pigs; ideally they should not even know that they are involved in an experiment.

The case against experimental public programming seems to be a strong one indeed. Evaluation researchers must acquiesce to the fact that the lion's share of government interventions are already in place and cannot be

Experiments with randomized controls: In a provisional tryout before the permanent intervention is adopted, targets are randomly divided into an experimental group, to whom the intervention is administered, and a control group—randomized controls—from whom the intervention is withheld (classic experiments).

Experiments with matched controls: Targets to whom a provisional tryout is given or who have been exposed to the permanent intervention are compared to a theoretically equivalent group, created nonrandomly through matching—matched controls—from which the intervention is withheld or which has been exposed to other intervention(s) (quasi-experiments).

Generic controls: Effects of a provisional or permanent intervention among targets are compared with established norms about typical changes occurring in the larger population not covered by the intervention.

Reflexive controls: Targets who receive or have received the provisional or permanent intervention are compared to themselves, as measured before the intervention.

Statistical controls: Participant and nonparticipant targets of the provisional or permanent intervention are compared, statistically holding constant differences between participants and people not covered by the intervention.

Shadow controls: Targets who receive or have received the provisional or permanent intervention are compared to the judgments of experts, program managers and staff, and of the targets themselves on what changes they believe would have happened should there have been no intervention.

Explanatory process evaluation: The development of the permanent intervention in its natural setting is traced step by step from decision to outcome to find out facilitating and constraining factors.

Note. A permanent intervention is a "real" intervention by contrast with a provisional tryout intervention.

Figure 23.4 *Evaluation research designs for illumination of impact*

Source: Adapted from Vedung 1997: 170.

subjected to small-scale provisional field trials. In these cases, evaluators must work with research designs that are more easily applied to existing political practice. More emphasis must be placed on reflexive, statistical and shadow controls, and above all process evaluations of a qualitative, case-study, mechanism-seeking type. On the other hand, experimental evaluation has made a strong comeback lately in the form of evidence-based medicine, and evidence-based social work. The debate continues.

EFFECTS ANALYSIS AS EXPLANATORY PROCESS EVALUATION

In real life, most effects analysis is carried out as process evaluation (modus operandi evaluation, process tracing). Process evaluation attempts to trace all kinds of intervention consequences, including intended effects, null effects, perverse effects, and side-effects, whether advertent or inadvertent. It adopts a broad, configurative, mechanism-oriented

approach to explanatory factors. Process evaluation seeks to establish a whole pattern of interacting mechanisms between adopted interventions, their implementation, addressee responses, contexts and outcomes.

Process tracing concentrates on evaluands in their natural surroundings. It is executed in close interaction with intervention managers, staff and participants. The evaluator seeks contact and interaction with those investigated, not distance and avoidance as in experimentation. Process evaluation does not shun hard statistical data, surveys, and questionnaires. But qualitative data assembly techniques like in-depth interviews, focus group interviews, textual analysis, and direct ocular observation through site-visits are favorites.

SEVEN BROAD FACTORS THAT MIGHT INFLUENCE OUTCOMES

The basic issue of explanatory process evaluation—as seen from a top decision-maker's

I. INTERVENTION FORMATION

1. Direction of proposed change
2. Political support
3. Symbolic politics
4. Participation of affected interests

II. INTERVENTION DESIGN

1. Clarity: indeterminate words, goal catalogs

III. DECISION-MAKER SUPPORT AFTER INSTIGATION
IV. IMPLEMENTATION

1. National agencies: comprehension, capability, willingness (public choice, divergent attitudes)
2. Formal intermediaries
3. Street-level bureaucrats: coping strategies

V. ADDRESSEE RESPONSE

1. Comprehension, capability, willingness
2. Formative moments
3. Zealots
4. Capture
5. Free riders

VI. OTHER GOVERNMENT INTERVENTIONS AND IMPLEMENTATION SYSTEMS
VII. MARKETS AND OTHER ENVIRONMENTS

1. Consumer power in the marketplace
2. Support of actors external to decision-making and formal administration
3. Mass media

Figure 23.5   *Explanatory factors in process evaluation*

Source: Adapted from Vedung 1997: 212.

perspective—can be formulated in the following fashion: (1) In what ways and to which extent does the outcome stem from the intervention?

Seven broad factors and mechanisms which may have impact upon outcomes of public interventions are arranged in Figure 23.5.

Intervention formation. The *direction of proposed change* may affect outcomes through addressee considerations or indirectly via considerations among implementing actors. Should the envisaged change point in a direction different from the one public officials and recipients are used to, it will become more difficult to carry out.

The outcomes will be influenced by the *political support* for the intervention in connection with its instigation. Partisan and pressure group disagreements create uncertainty about the future of a program, which will probably trigger reflections and reasonings and affect decisions in national agencies and among other actors in the implementation stage.

Symbolic politics may influence implementation and results. Symbolic politics means that the intervention is inaugurated for other purposes than to attain substantive results, i.e. to give an impression of being concerned without actually being so. Policy-makers may want to satisfy party opinion or strengthen their own party leadership, to keep party membership in line, to secure votes in general elections, or to facilitate government coalitions. Naturally, agency officials, low-level operators, and other official actors may perceive the symbolic content and devote less energy to implementation than they otherwise would have done.

Participation of affected interests in the preparatory work leading up to intervention adoption may well have an influence on intervention results. If those to be affected are allowed to participate in the formation, the intervention will acquire a legitimacy, which in turn will facilitate implementation.

Intervention design. Intervention obscurity makes it difficult for implementing officials and addressees to form a correct image of what policies are designed to achieve. *Indeterminate words* make intervention language ambiguous and vague. *Goal catalogs* consist of an array of goals with no priorities among them. In both cases, it becomes impossible to lay bare the overall purpose of the intervention as originally conceived. This provides enforcement officials with a broad latitude of discretion.

Decision-maker support after instigation. Decision-makers may back the intervention after its inauguration, for instance through repeated endorsements of the intervention, may influence the results.

Implementation. Implementation might impinge on results. Three problem levels are discerned: national agencies, formal intermediaries, and street-level bureaucrats.

Deficient administrator *comprehension* of intervention content may cause execution problems. The comprehension ingredient is important at all three implementation levels. For simplicity reasons, I shall mention it only at the national agency level.

Administrative capability may modify results. If intervention execution requires appropriations, personnel, talent, time, energy, and equipment unavailable to administrators, the probability of achieving successful results will be weakened.

Outcomes are affected by *administrative willingness.* Public bureaucracies may have agendas of their own, which may conflict with the faithful implementation of the principal's directives and recommendations. A much debated hypothesis says that bureaucrats are budget-maximizers. To enhance their personal reputation, salary, happiness, comfort, field of influence, and other self-serving resources, bureaucrats tend to expand their budgets.

A milder variation on the administrative-willingness theme is that civil servants may harbor doubts about the appropriateness of the intervention itself, which may hamper their preparedness to act.

Still another subcomponent of the larger implementation factor suggests that the comprehension, capabilities, and willingness of *formal intermediaries* may positively or negatively affect the outcomes. Formal intermediaries enter the stage as middlemen between national administrative agencies and target groups.

More and more non-governmental intermediaries are used to carry out public intervention objectives. One category is private business contractors and their interest organizations. Another is public interest organizations or voluntary local associations like home-owners' associations, sports clubs, or tenants associations.

Non-governmental intermediaries may be negotiating partners when agencies work out norms under a regulatory statute. They may be represented on agency boards. They may act as real implementors. They can participate in evaluations.

The use of non-governmental intermediaries may increase cost-effectiveness and avoid the build-up of large bureaucracies. Non-governmental intermediaries may enhance the program's legitimacy in the eyes of the recipients and the general public. Yet, intermediaries may also create drawbacks. The intervention may be diverted in directions not conforming with its stated original intentions.

Also *street-level bureaucrats*, "public service workers who interact directly with citizens in the course of their jobs", may influence outcomes through the multitude of decisions they make in interacting with clients. They consciously develop coping strategies like limiting the information about their services, asking clients and inspectees to wait, making themselves unavailable to contacts, making ample use of referrals of clients to other authorities or concentrating attention to a limited number of easy, well-defined cases.

Addressee response. Addressee comprehension, capability, willingness, organizational belongingness and general predicament may operate on outcomes. If clients neither know nor understand, the intervention cannot work. A grants program unknown to prospective applicants will not contribute to the results it was instituted to achieve.

An intervention's time adaptation to the decision situation of the addressees may explain the outcome. If the program arrives in a *formative moment*, it may produce rapid results, otherwise not. The willingness of individual recipients may also play a role. The program may be more efficiently complied with among some actors because of *zealots*, people who are strongly committed to the cause and who are willing and capable to devote their time and energy to it. If the zealots disappear to other activities, the desirable results may peter out.

The state often attempts to prompt action that addressees have little interest in taking or alter behavior that the addressees do not want to change. Regulatees may also try to *capture* the regulators (regulatory capture theory). Individual agency officials or the entire agency may be captured and start to defend the interests of those regulated against the public interest.

A different possibility is that the addressees on their own initiative have planned to implement the measures that the government wants them to do, but that they participate in the program anyway by applying for and getting economic support. Then the addressees are *free riders* on the government program. To elicit programmatic effects, these so-called deadweight effects must be subtracted, because they would have ensued even without the program.

Other government interventions, other government agencies. Outcomes may stem from other interventions and agencies in the same or in other policy sectors, either directly or via complicated interaction with the program activities under appraisal.

Markets and other environments. Consumer power in the *marketplace* may influence implementation and outcomes. In environment policy it has been noted that producers, due to strong consumer demand, feel forced to end production of a commodity before government regulations determine that they have to do so. Company management may also decide to dismantle environment damaging features in industry before they have to do so through government regulation or, even if they are not forced by government at all, in order to avoid

an anticipated critical public debate, which may damage the image of the firm and thereby in the long run hurt future sales.

Finally the *mass media*. A strong positive opinion in the mass media for a specific program will psychologically strengthen management and operators of overseeing agencies and make them act more strongly and persistently to discover infractions.

UTILIZATION

That evaluation findings should be useful and used is a dogma in the evaluation community. The pioneers of evaluation in the 1960s held an *instrumental* view on evaluation use. Evaluation findings are used if they are adopted by decision-makers and permitted to influence their actual decision-making and practical action. Findings could be about efficient means to reach given ends.

Conceptual use implies that evaluation findings are incorporated into the user's overall frame of reference, but not acted upon. Evaluation is used in action-relevant thinking but not in action. Politicians and other stakeholders receive cognitive, evaluative and normative insights through the evaluation. These insights may contribute to a thorough scrutiny of the intervention's premises, an illumination of its problems, and a deeper understanding of its merits and limitations. But neither of this is transformed into action.

There is also an *interactive utilization* of evaluation. Interactive means that utilization occurs in *dialogical* and *deliberative* exchange processes between evaluators and practitioners and between various groups of practitioners. Public policy designers are engaged in hobnob search processes with different actors, where evaluators constitute one group only and their insight just one set among many. Participants may include administrators, interest group representatives, planners, journalists, clients, political appointees, friends, party members and exercised citizens. All parties learn. The process from evaluation to future decision is not linear and unidirectional but unorganized, messy and interactive in a fashion that escapes diagrammatic representation.

Interactive use involves the application of evaluation-informed information in conjunction with other research-based data and forms of background like common sense, conventional wisdom, tacit knowledge, and recipients' own first-hand experiences. This is probably the most interesting type of utilization in short and medium-long time perspectives.

Instrumental, conceptual and interactive application are reasonable utilizations of evaluation. But there are two additional uses, which seem more problematic from a normative and ethical point of view.

In *legitimizing use*, evaluation is seized upon to justify established positions grounded in other considerations, such as political ideology, electoral hopes, coalition expediency or personal idiosyncracies. Evaluation is used to strengthen one's positive or negative stances on either issues or political adversaries and allies. The de facto task of evaluation is to deliver ammunition for political battles, where alliances are already formed and frontlines already exist.

Tactical utilization asserts that evaluation is requested to gain time, avoid responsibility, or establish an arena for manufacturing agreement. The important fact is not the eventual findings, but that an evaluation is appointed and under way. This observation reveals something crucial. What is used in instrumental as well as conceptual, interactive and legitimizing use is evaluative findings about the intervention. In tactical utilization it is not the findings that are used but the process of commissioning and exercising the evaluation. Evaluation is a process-product concept; not only the product, the findings, may be used but also the preceding processes of doing evaluation.

Strategies for Enhancing Use of Evaluation Findings

Four broad approaches to enhance the use of evaluation findings are outlined in Figure 23.6.

1. **Diffusion-oriented strategy**
   a. Reporting method
   b. Linkage method
2. **Production-oriented strategy**
3. **User-oriented strategy**
4. **Intervention-oriented strategy**

Figure 23.6 *Strategies to enhance use of evaluation findings*

The *diffusion-oriented strategy* is concerned with making dissemination of evaluation findings as effectual as possible. There is nothing wrong with evaluation as long as it is carried out with best available methodologies. The bottleneck is that the recipients must know the findings before they can use them.

Within the diffusion-oriented strategy, two sub-approaches are discerned: the reporting method and the linkage method. Concentrating on evaluation papers, tracts, and oral briefings, the *reporting method* attempts to broadcast evaluation output as widely as feasible and make it as recipient-friendly as possible, without compromising on either methodology or facts.

A collection of strategies for streamlining evaluation reporting is shown in Figure 23.7.

The success of the reporting method requires that evaluators are committed to utilization, locate the potential users, attempt to avoid unintelligible writing, shun no effort to fashion their papers and briefings in a user-friendly manner, and assume the role of ardent advocates of their findings.

The purpose of the *linkage method* is to promote dissemination by opening up channels to practitioners in an organized, systematic, and sustainable fashion. It involves permanent use of some intermediary agent between evaluators and recipients. Advisory commissions are one such possible intermediary agent, opinion leaders another. Another would be to engage an information transfer specialist.

However, just good reporting won't do. The *production-oriented strategy*, the second major approach to utilization improvement, suggests that evaluation findings should be made more

Process-reporting (primary and secondary, before the final report)

- Potential evaluation clients should be located early on in the evaluation process;
- Information should be disseminated about the evaluation's start;
- Findings and recommendations ought to be disseminated rapidly and continually to many audiences *before* the final essay is completed

Primary final reporting: designing and shaping of final reports

- A report should contain a highly visible abstract to enable potential users to decide whether to continue reading or not;
- A report should contain an executive summary, somewhat longer than an abstract, but still short and sharp;
- Reports should display some startling fact that makes people sit up and think;
- Reports ought to be pointed and brief;
- Each written report should be confined to one trenchant issue; if complex, the results should be presented in several brief reports instead of one comprehensive treatise;
- Written reports should be fashioned in user language rather than in jargon designed to make simple ideas difficult to grasp;
- Accounts of results should be accompanied by graphics, tables and other illustrations;
- Crucial results should be highlighted stylistically, through the use of clear headings, subheadings, and an appropriate overall organization of the analysis; substantive findings ought to be presented first, methods afterwards; the major substantive results should be stated in unequivocal terminology prior to reservations, not the other way around; it is important that the executive summary starts with the major substantive findings;
- Reasoning on methods should be reduced to an absolute minimum in the bulk of the report; instead methodological considerations ought to be appended as attachments;
- Reports should include recommendations for action;

Primary final reporting: handling of final reports

- Final reports should be prompt and timely;
- Appropriate managers and other stakeholders should receive hard copies of the final essay;
- Final reports should be disseminated through libraries, internet and databases to enable long-run use;

Secondary final reporting

- Final results should be communicated in person;
- Evaluators should become involved in the selling of their final findings;
- Evaluators should be around in case potential users may want to ask questions and talk;
- Evaluators should talk briefly and often;
- Evaluators should tell stories—performance anecdotes—to illustrate the points;
- Evaluators should engage in public debate;
- Evaluators should disseminate final findings by participating in meeting places, conferences, seminars, and dialogs;
- Evaluators should disseminate results long afterwards through contacts and networks.

Figure 23.7　*The diffusion-oriented strategy: the reporting method*

Source: Adapted from Vedung 1997: 281.

pertinent and of higher quality through efforts directed at the evaluation process.

Evaluators should conduct self-evaluation of her own evaluation, preferably the final report, before it is left to the commissioners. Self-evaluation amounts to quality control. Another stratagem is to encourage critical commentaries from enlightened but dispassionate scholars and evaluator colleagues.

Responsiveness to user worries is important. The responsive evaluator should care for the questions of potential users, not the questions of academics. Preferably, evaluators and the likely recipients should frame the questions together before they are left to the evaluators for investigation. Alternatively, recipients and evaluators should work together throughout the entire assessment process. Evaluations should be demand-led, not supply-led.

The use of *manipulable variables* as explanatory factors is commended. Users are only attentive to contingencies that can be influenced through human action, or more specifically, the user himself. Suggestions aiming at a complete restructuring of society should be avoided. Yet, the underlying notion is that evaluations must be theoretical to become practically applicable. There is nothing more practical than a good theory. Theory in this context stands for explanatory theory. Only when we know what factors condition a beneficial or detrimental outcome can the appropriate conclusions for the future be drawn.

Some people go even further and maintain that evaluators should focus on *feasible variables*. Suggested modifications must be politically and administratively acceptable.

A more far-reaching specimen of the production-focused strategy claims that the prospective recipients should be consulted by the evaluators throughout all stages of evaluation and utilization. In addition to problem identification, planning for data collection, actual data collection, data processing, conclusion drawing and report writing, cooperation should spill over into dissemination and utilization as well.

The stakeholder-consultation approach displays advantages. The chances of providing the right kind of information to recipients will increase. This will enhance the probability that the users become committed to the findings, which will make them more prone to use the findings or recommend others to do so.

Another merit is that learning may occur in the evaluation process, i.e. long before the publication of the final tract.

A drawback is that evaluators risk becoming involved in political processes. In choosing between objectivity and usefulness the latter may be preferred. From the point of view of academic research, it is important to separate objectivity and truth from usefulness and use. Invalid knowledge may be used, valid knowledge may remain unused. Evaluation should not be politicized.

An indirect production-oriented strategy would be *metaevaluation* in the sense of auditing

of the evaluation function. Metaevaluation of this type is often included in a larger evaluation management philosophy suggesting the following. Instead of actually carrying out substantive evaluations, senior management should concentrate on auditing the evaluation function in subordinate bureaus. Another variant is that lower levels perform self-evaluation and summarize their findings in an evaluation essay; the task of senior management would then be to evaluate and use the evaluation report.

The third major approach to utilization improvement, the *user-oriented strategy*, engenders making potential evaluation clients more susceptible to utilization. Users might be educated in evaluation. To be utilized evaluations need some champion in the recipient organization. The standard procedure in this area would be to incorporate evaluation into the management system of the organization. Evaluation should be institutionalized as an ongoing internal affair. Senior management must be strongly involved.

A fourth possibility is to adjust the policy formation process to the demands of evaluation research. This *intervention-oriented strategy* could be realized through a two-step style of public policymaking: first a provisional small-scale tryout accompanied by stringent evaluation, then inauguration across the board of the best alternative elicited through the tryout and pointed out by the evaluation.

FURTHER READING

Dale, Reidar (2004) *Evaluating Development Programmes and Projects*, London: Sage Publications, 2nd ed.

Furubo, Jan-Eric, Ray C. Rist and Rolf Sandahl, eds., (2002) *International Atlas of Evaluation*, New Brunswick, New Jersey and London: Transaction Publishers.

Owen, John M., with Patricia J. Rogers (1999) *Program Evaluation: Forms and Approaches*, London: Sage Publications.

Martin, Lawrence L. and Peter M. Kettner (1996) *Measuring the Performance of Human Service Programs*, London: Sage Publications.

MEANS Collection, (1999) *Evaluation of Socio-economic programmes.* Luxembourg: Office for Official Publications of the European Communities. ISBN: 92-828-6626-2. 6 volumes. 1. Evaluation design and management, 2. Selection and use of indicators for monitoring and evaluation, 3. Principal evaluation techniques and tools, 4. Technical solutions for evaluation with partnership, 5. Transversal evaluation of impacts on the environment, employment and other intervention priorities, 6. Glossary of 300 concepts and terms.

Pawson, Ray and Nick Tilley (1997) *Realistic Evaluation,* London: Sage Publications.

Rossi, Peter H., Mark W. Lipsey and Howard E. Freeman (2004) *Evaluation: A Systematic Approach,* Thousand Oaks, CA: Sage, 7th ed.

Stern, Elliot (2005) ed., *Evaluation Research Methods,* vol. I-IV, London: Sage Publications, Sage Benchmarks in Social Research Methods.

Vedung, Evert (2001) *Public Policy and Program Evaluation,* New Brunswick, New Jersey and London: Transaction Publishers.

24

Efficiency and Cost-Benefit Analysis

AIDAN R. VINING AND DAVID L. WEIMER

INTRODUCTION

Which public policies promote the good society? This central question of political philosophy must also be routinely confronted by practicing policy analysts. Comprehensive policy analysis requires the assertion and justification of goals that provide a basis for systematically comparing policy alternatives. Almost always, efficiency is among the relevant policy goals. It is the primary concern of welfare (normative) economics. Indeed, some economists even regard efficiency as the only appropriate goal for comparing alternatives in many substantive policy areas.

Cost-benefit analysis (CBA) is the primary method for comparing alternatives in terms of their efficiency impacts. CBA comprises the concepts, conventions, and techniques for assessing efficiency in practice. This essay reviews the evolution of thinking about the meaning of efficiency and the use of CBA as a tool for selecting policies. As Joe Grice notes in the preface to the Green Book, UK Treasury's guide to best practice in policy analysis (HM Treasury, 2003: v):

> Appraisal, done properly, is not rocket science, but it is crucially important and needs to be carried out carefully. Decisions taken at the appraisal stage affect the whole lifecycle of new policies, programmes and projects. Similarly, the proper evaluation of previous initiatives is essential to avoiding past mistakes and to enable us to learn from experience.

Certainly, there is increasingly widespread acceptance of CBA and related methods by national and sub-national governments in a broad range of policy areas, especially regulation. Hahn and Dudley (2004: 1) observe that: "Countries and states throughout the world are requiring extensive use of cost-benefit analysis and related tools as a way of informing key regulatory decisions and reforming the regulatory process." Many countries with primarily public health systems, such as Australia, the United Kingdom, and Canada, are attempting to use CBA and cost-effectiveness analysis to make important health resource allocation decisions (Drummond, 2004). Many countries also require that transportation infrastructure projects be subjected to detailed CBA.

Some observers object to CBA on the grounds that limited information and expertise make it impractical. Yet, even when performed well, critics of CBA oppose its use on grounds that it is fundamentally flawed. Some critics view placing monetary values on goods, such as lives saved, as inherently inappropriate (Kelman, 1981; Ackerman and Heinzerling, 2002). Other critics view its exclusive focus on efficiency as rendering it inappropriate as a decision rule in most policy contexts.

A definition of efficiency is a necessary starting point for understanding CBA. After briefly describing the neoclassical perspective on efficiency that underlies CBA, we consider three lines of criticism. First, the social choice literature raises technical issues about the limitations of various, indeed any, measures of efficiency. Second, the transaction cost literature challenges the conceptual basis for efficiency-enhancing policies and the measurement of opportunity costs. Third, the behavioral economics literature raises questions about how well individual choice corresponds to the axioms of rationality, and therefore about the appropriateness of traditional neoclassical measures of efficiency, especially as they apply to the treatment of decisions under risk and over time.

The discussion of efficiency sets the stage for an overview of CBA. The distinction between stated and revealed preferences in the measurement of benefits and costs is fundamental to understanding CBA in both theory and practice. Measurement based on stated preferences involves eliciting individuals' willingness to pay for the states of the world that they believe would be produced by alternative policies. It is attractive because it avoids many of the conceptual difficulties posed by risk acceptance, time preference, and altruism; it is challenging because it forces analysts to conduct surveys of samples of respondents whose responses can reasonably be used to make inferences about the preferences of the population. Measurement of revealed preferences, in contrast, requires analysts to make many judgments about the appropriate way to treat risk and time from the social perspective as well as deal with all the challenges of inferential social science.

Yet, even when efficiency impacts can be reliably monetized, the issue remains as to the appropriateness of CBA as a decision rule. Multiple goals and the problem of immoral preferences pose challenges to the use of CBA for selecting policies. Nonetheless, taking a realistic view of the functioning of representative democracy, and the role that CBA plays in that process, we argue that CBA can have, and does have, a constructive role in informing the policy-making process.

CBA has steadily evolved since its first use in the evaluation of water projects during the last century. Two developments are particularly important. First, the increasing demand for methods to value public goods, such as environmental quality, has resulted in the growing use (and sophistication) of contingent valuation, a method for eliciting stated preferences. Second, the increasingly common imposition of requirements that certain classes of policies be subjected to CBA raises a number of issues. These include questions about the circumstances in which the use of analytical resources for CBA is appropriate. It also includes questions about the ability of government agencies to conduct sound CBA in inherently political contexts.

PERSPECTIVES ON EFFICIENCY

What does "efficiency" mean? It is important to first distinguish between technical and allocational efficiency. First, consider allocational efficiency. C_{te} in Figure 24.1 shows the total cost of producing various quantities of a good given technical efficiency (see below). **B** shows the total benefits accruing to society at each level of output. Allocational efficiency is straightforward: it results when the output level that maximizes the difference between total benefits and total costs, Q_{te}, is selected.

Second, consider technical efficiency. C_{te} shows the total cost of producing various quantities of a good *assuming* technical efficiency. Technical efficiency requires that the total cost of the resources employed in producing the good is the lowest feasible amount at every level of output. If output is not produced using the least-cost combination of inputs, then a technically inefficient total cost curve, such as C_{ti}, results. Maximizing the difference between total benefits and total costs with this technical inefficiency would result in output level Q_{ti}. This output level is both allocationally and technically inefficient. It is allocationally inefficient because it results in too little output (Q_{ti} rather than Q_{qe}). It is technically inefficient because the output that is produced costs more than the minimal feasible amount (C_i rather than C_e).

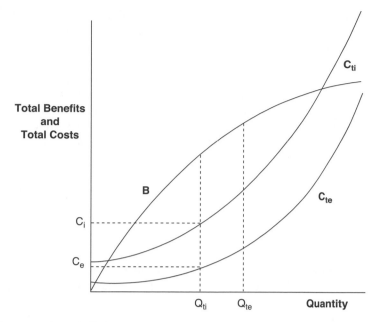

Figure 24.1   *Interpretations of efficiency*

Technical inefficiency is straightforward: an alternative way of producing the good at lower cost is available. For example, technical inefficiency results if refuse trucks are manned by three-person crews when the same work could be performed within established shifts with two-person crews. However, technical efficiency can be more complicated for two reasons. First, there may be trade-offs between various inputs—two-person crews can replace three-person crews, but only if loading equipment is added to the refuse trucks. An understanding of such trade-offs requires knowledge of the "production functions" for public agencies. Much work has been done on how inputs, such as class size, contribute to school outputs, including student achievement on tests (e.g. Hanushek, 1999), and increasingly work can be found on the technical efficiency of other publicly provided services (e.g. Drake and Stimper, 2003; Hammond, 2002; Vitaliano, 1997). Second, the prices the producer sees for the inputs may be incorrect from the social perspective—the salaries of the refuse workers may not equal the forgone value these workers could produce if employed elsewhere in the

economy, perhaps because of union rules mandating that the agency pay workers even when there is no work to do. Such cases require the estimation of shadow prices that indicate opportunity costs.

The issue of social pricing directly connects technical and allocation efficiency. More generally, economics deals with discovering the location of the curves in Figure 24.1. The benefits of a policy can be measured by the aggregate amounts that people would be willing to pay to obtain its effects (curve B in Figure 24.1). The opportunity cost of the resources can be measured as the aggregate amount people would have been willing to pay for the effects that would have been produced had the resources been employed in their next best use (curve C_{te} in Figure 24.1). CBA calculates net benefits (benefits minus opportunity costs) and uses net benefits to assess the relative efficiency of alternative policies. The efficient policy is the one with the largest (positive) net benefits (Q_{te} in Figure 24.1).

The application of the concept of allocational efficiency involves some controversy. One theoretical controversy, arising from the social choice perspective, centers around how well the neoclassical measures of willingness to pay appropriately measure benefits (curve B in Figure 24.1). Another theoretical controversy, arising from the transaction cost perspective, concerns the interpretation of opportunity costs (curve C_{te} in Figure 24.1). A practical controversy, arising from behavioral economics, concerns the extent to which individuals' apparent deviations form utility maximization affect the prediction and interpretation of their willingness to pay.

Neoclassical Perspective

Traditional welfare economics has its foundations in the notion of the ideal competitive economy. Under certain assumptions about individual preferences and technology, the model of the economy has an equilibrium (Arrow and Debreu, 1954; for an overview, see Weintraub, 1983). Defining efficiency in the sense of Pareto, specifically, that an allocation is efficient if it is impossible to make someone better off without making anyone else worse off, the fundamental theorem of welfare economics is that the equilibrium of the ideal competitive economy is efficient. Market failures result from violations of the assumptions so that the resulting equilibrium is not Pareto efficient. For example, the market failure of pure public goods occurs when the assumptions of the ideal competitive model that goods are rivalrous in consumption and exclusive in ownership do not hold.

The existence of a market failure indicates the possibility that a public intervention to force a reallocation could offer sufficient gains to permit compensations to be made so that a Pareto improvement, a change in allocation that makes at least someone better off without making anyone else worse off, could be achieved. In practice, however, it is almost never feasible for government to discover and execute the compensations required to make policies Pareto improving. Consequently, potential Pareto efficiency is the actual guide for applied welfare economics. Formalized in slightly different ways by Kaldor (1939) and

Hicks (1940), it basically asks if a change would generate sufficient net gains so that it would be possible, with costless redistribution, to achieve a Pareto improvement.

The most common justification of the use of potential Pareto efficiency assumes that its consistent application in the selection of policies will not only produce the greatest total net benefits but also make everyone better off in the long run because different policies will tend to have different winners and losers. Of course, this need not be the case in practice. Further, the theoretical reference of Pareto efficiency can itself be challenged in that it depends on the initial endowments of the members of society prior to the consideration of policies. Different initial endowments can result in different sets of Pareto efficient moves from the status quo.

The dependence of Pareto efficiency on initial endowments has led some to reject it in favor of an interpretation of efficiency as maximizing some social welfare function over the distribution of goods after the adoption of policies (Bergson, 1938). This approach, however, places a political and conceptual burden on the analyst to choose a specific social welfare function that appropriately incorporates distributional values. From a practical perspective, social welfare functions are often unworkable because they typically require extensive information, well beyond that provided by markets that often provide the basis for applying potential Pareto efficiency.

The guiding principle for measuring net benefits within the framework of potential Pareto efficiency is willingness to pay: how much money would someone be willing to pay to obtain the impacts of a policy? The resources required to implement a policy are valued in terms of their opportunity costs, the willingness to pay for what the resources would have produced in their next best uses. Willingness to pay is a "money metric" for persons' utility changes from policies that can be aggregated across persons to obtain the overall net benefits of a policy. If the net benefits are positive, then the policy offers a potential Pareto improvement. Efficiency calls for choosing the set of feasible policies offering the largest net benefits.

The actual measurement of willingness to pay can be based either on compensating or equivalent variation. Compensating variation is the amount of money that could be given or taken away from a person so that he or she has the same utility with the policy and compensation as he or she would have had with neither the policy nor compensation. Equivalent variation is the amount of money that could be given or taken away from a person so that he or she would have the same utility without the policy as he or she would have with it and no compensation. Although equivalent variation has some technical advantages (McKenzie, 1983), compensating variation is more intuitive and easier to apply, and therefore is most commonly used to assess willingness to pay.

Social Choice Perspective

Economists have long recognized that the sum of individuals' willingness to pay, as measured by compensating variation, is an imperfect welfare metric. A number of theoretical anomalies urge caution. For example, it is possible to construct examples in which the sum of compensating variations is positive for a move from one Pareto efficient alternative to another and is also positive for a move from the new policy back to the original one (Scitovsky, 1941). More generally, it can be shown that a positive sum of compensating variations is a necessary but not sufficient condition for a potential Pareto improvement (Blackorby and Donaldson, 1990).

These anomalies should not be surprising in light of Arrow's Possibility Theorem. Arrow proved that no social choice rule satisfying minimal standards of fairness can guarantee a coherent (transitive and complete) social ordering (Arrow, 1963). Ranking policies in terms of their net benefits is clearly a social choice rule. It can be shown that quite strong restrictions on individual preferences, specifically that individuals' demands for goods increase linearly with income, are required to guarantee that the sum of compensating variations will produce a coherent social ordering (Blackorby and Donaldson, 1985).

Applied welfare economists generally ignore the social choice critique for two reasons. First, while it is always possible that ranking policies in terms of their sums of compensating variations could produce an anomalous result, there is no reason to believe that such results are likely to be common. Second, any concern about incorrectly ranking policies because of the limitations of the social choice rule are almost certainly going to be dwarfed by the errors one encounters in actually measuring compensating variations. For those who have actually conducted cost-benefit analyses the second reason is very convincing.

Transaction Cost Perspective

Whereas the social choice critique of the neoclassical approach to efficiency is theoretically precise and valid, but not very relevant, the transaction cost perspective is less theoretically precise, but potentially quite relevant. The transaction cost approach has been advanced most prominently by Coase (1937, 1960) and Williamson (1985). Although often used without precise definition, the term transaction costs can probably be most usefully defined as "the resources use to establish and maintain property rights" (Allen, 1991). It is generally agreed among transaction cost theorists that the resource expenditures needed to establish and maintain property rights depends on uncertainty about contingencies and the actions of parties to transactions, though there is disagreement over whether the assumption of complexity-induced bounded rationality is a central component (Slater and Spencer, 2000). In a world with complete and fully effective property rights and rational decision-makers, all gains from trade would be realized. Indeed, the model of the idealized competitive economy assumes that property rights are complete and produces an efficient allocation that has realized all possible gains from trade. The challenge to the neoclassical view of efficiency arises when one moves away from the assumption of complete and fully effective property rights. Whereas neoclassical economics categorizes such deviations as inefficient market failures, transaction cost critics argue that such market failures do not necessarily imply inefficiency because, to avoid the "Nirvana Fallacy," the institutional arrangements that produce the market failure must be compared to feasible alternative arrangements rather than to the ideal (Demsetz, 1969).

Some critics challenge the whole notion of market failures as indicating inefficiency, arguing that transaction costs are ubiquitous because property rights are never perfectly complete and effective (De Alessi, 1983; Zerbe and McCurdy, 1999). This line of argument can become tautological: existing institutions are efficient because any possible gains from trade would be realized in the absence of transaction costs. There is also a tendency not to recognize the essential role of government in shaping property rights. For example, the private provision of lighthouses in England, cited by Zerbe and McCurdy (1999) in their attack on the notion of market failures, required substantial government involvement in supporting the collection of fees (Van Zandi, 1993). Others argue that Pareto efficiency is too ambitious a criterion in a world of transaction costs and that a simpler net profit test (which one may interpret as simply a net benefits test for public policy purposes) is more realistic and therefore more appropriate (Furubotn, 1999).

The transaction costs approach seems most useful in comparing alternative property rights arrangements, or what Williamson (1985: 2) calls the "comparative costs of planning, adapting, and monitoring task completion under alternative governance structures." An empirical literature has had some success in applying the theory to questions such as organizational form (for a review, see Shelanski and Klein, 1995). To the extent that resources must be expended to establish and maintain property rights, they should be included in any efficiency assessment. The proper perspective is not just the comparison of the costs and benefits of alternative final states of the world, but additionally the costs and benefits of moving from the status quo to these alternatives. In practical terms, this simply means that comparison of policies should take account of all their impacts, including any uses of scarce resources required to implement and maintain the policies.

The problem for those advocating the transaction cost approach is how to treat the costs of reaching political decisions to adopt policies. If one treats the costs of collective decision-making in comparing alternatives, then one risks sliding into the tautology that "what is, must be efficient"—if gains from trade were larger than the collective action costs of achieving them, then these gains would have been realized. In attempting to assess these political costs, one would ultimately encounter what has been called the "determinacy paradox": political economy models that fully endogenize politics would leave no room for giving normative advice about efficiency or other values (O'Flaherty and Bhagwati, 1997). Consequently, strong advocates of the transaction cost approach, who do not want to abandon analysis altogether, retreat to essentially the neoclassical approach of ignoring decision-making costs (Zerbe, 2001: 17–18).

Behavioral Perspective

Individual rationality is an axiom of neoclassical economics. Individuals are assumed to have coherent preferences characterized by transitivity (if alternative A is preferred to alternative B, and B is preferred to alternative C, then A is preferred to C) and completeness (all alternatives can be ordered), and they act as if they are seeking to obtain more over less preferred outcomes. Conceptually, preferences can be very broad, including not only individuals' assessment of impacts of alternatives on themselves (self-regarding preferences), but also assessments of the alternatives' impacts on other persons (other-regarding preferences) or the ways in which alternatives were selected (process-regarding preferences). In practice, neoclassical economics usually assumes that individuals are self-regarding for reasons of tractability. Nonetheless, it is conceptually possible to account for the more general preferences in CBA. A more conceptually challenging problem arises when individuals make choices that appear to be inconsistent with the rationality axiom.

Behavioral economics, which draws heavily on the experimental findings and theoretical perspectives of psychology (Rabin, 1998), integrates research about how individuals actually make choices into models of economic behavior. Among the important topics addressed by behavioral economics are complexities in the structure of preferences and judgment biases arising in situations involving uncertainty.

The various complexities in the structure of preferences that have been identified do not inherently violate the axiom of rationality, but do so if simpler utility structures are assumed. For example, there is considerable evidence people value goods more once they possess them—in other words, they experience an "endowment effect" (Kahneman, Knetsch, and Thaler, 1990). Though it is possible to posit utility functions that are consistent with the endowment effect, they would differ substantially from those commonly assumed in welfare economics. In applied work, the endowment effect usually manifests itself as a large divergence between the willingness of individuals to pay for marginal expansions of a public good and their willingness to accept marginal reductions of the same magnitude. In experimental settings, the divergence between willingness to pay and willingness to accept declines with experience, but does not disappear when the goods being considered do not have close substitutes (Shogren et al., 1994). Another complexity of preference structures is behavior that exhibits time inconsistency. For example, individuals may choose one option if payoffs are to be immediate, but another if the payoffs occur further in the future. Such choices are inconsistent with the conventional assumption that individuals discount at a constant marginal rate of time preference, although they may be consistent with a discount rate that declines over time (Laibson, 1997).

Cognitive psychologists have identified a variety of biases that result from heuristics that people commonly employ in situations involving uncertainty (Kahneman, Slovic, and Tversky, 1982). These biases clearly pose a problem for positive economics based on the assumption that individuals rationally use information to estimate probabilities and

apply them according to the expected utility hypothesis. Prediction aside, whether or not these biases pose a problem for the assessment of efficiency depends on the extent to which we believe people would make fully rational choices if they were fully informed.

COST-BENEFIT ANALYSIS

CBA provides the science and craft for ranking alternatives in terms of neoclassical efficiency. When efficiency is the only goal relevant to the policy problem being addressed, CBA provides a conceptually clear decision rule: choose the set of alternatives offering the largest present value of net benefits. It also provides a methodology for assessing efficiency in contexts where efficiency is one of the relevant goals.

A full exposition of CBA requires book-length treatment (see, e.g., Boardman et al., 2001; Dinwiddy and Teal, 1996; Zerbe and Dively, 1994; Gramlich, 1990). Briefly, the basic steps are as follows: First, identify the set of alternative policies, including the status quo policy, to be assessed (for convenience, alternatives are often assessed relative to the status quo policy so that common effects can be netted out). Second, decide who has standing (Whittington and MacRae, 1991). This involves choosing a jurisdictional scope (usually national because of the shared economy and constitution), but it may also involve deciding who within the jurisdiction (citizens, legal residents, illegal aliens) has their costs and benefits counted or whether all preferences (such as those for illegal activities) are counted. Third, comprehensively identify the impacts of alternatives, select units of measure, and project the impacts into the future. In the case of investment projects, the future is determined by the life of the longest alternative considered. Fourth, monetize all impacts. That is, put all the impacts into a common metric. Doing so will often require the use of shadow prices for goods not traded in efficient markets, such as statistical lives saved or commuting time avoided. Fifth, discount costs and benefits to take account of the preferences of people to consume sooner rather than later. Sixth, algebraically sum the discounted costs and benefits to obtain a present value of net benefits, which provides the basis for ranking policies in terms of their efficiency. Seventh, taking account of uncertainties in projecting and monetizing effects, select the policy with the largest present value of net benefits.

The discussion that follows highlights a few of the important conceptual and practical issues that arise in applying CBA.

Stated Preferences: Option Price

Most CBA relies on observations of past behavior, often in markets, to estimate people's willingness to pay for various outcomes that would occur from the adoption of alternative policies. Economists concerned about the valuation of policies with uncertain outcomes have introduced a conceptual framework for thinking about willingness to pay in terms of certain equivalents, or option prices, that can be compared to the usually certain costs of the real resources needed to implement policies (Graham, 1981). In this framework, each person is asked to state how much he or she would be willing to pay for the implementation of some policy—effectively combining steps three, four, and five outlined above. If an appropriate methodology could be developed for eliciting coherent and truthful responses, then the sum of the option prices stated by all people with standing would be the aggregate benefits of the policy.

Valuing impacts of policies using option prices is conceptually attractive for a number of reasons. First, taking individual choices as sovereign, option prices incorporate discounting for time and risk by the respondents. Thus, there would be no need to deal with issues such as social risk and social discounting. Second, as long as respondents are asked to value the policy fully, including all the states of the world it would produce and the processes by which it would reach them, the option prices would incorporate values representing the full range of individual preferences. It would include those preferences that

are other-regarding and process-regarding as well as private-regarding preferences for public goods that leave no behavioral traces to support observational valuation. It would thus provide a much broader basis for assessing efficiency than is possible in traditional revealed preference approaches.

Revealed Preferences: Expected Surpluses

Although option prices are estimated from samples in some contexts, which we discuss below, the more common approach is to value distinct policy impacts. Where impacts of policies can be interpreted as changes in undistorted markets, previously estimated elasticities of supply and demand can be used to predict changes in social surplus, the values consumers receive above the amounts they pay for goods plus the revenues producers receive in excess of their costs of supplying the goods. However, impacts that affect distorted markets require that analysts take account of the distortion in calculating changes in social surplus. So, for example, a policy that changes the consumption of a good with impacts on third parties should take account of changes in surpluses realized by the third parties as well as by the direct participants in the market. Many applications require analysts to value impacts on goods not directly traded in markets. A prominent example is a change in mortality risk. Although there is no direct market for mortality risk, people routinely confront decisions related to employment, the purchase of safety equipment, and recreational choices that require them to make trade-offs between money and risk. Such decisions provide a basis for estimating an average value in a population for a statistical life (Viscusi, 1993). These shadow prices for the statistical value of a life are most appropriate when applied to policies that have demographically broad effects, such as those related to highway safety (their use indirectly introduces an egalitarian value in the sense that the population averages underestimate the willingness of the wealthy to pay for reductions in risk and overestimate the willingness of the poor to pay for such reductions). In narrow applications, such as the comparison of policies with differential effects on different age groups, there is considerable controversy over whether group-specific statistical values of life should be used (Aldy and Viscusi, 2004).

A fundamental problem for the revealed preference approach arises when impacts do not have behavioral traces that can be used to estimate shadow prices. These impacts, called passive use benefits, are especially important in environmental applications of CBA (Vining and Weimer, 1998). One important category is option value, the amount people would be willing to pay to have the opportunity to consume some good in the future if specific contingencies arise (Weisbrod, 1964). Assumptions about the shape of individual preferences can sometimes be used to estimate option value (Larson and Flacco, 1992), which has the technical definition of the difference between option price and expected surplus. Another important category of passive use benefit is existence value, the willingness of people to pay for public goods, such as environmental quality, beyond any direct consumption value the goods provide (Krutilla, 1967).

Challenges to CBA as a Decision Rule

Conceptual and practical arguments can be raised against the use of CBA as a decision rule: goals beyond efficiency are relevant in the particular policy context; not all efficiency impacts can be appropriately monetized; and CBA is inconsistent with democratic principles.

Goals Other Than Efficiency

CBA ranks alternatives in terms of efficiency. In many policy contexts, however, other goals are clearly important (Okun, 1975; Myers, 2002). Nussbaum (2000), for example, argues that preservation of basic social entitlements often should be legitimately viewed as a separate goal. Okun (1975) argues that the efficiency-equity trade-off is the "big one." Yet several caveats deserve note in describing the

relationship between efficiency and equity as a trade-off. In the presence of market failures, many redistributive policies may be efficiency-enhancing (Aghion, Caroli and Garcia-Penalosa, 1999; Rogers, 2003). Thus, these policies involve no trade-off. The trade-off is likely to arise largely from incentive effects: equity requires redistribution, which necessarily transfers wealth from the more to the less wealthy. This reduces work incentives and aggregate welfare. However, the size, and therefore the policy significance, of this disincentive is unclear; it may be small in aggregate (Slemrod, 2000). Additionally, the relationship between inequality and economic growth (at least a partial proxy for dynamic efficiency, the improvement of productive capacity over time) is complex, suggesting that short run evidence on the existence of the trade-off may be deceptive. For example, "inequality can be associated with crime, riots, disputes and alike, which reduce productive activities and raise uncertainty" (Rogers, 2003: 119).

Weimer and Vining (1999) argue that if any goal other than efficiency is relevant, then the policy problem always becomes one of multiple goals. Take the case of equity. Even if one solely or mostly cared about redistributing resources to poorer members of society, few would argue that this should be done with Okun's "leaky buckets" (that is, inefficiently), if it can be avoided. Maximizing allocative efficiency (subject to the redistributive constraint) maximizes the resources available for consumption or redistribution; therefore, it potentially facilitates redistribution. The same logic applies to any other goal.

Moving to multi-goal analysis, however, means that CBA is not an appropriate decision rule. The argument that efficiency should also generally remain a goal, however, means that analysts still face the task of assessing the relative efficiency of alternatives. The techniques of CBA provide the science and craft for doing so. In the special case when efficiency and one other goal are relevant, and the impacts of policy alternatives on the other goal can be quantified, analysts may resort to cost-effectiveness analysis, ranking alternatives in terms of how much of the non-efficiency impact can be achieved per dollar of efficiency loss, or how many dollars of efficiency loss it takes to produce a unit of non-efficiency impact (Gold et al., 1996).

In some applications, it may be possible to disaggregate costs and benefits by groups so that it would be possible to apply distributional weights. That is, a dollar of costs or benefits accruing to members of some groups, such as those with lower levels of wealth or income, would be counted as more than a dollar. The weights might be based on assumptions about declining utility of income (Feldstein, 1972). As consensus on appropriate weights is unlikely, Harberger (1978) recommends that analysts present standard CBA along with weighted-CBA to make clear the implications of the assumed weights on policy rankings.

Non-Monetized Impacts

CBA requires that all efficiency impacts be monetized. Monetization can be stymied in several ways: impacts cannot be reasonably quantified, appropriate shadow prices cannot be found for quantified impacts, or analysts may not be willing to apply available shadow prices. Any failure to monetize prevents the use of CBA as a decision rule.

When an impact cannot be quantified or monetized, analysts may still find it useful to estimate the net benefits of all other impacts. The sign of net benefits by itself does not indicate whether an alternative offers potential Pareto improvement over the status quo. Instead, net benefits must be compared to the likely magnitude of the net benefits of the excluded impact. For example, estimates of the net benefits of public sports stadiums usually do not explicitly include the existence and option values some residents might have for the facilities. If the net benefits are negative, however, one could ask how large these benefits would have to be to make the overall net benefits positive. The answer for Camden Yards, for instance, would be approximately $11 million per year (Hamilton and Kahn, 1997).

It is quite common in the areas of health and medicine for analysts and decision-makers to be unwilling to monetize the value of statistical lives. Instead, change in either life-years or quality-adjusted life years (QALYs) is typically treated as a quantitative but non-monetized impact in cost-effectiveness analysis. Considerable controversy still surrounds the measurement of quality of life (Blomqvist, 2002), the extent to which cost-effectiveness rankings are consistent with welfare theory (Dolan and Edlin, 2002), and the extent to which quality of life measures should reflect the valuations of the public as well as those of directly affected groups such as patients (Ubel et al., 2000).

CBA in Political Context

Is CBA a threat to democracy? Faced with the choice of a world in which one was forced to choose either vibrant democracy or well-applied CBA as a basis for collective choice, we doubt that even many economists would choose CBA.

A more realistic question is whether society would be better off using CBA as a decision rule in those areas of policy where efficiency is legitimately the dominant goal and the full range of impacts can reasonably be monetized. Additionally, would society be better off using CBA to compare redistributive policies? The first point to note in addressing these questions is to recognize that, although CBA has increased in visibility and influence, rarely does it serve as a decision rule. Indeed, it is easier to find laments about its lack of ultimate influence (Anis and Gagnon, 2000; Jan, 2003; Drummond, 2004) than to document cases where it has been determinative.

We believe that the nature of representative democracy suggests that greater use of CBA would be beneficial. This argument rests on the observation that a major weakness of representative democracy is that it tends to favor concentrated and organized interests over diffuse and unorganized interests. As a consequence, many implemented policies are inefficient and inequitable. Because it aggregates costs and benefits over the entire population, the information provided by CBA often provides a voice for diffuse interests (Vining and Weimer, 1992). In this view, the information provided by CBA helps compensate for an inherent structural weakness of representative democracy. Indeed, one can conceptualize recent attempts by governments to institutionalize CBA-like analysis as an attempt to credibly commit themselves to efficiency-enhancing policies (this has the added advantage of discouraging future rent-seeking by interest groups, as well as encouraging efficient policies). All this is very worthy, but no easier than other difficult self-commitment exercises, such as quitting smoking. It is especially difficult for Parliamentary systems that have few mechanisms for credibly making long-term commitments.

Technical Frontier: Contingent Valuation

Economists continue to strive to find ways of making inferences about willingness to pay from data that can be observed, such as the travel costs people bear to visit recreational sites (Clawson and Knetsch, 1966) or the capitalization of environmental amenities into property values (Smith and Huang, 1995). Such efforts have moved the boundary line between use and passive use benefits. Simultaneously, economists have worked to improve methods for eliciting option prices for passive use benefits through surveys that ask respondents to value hypothetical, or contingent, goods (for a comprehensive review, see Bateman and Willis, 2000). Over the last twenty years elicitation of willingness to pay through contingent valuation (CV) surveys has become more sophisticated, expanding the range of policies that can plausibly be subjected to CBA.

An important factor in the methodological development of CV surveys is their use in environmental damage assessment. With U.S. courts giving CV surveys the status of "rebuttable presumption," plaintiffs and defendants have had an incentive to invest in developing better and more defensible methods (Kopp et al., 1990). Although CV surveys remain controversial, endorsement by a blue ribbon panel assembled by the National Oceanic and Atmospheric Administration has encouraged their use and further development (Arrow et al., 1993). Almost every issue of the *Journal of Environmental Economics and Management* and *Land Economics*, the two leading environmental economics journals, carries articles dealing with methodological issues. CV studies are being widely applied to evaluate health policies (Diener et al., 1998); increasingly other applications, such as the measurement of the existence value of sports stadiums (Johnson and Whitehead, 2000) and the valuation of Aboriginal artifacts (Boxall et al., 2000).

Aside from all the general problems of survey methodology, CV surveys must ensure that respondents understand the good being valued and that they are asked questions that elicit truthful (non-strategic) responses. If problems of representative sampling can be overcome, internet-based surveys offer the potential for providing more and different information to respondents to expand the range of public goods they can adequately understand (Berrens et al., 2004). The theory of mechanism design provides a basis for assessing the risks of strategic responses (Carson et al., 1999). In particular, only the valuation of public goods through referendum-type questions with dichotomous responses eliminate incentives for strategic answers. At the same time, considerable progress has been made in linking this elicitation format to utility theory (Hanemann and Kanninen, 2000).

Policy Frontier: CBA as an Intra-Governmental Accountability Mechanism

How useful are CBA and related economic evaluation methods as an accountability mechanism? Can these methods be used more effectively to achieve good policies? In the United States, the use of CBA for informing decisions about public investments can be traced back to the River and Harbor Act of 1902 (Steiner, 1974). Since then, CBA has been widely adopted by national governments, state and provincial governments, as well as by international agencies as a preferred form of analysis. CBA in the United States is mandated within the federal government across a wide spectrum of public policies. Both President Reagan's Executive Order 12,291 and President Clinton's Executive Order 12,886 require federal agencies to prepare impact analyses for regulations that are likely to result in significant economic impacts. The Clinton Executive Order requires that analyses identify social costs and benefits and attempt to determine if the predicted benefits of the proposed regulation justify the costs to society. Additionally, the Order "places greater emphasis on distributional concerns" than does previous Executive Orders (Hahn et al., 2000; 860). Congress has included requirements for CBA-like analysis in a variety of legislation, such as the Unfunded Mandates Reform Act of 1995. Even the federal courts in the United States are now utilizing a form of "cost-benefit balancing" where legislation authorizes them to do so (Hahn and Sunstein, 2002). Many states also require that regulatory initiatives include some form of cost-benefit analysis (Whisnant and Cherry, 1996; Zerbe, 1998).

Experience to date suggests that many federal agencies have had difficulty performing CBA well (and this is almost certainly generalizable to other governments). Two explanations seem important. First, in spite of the fact that it "ain't rocket science," there are difficult technical issues, some of which we have already discussed. These range from non-intuitive meanings of costs and benefits (Boardman, Vining, and Waters, 1993) to the difficulty of appropriate discount rates for intergenerational projects (Moore et al., 2004) and the problems of measuring costs and benefits that have few behavioral traces. As a consequence, good analysis takes scarce analytic capacity and therefore can involve large opportunity costs. Such capacity, both general and specific to particular policy areas, can take time to develop and often suffers during periods of budget cutting.

Second, and probably of more importance for the future of CBA within government, politicians, senior civil servants, or those trying to influence them often do not like the recommendations that result from high quality CBA, for self-interested reasons. Agencies, if they cannot avoid the requirement for analysis, may provide self-serving analysis. Boardman, Vining,

and Waters (1993) provide models of such behavior. There are two (not necessarily mutually exclusive) ways to produce biased analysis: incorrect application of techniques or inaccurate predictions.

Common incorrect applications of CBA techniques include failure to discount or the use of inappropriate discount rates, selective inclusion or exclusion of cost or benefit categories, double-counting of costs or benefits, and idiosyncratic definitions of standing, among other problems. These kinds of errors, however, are generally observable provided the analysis is available in some form to external review. Indeed, at least at the federal level, there is a growing trend for oversight agencies, think tanks, and academics to identify and criticize these analytic errors (GAO, 1998; Hahn et al., 2000; Hahn and Dudley, 2004) and to publicize cases where agencies are attempting to proceed with projects or regulations with negative net benefits.

The problem of prediction bias is probably more serious. Analysts have to predict *ex ante* how many motorists will use a highway or how many illnesses will be avoided by a specific immunization program. It is impossible to show that a given prediction is incorrect until the project is significantly under way or complete (Boardman, Mallery and Vining, 1994). Indeed, it is often even difficult for external reviewers to decide whether projections are plausible without access to detailed agency data. Nonetheless, there is considerable *ex post* evidence that agencies do underestimate costs or overestimate benefits in ways that inflate projected benefits of projects (e.g., Kain, 1990; Flyvbjerg, Holm, and Buhl, 2002; Seong and Mendeloff, 2003).

In view of all these barriers to effective use, what is the prognosis for CBA? Clearly, the efforts of scholars such as Robert Hahn and others to induce agencies to engage in sound and comprehensive economic analysis is useful. There is also some systematic evidence, although not from North America, that good analysis leads to good projects (Deininger et al., 1998; Vawda et al., 2003). In any event, unless agencies are required to publish in easily accessible format their complete analyses, including supporting data and assumptions, there will remain much room for both unintentional error and strategic behavior. For example, regulatory dockets, including agency CBAs and supporting materials, could be made available on the Internet—for a detailed proposal along these lines in the context of analysis of infrastructure projects in Canada, see Vining and Weimer (2001).

CONCLUSION

Economists generally argue that efficiency should be considered an important goal of public policy. The proper measurement and interpretation of efficiency are not without controversy. Nonetheless, economists continue to refine the science and improve the craft of CBA and related techniques for assessing the relative efficiency of public policies. Governments are increasingly demanding CBA be conducted by their agencies for important decisions. As CBA techniques continue to develop, the plausible range of application of CBA will almost certainly increase.

REFERENCES

Ackerman, Frank and Lisa Heinzerling (2002) "Pricing the Priceless: Cost-Benefit Analysis of Environmental Protection," *University of Pennsylvania Law Review,* 150(5): 1553–84.

Aghion, Philippe, Eve Caroli and Cecilia Garcia-Penalosa (1999) "Inequality and Economic Growth: The Perspective of the New Growth Theories," *Journal of Economic Literature,* 37(4): 1615–1660.

Aldy, Joseph E. and W. Kip Viscusi (2004) "Age Variation in Workers' Value of Statistical Life," National Bureau of Economic Research, W10199: January.

Allen, Douglas W. (1991) "What Are Transaction Costs?" *Research in Law and Economics,* 14: 1–18.

Anis, Aslin and Yves Gagnon (2000) "Using Economic Evaluation to Make Formulary Coverage Decisions: So Much for Guidelines," *PharmacoEconomics,* 18(1): 55–62.

Arrow, Kenneth J. (1963) *Social Choice and Individual Values,* 2nd Edition, New Haven: Yale University Press.

Arrow, Kenneth J. and Gerard Debreu (1954) "Existence of an Equilibrium for a Competitive Economy," *Econometrica,* 22(3): 265–290.

Arrow, Kenneth J., Robert, Solow, Paul Portney, Edward Leamer, Roy Radner and Howard Schuman (1993) "Report of the NOAA Panel on Contingent Valuation," *Federal Register,* 58(10): 4601–4614.

Bateman, Ian J. and Ken G. Willis (eds.) (2000) *Valuing Environmental Preferences: Theory and Practice of Contingent Valuation Methods in the U.S., EC, and Developing Countries.* Oxford, UK: Oxford University Press.

Bergson [as Berk], Abram (1938) "A Reformulation of Certain Aspects of Welfare Economics," *Quarterly Journal of Economics,* 52(2): 310–334.

Berrens, Robert P., Alok K. Bohara, Hank C. Jenkins-Smith and Carol L. Silva (2004) "Information and Effort in Contingent Valuation Surveys: Application to Global Climate Change Using National Internet Samples," *Journal of Environmental Economics and Management,* 47(2): 331–363.

Blackorby, Charles and David Donaldson (1985) "Consumers' Surpluses and Consistent Cost-Benefit Tests," *Social Choice and Welfare,* 1(4): 251–262.

Blackorby, Charles and David Donaldson (1990) "A Review Article: The Case Against the Use of the Sum of Compensating Variation in Cost-Benefit Analysis," *Canadian Journal of Economics,* 23(3): 471–494.

Blomqvist, Ake (2002) "QALYs, Standard Gambles, and the Expected Budget Constraint," *Journal of Health Economics,* 21(2): 181–195.

Boardman, Anthony E., David H. Greenberg, Aidan R. Vining and David L, Weimer (2001) *Cost-Benefit Analysis: Concepts and Practice 2nd,* Upper Saddle River, New Jersey: Prentice Hall.

Boardman, Anthony E., Wendy L. Mallery and Aidan R. Vining, (1994) "Learning from Ex Ante/Ex Post Cost-Benefit Comparisons: The Coquihalla Highway Example," *Socio-Economic Planning Sciences,* 28(2): 69–84.

Boardman, Anthony E., Aidan R. Vining and William Waters (1993) "Costs and Benefits Through Bureaucratic Lenses: Example of a Highway Project," *Journal of Policy Analysis and Management,* 12(3): 532–555.

Boxall, Peter C., Jeffrey Englin and Wiktor L. Adamowicz (2000) "Valuing Aboriginal Artifacts: A Combined Revealed-Stated Preference Approach," *Journal of Environmental Economics and Management,* 45(2): 213–230.

Carson, Richard T., Theodore Groves and Mark J. Machina (1999) "Incentive and Informational

Properties of Preference Questions," Plenary Address, European Association of Resource Economists, Oslo, Norway, June.

Clawson, Marion and Jack L. Knetsch (1966) *Economics of Outdoor Recreation*, Baltimore: Johns Hopkins Press.

Coase, Ronald (1937) "The Nature of the Firm," *Economica*, 4(16): 386–405.

Coase, Ronald (1960) "The Problem of Social Cost," *Journal of Law and Economics*, 3(1): 1–44.

De Alessi, Louis (1983) "Property Rights, Transaction Costs, and X-Efficiency: An Essay in Economic Theory," *American Economic Review*, 73(1): 64–81.

Deininger, Klaus, Lyn Squire and Swati Basu (1998) "Does Economic Analysis Improve the Quality of Foreign Assistance?" *The World Bank Economic Review*, 12(3): 385–418.

Demsetz, Harold (1969) "Information and Efficiency: Another Viewpoint," *Journal of Law and Economics*, 12(1): 1–22.

Diener, Alan, Bernie O'Brien and Amiram Gafni (1998) "Health Care Contingent Valuation Studies: A Review and Classification of the Literature," *Health Economics*, 7(4): 313–326.

Dinwiddy, Carolyn and Francis Teal (1996) *Principles of Cost-Benefit Analysis for Developing Countries*, New York: Cambridge University Press.

Dolan, Paul and Richard Edlin (2002) "Is It Really Possible to Build a Bridge Between Cost-Benefit Analysis and Cost-Effectiveness Analysis?" *Journal of Health Economics*, 21(5): 827–843.

Drake, Leigh and R. Stimper (2003) "The Measurement of English and Welsh Police Force Efficiency: A Comparison of Distance Function Models," *European Journal of Operations Research*, 147(1): 165–186.

Drummond, Michael (2004) "Economic Evaluation in Health Care: Is It Really Useful or Are We Just Kidding Ourselves?," *The Australian Economic Review*, 37(1): 3–11.

Feldstein, Martin S. (1972) "Distributional Equity and the Optimal Structure of Public Prices," *American Economic Review*, 62(1): 32–36.

Flyvbjerg, Bent, Mette Skamris Holm and Soren Buhl (2002) "Underestimating Costs in Public Works Projects: Error or Lie?," *Journal of the American Planning Association*, 68(3): 279–293.

Furubotn, Eirik G. (1999) "Economic Efficiency in a World of Frictions," *European Journal of Law and Economics*, 8(3): 179–197.

General Accounting Office (GAO) (1998) "Regulatory Reform: Agencies Could Improve Development, Documentation, and Clarity of regulatory Economic Analyses," Report to the Committee on Governmental Affairs, U.S. Senate, GAO/RCED-98–142, May.

Gold, Marthe R., Joanne E. Siegal, Louise B. Russell and Milton C. Weinstein, eds. (1996) *Cost-Effectiveness in Health and Medicine*, Oxford, UK: Oxford University Press.

Graham, Daniel A. (1981) "Cost-Benefit Analysis Under Uncertainty," *American Economic Review*, 71(4): 715–725.

Gramlich, Edward M. (1990) *A Guide to Benefit-Cost Analysis*, Upper Saddle River: Prentice Hall.

Hahn, Robert W., Jason K. Burnett, Yee-Ho I. Chin, Elizabeth A. Mader and Petrea R. Moyle (2000) "Assessing Regulatory Impact Analyses: The Failure of Agencies to Comply with Executive Order 12,866," *Harvard Journal of Law & Public Policy*, 23(3): 859–885.

Hahn, Robert W. and Patrick Dudley (2004) "How Well Does the Government Do Cost-Benefit Analysis?" Working Paper 04–01, Washington, D.C: AEI-Brookings Joint Center for Regulatory Studies, January.

Hahn, Robert W. and Cass R. Sunstein, (2002) "A New Executive Order for Improving Federal Regulation? Deeper and Wider Cost-Benefit Analysis," *University of Pennsylvania Law Review* 150(5): 1489–1552.

Hammond, Christopher J. (2002) "Efficiency in the Provision of Public Services: A Data Envelope Analysis of the UK Public Library System," *Applied Economics*, 34(5): 649–657.

Hamilton, Bruce W. and Peter Kahn (1997) "Baltimore's Camden Yards Ballparks," in Roger G. Noll and Andrew Zimbalist (eds.), *Sports, Jobs, and Taxes: Economic Impact of Sports Teams and Stadiums*, Washington, D.C.: Brookings Institution: 245–281.

Hanushek, Eric. A. (1999) "The Evidence on Class Size," in S. E. Mayer and P. Peterson, eds., *Earning and Learning: How Schools Matter*, Washington, D.C.: Brookings Institutions, pp. 131–168.

Hanemann, W. Michael and Barbara Kanninen (2000) "The Statistical Analysis of Discrete Reponse CV Data," in Ian J. Bateman and Ken G. Willis (eds.), *Valuing Environmental Preferences: Theory and Practice of Contingent Valuation Methods in the U.S., EC, and Developing Countries*. Oxford, UK: Oxford University Press: 302–441.

Harberger, Arnold C. (1978) "On the Use of Distributional Weights in Social Cost-Benefit Analysis," *Journal of Political Economy*, 86(2): S87–S120.

Hicks, John R. (1940) The Valuation of Social Income, *Economica*, 7(26): 105–124.

HM Treasury (2003) *The Green Book: Appraisal and Evaluation in Central Government*, London: TSO.

Jan, Stephen (2003) "Why Does Economic Analysis in Health Care Not Get Implemented More? Towards a Greater Understanding of the Rules of the Game and the Costs of Decision Making," *Applied Health Economics and Health Policy*, 2(1): 17–24.

Johnson, Bruce K and John C. Whitehead (2000) "Value of Public Goods from Sports Stadiums: The CVM Approach," *Contemporary Economic Policy*, 18(1): 48–58.

Kahneman, Daniel, Jack L. Knetsch and Richard H. Thaler (1990) "Experimental Tests of the Endowment Effect and the Coase Theorem," *Journal of Political Economy*, 98(6): 1325–1348.

Kahneman, Daniel, Paul Slovic and Amos Tversky, editors (1982) *Judgment Under Uncertainty: Heuristics and Biases*, New York: Cambridge University Press.

Kain, John F. (1990) "Deception in Dallas: Strategic Misrepresentation in Rail Transit Promotion and Evaluation," *Journal of the American Planning Association*, 56(2): 184–96.

Kaldor, Nicholas (1939) "Welfare Propositions of Economics and Interpersonal Comparisons of Utility," *Economic Journal*, 49(195): 549–552.

Kelman, Steven (1981) "Cost-Benefit: An Ethical Critique," *Regulation*, January/February: 33–40.

Kopp, Raymond J., Paul R. Portney and V. Kerry Smith (1990) "The Economics of Natural Resource Damages after *Ohio v. U.S. Department of the Interior*," *Environmental Law Reporter*, 20(4): 10127–10131.

Krutilla, John V. (1967) "Conservation Reconsidered," *American Economic Review*, 57(4): 777–786.

Laibson, David (1997) "Golden Eggs and Hyperbolic Discounting," *Quarterly Journal of Economics*, 112(2): 443–478.

Larson, Douglas M. and Paul R. Flacco (1992) "Measuring Option Prices from Market Behavior," *Journal of Environmental Economics and Management*, 22(2): 178–198.

McKenzie, George W. (1983) *Measuring Economic Welfare: New Methods*, New York: Cambridge University Press.

Moore, Mark, Anthony E. Boardman, Aidan R. Vining, David Weimer and David Greenberg (2004) "Just Give Me a Number!," *Journal of Policy Analysis and Management*, 23(4): 789–812.

Myers, Samuel L. (2002) "Presidential Address— Analysis of Race as Policy Analysis," *Journal of Policy Analysis and Management*, 21(2): 169–190.

Nussbaum, Martha C. (2000) "The Costs of Tragedy: Some Moral Limits of Cost-Benefit Analysis," *Journal of Legal Studies*, 29(2): 1005–36.

O'Flaherty, Brendan and Jagdish Bhagwati (1997) "Will Free Trade With Political Science Put Normative Economists Out of Work?" *Economics and Politics*, 9(3): 207–219.

Okun, Arthur M. (1975) *Equality and Efficiency: The Big Tradeoff*, Washington, DC: The Brookings Institution.

Rabin, Matthew (1998) "Psychology and Economics," *Journal of Economic Literature*, 36(1): 11–46.

Rogers, Mark (2003) "A Survey of Economic Growth," *The Economic Record*, 79(244): 112–135.

Scitovsky, Tibor (1941) "A Note on Welfare Propositions in Economics," *Review of Economic Studies*, 41(1): 77–88.

Seong, Si Kyung and John Mendeloff (2003) "Assessing the Accuracy of OSHA's Projections of the Benefits of New Safety Standards," Washington, D.C: AEI-Brookings Joint Center for Regulatory Studies, 03–8, July.

Shelanski, Howard A. and Peter G. Klein (1995) "Empirical Evidence in Transaction Cost Economics: A Review and Assessment," *Journal of Law, Economics, and Organization*, 11(2): 335–361.

Shogren, Jason F., Seung Y. Shin, Dermot J. Hayes and James B. Kliebenstein (1994) "Resolving the Differences between Willingness to Pay and Willingness to Accept," *American Economic Review*, 84(1): 255–270.

Slater, Gary and David A. Spencer (2000) "The Uncertain Foundations of Transaction Costs Economics," *Journal of Economic Issues*, 34(1): 61–87.

Slemrod, Joel B. (2000) *Does Atlas Shrug? The Economic Consequences of Taxing the Rich*, Cambridge, Mass: Harvard University Press.

Smith, V. Kerry and Ju-Chin Huang (1995) "Can Markets Value Air Quality? A Meta-Analysis of Hedonic Property Value Models," *Journal of Political Economy*, 103(1): 209–227.

Steiner, Peter O. (1974) "Public Expenditure Budgeting," in Alan S. Blinder et al. (eds.), *The Economics of Public Finance*, Washington, D.C.: Brookings Institution: 241–357.

Ubel, Peter A., Jeff Richardson and Paul Menzel (2000) "Societal Value, The Person Trade-Off, and the Dilemma of Whose Values to Measure for Cost-Effectiveness," *Health Economics*, 9(2): 127–136.

Van Zandi, David E. (1993) "The Lessons of the Lighthouse: 'Government' or 'Private' Provision of Goods," *Journal of Legal Studies*, 22(1): 47–72.

Vawda, Ayesha Yaqub., Peter Moock, J., Price Gittinger and Harry Anthony Patrinos (2003) "Economic Analysis of World Bank Education Projects and Project Outcomes," *International Journal of Educational Development,* 23(6): 645–660.

Vining, Aidan R. and David L. Weimer (2001) "Criteria for Infrastructure Investment: Normative, Positive, and Prudential Perspectives," 131–161 in Aidan R. Vining and John Richards (eds.), *Building the Future: Issues in Public Infrastructure in Canada.* Toronto: C.D. Howe Institute.

Vining, Aidan R. and David L. Weimer (1998) "Passive Use Benefits: Existence, Option, and Quasi-Option Value," in Fred Thompson and Mark Green, eds, *Handbook of Public Finance,* New York: Marcel Dekker, 319–345.

Vining, Aidan R. and David L. Weimer (1992) "Welfare Economics as the Foundation for Public Policy: Incomplete and Flawed but Nevertheless Desirable," *Journal of Socio-Economics,* 21(1): 25–37.

Viscusi, W. Kip (1993) "The Value of Risks to Life and Health," *Journal of Economic Literature,* 31(4): 1912–1946.

Vitaliano, Donald F. (1997) "X-Inefficiency in the Public Sector: The Case of Libraries," *Public Finance Review,* 25(6): 629–643.

Weimer, David L. and Aidan R. Vining (1999) *Policy Analysis: Concepts and Practice,* 3rd Edition, Upper Saddle River: Prentice Hall.

Weintraub, E. Roy (1983) "On the Existence of a Competitive Equilibrium: 1930–1954," *Journal of Economic Literature,* 21(1): 1–39.

Weisbrod, Burton A. (1964) "Collective Consumption Services of Individual Consumption Goods," *Quarterly Journal of Economics,* 78(3): 71–77.

Whisnant, Richard and Diane DeWitt Cherry (1996), "Economic Analysis of Rules: Devolution, Evolution and Realism," *Wake Forest Law Review,* 31(3): 693–743.

Whittington, Dale and Duncan MacRae, Jr., (1991) "The Issue of Standing in Cost-Benefit Analysis," *Journal of Policy Analysis and Management,* 10(1): 96–105.

Williamson, Oliver E. (1985) *The Economic Institutions of Capitalism,* New York: The Free Press.

Zerbe, Richard O., Jr., (2001) *Economic Efficiency in Law and Economics,* Northampton, Mass: Edward Elgar.

Zerbe, Richard O. (1998) "Is Cost-Benefit Analysis Legal? Three Rules," *Journal of Policy Analysis and Management,* 17(3): 419–456.

Zerbe, Richard O., Jr., and Dwight D. Dively (1994) *Benefit-Cost Analysis in Theory and Practice,* New York: Harper Collins.

Zerbe, Richard O., Jr., and Howard E. McCurdy (1999) "The Failure of Market Failure," *Journal of Policy Analysis and Management,* 18(4): 558–578.

25

Ethics and Public Policy

GARY BRYNER

Ethical issues permeate the design, implementation, and evaluation of many public policies, particularly those policies that regulate some of the most personal and intimate decisions individuals make, shape the distribution of essential resources, determine national and personal security, and influence the natural environment that makes life itself possible. We assume that such important decisions will be made rationally rather than arbitrarily, with a careful weighing of alternatives and selection of those that are most beneficial to those affected. One critical challenge for policy makers, policy analysts, and others who care about how policy making decisions are made, is how to integrate the analytic tools and approaches used in analyzing policy options with reasoning that is rooted in views about what actions are morally right and wrong. This chapter explores the intersection of policy analysis and moral reasoning by examining how cost-benefit analysis, the predominant methodology of policy analysis, can help illuminate ethical issues underlying policy choices.

THE PROBLEM: INTEGRATING COMPETING METHODS OF POLICY ANALYSIS

Public policy and ethics converge in a number of ways. At one level, ethical considerations are expected to guide the conduct of policy analysis. Policy analysts should conduct their professional activities with analytical integrity and provide objective advice about policy options and consequences and make predictions as accurately as possible, ensure the transparency of their assumptions, and clarify value choices, but leave such choices and trade-offs to policy makers. However, policy analysts are also responsible to their clients and expected to be loyal to their clients and represent their interests. Much like attorneys, policy analysts must not misrepresent data, purposely omit important information, or otherwise provide misleading analyses, but also interpret their analyses in ways that are most favorable to the interests of their clients. Analysts may also seek to use their analysis in ways that promote their conception of what kinds of public policies are most desirable and advocate changes in which they believe. Policy analysis is also expected to promote values such as consistency with constitutional standards and the rule of law. These expectations may clash in a variety of ways as the interests of clients may differ from those of objective analysis or personal value commitments. Since analysis almost always requires judgment about what data to use, what models and analytic methods to employ, what assumptions to begin with, how to characterize uncertainties, and other choices, analysts cannot escape the need to make ethical choices based on how they understand their role and what expectations guide them (Weimer and Vining, 1999, 47–53).

At another level, the kind of reasoning that people use to assess ethical choices surrounding moral issues—choices about what they believe to be right or wrong—may clash with analytic tools and methods used to evaluate policy options. Cost-benefit analysis (CBA) is the most widely used analytic tool in policy analysis. It appeals to common sense notions that the benefits of actions should exceed their costs, but its power lies in its claim that different factors can be translated into a common metric, usually dollars, and then compared. CBA is rooted in utilitarian, egalitarian values that policies should promote the greatest utility or happiness for the greatest number of people possible. The value of a policy is the sum of the utility it produces for each affected person. But policies may also be expected to promote other values besides utilitarian ones. Policies may also seek social justice and fairness, taking into account the differing circumstances that people find themselves in, compensating for past actions that have been discriminatory, and creating opportunities for those whose choices and chances have been limited in the past. Policies may also be aimed at preserving inherent rights such as personal autonomy and liberty that are to be honored regardless of whether they contribute to the aggregate happiness or utility. Protecting the rights of unpopular minorities may even diminish the overall utility of the majority but nevertheless be compelled by the value of preserving individual rights. Policies may seek to promote sustainability and ensure that future generations have at least the same options as the current one to meet their needs. Policy analysis may assess options in terms of the inherent rightness or wrongness of policy choices or whether their consequences are desirable or undesirable, however those terms are defined.

What are decision makers to do when confronted with the diversity of policy analyses? They may simply choose to make decisions based on one value—utilitarianism, social justice, preservation of individual rights,

sustainability, or some other distinction. They may review the results of a diverse set of analyses, somehow weigh and balance the competing conclusions, and then draw some conclusions. Or they may try to integrate these different ways of assessing policy choices and designing public policies into a more coherent, synthetic analysis. There are considerable challenges in seeking such an integration. Some decision makers may simply prefer to keep the analyses separate so that their strengths and advantages are preserved. An integration or synthesis may make the analyses hopelessly complex. But analysis that does not incorporate some kind of assessment of benefit and costs is likely to be significantly disadvantaged because of the convenience, clarity, and preciseness (albeit perhaps misleadingly) represented in CBA, where values are quantified and comparable within one overall indicator. Quantification and monetization of variables is often imprecise and incomplete at best. Nevertheless, in an economic system driven by markets, prices, and other economic indicators, a failure to engage in the debate using the dominant terms of discourse risks having those values ignored.

BENEFITS OF COST-BENEFIT ANALYSIS

In 1792, Benjamin Franklin, writing from London, offered this explanation for how he determined what course of action to take when confronted with difficult choices:

> When those difficult cases occur, they are difficult, chiefly, because while we have them under consideration, all the reasons pro and con are not present to the mind at the same time; but sometimes one set present themselves, and at other times another, the first being out of sight. Hence the various purposes or inclinations that alternatively prevail, and the uncertainty that perplexes us. To get over this, my way is to divide a half sheet of paper by a line into two columns; writing over the one Pro, and over the other Con. Then, during three or four days consideration, I put under the different heads short hints of the different motives, that at time occur to me, for and against the measure. When I have thus got them all together in one view, I endeavor to estimate their respective weights; and where I find two, one on each side, that seem equal, I strike them both out. If I find a reason pro equal to some two reasons cons, I strike out three. If I judge some two reasons con,

equal to some three reasons pro, I strike out five; and thus proceeding I find at length where the balance lies; and if, after a day or two of further consideration, nothing new that is of importance occurs on either side, I come to a determination accordingly. And, though the weight of reasons cannot be taken with the precision of algebraic quantities, yet when each is thus considered, separately and comparatively, and the whole lies before me, I think I can judge better, and am less liable to take a rash step, and in fact I have found great advantage from this kind of equation, in what may be called moral or prudential algebra (Gramlich, 1998, 1).

More than two hundred years later decision makers continue, like Franklin, to rely on a logical delineation of the pros and cons of alternative courses of action. CBA allows decision makers to rationally set priorities and allocate resources. Critics of government regulation, for example, argue that regulatory agencies fail to address the most serious risks, and that identifying the costs and benefits of alternative actions will help steer them towards the initiatives that promise to accomplish the most good with the resources expended. CBA is also championed as a way to avoid policies such as overly stringent regulations that impose major compliance costs but produce limited value and to ensure that only worthwhile projects are undertaken. Since the costs and benefits of different policy choices vary significantly, CBA can help ensure that risks are regulated and desirable actions encouraged in comparable, fair ways. CBA is ultimately aimed at producing efficient public policies—the kinds of decisions that markets would produce if they were fully functioning.

Identifying costs and benefits is only the first step; cost benefit analysis involves quantifying and monetizing variables so they can be more easily compared. Concepts and methodologies from economics are used to estimate the market value of variables for which prices do not exist, such as survey data that ask respondents to express their willingness to pay to ensure the preservation of ecosystems and species. Risk assessment is used to estimate the probability and seriousness of risks that might be avoided (and benefits produced) if preventative action is taken. Cost-effectiveness analysis permits decision makers to calculate the benefit-to-cost ratio of alternative courses of

action and select those with the greatest ratio, or choose the option that produces the desired outcomes or benefits at the lowest cost.

Both Democratic and Republican policy makers in the United States, and a great many public policy analysts and advocates, continue to have great faith in the power of cost benefit analysis to illuminate policy choices. Every president during the past 25 years has sought ways to require regulatory agencies to take greater account of the economic impacts of their actions through some form of cost-benefit analysis. These efforts have been motivated by a variety of concerns, such as reducing the cost of compliance with regulations in order to foster economic growth, and increasing the cost-effectiveness of regulation so that benefits are maximized. Congress joined the effort in the mid-1990s, as members introduced a variety of bills to mandate cost-benefit analysis in regulatory agencies. In 1995, Congress required that agencies *identify* the costs and benefits of major rules. It came close, but has not yet succeeded, in enacting the requirement that agencies *only issue* regulations whose benefits exceed their costs. Federal Courts have joined the debate over how agencies are to make difficult decisions. In one of the most far-reaching challenges to regulatory agencies it has ever considered, the Supreme Court rejected an industry challenge to the U.S. Environmental Protection Agency's national air quality standards for fine particles and ozone it issued in 1997, concluding that EPA use of cost-benefit analysis in formulating regulations requires express congressional approval.

The current debate in the United States over energy policy provides examples of the latest in a long line of disputes over how to think about and assess public choices. Bush administration officials have consistently argued that developing new energy supplies and constructing new power plants are the primary solutions to the energy crisis, and that modern technologies allow expanded oil and gas production "with minimal impact on our environment and wildlife" (McAllister, 2001). Cost-benefit analysis is expected to provide the analysis to guide decisions about protecting natural resources and promoting energy development.

President Bush, for example, said early in his administration that at least some national monuments should be opened to drilling for oil and gas: "there are parts of the monument lands where we can explore without affecting the overall environment. It depends on the cost-benefit ratio" (Soraghan, 2001). Critics reacted with dismay to the belief that preservation values could actually be reflected in a cost and benefit formula. Richard Fineberg, an environmental consultant in Alaska, argues that the concept of wilderness "is immutable. It is like perfection—there are no degrees to it. Oil development in a wilderness, no matter how sensitive, changes the very nature of it. It means it's no longer wilderness" (Friedman, 2001).

Proponents of CBA argue that it is an essential tool analysts should use in assessing policy choices, for several reasons:

- CBA is promoted as a solution to the problem of lack of sensible priorities. Critics of government regulation, for example, argue that agencies fail to address the most serious risks, and that identifying the costs and benefits of alternative actions will help steer them towards the initiatives that promise to accomplish the most good with the resources expended.
- CBA is championed as a way to avoid policies such as overly stringent regulations that impose major compliance costs but produce limited value. The analysis seeks to ensure that only worthwhile projects are undertaken and that imposing costs does not waste resources that could be put to productive use.
- The costs and benefits of different policy choices are believed to vary significantly, and CBA can help ensure that comparable factors are examined in comparable ways and options are selected that produce the greatest benefits. One variation of CBA, cost-effectiveness analysis, seeks to ensure that the option with the greatest benefit to cost ratio is identified.
- CBA is aimed at identifying the kinds of decisions markets would produce if they were able to function. Efficient allocation of resources is in the interests of everyone,

and CBA is a critical tool in ensuring that policies promote efficiency.
- Cost-benefit's bias against values that are not easily quantified need not be fatal. CBA can also lay out in qualitative terms the values to be compared; this systematic identification of the costs and benefits of alternatives can be a very useful decision making tool and help illuminate the consequences of policy choices. However, the inability of qualitative CBA to generate an unambiguous bottom line—whether the benefits are greater than the costs—makes it less useful, at least to some users.

Cost-benefit analysis' utilitarian roots make it attractive for a number of reasons. It calls for a distribution of benefits, opportunities, and burdens that generates the greatest welfare for the greatest number. It is consistent with economic efficiency; a failure to maximize benefits would be unjust, because of the unrealized potential for generating wealth and the consequential well-being. It seeks to maximize the economic value of goods and services or economic utility. It is also egalitarian: every person's utility or interests are given equal weight and reinforces democratic expectations of individual equality and majority rule.

Even ardent proponents of CBA may acknowledge the difficulties in achieving the expectations held for it. Many values cannot be easily quantified. More precise economic costs, for example, may be given more weight than imprecise estimates of the value of ecosystem health, ecological services, public health, or aesthetics. Others emphasize that CBA is not a neutral analytic tool in practice, but has been used to provide "objective" cover for decisions reached on questionable grounds. The Office of Special Counsel of the Department of Defense, for example, concluded that officials in the Army Corps of Engineers appeared to engage in a deliberate pattern of manipulating economic cost analyses in order to justify expansion of Corps projects (Grunwald, 2000). But, from this perspective, these are largely problems in implementation rather than a reflection of fundamental shortcomings with the methodology.

INDIVIDUAL RIGHTS AND
COLLECTIVE UTILITY

One important strand of criticism of cost-benefit analysis focuses on the clash between the aggregation of utility and the moral commitment to protect individual rights. Cost-benefit analysis may produce unfair outcomes as benefits largely accrue to one group while burdens are primarily imposed on others. Michael Sandel nicely lays out the conflict in vivid imagery: "If enough cheering Romans pack the Coliseum to watch the lion devour the Christian, the collective pleasure of the Romans will surely outweigh the pain of the Christian, intense though it be. Following Kant, Sandel argues that utilitarianism fails because it "fails to respect the inherent dignity of persons" and "treats people as a means to the happiness of others, not as ends in themselves, worthy of respect" (Sandel, 1996, 9).

The dominant American understanding of individual rights is that rights are so important that, in the words of John Rawls, they cannot be outweighed by majority will: "rights secured by justice are not subject to political bargaining or the calculus of social interests" (Rawls, 1999, 25). Rawls argues that rights provide a framework that ensures individuals have the freedom to pursue their own vision of the good life, as long as they respect the similar freedom of others. Government is to remain neutral towards specific ends in respecting the capacity of individuals to choose for themselves their own beliefs and values. Liberals, following Kant, argue that society should protect rights and liberties, rather than promote "good" values. No one way of life should be affirmed or mandated, but society should be neutral in terms of what values individuals choose to live. Individual rights are trumps that persons possess against the majority. Rawls' theory of justice is an alternative to the dominant role of utilitarianism as it calls for policies that remedy injustices that disadvantage those who are already less well off than others. Priority must be given to the status of the least well off, as long as this can be done without violating basic personal and civil liberties. People are disadvantaged by social structures for which they are not responsible. The more fortunate should only benefit from

political and economic arrangements if the less fortunate benefit even more.

Other definitions of justice suggest criteria for designing and assessing policy choices. Corrective or compensatory justice seeks to compensate victims of injustices in order to restore victims to the condition they were in before the injustice occurred or make her whole, to remedy the damage inflicted, or to provide fair recompense for the injury suffered. Obviously, some harms can be remedied and conditions restored. In the case of environmental policy, for example, hazardous sites can be cleaned up. But in many cases, where life or health has been lost, cash payments are a limited surrogate for making the victim whole. The repeated violation of treaties with Native Americans, the history of colonial exploitation, or slavery, for example, may trigger demands for compensatory justice that do not satisfy a cost-benefit test but are compelled by a sense of moral obligation.

THE DISTRIBUTION OF BENEFITS
AND BURDENS

Cost-benefit analysis may produce outcomes that are ethically objectionable in other ways. A cost benefit analysis is based on an *aggregate* of relevant costs and benefits, but these consequences may not be distributed equally. A facility that generates benefits to an entire community, for example, may also pose greater risks to some residents than others, such as those who live near enough to inhale toxic emissions. Even if the aggregate benefits clearly and strongly overwhelm the costs, it is hard to defend as fair such a mismatch between those who bear the burdens and enjoy the benefits of a particular activity.

Different definitions of egalitarianism challenge the outcomes of cost-benefit analysis. Perhaps the simplest notion is that benefits and burdens are to be distributed equally across all affected parties; everyone receives the same level of benefit, such as access to natural resources, and is exposed to the same level of environmental risk or pays the same cost. Alternatively, equality can mean that those who are similarly situated are treated the same, and those who are in different circumstances are treated differently. That is, there may be some factors that justify different treatment, although there should be consistency within each category. For example, those who benefit from a risky activity should bear the associated costs. Or equality can be understood to require a minimum level of equality or access to benefits or imposition of burdens or risks. A commitment to equality may conflict with simple utilitarian calculations and suggest different distributions to different persons, according to their merit, conditions, or needs. A collectivist formulation links benefits and needs: everyone is to receive the level of benefits consistent with their needs. In contrast, a merit-based approach requires that benefits be distributed according to effort or contribution and burdens. Correspondingly, those who make only partial contribution should receive partial benefits (Paul, 1995, 27).

The nature of risk is a complicating but important factor here. Risks that are voluntarily assumed and represent an informed choice pose less of a problem than risks involuntarily imposed on others. For example, the choice of individuals to live on the oceanfront and voluntarily accept the increased risk of damage or death from hurricanes and other storms does not pose a challenge to this notion of distributive justice. On the other hand, a decision to live next to a toxic emitting factory or incinerator is problematic, because it may be in only a very narrow sense "voluntary;" low-income persons may have few options besides choosing to live in economically depressed areas where prices are low and environmental risks are high.

QUANTIFYING COSTS AND BENEFITS

Critics of CBA argue that it inevitably is biased in favor of easily quantified values, such as industry compliance costs, and against more intangible and hard to quantify ethical values of biodiversity, environmental health, social equity and empowerment of politically disadvantaged groups, and public well-being. Others argue that values such as environmental quality, public health, personal freedom, and equality of opportunity are most powerfully defended by arguing that they are priceless, and that their protection is compromised by considerations of costs. Many values cannot be easily quantified in dollars; those values that can be more precisely and unambiguously quantified will be given priority over those that are less certain. More precise economic costs, for example, may be given more weight than imprecise estimates of the value of ecosystem health, ecological services, public health, or aesthetics. Cost-benefit analysis's bias against values that are not easily quantified can be overcome by resisting quantification and laying out in qualitative terms the values to be compared. This systematic identification of the costs and benefits of alternatives can be a very useful decision-making tool and help illuminate the consequences of policy choices, but its inability to generate an unambiguous bottom line—whether the benefits are greater than the costs—makes it less useful, at least to some users.

More fundamentally, neoclassical economic theory underlies the calculation of costs and benefits, but that theory is problematic, for several reasons. At one level, the problem is rooted in differences between private and social costs. Markets work well when private and social costs are equivalent, when prices include all the costs that matter to society and to the environment. But prices often fail to reflect the true costs of production and externalize rather than internalize costs in the pursuit of maximum profits. Producers and consumers often make choices that reflect their narrow economic interests at the expense of broader societal and environmental interests. There are often differences between the private and social benefits: the use of some resources may produce economic gains for some individuals, while other activities could bring much greater gains. Planting a forest creates some level of benefits for a landowner who eventually sells the timber, for example, but it also produces additional benefits of sequestering carbon, filtering air and water, and providing habitat. Geoffrey Heal nicely summarizes this fundamental limitation of markets: "Just as we will tend to do too much of the activities shows social costs exceed the private costs, so will we also do too little of those for which social benefits exceed private benefits" (Heal, 2000, p. 28).

The idea of the state of balance produced by the invisible hand of markets is rooted in the work of Adam Smith, Thomas Malthus, and David Ricardo, who sought to discover a set of natural laws of economics that mirrored the natural laws of Newtonian physics that came to dominate thinking in the 18th Century. Just as the universal force of gravity held the elements in balance, the natural law of economics ensured that individual economic actions would, without some overarching direction, ensure order and stability. Smith argued that the market's invisible hand was similar to the invisible force that caused a pendulum to oscillate in equilibrium or a liquid to flow through connected containers to reach its own level, a conclusion he drew not from empirical research but from metaphysical assumptions. Subsequent theorists also sought to imbue economics with the same kind of authority enjoyed by physical scientists who substituted economic concepts for physical variables developed in 19th-century physics (Nadeau, 2003).

Contrary to its theoretical underpinnings, however, markets are intimately intertwined with the natural world. Natural resources are exhaustible and natural systems are, overall, irreplaceable. In contrast, market ideology demands that costs and benefits that extend very far into the future are discounted and devalued. As a result, as Ophuls and Boyan (1992, 219) put it, "critical ecological resources that will be essential for our well-being even 30 years from now not only have no value to rational economic decision makers, but scarcely enter their calculations at all." Markets typically handle incremental change with relative ease but tend to break down when confronted with absolute scarcity or even marked discrepancies between supply and demand. In such situations (e.g., in famines), market collapses or degenerates into uncontrolled inflation, because the increased price is incapable of producing an equivalent increase in supply. Markets also fail to respond to problems of ecological scarcity

because scarcity "tends to induce competitive bidding and preemptive buying, which lead to price fluctuations, market disruption, and the inequitable or inappropriate distribution of resources" (Ophuls and Boyan, 1992, 200). Even if prices are carefully regulated to ensure they reflect true costs, the assumptions on which neoclassical economics rests are largely at odds with ecological science. Assumptions such as the following are recipes for eventual environmental collapse (Nadeau, 2003, p. 9):

• Markets are closed circular flow systems of production and consumption separate and distinct from the external environment,
• Inputs of raw materials from the environment are "free" unless costs associated with their use are internalized,
• Raw materials are inexhaustible or replaceable by other resources or by technologies,
• The external environment is a bottomless sink for waste materials and pollutants,
• There are no biophysical limits to the growth of closed market systems; markets will perpetually grow and expand.

Market ideology fails to reflect the larger community of land, resources, biomes, languages and cultures, and institutions in which economic activity is embedded and on which it depends (Daly and Cobb, 1989). The inherent dynamic of markets has produced a global environmental deficit, the "collective and mostly unanticipated impact of humankind's alteration of the earth's atmosphere, water, soil, biota, ecological systems, and landscapes;" this deficit has occurred because "the longer-term ecological, social, and economic costs to human welfare are greater than the shorter-term benefits flowing from these alterations" (Borman and Kellert, 1991, xii). Environmental deficits rob future generations as they permit profligate consumption by the current generation, who pursue their interests rather than ensuring that the needs of current and future generations are preserved.

Cost-benefit analysis has deep roots in natural resource policy making (Gramlich, 1990, 2). Much of the criticism of CBA has been developed in response to its use in environmental policy but similar criticisms can be made in other areas of policy sectors. Can policy options concerning whether or not to allow cloning and stem cell research, regulate genetically modified organisms in food, permit genetic manipulation of fetuses and disclosure of genetic predispositions toward certain diseases and disabilities, provide health care coverage to low-income persons, strengthen families and marriage by making divorce more difficult, restrict the availability of pornography, increase educational choice, and a host of other variables be quantified in terms of the costs and benefits of alternative actions?

THE SOLUTION: INTEGRATING ALTERNATIVE APPROACHES TO POLICY ANALYSIS

The plurality of analytic approaches to policy analysis is inevitable and desirable, since no one approach can sufficiently represent the variety of perspectives that are required for policy analysis of complex issues. A broader framework is needed that incorporates CBA with approaches rooted in ethical and moral analyses. One candidate for such an integrative approach is ecological sustainability. While it is aimed at environmental and natural resource issues and, at first blush, does not lend itself to a host of other policy questions, it is worth examining as an example of how CBA and other kinds of analyses can be brought together to illuminate and clarify ethical choices, give direction to policy making, and provide criteria for assessing specific policy options

Ecological sustainability emphasizes the interaction of ecological, economic, social, cultural, and other values, so that no one set of values, such as environmental or economic factors, can alone determine policy. Sustainability assessments can be used to organize factors and show their interrelationships and interactions. The methodology of sustainability builds on the idea of ecosystem services, but goes beyond to include several other additional criteria for assessing policy choices, including pollution prevention rather than treating emissions, sustainable yield of renewable resources, the precautionary principle and preservation of ecological values in the face of uncertainty, true-cost prices that internalize environmental costs in market exchanges, the development of economic indicators and measures that reflect depletion of natural resources, considerations of equity and distribution, and preservation of ecological conditions and options for future generations. It incorporates critical theories rooted in economics, ecofeminism, socialism, and other critiques of modern, industrial, high consumption societies and their foundational ideas of progress and materialism, that offer alternative visions of environmental and social ethics (Merchant, 1994).

Ecological sustainability holds that environmental preservation is a precondition for life itself. It places a major constraint on economics; only economic activity that is consistent with ecological sustainability is acceptable. Critical natural capital must be maintained so that the ecosystem services it provides are maintained; it cannot simply be harvested to generate economic wealth. Industrial activities, energy production, transportation, and consumption must be fundamentally transformed to avoid ecological disruptions and protect regenerative processes. Ecological survival simply outweighs economic growth as the primary public priority. Balancing environmental protection and economic growth is not enough; ecological values must come first, and must define and limit what kinds and levels of economic activity are acceptable. Policy goals such as free trade and economic efficiency are subordinated to preservation of biodiversity, protection of wild lands, and reclamation of damaged areas. Sustainability requires that, for precautionary reasons and because we do not know what the desires or utility functions of future generations will be, we should ensure the preservation of as much of the natural world as possible as we balance meeting the needs of current generation with preserving resources for future ones. Sustainability requires strong commitments to monitoring, feedback loops, and other means of ensuring that decision makers learn from experience and be able to make adjustments as learning occurs.

Part of what is most central here is an endorsement of the idea of true costs—prices should include the *real* or *true* costs of production, including the environmental and health consequences and impacts, rather than allowing sellers and purchasers to externalize those costs to others. In a system committed to markets as a way of allocating scarce resources, determining value, and making choices from competing needs and wants, it is critical that prices provide accurate information about the true costs of what is being sold. As real costs are better understood, those affected by them can have more of the information needed to make trade-offs and balance competing concerns such as environmental protection and economic development (Prugh, Constanza, and Daly, 2000, 28–29). Cost-benefit analysis can be useful in assessing policy alternatives, but the analysis requires information about true costs.

A central feature of ecological sustainability is its integration of ecological protection and economic activity with social equity and political empowerment. Sustainable development here gives priority to reducing poverty and helping the poor gain some measure of self-sufficiency through a more equitable distribution of resources. Sustainability is largely a concept of community, bound up with notions of strong democracy, participation, community, and those social characteristics are fostered through a scale of personal interaction. Political participation is a key ingredient in ensuring that decisions affecting economic and environmental conditions be made more inclusive. Sustainability is not an ecological concept alone, but also one of social justice, inclusion, fairness, community well-being, and political engagement. Sustainability requires new ways of thinking that integrate ideas of individual rights, community responsibility and accountability, material and spiritual well-being, and ecological health. It requires, from this view, a radical set of changes in order to ensure fairness in the distribution of benefits and burdens, a perpetual resource base and ecological services, and a social system that secures the interests of all persons. Sustainability focuses on comprehensive solutions that reflect the interconnections of ecology and respects the maxim,

"everything is connected to everything else," that is at the heart of ecology. So too is it a commitment to a land ethic. Aldo Leopold (1966, 238–39) defined a land ethic, sounding much like a proponent of sustainable communities:

> An ethic, ecologically, is a limitation on freedom of action in the struggle for existence.... All ethics so far evolved rest upon a single premise: that the individual is a member of a community of interdependent parts.... The land ethic simply enlarges the boundaries of the community to include soils, water, plants, and animals, or collectively: the land.

Ecological sustainability can be understood in terms of three core elements:

1. *Ecological integrity, ecosystem services, natural capital, and true-cost prices:*

Ensure economic activity is within ecological limits, maintain ecological integrity, protect key ecosystem services, ensure sustainable yield of renewable resources, preserve and regenerate natural capital base, internalize environmental costs in market exchanges, reduce subsidies that have harmful environmental consequences

2. *Equity, wealth, and consumption:*

Ensure inter-and intra-generational equity, carefully identify the equity consequences of costs and benefits, address interaction of poverty and environmental degradation, distribute resources in ways that increase opportunity, transfer and disseminate widely cleaner technologies that benefit all persons, not just the wealthy

3. *Democratic politics, community, and natural resource governance:*

Foster strong democracy and participation, provide economic and technical resources to ensure effective participation, strengthen community, civil society, and social capital, develop economic indicators and measures that reflect depletion of natural resources and pollution as costs, devise broader measures of social and economic factors.

Debates over the depth of sustainability permeate efforts to determine guidelines for public policy and private behavior. Questions over the scope of sustainability, and what behaviors should come within its reach are just as contested. If sustainability requires that the stock of nonrenewable natural resources be preserved for future generations, does that mean we have long since violated its basic premise? Does sustainability suggest a static goal of ensuring that future generations have the same level of resources and ecosystem services to rely on? How does sustainability make sense in light of the dynamic nature of biological evolution? The value of natural resources, in part, lies in their use, but human use has varied greatly. Uses of forests have changed dramatically, for example, from sources of strategic defense materials (wood for battleships) to watershed functions of cleansing water. What kinds of changes can and should be limited in the pursuit of sustainability? Perhaps most difficult is the question of whether sustainability is in the interest of the current generation. Is it more morally compelling for them to improve the quality of life of existing members of that generation and reduce the enormous disparities in wealth, or is it better to set aside resources for those not yet born? Sustainability seems promising as an idea for governing a community. The problem is how to extend the idea beyond our community. We may find that our own community is sustainable if we export our wastes or import unsustainable levels of resources. How does sustainability guide us in these circumstances?

Developing good answers to these and other questions is central to the viability of ecological sustainability as a way to integrate CBA, moral and ethical frameworks, and other approaches to policy analysis. The idea of sustainable development has firmly taken root in global, national, and local political discourse in a remarkably short length of time. Government agencies at all levels, transnational corporations, multilateral institutions, community-based collaborative groups, and many others have embraced the idea of sustainability. The impreciseness of sustainability makes it an attractive idea around which diverse expectations can congregate. But that impreciseness makes its use as a guide for decision-making problematic. The contested nature of the idea of sustainable development is rooted in two primary dimensions: the depth of sustainability and the level of change required, and the breadth of sustainability and the range of practices and behaviors it reaches. As these provisions are debated and refined, we can develop a clearer picture of what an ecologically sustainable technological society might look like. The development of sustainability-related methods and tools can also serve to replace assessments of discrete policy choices, now dominated by cost-benefit analysis, with a richer form of analysis that incorporates a more diverse set of values, perspectives, and objectives.

REFERENCES

Borman, F. Herbert and Stephen R. Kellert (1991) *Ecology, Economics, Ethics: The Broken Circle.* New Haven: Yale University Press.

Daly, Herman and J. B. Cobb, Jr. (1989) *For the Common Good.* Boston: Beacon Press.

Friedman, Thomas (2001) "Drilling in the Cathedral," *The New York Times* (March 8), A25.

Gramlich, Edward (1990) *A Guide to Benefit-Cost Analysis.* Prospect Heights, IL: Waveland Press, 2nd ed.

Grunwald, Michael (2000) "Shooting Pork in the Barrel," *The Washington Post* (March 2): A17.

Heal, Geoffrey (2000) *Nature and the Marketplace: Capturing the Value of Ecosystem Series.* Washington, DC: Island Press.

Leopold, Aldo (1966) *A Sand County Almanac.* New York: Ballantine Books.

McAllister, Bill (2001) "Norton praises oil-drilling efforts," *Denver Post* (April 5) www.denverpost. com/business/biz0405c.htm.

Merchant, Carolyn (1994) *Ecology.* Atlantic Highlands, NJ: Humanities Press.

Nadeau, Robert L. (2003) *The Wealth of Nature.* New York: Columbia University Press.

Ophuls, William and A. Stephan Boyan, Jr. (1992) *Equality and the Politics of Scarcity Revised.* New York: W.H. Freeman.

Paul, Ellen Frankel (1995) "Set-Asides, Reparations, and Compensatory Justice," reprinted in Kenneth A. Manaster, *Environmental Protection and Justice.* Cincinnati: Anderson Publishing Co., 27.

Prugh, Thomas, Robert Costanza, and Herman Daly (2000) *The Local Politics of Global Sustainability.* Washington, DC: Island Press.

Rawls, John (1999) *A Theory of Justice.* Cambridge, MA: Harvard University Press, revised ed.

Sandel, Michael (1996) *Democracy's Discontent: America in Search of a Public Philosophy.* Cambridge, MA: Harvard University Press.

Soraghan, Mike (2001) "Bush: National monuments have oil-drilling potential," *The Denver Post* (March 15) www.denverpost.com/news/news0315d.htm.

Weimer, David L. and Aidan R. Vining (1999) *Policy Analysis: Concepts and Practices,* 3rd ed., Upper Saddle River, NJ: Prentice-Hall.

26

Performance and Performance Management

GEERT BOUCKAERT AND JOHN HALLIGAN

Performance has become a defining feature of modern government. The age of performance has produced commitment to, but not necessarily clarity about, the universal objective of organisational and government improvement. Performance and performance management continue to be enigmatic concepts. There is a paradox too in that the adoption rate of performance approaches continues to expand despite the mounting critique. One limitation has been the failure to integrate performance and measurement within a broader system of management and within a conception of organisational life that invests practice with greater meaning.

Performance management lacks a coherent treatment that explicates its significance, analyses its several dimensions as a working system and challenges its shortcomings. The purpose of this chapter is to seek an understanding of performance and performance management as concepts as they are applied in practice and in relationship to public management. Performance management has to be located within a broader construction of organisational life, which recognises that performance management cannot be considered in isolation from other factors that make up public management and the more general public administration system. Our study is grounded in public administration tradition that recognises rationality and trust as two fundamental dimensions of organisational life. The performance focus not only has an impact on the key public management functions and components (HRM, finance, strategy, etc.) but also changes the nature of policy and management in the public sector in itself.

WHY PERFORMANCE MANAGEMENT?

The need for the systematic study of performance management is based on the increase in application and its current significance within OECD. The key debates have produced a burgeoning literature because they address core issues of public administration and policy, yet some ambiguities, even confusion, remain about the workings and standing of performance management.

The most striking feature of performance management is its continuing expansion over the last two decades, making this current period its international apogee. As will be discussed later, the antecedents of performance management – various approaches to performance and measurement – have a long lineage. But the high international commitment goes well beyond a resurgence of interest in measuring performance. Moreover, performance management is recognised to have evolved, to be different and to involve more sophisticated measures (Schick, 2001: 40).

International observers agree that something unusual was occurring internationally in the 1990s, with 'the rise and rise of "performance" as an issue in public sector theory and practice' (Talbot, 1999). Similarly a US observer reports that 'if there is a single theme that characterizes the public sector in the 1990s, it is the demand for performance. A mantra has emerged in this decade, heard at all levels of government, that calls for documentation of performance and explicit outcomes of government action' (Radin, 2000: 168). The penetration was significant by the mid-1990s: measurement was becoming 'more intensive, more extensive and more external' (Bouckaert, 1996); and key performance management questions were prominent in a ten-country survey by the OECD but stronger in the Anglo-American compared to the European (OECD, 1997, Bouckaert, 1997). This trend continues in the 2000s, with no indication that it is abating with 'performance measurement and reporting becoming even more important within most governments. "If you can't measure it, you can't manage it" has become a familiar refrain' (Thomas, 2004: 1).

Two big questions in public management during the last fifteen years – markets and performance – have attracted the most controversy in an era of unprecedented public sector reform. Both have recent origins in New Public Management (NPM), although their lineage is much longer, and reflect private sector ideas. Markets are examined in many other studies, but performance management remains something of an enigma and is lacking coherent meta-analysis.

One factor has been its centrality to public management. Performance management forms the core of public management, especially NPM: is it possible to envisage management in the public sector without due regard to the pursuit of results and the measurement of performance? This correspondence can readily be established through stock specifications of New Public Management features (e.g., Hood, 1991). When Behn (1995) writes about the 'Big Questions of Public Management' – micromanagement, measurement and motivation – he is essentially identifying questions about performance management. When Hood and Peters (2004) reflect on 'The Middle Aging of New Public Management' are they not writing for the most part about the side-effects of performance management?

The field has become the subject of debates about the value of performance, measurement and their management. Performance management has become a small growth area within public administration and management, centred on critiquing aspects of performance and measurement (e.g., Forsythe, 2001). Three types of argument can be mentioned. The first is about the impact of rhetoric on poor implementation ('What makes performance management so attractive in theory, yet so difficult in practice?' Thomas, 2004: 1); and the assumption of the performance management industry that an agency will be 'transformed by measuring its performance. This is the logic of GPRA' (Schick, 2001: 40, 43). A second critique explores the limits of rationality and unintended consequences. Managers are seen as functioning within the narrow parameters of performance management and an imperfect model that is rationally defined and deficient. A third type of argument points to apparent confusion. There is a lack of agreement on how to measure performance. Moreover, with performance measurement there are an 'array of buzzwords... reinventing government, new public management, performance management, results-driven government, results-based budgeting, performance contracting etc.' (Thomas, 2004: 1); and authors move casually between one concept and another (e.g., a discussion of performance management is really about performance measurement: Bovaird and Gregory, 1996: 239). For all these reasons there is a need to look at performance management more systematically and to ground it in analysis of its constituent elements.

TOWARDS CLARIFICATION OF PERFORMANCE AND PERFORMANCE MANAGEMENT

Several themes emerge from the literature, each associated with the core concepts of performance, measurement and performance management.

The first is *performance*. A broad conception of performance claims that it has always 'been an issue in government' and key goals, such as efficiency, economy and fairness are '"performance" goals as widely defined' (Talbot, 1999: 2). Performance is commonly conceived in either individual or organisation terms, and also as a combination of both. It may also be identified with an activity, program or policy (Talbot, 2005), the latter linking in with the evaluation movement. Talbot (2005) outlines the different dimensions of performance – as accountability; user choice; customer service; efficiency; results and effectiveness; resource allocation; and creating public value. 'Performance' is also commonly used as prefatory to other activities such as auditing and budgeting and more diffusely to 'improvement', 'orientation' and trajectories (Pollitt and Bouckaert, 2004: 341, 126).

Another literature focuses on *measurement*. Performance measurement may be defined specifically or broadly, an expansive definition being performance measurement (Thomas, 2004: 1), 'the regular generation, collection, analysis, reporting and utilization of a range of data related to the operation of public organizations and public programs, including data on inputs, outputs and outcomes'.

Factoring in *management* has become commonplace. One option is to view 'managing performance' as focusing on measurement (de Bruijin, 2001); another is to adopt a narrow conception of performance management as equalling the management of people (Flynn and Strehl, 1996: 14–17), whereas a broader conception would embrace individuals and organisations. The significance of the connection is registered through analysis of the role of management capacity in government performance (Ingraham et al., 2003). *Performance management* is now commonly distinguished as one of several management processes, alongside the familiar financial, human resource and strategic management (Halligan, 2001).

In seeking a definition of performance management we need to specify what it might encompass. Performance management can be represented as 'both about measurement and management, about information and action' (Bouckaert and Van Dooren, 2002), involving 'taking/allocating responsibility for the performance of a system and being accountable for its results' (Pollitt and Bouckaert, 2000). A standard meaning is: 'an integrated set of planning and review procedures which cascade down through the organization to provide a link between each individual and the overall strategy of the organization' (Rogers, 1990: 16). A performance management framework use 'interrelated strategies and activities to improve the performance of individuals, teams and organizations. Its purpose is to enhance the achievement of agency goals and outcomes for the government' (Management Advisory Committee, 2001: 14).

It is possible therefore to identify several elements that might be explicit or implicit in a definition: results and goals; means to achieving these ends such as integrated strategies; use of performance measurement; taking responsibility for performance and being held to account; and relationships between the elements (individual and organisational, etc.). In an ideal type of definition this may result in the financial function rotating from a horizontal to a vertical dimension and links to financial and other information; guidance and steering; from ex ante to ex post; new interactions between parts of the organisation and between the organisation and its environment; and cascading down of organisational objectives to an individual level.

For our purposes, it is helpful to distinguish performance measurement as a quite specific term that refers to tasks and techniques,

Table 26.1   *Four models*

	Model 1: *Traditional/Pre-* *Performance*	Model 2: *Performance* *Administration*	Model 3: *Managements of* *Performances*	Model 4: *Performance* *Management*
1. Measuring	Intuitive	Administrative data registration	Specialised performance measurement systems	Hierarchical performance measurement system
2. Integrating	None	Some	Within different systems for specific management functions	Systemically integrated
3. Using	None	Limited	Disconnected	Coherent, integrated, comprehensive, consistent
4. Limitations	Functional unawareness	Ad hoc selective	Incoherence	Sustaining complex system

managing performance as a generalised depiction of results-focused activity and performance management as a term that is best used where an effort has been made to systematise and give coherence to that activity. Other terms can either be discarded as lacking conceptual significance, the exceptions being forms of budgeting or other specific activity that might be a component of different managements of performance.

A FRAMEWORK FOR COMPARATIVE ANALYSIS OF PERFORMANCE MANAGEMENT

Most books in the field of performance management fall into one of the following categories: general public management with some (minor) reference to performance as such (Christensen and Laegreid, 2001; Wollmann, 2003); performance measurement (sensu strictu) (Hatry, 1999); and specific public management functions with some reference to performance (e.g., budget cycle, personnel, evaluation, contracts, etc.) (Miller et al., 2001). Other studies are based on either a single country or are organised around several classical management chapters like finance, personnel, organisation, strategy, etc. In contrast to the standard approach of focusing on specific

management functions (integrating performance information by the traditional functions), a crosscutting issues approach is favoured here. The analysis of performance management takes two forms: specification of its components and their relationships, and applications to different countries.

In order to make meaning of the diverse uses and combinations of performance, measurement and management, a framework has been developed with three components – performance measurement without management, management of performance of specific functions and performance management. Based on the logical sequence of, firstly, collecting and *processing* performance data into information; secondly, *integrating* it into documents, procedures, and stakeholder discourses; and thirdly, *using* it in a strategy of improving decision-making, results, and accountability, four 'pure' models can be constructed (Table 26.1).

The four models distinguished are: Traditional/Pre-Performance, Performance Administration, Managements of Performances, and Performance Management. Each represents an ideal type, and the four can be applied to the historical development of performance and management as a basis for analysing and comparing country orientations to performance and as a means for thinking analytically about performance management and its components.

Model 1 is termed **Traditional/Pre-Performance** and essentially recognises that 'performance' objectives in a generic sense can be found in most systems of public administration, but that many of them might be regarded as pre-modern management. In these cases, the expectation is that 'performance' would be generalised and diffuse, with goals not defined in terms of performance as such as it arises where measurement and management are present. Input driven and tax-collecting organisations, within law-based systems focusing on procedure and due process, may have a very implicit interest in performance. Scarcely available data may not have an information value, will not be integrated, and hardly will be usable. A pre-Weberian bureaucracy covers this model quite well.

Under Model 2, **Performance Administration**, a commitment to measurement and performance is expected, but the relationship may not be explicit or well developed and the application is often ad hoc. The Performance Administration Model's focus on measurement is inclined to be technically oriented but the level of coherence may depend on which generation of measurement system is under discussion. This type is therefore relevant to both early experiments with measurement and performance and to successive phases of greater sophistication, including focused applications in recent times. There is an intuitive and generalised concern for performance that is registered and administered. Measurement becomes another administrative procedure that may be part of an administrative and legal setting, not a managerial or policy context. Information generated from these administrative procedures is disconnected from improvement strategies. Sophisticated rules developed for registering and administering performance are not developed to generate information to affect managerial functions nor elements of a policy cycle. A classical Weberian bureaucracy fits this model.

Model 3 is an interesting and quite complex type, entitled **Managements of Performances**. This category is intermediate between Performance Administration and Performance Management and arises where management and performance have been linked but the connection between them is underdeveloped and concurrent systems operate. Managing performances includes performance measurement but goes beyond its administration. Management of performances implies different types of performances according to different and unconnected management functions. This results in a diverse range of managements of performances, like performances in personnel management, financial management (budgets, accounting systems, audits), strategic and operational management, customer management, communication management.

A diverging set of performance measurement systems is feeding information into a disconnected set of management functions, resulting in different performances for different purposes, which are not necessarily linked in a hierarchical and logical way. A symmetrical development of these function-based measurement systems make it not very consistent, coherent, comprehensive, and integrated between these functions. However, within some functions there may be a high level of sophistication and development, even up to driving an improvement and reform process in other functions. Performance-based financial cycles may drive contract cycles and personnel functions or vice versa.

The Model 4, **Performance Management**, is defined by the presence of distinctive features: coherence, integration, consistency, convergence, and comprehensiveness. It includes a solid performance measurement system beyond administration and proliferation. It includes an integration of performance information, which goes beyond ad hoc connectedness, for the purpose of using it in a coherent management improvement strategy. Performance management is conceived as a framework with system properties. It may also comprise several systems (a framework may require different performance measurement systems for different purposes: Bouckaert, 2004: 462), but they must be (hierarchically) connected to satisfy the criteria of Performance Management as a type. The Performance Management Model also requires an explicit policy on measurement and managing the different functions and their performances.

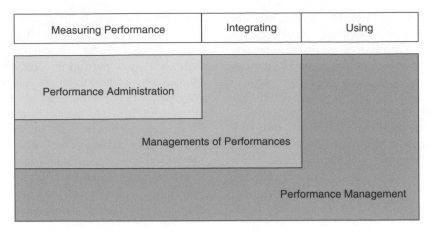

Figure 26.1   *Relationship between measuring, integrating, and using performance and the evolving models*

The relationship between the three performance models, and how each is successively nested within another, are illustrated in Figure 26.1.

One further question is the relationship between performance and management. What differentiates more developed systems is the application of management, but this is insufficient for fully-fledged Performance Management as an ideal type. In Table 26.2 the types in the first column are narrowly conceived in terms of either limited conceptions of performance or measurement or both. Whereas the two types in the second column are more comprehensive. The first line is more diffuse/less systematised; the types in the second line more integrated within their sphere (either measurement or management system).

HISTORICAL APPLICATION

The framework provides a basis for analysing the development of performance measurement and management. It requires the identification of the several elements and stages from concerns with performance measurement in the early decades of the twentieth century to fully developed performance management at the end of the century. This is done with reference to two closely-linked countries (Halligan, 2003; Pollitt & Bouckaert, 2004): the United States, which pioneered the early experiments and significant developments up to managing performances, and the United Kingdom, which illustrates the evolution of a system of performance management over several decades.

Early Measurement of Government Activities under 'Performance Administration'

The early history of performance measurement is mainly centred on the United States,[1] and is complex because of variations in terminology, differences of actors and the levels of government involved. The initial decades of the twentieth century resulted in many institutions focusing on mostly municipal efficiency, but a Bureau of Efficiency (1912), and the Institute for Government Research, the predecessor of the Brookings Institution (1916) were created at the national level.

First generation performance measurement was concerned with measuring government activities that were eventually to be defined in terms of service delivery. This was 'the earliest identifiable sustained effort to engage in performance measurement and productivity improvement' (Williams, 2003). In the first part of the 20th century the 'Government by

Table 26.2 *Performance and management*

Focus	Pre & proto 'performance' (lack of management)	Managing of performances
Unsystemic	Traditional performance	Managements of performances
Systemic	Performance administration	Performance management

the Good', changed into the 'Government by the Efficient': public administration and scientific management 'proclaimed a new gospel to a new deity: efficiency' (Mosher, 1968: 71, passim). There was a focus on economy and efficiency in a context of a division between politics and administration. Politicians should not be involved in administration since it is scientific and value-free, and aims at economy and efficiency, a conviction strengthened by the view that the activity was purely technical. Although efficiency was generally defined as obtaining a result with a minimum of resources, there was discussion from the beginning about definitions of efficiency, with terminology focusing on inputs, activities, outputs, and efficiency, but not much on results and outcomes. There was also an assumption that more efficiency results in more effectiveness, allowing administration to focus on the technical dimensions without having to get involved in effectiveness.

Broadening and Elaboration of Performance, Measurement and Productivity

A second generation of performance measurement activity emerged with post-World War 2 experiments, led by the US central government's interest in performance (in budgeting), measurement (more generally) and productivity. This resulted in the development of tools and techniques like PPBS, MBO, or ZBB, all including performance information. The first Hoover Commission (1949) recommended performance-based budgets and the second Hoover Commission (1955) on budgets, costs, and management reports. Economy and efficiency remained crucial, but a crucial driver for the innovations was not the search for a 'better government' but an explicit desire to reduce expenses. For that reason productivity

was on the budget agenda. The Bureau of the Budget started a productivity project in 1962 and the eventual report concluded that productivity could be measured and that there should be annual reporting to the President and Congress (Kull, 1978: 5). Presidents Nixon and Carter established a succession of national productivity commissions.

Although the interest in measuring productivity from an administrative technical point of view continued, savings and spending less tax money became the main issues in the 1980s. Under Reagan the President's Private Sector Survey on Cost Control, the Grace Commission, estimated yearly savings of $US 3 billion. The Commission was primarily concerned with efficiency, expressed as cost savings and operated within an agenda that sought minimal government. This debate had a technical and an increasingly dominant ideological angle, which ultimately led to New Public Management in the 1990s (Bouckaert, 1991).

For the United Kingdom, there were two decades (1960 and 1970s) of ad hoc experiments and dabbling in performance measurement during which programs were piloted but were eventually discontinued. The earliest cases of performance measurement have been traced to the 1960s and associated with cost benefit analysis, management by objectives and output budgeting, but only two remained significant in the 1970s. The two decades of discussing and piloting performance measurement yielded little that was convincing and durable (Bovaird and Gregory, 1996: 239–40).

The Advent of Managements of Different Performances

Two decades of pursuing performance, measurement and increasingly management followed (1980s and 1990s). Performance measurement became a growth industry in the UK following the launching of the Financial Management Initiative in 1982, which was designed to focus on objectives and to measure outputs and performance. A significant component of the approach was the use of performance indicators (PIs), Prime Minister Thatcher proclaiming in the 'manifesto of the revolution – that a thousand PIs should flourish' (Carter, Klein and Day, 1992: 2; Cave, Kogan and Smith, 1990). By 1987 departments had 1800 PIs (Pollitt, 1993: 54).

UK's FMI was only partly successful yet it laid the foundation for the next stage. During the 1980s the fundamental shift occurred from public administration to public management with the new philosophy and style being more receptive to and influenced by the private sector. Public management had already been identified in the US (Perry and Kraemer, 1983), although the more fundamental basics of new public management did not register until the 1990s. This management focus had major implications for the efficiency agenda, and provided the basis for the active implementation of performance and measurement. The move to management of performances was to emerge from this foundation with the management of individual and organisational performance becoming increasingly common. There were aspirations in both countries to manage individuals in the respective senior civil services through the use of performance-related pay (Pollitt, 1993). Eventually it became possible for the management of performances to assume a more integrated form as a construction of performance management. New Public Management has an interesting place in these developments and the progression towards performance management.

Public Management Trends Produce Fusing of Performance and Management

If the 1980s saw the flowering of performance measurement, the 1990s were years of performance expansion and management consolidation. Observers in the UK and US record the mushrooming of performance in 1990s,

agreeing that something exceptional was occurring (Talbot, 1999; Radin, 2000). For these developments to make a difference, it was necessary for performance to become embedded in management framed in comprehensive terms.

The Government Performance Results Act 1993 provided the main US impetus, eventually becoming mandatory for national agencies, and revolutionised the systemic implementation of outcome-related goals and performance measurement, planning and reporting. For the UK, the transition from Performance Administration to Managements of Performances occurred in the 1980s and was arguably the more complete move (of the two countries) to Performance Management in the 1990s.

APPLICATION OF TYPES TO COUNTRY PERFORMANCE MANAGEMENT

A significant element is contextual analysis of different performance management systems to enable comparisons to be made across countries, while recognising the importance of their cultural and administrative traditions. Three country approaches can be identified: those that have made a high commitment to performance management, where the interest is in how they frame their performance management systems to handle the limitations to this approach; countries that have sought to balance performance management with other features and how that plays out in practice; and countries that have sought to selectively draw on performance management techniques while operating within another type of system.

A purpose of the ideal types is to use them as a basis for examining the variations in the orientation of the public administration systems to performance management. Preliminary analysis indicates that Germany (at the national level) continues to operate without commitment to, and application of, performance, measurement and management principles, while France has made a major commitment to performance management but the relationship to management is tenuous

Table 26.3   *Ideal types and OECD country systems*

	Pre/Proto Performance	Managing Performances
Unsystemic	Traditional:	Managements of performances:
	Greece	Canada, The Netherlands, USA
Systemic	Performance administration:	Performance management:
	France, Germany	Australia, UK

(Table 26.3). Three countries in different ways approximate Managing Performances: Canada, the Netherlands and the United States. This means that, while performance management principles and practice may be fairly well developed, they are inclined to be neither integrated nor systemic. For the Performance Management type two countries, Australia and the United Kingdom, come closest to the stringent requirements, although there are weaknesses in both cases that make the fit less than optimal.

The criteria for performance management include an identifiable framework that must be sustained over time and formally supported by key actors (e.g. central agencies and cabinet); and the presence of attributes identified with Model 4: performance management must be comprehensive (systemic), integrated, coherent and consistently applied across agencies. This requires evidence of practice at the agency level, of how the 'system' as a whole is operating and of a capacity to review and absorb lessons. At the agency level, the prerequisites include a performance focus, measurement systems in place and a management approach and a coverage that includes individual, organisational, financial, etc. There also needs to be evidence of the use of performance measurement; taking responsibility for performance and being held to account; and relationships between the elements (cascades, individual, organisational, etc.).

One of these cases illustrates the features of the Performance Management type. Australia has been more committed to performance management than most OECD countries (see OECD, 1997). Two management frameworks have existed within which two generations of performance management can be distinguished (Halligan, 2002; McKay, 2003). The performance management framework encompasses most of the attributes referred to above, but there remain weaknesses in consistency of approach, reporting of information externally and meaningful applications of principles in practice.

A strength has been central and external oversight with a series of inquiries reviewing the principles and their application, but they have revealed a persistent problem: the credibility of performance management systems (APSC, 2004). The performance aspects of human resource management have attracted sustained interest because of fundamental issues raised by the transformation of employment relations under a highly devolved system. A prominent issue has been the subjectivity of management assessment of performance, and public servant motivation where remuneration is based on performance (e.g. O'Donnell and O'Brien, 2000).

SOME KEY ELEMENTS OF PERFORMANCE MANAGEMENT ISSUES IN A POLICY CONTEXT

Performance is relevant for (policies of) single organisations, for substantive policy areas (see especially Part III in this volume) and for the macro level of countries. The general purpose is to describe the link of resources with activities and outputs, to link outputs to effects of organisations and their policies, and sometimes even to link this to satisfaction or confidence in single organisations, policies or their institutions.

Essential information for policy makers is linking expenditure to effects and to confidence at all levels, if possible.

Comparing the macro level between countries is obviously a challenge. There are differences

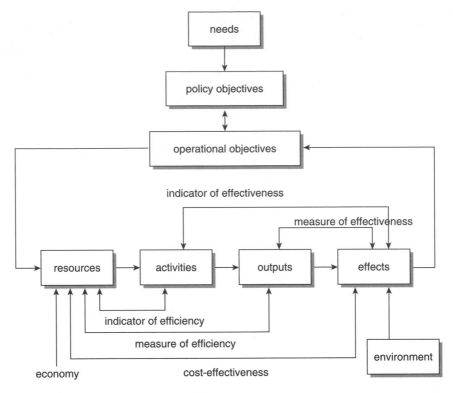

Figure 26.2   *Performance management in a policy context*

in institutions, definitions and registration procedures for data, and there are longitudinal inconsistencies. Also data are incorrect, preliminary, inconsistent, and incomplete. All these reasons are insufficient not to look for performance data and information, integrating and using this in policy decision-making, results upgrading, and enhancing accountability.

Figure 26.2 places inputs-throughputs-outputs-effects in a context of general and operational needs and embedded policy objectives that are interacting with environments. This scheme allows us to define the economy, efficiency/productivity, effectiveness, and cost-effectiveness of organisations, policies, and countrywide analysis. As a consequence the available performance information allows us to develop a policy focus on this economy, efficiency, effectiveness, cost-effectiveness, and even confidence. It is obvious that defining the responsibility for performance, however it is defined, will immediately determine who is accountable for that performance.

But this systemic approach also causes some significant problems affecting performance measurement and management of 'substantive' policies, and therefore requires a 'performance measurement and management' policy itself. It is clear that micro (single organisation), meso (substantive policy), and macro levels (government wide) are not necessarily harmonious and compatible (Figure 26.3). There are obvious conflicts between individual schools or hospitals (which may aim at maximising numbers of students or patients) and educational and health policies that want to control or even limit (and definitely audit) numbers of students and patients.

Also, well functioning and performing single organisations do not always guarantee a well functioning and good performing policy. Good performing micro levels are necessary but insufficient for a well performing meso level. Performance measurement systems should make this visible and performance management should take this into account by

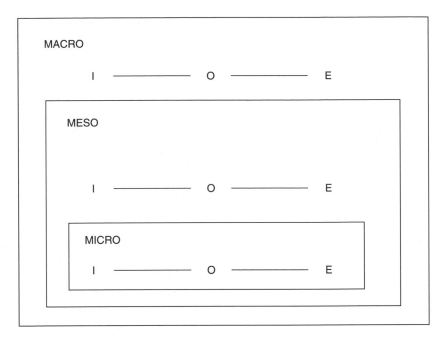

Figure 26.3   *Linking micro, meso and macro performance management. I: Input;*
O: Output; E: Effect

looking at micro, meso, and macro performance management.

Third, several and different single organisations may contribute to a general effect (see Figure 26.4). Environmental policies are implemented by a whole range of agencies (inspection, subsidies, direct intervention, communication, etc.), which may be disconnected. Micro performance should be consolidated at the policy level. But defining the level of attribution of separate well performing agencies to a general policy effect is impossible. Therefore, performance measurement systems should be developed at the level of a substantive policy field (meso), and at a single organisational level (micro). Obviously, government wide indicators (macro) are also indispensable and are developed in several OECD countries (US, Canada, Australia).

From a 'performance management' policy point of view this implies that an integrated micro/meso/macro performance focus is needed. New Public Management has concentrated more on the need to guarantee an optimal micro level than a meso level, even up to ignoring the co-ordination of single organisations in a substantive policy field.

This also requires a policy to integrate, to add or to consolidate the micro into the meso, and the meso into the macro level.

'Performance management' also requires a clear statement on how this performance information will be integrated into the financial cycle (budgets, accounts, audits), the contract cycle, and the policy cycle. It is crucial that performance based information is consistently integrated in a coherent way in the three related financial, contract and policy cycles. This is probably a requirement to guarantee evidence-based policies in all stages.

ASSESSING PERFORMANCE MANAGEMENT IN A POLICY CONTEXT

In the history of public management and public policy reform one of the common denominators has been to increase the level of performance information in order to improve the level of decision-making and the level of effectiveness (OECD, 2000; Bouckaert, 1994).

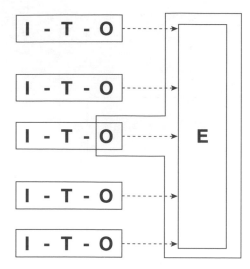

Figure 26.4   *Linking performance at micro level to effects at meso level. I: Input; T: Throughput; O: Output; E: Effect*

The general assumption of this sequence is that if and when we know what to do and how to do something we indeed will do it. Performance management in all its variations (for example, the latest generation of evidence-based evaluations) is derived from a rather naive scheme of thinking which is highly rational and resulted in many publications on how to measure performance in the public sector (Hatry, 1999; Morley et al., 2001; Liner et al., 2001; Bouckaert and Van Dooren, 2002).

At the same time, there is increasing evidence demonstrating the difficulties, and perhaps even the impossibility, of measuring performance and integrating this information in a comprehensive, coherent, consistent, and therefore functional way in policy and management cycles (Ammons, 2002; Hatry, 2002; Bouckaert and Peters, 2002). However, criticism (Radin, 1998) and counter-evidence have not stopped many of the reform machines. Also, evidence based on comparative data is lacking and evaluations of reforms are a missing link (Pollitt and Bouckaert, 2001; Jones and Kettl, 2003).

One of the most extreme reform positions in managing performance was the so-called New Public Management (NPM). Although it was restricted in space (mostly Australia, New Zealand and the UK) and time (mostly the 1990s), it influenced reform agendas of other countries. Even if NPM was mainly an Anglo-Saxon, partly Westminster featured phenomenon, it has been described as 'an international phenomenon' (Jones and Kettl, 2003: 2) with a generic narrative capacity (Barzelay, 2001), which fits the NPM normative and rhetorical strategy of a self-fulfilling performance management prophecy.

Other scholars have put NPM in a broader perspective of general public management reform (Pollitt and Bouckaert, 2000; Christensen and Laegreid, 2001) or even governance reform (König, 1996; Wollman, 2003).

Many countries have followed a more cautious and even a different 'managing performance' strategy. Reform results in four main patterns of practice: maintaining, modernising, of marketising, and minimising (Pollitt and Bouckaert, 2000). In reality there are combined and hybrid strategies which change over time, and also depend on the political context. Ultimately, the choice of a reform agenda includes implicitly an ideological choice for a state of law or a market state and is not just the integration of some management techniques as part of a public management policy. Whether country strategies are to maintain, modernise, marketise, or minimise, all emphasise the importance of performance measurement and management.

In reality it seems that performance management and its related reform agenda are not so obvious to realise in practice. The official win/win/win rhetoric seems not to be mirrored in reality. The picture that politicians win because they steer on strategic lines, that managers win because they are allowed and able to manage, and that citizens win because they get better service seems more complex, definitely conditional and perhaps even untrue in reality. Many advocates are disappointed about the lack of interest of parliaments in this reform, even if some countries have made serious efforts to increase the levels of accountability and have changed the budgetary procedures to facilitate a contradictory debate between the executive and the legislative, like, for example, in Canada (Improved Reporting to Parliament Project) or in Sweden (VESTA).

Implementation is difficult and even subject to obstruction. And executive politicians lose interest if the potential political yield is not obvious.

A major question is therefore what is going on in the practice of the reform agenda in general, of which the performance issue is a crucial common denominator, and how can we explain what is going on.

One key change has been the creation of autonomous agencies. These agencies and their guiding centres use a variety of tools and techniques like, for example performance budgeting, accrual accounting, performance evaluation and value for money auditing, personal and institutional performance contracts with rewards and sanctions, target setting, benchmarking and performance monitoring systems.

In any case, the general assumptions seem to be that more information is better than less, that comparative information is better than non-comparative information, that timely information is better than untimely information, that output and effect information is better than single input information, and that clear and quantitative objectives are better than opaque ones.

CONCLUSION: PERFORMANCE MANAGEMENT IN A CONTEXT OF POLICY EVALUATION

In practice the implementation of measuring performance attracts scepticism (Ammons, 2002), fallacies (Hatry, 2002), and even resistance (Bouckaert and Peters, 2002). Performance measures are Achilles' heel, and measuring performance is Sisyphus' job. However, from the history of performance measurement systems it is obvious that there is a learning cycle and progress is present (Bouckaert, 1995, 1996). The study of the history of measurement systems in the public sector can be useful for future strategy.

First, learning from history, for example, the progress in measuring performance could result in extrapolating the learning cycle. Could performance measurement become even more intensive, more extensive, and more external? There is still scope for a more extensive approach, i.e. an increased coverage rate in organisations and policy fields. The absorption of performance measures in financial cycles (budgets, accounts, and audits), in policy cycles (design, strategic plans, monitoring of implementation, and evaluation), in personnel functions, and in organisational intra- and inter-action still has potential for intensive expansion. Finally, a growing external dimension is also correlated to a developing accountability.

Second, just like the accounting adagium 'different costs for different purposes', a system needs different performance measurement systems for different purposes. Three main objectives of performance management include (re-)allocation of resources (of which savings is one specific variant), increase performance of the public sector as such, and enhance accountability. Performance measurement systems will have to cover all these objectives.

How to balance costs and benefits of performance measurement and systems of managing performance? A performance measurement/management Cost Benefit Analysis is always present, be it more implicitly than explicitly. Listing costs and benefits is not easy. Quantifying performance measurement/management costs and benefits is even more difficult. One key problem is that in general costs are more immediate, more tangible, and less conditional than benefits, which are less immediate, less tangible, and more conditional. Costs precede benefits because one needs to collect data and process this into information before one can collect the benefits of it. Also costs seem to be more tangible than the nature of the benefits, which are also and perhaps predominantly intangible. A focus on transparency, accountability, and trust are clear benefits but difficult to match to a monetary cost. Finally, costs are incurred almost as a fact of an accounting nature, whereas benefits depend on the functional use of this information in a policy and management cycle.

It is important to avoid measurement/management systems that are not used, that demonstrate failures (because of technical problems, illegitimacy, or dysfunctionality), or that clearly demonstrate a perverse effect (Bouckaert, 1995). Awareness of transitional problems like, for example, a temporarily doubling of red tape because of simultaneously reducing ex ante input controls and increasing ex post output and outcome controls, is also a key element.

Third, these performance measurement strategies need to put in a broader context, i.e. the 60-year-old Friedrich/Finer debate is relevant. The key question is whether there is a need for a system based on *subjective* elements (e.g., personal accountability based on integrity and trust – Friedrich's position) or for a system based on *objective* elements (e.g., rule-directed accountability based on compliance and performance measurement systems – Finer's position).

According to Friedrich (1940), professionals themselves provide 'fellowship', which regulates the behaviour of fellow practitioners, and their technical and situational knowledge allows them to have a deeper knowledge of the public interest. Pride-related arguments of these professionals allow for a subjective accountability mechanism derived from their values. According to Finer (1940), the track of objective accountability should be followed, since those within agencies are obliged to follow and implement the popular will as expressed by political officials and agency executives. Control could then be linked to performance-based elements.

How can this dichotomy be resolved? One option is to upgrade both positions. Balk proposes two fundamental positions to orthodox practitioner perception. The first raises subjective agency accountability to a formal level of visibility by providing an applied theoretical rationale. Then the realm of public administration discourse is extended well beyond conventional management philosophical domains so as 'to recognize employees as legitimate, proactive actors, citizens with a powerful commitment to the values and actions essential to democratic political institutions' (Balk, 1996: 13).

The second option is to choose one position as dominant. Gawthrop contends that there is a need to expand and implement the ethical imperatives for the 21st century through education, values and commitment in order to re-establish and rediscover democracy (Gawthrop, 1998). Education of the citizenry will empower citizens in a governance context and equilibrate bureaucratic values. Values are crucial and should not be replaced by facts and figures but balanced with these. Commitment and engagement imply that public servants know what to do and go beyond what they have to do.

A third option is the dominance of performance measurement/management systems that turn the whole system into performance budgets, accounts, audits, contracts, evaluations, etc. The cost of monitoring and compliance is considerable. Principles and agents will try to create disequilibrated information systems. The system would not use trust and integrity at all for its governing (Bouckaert, 1998).

A fourth option – balancing the two positions – seems to be desirable. A fair mix of trust and measurement, of integrity and compliance, of subjective and objective approaches is necessary. Upgrading the two positions and combining them seems to be a functional way to make things work. According to Balk 'professionals as key actors in the network of stakeholders in a democratic society, will develop mutually supportive relationships at the workplace in order to maintain their integrity and strengthen democratic political institutions. They can take the lead by acknowledging that principles of tentative trust and contingent loyalty need not threaten the benefits of, nor the necessity to respond to, appropriate hierarchical direction' (Balk, 1996: 190–1). This implies that performance-based systems should be combined with trust based systems in a dynamic way.

Fifth, there will remain tensions or contradictions between responsibility and the accountability on issues like output versus outcome and organisation versus policy and these often derive from the relationship between the civil service and the politicians. Performance measurement/management may clarify this but will never solve these tensions.

Sixth, the impact of introducing performance measurement/management in a Weberian context may lead to a neo-Weberian or a post-Weberian design of the public sector

(Pollitt and Bouckaert, 2004), creating a possible trajectory from our Model 2 to Model 3 or even 4.

Performance measurement/management is a comprehensive programme of organisational development that affects the whole organisation and its policy cycle. We would contend that the strength or weakness of the performance measurement system, and its integration and institutionalisation in the managerial and policy systems, determines the strength or weakness of the redesigned system. Having a range of new management practices in place with inadequate, or even counter-productive performance measurement and management systems, may be worse than no reform at all. It can provide a false sense of security and accomplishment. Performance management therefore becomes the Achilles' heel of the modernisation process itself (Bouckaert and Peters, 2002).

NOTE

1. The earliest practices in Britain appear to be the surveys and municipal statistics that reach back into the nineteenth century (Williams, 2004). More considered thinking about measuring performance existed, as indicated by Sidney Webb's 1901 call for an annual municipal competition to investigate municipal efficiency, by calculating 'statistical marks for excellence' (quoted in Cutler and Waine, 1994: 27).

REFERENCES

Ammons, David (2002) Performance measurement and managerial thinking. *Public Performance & Management Review*, 25(4): 344–347.

APSC/Australian Public Service Commission (2004) *State of the Service Report 2003–04*. Canberra: Commonwealth of Australia.

Balk, Walter L. (1996) *Managerial Reform and Professional Empowerment in the Public Service*. Westport, Connecticut: Quorum Books.

Barzelay, M. (2001) *The New Public Management*. Berkeley, CA: University of California Press.

Behn, Robert D. (1995) 'The Big Questions of Public Management', *Public Administration Review*, 55(4): 313–24.

Blalock Ann B. and Barnow Burt S. (2001) in Dall W. Forsythe (ed.) (2001) *Quicker Better Cheaper:*

Managing Performance in American Government. Ithaca, NY: Rockefeller Institute Press.

Bouckaert, Geert (1991) Public Productivity in Retrospective. In M. Holzer (ed.), *Public Productivity Handbook*. Marcel Dekker, New York, 15–46.

Bouckaert, Geert (1994) 'The History of the Productivity Movement', in M. Holzer and A. Halachmi (eds), *Competent Government: Theory and Practice. The Best of Public Productivity & Management Review 1985–1993*. Burke: Chatelaine Press.

Bouckaert, Geert (1995) 'Improving Performance Measurement', in A. Halachmi and G. Bouckaert (eds), *The Enduring Challenges in Public Management, Surviving and Excelling in a Changing World*. San Fransisco: Jossey Bass.

Bouckaert Geert (1996) 'Measurement of Public Sector Performance: Some European Perspectives', in A. Halachmi and G. Bouckaert (eds), *Organizational Performance and Measurement in the Public Sector*. Westport: Greenwood Publishing Group.

Bouckaert, Geert (1997) 'Overview and Synthesis', in Organisation for Economic Co-operation and Development, *In Search of Results: Performance Management Practices*. Paris: OECD.

Bouckaert, Geert (1998) 'Public Sector Performance Measurement in a Principal Agent Context', in A. Halachmi & P. Boorsma (eds), *Inter and Intra Government Arrangements for Productivity, An Agency Approach*. Boston: Kluwer Academic Publishers.

Bouckaert, Geert (2004) Institutionalizing Monitoring and Measurement Systems in the Public Sector', in Arthur Benz, Heinrich Siedentopf and Karl-Peter Sommermann (eds), Instituionenwandel in Regierung und Verwaltung, Festschrift fir Klaus Konig, Berlin: Duncker and Humblot.

Bouckaert, Geert and Guy Peters (2002) Performance Measurement and Management: The Achilles' Heel in Administrative Modernisation. *Public Performance & Management Review*, 25(4): 359–362.

Bouckaert Geert and Wouter Van Dooren (2002) 'Performance Measurement: Getting Results', *Public Performance & Management Review*, 25(3): 329–335.

Bovaird, Tony and David Gregory (1996) Performance Indicators: the British Experience, in Arie Halachmi and Geert Bouckaert (eds), *Organizational Performance and Measurement in the Public Sector: Toward Service, Effort and*

Accomplished Reporting. Wesport, Conn: Quorum Books.

Carter, Neil, Rudolf Klein and Patricia Day (1992) *How Organisations Measure Success: The use of performance indicators in government*. London and New York: Routledge.

Cave, Martin, Maurice Kogan and Robert Smith (1990) 'Introduction', in Martin Cave, Maurice Kogan and Robert Smith (eds), *Output and Performance Measurement in Government: The State of the Art*. London: Jessica Kingsley Publishers.

Christensen, Tom and Per Laegreid (2001) (eds), *New Public Management, The Transformation of Ideas and Practice*. Aldershot: Ashgate.

Cutler, Tony and Barbara Waine (1994) *Managing the Welfare State: The Politics of Public Sector Management*. Oxford/Providence: Berg.

de Bruijin, Hans (2001) *Managing Performance in the Public Sector*. London: Routledge.

Finer, Herman (1940) 'Administrative Responsibility in Democratic Government', in C.J. Friedrich (ed.), *Public Policy*. Cambridge, MA: Harvard University Press.

Flynn, Norman and Franz Strehl (1996) *Public Sector Management in Europe*. New York Prentice-Hall.

Forsythe, Dall W. (2001) *Quicker Better Cheaper? Managing Performance in American Government*, Ithaca, NY: Rockefeller Institute Press.

Friedrich, Carl J. (1940) 'Public Policy and the Nature of Administrative Responsibility', in C.J. Friedrich and Edward S. Mason (eds), *Public Policy*. Cambridge, MA: Harvard University Press.

Gawthrop, Louis C. (1998) *Public Service and Democracy: Ethical Perspectives of the 21st Century*. New York: Chatham House.

Halligan, John (2001) 'Comparing Public Sector Reform in the OECD', in Brendan Nolan (ed.), *Public Sector Reform: An International Perspective*. Hampshire: Macmillan.

Halligan, John (2002) 'Public Sector Reform in Australia', in Byong-Man Ahn, John Halligan and Stephen R.M. Wilks (eds), *Reforming Public and Corporate Governance: Management and the Market in Australia, Britain and Korea*. Cheltenham: Edward Elgar.

Halligan, John (ed.) (2003) *Civil Service Systems in Anglo-American Countries*, Civil Service Systems in Comparative Perspective Series. Cheltenham: Edward Elgar.

Hatry, Harry (1999) *Performance Measurement: Getting Results*. Washington, DC: Urban Institute Press.

Hatry, Harry (2002) Performance Measurement: Fashions and Fallacies. *Public Performance & Management Review*, 25(4): 352–8.

Hood, Christopher (1991) 'A Public Management for all Seasons?', *Public Administration*, 69(1): 3–19.

Hood, Christopher and Guy Peters (2004) 'The Middle Aging of New Public Management: Into the Age of Paradox?', *Journal of Public Administration Research and Theory*, 14(3): 267–82.

Ingraham, Patricia W., Philip G. Joyce and Amy Kneedler Donahue (2003) *Government Performance: Why Management Matters*. Baltimore and London: John Hopkins University Press.

Jones, L.R. and Donald Kettl (2003) Assessing Public Management Reform in an International Context. *International Public Management Review* (electronic journal at http://www.ipmr.net) 4(1): 1–18.

König, Klaus (1996) On the critique of New Public Management, *Speyer Forschungberichte* 155. Speyer: Institute fur Verwaltungs-wissenschaft.

Kull, D. (1978) Productivity Programs in Federal Government, *Public Administration Review*, 38(1): 5–9.

Liner, Blaine, Harry Hatry, Elisa Vinson, Ryan Allen, Pat Dusenbury, Scott Bryant and Ron Snell (2001) *Making Results-Based State Government Work*. Washington, DC: Urban Institute Press.

McKay, Keith (2003) 'Two Generations of Performance Evaluation Management Systems in Australia', *Canberra Bulletin of Public Administration*, No. 110, 9–20.

Management Advisory Committee (2001) *Performance Management in the Australian Public Service: A Strategic Framework*. Canberra: Commonwealth of Australia.

Miller, Gerald, Hildreth Bartley and Rabin Jack (2001) Performance Based Budgeting. Boulder, Co: Westview.

Morley, Elaine, Scott P. Bryant and Harry Hatry (2001) *Comparative Performance Measurement*. Washington, DC: Urban Institute Press.

Mosher, Frederick C. (1968) *Democracy and the Public Service*. Oxford: Oxford University Press.

O'Donnell, M and J. O'Brien (2000) 'Performance–Based Pay in the Australian Public Service', *Review of Public Personnel Administration*, Spring, 20(2): 20–34.

OECD/Organisation for Economic Co-operation and Development (1997) *In Search of Results: Performance Management Practices*. Paris: OECD.

OECD (1999) *Integrating Financial Management and Performance Management*. Paris: OECD.

OECD (2000) *Government of the Future*. Paris: OECD.

Perry, J. and K. Kraemer (1983) *Public Management: Public and Private Perspectives*. California: Mayfield.

Pollitt, Christopher (1993) *Managerialism and the Public Services*, 2nd ed. Oxford: Blackwell.

Pollitt, Christopher and Geert Bouckaert (2000) *Public Management Reform, an International Comparison*. Oxford: Oxford University Press.

Pollitt, Christopher and Geert Bouckaert (2001) Evaluating Public management Reforms: an International Perspective. *International Journal of Political Studies*, Spring 2001, 167–192.

Pollitt, Christopher and Geert Bouckaert (2004) *Public Management Reform: A Comparative Analysis*, 2nd ed. Oxford: Oxford University Press.

Radin, Beryl (1998) The Government Performance and Results Act (GPRA): hydra-headed monster or flexible management tool? *Public Administration Review*, 58(4): 307–16.

Radin, Beryl (2000) *Beyond Machiavelli: Policy Analysis Comes of Age*. Washington, DC: Georgetown University Press.

Rogers, Steve (1990) *Performance Management in Local Government*. Harlow: Longman.

Schick, Alan (2001) 'Getting Performance measures to Measure Up', in Dall W. Forsythe (ed.), *Quicker Better Cheaper: Managing performance in American Government*. Ithaca, NY: The Rockefeller Institute Press.

Talbot, Colin (1999) 'Public Performance: Towards a new model?' *Public Policy and Administration*, 14(3).

Talbot, Colin (2005 forthcoming) 'Performance', in Christopher Pollitt and Lawerence Lynn Jr (ed.), *Oxford Handbook of Public Management*. Oxford: Oxford University Press.

Talbot, Colin, Lyn Daunton and Colin Morgan (2001) *Measuring Performance of Government Departments – International Developments*, A Report for the National Audit Office. Abergavenny: Public Futures Ltd.

Thomas, Paul (2004) *Performance Measurement, Reporting and Accountability: Recent Trends and Future Directions*, Public Policy Paper 23. Regina: The Saskatchewan Institute of Public Policy.

Williams, Daniel W. (2003) 'Measuring Government in the Early Twentieth Century', *Public Administration Review*, 63(6): 643–59.

Williams, Daniel W. (2004) 'Evolution of Performance Measurement until 1930', *Administration and Society*, 36(2): 131–65.

Wollman, Hellmut (ed.) (2003) *Evaluating Public Sector Reforms*. Aldershot: Edward Elgar.

27

Argumentative Policy Analysis

HERBERT GOTTWEIS

INTRODUCTION

During the 1990s, argumentative policy analysis became a major strand in the contemporary study of policy making and policy theory development. The term *argumentative policy analysis* subsumes a group of different approaches towards policy analysis that share an emphasis on language as a key feature of any policy process and thus as a necessary key component of policy analysis. Argumentative policy analysis links post-positivist epistemology with social theory and methodology and encompasses theoretical approaches, such as discourse analysis, frame analysis, and interpretative policy analysis. Although these different approaches are hardly synonymous, they nevertheless share the special attention they give to argumentation and language and the process of utilizing, mobilizing, and weighing arguments and signs in the interpretation and praxis of policy making and analysis (Fischer, 2003). Argumentative policy analysis does not believe that policy analysis can be a value-free, technical project, and argues that both policy making and policy analysis essentially involve argumentation that needs to be at the center of policy studies.

Argumentative policy analysis has its roots in European philosophy and theory, originated as a policy approach in the United States during the late 1980s, and has since expanded considerably in both Europe and in the United States. Although policy analysis traditionally has not been a stronghold in Europe, argumentative policy analysis as a policy approach is especially prominent in Europe. The reasons for the particular strength of argumentative policy analysis in Europe are multifold. Unlike in the United States, European policy analysis developed relatively late; it was not until the 1980s that a new generation of European political scientists began to specialize in policy research and many universities established new chairs in policy studies. In most European countries, these policy scholars operated in the context of political science departments, and in dialog with multi-paradigmatic settings that were less shaped by the neo-positivist persuasion that had become hegemonic in USA political science during the 1980s at the latest. Whereas in the United States many out of those generations of political scientists who had grown up with the classical philosophical tradition were in the process of retiring, in Europe many political science departments continued to stay open-minded towards a broad tradition of political and social theory, or displayed a rather indifferent attitude towards new social theoretical and philosophical approaches. For many scholars in these institutions, the idea that language is important in politics linked well with what most educated people associate with the Greek philosophy tradition, but this was hardly seen as undermining any important epistemological positions. It was in this intellectual climate that from the late 1980s on important positions in policy analysis in countries such as in the United Kingdom, Germany, Austria, the Netherlands, and Denmark were taken by scholars working in the tradition of argumentative policy analysis.

At the same time, the European Union not only became a mounting challenge for political scientists to comprehend, but it also matured into a major force of research funding. New approaches to understanding Europe and the unprecedented challenges for European governance were asked for, which opened up the space for new theoretical avenues, such as constructivist policy and communicative planning approaches. Most scholars in the argumentative tradition emphasize their commitment to offer useful and more practical policy analysis than normally done by the traditional policy approaches. This type of concrete and specific analysis and advice was precisely what the European Commission was looking for in its various Framework programs. Thus, a new and important source of funding for argumentative policy analysis developed, and which helped further expansion.

ARGUMENTATION, SOCIETY, AND POLITICS

Argumentation theory has a long history that dates back to pre-Aristotelian philosophy. It is always connected to considerations and reconsiderations of the notions of logic, communication, and persuasion. Mobilizing, positioning and transmitting arguments also requires appropriate sociopolitical conditions: argumentation is the antithesis to revelation; it

is not about revealing a truth but attempts to convince (Breton and Gauthier, 2000: 3–5). The Sophists emphasized the importance of rhetoric in politics and the idea that facts are what we are persuaded of (Danzinger, 1995). Plato accused the Sophists of only dealing with the appearances of truth, whereas philosophy's role was to deal with establishing the true and the good (Meyer, 1994: 50–1). Aristotle, by contrast, attempted to accord a positive place to rhetoric by positioning rhetoric as part of dialectic, along with poetics and the study of topics (Meyer, 1994: 119–23). As Michel Meyer points out, rhetoric appears forcefully in times of crisis for the lack of directing principles in the settling of questions that are being submitted to controversial answers. In the absence of leading principles that could offer some definitive, unequivocal answers problems are bound to be disputed and solved 'equivocally'. Just as the Peloponnesian wars led in ancient Greece to a collapse of previous and well-established values and modes of thought and the rise of rhetoric, the upheavals of our times have led to a new reconsideration of rhetoric, argumentation, persuasion and its relationship to logic and communication (Meyer, 1994: 36–7). Rhetoric is a discourse in which one can hold opposite judgments on the same question. What is problematic remains so through the displayed multiplicity of judgments (Meyer, 1994: 52).

In contemporary times, the theory of argumentation was taken up and further developed by Stephen Toulmin (1958) and Chaim Perelman (1958) in the late 1950s, and the work of both had a lasting influence in the field of political science. Closely related to the development of argumentation theory was the rise of hermeneutics, phenomenology, structuralism and post-structuralism, not only in philosophy but also in the social sciences from the 1970s on. The ascent of argumentative policy analysis must be seen in this complex intellectual environment as a result of a political constellation of transformation and upheaval, when, during the 1980s, largely unanticipated by the international political science community, the Soviet Empire broke down, the 'end of history' was proclaimed, the European Union finally rose to the status of an international economic super power, and the traditional models of economic growth and the nature-society interaction came to be deeply questioned. The crisis of the major political metanarratives, powerfully analyzed by Francois Lyotard (1979), and the limits of growth and scientific progress seemed to call for new, more nuanced confrontations and understandings of the nature of policy making.

One of the key texts in contemporary argumentative policy analysis, Giandomenico Majone's 'Evidence, Argument, and Persuasion in the Policy Process' (1989) contextualizes the need for argumentative policy analysis by reference to the 'crisis of scientific expertise' in regulation policy, which began to become visible during the 1970s: 'Increasingly, public debates about regulatory decisions, nuclear safety, technology assessment, and similar trans-scientific issues tend to resemble adversary proceedings in a court of law, but with an important difference – the lack of generally accepted rules of procedure' (4). Majone then explicitly defines the ancient tradition of rhetoric as the obvious and necessary point of departure for modern policy analysis. 'The centuries-old tradition of humanistic disciplines, from history and literary criticism to moral philosophy and law, proves that argumentative skills can be taught and learned. Thus, if the crucial argumentative function of policy analysis is neglected in university departments and schools of public policy, this is due less to a lack of suitable models than to serious misconceptions about the role of reason in human affairs and about the nature of the "scientific method" … when mathematicians acknowledge that mathematics is not the antithesis of rhetoric … it should not be left to policy analysts to fight the last battles of positivism' (Majone, 1989: XII). Majone then goes on to discuss in great detail the virtues of rhetoric for policy analysis, and the 'argumentative character' of the policy process itself, which calls for systematic attention to the role and function of words in and the ways of 'doing things with words' (Majone, 1989: 7). 'Its crucial argumentative aspect is what distinguishes policy analysis from the academic social sciences on the one hand, and from problem-solving

methodologies such as operations research on the other' (Majone, 1989: 7).

In a similar direction, Deborah Stone's Policy Paradox (first published in 1988) constituted a sweeping critique of the (neo-positivist) rationality model of policy making and its attempt to provide unequivocal, value-free answers to the major questions of policy making today. Stone's understanding of policy emphasizes the importance of language in the policy making process, and views policy as an element of a never-ending political struggle over the criteria for classification, the boundaries of categories, the definition of preferences that shape the way people behave, and the importance of persuasion in political life. According to Stone, neutral facts that could 'decide' conflicts do not exist: 'Facts do not exist independent of interpretive lenses, and they come clothed in words and numbers' (Stone, 1988, 307).

Both books, Majone's 'Evidence, Argument, and Persuasion', and Stone's 'Policy Paradox', set the tone for a new way of argumentative policy analysis in the late 1980s, provided a novel conceptual framework of analysis with language and argumentation at its center and had a large impact on the field of policy studies. But it was not before Frank Fischer's and John Forester's 'The Argumentative Turn in Policy Analysis and Planning' (1993) that 'argumentative policy analysis' became a clearly recognizable movement and tendency in policy studies with a clearly articulated research agenda. The publication of the Argumentative Turn had been preceded by a number of other writings by Fischer, Forester and others (Fischer 1980; Forester 1985) that had begun to outline the map the key features of the argumentative turn. While Majone's and Stone's book remained, in many respects, singular events that nonetheless changed the field of policy studies without mapping a clear agenda for broader change, the 'Argumentative Turn' offered a more systematic, more epistemologically argued, but also 'pluralistic' agenda for a new, argumentative policy analysis. The range of contributions stretched from more Foucault- to more Habermas-oriented contributions and encompassed diverse approaches from rhetorical analysis to frame analysis. It is in this volume that the emerging project of argumentative analysis, a particular linking of epistemology, methodology, policy theory, and policy practice clearly began to take shape. Both editors of the 'Argumentative Turn', Fischer and Forester, had in quick sequence several monographs to follow that set the standards in argumentative policy analysis and developed sophisticated and comprehensive framework of analysis (Fischer, 1995, 2000, 2003; Forester, 1993, 1999). The central idea of the book was unequivocal: since both policy making and policy analysis fundamentally involve argumentation, policy analysis needs to move argumentation at the center of its analytical and epistemological project.

ARGUMENTATION: EPISTEMOLOGY AND METHODOLOGY

Argumentative policy analysis could hardly claim to offer an especially innovative and different approach in policy analysis if its feature of distinction were mainly the emphasis on the importance of language in the policy process. There are a number of contemporary policy approaches that highlight the importance of ideas in the policy process, such as versions of neo-institutionalism (Hall, 1986), the policy paradigm tradition (Braun and Busch, 2000), and the issue network and the policy learning tradition (Sabatier, 1988). Despite attributing considerable importance to language and language-related phenomena, such as learning and policy ideas, these approaches tend to conceptualize language as one variable next to others that take their influence on policy making. Argumentative policy analysis takes a different approach. In its view, language is not only an instrument of communication, it is also constitutive of policy (Benveniste, 1972), and this has serious implications for policy analysis.

First, if language is constitutive of policy, its usage as an instrument to describe and analyze reality needs to be reconsidered. There is no such thing as a theory-neutral observation language. Numerous philosophical influences have shaped this view in argumentative policy analysis. The later work of Ludwig Wittgenstein undermined the empiricist epistemology of logical positivism, which took as a given the atomistic nature of the relationship between the objects of 'the world' and their meanings as expressed in elementary linguistic expressions. Wittgenstein contended against this view, that to understand reality through language was to engage in complex social practices that defied the atomized logic. According to Wittgenstein, one should not concentrate on the logical independence of things, but on the systemic relationship between them, which invests them with social meaning. For Wittgenstein, language was not an exclusively descriptive medium, but something active that can be used to give meaning to the things, which, in turn, is to constitute social reality (George and Campell 1990, 273). Another important influence was J. L. Austin's performative speech act theory, most famously developed in his 'How to Do Things with Words' (1962), in which he interpreted sentences as forms of actions. Whereas the (neo-positivist) representationalist/correspondence theory of truth believes that there 'is a truth out there' that can be represented through the neutral medium of language, argumentation theory follows the neo-pragmatist line of reasoning, rejecting such a 'picture theory' of language in which the physical properties of the world are considered fixed while language is in the business of meeting the needs of their description. As Richard Rorty, one of the most influential philosophers in the late 20th century put it, 'Truth cannot be out there – cannot exist independently of the human mind – because sentences cannot so exist, or be out there. The world is out there, but descriptions of the world are not. Only descriptions of the world can be true or false. The world on its own – unaided by the describing activities of human being – cannot' (Rorty, 1989: 5). Hence, we can say that there might be all sorts of things 'out there'. There is absolutely no reason to deny the existence of a reality, let's say of the reality of an economic crisis. But if we get humans into our picture, we need to understand that humans tend to interact with 'this reality out there', which for them is neither just there nor is this reality the simple outcome of human activity (Yanow, 1996: 4–9). Many policy studies approaches follow the recommendation of neo-positivist epistemology to engage in hypothesis testing, with the goal to find causal generalizations that are quantitatively testable. In this perspective, language is viewed as a neutral medium to record observation. This conceptualization of language and the idea to search for universally generalizable findings is questioned in the post-positivist, neo-pragmatic perspective of argumentative policy analysis (Fischer, 1998). With it, philosophical realism, the idea that objects, properties, and the relations the world contains exist independently from human thoughts or perceptions of them, is put in doubt, or rejected. It is at this point that the relatively harmless assertion that language is important in the political process is epistemologically 'radicalized' and becomes a sharp dividing point within policy studies: although it is safe to assume that most policy scholars will attribute at least some importance to the role of language in policy, many will be hesitant to give up on philosophical realism, the idea that 'things out there' exist independent of the human mind, a view which also tends to be broadly shared within the more general political science community.

Although philosophical neo pragmatism and anti-representationalism (Rorty) seem to unify the various approaches in argumentative policy analysis, a great deal of variation exists, however, due to the fact that a number of additional philosophical and sociological traditions have taken their impact on argumentative policy analysis. The intellectual roots of the post-positivist movement in political science trace as far back to German sociology and social theory of the late nineteenth century and early twentieth century, in particular to the work of Max Weber, Edmund Husserl, and Alfred Schutz. In sociology, their work constituted an important influence on the evolving sociological schools of symbolic interactionism, critical phenomenology, and ethnomethodology, as developed by Erving Goffman (1974) and Harold Garfinkel (1967). Many scholars have taken up these sociological

traditions in argumentative policy analysis. Whereas positivist social science was searching for universal laws or empirical regularities of human behavior, interpretative approaches were more interested in the unique capacities of the human capacity for creating, communicating, and understanding meaning, which is seen to be located in social practices and texts (Yanow, 1996: 4–9). The hermeneutic approach to data collection provides access to facts *via* the understanding of meaning, which can be reconstructed on the basis of the interpretation of written or spoken texts (*Verstehen*). Thus, the researcher may come to understand the actors' motives to act (both the reasons why and the intentions with which to act), and their interpretation of their own actions and of those of others (Gadamer, 1977). A further key influence on argumentative policy analysis is in the Critical Theory of Jürgen Habermas, who, in his *The Theory of Communicative Action* (1985), had developed a universal pragmatics through a grand synthesis of the major traditions of social theory and philosophy. In particular, Habermas' normative concept of communicative rationality, the process of problem solving and conflict resolution through open discussion, should turn out to be a key inspiration for a number of the authors working in argumentative policy analysis.

Within argumentative policy analysis, there is another strand of reasoning that explicitly wants to go beyond an exclusive focus on how particular actors understand their social worlds and each other. Discourse theory in the tradition of Michel Foucault and others emphasizes that discourse is not just a system of words, but an entity that operates in contexts, in social, economic, or in political contexts. Discourse is a historically specific system of signification in which human and nonhuman phenomena are given meaning and context. In this more structuralistic view, the idea that actors are 'unified subject' who encounter decision-making with an identity already formulated in terms of his or her preferences are rejected. Instead, the notion of actor is questioned in a radical way. Discourses are seen as constitutive of identities, subjects, and objects and thus part of the structure that organizes life (Howarth and Stavrakakis, 2000: 6).

The Foucauldian influence in argumentative policy analysis is historically related to classical structuralism, as paradigmatically developed in the work of Ferdinand de Saussure that, in general, constitutes a key departing point of structuralistic and post-structuralism's critiques of language and meaning. Saussure developed his notion of structure through the analysis of language (Frank, 1989: 20–33; Welsch, 1996: 245–255; Derrida, 1976). For Saussure, structure refers to the ordering principle according to which the lexicon of a language is articulated. This is done in such a way that it can be recognized and mastered as the lexicon of one and the same national language. This process happens in acts of differentiation and connection; that is all elements of expression that make a sign audible and legible must be clearly distinguishable from another, I must be able to distinguish between signs. But, according to Saussure, this is not immediately possible merely based on the meaning of signs, but rather by means of their expression. Meaning itself is amorphous, lacking a clear profile. Therefore, in order to be able to distinguish among meanings, I can do this only by differentiating between sound images or written images – the signifiers (acoustic or written image as opposed to the signified, the concept). Hence, structure is a system of pairs meaning-expression, that is, signified/signifier – such that one and only one signified is assigned to every signifier. The individual signs are exact applications of an invariable law to which they are related, they cannot proliferate out and become uncontrollable (Frank, 1989).

But it is exactly the concept of uncontrollability that post-structuralism brings into the debate. Post-structuralism has taken influence on a number of policy analysis scholars, such as Jacob Torfing (1999) and David Howarth (2000) who, in the context of the 'Essex School of Discourse Analysis' have begun to use the theoretical framework developed by Ernesto Lacalu and Chantal Mouffe (1985) for the purpose of policy studies. In this context, the work of French philosopher Jacques Derrida plays an especially important role for a new reading of language and discourse (1976). For Derrida, the idea of a closed structure reflects metaphysical thinking and a desire for control. Structuralism searches for general ordering principles and universal regularities which make the world capable of technological and scientific mastery, which give clear orientation in a world which otherwise would seem to be out of control. According to Derrida, Saussure has taken an important step in his critique of language by rejecting the idea that words are somehow images of prior existing ideas; by pointing at the phenomenon that meaning is constituted solely by differences between signifiers within a system of interrelations; that we can only think about the redness of an apple in relationship to yellow apples and green pears. But Saussure had insisted on the existence of something like a structuring principle of language. This, argues Derrida, constitutes a move in the language game of metaphysics. Metaphysics not only believes in a transsensual world, it also offers orientation in the form of control and domination, for example by searching for general ordering principles and universal regularities. Derrida contests that structures can decompose, that we are entangled in structures and have no possibility of getting beyond our 'Being-inside-structures'. He says, 'Everything is structure', but he does not mean 'everything' is taxonomy, but, rather, every meaning, every signification, every view of the world is in flux; nothing escapes the play of the differences and thus nothing can be tracked down and fixed in its meaning (1976; Frank, 1989).

Obviously, in this tradition of reflection the relationship between actors and structures is interpreted in a different light than in the hermeneutic tradition. In argumentative policy analysis this has led to a strong interest in phenomena beyond individual interpretations of meaning, such as discourses, narratives and other 'structures of culture' that were seen to play a key role in the shaping of policies (mentioned below). There are, for example, striking differences how in different countries embryo experimentation, cloning, and stem cell research are approaches on the regulatory level. In argumentative policy analysis such differences are not simply explained by reference to differences in political culture, such as between Germany and the United Kingdom, but it is studied how historically grown systems of meaning are interpreted and also reinterpreted into new configurations of meaning and shape policy making (Gottweis, 2002).

If language cannot be used like an instrument to describe reality and the goal of social science is not to produce generalizable findings, what is the knowledge goal of argumentative policy analysis? Although a number of currents occur in argumentative policy analysis, the different approaches share the position that the ontology – epistemology distinction that characterizes the conventional (neo-) positivist inquiry paradigm is mistaken. This view implies that the social sciences deal with multiple realities that are constructed in context; a view that holds obvious implications for the methodology of social inquiry. As a result, in the act of inquiring, discovery and verification are two sides of the same coin (see for instance, Berger and Luckmann, 1967). This insight has implications for the organization of an inquiry process, from the selection of methods to the presentation of the research findings.

Methodologically, in argumentative policy analysis, there tends to be a focus on entering in a 'dialogue with the data', researchers may identify particular instances of empirical reality as exemplars of some conceptual category of social phenomena, tying them together on a higher level of abstraction: a 'grounded' approach to generating theory (Glaser and Strauss, 1967). Though there is no shared methodology in argumentative policy research, the idea of 'grounded theory' explicitly or implicitly plays an important role in much research in the argumentative tradition. 'Grounded theory' means to develop theory inductively from a corpus of data. Typically, a textual corpus (such as field notes) are studied to identify variables and their interrelationships. In this approach, theoretical concepts are elaborated at the onset of a research project, in the form of a conceptual lens and further elaborated and refined in the course of a research project in a close interplay with the progress made in empirical investigation. In a similar way, Flyvberg has spoken of 'contextualism' (Flyvberg, 2001) as an important feature of social science research. Contextualism is considered the solution to the seeming polarity between the idea of reproducible, objective truth that compels universal validity, on the one hand, and sheer relativism ('any interpretation is as valid as the next') on the other. Contextualism implies that the data collected in a case study must be understood in terms of the studied phenomenon's own context, history, and sociality. It features a focus on 'text in context', that is, on *practice* (Flyvberg, 2001: 115). The research does justice to the particulars of the situation under scrutiny as well as to the meanings produced and conveyed by the actors in that situation. Such a focus on practice and 'contextualism' is central in recent developments in 'interpretive' or 'phronetic' social science (Flyvberg, 2001).

Thus, argumentative policy analysis does have a strong commitment to theory development, rigorous testing of prepositions, and the study of the interplay between text and context, the praxis of policy making embedded in its complex social, cultural and economic configurations. But it rejects abstractionism, what it regards as the pursuing of imaginary goals, such as finding insights of general validity or identifying 'laws of society'. Argumentative policy analysis has an interest in variables and their relationship but takes a cautious approach towards questions of causality, dependence, and independence of factors, and it views policy as a complex configuration in which the material (such as industrial production or unemployed workers) is inextricably linked with the immaterial (such as statistical data and representational strategies) in a complex scenography (Maingueneau, 2002: 71–73) located in space and time.

ARGUMENTATION: VARIATIONS ON A THEME

The phenomenon of argumentation is at the core of argumentative policy and gives it its name. But, despite a certain shared philosophical and epistemological heritage, there is hardly one shared notion of argumentation dominant in argumentative policy analysis (Fischer, 2003). This is a strength, but also a weakness. The many variations on the theme of argumentation display the plurality of approaches in argumentative policy analysis, but the fact that different scholars use different notions of argumentation has also occasionally created some confusion and might have hampered the diffusion of argumentative policy analysis.

Majone, for example, defines argument as 'the link that connects data and information with the conclusions of an analytical study. The structure of the argument will typically be a complex blend of factual statements and subjective evaluations' (Majone, 1989: 10). For Majone, this definition of argument and argumentation is crucial, because it determines his project of policy analysis: the task of the policy analyst is not the one of the nonpartisan, technical problem solver but as a producer of policy arguments; the analyst needs to probe assumptions critically and produce and evaluate evidence.

But Majone, and this is a great element of the elegance in his approach, does not seem to attempt to embed his concept of argumentation in any other theoretical context than the classical Greek tradition of rhetoric. Within argumentative policy analysis, an important strand of scholarship has begun to locate its understanding of argumentation in the tradition of the theory of narration and discourse theory. Narrative and discourse are structural phenomena that underscore that the boundaries of politics, science, and technology are always drawn within the larger semiotic context of the different stories that give a society its identity and hold it together. Theories of narrative and discourse have played an important role in the further development of argumentative policy analysis by providing a new, sophisticated and elaborated theoretical approach for linking argumentation with social, literary and linguistic theory. They specify the Argumentative Turn's doubt in the idea of the omnipotent, rational, utility maximizing human actor, and show how deeply embedded political actors are in complex structures of culture, language and symbolic orientation.

But what precisely is a 'narrative', one of these much used and often little understood terms? 'The narratives of the world are numberless', Roland Barthes begins his famous essay on narrative theory. Narrative is present in myth, legend, novella, cinema, weather reports, government documents, political speeches, and articles about molecular biology. News of the world comes to us in the form of 'stories', our dreams narrate about the subconscious, and for each of us there is a personal history, the narratives of our lives, which enable us to construe who we are and where we are going (O'Neill, 1994: 11) However, it is only recently that the study of narratives has emerged as a field of interest for a variety of fields in the social and human sciences, from literary theory to philosophy, economics, ethnography, and, more currently, political science.

This 'narrativist turn' must be contextualized as part of the broader anti-representationalist (Rorty) movement identified above as the breakdown of the logico-deductive models of reason and knowledge and of transcendental truth claims. The anti-representationalist perspective asserted that there is no objective reality that can be universally represented through a neutral medium of language. The methods of natural science, as interpreted by logical positivism, were seen as inadequate for an understanding of society and culture. This development opened the way for new approaches, one of which is narrative analysis. As Wallace Martin states, 'Mimesis and narration have returned from their marginal status as aspects of "fiction" to inhabit the very center of other disciplines as modes of explanation necessary for an understanding of life' (Wallace, 1986: 7).

The exact nature of narratives and their relationship to politics requires explication. On the most general level, narrativity is the representation of real events that arise out of the desire to have real events display the coherence, integrity, fullness, and closure of an image of life that is and can only be imaginary (White, 1981: 23). Narratives bring elements of clarity, stability, and order into what usually tends to be the complicated and contradictory world of politics. This power to create order is an attractive quality that makes narratives essential for the shaping of policies, the settling of conflicts, or the securing of legitimacy for political action.

Narratives can function as 'networks of meaning', which establish relationships between varieties of different entities. They problematize, enroll, and mobilize persons, procedures, artifacts, and representations in the pursuit of a particular policy goal. Thus, they do not only describe realities, they are also part of the process of persuasion (see, for a critical view of this, Fischer, 2003: 181). The most important features of a narrative require further clarification. First, events of some sort, such as the October Revolution in Russia, are a central necessity if we are to speak of a narrative. These events constitute the raw materials of narratives, which arrange them in a temporal and causal order. Times, places, and characters interact in a complex fashion in the narrative transaction. Narrative events are a function of time, setting (place), and characters of both time and place (Wallace, 1986: 124). Narratives depend on texts. Text is a concrete and unchanging product, words upon a page. It is only through the text that we acquire knowledge of the narration. At the same time it is through narrative that the text manages its articulation in time and orchestrates the relations of its writers and readers. The sentence 'Bangkok is one of the most polluted cities in the world' constitutes a text or statement. Set into the context of a report on new strategies for pollution control drafted by the Thai government, the sentence becomes part of a narrative and assumes narrative character. As soon as any story becomes a story by being told, it gives rise to a proliferation of possible intersecting meanings and enters the realm of textuality. Textuality refers to the voluntary and involuntary interactivity of authors, readers, and texts, the phenomenon of intertextuality (O'Neill, 1994: 23–25; Wells, 1996). Two critical articulations of narrativity in political discourse are political metanarratives and policy narratives, a notion that has been broadly taken up in the argumentative policy analysis literature. (Stone, 1997; Roe, 1994; Hajer, 1993; Fischer, 2003).

Political metanarratives describe general concepts and values of the social order, and provide for individual orientation and location in the symbolic universe. Metanarratives offer a conceptual framework that provides a polity and its subjects with an imagined collective political identity situated in historical time. In this way the discourse of modernization, dominant state projects such as welfare state or neo-liberalism, or the idea of democracy can be construed as elements of the political metanarrative. Though rather broad and general in content, metanarratives are nevertheless also specific. For example, though seemingly universal, the idea of modernization has rather different meanings for example in China and in France. This is a function of the intertextual nature of metanarratives, which are always linked to specificities of historical experience and culture. Metanarratives are not simply 'out there'. They are performative practices; they do things with words; they are always written, rewritten, read and reinterpreted. Thus, there cannot be any 'general theory' of political metanarratives. The study of political metanarratives is always the study of interwoven practices taking place in contexts of time, space, and sociality. Therefore, the analysis of political metanarratives requires careful empirical examination of specific settings, such as modernization narratives in France in the 1950s or in China in the 1990s. The ensemble of the metanarratives dominant in a particular society constitutes the political imaginary. Individuals see and experience the world through a political imaginary, a cognitive mapping and its accompanying values. The political imaginary is a social construct that is part of the available repertoire of political visions and identifications in one's social situation. It consists of the configurations of the most common representations, stories, ideals, and so on defining a particular social space and its boundaries. (Keller, 1989; Baudrillard, 1976). Roe uses the concept of the metanarrative in related but altogether different fashion: he views the policy analyst's task to generate metanarratives by comparing conflicting narratives in policy conflict and to identify ways how opposite narratives can still relate to each other. The purpose of this exercise is to determine how a metanarrative recast a problem in such a way as to make it possible for opponents to act on an issue over which they still disagree (Roe, 1994: 156).

Policy narratives are more specific and describe the frames or plots used in the social construction of the fields of action for policy making, for governmental activities from environmental to technology policy. These frames or plots are principles of organization that govern events and give orientation to actors in a policy field (Gottweis, 1998). Narratives describe a structure of relationships that endows the events contained in the account with a meaning by integrating these events into a narrative. Policy narratives or frames are constructed and used to make sense out of events. Their 'raw material' are the dispersed events, such particularly exciting and economically promising research in a sub-field of genetics that takes place in the laboratories of a number of important medical schools in a particular country, the pharmaceutical industry of this country, the world economic situation, and financial resources of the country's Ministry of Research. A policy narrative might begin to take shape when the Ministry of Research argues in an internal paper that special support should be given to researchers working in the newly emerging genetics sub-field because they are working in such a promising area with high economic potential that might eventually help the international competitiveness of the country. The construction of such a narrative would also typically involve references to certain metanarratives, such as statements about the importance of industrial policy for capitalist development, the importance to do everything for the health of the nation, or about the general character of capitalist development. Political metanarratives endow policy narratives with a higher authority and legitimacy as they tie policies to the revered hold systems of values and identity codes of a community.

But, like with many concepts in argumentative policy analysis, there is also not one broadly shared notion of narrative in argumentative policy analysis. Hajer speaks of storylines as a generative sort of narrative that allows actors to draw upon various discursive categories to give meaning to specific phenomena (Hajer, 1993: 56). The focus in his concept of narrative qua storyline is less on narratives as sources for attributing meaning and sense to a complex policy setting, but as a semiotic tool for the creation of what he calls 'discourse coaltions'. Once a discourse is formulated, ' … it will produce story lines on specific problems, employing the conceptual machinery of the new discourse (e.g. Sustainable development). A discourse coalition is thus the ensemble of a set of story lines, the actors that utter these story lines, and the practices that conform to these story lines, all organized around a discourse' (47). In this respect, Hajer's concept of the story line is more distant to narrative theory, and closer to Laclau and Mouffe's (1985) and the Essex School's notion of the 'empty signifier', that refers to the fact that important notions, in political struggle, such as environment or nation are not characterized by special density of meaning, but, on the contrary, by a certain emptying of their content which strengthens their role in the discursive struggle (Torfing, 1999: 98). Hajer exemplifies his concept of discourse coalition by showing how in the United Kingdom the acid rain concept and the story line to which it gave rise brought a variety of actors with very different background and beliefs together and thus created a new dynamics in environmental policy making. Roe gives special attention to how narrative policy analysis can be constructed as to examine competing narratives in policy controversies (Roe, 1994). Rein and Schön speak, in vicinity to Goffman's terminology, of frames as 'policy positions resting on underlying structures of belief, perception and appreciation that define what counts as fact or argument and that are resistant to resolution by appeal to facts or reasoned argument' (Schön and Rein, 1994: 23). In their key study 'Frame Reflection,' 'they develop an elaborated framework of analysis for policy analysis and show how policy makers use frames for dealing with problems, manage solutions and find compromise. An explicit goal of frame analysis in the tradition of Rein and Schön seems to be to somehow transcend frames via what they call frame-reflection, a process guided by Kuhn, Habermas, Foresters and others to somehow arrive at viable solutions for policy problems through the process of "thinking through" the constraining and often confusing nature of frames in a struggle to avoid the "relativist trap" ' (38–49).

An obvious question arising from narrative policy analysis is where do political metanarratives and policy narrative come from? Apparently, narratives could be construed as 'tools' used by policy actors in policy controversy. But are political narratives just vehicles and instruments for skillful actors and interests in the game of power? There is a strong tendency in argumentative policy analysis for a more 'structuralist' interpretation of narrative. Discourse, in particular historical and political discourses, are endowed with 'narrative structure' They are narrativizing discourses, as Hayden White puts it, discourses without a narrator. No one seems to speak and the events seem to speak for themselves (White, 1987: 202). Narrativizing discourse refers to the numerous kinds of narratives that every culture disposes for those of its members (such as administrators) who might wish to draw upon them for the encodation and transmission of messages (e.g., about pollution control). In other words, there are people and interests behind narratives who bring narratives into the world. But these individuals give birth to narratives only within the confinements of the available discursive possibilities. Actors cannot freely choose the narratives they deploy. The given discursive possibilities describe the large reservoir of narratives, which can be mobilized for political purposes. For example, whereas it had certainly been for decades within the realm of discursive possibilities to craft neo-liberalism into a new political metanarrative, it was not before the 1980s that neo-liberalism actually achieved the status of a new political metanarrative in many countries. In this context, Foucault has emphasized the importance of the archive, the general system of the formation and transformation of statements existing at a given period within a particular society. This archive determines what may be spoken of in discourse, which statements survive or are repressed and what individuals or groups have access to particular kinds of discourses (Smart, 1985: 48). However, it is important to see that the regulated and systematic character of a discourse does not imply a sense of closure. The rules delimiting the sayable or thinkable are not just those internal to discourse, but include rules of combination with other discourses. In the European Community during the 1980s, for example, the rise of neo-liberalism to the status of a political metanarrative was closely connected to a discourse of 'Europessimism', the creation of an image of Europe that was increasingly unable to compete with nations such as Japan and the United States. In fact, the systemic character of discourse implies its articulation with other discourses.

In this way it could be stated that discourse is always caught in a web of materiality that is a historical product. Discourse is not just a system of words, but an entity that operates in contexts – in social, economic, or in political contexts. But discourses are not simply reflections of these contexts; rather, they are complex mediations between various codes by which reality is to be assigned possible meaning (White, 1987: 202). For instance, political discourse on industrial development that discusses different strategies for industry support cannot be separated from practices in companies to which it refers. At the same time, the objects of this discourse do not coincide with the range of activities and phenomena they systematize as central to specific discourses, though they bear relations to them. For example, industrial development discourse is not equivalent to the investment and product development decisions of companies, though there is a specific relationship between these two domains of the theoretical and the material. We can say that, to some extent, context is already in discourse, that discourse bears the traces of content, and that the study of discourse involves the question as to what extent discourses are able to come to terms with contexts and vice versa. Discourse should be seen as a practice of production that can be characterized as material, intertextual and complex, always inscribed in relation to other discourses and thus part of a 'discursive economy' (Henriques, Holway, Urwin, Venn and Walkerdine, 1984: 105–106).

Industrial production, for example, is governed by a proliferation of discourses and it cannot exist prior to or outside of its articulation with a set of other social and political discourses in concrete historical conjunctures (Daly, 1991: 100). Discursive formations like modern biotechnology are intertwined with other disparate factors, such as institutions or economic forces, which establish flexible relationships and interactions that merge into a single apparatus (Dryfus and Rabinow, 1983: 121). The fact that one discursive formation gains influence over another, that it becomes hegemonic, is related to the degree of congruence and complementarity that this discursive formation has within a given discursive constellation and within an apparatus or historical bloc. Rising unemployment rates, lack of success in high-technology fields such as in information electronics, and the discourse of Europessimism are examples of such a constellation in Europe, in which neo-liberal narratives began to gain political currency.

By introducing the concepts of discourse and narrative in argumentative policy analysis (Fischer, 2003: 73–94; 161–180), the 'Argumentative Turn' has contributed significantly to reshaping the agenda or rhetorical analysis in argumentation theory. Discourse and narrative provide crucial and sophisticated conceptual tools for argumentative analysis and link micro- and macro-levels of analysis, structure with action, culture with citizen, and institutions with everyday life practices. They bring the notion that 'language matters' to life by introducing an array of analytic techniques to deal with phenomena like language, symbols, talk, and interaction and their role in the play of power.

THE POLITICS OF ARGUMENTATION

One of the key characteristics of argumentative policy analysis is its conceptualization of the role of policy analysis and the policy analyst in the policy process. As already shown, argumentative policy analysis sweepingly rejects the idea of the 'neutral' 'objective' policy analyst qua social technician and, rather, espouses the idea of the policy analyst as something like a lawyer (Majone), advocate, deeply engaged in the policy process itself. Although authors such as Majone and Stone have not gone further than rejecting the 'objectivist' idea of the policy analysist, in the wake of Fischer and Forester's 'Argumentative Turn' and Dryzek's 'Discursive Democracy' the notion of argumentative policy analysis as fostering and encouraging political participation and deliberation has become very influential. With the departure of the idea that the main task of the policy analyst is to identify solutions for objective problems, the image of the professional expert is reconstructed as one of the facilitators of public learning and political empowerment (Fischer, 2003). Torgerson argues that 'just as positivism underlies the dominant technical orientation in policy analysis, so the postpositivist orientation now points to a participatory project' (Torgerson, 1986: 241). Forester (1999), Healy (1997), and Innes (1999) have advocated communicative policy analysis, the idea that the main task of the policy analyst is to facilitate process of deliberation and to help planners to critically reflect on their own discursive practices. Underlying this 'policy model' is an approach towards communication and argumentation strongly influenced by the late work of Jürgen Habermas. In his 'Theory of Communicative Action', (1985, originally in German, 1981), Habermas has developed a notion of 'communicative rationality', which defines as rational what is communicatively, intersubjectively justified or justifiable. Rationality comes into existence via intersubjectively grounded argumentation. This advocacy for a 'communicative policy analysis' is in most detail elaborated in Dryzek's 'Discursive Democracy', which discusses Habermas's critique of instrumental rationality, the idea to devise, select, and effect good means to clarified ends, and the alternative model of a communicated rationality, oriented towards the coordination of interactions via communication

(Dryzek, 1990). This idea of policy analysis as a deliberative, participatory, communicative project can be followed from Torgesen, via Dryzek, the 'Argumentative Turn' and, most recently, in 'Deliberative Policy Analysis' by Hajer and Wagenaar (2003), who bluntly state that policy analysis *is* deliberative (21). Clearly, this 'politics of argumentation', the advocacy for a particular political engagement of policy analysis, is consistent with the dominant identification of the nature of policy analysis as being engaged in the clarification of argumentation, a process that by definition is open-ended and can hardly be defined as monopolized by any form of expertise. On the other hand, it cannot be ignored that an interesting tension exists between the basically idealistic idea of communicative rationality, the idea that, given the right domination-free circumstances, individuals are capable of making reasonable, informed, independent decisions benefiting the common good, and the embrace of the work of Foucault and other post-Enlightment thinkers by many authors in argumentative policy analysis. Traditionally, the Derrida/Foucault tradition of discourse analysis has been rather critical towards the last heroic efforts of the Frankfurt School personified by Jürgen Habermas to save the Enlightment project and the idea that reason can be brought into the world through discussion and communication. Although the comprehensive work of Jürgen Habermas in the field of language, argumentation and pragmatics has been to a considerable extent ignored in argumentative policy analysis, his idea of communicative rationality and, in particular, the underlying human model and political philosophy, have been highly influential on it. This has led to the following paradox: on the one hand we see in argumentative policy analysis a considerable influence of a Foucault-inspired understanding of discourse as far as epistemology goes, but great reluctance to deal with the underlying rather more pessimistic Foucaudian/structuralist critique of the idea of the human subject and the potential of humans for free, domination-free interaction when it comes to normative-political positions. It seems that quite a number of authors writing in the argumentative tradition can relate well to a structuralist relativization of the autonomy of human action for the purpose of discourse analysis per se, without being prepared to consider the corresponding normative-political consequences. The very optimistic approach towards 'collaborative and participatory policy making' of many proponents in argumentative policy analysis seems to be especially problematic in a situation, when, like at the beginning of the 21st century, many Western and non-Western governments have enthusiastically embraced the idea of participatory democracy as a new material and symbolic method to create political stability and, to paraphrase Ian Hacking, 'to make up' a participatory citizenry as part of its governance agenda.

Via the Habermasian 'Communicative Action' model another important feature of argumentative policy analysis has been introduced in argumentative policy analysis: a certain tendency towards cognitivism. Discourse ethics in the Habermas tradition starts from the assumption that moral problems are capable of being solved in a rational and cognitive way. However, students of rhetoric and persuasion in politics can hardly subscribe to the notion that policy disputes are always solved or settled by appeal to reason. Although argumentative policy analysis clearly recognizes this phenomenon, much analysis in this tradition tends to pay only scant attention to phenomena such as passions and emotions in policy making, probably because of an understanding of discourse and argumentation that tends to reduce argumentation to the operation of logos than to pathos and ethos, which, in the tradition of Greek rhetoric, have received much attention. In fact, there seems to be a tendency in argumentative policy analysis to confine reasoning to deliberative and judicial reasoning as apart and separated from manipulative, negative rhetoric. Propaganda is clearly differentiated from 'genuine argumentation', and in this respect argumentative policy analysis seems to be closer to the Platonic ideal for science as a search for truth than to the Aristotelian/Sophistic tradition (Turnbull, 2003). In its attempt to avoid what is seen as one of the main mistakes in neo-positivist policy analysis, namely the confusion of reason with instrumental rationality, the communicative model suggests communicative rationality as the democratic version of bringing reason into the world. But the underlying construction of the policy process is guided by rationality assumptions, in particular by the idea that the policy process needs to be structured in a way to allow for the operation of communicative rationality. This, however, constitutes a new form of constraint for the notion of reason. There is a line in reasoning about politics from Plato to Kant and Hegel that emphasizes reason as the sound foundation of politics, versus uncontrolled, passionate behavior leading to disaster. Historically, the image of the wild and uncontrolled passions as a deep threat to humankind and civilization is deeply rooted in Western philosophy. For Plato, passion is the name of a problem for which reason is the answer (Meyer, 1991: 38). Deep philosophical suspicion concerning the dark powers of passion continue in the history of thought also in philosophers like Kant or Hegel, for whom reason was describing the path to freedom and truth, and passion threatened the moral and society order (Meyer, 1991; Svasek, 2002: 13). However, we might also interpret passions in a more benign fashion. And this conceptualization of passions also has important implications for argumentative policy analysis. For Aristotle, emotions were 'all those feelings that so change men as to affect their judgement' (Aristotle, 1995). For Aristotle there was no contradiction between reason and emotion. Aristotle construed thought and belief as the efficient cause of emotion and showed that emotional response is intelligent behavior open to reasoned persuasion. As W. W Fortenbaugh puts it in his classical study on Aristotle and Emotions: 'When men are angered, they are not victims of some totally irrational force. Rather, they are responding in accordance with the thought of unjust result. Their belief may be erroneous and their anger unreasonable, but their behavior is intelligent and cognitive in the sense that it is grounded upon a belief which may be criticised and even altered by argumentation' (Fortenbaugh, 1975: 17). Thus, it might be useful to return to a close reading of the Classical tradition of rhetoric in order to advance a more comprehensive model of argumentation.

Much later, in Western philosophy, this tradition of reasoning was further developed by David Hume in his 'Treatise on Human Nature, (1739). Hume famously argued that reason itself could never motivate us to act and, further, that it could not oppose the only true motive of the will, our desires, or what Hume calls the passions. No doubt, despite its negative image in the history of philosophy, emotions have figured largely as a topic of interest in a variety of scientific contexts, such as in psychiatry and psychology. But much of the work on emotions in this direction has been characterized by an essentializing attitude towards emotions as they are conceptualized as predictable outcomes of universal psychobiological processes or 'things' the social systems must deal with (Abu-Lughod and Lutz, 1990: 2–3) In contrast, emotions could also be conceptualized as a discursive practice. Emotions belong to the repertoire of rhetoric, and emotional display and the language of passion may very well coexist with argumentative and ethical discourse. This rhetorical view of emotions allow us to explore how speech and language provide the means by which local views of emotions have their effects and take on significance. Thus, this view emphasizes the interpretation of emotions as pragmatic acts and communicative performances, and thus as modes of argumentation. Emotions, then, should not be seen as 'things' being carried by the vehicle of discourse and rhetoric, but as a form of rhetorical praxis that creates effects in the world (Abu-Lughod and Lutz, 1990: 11–3; Lutz and White, 1986).

Emotional discourse is always bound up with structures and hierarchies of power. It is part of complex scenographies in which argumentation takes place. Power relations determine what or what not can be said about self and emotion, and emotional discourse can establish, assert, or reinforce power or status differences (Abu-Lughod and Lutz, 1990: 14). When, in a parliamentary debate about the pros and cons of human embryonic stem cell research, a member of the US Senate tells moving stories about his son who suffers from diabetes, scientists invite wheelchair-bound Christopher Reeve to tell an audience his story of despair and hope, or when pro-life advocates talk about baby farms producing organs, we see not only the classical instruments of rhetoric being used to move the passions of audiences, but also efforts to stabilize or destabilize existing structures and practices in research and medical practice. Policy analysis needs to pay attention to such aspects of political decision-making. To some extent in subfields of political science, such as in public opinion or electoral research, doubts are few that emotions and persuasion matter in politics. However, as uncertainty becomes more pronounced in many policy fields, it might be useful to reconsider pathos and emotion not as a 'force' on its own, as a 'fact' of political life', but as being intrinsically linked to the everyday practice of policy making, as a rhetorical device that takes considerable impact in many policy areas and is a key element of policy argumentation.

PERSPECTIVES

Since the late 1980s, argumentative policy analysis has become an influential tendency in policy analysis. While argumentative policy analysis is a pluralistic movement, inspired by not necessarily synonymous philosophical schools such as hermeneutics and structuralism, it nevertheless is united by an epistemological perspective critical of philosophical realism and a common focus on language and argumentation as the foundation of the policy process.

The pluralistic character of argumentative policy analysis has led to a growing number of approaches and theoretical conceptualizations, a development that has not always helped the building of a 'core approach' in this field. There is a clear hesitation in argumentative policy analysis to develop 'models' of the policy process. This is not surprising, since a contextualist understanding of social science, the emphasis on meaning and interpretation, and the critical attitude towards 'generalizable'

findings constitute a natural obstacle to abstract and universal modes of explanation. By contrast, there has been much emphasis on more ethnographic kinds of studies that convey a close sense of context. It is a common assessment in the policy literature that argumentative policy analysis has focus much on a 'critique of neo-positivism' and the expense of the development of more finely grained conceptual frameworks of analysis. It could be added that, in the recent literature, the focus on the ethnographic richness of studies, together with the emphatic promotion of deliberative democracy, has led to a further concentration of analysis on dimensions that are probably neither key nor necessarily positive for the further development of argumentative policy analysis. Although ethnographic richness might easily lead to studies in which too many trees hinder the sight of the wood, neither detail nor political orientation can substitute for better-clarified conceptual frameworks of analysis. At the same time, there is a certain ambition in argumentative policy analysis to link up policy analysis with political and social analysis. It might, however, be helpful to withstand 'grand social theorizing' to some extent and, instead, focus more on the development of 'middle range theory' and the further elaboration of a conceptual framework of analysis, just it has been done so successfully in the work of Majone (1989) Stone (1997) and Fischer (1995).

Simultaneously, we see a strong influence of planning theory in argumentative policy analysis that might have been an important reason for the dominant role of communicative policy making and deliberative policy analysis as the normative orientation of choice for many scholars in argumentative policy analysis. Whereas, in the context of planning, the local level is highly important and lends itself well to participatory modes of policy making, considerations of policy making processes on other levels of policy making, such as on the national, European, or global level, seem to call for new or additional normative orientations. It is simply rather unlikely that anything of significance will be decided on a global or EU level via deliberative planning

Figure 27.1

mechanisms. Furthermore, it can be hardly denied that policy making typically cannot be reduced to communicative action in a Habermasian sense; instead it also involves other forms of persuasion, such as manipulation, the mobilization of fear, trust, and hope. It seems that in many ways argumentative policy analysis, with its tendency towards cognitivism, has turned a blind eye on such phenomena, and it might be useful to leave behind this Platonian tradition of reflection on argumentation.

It is precisely Greek rhetoric, in particular the tradition of Aristotle, re-read by Perleman, Meyer, contemporary linguistic theory (Maingueneau) and neopragmatism that might offer an interesting conceptual approach for a broader conceptual framework for argumentative analysis.

If we look at a political discourse, as shown in Figure 27.1, we can understand its mode of argumentation as being dominated by one of the three elements – logos, ethos, and pathos – that take on different weight in the argumentation (Adam, 1999). In the Aristotelian tradition, logos instructs and applies reason, ethos refers to the 'morality' of the speaker, and pathos has the function to move and refers to the passions. Any text or genre of discourse can be analyzed with respect to its dominant modes of argumentation and related dominant constructions and presentations of individual and collective selves. Although a mode of argumentation dominated by logos is characterized by reasoning, the presentation of facts, evidence and empirical proofs, pathos

operates with empathy, sympathy, sensibilities, and ethos with trust, respect authority, honesty, credibility, and considerations of the desirable. Any communication or speech act combines elements of logos, pathos, and ethos, though different weight might be put by a speaker on these three elements of persuasion. The concept of ethos plays an especially interesting role in this elaboration. Maingueneau suggests that, with the concept of the ethos, the archive (in the sense of Foucault, as the organization of the discursive practices in a society) takes on a 'bodily form'. Thus, ethos is not only defined as by a discursive position, but as a 'translation' of this discursive position as body, voice, sound, and gesture, and it opens itself up to a series of identifications (Maingueneau, 1991: 183–4). In this perspective, argumentative policy analysis introduces the rich scenography (Maingueneau, 2002) of studying 'real people' and their rich repertoires of performance and interaction during the praxis of policy making. Such a move is as much in tune with Greek philosophy and, for example, its study in oratory, as with contemporary sociology, such as the work of Ervin Goffman and contemporary linguistics (Adam, 1994; Meyer, 1986, 1991, 1994).

For policy analysis this could mean a further reconsideration and extension of the notion of argumentation. Deliberative democracy models are essentially based on the assumption of a dialogical model for arriving at a truth consensus. There is nothing wrong with this, but the tradition of rhetoric brings back to our attention crucial factors of the political, such as emotions and ethos as elements of the policy process, in which decision-making is not only a matter of constructing realities and identities but also an interactive, situated process in which truth is not only a matter of construction, but also of credibility, emotional state and belief in personal qualities. If politics, and, implicitly, policy making is about 'who gets what, when, and how, to paraphrase Harold Lasswell, then Lasswell's 'how' question can be understood as an invitation to acknowledge the rich complexities of the policy process and to analyse them in this richness, that, among other things involves such disperse phenomena as fear, anger, trust, and respect. We then have to pay close attention to the performative and situated dimensions of persuasion (Hajer, 2005), a key element in the decision-making process, and try to better understand the intermediation of pathos, ethos, and logos, or, in other words, the intersecting of argumentation, feelings, and status of speakers. What thus comes into view is the complex scenography of policy making, its argumentative performativity and location in time and space. Such an approach is certainly compatible with the idea of deliberative policy analysis but also opens up new avenues of analysis for policy making beyond the local level and for the broad variety of strategies being used in policy making. The role of the policy analyst would still be the one of the 'clarifier' of issues of public deliberation, as envisioned by Lasswell, without being limited to the (typical local) role of the 'deliberative practitioner' (Forester). This approach would also open up the normative horizon for the consideration of political innovation beyond participatory democracy. One of the classical questions of liberal democracy, namely how to cultivate appropriate compassion, and to link emotions and passions with the polity (Nussbaum, 2001: 422–423) might have to be asked anew by a policy analysis that has at its core a comprehensive understanding of argumentation.

REFERENCES

Adam, Jean-Michel (1999). *Linguistique Textuelle et Analyse des pratiqueses Discursives*, Nathan: Paris.

Aristotle (1995). *The Art of Rhetoric*. London: Penguin.

Abu-Lughod, Lily and Lutz, Catherine (1990). 'Introduction: Emotion, Discourse, and the Politics of Everyday Life', in Abu-Lughod and Lutz (eds), Language and the Politics of Emotion. Cambridge: Cambridge University Press, 1–23.

Austin, John, L. (1992). *How to do Things with Words*. Cambridge, Mass.

Baudrillard, Jean (1976). L'échange symbolique et la mort. Paris: Gallimard.

Benveniste, Emile (1972). *Problèmes de linguistique générale*, Volume II. Paris : Gallimard.

Berger, Peter L. and Luckmann, Thomas (1967). *The Social Construction of Reality: A Treatise in the Sociology of Knowledge*. London: Penguin Books.

Braun, Dietmar and Busch, Andreas (2000). *Public Policy and Political Ideas*. London: Edward Elgar.

Breton, Philippe and Gauthier, Gilles (2000). *Histoire des Théories de l'Argumentation*. Paris : La Decouverte.

Daly, Glyn (1991). The Discursive Construction of Economic Space: Logics of Organization and Disorganization. *Economy and Society*, Vol. 20, 79–102.

Danzinger, Marie (1995). "Policy Analysis Postmodernized: Some Political and Pedagogical Ramifications." *Policy Studies Journals* 23, No. 3, 435–50.

Derrida, Jacques (1976). *Of Grammatology*. Baltimore: Johns Hopkins University Press.

Dryfus, Hubert L. and Rabinow, Paul (1983). Michel Foucault: Beyond Structuralism and Hermeneutics. Chicago: Chicago University Press.

Dryzek, John S. (1990). Discursive Democracy: Politics, Policy, and Political Science. Cambridge: Cambridge University Press.

Fischer, Frank (1980). *Politics, Values, and Public Policy: The Problem of Methodology*. Boulder, CO: Westview Press.

Fischer, Frank (1995). *Evaluating Public Policy*. Chicago: Nelson Hall Publishers.

Fischer, Frank (1998). 'Beyond Empiricism.' *Policy Studies Journal* 26, 129–146.

Fischer, Frank (2000). *Citizens, Experts, and the Environment: the Politics of Local Knowledge*. Durham: Duke University Press.

Fischer, Frank (2003). *Reframing Public Policy: Discursive Politics and Deliberative Practices*. Oxford: Oxford University Press.

Flyvberg, Bent (2001). *Making Social Science Matter. Why Social Inquiry Fails and How it can Succeed Again*. Cambridge University Press.

Forester, John (1985) (ed.). *Critical Theory and Public Life*. Cambridge, MA: MIT Press.

Forester, John (1993). *Critical Theory, Public Policy, and Planning Practices*. Albany: SUNY Press.

Forester, John (1999). *The Deliberative Practioner: Encouraging Participatory Planning Processes*. Cambridge, MA: Cambridge University Press.

Fortenbaugh, W.W. (1975). Aristotle on Emotion. London: Duckworth.

Foucault, Michel (1972). The Archaeology of Knowledge and the Discourse on Language. New York: Pantheon.

Frank, Manfred (1989). *What is Neostructuralism?* Minneapolis: University of Minnesota Press.

Gadamer, Hans (1977). Philosophical Hermeneutics. Berkeley: University of California Press.

Garfinkel, Harold (1967). Studies in Ethnomethodology. Englewoods Cliff, NJ: Prentice Hall

George, Jim and Campell, David (1990). 'Patterns of Dissent and the Celebration of Difference: Critical Social Theory and International Relations.' *International Studies Quarterly*, Vol. 34, 269–293, 273.

Glaser, Barney G. and Strauss, Anselm L. (1976). Discovery of Grounded Theory: Strategies for Qualitative Research. Chicago: Aldine.

Goffman, Erving (1974). Frame Analysis. Cambridge, MA: Harvard University Press.

Gottweis, Herbert (1998). Governing Molecules: The Discursive Politics of Genetic Engineering in Europe and in the United States. Cambridge, MA: MIT Press.

Gottweis, Herbert (2002). "Stem Cell Policies in the United States and in Germany: Between Bioethics and Regulation. *Policy Studies Journal* 30, 444–469.

Gottweis, Herbert (2003). Theoretical Strategies of Post-structuralist Policy Analysis: Towards an Analytics of Politics, 247–265. In Hajer and Wagenaar, 2003.

Habermas, Jürgen (1985). Theory of Communicative Action, Vols. 1 and 2. Boston: Beacon Press.

Hajer, Maarten A. (1993). "Discourse Coalitions and the Institutionalization of Practice: the Case of Acid Rain in Britain," in Frank Fischer and Jon Forester (eds.), *The Argumentative Turn in Policy Analysis and Planning*. Durham: Duke University Press, 43–76.

Hajer, M. A. and Wagenaar, H. Eds. (2003). *Deliberative Policy Analysis: Understanding Governance in the Network Society*. Cambridge: Cambridge University Press.

Hajer, M. A. (2005). Setting the Stage: A Dramaturgy of Policy Deliberation Administration & Society, 624–647.

Hall, Peter (1986). *Governing the Economy: The Politics of State Intervention in Britain and in France*. New York: Oxford University Press.

Healey, P. (1997). *Collaborative Planning: Shaping Places in Fragmented Societies*. London: MacMillan.

Henriques, Julian, Holway, Wendy, Urwin, Cathy, Venn, Couse and Walkerdine, Valerie (1984). Changing the Subject: Psychology, Social Regulation and Subjectivity. London: Methuen.

Howarth, David, and Stavrakakis, Yannis (2000). *Discourse Theory and Political Analysis: Identities. Hegemonies and Social Change*. Manchester: Manchester University Press.

Hume, David (1739). *A Treatise on Human Nature*. Mossner, Ernst C. editor, Viking Press, 1986.

Innes, J. E. (1996). 'Planning through Consensus Building.' *Journal of the Americam Planning Association* 62, 460–472.

Innes, J. E. and Booher, D. E. (1999). 'Concensus Building as Role Playing and Bricolage: Toward a Theory of Collaborative Planning.' *Journal of the American Planning Association* 65, 9–26.

Keller, Douglas (1989). *Jean Baudrillard: From Marxism to Postmodernism and Beyond*. Stanford: Stanford University Press.

Lacalu, Ernesto and Mouffe, Chantal (1985). *Hegemony and Socialist Strategy. Towards a Radical Democratic Politics*. London: Verso.

Lasswell, H. D. (1951). 'The Policy Orientation.' The Policy Sciences. H. D. Lasswell and D. Lerner. Stanford: Stanford University Press.

Lasswell, H.D. (1971). *A Pre-View of Policy Sciences*. New York: American Elsevier.

Lutz, Catherine and White, Geoffey M. (1986). 'The Anthropology of Emotions'. *Annual Review of Anthropology*, 15, 405–35.

Lyotard, Jean-Francois (1979). *The Post-Modern Condition*. Manchester: Manchester University Press, 1984.

Maingueneau, D. (1991) L'Analyse du Discourse. Paris: Hachette.

Maingueneau, Dominique (2002). *Analyser Les Textes de Communication*. Paris : Nathan.

Majone G. (1989). *Evidence, Argument and Persuasion in the Policy Process*. New Haven, Conn: Yale University Press.

Martin, Wallace (1986). *Recent Theories of Narrative*. Ithaca: Cornell University Press.

Meyer, Michel (1986). *De la Problématologie. Philososphie, Science et Langage*. Bruxelles: Pierre Mardaga.

Meyer, Michel (1991). *Le Philosophe et les Passions: Esquisse d'une histoire de la nature humaine*. Le Livre de Poche, Paris.

Meyer, Michel (1994). *Rhetoric, Language, and Reason*. University, Part: The Pennsylvania State University Press.).

Nussbaum, Martha C. (2001). *Upheavals of Thought. The Intelligence of Emotions*. Cambridge: Cambridge University Press.

O'Neill, Patrick (1994). *Fictions of Discourse: Reading Narrative Theory*. Toronto: University of Toronto Press.

Perelman, Chaim and Olbrechts-Tyteca, Lucie (1958). *Traité de l'argumentaion, la nouvelle rhétorique*. Paris : Presse Universitaire de France.

Roe, Emery (1994). *Narrative Policy Analysis: Theory and Practice.* Durham: Duke University Press.

Rorty, Richard (1989). *Contingency, Irony, and Solidarity.* Cambridge: Cambridge University Press, 5.

Sabatier, Paul A. (1988). 'An Advocacy Coalition Framework of Policy Change and the Role of policy-Oriented Learning Therein'. *Policy Sciences* 21, 129–88.

Schön, Donald A. and Rein, Martin (1994). *Frame Reflection: Towards the Resolution of Intractable Policy Controversies.* New York: Basic Books.

Smart, Barry (1985). Michel Foucault. Chichester: Ellis Horwood Limited.

Stone, Deborah (1997). *Policy Paradox: The Art of Political Decision Making.* New York, London: W.W. Norton & Company.

Svasek, Maruska (2002). The Politics of Emotions. Emotional Discourse and Displays in Post-Cold War Contexts, '*Focaal – European Journal of Anthropology*', No. 39, 9–27.

Torfing, Jacob (1999). *New Theories of Discourse: Laclau, Mouffe and Zizek.* Oxford: Blackwell Publishers.

Torgerson, D. (1986). Between Knowledge and Politics: The Three Faces of Policy Analysis, Policy Sciences, 19, 33–59.

Toulmin, Stephen (1958). *The Uses of Argument.* Cambridge: Cambridge University Press.

Turnbull, Nick (2003). 'The Implications of the Division of Logic and Argumentation for Policy Theory'. Paper given at the 2nd ECPR Conference, Marburg, 18–21 September 2003.

Marin, Wallace (1986). Recent Theories of Narrative, Cornell University Press: Ithaca.

Wells, Susan (1996). *Sweet Reason. Rhetoric and the Discourses of Modernity.* Chicago: Chicago University Press.

Welsch, Wolfgang (1996). *Vernunft. Die zeitgenoessische Vernunftkritik und das Konzept der transversalen Vernunft.* Frankfurt am Main: Suhrkamp Verlag.

White, Hayden (1981). 'The Value of Narrativity in the Representation of Reality,' in Mitchell, W.J.T. (ed.), *On Narrative.* Chicago: University of Chicago Press.

White, Hayden (1987). *The Content of the Form: Narrative Discourse and Historical Representation.* Baltimore: Johns Hopkins University Press.

Yanow, Dvora (1996). *How Does a Policy Mean? Interpreting Policy and Organizational Action.* Washington, D.C.: Georgetown University Press.

28

Disciplinary Perspectives

JON PIERRE

Richard Rose once described the study of public policy as "disciplined research but undisciplined problems".[1] While academics think and act very much within disciplinary boundaries, real-world problems are rarely understood by one academic discipline. Almost all policy problems have political, economic and social dimensions – we could easily add several more – which means that our academic understanding of those problems require some degree of inter-disciplinary work. As a result, the study of public policy has almost always been more or less multidisciplinary. In the Introduction to this volume we discuss the eclectic nature of policy research, and it is safe to say that no single academic discipline can claim monopoly on policy research. Public policy is an umbrella concept for government actions to address vastly different kinds of societal problems. Given that government policy includes such different policies as housing policy, economic policy and defense policy, it should not surprise anyone to see that an academic understanding of public policy almost by design must incorporate theories and framework from several different academic disciplines. However, different disciplines represent different discourses, draw on different theories, focus on different economic, social and political phenomena and are geared to solve different types of problems.

Applying a strict economic analysis when designing a policy towards homelessness is probably not a recipe for appropriate public policy; nor would sociology probably have very much to offer in terms of advice in the foreign policy field.

To understand the contributions of different academic disciplines to public policy analysis we must also remind ourselves that these disciplines are not only tools for research but are also present in the process which is analysed. Policy makers acquire advice from academics both inside and outside the institutions of government and civil servants usually have an academic degree in the social sciences or economics. Moreover, think tanks and independent research institutions are omnipresent in the political debate, presenting reports and policies with which they try to influence elected officials. Here, too, we can see how public policy is evaluated, and how alternative policies are propagated, from an academic viewpoint.

This chapter will discuss the contributions of three academic disciplines – economic theory, political science and sociology – to the analysis of public policy. Thus, we are leaving aside, for the most part, the role of these disciplines within the policy process. It is not very difficult to see, for instance, how the *Zeitgeist* of the 1960s and 1970s, with its emphasis on political solutions to most or all societal problems, made sociologists and political scientists attractive policy advisors, whereas the more market-embracing policy style of the 1980s and 1990s gave economists a privileged position in the policy process. Bearing these caveats in mind, the overarching question which this chapter will address is what types of knowledge and information that the three academic fields can produce, given the core focus of the disciplines and the typical research questions which are raised within the disciplines. To what extent can these disciplines help the observer uncover the logic of public policy and explain the policy process and its outcomes?

Before we embark on that analysis, three general comments need to be emphasised. First, given the eclectic nature of policy research, scholars face a significant problem in applying the wrong discipline to a given policy. In the ideal world, there should be some degree of correspondence between the causal model sustaining a policy on the one hand, and the academic theory used to analyse the policy on the other. A policy which is aimed at increasing the number of new businesses, for instance, departs from some model of what discourages potential entrepreneurs from launching new business ventures and seeks to remove those obstacles. These problems could be assumed to be primarily economic in nature, hence, economics should be the preferred – although not necessarily the only – analytical model to employ in the policy analysis. Sociologists and political scientists would probably be able to offer some useful contribution to the analysis, but if the problem is construed as primarily an economic or financial problem, that is where we would expect the most rewarding analysis to come from.

Secondly, we need to realise that the notion of a policy process guided by scientific logic and causal models is a somewhat idealised representation of policy making. In order to understand policy design or policy change we need to not only look at public policy in and of itself but also at the politics of policy (Gourevitch, 1986). Politicians and political parties have strategic goals and long-term visions and manoeuvre tactically to promote those objectives and to cater to their constituencies. This pursuit tends to place more emphasis on the interests and goals of the actors than on the role of analysis and causality in designing the policy. Also, policy makers are sometimes guided almost entirely by political or economic necessity. During time periods of extensive cutbacks, policies tend to be assessed in terms of their economic potential, regardless of whether that was the theory which guided the initial design of the policy.

A final introductory observation is that there has for a long time been some degree of rivalry between different academic disciplines with regard to their purported values, both in understanding public policy and also the quality of the advice they can offer to policy makers. Economists from time to time tend to think that social scientists rely too much on "soft data" and fuzzy theories and therefore fail to produce good scientific explanation. Similarly, political scientists and sociologists sometimes accuse economists for using unrealistic models of rationalistic, utility-maximising actors in their research; for instance, Peter Self (1977) once referred to cost-benefit analysis – and economics more in general – as "nonsense on stilts". Given the growing interest among political scientists in rational choice-based models of political behaviour, some of the antagonism between political science and economics may have faded, but even so we need to be aware of the tension that exists between these different academic camps.

APPROACHES TO PUBLIC POLICY

Economics, political science and sociology offer three different analytical vantage points for policy analysis. Before we embark on a more systematic comparison of the three disciplines we should first briefly go over the main feature of the three perspectives on public policy.

Economic Theory

In order to forestall the impending attack from economists, it must immediately be noted that there is no single "economic theory"; there are theories at the micro, meso and macro levels of society just as there are economic theories that highlight different policy areas. In addition, economic theory is beginning to pay greater attention to the role of institutions and the consequences of different institutional arrangements. Indeed, constitutionalism – a research field that attracts both political scientists and economists – is an area of research which seeks to assess the macro-economic consequences of institutions for political representation and policy implementation.

An important contribution of economics in understanding public policy is the analysis of how markets can be employed to enhance allocative efficiency. Neo-classical market theory is a powerful analytical tool in this research. Applied more specifically on the public sector, public choice – the so-called Chicago school – helped understand some problems in tax-financed service provision. It might be argued that economists do a better job at describing these problems than actually explaining them – largely because political agency and institutional inertia are phenomena that are difficult to accommodate in economic models – but even so it remains clear that economic theory delivers an important contribution to policy studies.

Even more importantly, economic theory is the keystone of cost-benefit analysis, an approach which probably is the most significant contribution of economic theory to public policy. Cost-benefit analysis, which has developed into a key analytical model in policy analysis, accords values to different policy options and hence provides an elegant model for assessing alternative policies in addressing policy problems (see Vining and Weimer, this volume).

Economics as a cluster of theories rests firmly on an assumption of rationality. There is a distinct focus on agency, and the notion of the rational actor has become a powerful predictive analytical model. While much of the focus is on individual market behaviour, the model has also been immensely useful in studies on collective action and the "free-rider" problem (Olson, 1965). This research, in turn,

has helped us better understand a number of complex policy-related issues such as tax evasion and the consumption of collective goods. To be sure, given that political solutions to societal problems nearly always tend to be collective solutions, the nexus of collective action and individual rationality offers a host of important research questions.

That having been said, we should also note that the agency-focus which is typical to much of economic analysis creates problems in accounting for the role of institutions. Furthermore, if we allow institutions to incorporate not just structure but routines and practices as well, we can see that economics, in the form of neo-classical micro-economic theory, has problems conceptualising or explaining behaviour which is guided by non-rational consideration. Douglass North, one of the founding fathers of the institutional school of economic theory, bemoaned these shortcomings and delivered a powerful attack on neo-classical economic theory based on an institutional approach to economic development. Development economics, North argued, had failed to produce explanations to cross-national variations in economic growth and was simply "not up to the task" (North, 1990: 11).

Essentially, North's criticism of not just development economics but much of the neo-classical market theory as well takes aim at the inability of these theories to account for cooperation and institutions. The argument is that theory does not take real-life factors into account and hence cannot provide a useful framework for empirical analysis. This debate among economists has probably helped move the discipline towards greater policy relevance and understanding.

Political Science

Public policy is to a very large extent a political phenomenon and, as such, a field of expertise for political scientists. In particular, political science can account for not only the substantive side of policy but also the politics of public policy, i.e. the compromises among political actors and the trading of support for different policy proposals as well as an understanding of the institutional dimension of public policy. Thus, political science uncovers the process through which policy evolves and what factors drove policy design and choice of policy instruments.

Political science also has much to offer in terms of understanding agency as well as institutions, although the combination of the two seems to be somewhat of a weak spot; policy studies typically focus either on institutions or actors. The stages model allows for analysis which takes into account both institutions and actors and the interplay between these two variables (see Hill and Hupe, this volume). The institutional dimension of public policy has been the dominant field of public policy research over the past couple of decades. Alongside that research there has also been a rapid growth in the application of rationalistic models of political behaviour and decision-making. Interestingly, however, so far rational choice has made rather few inroads into policy research.

Futhermore, political science appears to be geared to provide an understanding of how some types of public policy are shaped by intergovernmental relations. Decentralisation has a profound influence on the state's ability to impose policies on subnational institutions and to ensure equal standard (or equalisation) across the nation. Intergovernmental relations appear to a growing extent to be negotiated rather than hierarchical, and the state finds itself increasingly often playing the role of a mitigator between transnational and subnational institutional systems and ditto actors and interests. The resulting multi-level governance, as shorthand for contextually defined and negotiated institutional relations, has gained much attention in recent research, not least because it highlights significant limitations to state power and centrality (see, for instance, Bache and Flinders, 2004).

A final stronghold of political science in public policy research is the discipline's focus on power and allocation of public goods. While policy scholars frequently note the contextual and ad hoc nature of policy processes (see Kingdon, 1995), it is difficult to ignore that

political power and the institutions where it is vested remain the key players in the policy process. Certainly, actors are framed by institutions and previous policy decisions, but history is replete with examples of how the exercise of political power has made an autonomous and decisive impact on the course of events. Politics, and public policy, is to a great extent about "who gets what, when and how", to quote Lasswell's (1936) classical book title, and political science remains the discipline most unambiguously devoted to study of those issues.

All of that having been said, political science also has several shortcomings in understanding public policy. One significant problem is related to the previously mentioned tension between structure and agency and the complexities of bringing the two together in an analytical framework. While most political scientists probably agree that the interplay between structure and agency harbour much of the explanation to public policy issues, very few have been able to provide ideas about how to integrate them into a common framework or theory.

Another potential problem with the political science approach to public policy is its state-centric view on governance. Although the state-society literature has helped us understand the often complex relationship between policy makers and policy targets, political science as a whole still seems to take comfort in the notion that once a policy has been decided by political institutions there is an immediate and appropriate societal response to that policy. Implementation research has, from time to time, been successful in disturbing that comfort by showing the frequently rather meagre outcome of policy (Winter, 2003). And, more recently, governance scholars have convincingly argued that the state-society nexus is a two-way street and public policy is in no insignificant measure shaped by actors outside the state (Pierre and Peters, 2000; Rhodes, 1997). While there is much to suggest that the state remains the undisputed centre of governance, we need also be prepared to acknowledge the increasing societal complexities and how they shape much of contemporary governance (Pierre and Peters, 2005).

A third potential problem, finally, in the political science approach to public policy is a tendency to focus too much on interests and objectives while ignoring the significance of political ideas, ideology and vision. It is easy to argue that politicians are driven by strategic and tactical goals such as power, perks, prestige, success, and re-election. The notion that people sometimes choose to become involved in politics because they have a vision about how to transform society is, while intriguing and far from unlikely, far more difficult to fit into an analytical model. Goal-oriented (teleological) explanations are tricky – politician X did what she did because she wanted to, where goal and action become circular evidence – and are also not conducive to theory building. For successful and hugely influential politicians like Margaret Thatcher, Francois Mitterand, John F. Kennedy and Olof Palme, power and political office was probably more a means towards an end rather than a goal in itself, yet much of the political science analysis has remained focused more on strategy than on sheer political passion. The recent interest in the "ideational" approach which highlights the significance of ideas and beliefs in shaping politics (see, for instance, Berman, 1998) holds some promise in ameliorating this problem.

Sociology

Sociology was once argued by two prominent sociologists to "not apply" to any areas of public policy (Scott and Shore, 1979). These two scholars appear to have underestimated the value of their discipline for helping to solve policy problems such as crime, poverty, and the disintegration of family structures. Sociology has tended to address these issues as social problems, but attempts to understand the social causes of these conditions may be crucial for designing policies to ameliorate them. Thus, sociology's perhaps main contribution to public policy lies in its ability to identify and analyse social problems. Again, however, there is to some extent a trait in sociology not to identify social problems as political problems – that is to say, problems which are conducive

to a resolution through political means – but rather as problems which are derived from social dynamics or from the relationship between social and economic organisation.

If treating economics and political science as homogenous academic projects is problematic, this becomes even more difficult with sociology. This discipline displays the full range of different ontological and epistemological traditions. Some sociologists are anchored in methodological positivism and conduct their research using mass data. Others employ a more deductive, theoretical approach and use empirical data basically to drive home a theoretical argument. Yet others are almost exclusively concerned with the development of social theory. Sociological theory is equally heterogeneous. The classical focus on structure-agency problems has spun off a wide variety of approaches such as neo-Marxism, institutional theory and theories focused on sociological issues such as power and powerlessness, alienation and similar issues. Thus, sociology has much to offer to public policy, both in terms of presenting and describing social problems and also in measuring the effects of policy implementation.

Much of sociology has, with massive simplification, a conceptualisation of the state, which to some extent tends to obscure the potential role which public policy may have in addressing social problems. Sociologists with a neo-Marxist orientation argue that the state is a captive of the ruling class in society and/or that there is little the state can do to mitigate the social ramification of the capitalist economy (Therborn, 1978). A related perspective is that the state caters to economic interests and therefore public policy is design to fulfill "reproductive" functions within that economic order. Alternatively, the state is seen as a set of structures controlled by the political elite. Either way, policy design is divorced from social problems per se, hence the lower social classes have little to expect from the state or public policy in terms of support or welfare.

Further, the sociology of organisations is important for understanding policy implementation. Implementation scholars tend to focus just as much on the organisational context within which implementation takes place as on policy objectives or design when accounting for the degree of success or failure in policy implementation (see, for instance, Pressman and Wildavsky, 1984; Winter, 2003). To be sure, sociology, particularly sociological institutionalism, thus seems to have much to offer in terms of understanding consequences of organisational design and of changes in regulations. Much of the institutional theory that has become mainstream political science, and which more recently is making inroads into economics, has its intellectual roots in sociology and the structure-agency problematic as it is treated by sociologists.

The most important contribution which sociology has made to public policy research is probably its analysis of framing. Sociologists typically argue that, throughout the policy process, issues need to be framed in certain ways in order to receive attention and to be successfully resolved. The important point here is that what matters is not so much issues per se but rather how those issues are described and politically packaged, which to a large extent determines the future political handling of them. More recently, framing has found its way into public policy through the constructivist approach to public policy (see Gottweis, this volume).

There are also some significant shortcomings with regard to the utility aspect of sociology in public policy analysis. First of all, sociology tends to portray and conceptualise power in ways which makes it difficult to employ in a meaningful way in public policy. To most sociologists, power or control is derived from (nominally) non-political variables such as the economy or social status. Thus, power is rarely seen as something coming out of the policy process. That said, there may certainly be some value in the insight that political power is not the only source of influence and control in society but it might not be useful when designing public policy.

Another aspect of sociological theory which to some extent obstructs its utility in public policy is that it is not a discipline directed towards choice, options and decision-making.

Public policy is to a large extent a matter of choice. Policy making, for the most part, is less about whether or not a policy should be created towards some political objective but rather more about incremental adjustments in terms of spending and organisational design. Sociology performs rather poorly in assessing options or in understanding decision-making process.

It almost goes without saying that this somewhat rhapsodic review of three major academic disciplines can hardly do justice to any of them. The purpose of this quick review has been to point at some strengths and weaknesses in the three disciplines with regard to their contributions in understanding public policy.

CONTENDING THEORIES AND THE STAGES MODEL

We will now go into some more detail by discussing the strengths and weaknesses of the three disciplines at different phases of the policy process. We have already had some remarks on these issues; now is the time to look more closely at them.

Agenda setting

A number of observers have pointed to control over the political agenda as one of the most powerful ways to control the political process, (see e.g. Kingdon, 1995; Schattschneider, 1960). The three disciplines discussed in this chapter perform rather differently with regard to their utility in public policy analysis. Quite some time ago now, Bachrach and Baratz pointed out that "there are two faces of power, neither of which the sociologists see and only one of which the political scientists see" (Bachrach and Baratz, 1962: 947). Their argument, in brief, was that political scientists tend to focus their analysis on power in the decision-making context, forgetting that the power to keep issues off the agenda is an equally important expression of power and control. Sociologists fail to see both of these manifestations of power and control, according to Bachrach and Baratz. While that was probably a correct observation at the time of writing, sociology has since then made some significant contributions to our understanding of the power dimensions of the agenda-setting stage of the policy process. Steven Lukes' (1974) analysis of power as an instrument of influencing the basic images and perceptions of personal efficacy and social structure is a significant contribution to the power literature at large and to the study of agenda setting in particular.

Bachrach and Baratz' conclusion that sociology is basically oblivious of the power associated with agenda setting is somewhat harsh. To be sure, one of the strengths of sociology is its research focus on social problems which do not make themselves easily visible to the political and administrative elite. More importantly, sociology is highly useful for an understanding the framing of issues, something which can be decisive in whether or not an issue finds its way on to the political agenda (Schon and Rein, 1994).

Economics can make a contribution to understanding agenda setting, but we should acknowledge that this is not an area of expertise for economists. For both sociologists and economists their overall contribution to agenda setting lies in the normative dimension of the actual state of affairs, to paraphrase the German philosopher Fichte; by drawing the attention of politicians to social problems or misuse of public resources, these disciplines can exert substantive influence over the policy agenda.

Given its overall focus on the political process, political science should be geared to understanding the agenda-setting phase of the policy process. Interestingly, however, political scientists tend to draw on the work of scholars from other disciplines, like, for instance, mass communication, when approaching the agenda-setting phase of the policy process (see McCombs, 2004). Alternatively, research on agenda setting tends to focus on contextual richness more than theory building (cf. Kingdon, 1995).

In sum, our knowledge on agenda setting is rather scattered and eclectic. There is no predominant theory of agenda setting available today. At the same time, however, we can see that politicians seem to be increasing attention to controlling the political agenda and putting a positive "spin" on issues on the agenda. Thus, politicians are probably more aware of the significance of controlling this phase of the decision-making process than are most academic observers of the process.

ASSESSMENT OF POLICY OPTIONS

The evaluation of decision alternatives is the next phase we will discuss. Here, it appears as if all three disciplines have some help to offer, although each discipline can only produce a somewhat limited and uni-dimensional assessment of the policy options. One of the key problems in assessing policy options is that such an assessment will almost by design have to reflect the multi-dimensional nature of many policies. Thus, for instance, most regulatory reforms have some economic, social and political or institutional ramifications, hence an assessment of such a policy option must be conducted against the backdrop of the stated objectives of reform. Some regulatory reforms may be costly but will be implemented regardless, since they serve other objectives than simply saving public resources.

Economics have much to offer in terms of assessing different policy options. Cost-benefit analysis is a powerful approach in policy choice analysis (see Vining and Weimer, this volume). Again, however, economists have problems accounting for those types of benefits which do not lend themselves to measurement which is compatible to financial costs. True, most economists seem to agree that you can, indeed, measure the benefit of clean air or consumption of culture or personal safety, but not everyone would probably agree with that.

Political scientist E. E. Schattschneider once suggested that "the definition of the alternatives is the supreme instrument of power" (Schattschneider, 1960: 68). While that is a congenial observation, it has not left any noticeable traces in the political science literature. To some extent, political scientists share some of the economists' problems with quantitative assessment of decision alternatives. The typical criterion advanced by political scientists would be goal attainment – i.e. the extent to which the different options mean reaching the goals and objectives of the policy – which certainly is useful information, although it says rather little about policy substance. Sociologists, finally, can also assess policy options according to their consistency with the policy goals and are also well equipped to assess both the likely outcomes of policy options as well as assessing potential implementation problems.

To sum up, all three disciplines – but probably most economics – can help us understand the phase of selecting policy options. A significant problem, however, is that this selection often is a multidimensional task, where variables such as probability of successful implementation, costs and predicted outcomes, must be weighed against each other, and the three disciplines tend to only be capable of assessing one or very few of these variables.

Decision-making

Political science – if we stick with Bachrach and Baratz' portrayal of the social sciences and political power – does capture one aspect of power but it is not the type of power which manifests itself in control of the political agenda. Instead, they argue, political scientists have a strong expertise in understanding one "face of power" – decision-making. It is difficult to take issue with that argument; political science is a discipline which directly and indirectly is geared to enhance our knowledge about how decisions are formed. David Easton's (1971) definition of politics as the "authoritative allocation of values" strongly suggests that political science is first and foremost a discipline about decision making. Similarly, Harold Lasswell's (1958) classical book title "Politics: Who Gets What, When, How" also points at decision-making as the

critical phase of the policy process and the key focus of political science.

That having been said, we should also note that there is little agreement among political scientists about how to approach decision-making. Influenced by economic theory, organisation theory and decision theory, political science today displays the full range of theories of decision-making, from rational choice theory to the "garbage can model of organizational choice" (Cohen et al., 1972). The fact that these contending views of these issues sit at the predominant line of skirmish in the discipline today is a somewhat paradoxical proof of the significance of decision-making in political science. Thus, while decision-making in principle should be perhaps the main stronghold of political science, there is little agreement about which theory, or theories, is best at conceptualising and explaining such decision-making.

Understanding decision-making is a matter of understanding both the substantive process but also the strategy of the actors involved in that process. Decision theory provides an excellent base for understanding the strategy of the actors but says very little about the substantive aspects of the decision-making.

One might argue that economics, at least micro-economic theory, should be a theory of decision-making, since this is a theory which deals extensively with preferences and choice, broadly defined. However, this theory says surprisingly little about decision-making *strictu sensu*. Choice – the process of choosing – is not given much attention, presumably because choice is believed to stem automatically from preferences and objectives. Economic man never makes irrational decisions, hence little need to focus on decision-making. Once the alternatives and preferences are known, choice will follow suit.

Sociology too is rather quiet when it comes to understanding decision-making. Its main contribution probably comes from organisational sociology, which is focused on organisational behavior, including decision-making. Also, decision theory is influenced by organisational sociology; Herbert Simon's seminal analysis of bounded rationality grew out of work conducted by economists, sociologists and political scientists (Simon, 1967).

IMPLEMENTATION

If sociology has fairly little to contribute to an understanding of the decision-making phase of the policy process, it has substantively more to offer when it comes to understanding implementation. Policy implementation is normally an interorganisational process, frequently transcending the border between the state and the surrounding society. Implementation can also be conducted at the regional and local levels of the public sector, something which again highlights the need to ensure that different organisations interact efficiently.

Political science too has – at least from time to time – had a significant interest in policy implementation (see Winter, 2003). Much of the initial wave of implementation studies followed on the growth of policy programs in the United States during the late 1960s and early 1970s (Pressman and Wildavsky, 1984). When the outcomes of those policies proved to be rather meagre, scholars turned their attention to the implementation phase to see what types of obstacles explained that pattern. Since then, implementation research is an established subfield of political science. This research typically argues that policy design is a key variable in understanding the success or failure of policy implementation. Policy design, which does not take into account the institutional context within which the policy is to be implemented, runs a significant risk of being inefficient because it is not very likely to be properly implemented. Closely related to matters of policy design is the cluster of issues on policy instruments. The selection of policy instruments is an important factor in understanding policy implementation. To a significant degree, this argument relates to economic theory (Kirschen et al., 1964), although lately this area of research has become more integrated in the political science literature on public policy and implementation (Salamon, 2000).

Economic theory is not directly focused on the complexities of policy implementation, at least not as far as the organizational dimension of implementation is concerned. However, economics has proven to be useful in those cases of policy implementation which involve economic incentives as a means of altering social or market behaviour. Significant segments of environmental protection policies draw on incentives as a policy instrument. Similarly, financial incentives is a frequently used policy instrument in industrial policy, and there are many features of the tax system of many countries which effectively serve as incentives to reward a certain behaviour.

To sum up, implementation is for the most part an interorganisational process, and disciplines geared to understanding that problematic will also be helpful in understanding implementation. Moreover, by linking implementation to policy design, particularly the use of economic incentives, economic theory has much to contribute to the analysis of policy implementation at the micro level.

EVALUATION

To assess the utility of the three disciplines in policy evaluation, it is useful to make a distinction between process evaluation and outcome evaluation. Although most evaluation seeks to measure different types of policy outcome – the effects of the policy – process is sometimes also evaluated in order to generate knowledge (what organisational theory calls second-loop learning) about the efficiency of the process in devising appropriate policy. All three disciplines can make important contributions to policy evaluation. Economics can assess the efficiency and effectiveness of the policy, e.g. to what extent the same outcomes could have been achieved at a lower cost. Political science is good at process tracing and can link outcomes to input and also generate explanation to the degree of policy success or failure by bringing political and institutional variables into the analysis (see Vedung, this volume). Sociology, finally, has a stronghold in analysing social problems and the extent to which they have been ameliorated by a particular policy.

Policy evaluation is sometimes part of the legitimation process of public policy. By making evaluation an integrated part of the policy itself, policy makers provide critics with a channel to voice their discontent with either the policy process or with the policy outcomes. Evaluation in this perspective is a means of institutionalising a feedback loop in the policy process. Sociology and political science have a great deal of input on these issues, which arguably are more salient to policy analysts than they are to policy makers.

CONCLUDING DISCUSSION

Looking back at the discussion thus far, it appears as if there are a couple of more overarching features of the three disciplines which to a large extent determine the utility of them in understanding public policy. Economics, in this context, is first and foremost the art and craft of optimising; economic theory is outstanding in identifying allocative inefficiencies. That having been said, optimising the use of scarce resources can be problematic in policy as it is not the only criterion which policy makers take into consideration when policies are designed.

Political science, on the other hand, might be able to tell us more about these trade-offs between conflicting policy objectives. If economics is about optimising, political science deals to a large extent with issues of satisficing and democratising. Political science is weary of optimising because it draws on a rationalistic idealisation of the policy process. Satisficing – Herbert Simon's model of bounded rationality in organisations – seems to capture much of political decision-making under uncertainty and complex contingencies. Equally important, democratising is a process through which policy, is perceived as a collective project, with all that entails in terms of transparency,

electoral input and political and administrative accountability.

Turning to sociology, it is the unrivalled discipline in terms of contextualising; the key sociological contribution to policy analysis is that it uncovers the significance of the institutional and organisational within which policy is designed and implemented. Questions about why policy evolves in the fashion it does, or why the implementation of a policy was success or a failure, cannot be fully answered without taking these contexts into account. These contexts represent much of the backdrop against which economists and political scientists try to make sense of the assessment of policy options or the actual decision-making.

To these three disciplines we should also add decision theory as a means of understanding strategising. This approach to public policy is entirely focused on the politics of policy making and the behaviour of decision makers. It says virtually nothing about the substantive dimension of policy but it is certainly valuable in terms of understanding agency in the policy process. However, the analysis of policy substance cannot be divorced from the analysis of policy strategy; since policy makers pursue both substantive and strategic interests in the policy process, decision theory can be of indirect use in understanding why the process generated a particular outcome.

We could certainly have added more disciplines to the analysis. Law has probably become more and more important, along with the increasing significance of courts in policy implementation and intergovernmental relationships. Statistics crops up at every phase of the policy process as a prerequisite for good policy advice. Philosophy – particularly normative philosophy on state power versus individual freedom – provides the point of departure for much of policy theory and social theory, just to mention a few additional academic disciplines, which directly or indirectly speak to public policy. Again, this is proof of the eclectic and inter-disciplinary nature of public policy.

Policy makers have looked at these disciplines with changing degrees of affection or hostility during the post-war period. U.S. President Wilson is once said to have asked for advice from a one-armed economist to escape the "on the one hand, but on the other hand" type of analyses that economists sometimes are accused of delivering. During the harsh economic situation of the 1990s, economic considerations played a key role in the policy process in most western democracies. Given that policy objectives such as balancing the budget, curbing inflation and cutting taxes were overriding political goals, economic criteria became the main yardstick with which policy proposals were assessed.

Seen in a longer time perspective, however, one cannot escape the notion that it is awkward to believe that the answer to the question of what is good policy sits at the end of an economic formula. The "New Deal" and the "strong society" in the United States and the extensive welfare states in many Western European countries were huge political projects that were launched, not because they were believed to be economically sound but because they were seen as politically desirable and socially justified. Economics has little to offer in terms of a deeper understanding of why politicians behave the way they do. Instead, a deeper understanding of policy rests to a large extent on an appropriate employment of all the disciplines discussed in this chapter. Public policy, to reiterate a comment from the Introduction to this volume, is an eclectic and multi-disciplinary challenge.

NOTE

1. I am, as ever, indebted to Guy Peters for valuable comments on an earlier version of this chapter.

REFERENCES

Bache, I. and M. Flinders (eds) (2004), Multi-level Governance (Oxford: Oxford University Press).

Bachrach, P. and M. S. Baratz (1962), "Two Faces of Power", *American Political Science Review*, vol. 56: 947–52.

Cohen, M. D., J. G. March and J. P. Olsen (1972), 'A Garbage Can Model of Organizational Choice', Administrative Science Quarterly 17: 1–25.

Beman, S. (1998), *The Social Democratic Moment: Ideas and Politics in the Making of Interwar Europe* (Cambridge, MA: Harvard University Press).

Easton, D. (1971), *The Political System: An Inquiry into the State of Political Science* (Chicago: The University of Chicago Press).

Gourevitch, P. (1986), Politics in Hard Times: Comparative Responses to International Economic Crises (Ithaca: Cornell University Press).

Kingdon, J. W. (1995), *Agendas, Alternatives, and Public Policies* (2nd. edn) (New York: Harper Collins).

Kirschen, E. S. et al. (1964), *Economic Policy in Our Time* (Chicago: Rand McNally).

Lasswell, H. D. (1958), *Politics: Who gets What, When, How?* (New York: Meridian Books).

Luke, S. (1974), *Power: A Radical View* (Basingstoke: Macmillan).

McCombs, M. (2004), *Setting the agenda: Mass Media and Public Opinion* (Oxford: Polity Press).

Meehan, E. J. (1982), *Economics and Policymaking: The Tragic Illusion* (Westport, CT: Greenwood Press).

North, D. A. (1990), Institutions, Institutional Change and Economic Performance (Cambridge: Cambridge University Press).

Olson, M. (1965), *The Logic of Collective Action: Public Good and the Theory of Groups* (Cambridge, MA: Harvard University Press).

Ormerod, P. (1994), *The Death of Economics* (London: Faber).

Pierre, J. and B. G. Peters (2000), *Governance, Politics and the State* (Basingstoke: Palgrave).

Pierre, J. and B. G. Peters (2005), *Governing Complex Societies: Trajectories and Scenarios* (Basingstoke: Palgrave).

Pressman, J. L. and A. Wildavsky (1984), *Implementation* (3rd edn) (Berkeley: University of California Press).

Rhodes, R. A. W. (1997), *Understanding Governance: Policy Networks, Governance, Reflexivity, and Accountability* (Buckingham: Open University Press).

Salamon, L. M. (2000), *Handbook of Policy Instruments* (New York: Oxford University Press).

Schattschneider, E. E. (1960), *The Semi-Sovereign People* (New York: Holt, Rinehart & Winston).

Schon, D. and M. Rein (1994), *Frame Reflection: Toward the Solution of Intractable Policy Controversies* (Cambridge, MA: MIT Press).

Scott, R. A. and A. R. Shore (1979), *Why Sociology Does not Apply: A Study of the Use of Sociology in Public Policy* (New York: Elsevier).

Self, P. (1977), *Econocrats and the Policy Process: the Politics and Philosophy of Cost-benefit Analysis* (Basingstoke: Macmillan).

Self, P. (1999), *Rolling back the Market: Economic Dogma and Political Choice* (Basingstoke: Macmillan).

Simon, H. A. (1967), *Administrative Behavior: A Study of Decision Making in Administrative Organization* (New York: Free Press).

Therborn, G. (1978), *What does the Ruling Class do When it Rules?: State Apparatuses and State Power under Feudialism, Capitalism and Socialism* (London: Verso).

Winter, S. (2003), *Handbook of Public Administration*, edited by B. G. Peters and J. Pierre (London: Sage).

Index